THE FAR EAST
A Modern History

The University of Michigan History of the Modern World

Edited by Allan Nevins and Howard M. Ehrmann

THE
FAR EAST

A Modern History

BY NATHANIEL PEFFER

Ann Arbor : The University of Michigan Press

Contents

THE FAR EAST
A Modern History

CHAPTER I

Introduction

The history of any people at any time is social history, cultural history, the chronicle of how they have developed the institutions in which they order their lives and the beliefs and moral values by which they live. Of no people and at no time has this been more true than of the inhabitants of the Far East in the last hundred years. The consequences of the impact of the new and freshly invigorated West on the old and static East have been felt in the daily lives of the Far Eastern peoples, in the way they earn their livelihood, in the way they live together, in their thoughts and feelings and attitudes, and, of course, in the conventional stuff that is known as history—politics, revolutions, wars. The struggle that engulfed all Asia after the Japanese attack on Pearl Harbor, the fall of China to the Communists, the nationalistic uprisings against Western empires throughout Southeastern Asia—these are but the latest and most dramatic incidents. The history of the modern Far East is a study in comparative culture—the relation between one form of life and another.

In one sense this is not peculiar to the Far East. It may be that the West, too, is suffering from the impact of a new scheme of life on its traditional institutions, and that the modern history of the West, too, is a study in comparative culture. For what we now call Western, by contrast with the East, is really the effect of scientific discoveries applied to production and distribution through the use of machinery. And this was as new to the West 150 years ago as it is to the East now. From the internal combustion engine to the atomic bomb, science and the scheme of life founded on it—industrialism and the machine age—have unhinged our institutions and disturbed the balance of both collective and individual life, and the consequences are now being recognizably felt.

The world wars—the effect as much as the cause of our instability—

the economic depressions, the weakening of old moral sanctions, the loosening of the hold of the family and the church are all the consequences of the impact on us of the machine age. But it is a less dramatic consequence than that which is felt in the East. For one thing, machine industrialism came at our own option and at our own pace. There was at least some opportunity for adjustment of institutions to the new forces they had to contain. In the East, on the other hand, machine industrialism came from without by imposition of the invigorated power of the West, power deriving from the energy released by the machine, if only in the form of weapons. There was no option or opportunity for adjustment or adaptation. Most of all, the imposition of Westernism was accompanied by political and military conquest or at least domination. The East lost all control over its own destiny, which is itself enough to generate a complication of social ills.

For at least 500 years before the nineteenth century Eastern Asia (a more accurate designation than the more commonly used Far East) had been reasonably stable. There had been wars, internal upheavals, natural catastrophes, after the fashion of nations and races everywhere; there had been the unparalleled cataclysm of the eruption of Genghis Khan. But on the whole, compared to Europe in the same 500 years, Eastern Asia had been peaceable and orderly. Not only politically but socially and culturally—in institutions, customs and conceptions of life —there had been little, if any change. Europe at this time witnessed the passing of feudalism and the onslaught of the commercial revolution and capitalism. The Reformation and the religious wars followed, and also the development of nationalism, which was equally important as a force molding the West. There was nothing comparable in Eastern Asia. And if Eastern Asia had in addition to the disadvantage of a static system the disadvantages of rigid conservatism that were to be disastrously felt in the nineteenth century, it also had the advantages. There was a minimum of the cruel toll that fundamental change always takes of men.

The foundation of mundane existence was secure; the orbit in which men and society moved was fixed. The "Unchanging East," Western writers of the nineteenth century used to call it, and they were right, although they often drew wrong conclusions therefrom. If the East was conservative, it was not altogether out of obscurantism or cultural self-infatuation, though there was much of both. For one thing, conservatism was not unique. While the West had changed more, since its culture and society were in an earlier stage of development, basic changes even in the West were infrequent and did not come by volition. At bottom, the ordering of social life was static everywhere before the nineteenth century, though there were differences in degree and the West was less static than the East. Men who went to the East from Europe and America were inclined to judge by the standards of the nineteenth century alone, which was shortsighted. The fact is that there had been little reason for the East to change.

If the Chinese, Japanese, or Koreans had been objective about their scheme of life, which of course they were not, and had consciously set out to measure it against what could be seen in Europe or America or elsewhere in Asia, they could have told themselves without racial or cultural arrogance that there was nothing to gain by changing. In the intangible aspects of a culture, that is, in the arts, in philosophy, in religion, in the amenities of social intercourse, they did not suffer by comparison. Their political and administrative system was as highly developed as any in the West. In what is known as law and order they were advanced by comparison with the West: less outlawry and less crime against person or property occurred in the capital of China in the middle of the eighteenth century than in the capital of England. Even in the technology of production, that which has become the highest criterion for the West—and, perhaps, for America the only criterion—the peoples of the East had little to learn from the West until the latter part of the eighteenth century.

The whole idea of the "backwardness" of the East, universally held in the West, is of recent origin. In the political and philosophical literature of Europe in the eighteenth century China was held up as a model for emulation. It was idealized, no doubt, but what is significant is that Europe in one of its culturally highest periods did see in China an ideal. What we mean when we say that the East is backward is that it lacks machinery and the other accompaniments of applied science—modern medicine, prevention of disease, ease of transportation and communication, cheap printing, and literacy for the masses. In all its economic processes it functions as it always has (except in Japan in the last forty or fifty years) and as Europe and America functioned until some 150 years ago. In this respect only is the East now, or has it ever been, backward. The West made its break with the past between 150 and 200 years ago; the East is only now beginning to make it. The contrast in the life of the two hemispheres lies in a time factor, not in the peculiar essence of the life of either.

The East is making its break, however; or rather, the break has been forced on it. And in that fact lies the whole of the modern history of Eastern Asia; that fact, too, will shape its future. The history of modern Eastern Asia, in short, is the story of the intrusion of Western forces, the way in which those forces have operated, and the effects of their operation.

CHAPTER II

The Traditional Chinese System

It is necessary first of all to say what constitutes the Far East or Eastern Asia. This cannot be done with precision. In Asia as in Europe there are no exact regional demarcations. But one thing must be observed. What we in the West have always meant by the East is an artificial abstraction with no validity except as a convenience in discussion. Otherwise it has no reality. There is no distinct single entity that can be called the East. There are as many differences within the so-called East as there are in Europe. Between Turkey and China, both in Asia, there is at least as great a difference as between Latvia and Italy. Even between India and China there is a greater difference than between Germany and France; Germany and France have in common the heritage of Greece, Rome, Christianity, and the Renaissance. In Europe west of Russia there is a greater cultural unity than there is in Asia. The various Asian countries have only three things in common: their inhabitants are not white; all except Japan are not yet industrialized; and they all resent the domination by Western Powers that has been their lot in modern times, again except Japan. And of these the last fact is the most important, for it has precipitated the dramatic upheavals of the last generation in that part of the world. Beyond these three points of similarity there is nothing fundamental that can be called uniquely Eastern in contrast to other parts of the world and other parts of the human race.

There is, however, within Asia one fairly definite line of demarcation setting off a generally homogeneous region. In this region lie Japan, Korea, and China. They can be grouped not only because of geographical propinquity but because of a common cultural and institutional development. On the margin of this region are French Indo-China, Siam, Burma, and perhaps even the Philippines and Indonesia and Malaya, which also have come under its influence, although that which these areas have in common with China, Korea, and Japan is less than that which separates them. For practical purposes, certainly, and perhaps logically and culturally as well, the Far East or Eastern Asia consists of Japan, Korea, and China. It will be so considered in this book.

This is in turn to say that Eastern Asia is in effect China, with some marginal lands. It was so in ancient times and up to the modern era, it was so in the period between the opening of China by the West in the middle of the nineteenth century and World War II; essentially it is so now. The reasons are simple and obvious. China is, like Russia and the United States, a continent rather than a country. It has the largest population in the world and probably always has had. India alone is comparable. Furthermore, China has one of the oldest cultures in the world; in fact, at the middle of the nineteenth century, it was the oldest still surviving and functioning in the traditional mode and spirit. The Indian culture is as old but has been subjected to more modification as the result of alien conquests. And China has definitely set, in one measure or another, the cultural pattern in all its environs as far as Central Asia.

It has long been a truism that as China goes so goes at least half of Asia. There is both theoretical justification and historical evidence to substantiate the truism. The struggle for control of China has been the stuff of international politics in Eastern Asia for a century. It was China that was the object of Occidental maneuvers and manipulations until World War I, when Japan took precedence over all other Powers, since they were then absorbed in that first great internecine struggle of the West. And even Japan's importance and its potential menace derived, not from its own properties or powers, but from the power it would obtain from control of China. Without China it would remain a second-rate Power; with China it would become an aggregation of might that could imperil the world. Even in Japan's fleeting moment of glory China, not Japan, was the focal point of Eastern Asia. The core of Eastern Asia culturally, politically, economically was, is, and probably will be China.

What, then, was the social system, the culture, the way of life of China, which, it has been said, set the pattern of life for the whole region until they experienced the impact of the West? Before this is discussed, however, a word of caution must be expressed.

Much too much emphasis has in the past been given to "the Soul of the East," "the Spirit of the East," the indefinable, enigmatic, almost mystical something, unfathomable to men of the West. In this there is a good deal of myth, if not of empty rhetoric, spun by Europeans and Americans in the East who made little effort to understand the East or see it from its own point of view and who also enjoyed nourishing a romantic conception of themselves as living in a mysterious, exotic setting, with a little fillip of danger. The result has been the dissemination of a romantic but warped idea of the East, its inhabitants, and their life. The fact is that the East is no more "colorful," no more spiritual than the West. There are aspects of the life and environment of both that are colorful and aspects that are drab. In both the spiritual and material are to be found, and no doubt men are more material than spiritual everywhere.

The differences, such as they are, lie in the institutions in which the human relationship is organized. And in fundamentals the differences between the institutions are no greater than the likenesses.

It has already been said that a time factor accounts for much misapprehension. In the last hundred years or more, contrasts between East and West have become more pronounced and, of course, more easily recognizable. And men of the modern West are inclined to make their judgments on a narrow time span, the more so because on a narrow span of time judgment will be more favorable to themselves. It is true that the application of science in the form of industrialism, in emancipation from disease, in emancipation from labor, in mitigation of the harshness of nature, has created a great gulf between East and West. But for that matter it has cut a great gulf, too, between the West in the twentieth century and the West in the eighteenth century. That we ourselves forget, perhaps because it ministers to our self-esteem to do so. But as we look at ourselves now and at those parts of the world that are still at the mercy of nature, unshielded by what the machine age has given us, the contrast is glaring and appears to be eternal.

Until a recent historical period men were at the mercy of nature everywhere. The majority of human beings were peasants, wresting a meager livelihood from the soil by the sweat of the brow, or artisans making things of use by hand and simple tools. And between the condition of the peasant on the Yangtze or the Ganges and that of the peasant on the Rhine or Danube there was not much difference. They could have understood each other's problems without much difficulty, perhaps with less difficulty than would be experienced by an Iowa corn farmer of today and his sixteenth-century English yeoman ancestor.

The most pronounced distinguishing characteristic of Chinese culture is its age. Nowhere else in our time does the life of a people correspond so closely to its life a thousand years ago. Until recent years, certainly until 1911 and perhaps until 1950, the Chinese lived in all the essentials very much as their forefathers did in the tenth century. Their institutions were much the same; their fundamental beliefs were much the same; so, too, were their ways of earning a livelihood, their recreations, and their habits. A Chinese of the tenth century, resurrected in the nineteenth, would not have had much strain in adjusting himself.

The land has been overrun time and again by rude, more virile tribes from the north, and alien dynasties have occupied the throne, but the institutions have not changed, nor has the way of life. Because Chinese culture was already fixed and highly developed and the conquerors were always of a lower order of civilization, usually very much lower, it was they who conformed to the Chinese way rather than the reverse, and Chinese life went on the normal course though the country was ruled by alien conquerors. The Manchus, sweeping down from the north in the seventeenth century, like earlier invaders, ruled the country for more than 250 years. They compelled Chinese men to wear queues, but, almost literally, the Chinese people were not affected under the scalp. The Chinese spirit was not touched, nor was Chinese thought or even custom and habit. Within fifty years after their advent the Manchu emperors were ruling in accordance with Chinese traditions and within Chinese institutions. The Manchu emperors were sometimes more Chinese than the Chinese themselves. And a decade after 1911, when they were thrown out, it was as if they had never been.

It has been so through Chinese history, and this has given rise to the common belief that the Chinese always absorbed their conquerors. This happened because Chinese culture was deeply rooted and highly developed, while that of the conquerors was simple and rude, the con-querors themselves inferior in everything except fighting capacity. They were physically stronger, but culturally, even technologically, of lower vitality. But it does not follow that the Chinese must always absorb their conquerors. For today, with distance shrunk by invention, they perforce have contact with cultures of equal vitality, higher efficiency, and technological superiority—for example, Europe, Japan, and Russia. And this comes about just when the authentic, ancestral Chinese culture is more depleted, more shaken, more riven by intrusions from without than it has been for some 2000 years. Now its conquerors, if there are to be any, will not have to conform to the Chinese way of life, since it no longer is demonstrably superior.

The continuity of Chinese culture and the conservatism that both caused it and followed from it rested on a firm base of tradition, one of the most fully formed, fixed, and binding the world has known. For almost 2000 years there was universal acceptance of what things were good and what evil, what was true and untrue, what constituted propriety in the relation of man to man, and man to the state and society. The tradition was formed from the teachings of Confucius (born in the sixth century B.C.) and his disciples. These teachings were amended and emended, interpreted and reinterpreted in succeeding centuries according to the temper of the time, as has been every religion or controlling philosophy; yet the core remained intact and it has given the stamp to Chinese life and in some degree to the life of surrounding peoples.

Despite a widely prevalent belief Confucianism was not a religion but a social and political philosophy and a code of ethics. It did not deal with man's relation to the universe or with the afterlife or even with a Supreme Being. By inference Confucius disclaimed any such intention, saying indirectly that since he had not yet mastered the problems of this sphere and this life, he was not qualified to pronounce on other spheres and the life after death. From that day to this the Chinese have been less occupied with cosmology and metaphysics than any other civilized people. It may be the influence of Confucius that has given the Chinese the rationalism and the humanism that characterize them. The rule of reason is considered the supreme way and the well-being of man the highest good. In all that concerns religion and earthly ideologies they have been uniquely tolerant. On the rare occasions when they have persecuted men of other faiths—and they have been rare indeed—the ground was not so much religious or philosophical as political. It was a matter of defense. Conversion to Christianity was neither forbidden nor punished until the European Powers had begun their military conquests on the Asiatic continent. The Chinese could not distinguish between the religious West and the military West: naturally not, since the Church was then inseparable from the State, or so nearly inseparable that the Chinese believed the Church was the spearhead of the State for military penetration in Asia.

The primary preoccupation of Confucius was good government. Given good government, the state would be secure, society stable, and the people happy. Without good government, the foundations of society would be sapped, the people would be rebellious, and anarchy would ensue. Asked once by a disciple what were the essential functions of the government, he replied that it must provide sufficient food, it must have weapons, and it must have the confidence of the people. Asked which of these could be dispensed with first, he answered, first weapons, then food, and last the confidence of the people. "For, from old, death has been the lot of all men, but if the people have no confidence in the government, the state cannot stand."

The highest aim of government was the welfare of the whole people, and this could come about only when the administration of the government was in the hands of the ablest men, when administration was "open to the talents." Since ability, the main qualification, was not confined to any social stratum, the men who governed must be chosen from all classes—noble and peasant alike. And ability was the product of character and knowledge, which in turn were developed only by education. Not even in modern times has there been a more ardent advocate than Confucius of education—education open to all who were qualified to assimilate it, education of both character and intellect. Not all men could or should be educated, of course, but all should have the opportunity if they had the native capacity and the diligence. And if the properly educated carried out the functions of government in accordance with the dictates of their education, they would by precept and example inspire similar conduct in those whom they governed. This, indeed, was the responsibility of those who governed: to inspire and uplift the people.

Therefore there was great emphasis in the teaching of Confucius on propriety—using the word in its broadest sense: the conduct of a man superior in intellect, in character, in sense of responsibility and obligation to duty, in feeling for accepted ceremony and manners, the last by no means least. *Noblesse oblige* comes perhaps closest to what is meant. Confucius used the word *chün-tze* to convey his meaning. This can be translated as "superior man" or "gentleman." The *chün-tze* would undertake the obligation of serving the state, taking as his highest aim the welfare of the people, and in the five primary relationships —prince-subject, father-son, husband-wife, brother-brother, friend-friend—he would know by instinct how to act and by his conduct induce others to follow his example. This, then, was the central problem of earthly life: how to govern men. If they were well governed they would be happy, the state would be secure, and society would flourish. The prime cause, and hence the highest object, was the happiness of men. If this has a modern ring, that may not be only because Confucius was one of the great philosophers and prophets of all time; it may be also because truth is universal and timeless.

This political philosophy was pointed up and underlined almost 200 years later in a postscript by Mencius, the foremost expounder of Confucius and second only to him in the development of Chinese thought. Mencius made explicit what was latent in Confucius by evolving a kind of rationale of revolution. The first charge on a ruler is to give good government. Furthermore, nature was essentially good. The emperor, the Son of Heaven, was accountable to Heaven (which is not to be confused with the Christian idea of Heaven, since it is much more abstract and immaterial and denotes rather the scheme of things) for his trusteeship in his high office. If he misruled, if under him the lot of men was wretched, then not only was he unfaithful to his trust but he ignored, even violated, the principles of nature. By definition, then, he was a usurper and there was not only the right to overthrow him but almost a moral obligation. As the Chinese came to put it in later years, he had forfeited the mandate of Heaven and had to go. Tacitly this has underlain political thought ever since. It was exemplified in the overthrow of Chiang Kai-shek and his Nationalist regime by the Communists in 1949. The Chinese people did not make a deliberate or even willing choice of the Communists. They had only withdrawn their support from the Chiang Kai-shek government and thus demonstrated their rejection of it. By its misrule, its exploitation and spoliation it had violated the moral law. Hence its mandate was forfeited, and against such a usurper there was a right to revolt. What succeeded it is secondary. It, too, will be submitted to the test: does it fulfill the obligations of rule in accordance with the principles of nature?

By a loose and derived construction this can be called the political theory of government by consent of the governed. It operates slowly and painfully, since a regime must transgress egregiously before it falls into a vacuum of disloyalty and then generates opposition strong enough to overthrow it; but the principle is there. This view, innate in Confucian teaching and a cardinal principle of Chinese thought, illustrates the maturity of even early Chinese political philosophy. And it must be borne in mind that, however unavowedly and slowly, it was operating in the centuries when Europe was still in the grip of a politically primitive personal absolutism.

One other tenet of the Confucian philosophy has left a permanent impress on Chinese life: the emphasis on education. Education was the prerequisite of the governing class and the mark of the elect, of the well-bred. Over the centuries the scholars constituted both aristocracy and governing class. No other race has ever similarly exalted education in the scale of human values or put so high a premium on culture. To this day to say of a man that he is an uncultured person, meaning not only that he is ignorant but that he cannot conduct himself with propriety or good manners, is to put on him the most opprobrious stigma, whether for personal association, public office, or business. And among no other people has the sanction of the educated class carried so much weight. This had a striking illustration in the most historic development of recent Chinese history—the accession of Communists to power. It was the withdrawal of support by the men of the universities, both professors and students, and of the liberal professions that started the weakening of the Nationalist government of Chiang

Kai-shek which allowed it to be swept off the continent in less than three years.

The emphasis on education had two concrete manifestations. The first was the examination system by which officials were chosen. The examination system was abandoned in 1911 after the revolution that overthrew the Manchu dynasty and the old order, but for almost 2000 years before that men could be admitted to public office only on passing examinations. The rule was subject to some violation, especially in periods when dynasties were on the decline and there was general instability, but on the whole the rule was honored in the observance. The examinations were held every year, locally, provincially, and nationally, on three scholastic levels, for what were roughly the equivalents of bachelor's, master's, and doctor's degrees. They were based on the classics, the Confucian school in particular, and consisted in exercises in philosophy, ethics, literature (both prose and verse), and art, especially calligraphy, which is considered by the Chinese the highest of the arts. They were conducted with no little ritual and were perhaps the most important lay ceremony of the year. The posting of the results was awaited almost with as much eagerness as the result of elections in modern democracies. Success in the examinations was the passport to an official career, the highest activity to which a Chinese could aspire. And to have a son who passed the examinations with distinction was coveted by a family as the highest honor that could befall it. Furthermore, the examinations were open to men of all classes, a few occupations such as actors and barbers alone being excluded. No doubt the poorer families were under a handicap and in practice did not often have candidates, since they could not afford tutors for their sons; yet a principle of equality was established and it, too, has been reflected in Chinese society. Easy mobility between classes is rare in any fixed society, but in no such society have the lower orders been officially less excluded from the upper ranges of society by virtue of their origin.

Perhaps because the examination system was a passport to political office and was so centered on the classics, education in China became frozen and uninspired, closed to fresh and reinvigorating ideas. Toward the end there was indeed a dead and dreary classicism. To acquire by rote was enough, and to do more than embroider by commentary was not only unnecessary but suspect. There was a penalty on originality, and this may have had something to do with the undoubted fact that for a country with such a heritage, China has for centuries been singularly unproductive of new ideas or new forms of expression, even of significant expression in ideas, in the arts, in science. Intellectually it has been stagnant for centuries, not decadent so much as repetitive.

The second concrete effect of the emphasis on education was the conservation and transmission from generation to generation of the tradition that gave the Chinese people and their culture the homogeneity and continuity that distinguished them from others. Now, it is true that very few Chinese were formally educated. Even in recent years only about one in ten of the population was literate. Yet, precisely because it was only by a command of the body of Confucian thought that one could aspire to a successful career and rise in the social scale, even those who could not partake of it directly sought to absorb it and were influenced by it. And since it comprised not only knowledge but moral values, proprieties, and the concepts of dignified deportment, it set a pattern to which all sought to conform. The peasant could not teach his son to read, but he could give him the moral maxims, the rules by which men conducted themselves in their relations with one another, the canon of what was done and what was not done. And thus was handed down from son to son a body of sanctions that guided the race through life and molded it both in inner being and external act. Dignity, poise, an instinctive feeling for carrying off a situation with assurance and finesse, are traits that cut across class lines and are to be found in every range of the social scale. No Western traveler in China has failed to be struck by something in the bearing of the poorest peasant in a bedraggled hovel or the apprentice in the poorest quarter of a town that marks him as superior to his material estate. Something indefinable marks the race at every social level as possessing that which for lack of a better word can be called culture. And this is the inheritance of Confucianism, carried down through the ages by education.

Something must be interjected here about the Chinese language, since it has been the subject of so much misapprehension. It is commonly said that each district in China has a different language and two Chinese from different parts of the country cannot understand each other. That is a myth. As a matter of fact, three-quarters of the country, measured in area, speaks the same language (two-thirds of the country, measured in population). This is what is known as Mandarin, or the language of the former court. Indeed, this language is spoken by more people than any other in the world, with the possible exception of English since in the last few decades the population of the United States has increased so materially. There are three main variants from Mandarin—Cantonese, spoken by the inhabitants of Kwangtung Province; Fukienese, spoken only by the inhabitants of Fukien; and what is known as the Shanghai dialect, spoken in the environs of that metropolis. All of these are on the coast, and since it was to the coast that the first foreigners came, they concluded that all parts of the country spoke a different language, and the myth that no two Chinese born a hundred miles apart can understand each other has persisted. There are, of course, local dialectical variations, so that some time for adjustment may be necessary, especially in rural areas; but these are no greater within each linguistic group than they are between northern and southern Italy or between Hamburg and, say, a Bavarian village. Between Peking and Kunming, for example, a thousand miles apart, the difference is no greater than between Maine and Alabama.

Whatever may be true of the spoken language, the written language— the one in which the classics are written—is uniform throughout the country. A man in Canton might pronounce each character differently from a man in Peking, but both understand exactly the same thing by that character. Thus there has been no barrier in the repository of Chinese thought to any Chinese who could read, no matter what part of the country he came from. For lasting and important purposes, therefore, there was and is only one Chinese language.

Note should also be taken of two other influences that entered into the making of China, though in a subordinate role. They are Taoism and Buddhism. Taoism is the doctrine of Lao Tze, an enigmatic figure roughly contemporaneous with Confucius. It is a tenuous, mystical doctrine, difficult to fathom and therefore subject to contending interpretations. Its main tenet is one of passivism or quietism. There is a Way—Tao means way—and he who finds the Way and submits to it, letting it carry him rather than following it—will lead a happy life. Philosophically this means a life of inaction, or rather nonaction, but since it is a recondite philosophy, in practice it has operated in Chinese life as a set of superstitions and magical rites that have become progressively more discredited except among the most ignorant. Except in those individuals who have a genuine feeling for the mystical—and their number is small among Chinese, who are above all rationalistic and naturalistic—its impact on Chinese thought has been slight.

Much more is to be said for Buddhism. It made its way into China from India shortly after the beginning of the Christian Era but did not find a secure foothold until a few hundred years later. While Confucianism is worldly, rationalistic, and humanistic, occupied with the things of this planet and this life and concerned with the proper ordering of this world's affairs and man's relation to man, Buddhism almost repudiates this life as a small span in the eternal scheme, a moment in time. In depth and compass it is not to be compared with Taoism; it is one of the great cosmological schemes sprung from man's spirit. But it too is a denial of the world and of life, essentially a renunciation of the instincts as the way to peace and happiness.

Whether there is something in the Chinese genes that found the true essence of Buddhism uncongenial, or whether the earthy humanism of Confucianism had already conditioned Chinese thought, the reality of Buddhism never struck very deep in the Chinese. That which the intellectualism of Confucianism left unsatisfied, however, Buddhism does seem to have supplied. For the generality of the population it has done so in the form of idols and rituals; for others, the small minority, in its pure message. But it does not seem to have put a heavy stamp on China. Like everything else that has entered China from without, it has been transformed by the Chinese to their own taste and temperament. A true Buddhist would find the religion as practiced in China difficult to recognize, and perhaps also repellent. The Chinese philosophers of the early part of the second millennium after Christ, those who gave Confucianism the kind of reinterpretation that all philosophies and revelations have undergone, were, if only unconsciously, influenced by Buddhism and did weave some of its concepts into Confucianism. But its most definite effect has been in the arts, especially in painting. There it is clearly recognizable. That in Chinese painting which is highly wrought in detail, almost over-wrought, is Indian in origin and spirit rather than Chinese. Yet despite these influences the dominant force by far in shaping the spirit and material life of the Chinese people has been Confucianism—its scheme of thought and its moral concepts.

How within these traditions was Chinese life organized, in what institutions, and how did it function? The first thing to be said is that it had all the characteristics of an unindustrialized society; in other words, it was a society without integration or effective centralization. A country predominantly of small trading towns and peasant villages, of officials, merchants, handicraft artisans, and farmers, it had no need to be integrated or centralized. Highly articulated systems, with arterial centers to and from which the lifeblood of the system flows, are to be found only where there is advanced industrialization. This may be platitudinous, but the truth of the platitude was forgotten in the nineteenth and early twentieth centuries, when we of the West were making comparisons between ourselves and China and other Eastern countries and coming to drastic judgments about the East. We forgot that the East was not yet a part of our nineteenth century and could not be judged by our nineteenth-century standards.

China could until very recent years be described as an agglomeration of small cells, contiguous to one another, but loosely connected if at all. If each cell can be taken as a market town with its surrounding villages from which it bought food and to which it sold implements and handicraft products and a few staples such as salt, then it can be said that each cell was for practical purposes self-sufficient. Practically everything it made or grew was consumed within its own borders; just as everything it consumed was produced within its own borders.

A society so organized has advantages as well as disadvantages. On the one hand, it cannot be paralyzed by a stroke at its nerve centers. If, for example, China was beset by war, one province could be besieged or overrun or devastated while an adjoining province was unaffected, whereas in modern Europe or America, if the capital city and a few industrial centers or transportation centers were destroyed, the whole country would be crippled or numbed. One has only to think what would happen in the United States if New York, Chicago, Detroit, and Pittsburgh were wiped out by hydrogen bombs. On the other hand, in a decentralized society each local city exists under the limitation of its own resources. If drought and famine afflict one province, that province is helpless and people starve, although there may be plenty in the adjoining province. There is no easy and therefore economical means of transportation to bring to the stricken area the surplus of the one adjoining. This has been amply illustrated by the numerous periodic famines in China in our own time. Furthermore, the whole power of the country can never be mobilized to meet threat from an external enemy, an internal enemy, natural catastrophe, or even the uneven distribution of natural resources. In general, a country not organized as an industrialized country cannot act or think of itself as a single entity except symbolically or abstractly, that is, as something having a common heritage and common beliefs. It is not and cannot be a nation in the modern sense.

In such a society, too, government in the modern sense of the word is of lesser importance. This was conspicuously true in China. Government was symbolical and titular. There was an emperor, the Son of Heaven, and he was in theory not only absolute but omnipotent. In actuality his power was felt by the people only indirectly, if at all. He reigned, but he did not rule. There was an imperial court, with ministers of a sort (also more symbolical than real), and there was a bureaucracy, highly organized from a base of lower officials in local areas to the apex at the court; but their functions, while nominally unlimited, in actuality touched the people but little except in the matter of taxation. The only official of whom the people were at all aware was the magistrate of a district, roughly the equivalent of a county. He, too, was theoretically absolute in his district, but he, too, in actuality interfered little except by levying and collecting taxes. He was executive, legislature, and judiciary in one. He was responsible for maintaining order, supervised such public works as there were, and adjudicated civil and criminal cases if brought before him, as they seldom were. But he did very little except collect taxes. For the rest he left the people of the district to their own devices. He could do so. The Chinese people could go on, in public and private relations, as it had been fixed by tradition that they should.

Government as we know it was not necessary, yet any society not primitive has to be managed. In China there were two agencies that exercised the functions of management. They were the guild and the family. These were the basic institutions on which the structure of the society rested, and they regulated man's relations with his fellows—again, under the principles bound in an unwritten tradition. In any society these relations fall broadly into two categories. There is first what may be called the public or impersonal relationship, that which has to do mainly with the production and distribution of the necessaries of life and the uses of property—the economic, in short. Second is the private or personal relationship, having to do with the conduct of men in intercourse with one another—safety of person and property, preservation of order, marriage and the parental-filial relation. Under these two headings falls practically everything necessary to order a society.

The economy was regulated by the guild. The Chinese guild was in essentials like the European guild of the Middle Ages. If there was any difference, the role of the Chinese guild was the more powerful, its rule of the economy more nearly absolute. It was an association of all those engaged in the same occupation in a community—merchants, craftsmen, and those in personal services, from bankers to cooks, boatmen, even beggars had their guilds. Scholars and peasants alone were not so organized; but peasants lived in villages, which generally were inhabited by the members of one or two clans and the clan organization served the same purpose as the guild. In each occupation or trade the guild control was close, detailed, and supreme. Here government was not symbolical or titular, but positive, direct, and inescapable.

First of all the guild was both intermediary between the community and district magistrate and, especially in urban centers, buffer between people and official government. When the magistrate had in mind measures affecting the district, especially the town which was the center of the district, he communicated first of all with the representatives of the guilds. This was especially true if the measures involved taxation. If the guild representatives were convinced that the magistrate's proposals were justified, they gave assent, more generally tacitly rather than formally. Then the measures were put into effect and enforced. If, on the other hand, the proposals were so unreasonable as to threaten injustice or hardship, the guilds demurred, there were negotiations, and in extreme cases the guilds could take reprisals. If all attempts at compromise failed, they could declare a boycott, which was tantamount to a general strike. All economic activity ceased, except on the soil, and the life of the community was paralyzed. The confusion that resulted, sometimes culminating in disorder, inevitably came to the attention of the magistrate's superiors and he was penalized, generally being removed. There was a prima facie case against any official in whose jurisdiction there was trouble. He had violated the unwritten bureaucratic law under which any event or condition anywhere that forced higher officials to disturb the even tenor of their ways was charged against the official immediately concerned, and the penalty was visited on him. This the district magistrate knew, and he took pains not to antagonize the guilds beyond their sufferance. He had a margin of time in which he could enjoy immunity, but when that was passed there would be an accounting in which he no less than the community suffered. It was an unofficial and unavowed exercise of the sanction of public opinion, of government by consent—indirect and delayed but in time, and in its own way effective. Against the only official with whom the people had any contact there was a check. It was imposed by the guilds, and this was one of their most important functions.

In the economy itself the most direct intervention consisted in fixing prices—not the maximum price but the minimum. A merchant could charge as much as he could get for a commodity, for under the system of *caveat emptor* it was assumed that if a buyer were so unskillful a bargainer as to pay too much, that was his loss; but no merchant could charge less than the minimum established by the guild. In an overpopulated country with a static economy free competition was a luxury none could risk. If an exceptionally enterprising or efficient merchant or handicraft producer could sell his wares below others' cost of production, buyers would gain and he would get all the trade, but others in the same occupation would go under. The rice bowls of their families would be empty. In China the margin of survival has always been precarious. It was necessary therefore to restrain competition in the interests of all. Price cutting was forbidden below a certain level and the injunction was rigorously enforced. An offender was penalized. If offending often enough, he could be expelled from the guild, thereafter blacklisted and unable to earn a living. Therefore the offense was seldom if ever committed. This, parenthetically, must be borne in mind in trying to understand the Chinese attitude to communism. Whatever they may think of it in other respects, restraints on free enterprise do not shock them. They have never had free enterprise.

The guild fixed standards of weights and measures for its own trade, determined wages, working hours, apprenticeship rules and all other aspects of labor relations, regulated credit conditions, procedures in bankruptcy and trade practices generally. Taken together, the guilds constituted legislature and judiciary for the economic system. They made its laws, enforced them, and adjudicated disputes arising under them. Trade disputes were uniformly settled by the guilds. If the disputants were members of the same guild, an arbitral committee sat on the case, heard both sides, then delivered a judgment from which there was no appeal and no escape. Failure to abide by it would result in expulsion from the guild. That situation never arose; the sanction was universal and unchallenged. If the disputants were members of different guilds, representatives of each met and attempted to negotiate a compromise. If they failed, the dispute was referred to a third guild for arbitration, and its judgment, too, was final. The alternative of resorting to the district magistrate's court was almost never chosen. The guild was in common acceptance the agency for administering justice in economic matters. Government officials were suspect; they did not understand, and, besides, bribes might be more convincing than evidence.

The guilds were democratically controlled, at least in principle. Policies were laid down and administered by officers elected by the whole membership. The officers were more generally the wealthier members, since in the nature of things they were more influential and, furthermore, had more time to give to the affairs of the guilds.

In short, in all the activities by which men make a livelihood, the guilds were the government, exercising the functions of the state and doing so efficiently, honestly, and in accordance with the needs of the community and the will of those concerned. It was, in a word, good government. But we of the modern West, accustomed to thinking of government as a designated political arm, saw only the monarchy and and the mandarinate, and seeing them as ineffectual and venal, concluded either that China had no government or that what it had was worse than none. The error lay in judging by criteria drawn from our own environment and therefore judging falsely. We did not recognize the seat of government, let alone understand its processes.

That which did not fall under the jurisdiction of the guild fell under the jurisdiction of the family. Without understanding the role of the family it is impossible to understand China at all. Among no other people has the family had the same significance and the same power.

It was the foundation of the society. On it the whole structure rested and around it life was organized, not only biologically but economically, socially, morally, spiritually. It gave unity and meaning to life.

Much has been written and said about the difference between East and West. But, deep down, what differentiates the West from, at least, China is the relative importance accorded the individual and the family. Among us life is centered on the individual: the unit of measurement is the individual, values are set according as the individual is affected. The reason cannot be assigned with certainty. Probably it is religious: the Hebraic-Christian tenet that the individual soul is an entity sufficient in itself and to each is awarded salvation or retribution in accordance with his deserts. To this religious tenet must be added the effect of the movement of thought in the Western world in the last 200 years or more: the elevation of the dignity and interest of the individual above the whole. The revolt against this in recent years by the totalitarianism of Left and Right and the resistance to the revolt testify to the strength of that thought as a governing principle for Western man. Whatever be the reason, the individual is the center in the Western scheme of life.

In China the family is the social unit, but the family in the Chinese sense—not only the immediate group of one generation and its off- spring but three or more generations and collateral lines. By custom the family comprised father, mother, their sons, the sons' wives and their children, all living in the same household. A daughter became a member of her husband's family and thereafter lived with it. There was con- siderable variation in this respect, however. Among the poorer classes, especially on the land, the household was likely to consist of father, mother, their children, and perhaps the father's parents. One or two sons at most might also remain under the same roof. So small were the holdings of the poorer peasants that the land could not support the larger family, and the same was true of poorer urban workers. But whether under the same roof or not the family tie was tightly binding. All were members of the same clan, and within a clan even a remote relationship constituted a bond. In fact, the line between family and clan was hard to draw. As has already been said, the large majority of villages were inhabited by a single clan or by two at most. The strength of the bond within the clan varied with the closeness of the relationship, but some bond there was.

The family, whether in the smaller dimension or as clan, was ruled by the male elders, the patriarchs. In a village with only one clan there was a kind of informal council of elders which was actually the govern- ing body of the village, managing communal as well as personal affairs. This was in fact the counterpart of the guild in the town. In a lower degree it was intermediary between the farming community and the official government—the magistracy—just as the guild was for the urban community. If there were two or more clans in a village, elders representing each were in the council. The family was almost a collective. Property was held in common, income was pooled, expenditures were allotted from a single purse.

More important, no member of the family had full power of decision over his own life. By the family, meaning the elders, whether parents in a small household or the informal council of elders in a large one, it was decided who should be educated and who not, what occupation each member should follow, when each should marry and whom. Young men and women had no voice in choosing whom they married and in most cases did not even know their prospective mates until the wedding. Arrangements for marriages were made by the two families through a middleman. There was little in the life of any Chinese, at least until middle age, that was left to his own discretion and decision. All that concerned him was decided by a kind of collective judgment.

This necessarily carried with it the family's collective responsibility for all its members, whether for acts of misconduct, debts or any other form of obligation. The whole family could be held for fulfillment of a contract or other agreement made by any one of its members or for retribution for any deed by any one of them so flagrant as to come to the attention of government officials—violent rebellion, banditry, or the like. Any lesser infraction was dealt with outside the official law, as in the business life of the towns. If members of two different families got into a dispute, whether the result of personal attack or a disagreement over property, representatives of the two families met to arrange a settlement. If this failed, a neutral person was called in to arbitrate. Here, too, there was seldom recourse to a law court. Thus, maintenance of law and order, both civil and criminal, was in the jurisdiction of the family.

The inverse of collective family responsibility was collective obligation to every member. Every person in the family had a claim on the family for support, no matter what the circumstances. He was given food, shelter, and clothing when out of work or unable to work. Even if he had left the household to live or work elsewhere, he could return whenever he wanted to and find a home whether he had means or not—this as a matter of right and not charity. The aged and infirm had to be cared for as a matter of course. Aged parents, indeed, had the position of honor in the household. To Chinese there has also been something shocking in the Occidental custom of letting aged parents live by themselves, acquitting obligations to them by giving them an allowance. Thus the family constituted a system of social insurance, providing security for everybody insofar as the general poverty of the country, in common with all Oriental countries, made security possible for anybody.

One more characteristic of the family system should be pointed out. This is what is called ancestor worship and its corollary, filial piety. The two together made up the first article in the Chinese moral code. "Worship" is probably the wrong word. Man's highest obligation was due the whole line of one's forebears, not only materially but spiritually. As they were conscious of all one did, so one was accountable to them for one's whole bearing throughout life. Disobedience to one's parents or disrespect to one's ancestors was the highest transgression. The myths of the race were formed not around deeds of martial valor but deeds of sacrifice for one's parents. This, too, stems from the Confucian system. It was this principle that Confucius sought most unremittingly to inculcate in his disciples. It is both the foundation of the family system and, in turn, its most definite product. By reason of the principle of ancestor worship there was a premium on numerous progeny in order to be assured of one's due after death. Not to have sons was the highest misfortune that could befall one, but not to have children at all was sin, cardinal sin. If a woman was barren, one was justified in taking a concubine or secondary wife. If a man was sterile, he was obliged to adopt sons.

From the family system and its place in Chinese society certain practical consequences followed. The natural result of ancestor worship was an exaggerated adulation of the past. It has already been pointed out that Confucianism in itself made for extreme conservatism through the rigid classicism of the education founded on it and the very fixity of the tradition. This was accentuated by the enforced respect for old age per se, and the veneration of progenitors because they were dead. It was only natural that there should develop an unquestioning belief that all wisdom reposed in sages long dead, that the past contained everything that bore on present and future, and that a people so believing should turn backward in their whole outlook on life. And this has been one of the pronounced weaknesses of the Chinese people. A handicap has been put on freshness of thought and imagination, and the burden of proof has lain against anything different from what has been. It has made them abnormally resistant to change, and, when forced by circumstances to change, somewhat unstable and unbalanced. Unaccustomed to moving, they have difficulty in finding a sure footing when thrown off balance and are prone to ill-considered and perhaps irresponsible motions intellectually and politically. This has been conspicuously true since the fall of the monarchy in 1911.

Another consequence was the narrow localization of Chinese loyalties. The family or clan was the social unit and also the boundary of loyalty and obligation. There was also—and still is—a sense of provincial kinship, but this is much looser. Thus has arisen the common belief that the Chinese by nature have no feeling of patriotism or national loyalty. This is a great exaggeration. For one thing, what we now call patriotism is of relatively recent origin even in the West. In the intensity that now prevails it dates only from the Napoleonic era, and until the formation of nation-states only a few centuries before it did not exist at all. Furthermore, the Chinese cannot be said to be wholly without national feeling. There is a distinct consciousness of being Chinese, if only culturally. There is a definite sense of uniqueness, of differentiation from others. That sense is at least as pronounced as in any other people in the world. Indeed, there is a deep, unshakable pride in themselves, their history, their culture—their race, it may be said—that is exceeded by no others. But this is more remote and less articulate than conventional contemporary patriotism. The immediate active loyalty and acknowledgment of obligation has been to the clan, the local community and, more distantly, the province. But, as will be seen later, even this has changed since the early years of the twentieth century. There has set in now an active national consciousness not far different in content and expression from the Western prototype.

The family system had, too, the effect of stifling personal initiative. There was no incentive to enterprise or to departure from routine since there was assurance of security anyway. There was no opportunity to exercise personal initiative, since the family decided everything in the life of each individual and therefore there was no opportunity to develop personal initiative. There was no encouragement of expression of the personality in action or thought that led to action; on the contrary, there was almost a penalty attached to it. It was both necessary and easy to drift, and inertia was the rule rather than the exception. Combined with veneration for the past as past, this reinforced the tendency to conformity, to repetitiveness, to sterility in idea and imagination.

In the external life of China the family system had one clearly baleful effect. It made for nepotism, in government especially and to a lesser degree in business. That there was nepotism in government was clear on the most casual observation. A man newly appointed to a magistracy or any other political office in a short time brought into his office numerous relatives, whether of near or remote kinship, regardless of qualification or ability. The same was true in business. Indeed, if one engaged a Number One boy for one's household, it could be taken for granted that very soon the cook, ricksha puller, and gardener would turn out to be his brothers or cousins or relatives by marriage. The explanation is simple. If a man is compelled to support the members of his family anyway, no matter how numerous and how remotely related they may be, it is better to put them on the public payroll, regardless of their fitness. It was tempting, conventional, and almost obligatory. It was a spoils system, based not on party affiliation but on blood kinship. And it made for bad government—inefficient, wasteful, and frequently venal. It has been historically one of the main causes for governmental maladministration, and sometimes has contributed most to political disintegration and collapse.

Such, then, was the scheme of life in China for more than 2000 years, until the newly acquired power of the West intruded in such a way as to undermine its foundations. The attacks China had suffered from the virile tribes of the north, as has already been said, implanted alien rulers on its throne and quartered alien troops in its principal centers but did not tear through or seriously affect the scheme of life. The Chinese people followed their accustomed course, little aware of the rude invaders who had nominal control of their land.

China was a country with an old, sustained, highly advanced culture, most of the time as advanced a culture as existed on the planet. It was a static culture, a static society, a static scheme of life, such as existed almost everywhere in the world until the eighteenth century. The huge majority of its people lived on the land, cultivating the soil with simple implements and muscular labor, as did people all over the world. Things of use were made by hand and simple tools, also as all over the world. The people lived in villages, self-sufficient and self-contained, ordering their lives by ancestral precepts, not codified in law, not written down, but handed down from generation to generation and having more binding force than written law. And under these precepts they were for all practical purposes self-governing in their villages.

They were at the mercy of nature—the universal lot of man until modern times. Yet they were as far advanced in technology as any on earth, far more than most. Their city walls, their irrigation works, their canals were as efficiently built and as efficiently operated as any the world had known until the last 200 years; their imperial palaces had more grandeur and majesty and were more nobly planned and artistically executed in design and treatment than their counterparts elsewhere. Among the poor there was dignity, among the rich there was elegance both in manners and in the appurtenances of living.

The Chinese were not well governed, if the test of good government be the highest welfare of the largest number of men; but by that test no people have been well governed. If country be measured against country, however, over the 2000 years before the nineteenth century no people were better governed. Privilege and perquisite were to the few; so was it elsewhere. But justice was achieved probably more than in other lands. Public order obtained longer than in other lands; or, perhaps more accurately, there was less disorder than in other lands. And China was a great empire, for long periods the greatest in the world. It was—and is —the most populous in the world; there are more Chinese than there are people of any other breed in the world. And by none other has a greater contribution been made to man's ascent from the primitive to the civilized. This, indeed, is what was distinctive to China: the age, consistency, and quality of its culture and the extent to which it was disseminated through the race.

Such is the China that was and is no more. It began to pass at the beginning of the twentieth century and now has passed—to become, no one knows what.

CHAPTER III

The Traditional Japanese System

The life of the Japanese is, at least in theory, organized on the model of China. Yet the divergencies are so wide that Japan must be considered separately. Japan is a country so peculiar in its history and development as to be almost unique. Certainly it is a variant from type among nations in both the Old and New World.

Of the origin of the Japanese little can be said with precision. They are a mixture of continental Asiatic people in the main with some infusion from the islands off the southeast Asian coast, of Malay stock principally. How and when they arrived in the Japanese islands is not known, but arrive they did and slowly drove the aboriginal Ainus northward. By the beginning of the Christian Era they had taken over what are now Japan's main islands. They were by then already organized in the semblance of a state in a peninsula off what is now the main island of Honshu, in what was called Yamato, the poetic name the Japanese still attach to themselves and their land.

Around Japan's early history there has gathered a body of myths, deliberately created and sedulously fostered by the Japanese themselves. The quaint legend that their islands were born of the gods Izanagi and Izanami and their first emperor was the grandson of Amaterasu-no-Mikami, deputed by her to rule the earth, is not far different from the legends held by other older peoples, but nowhere else has it been given such seriousness and credence. This, incidentally, is the basis for the popular belief in the divinity of the emperor. All peoples surround their origins with a certain amount of fanciful embroidering; but nowhere else has there been so complete and so commonly accepted a distortion of history. The grandson of the Sun Goddess, the first emperor, is supposed to have founded the dynasty in 660 B.C., and the 2600th anniversary of its founding was solemnly and officially celebrated in 1940. Yet it is known that all this was fabricated and set in writing in two documents completed in the eighth century A.D., known as the Kojiki, or Record of Ancient Matters and the Nihongi, or Chronicles of Japan. There is in fact little authenticated history of the Japanese people before the Christian Era. The hold of the mythology on their peoples testifies to an extraordinary feat of indoctrination and nothing more.

On such evidence as exists, from Korean and Chinese sources principally, Japan appears to have been fairly primitive until after the beginning of the Christian Era. It consisted of a number of clans, of which the one that subsequently became the imperial family was the highest in rank, already enjoying a kind of titular supremacy, although for practical purposes all of them were independent. In addition to the clans and outside them were associations of those engaged in the same occupation, associations similar to guilds except that membership was hereditary. Hardened caste lines, not wholly broken even in modern times under a modern economic system, had already formed. The people tilled the soil by the most rudimentary implements, drew fish from the sea, and made by hand only the simplest things of use. These things were not only limited in number but apparently crude in quality. It was an already organized but still rude form of life, with few of the embellishments and refinements of culture.

Soon after the first century of our era Chinese influence began to enter by way of Korea, and there set in the process of transformation on the Chinese pattern which was to be made official and complete by the seventh century. Chinese script was introduced; before then Japanese writing had been rudimentary. Through Chinese script access was gained to Chinese literature and therefore to Chinese thought. Through the same medium and by way of pilgrimages came Buddhism, which, definitely established by the sixth century, has had from the beginning greater attraction for the Japanese and exercised correspondingly greater influence than in China. Korean and Chinese immigrants, who arrived in considerable numbers, brought with them a knowledge of the more advanced arts and crafts of the continent and introduced both technical knowledge and skill. Through them, too, came the greater refinements and more cultivated manners of the continent. The remolding of Japan on a Chinese design proceeded at an accelerated rate in the fifth and sixth centuries, and in the seventh century the reforms, introduced on the order of the Imperial Regent Shotoku Taishi, were definitely and consciously based on the Chinese scheme. Confucian thought and Buddhist thought were made official or semiofficial. Chinese books were systematically studied. Chinese arts were cultivated. Chinese institutions were sanctioned and adopted.

The most formative element in Japan, then, is Chinese. Nevertheless, one of the most revealing of its characteristics is its difference from the Chinese. Here a note of warning must be sounded against the hackneyed notion that the Japanese are only imitators. This is definitely not true. They have indeed been borrowers throughout their history. There is little that is original or indigenous in the components of their life. In fundamentals they have been on the whole uncreative. But they have not copied only. They have been singularly skillful in adapting to their native instincts and desires whatever they borrow. And on whatever they have taken they have put a stamp of their own—an unmistakable and distinctive stamp—whether it was taken from China in the seventh century or from the West in the nineteenth.

That it was so in the first instance is unfortunate for themselves and the world. They took the outer forms of China but not the spirit. That which was most distinctively Chinese was strained out. The Chinese, as we have seen, formed their concepts, their institutions, their way of life, and their manners on Confucianism—not always faithful to it, as we have said, but yet holding it as aspiration and trying to guide themselves by it. The humanism, the rationalism, the moderation, the obligation of ruler to rule for the welfare of the ruled, the elevation of the interests of the people above those of the state and the emperor himself, the imperative on those who governed so to conduct themselves as by their example to inculcate proper conduct in those they governed, the application of education as the test of excellence and the indispensable qualification for governing, the disparagement of the warrior and the military arts: to all these Japan, while professing Confucianism, gave lip service and nothing more.

The Chinese, for example, chose their officials by examinations based on history, philosophy, literature, and art, examinations open to all, regardless of family or social status. The Japanese, while theoretically taking over the Confucian theory of government, reserved official place for the sons of those who already held office, men whose qualifications lay wholly in the military sphere, if they had any qualifications at all besides heredity. They took over Confucianism, but even in profession there was no consciousness of the welfare of people or of people at all. Outside the aristocracy and the military caste, if they were not identical, human beings were hewers of wood and drawers of water or, more accurately, growers of rice and other necessities that the aristocracy and their henchmen consumed. Education was an agreeable ornament, giving cachet as one who was superior by virtue of having Chinese learning, but it signified nothing else. Certainly it conferred no higher place in the political and social scheme. The sword was the emblem of the superior man and war was the highest activity, proficiency in its arts conferring the highest honors a man could bear and the highest rewards. The Chinese arts were practiced with high skill and creative force, and the family system was followed with some fidelity. But otherwise, under the Chinese veneer, Japan remained a tribal warrior society, though one with rare aesthetic sensibilities and unusual gifts of aesthetic expression.

There has been something unnatural in Japan's development almost from the start, something that has made the Japanese perhaps a psychologically unhealthy people. The normal advance of any people from the primitive to the civilized is slow, so slow as to be imperceptible at any one time. It is evolution rather than change, and only after the passing of centuries can the difference between one stage and another be detected. It has not been so with the Japanese. They have twice in their history made sudden leaps from one stage to another, leaps spanning centuries—once when they passed in a short period from the near primitive to one of the highest forms then known to man, the Chinese; and again in the nineteenth century, when they passed directly from a medieval, military feudalism to the world of modern science and free inquiry. Both came about not so much in a natural process as by deliberate choice and fiat. The first, as we have seen, was not so sudden and rapid as the second. Chinese influence had been penetrating for some time before the conscious adoption of the whole Chinese system in the seventh century. Nevertheless, there was an irreconcilable difference between China as it then was and Japan as it then was. The two were of such inherently different inner content that they could not possibly be fused or even blended. It is not unnatural, then, that Japan should have taken on a veneer only, that very little of the real China was absorbed, and that under the surface Japan remained much as it had been.

The same was true after the middle of the nineteenth century. The samurai rode in railway trains and automobiles, talked on the telephone, ran shipping lines, and manufactured complicated machine tools with electric power—and flew Zero fighting planes—but though he had divested himself of his two swords, he was still a samurai. He was a man of affairs, as if in London or New York, or a man of modern industry, as if in Birmingham or Chicago, but his innermost responses to life were still those of a medieval clansman, the code of the knight-at-arms his set of values. Or rather—and this was worse—he was both. He inhabited simultaneously two worlds—two worlds on wholly different levels and of irreconcilable spirit and content. His reactions were first of one, then of the other. He was torn within, not wholly of one world or the other, unstable in either, unstable in his whole being.

This may account for the Japanese inclination to extremes, for the violent fluctuations in thought and action, for the proneness to crazes and fads to which the Japanese people have been so conspicuously addicted in recent years: fads in political ideas or music or architecture, now liberal and democratic, now arch-conservative and fascistic, now wildly militaristic and chauvinist—in one year of superman pretensions and the next year of unexampled abasement, as after the surrender in 1945. It may also account for the fact that their extreme politeness and kindliness in one setting may be immediately followed by brutality and violence in another. The historical development of the Japanese has been unnatural, and therefore they may be an unhealthy people.

If Japan had to be characterized in a single phrase (which is always tricky and never wholly accurate), it could be called a military feudalism. This is the note that has remained a constant throughout its history. It was avowedly and formally a military feudalism until its emergence from seclusion after the arrival of Commodore Perry and his American ships, and has actually been one ever since then. The adoption of Chinese forms had had little effect in this respect. After the seventh century Japan remained a loose association of feudal clans under the nominal supremacy of one of them—the emperor's. True, a capital city was erected (a smaller model of the Chinese capital of the T'angs), first at what is now Nara and later at what is now Kyoto. A central government, also copied from the T'ang system, established ministers at the capital and a division of the country into provinces and prefectures, but the men named to office in each were those who already were in control by hereditary right. The central government and its local ramifications were in effect a superstructure made of paper.

In the succeeding centuries, despite the theoretically centralized government, the clans gained in strength rather than lost. This was facilitated by the system of land taxation taken over from the Chinese. Powerful landed families remained immune to taxation and, by extending the same immunity to weaker families and peasants, gradually acquired direct or indirect control over them and their lands. There was thus a coalescence into a few great clans, which steadily aggrandized their military strength by adding to their military retainers, and which sooner or later were bound to vie for supremacy.

At the same time there developed a theory and practice of government, one of the distinguishing features of government in Japan until our own time. With the adoption of the Chinese philosophy of government the imperial family had been elevated to a status befitting its title, but at the same time it began to diminish in actual power, if not in prestige, a condition that prevailed until 1868. It retained a quasi-religious, semi-mystical position, a symbol of the divine origin of the race, but in the mundane affairs of the country it was not only powerless but negligible, at times ignored with what was little short of contempt. Even the proprieties and worldly concerns of the imperial family drifted into the control of a clan known as the Fujiwara, who for practical purposes acted as the imperial family in a status not formally defined but actually unchallengeable. By political manipulation and marital politics they came to control the dynasty. The emperor married a Fujiwara; the Fujiwaras occupied high offices at the court and elsewhere, and most of the time the emperor was persuaded to abdicate at an early age, naming, not always of his own volition, a Fujiwara as regent. Just as succession to the throne went by heredity, so succession to the regency went by heredity. There was thus an imperial family in name and one in actuality. The emperor was a figurehead before the real seat of power.

The practice under which one man carries a title and another holds power has run through all Japanese life, in business not much less than in government. It was not by a process of usurpation that the military came to control government in the decades before World War II. They were acting in the tradition. Ostensibly at the pinnacle were the emperor, a cabinet, and a Diet. They went through the motions of deciding on policy, they spoke officially and participated in governmental ceremony. The Foreign Office deliberated and carried on negotiations with other governments through its ambassadors and ministers; but the army and navy decided and acted sometimes without notifying the Foreign Office in advance. The emperor, cabinet, and Diet were the ornamental and dignified figureheads the system called for; the reality lay in others, as the system also called for. In most recent times these were the leaders of the army and navy.

Outside the system of emperor and regent the powerful military clans continued to develop, however, and since both the instruments and tokens of power were force of arms, they came into collision, the prizes being more land, more knightly retainers, more wealth, more influence. These skirmishes coalesced, too, into major conflicts between the strongest factions, and war became chronic, if not continuous. The two main contenders at first were the Taira and Minamoto clans and their allies. Victory fell to the Minamotos in the twelfth century. They became the actual rulers of Japan, calling themselves by the title of shogun, meaning roughly military commander. The shogunate survived until 1868. The imperial government remained, with the regent usually acting for the emperor, but there was a parallel and real government exercised by the shogun. With the shogun, which was a hereditary office, it was as with the emperor: the shogunate, too, became a titular office, while an unofficial regent usually acted for the shogun. The shogun, too, became a figurehead with the real agent of his power behind him; he, too, was for a long period of the Tojo family. Thus there was an emperor who was a figurehead with someone behind him who exercised his powers, and then a shogun who in the exercise of government superseded both but who was himself a figurehead for someone who exercised his power. There were three figureheads before the reality.

The shogunate was too great a prize, however, to allow stability, and the centuries from the twelfth to the beginning of the seventeenth saw war as the rule rather than the exception. The country was broken up into hostile principalities making alliances and going to war, which usually ended in a fitful and transient peace until new combinations were formed to start new wars. It was one of the bloodiest periods in the history of any people, and it continued until the end of the sixteenth century, when a series of great conquerors began to unify the country by force, a process completed early in the seventeenth century under the great Tokugawa leader Iyeyasu, who brought the whole country under his dominion and established the Tokugawa shogunate, which was to rule peacefully and beyond challenge until 1868.

In the two and a half centuries of Tokugawa rule the Japanese took on the form and identity that we now know. It was the time of maturing. For one thing, there was a long period of unbroken peace, that which Japan had not known for some five hundred years. For another, Japan was locked off from the rest of the world, not only from external ideas and influences but from physical contact as well. All aliens were forbidden to set foot in the country; Japanese were forbidden to leave the country; it was forbidden even to build ships large enough to venture on the high seas far from home ports. Occasional Chinese traders were allowed to enter and the Dutch retained a tiny trading post on an island off the port of Nagasaki, where their merchants were held practically as prisoners. Otherwise Japan was sealed off. The reasons will be dealt with in detail later. Here it is sufficient to say that the main reason was fear of Europe, which had begun its historic expansion into Asia. In Japan's case the immediate occasion was the presence of Catholic missionaries, who were regarded as the spearheads of European states, since the Catholic church was so closely interrelated with European dynastic families. For Japanese, as for other Asians, it was difficult to distinguish between one European and another, between a soldier of the church and a soldier of the king. At any rate, Japan went into seclusion and became wholly inward-dwelling both as a country and a people. The third element in Japan's stratification was the regimentation imposed by the Tokugawas, a regimentation closely akin to the totalitarianism of our own time. In the years before World War II, when Japanese militarism was on the rampage and a tight control was exercised on thought and action, it used to be commonly said that Japan had become converted to fascist doctrines. This was a superficial reading of Japanese history. In point of regimentation—*gleichschaltung*—Japan had little to learn from Nazi fascism, in point of methods of the police state little to learn from Russian communism. It had practiced both with high proficiency in the 250 years of the Tokugawa regime.

The Tokugawas set up the capital of the shogunate at Edo, now Tokyo, leaving the imperial capital at Kyoto, with its figurehead emperor and his court, in ceremonial vacuity. At Tokyo a really centralized government was established, though of a unique kind. Here a bureaucracy really functioned. The Tokugawas and their subsidiary clans themselves ruled directly a large part of the country, probably more than a quarter. Much of the rest was ruled by the daimyo—the feudal lords—of other clans who had been associated with the Tokugawas in their struggle for power. The remainder came under the daimyo of still other clans which had accepted Tokugawa supremacy because they were unable to resist. Each of the clans was left in substantial autonomy under its daimyo for most purposes, with a tight and ingenious system of checks designed to keep him submissive and unable to harbor any idea of revolt or to intrigue with allies for purposes of revolt. There were restrictions on the size of castles lest they serve as fortifications. Movement in and out of districts was under close supervision. Most of all, each of the daimyo had to leave part of his family in Edo as a kind of hostage and he himself was compelled to maintain an elaborate residence in Edo and to spend part of each year there. As an incidental, the expense of these pilgrimages, made in great state and attended by innumerable retainers, both military and civil, kept the daimyo from husbanding enough surplus wealth to be dangerous. In addition the shogunate maintained a network of espionage by which little or nothing could be unknown to it.

Another device was the complete stratification of the society. There were four fixed orders: the soldier, the artisan, the peasant, and the merchant, in that rank. In reality there were two divisions: the daimyo and the samurai—the knightly retainers—in one, and the rest of the populace in the other, which was much lower both in power and prestige. It would be exaggerating to say that there could be no movement from one stratum to another, but those who raised themselves in the social scale were the exceptions that proved the rule. Under the rigid Tokugawa supremacy the warrior was master. He did not work; work was demeaning. And since there was peace and he had no opportunity to fight, there was nothing for him to do, and idleness bred decay. The daimyo lived in luxury (modulated by the shogun's exactions) off the produce of their lands; the samurai were paid in a rice allowance, also provided by the hard-wrung peasantry. The peasants lived in abject poverty, their status being that of units rather than persons. It was then that there flowered the warrior code, the code of the samurai, later known as *Bushido,* the way of the knight. This was almost a rite, its prescriptions and proscriptions laid down with a nicety of precision. Its survival, much more living than vestigial, could be seen in the war of 1941–45: the fight to extinction; death rather than surrender, however hopeless resistance might be; suicide in the last stage of desperation, the kamikaze or suicide pilots, the stoic self-sacrifice that sometimes seemed to those brought up in another spiritual setting more like the submissiveness of cattle in a pen. But in the Tokugawa era this code governed the lord and knight only. They alone had the dignity of bearing the sword.

It was not only conduct that was prescribed, however. All else in life was laid down in detailed rules—style and size of house, furnishing, costume, manners. By a kind of extension this has had the result that all Japanese life has become stylized beyond that of any other people known to history. Even conversation is by formula: greeting, farewell, expression in certain situations almost by stipulated gambit. If ease and spontaneity and naturalness appear to be lacking in the Japanese as others first see them, it is because those qualities were strained out of them in the generations of rigidity under the Tokugawas, if not before. They are, indeed, the most repressed people on earth. And by the same token, when repression is lifted, as by a removal to some other environment—China or Manchuria or the Philippines—or by the incidence of some unprecedented event—as, for example, a war—all restraints break and they are prone to act without any self-control at all, even to go amok. Atrocities are only one symptom.

As Confucianism was the formative influence in China, so feudalism and militarism were the formative influences in Japan, and there is little cause for surprise that it should have followed the course it did in the decades before Pearl Harbor, when it had acquired the power industrialism yields. There would have been more cause for surprise had it done otherwise. In the first place, militarism has been the normal state since the beginning of Japan's existence as a nation—even before its existence as a nation, in fact. For those classes that counted, that made decisions for the race and set its forms of expression, it was the highest activity, the only respectable activity. And since it was associated with the classes at the apex of the Japanese order, the practice of arms and the arts of war naturally denoted the loftiest aspiration for all Japanese. It was not the Tojos and their like that made Japan militaristic; it was Japanese history that made the Tojos and a people that not only followed but admired and emulated the Tojos. Militarism is the natural expression of Japan's history, its institutions, its spirit.

Of those institutions, the one that had most effect was feudalism: inevitably so, since it was the principle on which Japanese life was organized. There were the feudal lords, and there were the samurai, and they alone mattered. The mass of the people were tributaries. This was a starker, more stringent feudalism than Europe had known. Probably because of the influence of Christianity and the Church European feudalism was a little more humanized. Human beings did count more than anywhere in Asia, also because of Christianity and the influence of the Church. The Church could and did act somewhat as buffer for the mass of the people, protecting them against the worst exactions and the too egregious abuses of conscienceless feudal lords. The Church had penalties to impose and latent sanctions served as discipline. European feudalism was thus somewhat softened. There were abuses, no doubt; but the obligation toward the serf implicit in the feudal institution was at least recognized and on the whole honored in the observance more often than in the breach.

In Japan there was no source of discipline from which sanctions could be imposed. The feudal lord was omnipotent, absolute. The peasant existed for his use. If any obligation to the peasant was ever felt and exercised it was by the accident of a kindly individual temperament. The unquestioning loyalty of the Japanese people, their obedience, their docility even, to their rulers have often been wondered at. It would be curious if the Japanese were otherwise. The essence of the feudal relationship is obedience and loyalty. Theoretically there is a compensatory sense of obligation for protection. But fulfillment of the obligation cannot always be exacted if those to whom it is owed have no power, while obedience can be, since those to whom it is due do have power. In Japan the question was never raised. Obedience was in the natural order. And this lasted long after the institution of feudalism was formally abolished after the Restoration in 1868. Whatever the nominal form of government and social organization after the abolition of feudalism, the instincts rooted in centuries past were not and could not be quickly exorcised. Whatever the Japanese people might have thought of the insensate adventurings of the Tojos, however much they might have been aware that Japan was reaching beyond its capabilities and inviting disaster, it never occurred to them to challenge. They might inwardly question, but they obeyed, and they obeyed silently. So it always had been; so it still was. Constitutions and parliaments were things of paper. Recognition of the master's inherent right to mastery was the reality, the essence of nature's plan as they knew it.

What has been discussed so far is the society of China and Japan before the advent of the West, but in Japan's case it may reflect much
light on the pre-Westernized Japan to anticipate in summary form and
give something of the first impact of the West and its results internally.
As has already been said, Westernization touched fundamentals very
little; nor could it have. The manner of its adoption was characteristic.
As in the seventh century, it was by fiat handed down from above, and
though it made the sharpest break with the past ever made by a people,
it was accepted with only scattered traces of resistance. It had been
decreed that the Japanese people change their way of life, so they
changed it. What followed thereon was a prodigious material accomplishment. The social face of Japan was made over. Men were dispatched
throughout the West to learn the ways of the new world. This will be discussed in greater detail later. Here it is necessary to say only that railways were laid, factories were erected, steamships were built and sent
plying all the seas, a school system was established providing universal
education, a modern army was organized based on conscription, a
modern navy was built, a new administrative bureaucracy was set up,
feudalism was abolished, and real power was given to the emperor and
a central government. Twenty-one years after the Imperial Restoration
a constitution was drafted (and handed down by the emperor as a grant)
providing for a cabinet and a parliament and all other accompaniments
of modern constitutional government.

Feudalism was abolished, but the same groups that wielded power
before continued to wield it, and their authority was unchallenged. The
daimyo turned over their landed domains to the emperor and received
in return titles of nobility, appointment as civil officials in the areas
they had held as fiefs, and salaries equivalent to one-tenth their former
income. Later the salaries were commuted by payment of a lump sum
in government bonds, calculated at a rate excessively liberal for a poor
country. The samurai lost their privileged status and their occupation
and were similarly pensioned, their pensions also being commuted later
in a lump sum but on much less generous terms. Posts in the new government went to the feudal lords and, more particularly, to a group of more
energetic younger samurai, those who had led in the movement for the
overthrow of the shogunate and the restoration of the emperor.

This was a truly extraordinary group of able and farsighted men, one
of the ablest anywhere in the nineteenth century. They estimated their
world with acumen and insight. They recognized that it was hopeless
to withstand the Western world. They saw what was happening elsewhere in Asia, especially in China, and they realized the West was irresistible on the terms then prevailing. It was necessary first of all to

strengthen Japan. But in contrast with all other Eastern peoples, they perceived that this required not only modern weapons but the kind of economic system, the social system even, that made possible the production of a military establishment with such weapons—in a word, industrialization. They resolved upon industrialization, proceeded to execute it and did so with conspicuous success in the course of the next fifty years.

They kept power in their own hands, however. It was they who decided, they who carried out decisions. Also it was they who enjoyed the material advantages that accrued therefrom. In order to accelerate industrialization, factories which were started received government subsidies, but in the nature of things those who started factories were those who alone had capital, and they were of the former upper classes—the feudal nobles, some of the more important and better-connected samurai, and some families which already before the Restoration had passed out of the class of lesser nobles and samurai into the commerce which had been developing in preceding generations. Thus it was the favored few who enjoyed special privileges in the process of modernization, who got in on the ground floor in modern big business. They were the few who always had been favored. The old oligarchy had become the new oligarchy, with a change in names, faces, titles, and methods.

Militarism was, if anything, reinforced. Conscription was adopted early in the 1870's and an army was organized on the Prussian model. This had a deep and lasting result. In the preceding centuries, as has been pointed out, the right to bear arms was restricted to the daimyo and samurai. To this dignity all Japanese of any class were now elevated. At first there were protests at being taken from their tools and their ploughs, but after a period of skillful indoctrination in the services it dawned that all were now on the same level. The practice of arms, the highest activity, was now open to all. While Europeans in the nineteenth-century period of the *levées en masse* looked on their compulsory term in the army as a disagreeable task that could not be escaped, something to be taken fatalistically like taxes and the weather, to the Japanese people as a whole it was a step upward in the human scale, a direction to which they were not accustomed and therefore all the more satisfying.

It was scarcely surprising that after Japan became a World Power and set off on conquests the army should have enjoyed the esteem it did, the esteem and loyalty and willing compliance. Ingrained in the past, militarism struck even deeper in the decades of modernism and constitutionalism. Militarism and feudalism, fused into one another as they were, were so large a part of Japan, so nearly the whole of Japan, that they survived and had to survive even when Japan officially moved into a new form of life.

Something should be said, too, about two other strains that have entered into the making of Japan. One is emperor-worship, the other is Shinto. Of these two the first is, despite common belief, the less genuine. It is in fact somewhat meretricious. Throughout nearly all of Japan's history, it will have been observed, the emperor has been a shadowy, negligible figure, never commanding respect and sometimes treated with contempt. In any analysis of the major elements in the composition of the Japanese scheme the emperor deserves a minor place. Only in recent times has he counted in the Japanese scheme. In 1868 he was for the first time given imperial prerogatives and imperial status. But that was not all. The young men behind the Restoration, it must be emphasized again, were resourceful and intelligent. They knew that a people, any people, must have a central point of loyalty. With the abolition of feudalism and the disestablishment of the daimyo, that point had disappeared in Japan. Also it had never been a truly centralized point, one denoting all Japan and therefore suited to a genuinely centralized country, as Japan had to be if it was to survive against the dynamic, thrusting West. A new point of loyalty had to be created, since vacuum was dangerous. The imperial myth was fabricated. The materials, it is true, were old and genuine. They were part of the legend of the divine creation and the Sun Goddess. But the finished product was synthetic.

The loyalty once owed and given to feudal nobles, each in his own area and confined to him, was gathered, concentrated, and transferred to the emperor as the symbol of the re-created Japan. Systematically and with high skill the myth was instilled into the Japanese people: the emperor was divine, sacred, immanent, and untouchable—and always had been, though any who knew Japanese history knew that only a few decades before he had been a person immured in his Kyoto castle to whom no attention had to be paid. It was a synthetic creation, but it testifies more to the skill of Japan's Restoration leaders and the docility of the Japanese people than to the intrinsic content of the emperor cult. It served its purpose, however. It acted as amalgam that bound together a people theretofore disparate, sectional, and given to fratricidal struggles. It gave Japan, for the first time in its history, a real sense of unity. And it represents one of the most remarkable feats of indoctrination, of "public relations," in modern times. In the latter part of the nineteenth century Japan's leaders did not know and had never heard of advertising techniques; they did not need them. They brought about in Japan in a little more than a generation an other-worldly veneration usually reserved for entities more than human. But once again, its importance lies in what it reveals of Japan's past, of the psychological make-up of the Japanese people, of the institutions that had predisposed them to credulity and submissive acceptance.

About Shinto there has been a great deal of misapprehension outside Japan. It is of authentic origin and predates Japan's written history, although refurbished in the nineteenth century to serve the same purpose as the emperor cult. Shinto—the Way of the Gods—is essentially a form of animism, or rather, of nature worship, deifying both natural phenomena and things of habitual use. The sun, the moon, mountains, streams, flowers, and household objects were endowed with being and given their meed of respect. If in origin it was simple, even primitive, it also had beauty. But it never had the hold of revealed religion, never appealed to the Japanese people as Buddhism did, and it acquired the semblance of religion only in the nineteenth century, a feat of indoctrination of the same order as the making of the emperor cult. Then something known as State Shinto was fabricated, a compound of which all the elements may have been authentic but the whole was meretricious. Both animism and ancestor worship after the Chinese pattern were included and thereto was added a dressing up of the old myth of the divine origin of the Japanese islands and the imperial family, the sanctity of the Japanese state and the Japanese "polity," and a fevered hyperpatriotism. In origin Shinto was genuine; in its manifestation in the decades before World War II it was spurious. But though spurious, it came to exercise a tremendous force in those decades. It gave moral driving power, spiritual content even, to Japan's fling for greatness before it came to disaster on the U.S.S. "Missouri" on September 2, 1945.

One more conditioning characteristic of Japan must be taken into account. This is its natural poverty. Few nations in the world have had such a niggardly natural endowment. The Japanese islands, less than 150,000 square miles in area, are smaller than California. More important, they are topographically disfavored, being mountainous in large part, so that only about a sixth of the area is arable. Further, it has a most meager supply of the natural resources that yield wealth, either in the preindustrial or in the industrial era, but most of all in the latter. Throughout Japanese history the Japanese people have had to toil unremittingly for the bare necessities of livelihood, making up for nature's niggardliness by ingenuity, backbreaking labor, and self-denial. The lack of raw materials played a decisive part in the period following Japan's industrialization and will be dealt with when that period is discussed; but even more it put a limit on the population which could survive in the islands. In the years before Westernization population never exceeded 30,000,000 and was kept to that figure by drastic methods of birth control or postbirth control—the surplus was removed by abortion or infanticide when not taken care of by wars, plagues, and natural disasters in accordance with the Malthusian law. But the most direct and significant effect of this natural condition made itself felt only after Japan entered the modern industrial scheme, in which natural resources are indispensable to survival, though always it has been, in one degree or another, a governing factor in the life of the Japanese people.

Such was Japan historically: Eastern and yet not of the East; of Chinese cultural heritage and yet not Chinese in spirit or action; a people unique—not comparable with any other in growth or development; insular not only with respect to continents but with respect to the planet, and yet destined to play a decisive part in the affairs of the planet in the modern age.

CHAPTER IV

The West Reaches Out

The phrase "advent of the West" has been used thus far with the connotation of something that came about in the nineteenth century. For international political purposes and for purposes of political, social, and cultural change in the East this is true. Not until the nineteenth century was the West able to register its power and influence in Eastern Asia to such an extent as to generate explosive international rivalries in the West or to affect the life of Eastern Asia under the surface. But this is not to say that there had not been some contact between East and West before. There had been for centuries—definitely and increasingly in the last three hundred years before the nineteenth century and sporadically since the beginning of the Christian Era.

Eastern Asia and Europe were first joined, literally, by a silken thread. It used to be written with poetic flourish that the togas of the Caesars were woven with silk spun from worms that fed on the mulberry trees of China. This is true as well as poetic. Both by caravan, on the land route from the China coast across Central Asia to Eastern Europe —called the Silk Road to this day—and by ship, along the coast of Asia through the South China Sea, Indian Ocean, Persian Gulf, Red Sea, and Mediterranean, Chinese silk was borne to Rome. The lure of the luxuries and riches of the East, it will be seen, began to exercise its pull early in European history. Its attraction has grown with the centuries.

There was trade, too, with the Arabs very early, a colony of Arab traders having settled in Canton in the fourth century. Also the first Christians began to arrive as early as the seventh century, when the Nestorians made their way from Persia. They were hospitably received and for at least two hundred years well treated. Likewise small companies of Jews arrived, though exactly when is not certain. They, too, were well treated and have been entirely absorbed by the Chinese, now being indistinguishable from Chinese although until after the beginning of the present century they were conscious of themselves as a different people and the last synagogue was still standing in Kaifeng, in Central China. It is interesting to observe, in parenthesis, that the Chinese are the only people to have fully absorbed the Jews. They are also the only people to have treated them without discrimination. There may or may not be a cause and effect relation here. It may be that the physical and cultural vitality of the Chinese gives them greater assimilative power than other peoples or it may be that the Jews were willing to assimilate when well treated. In any case the fact is worth noting.

Beyond this, however, there was little intercourse between East and West until the Middle Ages. About the thirteenth century Europe began to take a more active interest in the East, perhaps as a by-product of the Crusades. A number of travelers, emissaries either of the Church or of European monarchies, attempted the perilous journey across Asia, not all of them getting as far as China. But they learned enough about the mighty Asian empire to whet Europe's interest. So in the same way did another historic travel exploit, though one of another order and not exactly representing East-West intercourse. This was the prodigious sweep of the Mongol hordes across the Eurasian continent from the shores of the Pacific to the Hungarian plains, first under Genghis Khan and then under his grandson Kublai Khan, who brought China under his sway in the thirteenth century and established the Yuan dynasty, destined to last a hundred years. By making a kind of bridge between East and West, though a bridge of corpses and ruins, the Mongols added to Europe's awareness of the East, especially China.

In the thirteenth century also came the most famous visitation of all, that which was really to open Europe's eyes to China and help to generate the eagerness and curiosity that produced the great explorers who opened the unknown world. This was the legendary journey of Marco Polo, who came to China, traveled all over the country, and became an official under Kublai Khan. After a second journey to China he went back to Europe and wrote his famous book reporting on his experiences —probably the most remarkable travel book in history. Marco Polo made an immeasurable and lasting impression on the Western world in his time and after. His book is a glowing account of wonders to behold. He came, it must be remembered, from Venice when Venice was at its height and exemplified what was best in European culture at the time. And coming from Venice he was astounded by the marvels that he found in China—cities of unparalleled magnificence, impressive public works, law and order, efficient government, lavish wealth, luxury, an atmosphere of culture and refinement, elegance in houses and private grounds, in costume and manners. He might well have been. Compared with Hangchow, Soochow, and Canton, the cities of Europe were provincial, if not backward. The Europeans were somewhat incredulous but also dazzled and, still more, tempted.

It is in the light of this attitude of Europe that one must try to understand China's state of mind and actions later. The comparison was one of which the Chinese, too, became conscious, and if later they were to manifest airs of superiority to the West, manifest them openly and even with contempt, it was not only out of conceit and arrogance. There was arrogance no doubt, but it also had some basis. When East and West first came together, the East really was superior in all the things by which excellence is measured—culture, wealth, refinement, efficiency, public order, good government, technological grasp. Unfortunately the Chinese assumed that the world was static and immutable and were so indurated in certitude and complacency that 500 years later they could not perceive that the balance had shifted, and they still bore themselves to the white man as if Europe were still the Europe of the thirteenth century.

It was at the end of the fifteenth century, when the sea passage to the East had been found, that the great voyages began and with them the real impingement of one half of the world on the other and the extension of the horizon of history. The Portuguese came first, Vasco de Gama getting to Calicut in India in 1498. Portuguese traders followed. They got to Malacca in 1511 and then worked eastward to Siam, the East Indies, and the China coast, arriving in Canton in 1517. Still others followed, and the manner in which they comported themselves everywhere on the Asiatic coast, the Portuguese especially and to a lesser degree the Spanish and Dutch who came after them, made the opening of relations between East and West inauspicious. Therein may be found in some part the reason for the hostility of both Chinese and Japanese to the white man for centuries afterward and the desire to keep him at bay.

The traders came to trade and remained to plunder. They robbed, looted, terrorized. They conducted themselves as unrestrained marauders, and the native peoples in and near ports where they landed were helpless. As a matter of fact the first Portuguese traders who came to Canton were welcomed by Chinese merchants and encouraged to return. A Portuguese envoy designated to the Court at Peking, who came on the same ship, was permitted to proceed to the capital. But a second ship brought a crew that acted on the pattern that was to be followed for long. Their conduct outraged the Chinese, who retaliated by imprisoning the envoy, driving the ship out of the port, and forbidding Portuguese ships to enter thereafter. The Portuguese did succeed, however, in establishing in 1557 a permanent outpost in Macao, on an island off the south coast, where they still are.

The lasting effect of the misconduct of the first Europeans in Asia should not be underestimated. It shocked not only the peoples of Asia. There is impressive testimony in a much quoted statement by St. Francis Xavier, who arrived in 1542 in Goa, the island off the South India coast, where the Portuguese had already established a colony. He wrote:

> There is a power here, which I may call irresistible, to thrust men head-long into the abyss, where besides the seduction of gain and the easy opportunity of plunder their appetites for greed will be sharpened by having tasted it, and there will be a whole torrent of low examples and evil customs to overwhelm and sweep them away. Robbery is so public and so common that it hurts no one's character and is hardly a fault. . . . Everywhere and at all times it is rapine, hoarding and robbery. The devices by which men plunder, the various pretexts under which it is done, who can count? I never cease wondering at the number of new inflections which, in addition to all the usual forms, have been added in this lingo of avarice to the conjugation of that ill-omened verb, "to rob."

Nor did the native peoples cease to wonder—or to remember. It has already been remarked that it was not only out of arrogance that the Chinese were condescending to the white man, since the white man himself was at one time awed by the splendor of Chinese civilization. Nor was it out of arrogance that they looked on the white man as a barbarian, since the first white men with whom they had any experience did act barbarously. The generalization may have been unfortunate and unfair. The first white men they saw were unrepresentative, no doubt. But that they had no way of knowing. They could only judge by their own observation, and what they observed did warrant the judgment they formed. It gave good ground for the mixed contempt, resentment, and fear that they did not lose for centuries—if they can be said to have lost them yet.

The traders were followed by the missionaries, who, though in a different way, also were guilty of what would be, at least in the eyes of cultivated men in the East, offensive. The first missionaries, too, were Portuguese. They settled at Goa and soon had going a kind of religious terrorism. With the sponsorship of both the Church and the Portuguese Throne, Dominicans, Franciscans, and later Jesuits set out to Christianize the East. They proceeded to do so by force. They destroyed Hindu temples and persecuted those who would not follow their adjuration. Among the other accompaniments of their religious activities was the introduction of the Inquisition, with all its excesses. A kind of ecclesiastical despotism was established, with the corruption inseparable from despotism. Many of the missionaries themselves were outraged by some of the current practices, as, for example, St. Francis Xavier, and the atmosphere was in certain respects like that of Europe, where the revulsion ultimately took form in the Reformation. In the eyes of the East, however, the religious connotations were not recognized. Those who did not know the European environment could detect only the excesses of absolutism. With such excesses they were familiar enough in their own environment, but, in the first place, they did not associate them with the worship of God, and besides, these were committed by uninvited strangers. In his religion, too, the white man did not put the best face on himself and what he stood for.

In the next 150 years there was a steadily increasing European movement to the East. The Spaniards came to China but stayed permanently in the Philippines, with which China had considerable trade, and settled in Manila in 1571. A little later the Dutch came to the East Indies, where they held full sovereignty until 1949. They tried to start trade with China, but the Chinese refused, in part owing to Portuguese instigation. The rivalry between European states in the East is as old as Europe's relations with the East. The Dutch set up a trading post in the Pescadores and later in Formosa, and from Formosa they made periodic forays against Portuguese Macao. The first British ship did not arrive in China until early in the eighteenth century, when the East India Company sent out one of its vessels. The French came still later. But the Chinese remained adamant, and while there was some sporadic exchange with outlying foreign trading posts, they steadfastly refused to regularize trade with the outside world.

The West did penetrate through another channel, however. In the middle of the sixteenth century the missionaries won a foothold in both China and Japan. The Jesuits were first in the field and most successful. They were followed later by Dominicans, Franciscans, and Augustinians. In 1549 St. Francis Xavier landed in Japan. Both he and the Portuguese traders who preceded him received a cordial welcome. Xavier stayed only two years and then died on his way to China, but he laid the foundation in Japan for the most successful achievement of proselyting in the history of Christian missions. In thirty years Japanese converts to Christianity numbered approximately 150,000, principally in western Japan. Not only were the missionaries not obstructed; they were given encouragement and assistance by some of the leading daimyo.

In China there was success of a different order. Converts were few, but the influence exercised was tremendous. The Jesuits discerned quickly the high esteem in which learning was held in China and sent a group of men distinguished for their scholarship, the famous Matteo

Ricci, an Italian, being the first. He arrived in Peking in 1601 and re- mained until his death in 1610. He and his successors introduced to the scholarly and official world in the capital the scientific knowledge of the Western world—mathematics, astronomy, geography, mechanics and mechanical devices. At the same time, and discreetly, they expounded Christian doctrine and made some converts. Parenthetically, they also did much to acquaint Europe with the high state of Chinese civilization and were in large part responsible for the vogue of Chinoiserie, both in objects and ideas, that later swept Western Europe (in the eighteenth century).

The essential point is that in both China and Japan, and more par- ticularly in China, there was tolerance toward the alien faith. Both were willing to listen to Christian doctrine and weigh it on its merits. If this turned to rejection and suppression, it was not on doctrinal grounds or out of bigotry. It came about because of rivalries between factions within the Church and the overweening pretensions of the Catholic orders. To these were added the manifestations of a tendency on the part of both the Church and the European states to intervene in intra-Church dis- putes within China. The fratricidal sectarianism to which Christianity has traditionally been prone was conspicuous in the East as well as in Europe. This is something that the non-Christian peoples of the East have never been able to understand and that has weakened Christianity in their esteem.

The Jesuits were the first to come to China and Japan, as has been said, and they had the field to themselves for decades. After representa- tives of the other orders came there soon arose theological disputes turn- ing mainly on the interpretation of Christian doctrine as applied within China: the proper Chinese translation of the word God; whether Chi- nese converts should be permitted to do reverence to the tablets of their ancestors and to the tablets in the temples to Confucius; and other more abstruse theological refinements. The Jesuits were for a freer construc- tion, one which compromised with certain Chinese traditions and cus- toms; the others were for forbidding all such practices to converts, thus compelling them to cut themselves off not only from their former re- ligious beliefs but from their customs. The controversy sharpened with the passing of the years, the dispute being fought with all the ferocity of theological controversy in the Middle Ages. The Vatican was called upon to rule, and it ruled in favor of strict construction. The Emperor of China, then the Manchu K'ang Hsi, one of the most enlightened rulers of modern times, also was called upon to rule, and he ruled, naturally, in favor of the free constructionists and accommodation to Chinese cus- toms. The warning of the appeal to the pope was not lost on the Chinese.

Combined with all the other indications in Asia that Europe had purposes other than religious proselyting, that its advance was steady and fraught with peril to the countries of Asia, and that the Church was as much political as spiritual, the Chinese decided it was better to be circumspect, as did the Japanese. They resolved early in the eighteenth century on the expulsion of all the missionaries, a few being permitted to remain because of their scientific attainments. But again, this was not religious persecution. It was a precautionary measure of self-defense.

In Japan the same happened. There were even closer connections between the missionaries in Japan and European authorities, both secular and clerical, than there were in China, and the missionaries were much more presumptuous, in places seeking to assume quasi-political privileges. Spanish priests had come to Japan from the Philippines, and the friction between them and the other priests was even more venomous than in China. The Japanese finally came to suspect the missionaries of trying to override local political authority, and the suspicions may have had some ground. Tokugawa Iyeyasu, who had assumed the shogunate in 1600, was in no mood to risk the resumption of internal dissensions arising from insubordination to authority, and the moderate checks already imposed on the activities of the missionaries were strengthened and then changed to outright expulsion. At first foreign priests were driven out, but Christians were permitted to continue worshipping according to their faith. Later the practice of Christianity was forbidden altogether, and a relentless persecution set in, thousands of Japanese Christians being tortured and massacred. But here, too, political fear and not religious bigotry was the motive. Indeed, so great was the fear that the Tokugawas thought it would be safest if all the rest of the world were shut out, regardless of activity or interest in Japan, and Japan went into its historic seclusion.

Aside from religious channels, both China and Japan held themselves aloof from the West through the sixteenth and seventeenth centuries. For a few years the Dutch kept their trading post in Formosa, but were then driven out. Their trading post on the island of Deshima, near Nagasaki, they were allowed to retain, however, although their movements were as restricted as if they had been prisoners. Not until the end of the seventeenth century did the Chinese establish formal relations with an Occidental Power, and that was Russia, which then as now was Asiatic as well as European, both ethnically and culturally. In 1689 the Treaty of Nerchinsk was concluded between China and Russia, fixing the boundary between Manchuria and Siberia. The Manchu dynasty was then on the throne in Peking, and China was therefore even more than usually concerned with its northern frontiers.

The Russians were already beginning their remorseless thrust to the East, and the Chinese thought it prudent to regularize the position. The Russians have always down to our own day been more adept at dealing with the Orient than purely Western countries have been, and they soon succeeded in winning consent to the setting up of trading posts along the frontier. In 1727 they obtained an agreement allowing them to send a trading mission to Peking itself every three years, to establish a Russian Church in Peking, and to keep a limited number of missionaries there.

The West was finding itself, however, and was not to be denied much longer. Pressure on China was growing by the end of the seventeenth century and became insistent in the eighteenth. England and France were already in India and were eager to push farther, England especially. More ships were setting out for China, not only English and French but from other European countries and last of all from America. The "Empress of China" sailed from New York for Canton in 1784, inaugurating American commerce in East Asia, which is therefore, it will be noted, almost as old as the Union. The desire of all was to set up a regular trade and formal political relations with China, but China still stubbornly refused.

The English were coming to their ascendancy on the seas and they took the lead in the effort to open China to foreign ships and wares. They got added impetus from the growing wealth and power of the East India Company in India. Through most of the eighteenth century there was a kind of compromise, a *modus vivendi,* an arrangement satisfactory to neither party but accepted as the best that could be got at the time. For a long time, it will be remembered, there had been desultory trade with China, or rather with the fringes of China. Partly because Canton was the natural port of entry to China from the West and partly because from the days of the Roman and Arab trade it was the point of China most nearly open to the outer world, it became the place of exchange for such trade as there was. But in order to keep the trade and the foreigners engaged in it under strict control the Chinese government created a monopoly through a kind of franchise to certain Cantonese merchants for the conduct of the trade. They and only they—at first twelve of them then later thirteen—could deal with the foreigners of whatever nationality. They were a kind of foreign trade guild organized to serve as intermediary between the Chinese Empire and the Western world. The Co-hong merchants, as they were called, bought everything the Western ships brought and sold everything the Western traders wanted to take back with them or needed for their own use while in the port between voyages. Foreign ships put in at

Whampoa, an anchorage twelve miles below Canton, and sent their cargoes up to the city to warehouses known as the factories, where the Co-hong merchants took delivery. The foreign crews and merchants themselves could not live in the city proper. They stayed in a small secluded area outside the city walls while their business was being transacted, their movements limited, dependent even for their food on what the Chinese delegated by the Co-hong merchants provided for them. When not transacting business they went to Macao to stay.

As the trade progressed, permanent foreign agents were assigned to it, but they could not stay even in the restricted area all the time. They were compelled to retire for part of every year to Macao. There they had to keep their families all the time, since only the foreign representative himself was permitted to come to what was in effect a foreign traders' detention camp. At the same time the foreign trader was being bilked by exaction of all kinds—tariff duties, other taxes, imposts of all kinds. He was completely in the hands of the Co-hong merchants, but they in turn were responsible to the Chinese government for the good conduct of the foreigners and had to transmit to Peking a certain amount of revenue on the trade. Some of the Co-hong proprietors were reasonable men who had to make the best of a situation they themselves recognized as anomalous, but since they had the responsibility and the foreign merchants were completely at their mercy, the majority made the most of their powerful position and the foreigners had to swallow both being mulcted and being humiliated.

This was the situation for almost a hundred years, until well into the nineteenth century. But this was the time when England was rising to world supremacy, when all Western Europe was acquiring unprecedented might, and when the industrial revolution was getting its impetus. The situation was therefore untenable for very long. Sooner or later it had to break and by one means or another a new situation instituted and a new relation established. And given the conditions on each side—China and Europe—given the psychology of both, it could not have been expected that the situation could be resolved peaceably, and it was not. Almost a generation was required for the crisis to develop, but events marched steadily and irresistibly toward it, since the objects, desires, and positions of the two parties were irreconcilable. This is so important as setting the spirit and direction of subsequent relations between China and the West that it should be discussed in some detail.

CHAPTER V

The West Strikes

The fundamental issue was whether China could continue to shut itself off from the world. The Co-hong system, it is true, had made an aperture in its walls through which the foreigner might peep and exchange his wares for Chinese wares, but for practical purposes he was barred. This was galling to pride and injurious to economic interest, a dangerous combination. Because of its command of the sea and its position in world trade and world politics after the Napoleonic wars, England chafed most. It began to press seriously for regularization of relations on the basis regarded as normal among Western states. It wanted diplomatic representation at the Court of Peking, with an exchange of accredited ministers, so that questions at issue between the two countries could be negotiated between government and government. It wanted to trade at Chinese ports with whoever wanted to buy and sell and to do so without the vexatious, humiliating, and costly exactions of the Co-hong system. The official representatives who had been sent to Canton, at first representing the East India Company, had received no recognition from the Chinese and could deal only with the Co-hong merchants. This was not enough.

The first formal diplomatic mission sent from London arrived in China in 1793, headed by Lord Macartney, who had had long experience in India and therefore presumably knew the East. His object was to conclude a treaty providing for exchange of diplomatic representatives, the opening of certain ports to British trade, and a fixed schedule of tariff duties and other imposts to be applied uniformly at all ports. Macartney and his mission proceeded to Peking in great state. He was received with elaborate ceremonial and lavish hospitality, but he achieved nothing. Only one concession was offered him. He was not compelled to make the kotow to the emperor. The kotow subsequently became a point of honor to both sides, the British rigidly refusing on the ground that it was insulting to a representative of the British Crown and the Chinese as rigidly insisting on the ground that it was the emperor's due from all men, whether foreign or Chinese, and regardless of rank. The Chinese attitude toward the British in general and the Macartney mission in particular was revealed when the boats on which Macartney and his suite were brought on the last stage of the journey to Peking bore banners reading "Ambassador bearing tribute from the country of England." Macartney went home defeated. A second attempt was made by England in 1816, when Lord Amherst was sent to China with the same object as Macartney. He fared even worse. He got as far as Peking, where the Chinese firmly demanded that he promise to perform the kotow. He refused and was then subjected to calculated humiliation amounting to insults. When he protested he was hustled out of Peking and packed off to Canton.

That was the end of formal efforts to establish normal relations with China. As a second best the British appointed Superintendents of Trade at Canton, especially after the abolition of the East India Company's monopoly of the China trade in 1834. The superintendents were intended to have quasi-diplomatic status, negotiating on equal terms with the viceroy of Kwangtung Province, the highest civil authority in South China. They, too, were frustrated. The viceroy even refused to receive a letter from Lord Napier, one of the commissioners, and in his written refusals referred to Lord Napier only as "the barbarian headman." It was clear, then, that the Chinese were unrelenting and that the British would have to continue fragmentary trade under humiliating conditions, or withdraw from China entirely, or use force to batter down China's gates.

The reasons for the impasse are worth analyzing. They lie deeper than desire for profit on one side and intransigence on the other. The Chinese had not lost either their fear of the Western foreigner or their contempt of him. They really did look on him as a barbarian. To a great extent this was founded on arrogance, insularity, and racial conceit, but, as has been said before, there was some foundation for those traits. China was at the height of its power just then. The expanse of territory over which it ruled was probably the largest in the world under a single sway. The Manchus had occupied the throne since 1644, and from 1662 to 1796, with an interval of only a few years between, only two emperors had occupied the throne, each reigning sixty years. They were K'ang Hsi and Ch'ien Lung, and they happened to be among the greatest rulers of modern times in any country. Both were men of strong character, marked personality, enlightened, cultivated, and able as administrators. It was a time of flowering for China, perhaps its last time. There was peace, order, and relative prosperity. It was the time, too, when European intellectuals were urging that China be emulated. China appeared to be unshakably secure, and in those two centuries it was. Matching China from the end of the seventeenth century to the end of the eighteenth with England, France, Prussia, or Austria, it would be difficult to say which was on a higher level of enlightenment, of order, of good government. Probably the verdict would be in China's favor. And with K'ang Hsi and Ch'ien Lung matched against Louis XIV, Louis XV, or Frederick the Great, it would be difficult not to find that the two Chinese were the greater by any criterion. And the comparison becomes biting when it is borne in mind that the letter Macartney carried was from George III to Ch'ien Lung.

Ch'ien Lung's answer to that letter, since become famous, is both illuminating and revealing. "You, O King," he writes to a British monarch not many years before Trafalgar, "live beyond the confines of many seas; nevertheless, impelled by your humble desire to partake of the benefits of our civilization, you have dispatched a mission respectfully bearing your memorial . . . the earnest terms in which it is cast reveal a respectful humility on your part, which is highly praiseworthy."

Then with reference to the object for which the Macartney mission has been sent he says:

"If you assert that your reverence for our Celestial Dynasty fills you with a desire to acquire our civilization, our ceremonies and code of laws differ so completely from your own that, even if your Envoy were able to acquire the rudiments of our civilization, you could not possibly transplant our manners and customs to your alien soil. Therefore however adept the Envoy might become, nothing would be gained thereby."

With respect to England's desire to open regular trade:

"Swaying the wide world, I have but one aim in view, namely, to maintain a perfect governance and to fulfill the duties of the state; strange and costly objects do not interest me. I . . . have no use for your country's manufactures. . . . Our Celestial Empire possesses all things in prolific abundance and lacks no product within its own borders. There is therefore no need to import the manufactures of outside barbarians in exchange for our own produce."

Still, he goes on, if the tea, silk, and porcelain which China produces are absolute necessities to the British and other Europeans, he is willing to let them go on buying them at Canton as they have.

Bertrand Russell, in a book written in 1922 after a visit to China, says of this letter: "What I want to suggest is that no one can understand China until this document has ceased to seem absurd." This remark is both apt and conclusive. Arrogance and self-complacency are no doubt vices. Assurance of one's own superiority is similarly a vice, but it is one of which all peoples are guilty, and it should be added that over the whole span of history few have had as much justification for it as China, or perhaps it is better to say that most have had even less justification for it than China. And the truth is that China did need nothing from the Western world then and had no desire to profit by the exchange of goods with it, whereas the West, even if its need for China's products was not vital, did desire to profit from what China offered. Not for nearly a hundred years was China to lose this complacent assurance of superiority, not till long after it had lost the right to it, at least as the world measures superiority.

There was also a principle involved, one of which China was oblivious, if not ignorant, perhaps because it never had been relevant until the time when the issue with the West was pressed. The principle was this: has any nation a moral right to shut itself off from the world? Are nature's riches the exclusive possession of those born where the riches lie, to be denied all others even if others are willing to make return for what they obtain of them? Are not the world and mankind one, nature's bounty to be shared by all, so long as the shares be determined equitably and by mutual agreement? Can any race or nation be permitted to act the dog-in-the-manger? In principle and on consideration of the abstract alone, the Chinese were probably in the wrong and had neither the moral nor social right to immure themselves and deny the greater part of the human race entry to a large part of their own planet to exchange goods for goods. But the abstract had a concrete face and the principle a concrete manifestation. In principle the right to trade could not justly be denied, but it should also be asked, the right to trade in what? The British and the other foreigners as well, Americans included, considered the issue the right to trade as such; the Chinese contended against the right to trade in opium. It was unfortunate that the issue should have been blurred by the regrettable form given it.

In the earlier historical writing on opium in China there was a high degree of oversimplification. There was a tendency to present the conflict growing out of it as a melodrama with a too pure hero—China—and a too sinister villain—England. The conflict was more mixed than that, of course. There was wrong on both sides. Yet, on the most impartial weighing of the evidence the conclusion is inescapable that a heavy guilt lies on the white nations, on England mainly but not exclusively. The whole record of the white man in the East until very recent times was reprehensible enough, and if the memory of it still rankles in the minds of Eastern peoples, that is understandable. But in the whole history of East-West relations nothing was so culpable, so squalid, and so nearly unforgettable as the opium evil forced on China. The foreigners were not barbarians, as Ch'ien Lung and his subordinates called them, but they could hardly have been called moral. It was, in short, a sordid episode, and it has left its mark on East-West relations ever since. Unfortunately, it is those who have transgressed whose memory is short, and those who have been transgressed against whose memory is long. It would conduce to greater harmony in human relations in general and East-West relations in particular if the reverse were true. And this holds even now for other parts of Asia where opium is not involved, but where other memories cannot die—India, Indonesia, and Indo-China, for example.

The history of the opium traffic is a long one. Opium had been known to the Chinese for centuries and had long been used by them for medicinal purposes. But as a habit-forming drug it was introduced into China by the white man. Tobacco had been brought to the East by the Spanish when they came to the Philippines, and the Dutch had learned to mix tobacco with opium for its curative effects in intestinal disorders. They used it thus in Java and Formosa in the years when they had a trading post in Formosa, and from there tobacco came into China. The first opium in quantity was brought to China by the Portuguese from Goa, and the Chinese learned to smoke it without tobacco or any other ingredient. Early in the eighteenth century the habit had grown enough to be noticeable, and in 1729 the first imperial edict was issued providing severe penalties for the sale of opium or the maintenance of establishments for opium smoking. By then it is recorded that some 200 chests of opium were being brought into China every year—about 20,000 pounds.

From then the traffic increased steadily and sharply and the use of opium increased in proportion. By 1800 some 4,000 chests were being imported annually; ten years later it was 4,500 chests annually; ten years after that 9,700 chests and after another ten years 18,000 chests. As the habit spread, the demand for opium became greater; the supply kept pace and still more became addicted. China was becoming an opium-besotted nation. For a long period most of the opium was grown in India and the rest in Persia and Turkey, but the Chinese soon began to cultivate the poppy plant themselves in order to get the opium cheaper. There was also a high profit on the crop, which provided an extra temptation. The real center of the traffic, however, lay in India, where it was a monopoly of the East India Company. Since the East

India Company was also the government of nearly all India, the profits on opium helped to defray the cost of government and by so much added to English profits from the exploitation of India.

In 1800 there was another and more stringent imperial edict forbidding both the importation of opium and its cultivation in China. In deference to that order the East India Company ceased shipping opium in its own vessels, but it did nothing to discourage the cultivation of opium in India: it continued to sell the product at official auctions, it permitted private ships of any nationality to load cargoes of opium at Indian ports and sail for China, and it continued to pocket the profits. While all nationalities shared in the profits, it was in the main an English enterprise, and the onus of the opium traffic and resulting curse of the opium habit has fallen mainly on England—in the eyes of Chinese and all other Asians, justly so.

After 1800 the whole opium traffic became illicit—a bootlegging enterprise like liquor in the prohibition era in the United States, and equally successful. Ships of all nationalities smuggled the drug into the country, using Portuguese Macao as a base. Again it should be repeated that while the majority of the ships were English, the flags of nearly all countries having merchant marines were represented, not excepting the American. And they had the complicity of venal Chinese officials, without whose aid the drug could not have entered. To that extent China itself shares with Western countries the guilt for the country's poisoning. The Co-hong merchants, the official monopolistic intermediaries in China's foreign trade, abstained from the trade, as did the equally monopolistic and quasi-official East India Company. But other Chinese merchants met the opium ships outside Canton, took delivery on shipboard, and paid. Then the opium was repacked in smaller bags and put on small, fast boats—like the American prohibition rum-runners—and run into the port, where the merchants took care of the necessary official bribes. As the trade became increasingly successful and equally profitable, some foreign shippers became bolder and had their own fast boats to do the opium running, thus adding to their profits. The ships that brought the opium to China left with a return cargo consisting principally of silk and tea, and later silver specie, when opium imports far exceeded what China could export. But it must be made clear: without both foreign opium dealers and shippers and Chinese merchants and corruptible officials the traffic could not have survived. And it should be observed further that among the Chinese officials that could be bribed into connivance were some of fairly high rank.

At the same time there was mounting alarm among influential classes in China, especially at the capital. The Chinese people were becoming besotted. Large areas which always had been given over to raising food crops were now being planted with poppy. Silver, the basis of China's currency, was being drained off. There was some agitation for legalization of both the importation of foreign opium and cultivation of the domestic, in order that both might be more easily controlled. But the imperial government could not bring itself to this. There was too much opposition from many who were highly placed and who based their opposition both on the intrinsic moral issue and on the harm that was being done to the Chinese people physically, socially, and morally. By 1830, when the trade was rampant and smuggling and the attendant bribery were in full, flagrant course, events were moving to a climax. It was clear that either opium had to be legalized or stern measures would have to be taken to suppress it entirely. And if the latter, they would have to be such measures as would carry with them potentialities of open conflict with foreign nations, especially with England, the world's first Power in foreign commerce, on the sea, and in international politics.

At first the authorities at the capital sought to deal with the question locally. The viceroy at Canton was instructed to take vigorous measures to stop the traffic. This proved ineffectual, since he had to deal with foreigners who would brook no interference with their profits and Chinese, both merchants and officials, who had a vested interest in continuing the traffic. All that resulted was a number of incidents. There were disorders, arrests, violations of law and custom on both sides. Conflicting conceptions of justice were brought into opposition. The Chinese, when they arrested a foreign sailor for whatever offense, dealt with him on the basis of his being a foreigner and not on the basis of the offense charged to him, and he was guilty before trial. There were in consequence shocking miscarriages of justice that outraged all foreigners. And when Chinese officials brought charges against a sailor not yet apprehended and demanded that he be turned over to them for trial, the foreign officials or ships' captains naturally refused, thus adding to mutual resentment. But the merits of single issues no longer counted. The central conflict, which turned on opium, overrode all else.

At length the imperial government decided on strong action. It appointed a High Commissioner to go to Canton and deal with opium once and for all, which meant in effect to suppress it altogether. The commissioner was Lin Tse-hsu, a former viceroy in central China and a man of strong character, aggressive, obstinate, with nothing in him of the pliancy the foreigners had become accustomed to in Chinese officials. Moreover, he felt strongly about opium and was also antiforeign. He took his instructions literally and seriously. He had been sent to stamp out opium and he meant to do so.

Lin arrived in Canton in 1839. Within a few days he began the first of a series of electrifying pronouncements. He ordered the foreign merchants to surrender to the government all the opium stocks on board their ships and in their warehouses. Also he ordered the Chinese merchants to turn over all they had. The opium gathered from any source was to be destroyed. Furthermore, all foreign merchants would be required to post a bond in pledge that never again would their ships bring opium into the port. If the pledge were violated those guilty would suffer the extreme penalty, which in Chinese practice meant an unpleasant death. Meanwhile all foreigners were forbidden to leave the factory district at Canton for Macao. They were in effect prisoners, as Chinese troops and armed boats were brought up to surround the factory district.

Faced with unshakable determination and a show of force—for the first time—the English Superintendent of Trade, Captain Charles Elliott, who was the highest English authority on the scene, offered compromise. He turned over 20,000 chests of opium, estimated to be worth $6,000-000 at the going price. The opium was chemically treated to make it useless and then dumped into the sea, probably the most dramatic episode of the time. High Commissioner Lin was plainly a person to be reckoned with—a Chinese official who meant what he said and could not be reached in the usual way.

Captain Elliott yielded as far as the opium was concerned, but he was unyielding on the bond that Lin had also required. The matter had gone too far for negotiation, however. For one thing, Lin Tse-hsu, having tasted success, found in it further impetus. The usual Chinese instinct for compromise, for compensatory concession when a point has been won, if only to save the loser's face, was wanting in him. There were more incidents. The British merchants evacuated the factory district, retiring to Macao. They would have been permitted to trade in commodities other than opium, but they decided to withdraw entirely, which further irritated Lin. Disorders became frequent. In one, a riot involving English and American sailors, a Chinese was killed. Captain Elliott tried the sailors accused and sentenced them, though for rioting and not murder, since no evidence on that could be found against any of them. Lin, however, demanded that the sailors be turned over to him. This meant, of course, that they would be found guilty before trial and executed, probably with tortures. Naturally Captain Elliott refused. In retaliation Lin ordered all food and other supplies cut off from the foreign community at Macao. The English were forced to leave for

Hongkong, then a barren island with two English men-of-war lying offshore. Not yet satisfied, Lin sent ships to seize the sailors, instructing them to destroy any English ships that obstructed. They proceeded to do so. The English men-of-war warned them to come no farther. They did, with evident preparations to fight. The English fired. The Chinese ships, all of them small junks lightly armed, were sunk or dispersed. The first Western-Chinese war was on.

And the modern history of the Far East had begun.

CHAPTER VI

China Is Forced Open

The Anglo-Chinese War or the Opium War, as it is better known, can be called a war only by convention. There was not much occasion for fighting, for the Chinese had nothing to fight with, being armed only by their indignation at opium, their irritation with the foreigner, their ignorance of the foreigner's military might, and courage as well. Of the last they gave unmistakable evidence, for at some of the ports on the coast the Manchu garrisons fought almost to the last man, at some places killing their wives and children at the end to prevent their falling into the hands of the foreigner. But courage was not enough against the mistress of the seas. They were without effective weapons and they were poorly led. The British had little difficulty. They sent a squadron of ships and a few thousand men, and after a few engagements that could hardly be called battles in point of actual fighting, they blockaded and then bombarded Canton, which submitted and paid a ransom to escape further punishment. Then the British moved up the coast to the Yangtze River, taking ports as they went. They stood off Nanking, the most important city in central China, and prepared to bombard it. In 1842 China capitulated and accepted the terms Great Britain had stipulated two years before. The Treaty of Nanking, concluded August 29, 1842, and supplemented by the Treaty of the Bogue, concluded October 1, 1843, laid the basis for China's relations with the West for almost a hundred years.

The two treaties provided an indemnity of $21,000,000, which included $6,000,000 as compensation for the opium destroyed by Commissioner Lin, $12,000,000 for war costs, and $3,000,000 for debts owed to British merchants. The island of Hongkong was ceded to Great Britain in perpetuity and five ports were opened to foreign trade, with the right to station consuls there. They were Canton, Amoy, Foochow, Ningpo, and Shanghai. China agreed to a uniform tariff fixed at 5 per cent ad valorem, to be changed only by mutual agreement. It was this last provision, the implications of which China did not grasp at the time, which held the Chinese government in constricting bonds until well into the twentieth century, for thereby China lost tariff autonomy and, in result, control over its national revenue. Also there was a provision in the second treaty that was later elaborated into the full privilege of extraterritoriality or the exemption of foreigners from Chinese legal jurisdiction. Great Britain obtained, too, most-favored-nation status, under which any right, privilege, or concession extended in the future to any other country would automatically accrue to Great Britain. Not least, the Chinese agreed to set aside, in each opened port, areas where foreigners could reside. Neither side then realized that this would in time come to mean the whole system of foreign settlements and concessions, each of which constituted a foreign city under foreign government at geographically and economically strategic points in almost all parts of the country.

Great Britain had been the vanguard and had had the burden as well as the onus of breaking through China's gates and forcing it to submission, but it was not to have a monopoly of the advantages gained thereby. It was followed in short order by other Powers, first, significantly, by the United States. Americans had been active in the China trade since the "Empress of China" set sail for Canton in 1784. Only the British were more active. From New England ports and New York and Philadelphia ships sailed regularly for Canton, at first taking mainly furs from the Northwest coast and ginseng—a root highly prized by the Chinese for medicinal purposes—and returning with tea and silk. Later the exports to China were more diversified. Several firms were permanently established in the Eastern trade, with warehouses in the factory district at Canton, and the trade was of some importance as trade and industry developed on the northwestern seaboard.

Throughout the period before the Anglo-Chinese War the bulk of the China trade was British and carried in British bottoms, but the nearest to real competition came from the Americans. While American merchants and ships also had been engaged in the smuggling of opium, this was the lesser part of American commercial activities, and there was no official support for those engaged in the opium trade. On the contrary, some efforts were made to restrain them, and the opium traffic itself was highly unpopular in the United States. It was mainly for this reason that sympathy in this country was on the whole on China's side in the war.

At Canton itself relations between American traders and Chinese authorities were never satisfactory, since the Americans were under the same restrictions as the British, but there was less friction than between British and Chinese. The Americans were of less importance Also, they were not so deeply involved in opium, and besides, they were not so aggressive as the British in pushing for greater rights and privileges and for the general levelling of all Chinese barriers. It may be, too, that the British, already having extensive territorial holdings in Asia, had corresponding imperial ambitions and the psychology inseparable from an imperial position. They really were more overbearing than the Americans and those of any other nationality, and as a matter of fact there was no little friction between British and Americans, partly because the Americans were competitors and partly because the British were overbearing to the Americans, too. At any rate while there were numerous unpleasant incidents between Americans and Chinese, they never took on the same asperity as those between British and Chinese, if only because the Americans were more conciliatory. But the Americans chafed nevertheless, and there were recurrent demands not only from those actually at Canton but from commercial quarters in the United States for government action to obtain from China recognition of equality and a more normal opportunity for trade. When the war broke out in 1839 Americans remained at Canton, but they did give moral support to the British and sometimes acted as buffers for their properties and interests, especially after the British left the factory district.

America was neutral in the war but alert to the new situation it was creating and the potentialities raised for American commerce. There had been for some years an awareness of the Far East and its economic promise. Influential groups in New England, an area then more influential in the nation than later, were involved in the Eastern trade and their vested interest in it was not inconsiderable. However detached from Europe the United States might feel and however it resolved to have no part in the "primary concerns" of Europe against which Washington had warned, there was already an active consciousness of the Far East, a consciousness that portended much—but a consciousness that was economic rather than political. There had already been a good deal of discussion in the public prints, in Congress and in government reports before and during the war, and as soon as the war was drawing to a close, and China's submission was foreshadowed, there was a demand that the government bestir itself.

Before the government acted, however, measures had already been taken in China. After the outbreak of war an American naval squadron was sent to Far Eastern waters under command of Commodore Lawrence Kearny. Kearny had kept developments under close scrutiny and had a grasp of the questions at issue. In 1842, immediately on the signing of the Treaty of Nanking, he approached the Chinese authorities with a reminder of the importance of American trade at Canton and formally expressed the hope that American merchants would be put on the same footing as those of any other nation—meaning, in this case, Great Britain. He received in reply assurances that this would be done, assurances repeated in subsequent interchanges between himself and the Chinese. Thus was achieved, though not yet legally confirmed, the most-favored-nation status that the United States has enjoyed and insisted on ever since, a status expanded and made clear in the Open Door pronouncements of 1899, and which later became one of the fixed points in American foreign policy. Yet it must be pointed out that this was not a right wrested from the Chinese. They had granted it willingly to the British. There is even evidence that they initiated it, believing perhaps that safety lay in setting up rivalries among the foreigners and playing off one barbarian against another. As a matter of fact, this became and remained one of the fixed points of China's foreign policy.

Meanwhile the government at Washington was making preparations for more formal and official overtures to China. Soon after news of the Treaty of Nanking was received, President John Tyler proposed to Congress that a commissioner be sent to China to enter into negotiations for a treaty. It is not without interest that the initiative in this was taken by Daniel Webster, then Secretary of State, with a long record as a Massachusetts senator sensitive to New England's economic interests. And the man chosen to head the commission to be dispatched to China was Caleb Cushing, a Massachusetts lawyer. There was some precedent for such commissions. One headed by Edmund Roberts of New Hampshire had been sent earlier to the East, and in 1833 Roberts succeeded in signing treaties opening trade relations with Siam and Muscat. But this was the most ambitious to be attempted or even to be considered.

Caleb Cushing arrived in Macao February 24, 1844, on an armed ship and escorted by two other armed ships. His instructions, set down by Webster in some detail, were to be firm but courteous, by his conduct and his arguments to draw attention to the contrast between the United States and Great Britain, the one having no colonies and no aspirations for any in dangerous proximity to China, the other being already established in India and perhaps aspiring to further expansion. From the United States, he was to point out, China had nothing to fear, for it wanted nothing except the right to exchange goods. Also he was to dissociate himself from the opium traffic, disavowing any intention of the American government to protect opium smugglers. Mainly he was to obtain for the United States regular relations with China on a basis of equality and the right to trade on the same basis as any other country.

The Chinese sought to temporize, as was their wont. They pointed out that through Commodore Kearny and in other statements the Chinese government had already agreed to give all countries the same privileges. What, then, was there to negotiate about? But Cushing had been instructed to get a treaty and he made it clear that he meant to get it. On Cushing's demand that he be permitted to go to Peking for an audience with the emperor the Chinese were adamant, and perhaps by way of compromise they proceeded to negotiate a treaty, thus testifying to Cushing's Yankee shrewdness as a trader.

On July 3, 1844, a treaty was signed and relations were opened between the United States and China. The treaty was in general on the lines of the British, but was clearer and more definite. America won the right to trade at the five newly opened ports, to consular representation, to most-favored-nation status, and to full rights of extraterritoriality for American citizens, that which was only implicit in the British treaty. Also if American goods were landed at one port and customs duties paid on them, they could be reshipped to another port without payment of additional duties, thus giving Americans and therefore all foreigners an entering wedge in Chinese coastal trade. Americans were permitted to reside in areas set apart for them by mutual consent at all the open ports and they were to be permitted to employ Chinese teachers and learn the language, that which the Chinese government had forbidden before. Cushing's treaty or the Treaty of Wang-Hia, as it was subsequently known, served as a model for subsequent treaties between China and other Western Powers.

Immediately after the treaty with the United States a Franco-Chinese treaty was signed in October, 1844. It had one new and distinctive provision. This was the right of Catholic missionaries to proselyte in China and of Christian converts to worship according to their faith. France was acting in accordance with its historic role as protector of the Church the world over, but in China this had special implications. There had been Protestant missionaries, both American and British, in and around Canton since the beginning of the nineteenth century, but they were kept at a distance no less than the traders. As it happened they were of considerable service, first to the traders and then to their government representatives, since they knew the Chinese language. In the official negotiations they acted as interpreters and at times as advisers because of the greater knowledge of Chinese customs and ideas they had acquired through study of the language. Now the most-favored-nation principle was to assert itself in religion as in trade. What had been granted to Catholics the Protestants claimed for themselves and received. Ch'i Ying, the viceroy and commissioner for negotiations with foreigners, conceded willingly and with a touch of patronizing amusement. He had not been aware, he said, that the Western foreigners, all of whom seemed to be the same, had such differences in their religious beliefs and practices. The Chinese were to learn that unmistakably and painfully enough in subsequent decades, but they never quite came to understand why, since all foreigners professed the same religion, there were such virulent religious hostilities among them. That has puzzled Chinese to this day; but it has not always been just a matter of theological speculation to them. It has had consequences serious for them and as difficult to relate to the worship of God as were some of the episodes three hundred years before.

France was followed by Belgium and the Kingdom of Norway and Sweden. Belgium obtained in 1845 the right to trade but no treaty, while in 1847 Norway and Sweden obtained a treaty on the lines of the Treaty of Wang-Hia. China's gates had at length been battered and its walls breached, but fundamentally nothing was changed. There was no new and stable relation between China and the Western world. One kind of friction had ended, another kind was to begin—one no less irritating, no less productive of rancor and no less unendurable.

China had lost the war and its government had signed under duress a treaty acknowledging the foreigners' right to enter five ports for purposes of residence and trade, but nothing had changed in China's attitude. The signature to the treaty was nothing but a temporizing measure, its object to induce the British to withdraw their fighting ships and troops. The Imperial Government at Peking was too far removed from the scene of action to realize what the defeat signified. The Chinese people in and around Canton were still irreconcilably antiforeign. Neither recognized the full import of the West's superiority in power or even that such superiority existed. The foreigner was still just a barbarian to be scorned and ignored, certainly to be kept off Chinese soil. All that had been in the years before 1840 was to resume.

It did resume almost immediately after the treaties were signed with the three major Powers. At four of the five ports—Amoy, Foochow, Ningpo, and Shanghai—there was little difficulty. But at Canton friction was, if anything, worse than before the war. The foreigners, led by the British, demanded admittance to the city with full right of residence, as was their due by the treaty. The local authorities agreed, but the people, goaded by unofficial but influential leaders of the community, refused and attacked them when they attempted to enter. There were recurrent incidents, mounting in intensity. A group of foreigners would try to enter the city or go walking or hunting in its environs. They would be hooted and stoned and sometimes attacked. In some cases they escaped without injury, in others they would be injured and on occasion one or more were killed. On the part of the British there were protests and threats of reprisals and sometimes actual reprisals, with minor pitched battles being fought and casualties on both sides. Meanwhile British traders were prevented from setting up establishments to pursue their business and could enter the city only at their peril.

An anomalous triangular relationship ensued. There were the foreigners, led by the British; local Chinese authority, represented by the viceroy; and the Chinese populace. The imperial government still had nothing to do with the question. In actuality it, too, was obstructive and saw no reason to make concessions to the foreigner. It could be obstructive with impunity. It was safe from the pressure of the foreigner and his military might and could comfortably delegate responsibility to the viceroy at Canton. The viceroy, still Ch'i Ying, who had conducted the treaty negotiations, acknowledged that the foreigners were within their rights and at times made formal public exhortations to the people to comply with their legal obligations. The people, led by the gentry, the well-to-do, and the scholar class, responded by reviling him. On one occasion a local official who too vigorously reprimanded the people for their recalcitrance was himself attacked and his official headquarters was burned down by a mob.

Matters stood at an impasse. The mob was inflamed and the Chinese authorities were powerless. The local British community called on the home government to use its power but London was reluctant. Rather than force the issue it authorized Sir John F. Davis, highest British official on the spot, to make an agreement with the Chinese postponing British entry into Canton but explicitly reserving the right to do so. This was in 1846, four years after the signing of the Treaty of Nanking. The British concession by no means worked toward conciliation. On the contrary, it sharpened friction. The British were embittered, the Chinese emboldened. There were more serious clashes. Mobs attacked; goaded, the British sometimes responded with firearms. After a more serious clash in 1847 British ships were sent from Hongkong to attack the outer forts of Canton, and on a British ultimatum Viceroy Ch'i Ying agreed to full entry into Canton by 1849. When 1849 came, it was still impossible to enter. The Chinese mobs, worked up by inflammatory statements, refused to obey their officials, and without a permanent British garrison to protect them it would have been fatal for Britons to attempt to live in the city. There was a complete deadlock, one which lasted years longer.

As before 1840 there was right and wrong on both sides. The Chinese were ignorant of the world, obscurantic, stiff-necked and recalcitrant no doubt; but they were also moved by fear. They resented the white man not only as a foreigner but as a source of danger to the country. While they could not fully comprehend their helplessness before his might, if he chose to invoke it, they did perceive that the white man's countries were bent on encroachment in Asia and that the Britons' trade might be a spearhead of the white man's conquest of China as well as other parts of Asia—as indeed it turned out to be, whether or not originally so intended. To a certain extent also white men were guilty of the same abuses that had characterized them in the earliest years of European contact with the East. While the majority were respectable and law-abiding, there was a large enough element of adventurers, ne'er-do-wells, and ruffians, and the men off the ships that arrived in steadily increasing numbers were far from peaceable. Among the worst, it should be noted were Americans. Through the nineteenth century the American tramp and beachcomber on the China coast gave America an unenviable reputation in that part of the world. Under the extra-territoriality provisions of the treaties, which the Chinese did abide by, foreign nationals could not be brought under the jurisdiction of the Chinese authorities. No matter what offenses they committed they could be dealt with only by representatives of their own governments. Not for years did those governments set up a regular system for dealing with offenders among their own people, and besides, with Chinese acting as unreasonably as they did, it was natural for foreign officials to temper justice with charity to their own nationals where Chinese were victims or claimants for redress. It was a condition inevitably productive of injustice on both sides.

Also the opium traffic flourished without hindrance. In 1840 there were 20,000 chests imported into China; by 1850 this had risen to 52,000, almost all of it coming from India. But again, while all of this was brought in foreign ships, the Chinese, too, were engaged in the opium trade, profiting not much less than the foreigners. Naturally it was easier to blame the foreigners.

A new factor began to enter at this time, one which was to rasp as much as anything else. This was the coolie trade. The African slave trade had been outlawed, but cheap labor was still in demand in many parts of the world where the new plantation system was being established. Chinese peasants and unskilled urban workers were shipped out on contract, at what seemed to the Chinese coolie good pay when stated in cash sums to which he was not accustomed, but was in fact outrageous exploitation. Most of them went to the West Indies. The worst aspect of the trade lay in the conditions under which the coolies were transported. These were, in a word, barbarous. Men were packed in foul, airless holds like animals, and thousands died before the ship arrived at its destination. Chinese officials were scandalized at reports that seeped back and tried to stop or regulate the traffic, but their efforts had little effect. Like opium, the traffic was too profitable—and, like opium, some Chinese profited by it, too. Another grievance was added on the Chinese side of the accounting, one that was not balanced by Chinese recalcitrance on permission to trade. It must be said, too, that the Portuguese colony of Macao was the headquarters of the coolie trade, as it was of much that was abhorrent on the China coast after the middle of the nineteenth century, but in this, too, British and Americans had a part.

Piracy, which is endemic on the China coast, gave rise to still another abuse and cause of grievance. Foreign ships, being well-armed, offered themselves for hire to Chinese owners of cargo-bearing junks to protect them against pirates. The practice itself was unobjectionable, advantageous to both sides in fact, but plainly it lent itself to racketeering. The charge for convoying became higher and higher, and, as with the "protection" offered to store proprietors by American gangsters, convoying tended to become an enforced exaction. A Chinese junk which refused it—and the high fee demanded—was subject to pillaging not only by pirates. Indeed, it was not certain sometimes which was more predatory—piracy or convoying. In this, too, the Portuguese were the worst offenders. Foreign officials tried to put a stop to the practice or at least to prevent the abuses, but too many foreign ships and unscrupulous shipmasters were engaged in it to be brought under official control. Another item was added to China's score against the white man.

All in all, it was a situation no more tenable than the one before 1840. In one way or another it had to be resolved. An occasion was to arise in the natural course, for it had been provided in both the American and French treaties of 1844 that they were to be subject to revision in twelve years. As the time approached both countries proposed the opening of negotiations. Great Britain then had recourse to the most-favored-nation clause in its own treaty and similarly asked to negotiate on revision. But while the American treaty envisaged negotiations only for the "inconsiderable modifications . . . requisite in those parts which relate to commerce and navigation," the British demanded a more comprehensive review and changes which would regularize relations between the two countries on a stable and durable basis. To this end they asked numerous concessions—the right to navigate the Yangtze River and trade in the cities of the lower Yangtze Valley, legalization of the opium trade, residence of a British diplomatic representative at the imperial capital, suppression of piracy, and regulation of the coolie trade. The efforts of all the Powers to open negotiations had the same effect as before 1840. The Chinese refused, promised, postponed, temporized, evaded on one pretext or another; but they did not negotiate. Again it was clear that the foreigners would have to recede, losing much of what they had gained after the first war, or resort to force again, even if that meant another war.

Then in 1856 an incident supervened on the deadlock which was to resolve it. For some time the British in Hongkong had been allowing Chinese ships to take British registry. This helped build up that British port and added to British trade. But it also could lend British prestige and protection to such dubious activities as smuggling, opium running, and worse, since all British vessels flying the British flag were safe from Chinese inspection or interference. In October, 1856, one such Chinese ship with British registry—a lorcha called the "Arrow"—was off the port of Canton. The Chinese authorities there, charging that a pirate was among the Chinese crew of the lorcha, boarded it, hauled down the British flag, and took off twelve of the crew.

The British protested what was clearly a violation of international maritime law but the Chinese refused to heed. They maintained that the lorcha was a Chinese craft despite its registry, and besides, it harbored a pirate whom Chinese officials had been seeking to apprehend. The British nevertheless demanded an apology and the release of the twelve men. Viceroy Yeh Ming-chin, who had succeeded Ch'i Ying at Canton and who was even more stiff-necked than his predecessor, refused to apologize on the ground that the British flag had not been hauled down, but he did hand over nine of the crew. On the stern demand of Harry Parkes, British consul and a man as stiff-necked as Yeh, the latter at length handed over all twelve of the crew, but still refused to apologize. Parkes called for British ships. The ships started firing on the Canton forts. The viceroy responded with a proclamation calling for the "extermination" of the British. The second war was on.

In this war, however, the British had the support of the French. The latter had a special grievance of their own. A few years earlier a French missionary who had entered Kwangsi, the province west of Kwangtung—without any legal right to do so, incidentally—had been arrested by Chinese authorities, together with some of his Chinese converts. This was a legal violation on China's part, since the Frenchman, being protected by extraterritoriality, should have been turned over to the French consul. At any rate the French priest and some of the converts were tortured and then put to death. This aroused the French, who made demands but received no satisfaction. There followed consultations between the British and the French, who had already agreed to a joint demonstration of force even before the lorcha affair gave a more direct cause for action.

These were the incidents, or rather, accidents, that led to war. They were not the cause. There was an irrepressible and irreconcilable conflict. The foreigners still insisted on the right to enter China for such purposes as they desired; the Chinese still refused to have anything to do with them. One or the other had to yield or they had to fight. They fought. The incidents that served as precipitants hardly justified a war in themselves, and in themselves they do not put the foreigners, the British especially, in a very favorable light. Morally the foreigner does not come off very well in the whole train of events. It is a chapter in history that reflects no great credit on the Occidental. But more was involved than single events and disputes. There was at issue the fundamental relation between two parts of the world, two parts of the world still incompatible in their outlook, so incompatible that only force could be called to arbitrament.

CHAPTER VII

China's Decline Sets In

From the military point of view the second foreign-Chinese war was of little greater consequence than the first. The Chinese had as little power to resist as before 1842—less, in fact, for reasons that will be explained later. The British, too, were handicapped, since in 1857 they were engaged in putting down the Indian mutiny and not until the end of that year did action begin. British and French troops joined in attacking Canton and the city fell in short order. Viceroy Yeh was made a prisoner and sent to India, where he died a year later. The government of the city of Canton was taken over by the British and French.

The British and French then demanded formal negotiations for a new treaty, being joined in this by the representatives of Russia and the United States, both of which, however, had held aloof from the war. They sought as usual to conduct negotiations at the imperial capital or at least with emissaries of the emperor but were told as usual to deal with local officials in Canton. This time they refused, and an Anglo-French expedition moved up the coast first to Shanghai and then to the mouth of the Peiho, the river leading to the port of Tientsin. The viceroy of Chihli, the province in which both Peking and Tientsin lay (now called Hopei), was appointed to discuss the terms of the new treaties with the four Powers. Again the British and French refused, this time on the ground that the viceroy lacked sufficient authority. They insisted on proceeding up to Tientsin and therefore demanded the surrender of the forts of Taku, at the mouth of the river, lest they be trapped as they proceeded. When the Chinese refused to yield the forts the British and French attacked and took them in a matter of hours. Then they moved on to Tientsin and at length the negotiations took place. Treaties were signed with all four Powers, though separately, within a few days in June, 1858.

This was not the end, however. The treaties stipulated that ratifications were to be exchanged in Peking and on this understanding the British and French left Tientsin. The Russian minister proceeded to Peking and ratifications were duly exchanged. John E. Ward, the American Minister, was permitted to get as far as Peking but there the Chinese insisted as usual that he perform the kotow, which he refused, and he quit the capital. Ratifications of the American treaty were exchanged at Peitang, near the Taku forts. In June, 1859, the British and French arrived at the Peiho again, expecting to proceed up to Peking by way of Tientsin for the ratification ceremonies. They found instead that the forts had been strengthened in their absence and the Chinese refused to let them move up the river to Tientsin. British and French forces again attacked the forts, but this time they were unsuccessful and they returned to Shanghai to await reinforcements. It was in this engagement that there occurred the episode, subsequently legendary in the Far East, in which Commander Josiah Tatnall on an American ship went to the assistance of a British ship though America was not in the war, explaining his action later with the statement, "blood is thicker than water," a sentiment that did him great credit no doubt but would not be countenanced in international law and would have caused America no little embarrassment in any other situation.

The reinforcements came up to the Peiho in August, 1860, and the British and French demanded passage to Tientsin, an apology, and indemnity for the previous clash. The Chinese rejected the demands and the British and French attacked, quickly reducing the forts, and began the advance on Peking. There were recurring parleys on the way, the Chinese seeking delay, the British and French laying down conditions for their reception in Peking and the subsequent transactions. On one occasion a group of British and French participating in such a parley under a flag of truce were taken prisoner by the Chinese, removed to Peking and there incarcerated, and in addition subjected to cruel mistreatment. Included in their number was Harry Parkes, the British consul at Canton. Of the thirty-nine so imprisoned only eighteen survived their treatment. The Anglo-French expedition now speeded up its advance and the emperor and his court fled to Jehol in Inner Mongolia. The expedition stormed the gates of Peking with ease, and when it was discovered what had happened to the British and French who had been imprisoned it was decided, mainly on the urging of Lord Elgin, British representative, to take revenge and teach the Chinese a lesson. The lesson took the form of the deliberate destruction of the Imperial Summer Palace outside the city known as the Yuan Ming Yuan, one of the most beautiful of the palaces of that majestic capital, beautiful in itself and containing innumerable irreplaceable art objects. Some of these objects had already been looted by British and French soldiers, but that may be called one of the unfortunate accompaniments of war everywhere. Now, however, the palace was willfully and deliberately burned, a consciously planned act. Its ruins still stand, a memento of Occidental ideas of pedagogy. The lesson no doubt was graven on the Chinese mind and is still remembered; but what it taught was not what the British and French had intended. Indeed it only added another item to the score that the Chinese held against the white man—the score they were to call up with incisive commentation when the time came for reckoning against the Western Powers after World War I.

The Chinese, now at last, were forced to submit. A foreign army at the imperial court, with the Son of Heaven himself in ignominious flight, had demonstrated irrefutably the foreigner's superior might and, with whatever mental reservations, the Chinese bowed to their fate, at least for the time. They accepted the terms demanded before the war began and signed treaties with all four Powers and ratified them in Peking as originally demanded. By so doing they changed the status of China in the world for almost a hundred years, whether they recognized the fact or not.

The four Powers won the right to maintain diplomatic representatives in Peking. Their citizens could travel anywhere in the interior of China, carrying the protection of extraterritoriality with them. Ten more ports along the coast and up the Yangtze River as far as Hankow were opened to foreign trade and residence. Among them was Tientsin, in the shadow of the capital. Foreign ships were to be permitted to navigate the Yangtze River. There were two more provisions. Opium was legalized and the right of missionaries to preach Christianity was recognized, the latter including the right of missionaries to own property anywhere in the interior, a right denied to other foreigners, who could travel in the interior but not reside there. Opium and the Gospel: they were imposed together by a war that included the sacking of one of the world's most beautiful structures. The chapter of human history that deals with the relations of East and West has many sardonic twists, and this is perhaps the most sardonic. For the white man came to China bearing the Cross and the opium pipe, imposed them together at the mouth of cannon, and has prided himself ever since on the high purposes and fine fruits of his civilizing mission. The Chinese could see only the sardonic and what they naturally thought the pharisaical, and where it did not move to satire it moved to bitterness. But in any case the West had had its way and China was never to be the same again.

In the second war there had entered a new factor, one which was extraneous to the Chinese-Western issue but had complicated the war and influenced its course. This was the internal upheaval known as the Taiping Rebellion, which coincided with the period of friction over Canton and the war itself. It was more than a rebellion and a civil war. It had all the force of a cataclysm of nature and was as destructive. A large part of China was devastated, and while no exact figures were ever computed—they seldom are in the East—the lowest estimate of human losses was 20,000,000 and probably there were more. It was while the rebellion was at its height that the government was trying to keep the West at bay and then to defend the country against the attack of Anglo-French forces. And the most incongruous aspect of the whole period was that while the foreign Powers, led by Great Britain, were beating the imperial government into submission, they were simultaneously helping it to suppress the rebellion. So important was the Taiping Rebellion in its effect not only on Chinese-foreign relations but also on China's subsequent history that it must be dealt with in some detail.

The rebellion might be called accidental in origin in that it was the fortuitous product of the birth of a single individual, one who combined in himself the traits of madness and genius, a combination that has appeared at intervals in the annals of the human race and has generally devastated parts of the earth, the latest example being Hitler. But always when individuals have made or precipitated such cataclysms by sheer force of personality, a favorable combination of circumstances is necessary to give them opportunity and scope. There was such a combination in China at the time. The cyclical movement of Chinese history was in progress: a powerful individual who founds a dynasty and ushers in a period of vitality, growth, and a satisfying life for the people; one or two successors who carry on in his momentum; and then a decline, first slow and then at accelerated tempo. The end of the seventeenth century and the whole of the eighteenth, under the Emperors K'ang Hsi and Ch'ien Lung, had been periods of flowering, as has been said. With the nineteenth century the downward sweep of the cycle had begun. There was a succession of weak emperors, whose weakness was reflected in the court around them—the sycophantic, the incompetent, the mercenary, the parasitic. This was in turn reflected by the character and quality of men in government, and this by social and economic conditions throughout the country, if only because corruption took a heavier toll from the mass of the people.

Discontent had begun to gather, though not yet overt and expressed. Discontent was most acute among the peasantry, as always in China at critical periods. There were—as there always have been—too many people for the land to support, given the means of production then known. This made for abuses in the system of land tenure and cultivation: too many farm tenants, too high crop rent, too many impoverished families and thus egregious usury which impoverished still more, too much exploitation of the poorest by manipulation of the price of produce, and excessive taxation. The peasant was oppressed and murmuring. Alone, he was helpless and inert, but he was ready for the call of one who offered leadership on the way to betterment of his lot, meet for the manipulation of one who had the gift of tongues and could hypnotize masses.

There was also the fact that the Manchus were after all alien conquerors and the Chinese have never reconciled themselves easily and long to subjection to an outsider. Their compliance is forced, their patience deceptive. Many have come to false conclusions from the appearance of acceptation and submission—as, for example, did all men of the white race until the end of World War II. They saw how little the Chinese seemed to protest against the rule of their cities by the white man and the deference to him paid by their government, and they assumed that the Chinese did not care or fitted themselves contentedly to the yoke or were too spiritless to resist. And they concluded that it must have been divinely planned that the supremacy of the white man be eternal—God's chosen were ordained to rule Kipling's lesser breed. And suddenly the Chinese arose in unity and passion, desperate and determined, and in a few years white supremacy and the era of imperialistic control passed. So it was in the middle of the nineteenth century. The Manchus were outwardly accepted and submitted to; but deep within the Chinese the rankling had never ceased.

This was not lessened by the humiliations forced on the country by the white intruder. So long as the Manchus could maintain the country's integrity and safeguard its pride and position toward the outer world, they had some claim to respect, though, in Chinese eyes, they were usurpers. But when they proved themselves incapable of defending the country against external enemies, when they could not prevent intrusion from without, they forfeited even the prescriptive right conferred by superior power. He who rules by force and force alone must always validate his claim to rule by proof of his power. And it was not wholly by coincidence that the Taiping Rebellion started in the environs of Canton, where the foreigner's inroads had begun, that the half-mad genius who inspired and led it was a Cantonese, and that he had himself come into contact with the foreigners and in one special way had fallen under foreign influence.

Thus the Taiping Rebellion, however fortuitous its origin, magnetized and concentrated all the forces within the country making for disruption. It did not generate them; it brought out, brought together, and gave them driving power. It was a rebellion in that it did not succeed; but it was the beginning of a gigantic revolution, the end of which has not yet been seen, even by the middle of the twentieth century, a hundred years later.

In 1813 a son was born to a small farmer in a country district a few miles from Canton. He was Hung Hsiu-ch'uan. The boy grew up studious and ambitious but several times failed to pass the provincial examinations and thus qualify for an official post. After one failure he had a breakdown and began to see visions. He had already come into contact with a Christian missionary and had received some tracts which he began to study. In 1847 he became a sort of pupil of an American missionary for instruction in the Christian faith. He was converted, but by himself and to his own translation of Christianity. He founded a new religion: God the Father, Jesus the Elder Brother, and himself the Younger Brother. His visions instructed him to conquer for the new faith. He organized the Society for the Worship of God and set out; his first aim was to destroy all idols and put an end to idol worship.

Hung quickly won a few followers (not a very difficult feat in the disturbed atmosphere of the time) and began to spread out, attacking Buddhist and Taoist temples as he went. He moved into Kwangsi, the adjoining province to the west. This was in 1850. There his activities aroused the apprehensions of the authorities and they sent troops to suppress him. The troops were unsuccessful and Hung now, with a considerable following, started a march northward. He advanced into Hunan Province and laid siege to Changsha, the provincial capital, for more than two months. He failed to take it but moved on farther north to the Yangtze River and did succeed in capturing Wuchang, the capital of Hupeh Province and the most important city in central China. This was in January, 1853. From then on the movement gathered quick momentum. Adherents flocked to it by the tens of thousands. Imperial troops fled before it. Hung and his armies swept down the Yangtze Valley, capturing Nanking in March, 1853, and making their way to Shanghai, though they never succeeded in holding the actual port where the foreign settlement was. Another army, swinging north from the Yangtze, came within a few miles of Peking. But wherever they went, Hung's armies plundered and slaughtered, leaving ruin and desolation in their wake.

In Nanking Hung set up his capital, proclaiming himself the Tien Wang or Prince of Heaven and his dynasty the Tai Ping or Great Peace dynasty, whence the name Taiping Rebellion. With all the rapine and slaughter, the barbaric perversion of religion, and the subsequent corruption and degeneration, there was another side to the Taiping move-

ment that helped explain its success. There was a program of social reform, principally land reform, which did as much to win the populace
as the promise of the overthrow of the Manchus and certainly more than
the religious message, which seems to have made little or no impression.
Indeed, more than anything else, the Taiping Rebellion was an unsuccessful agrarian revolution.

The program was not practicable nor even thought out. There was a
vague plan of a sort of communism but a much more definite plan of
land redistribution on a principle of equalization. Communal ownership
and use peasants might not understand or even desire; enough land to
sustain them they did. And though nothing ever came of the program,
for energies were spent in conquest, dissipation, and then defense, it revealed the inner state of the country, the instability of its foundation, and
the ways by which the Chinese people might be won.

With the loss of Wuchang and Nanking and the narrow escape of
Peking, the imperial government awoke to the danger and girded itself
to overcome the rebels and save the dynasty. The Manchu leaders were
themselves of little use, but Chinese men of force and character emerged,
notably two of whom much was to be heard later. They were Tseng
Kuo-fan and Li Hung-chang. They were not only strong personalities but
had glimpsed something of the significance of modernism. They organized and trained armies; still more, they had the insight to recognize
that the same Western military superiority that led to China's undoing
in relation to the West might be put to use against the rebels. They
engaged the service of two foreign military men—Frederick Townsend
Ward, an American, and Major Charles George Gordon, a Briton known
in after years as Chinese Gordon and destined to come to a tragic end
at the hands of fanatical Moslems in the Sudan. Slowly the imperial
forces closed in on the Taipings, but it was not until 1865, fifteen years
after their eruption from the southeast, that they were finally crushed
and Hung Hsiu-ch'uan was forced to kill himself in flight. It was a
bizarre episode, but it was a portent. It revealed fissures in the Chinese
system, which were not closed, but widened through the decades until
China all but broke up and fell apart.

The foreigners were involved in the Taiping Rebellion in more ways
than the efforts of Ward and Gordon. The foreign relation to it also had
its bizarre aspects. The reaction of the foreigners was mixed. The missionaries were, of course, enthused at first, since they saw in it the
herald of the victory of the Cross in Asia. They soon became disillusioned when they perceived the mongrel infusions in the Taiping version of Christian doctrine and the moral practices of the Taiping leaders,
Hung Hsiu-ch'uan included. The attitude of the Western diplomatic

officers and traders was divided. Some saw in the rebellion an opportunity to get the obscurantic Manchus out of the way once and for all or to see them so weakened that they would have to be more pliant, especially since Hung Hsiu-ch'uan at first seemed to be sympathetic to the foreigners and willing to be co-operative. Others were frightened from the beginning, and all finally became shocked by the excesses of the Taiping leaders and the demonstration of their inability to function as a real government. And naturally all foreigners benefited by the imperial government's preoccupation with the rebellion, which made impossible any real mobilization of China's resources for effective resistance to the West in the 1850's.

There were also some more concrete by-products. When the Taipings arrived at the outskirts of Shanghai in 1853 and a subordinate rebel force took the Walled City, outside which lay the foreign residential area, there was confusion which was reflected at once in the course of foreign trade. The Chinese government had set up a customs house for the collection of the 5 per cent tariff duty agreed to in 1842, but the Chinese collectors fled on the arrival of the rebels, leaving foreign trade paralyzed, since cargoes could not be entered for payment of duties and clearance. As a temporary expedient the British and American consuls decided to collect the duties themselves and hold the amounts to the credit of the Chinese government pending restoration of order. When it was apparent that this would be long delayed, the situation was regularized by an agreement between the Chinese authorities and the British, American, and French consuls under which a joint foreign inspectorate of customs was set up to supervise the collection of tariff duties and administer the amounts accumulated.

The system worked well and was extended in scope in the ensuing years, a foreign staff being employed to supervise the operations. It worked so well and so much larger sums accrued to the imperial government by reason of greater efficiency and honesty that in 1858 another agreement was concluded under which the system was extended to all the ports where foreigners traded. A British Inspector General was appointed, more foreigners were engaged, and out of this developed the foreign control and management of China's maritime customs which lasted until after the nationalist revolution in the 1920's.

Under a British Inspector General foreigners collected tariff duties, deposited the funds in foreign banks, and administered the funds until receipts, less administrative expenses, were released to the Chinese government at regular intervals. This crucial part of China's administration, that which yielded the larger part of the Central Government's revenue, was under foreign jurisdiction and management for more than half a century. It was a glaring violation of sovereignty, but for China there was some advantage in that in the decades of decay, civil war, and breakdown there was a larger sum available to the government than there otherwise would have been, since the customs service remained intact and immune from governmental overturns.

There was another significant development in Chinese-foreign relations in these years. Great Britain had taken the lead in beating down China's barriers against the world from the coast, but meanwhile another Power had been assiduously but more quietly working in from the north. This was Russia. It has not been only in the twentieth century that Russia has been an active contender for priority, if not hegemony, in China. Russia had begun centuries before and though with less show of force than other Western Powers, with less drama and fewer overt acts and incidents, it probably has made more progress from the very beginning.

The Russian advance across the Ural Mountains into Eastern Asia began in the sixteenth century. It has never ceased. Remorselessly, slowly but persistently, it has pushed on. In the seventeenth century it had reached the undefined boundaries of the territory claimed by China. After minor clashes between forces representing the two countries, in which Russia did not always come off better, a treaty was signed in 1689 at Nerchinsk, east of Lake Baikal. This, the first treaty with a Western Power to be entered into by China, set the boundaries at the watershed north of the Amur River, a reversal for Russia.

There were minor incidents and modifications of the relations between the two in the ensuing century and a half, and meanwhile Russia advanced steadily eastward, its explorers, soldiers, adventurers, refugees, and pioneers in search of new land, carving paths and forming settlements after the fashion of pioneers in all new and uninhabited regions. By the middle of the nineteenth century Siberia was fairly well marked out and ready for development. This was just when European Powers were hammering at China's gates to the south and making breaches in them, all of which worked to Russia's advantage. Like the other Powers, Russia pressed for a revision of relations and concessions, though in a different region and in a different way. Russian representatives, it has been seen, participated in the negotiations accompanying the "Arrow" war, but it was a "parallel" participation, as was America's, though Russia played much more of a lone hand than did America.

In 1858 the Russians in separate negotiations at Aigun, far to the north, demanded a redrawing of frontiers much more to their favor. The Chinese protested but just then, with the British and French at Tientsin, they were helpless. The Treaty of Aigun was signed, ceding to Russia all the territory on the north bank of the Amur and providing joint control of the territory between the Ussuri River and the sea, now the Maritime Province of Siberia. But China refused to ratify this treaty as it did the Treaty of Tientsin with the British and French, and the Russians resorted to combined threats and blandishments. They alternately threatened to join the British and French and promised to intercede with them in China's favor. This was to become a familiar tactic in Russia's relations with China; it was still in use after World War II. With the imperial court in flight before the British and French and the government completely demoralized, the Chinese had no alternative. They yielded and in 1860 signed another treaty with Russia, as they did with other Western Powers. The boundaries were fixed as Russia demanded. All Eastern Siberia became Russian, including the part in which Vladivostok now lies, which is within striking distance of Japan and at the door of Korea and which dominates the whole northeast coast.

Thus the decade of the 1860's closed an epoch in both China's internal and external relations. The downward sweep of a cycle was in motion. It was not to reach its lowest point for almost a century.

CHAPTER VIII

Japan Opened to the World

In the twenty-year period in which China's foundation as a state was being sapped, Japan, too, was undergoing a fateful transformation, and attention should be turned now to that country.

One point must be cleared up first of all. The earlier notion that Japan lay dreaming placidly in a kind of Sleeping Beauty trance until rudely jolted awake by Commodore Perry in 1853 is oversimplified and untrue. The fact is that the Tokugawa system that had prevailed throughout the period of seclusion was loosening and cracking in all its parts. It would not have survived even if Perry had not come. In the nature of the forces of the nineteenth century Japan would have had to re-enter the world in any case. At the time the West gave Japan no choice, but neither would its own inner development have given it a choice.

The rigid symmetrical pattern of the Tokugawa scheme could no longer contain the forces pent up within it. The nice balance of the Tokugawa clan, the lesser feudal lords and their attendant samurai, the peasants, artisans, and merchants could be kept steady only as long as all the weights in the scale were held even. But in Japan, as in Europe in the preceding centuries, a new estate had emerged. This was the commercial class, the equivalent in Japan of the European *bourgeoisie*. Although this class had been the lowest class in the social system, it steadily became more important in the social composite through the eighteenth century and the first part of the nineteenth. In a simple feudal society in which land was the basis of wealth and rice was both the main product and the measure of value, equilibrium could be maintained as long as production was sufficient to satisfy needs. Production was not, however.

The feudal lords were compelled to maintain expensive establishments and to support their samurai with annual payments in rice. As has already been pointed out, they were also compelled by the Tokugawa shoguns to live on an extravagant scale, to spend large sums for travel back and forth between their own fiefs and Yedo, the Tokugawa capital, and to construct public works on command of the shoguns. No matter how grinding the taxes they levied on their peasants, they still could not make both ends meet. They were at times in arrears in their payments to the samurai and in some cases had to turn the samurai off. These became roving bands of unattached warriors—the ronin, as they were called—and sometimes they turned to outlawry. Before the end of the period they were to become a seriously disruptive influence. The daimyo fell deeper and deeper into debt, and for many of them there was only one recourse. This was to borrow.

There was only one quarter from which to borrow—the merchants. By the end of the eighteenth century trade had assumed considerable importance, if only because the demand for luxuries had grown, and firms of some magnitude had been established. The steady intrusion of the money economy and the growth of cities expanded their importance and enlarged their role in the society. As in Europe, life became polarized toward the cities. The merchants made loans to the daimyo and thus gradually obtained a measure of control over their properties, if not over them. The richer merchants were organized in guilds which steadily acquired a greater measure of power. The balance of Japanese society was shifting, but in such a way as to inject something inherently anomalous into the society.

The men of the merchant class, however extensive their interests might be and however rich they themselves were, still lay under a stigma of social inferiority. They were still under restrictions and restraints, not only as to their property but as to the use of their wealth. The humiliating sumptuary legislation, prescribing details of daily living and proscribing certain enjoyments of their income, was relaxed at times and sometimes politely overlooked, but it was still in effect. A class which had power was thus simultaneously subjected to humiliation and repression. It was an incongruity which inevitably generated disruptive force. Eventually the merchant class contributed materially to the strength of the movement for the overthrow of the Tokugawa shogunate, the opening of Japan to the world, and the restoration of the emperor to substantive power.

There was still another disruptive influence, though probably less serious. This was the ever sharpening popular discontent. The life of the peasants had never been more than just bearable. Everywhere in Asia the peasant was a beast of burden, but nowhere was he more driven and with less to sustain him than in Japan. And in the decades before 1853 his lot was becoming steadily worse. As the daimyo became poorer and their debts pressed on them, they themselves bore down more heavily on their peasants. Taxes and crop rents ground the peasants to the sheer edge of existence, sometimes to the point where existence was all but impossible. There were other exactions—forced labor and service, for example. The peasant, too, was forced into debt to meet taxes and crop rent, especially in years of poor yield, when what was left him after payment of taxes and rent was too little to live on. As always among poor peasants, especially in Asia, he had to borrow at usurious rates of interest. He borrowed from rich merchants and those of the daimyo who had surplus wealth, and in many cases he lost his land to them. He was then ground still harder, and when enough like him became desperate beyond endurance they resorted to violence. There were periodic peasant risings in various parts of the country through the latter part of the eighteenth century, and they became more numerous in the nineteenth. The basis of the Tokugawa shoguns' power lay in their ability to maintain internal peace after centuries of bloody strife. Now they were no longer able to guarantee public order and their hold on the country was correspondingly weakened.

Still another class became disaffected, an upper class composed of two groups dissident for different reasons. One was working for a renaissance of what it believed to be authentically Japanese; the other had become aware of the West, had acquired some knowledge of Western ideas and some intimation of Western power, and therefore was coming to believe that Japan would have to open its doors to the world, so that it could partake of the advantages that Westernism conferred. Both acquired increasing influence as the years moved toward the arrival of Commodore Perry.

With the progressive decline of Tokugawa power and prestige, men's minds began to turn back to the time before the Tokugawas, and among the better educated a critical, analytical spirit developed. This took concrete form in a school of historical studies, with emphasis on the old and presumably authentic institutions of Japan. In the mood of the time this in turn inevitably led to an idealization of the past and a desire to reconstruct the "pure" Japan. It also revived interest in the old myths about the country's divine origin and the sanctity of the imperial family, this last a matter that had to be treated with some discretion, since by inference it reflected on the Tokugawa shoguns as usurpers. Legitimism in the nineteenth-century European sense was becoming an issue tacitly but effectively nevertheless. A ferment was working in influential groups of the upper class, and a spirit was to rise that would eventually array many of that class against the shogunate and in favor of imperial restoration.

Western influence was stirring a similar ferment. It is not true, as once used to be written, that Japan was hermetically sealed off from the world during the whole period of seclusion. Through the aperture cut by the Dutch trading post on the island of Deshima something of the outer world could and did penetrate. For more than a hundred years after the beginning of the Tokugawa shogunate it was forbidden under drastic penalties to translate or even to read European books, but this prohibition was lifted early in the eighteenth century. There remained nevertheless difficulties that were almost insuperable. There was antiforeign prejudice. There was suspicion of everything from without. It was a risky enterprise to undertake studies in foreign learning or even to show too much interest. Further, there was the inherent conservatism, blended of Japanese insularity and the superciliousness of Confucian scholarship transplanted in Japan. It was a prodigious task to learn foreign languages from the meager supplies of books brought in by way of Deshima, and everything had to be seen through Dutch lenses.

What came through over the obstacles was only a smattering. It gave not so much knowledge or understanding as awareness. But this was of high potential consequence at a time when the West was coming into a new dispensation by way of the scientific revolution. If it did nothing else it gave the Japanese very early a sense of the power the West was acquiring through the instrumentalities of science. Because it opened Japan's eyes to the latent possibilities of accumulating wealth through the application of science to production and the immeasurable increase in trade, it gave the new commercial classes an incentive to reincorporate Japan into the world. And thus were shaken the complacency and obscurantism which the Japanese might otherwise have shared with the Chinese. Indeed, knowledge of the West had much to do with the contrast between the way China faced the test of the West's intrusion and the way Japan faced it. The Chinese remained ostrich-like until blasted out by the West's guns. The Japanese recognized the need of accommodation and began to adapt themselves to Westernism in order to meet the West on more nearly even terms.

Long before the opening to Perry's imperious knocking, conditions had thus been prepared for the abandonment of seclusion and the adoption of modernism. The shogunate was undermined by the West working through the Japanese themselves, and to this extent Japan began the task of social and cultural transformation in a healthier frame.

Perry's, it should be understood, was not the first attempt to force Japan open. It was only the most successful, since it came at the most propitious moment. There had been other attempts, and if they did not succeed it was because neither the circumstances in the world outside

Japan nor the conditions within Japan were conducive to success. But now, in the middle of the nineteenth century, the West had begun its definite, forceful incursion into Eastern Asia. It had the power to do so, and it was determined to use its power. It had succeeded in gaining a foothold in China and had derived increased confidence therefrom.

Now Japan also was open to encroachment. There was no longer any genuine belief in seclusion. There was lack of confidence in the repository of power, which was the shogunate. There were divided loyalties. Some of the clans of Western Japan, never wholly reconciled to Tokugawa overlordship, were restive, and opportunity seemed to beckon. If they were not overtly allied, a tacit understanding seemed to develop among them. For the West there was no feeling of welcome. There was even fear of it. But Westernism was attractive, if only for the power that it carried with it. Not only the ability to withstand the more aggressive West was lacking but also the resoluteness with which previous attempts to open up the country had been stood off.

Sporadic efforts had, indeed, been made in the past by one Western country after another to open relations with Japan, the Russians being most persistent. The Russians had got to the Kuriles early in the eighteenth century and by the end of the century began to reach toward Japan itself. Three successive expeditions were launched between 1792 and 1811. The Japanese were adamant; all were turned off or beaten off. The Russians chose not to force the issue. For one thing, the Napoleonic wars were in progress. The Russians were followed by the British. They, too, made several attempts in the first half of the nineteenth century, but they had no more success than the Russians. Within Japan a perceptible decline might be setting in and disruptive forces perceptibly gathering. Some Japanese groups might have become restless, penned up within the walls of self-imposed seclusion. But the country as a whole was not yet disposed formally to open its doors to the West and resume intercourse with the world. Xenophobia was still too general and racial egoism too unshaken.

After the defeat of China in 1842, the treaties imposed by the three principal Western Powers opening the country to foreign trade, and the subsequent establishment of foreign colonies in coastal ports, all was to change. There was an end to halfhearted and sporadic Western efforts for entry into all Eastern Asia. The walls had been breached. They were to fall everywhere. With the Dutch alone had the Japanese had even a faint semblance of relations through the trading post at Deshima, and twice in the 1840's William II of the Netherlands sent communications to the shogun apprising him of what was happening in China and warning him that Japan, too, was not immune. In fact, when the American government had decided to dispatch the mission of Commodore Perry it informed the Dutch government of its intention and asked it to transmit the information to the shogun. Both indirectly from what they knew of what had occurred in China and directly by way of the Netherlands the Japanese were forewarned; but they were not yet impressed enough by what they knew of Western might or shaken enough within to take any measures to forestall the impending shock or soften it by yielding in advance.

With regard to Japan as with regard to other parts of East Asia, the United States, while not so active a participant as Great Britain or even Russia, was not without interest or activity. The United States, too, had had its eyes on Japan. Its vessels, too, needed harbors into which to put for repairs and supplies and, like the British, French, and Russians, its vessels had picked up shipwrecked Japanese sailors from time to time and had sought unsuccessfully to repatriate them. And it was no less tempted to open up still another avenue for trade. But between America's attitude toward the opening of China and its attitude toward the opening of Japan there was a notable difference.

In the decade since the opening of China much had changed within the United States to account for the difference. The victorious war with Mexico had carried the Republic across the continent. The discovery of gold in California had begun to draw settlers to the Pacific coast and promised the early integration of the coastal region into the country, with a corresponding increase in interest in the Pacific and the lands on the other side of the Pacific. Already there had been consideration and discussion of a canal through the Central American isthmus to connect the two oceans, and the Clayton-Bulwer treaty concluded in 1850 between Great Britain and the United States providing for joint control of such a canal gave the project concreteness, even if it was not to materialize for some sixty years. Steam navigation had created greater opportunities for foreign trade and stronger incentives to seek it.

Events in Hawaii had also served to draw the country's attention to the Pacific and its commercial prospects. Throughout the 1840's both Great Britain and France had resorted to recurrent maneuvers to get control of the Sandwich Islands, the name by which Hawaii was then known. To every such attempt the United States interposed objections, sometimes stating its objections in the form of barely concealed threats. In 1842 Daniel Webster, then Secretary of State, warned officially that the United States would not consent to any other Power's taking control of those islands. In 1849 Webster, again Secretary of State, this time under President Taylor, said significantly: "The United States can never consent to see these islands taken possession of by either of the great commercial Powers of Europe." The significance lies in the word commercial.

Still more pointedly, President Fillmore, Taylor's successor, explaining in his message on the State of the Union why his government had recognized the independence of the Islands after France had run its flag up and hauled it down again on American insistence, said that the government was motivated "by the consideration that they [the Islands] lie in the course of the great trade which must at no distant day be carried on between the Western coast of North America and Eastern Asia. . . . I need not say that the importance of these considerations has been greatly influenced by the sudden and vast development which the interests of the United States have attained in California and Oregon, and the policy heretofore adopted in regard to those islands will be steadily pursued." The last words meant, of course, that all other Powers would be kept out of Hawaii by any means required, and so it turned out. And, it should be emphasized, it was not the intrinsic importance of Hawaii but the prospect of the trade with Eastern Asia, always in American consciousness and more alluring by virtue of the opening of China and the expansion of the United States to the Pacific coast, that impelled Fillmore to take his strong stand.

One thing more must be noted. It was between the middle of the 1840's and the middle of the 1850's that the movement began for a transcontinental railway with government subvention. There was protracted public debate, with much organized propaganda. Petitions were circulated, resolutions were passed by both public and private bodies, memorials were sent to Congress, and hearings were held and resolutions passed by committees of both houses of Congress. It is noteworthy that the argument most frequently advanced and counted on as most cogent was that the transcontinental railway would bring the agricultural West and industrial East nearer to the markets of Asia and thus give the United States a competitive advantage over European trading nations. It was as if the main purpose of such a railway were easier access to Asiatic markets, and the linking of the two shores of the country an incidental effect, rather than the reverse. This may not have been generally or even genuinely believed, and the appeal of Asiatic trade may have been used only as a talking point; but that it was considered a good talking point, an argument that would weigh with the government and public opinion, itself testifies to the thought of the country and the direction of its interest.

The United States, in short, was acutely concerned with the Asiatic shore of the Pacific before Japan was opened, more concerned than it was to be again until the end of the nineteenth century. It was out of this concern that Perry's mission was dispatched, and there was a sense of urgency, lest Great Britain act first in Japan, as it had in China. Again it must be pointed out that the United States was Great Britain's closest competitor for trade in East Asian waters in the first half of the nineteenth century.

As has been said, America had not been inactive before 1850 in the effort to open Japan. American ships had attempted to enter its ports for trade, just as British and Russian ships, and with as little success. The "Morrison," bearing three shipwrecked Japanese sailors, put in at Uraga in the Bay of Yedo in 1837. There were also some missionaries on board who sought to land to carry on teaching. The "Morrison" was first denied entry and then fired on to speed its parting. It had to withdraw, taking the Japanese sailors back with it. Another ship, the "Manhattan," also bearing shipwrecked Japanese sailors, was allowed to land in 1845 and to remain a few days but denied intercourse for any purpose. Two more vessels, under command of Commodore Biddle, arrived in the Bay of Yedo in 1846 and formally asked to enter into negotiations for a treaty opening Japanese ports to trade. The request was brusquely refused. In these years, too, American ships were coming to grief in the vicinity of Japanese waters and had to put in at Japanese ports for refuge. There the crews were imprisoned and in some cases brutally maltreated. Combined with the growth of American interest in the Pacific generally, these incidents only served to stimulate a resolve to force the issue and do in Japan as Great Britain had done in China. However, the Americans never seem to have faced the question whether to resort to war if necessary, as the British had in Canton, though Perry did make it clear that he was prepared to use force if the Japanese were recalcitrant. For one thing, there was no such issue as opium to provide the cumulative rancor that made compromise impossible in China.

In 1851 the decision was taken to make a formal effort to open Japan. Webster authorized the commander of the naval squadron in China to prepare to proceed to Japan for the purpose. Webster's original instructions were moderate. They asked only for friendly intercourse between the two countries: the right to buy coal for American ships in need of fuel, protection for shipwrecked sailors, and the opening of one or more ports for normal trade. Commander Aulick, the officer originally chosen for the expedition, became ill and Commander Matthew Perry was chosen instead. Webster, too, became ill and Acting Secretary of State C. M. Conrad drew up a new set of instructions for Perry, more explicit and sterner than Webster's. They included the following paragraph in accordance with the spirit of the time:

"Recent events—the navigation of the ocean by steam, the acquisition and rapid settlement by this country of a vast territory on the Pacific, the discovery of gold in that region, the rapid communication across the Isthmus that separates the two oceans—have practically brought the countries of the East in closer proximity to our own; although the consequences of these events have scarcely begun to be felt, the intercourse between them has already greatly increased and no limits can be assigned to its future extension."

Something is to be learned, too, from a statement by Commodore Perry while on his way across the Pacific, expressing sentiments that could not have been evolved out of his own consciousness but must have been produced by his reflections on discussions in Washington before he departed and therefore bespoke the spirit in which the mission was decided upon. He wrote:

When we look at the possessions in the east of our great maritime rival, England, and of the constant and rapid increase of their fortified ports, we should be admonished of the necessity of prompt measures on our part. By reference to the map of the world it will be seen that Great Britain is already in possession of the most important points in the East India and China seas. . . . Fortunately the Japanese and many other islands of the Pacific are still left untouched by this unconscionable government [England]; and some of them lay in a route of a great commerce which is destined to become of great importance to the United States. No time should be lost in adopting active measures to secure a sufficient number of ports of refuge. And hence I shall look with much anxiety for the arrival of the Powhatan and the other vessel to be sent me.

None of this was explicitly put in Perry's instructions, however. He was to seek only the objects assigned to Aulick, to be firm but also conciliatory. The United States wanted only to live in peace and friendship with Japan and therefore "Japan should change her policy and cease to act toward the people of the United States as if they were her enemies." If the conciliatory approach produced no effect, he was to be stiffer and to warn the Japanese that if there was any more mistreatment of American sailors in the future, punitive measures would be taken. But he was not to use force at all except in self-defense, that is, if his ships and men were attacked. As a token of good will Perry took with him a large assortment of presents, including a miniature railroad, with a locomotive, tender, a small car and tracks, and telegraphic instruments, rifles, pistols, and a generous quantity of liquor. The presents aroused almost as much excitement among the Japanese as his ships.

Perry arrived off Uraga on July 8, 1853, with four fighting ships, ready for any eventuality. He asked at once for the right to present President Fillmore's letter, which, incidentally, was addressed to the emperor. The Japanese sought to temporize, much as the Chinese once did, but they did not fire on his ships, as they had on foreign vessels before. They were too impressed by Perry's display of force. They knew now what had happened at Canton and were circumspect. They attempted to send minor officials to treat with Perry, but he refused to receive them, insisting that an official of appropriate rank be sent. They asked him to go to Nagasaki to wait; he refused. They put out a guard of small armed boats around his ships and he ordered them off on penalty of being driven off if they did not go voluntarily. They went. When the Japanese refused to send somebody of high rank to receive his letter Perry threatened to land with armed forces and deliver it himself. Then two Japanese of princely rank agreed to receive him on shore and to them he made his addresses and delivered his letter. He was then ordered to depart and refused, but after moving his ships in the direction of Yedo by way of demonstration he voluntarily departed, notifying that he would return the following spring for his answer and leaving no doubt that it would be to Japan's interests to make the answer favorable.

He returned to the Bay of Yedo in February, 1854, earlier than he had expected, since he had had word that a Russian fleet was in Japanese waters, and he did not want to be anticipated. After some more Japanese temporizing maneuvers, Perry was received at Yokohama and there informed that the shogun's government was willing to negotiate. At first it was proposed to open the port of Nagasaki to Americans on the same terms as those accorded the Dutch, which was tantamount to semi-internment or something like the conditions under which foreign traders had lived outside Canton before 1842. Perry summarily refused. The Japanese then yielded with as good grace as they could to what they recognized as the inevitable and signed a treaty on March 31, 1854.

Perry did not get all he had asked. Only two ports were opened to foreign ships—Hakodate in the north and Shimoda, near the Bay of Yedo. Neither was of much use for trade, but a principle had been gained. An American consul was to be allowed to reside at Shimoda but nothing was said about permanent residence for traders. Also most-favored-nation status was granted and better treatment was assured American sailors who were forced to land in Japan. The right of extraterritoriality was not asked, an act of restraint which was to stand to America's credit, since thereby Japan was spared the humiliation meted out to China. Neither side could claim complete victory. Japan had had to lower its barriers to foreigners; Perry had not obtained all he demanded. But on the American side, though victory was a partial one, even that much had been won by persuasion rather than force. On the Japanese side, by foregoing obscurantism humiliation had been escaped.

Compared to what had happened in China, the episode reflected credit on both sides and was to accrue to the advantage of both later.

As in China, the first Power to pierce the gates was soon followed by others. The British obtained a treaty at Nagasaki in October, 1854, and the Russians at Shimoda in February, 1855. The Dutch obtained one in January, 1856, being released from their earlier confinement and given the same rights as the other three Powers. Under the most-favored-nation provision, which all four treaties carried, the original conditions were extended. The Powers could obtain supplies at Shimoda, Hakodate, and Nagasaki. They could appoint consuls at both Shimoda and Hakodate. They could trade, with certain official restrictions, at all three ports, and male foreigners could reside at Nagasaki. Also a measure of extraterritoriality was won in the later treaties.

Thus Japan's seclusion was ended. For practical purposes a new life had begun for Japan.

Before leaving this episode in American history, one of the most important in its history as it turned out, it is necessary to recount some of the incidental events that were also to play a part, if only a negative one, in subsequent developments in the Pacific. As can be seen from the Perry statement already quoted, his ideas extended beyond Japan and he saw his problem as more than naval. He was attempting to think through a philosophy of America's status in the Pacific and his thoughts were not confined to his time or to strategic problems. They had a certain grandeur, if not grandiosity.

Perhaps out of that rivalry with the British which is well established in the American naval tradition, Perry was looking for points at which to counter British influence, politically and commercially as well as strategically. He proposed formally that he be permitted to occupy the Ryukyu (Liuchiu) Islands (of which Okinawa is one), the Bonin Islands (of which Iwo Jima is one), and Formosa. The United States could not escape the responsibilities "which our growing wealth and power must inevitably fasten upon us. The duty of protecting our vast and rapidly growing commerce will make it not only a measure of wisdom but of positive necessity to provide timely preparation for events which must, in the ordinary course of things, transpire in the east." Hence he foresaw the necessity of acquiring bases or posts or settlements, not for military purposes but for trade. Conventional naval thinking or historical foresight, even premonition? One cannot say; but it is worth recording, and inevitably it was recalled in the years between 1941 and 1945 when the Ryukyus and the Bonins were the scenes of memorable battles and cruel losses in men to obtain what Perry wanted and could have taken. It was recalled, too, after 1949, when Formosa became a kind of symbol on which a bitter internal political controversy was waged in this country, both in the government and in public opinion. Perry had landed in both the Ryukyus and the Bonins and lodged temporary establishments there, meanwhile proposing to the government at Washington that he be permitted to run up the American flag. With regard to the Bonins there was the beginning of a diplomatic brush with the British, who, if they did not have a counterclaim to those islands, at least looked with disapproval on American possession of them. But before that issue could even take form, the Department of State on President Pierce's order vigorously vetoed the whole project. The acquisition of outlying territory did not yet enter into American thinking or comport with its tradition or its conception of its role in the world.

A few years later Dr. Peter Parker, an American missionary who had come to China almost a decade before the opening of China, was appointed Commissioner to China. This was in 1855, just before the second war with China and the culmination of Western impatience with Chinese obstruction. Parker also conceived grandiose designs, among them no less than the annexation of Formosa. Perhaps because he was politically naïve and perhaps because he was overawed by his sudden exaltation to diplomatic status, Parker worked himself up into a fury of agitation and indulged in maneuverings which in a more normal political atmosphere could have had serious consequences. He made plans for a naval expedition to Formosa, and for a time American traders, without Parker's approval to say the least, ran up the American flag at Takao, a port on the southwest coast. Meanwhile a stream of urgent and hortatory dispatches was sent flowing to Washington and Parker gathered his forces, material and immaterial, for an act of conquest and expansion. Finally the answer came back from Washington. President Pierce's government cursorily and peremptorily rejected the whole idea, not without accents of reproof to Parker for his impetuosity.

Thus there was laid down, early in America's participation in Far Eastern affairs, a self-denying ordinance with regard to territorial acquisition. America wanted trade in the Far East, not territory; but trade without any unfair handicaps laid by the political measures of competitors. When James Buchanan, who succeeded to the presidency in 1857, sent William B. Reed to China as minister, the instructions given Reed were explicit and forceful. They read in part:

"You will not fail to let it be known to the Chinese authorities that we are no party to the existing hostilities, and have no intention to interfere in their political concerns, or to gain a foothold in their country. We go there to engage in trade, but under suitable guarantees for its protection.

The extension of our commercial intercourse must be the work of individual enterprise, and to this element of our national character we may safely leave it."

And so the United States did leave it for the rest of the nineteenth century, unique in the Western world's relations with the East, and to that may be attributed the high esteem in which the United States was held in Eastern Asia, the faith which the peoples of that part of the world had in its purposes and principles. Not until 1898 did the United States depart from its rule of action by taking Hawaii and the Philippines, but since the Philippines was to be prepared for self-government and then given independence and Hawaii was to have the status of an autonomous territory, they were acquisitions of a different order from the conventional Western expansion in the East. Only after 1945 did the United States make a clear, categorical break from its historic practice of restraint in territorial aggrandizement.

CHAPTER IX

Japan Accepts the New Dispensation

Japan was opened to the world, but there, as in China after the battering down of the gates, a period of confusion ensued, though with the difference that in Japan internal conflict was added to resistance to external intrusion. The recalcitrants against intercourse with the foreigner, while not so numerous, widespread, and uncompromising as in China, were strong enough to cause trouble for years. Also, and more important, the question of the declining shogunate had to be resolved. Submission to the foreigner had diminished its prestige still further and made its position even more unstable. Indeed, from the signing of the treaties with the Western Powers the days of the shogunate could be said to be numbered. On it was laid responsibility for the decision and blame for the consequent humiliation, illogically so because the shogun could not help himself and, moreover, the first treaties with the West, while negotiated by the Bakufu (the shogun's government) had been approved by the emperor's court in Kyoto. The imminent necessity of choosing a successor, since the ailing incumbent shogun was without heir, precipitated a struggle within the Tokugawa clan, which did not smooth the course of domestic politics or solidify the position of the shogunate.

The opening of relations with the West drove the contending factions further apart, both within the shogunate and between the partisans of the shogunate and the partisans of imperial restoration. The Western countries were not satisfied with treaties alone. As in China, they wanted fulfillment in act, and this meant the right of residence and the uninhibited right to trade. And, like the Chinese, the Japanese sought to temporize and obstruct. America took the lead again. The government appointed as its first consul to Japan a man named Townsend Harris, a New York merchant who had already been engaged in the Far Eastern trade. Harris was to prove a unique figure in American diplomatic history and one of the most distinguished figures in American diplomacy.

He left an impress on Japan as has no other foreigner, and a whole body of Japanese legends has gathered about his person. He was so completely a variant from the type of Occidental who went to the East in an official capacity as to be almost of a different species. When he said he was in Japan as a friend of the Japanese people it was not a diplomatic manner of speaking. He meant it and he lived up to it.

Harris arrived in Japan in August, 1856, and took up residence in Shimoda, the port partially opened by the Perry treaty. His mission was to negotiate the first commercial treaty between the United States and Japan, one which would assure normal rights of residence and trade. His earliest experiences in a remote and unfamiliar land were a trial of the flesh and the spirit. He lived alone in a small, poor, desolate port, housed in a shabby Buddhist temple, without the amenities, comforts, even necessities of the normal life of an Occidental. He was deprived of normal human intercourse.

The Japanese kept him at a distance, spied on all his movements, frustrated him by all the devices known to them, which were not few or unskillful. They sought thus to wear him down and by isolation, frustration, and discomfort force him to surrender and go home. They failed. Harris was patient, tolerant, and understanding. He perceived that their tactics arose from unfamiliarity rather than enmity. And by his forbearance and courtesy and the determination by which they were stiffened, he finally won the confidence of the minor officials sent to watch over him. He did so by patient conversations with them, by reasoning, by earnest and didactic disquisitions on the world into which they had entered, and by tokens of his own good faith. In a little more than a year his efforts were rewarded. Preliminary conventions were signed giving Americans the right to reside at Shimoda and Hakodate, to buy supplies at Nagasaki, and to enjoy complete extraterritoriality for criminal offenses, the latter having been embodied in principle in earlier treaties, especially the Dutch and Russian.

With that accomplished, Harris now pressed for permission to proceed to Yedo, the seat of the Bakufu, to give the agreement the formal status of a treaty. Again dilatory measures were resorted to. The situation was, though in lesser degree, of the same kind as that produced by the request of the foreigners for audience with the emperor of China fifty years before. Sanctity was being violated. For nearly 250 years no Occidental had been received by the shogun. But Harris won, thanks in some measure to enlightened men around the shogun, who knew that their world was changing and, perhaps of even greater weight, knew what had happened in China and could profit by the lesson. Harris proceeded to Yedo early in December, 1857, and was received by the shogun. He records in his diary how to the amazement of the shogun's court a foreigner could "look the awful Tycoon in the face, speak plainly to him, hear his reply—and all this without any trepidation, or 'any quivering of the muscles of the side.' " Harris did so and won his point— by persuasion, not threat.

With so much gained, Harris proceeded to his main object—the conclusion of a normal treaty of amity and commerce between two countries. Thus began a long course of negotiations, which consisted of discussion as much as negotiation and at which Harris was at his best. He was expository and didactic rather than conventionally diplomatic and demanding. In a long series of meetings lasting two months he explained customary usages between countries, the condition of the Western world and its strength compared to the weakness of the East and the resulting relation between the two. And he dwelt with emphasis on what was happening in China, where in that year of 1858 Great Britain and France were making war again. This was the fate in store for Japan unless it seized the opportunity to establish relations with the outer world on a normal basis voluntarily and at once. In that case it could obtain a status as near equality as was possible in the circumstances, whereas if it did so only under forcible pressure, the example of China was eloquent. Furthermore, if it did so first with the United States the terms would set a precedent for more favorable treatment, since the purposes of the United States were without national political self-interest, in contrast with those of the European Powers. It wanted trade, not territorial possessions or power, as events in China in the preceding fifteen years bore witness.

Harris' arguments were persuasive and a treaty was drawn up at the end of February, 1868, with provision for final signature on April 21. It was not to go so simply, however. Antiforeign recalcitrance was galvanized by the new concessions to the West. A number of the daimyo were against further compromise and they were supported by a faction of court nobles around the imperial court in Kyoto. There was alarm in Yedo, where there was more understanding of the foreigner's power and his resolve to brook no further obstruction or procrastination. Lord Hotta, an influential daimyo at the shogun's court, went to Kyoto to plead for acceptance of the treaty as the dictate of fate in lieu of something worse if the country remained intransigent. It should be observed here that so far had the shogunate already declined in prestige and the imperial court correspondingly gained that it was deemed advisable to reconcile the imperial court as well as the extremist daimyo. Lord Hotta argued urgently, but when mid-April and the date for the signing of the treaty approached he had made little progress. He had to return to Yedo and ask for an extension of time until September. Harris, sensibly and with characteristic patience and understanding of the internal difficulties, agreed.

He did not have to wait so long, however, for events in China forced the issue. Word arrived of China's complete defeat by the British and French and of the treaties forced on China, treaties far more stringent than those of 1842 and after. The message was brought to Harris at Shimoda by an American warship. This was followed by the arrival of a Russian ship and reports that a combined Western fleet would soon arrive to impose terms. Harris embarked at once on the U.S.S. "Powhatan," proceeded to the port of Kanagawa and from there communicated with officials of the Bakufu. This was at the end of June and the men around the Bakufu were duly impressed. They decided to yield against the imminent threat. It was better to deal with Harris, of whose moderation and friendliness they were sure. On July 29 the treaty was signed on board the "Powhatan." Harris had won, and Japan had formally admitted the West to regular intercourse. But Japan had not entirely lost, for in yielding to Harris it probably escaped a worse lot.

The treaty provided for exchange of diplomatic representatives, the stationing of American consuls at the ports opened to trade, the opening of additional ports, extraterritoriality in both civil and criminal cases, and a conventional tariff with fixed rates subject to change by treaty only—the rate was subsequently fixed at a uniform 5 per cent. Also America won freedom for its citizens to practice their religion and, as in China, most-favored-nation status. As after Perry's coming, Harris was soon followed by representatives of the other Powers. Within a month the Dutch, British, and Russians had signed treaties almost exactly like the American, and in October the French did likewise.

The treaties were signed and a principle won, but the antiforeign elements were not reconciled. On the contrary, their bitterness was exacerbated, and it soon manifested itself in acts. With the slogan *San No Jo I* —revere the emperor, expel the barbarian—their forces gathered and, after the old Japanese manner, resorted to violence. Again it should be pointed out that it was the emperor who was to be revered, not the shogun. Thus far had the anti-shogunate movement advanced, and the concessions to the West played into its hands. They were taken advantage of by many for domestic political purposes, apart from the merits of the question of continued seclusion. It was therefore around the court at Kyoto that the antiforeign groups coalesced. These included not only antiforeign fanatics but influential daimyo who, whether antiforeign or not, were anti-Tokugawa. Among the latter were the four powerful Western clans which were to play so decisive a role in the decade after the restoration of the emperor. They were the Choshu, Satsuma, Hizen, and Tosa. It was on the combination of Choshu and Satsuma that Japanese militarism was based until after World War I, Choshu controlling the army and Satsuma the navy.

Direct action set in after 1868. It took the form of attacks on the persons and property of foreign nationals, a number being killed in the years immediately following. The British and American legations were attacked and burned down. C. H. Heusken, who had been serving as Harris' interpreter, was murdered. Not all this was wanton. There were provocations too. Unfortunately, many foreigners were inclined to take in Japan the overbearing attitude that had marked the conduct of Occidentals everywhere else in the East since they first had arrived, an inclination not weakened by the fact that many of the first to come to Japan after 1854 came from China, where the attitude was being manifested at its worst. Fanaticism and provocation make a dangerous combination in any circumstance, and a particularly dangerous one among a people as warlike as the Japanese and at a time as turbulent as the 1860's. In any case, the incidents continued to occur until a climax was precipitated by one of particular seriousness.

This was the murder on September 14, 1862, of C. L. Richardson, a British subject who had come to Japan from Hongkong. He and three other Britons, one a woman, were riding horseback on a main road near Yokohama on which a procession bearing the daimyo of Satsuma was passing on the way to Yedo. By Japanese custom all men were obliged to dismount when such a procession passed, the penalty for failure to do so being death. Richardson, accustomed to Chinese usages and Chinese compliance, refused. He and his party were at once set upon by the samurai attending the daimyo. Richardson was killed and the others were wounded.

This brought on a general outcry for reprisals and focussed the whole question of the foreigners' status. The British decided that the time had come to act. There were demands by many Britons for immediate punitive measures, but the British government preferred a more moderate course for the present. In April of the following year a British admiral arrived with a set of demands that had the ring of an ultimatum, since failure to meet them would be followed by naval action. The demands called for an official apology, an indemnity of £100,000, and the execution of the men guilty of the murder. The Bakufu asked for an extension of time on the demands and it was granted. But while the British were waiting for an answer, the antiforeign groups in Kyoto persuaded the emperor to issue in June an order closing all ports to foreign ships—in effect expelling foreigners. Knowing that such an order would precipitate action by the British, who would also be sure to have French support, the Bakufu quickly accepted the British demands.

The officials around the shogun recognized the foolhardiness of trying to enforce the exclusion decree, which was to go into effect on June 25, and made it clear that they would not do so. But the strong-minded men of the Western clans were not inhibited by caution. The day after the expulsion order was to go into effect the daimyo of Choshu, in the southwest corner of Honshu, ordered the guns of his forts at Shimonoseki and the ships in the harbor to fire on the American trading vessel "Pembroke." In the two weeks following, British and Dutch naval vessels also were fired on, but even before those incidents an American warship was on the way to Shimonoseki to inflict punishment. When it arrived off the port it, too, was fired on and in reply it bombarded the port and destroyed the ships that had fired. Immediately after that a French ship arrived, landed a small force, destroyed some of the shore batteries, and burned a village.

Meanwhile the British demands in the Richardson case had not been entirely satisfied. The separate indemnity which the Shimadzu family, senior family of the Satsumas, was to pay to Richardson's survivors had not been handed over and the guilty men had not been punished. In August, 1863, the British sent a squadron of seven ships to Kagoshima, on the southern tip of Kyushu, the southernmost island. They were fired on and a battle was fought in which the British suffered some casualties, but the port was bombarded and severely damaged and several Japanese ships were sunk. The Satsuma then yielded, paid the indemnity, and agreed to execute the guilty men. As an interesting appendix, in the negotiations over the settlement the British were induced to help the Satsumas to purchase a naval vessel in England, thus starting the Satsumas' interest in navies, one which they held until after the early part of the twentieth century.

While these retaliatory measures were deemed sufficient for individual incidents, the Western representatives were coming to the conclusion that something more formal and general was required to give the treaties substantive and lasting value. There were proposals for a larger allied expedition to demonstrate once and for all to the most fanatical that Japan's engagements would have to be fulfilled and that foreigners, being entitled by treaty to enter the country, would have to remain unmolested. It might have been urged on the other side that duress had entered into the making of the contract and thus impaired its validity, but that was an abstract point as long as the Western states had the power to pronounce and execute judgment; furthermore, the Japanese at the seat of authority, which was the Bakufu, were themselves convinced of the necessity of accepting the new status.

The last consideration was not without force in the final outcome, since, as has been said, Japanese dissension on the position of the foreigners was inseparably intermingled with internal politics—the shogunate versus the imperial court and the groups working for imperial restoration. It was the latter who were intransigent and who were seeking to nullify agreements made by the Bakufu, if only to embarrass the latter. To a certain extent therefore the Bakufu was not unwilling to see the strong measures taken by the allied Powers against the Western clans and their supporters in Kyoto. In short, it wanted the Western clans and their supporters in Kyoto put in their place.

In any case the Western Powers decided to act. A fleet of British, French, and Dutch ships, with one American ship, was assembled and proceeded to Shimonoseki in August, 1864. There is evidence that this had not been sanctioned by the home governments, even that the British government disapproved; but under the strong leadership of the British Minister Sir Rutherford Alcock, who had served in China and perhaps acquired the habit of strong action there, the expedition proceeded anyway. Arriving off Shimonoseki, the ships went to work without preliminary palaver. They bombarded the port and silenced the forts. Then landing parties were sent ashore to destroy the guns. Early in September the Choshu leaders acknowledged defeat and entered into negotiations. The terms imposed were harsh. An indemnity of $3,000,000 was to be paid, the Straits of Shimonoseki were to be opened to passage of ships and to remain unfortified, and foreign ships were to be permitted to stop at Shimonoseki and purchase supplies.

One more effort was needed, however, to suppress opposition entirely. When delay ensued in payment of one installment of the indemnity the British and French saw an opportunity that could be capitalized to put down all obstruction. They proposed to send another joint naval expedition to Osaka, the port near Kyoto, to enforce their will. Their demands were the immediate opening of Osaka and Hiogo, instead of in 1868 as originally stipulated; the reduction of the tariff to a uniform 5 per cent; and imperial ratification of the treaties. In return, two-thirds of the Shimonoseki indemnity would be remitted. Incidentally, the United States returned its share of the indemnity in 1883 to pay the cost of constructing a breakwater in the harbor of Yokohama, which was to become Japan's principal port. The expedition never had to be made. Before it was undertaken the imperial court yielded; the lesson of Kagoshima and Shimonoseki had sunk in. The ports of Osaka and Hiogo were not opened until 1868 and therefore the full indemnity would have to be paid, but the emperor agreed to ratify the 1868 treaties, which was most important. There were still to be incidents in which foreigners were to be attacked and in some instances murdered, but essentially antiforeign resistance was broken. The last vestiges of the unreconstructed submitted. They had been convinced, by demonstration of ineluctable force, that their hopes were vain.

On the foreign issue the shogunate had triumphed over the imperial faction and paradoxically this hastened its downfall. For the imperial faction had demonstrated its strength and, furthermore, the adherence to it of the Western clans had cut a deep fissure within the shogunate. It was by keeping the powerful clans in submission by the devices already described that the shogunate could maintain unchallengeable control; but now it had been demonstrated that it could no longer keep them in submission. The power of the West, not the power of the shogunate, had subdued them.

Even among the closest supporters of the Tokugawas there were schisms. Dispute over the right of succession as shogun had left its mark. The Bakufu was forced to resort to ever more stringent measures to keep down opposition. Here, too, characteristically Japanese violence was employed. There were purges, assassinations on both sides, arrests, banishments. At the same time economic difficulties became aggravated, in part because of exports of staple commodities such as silk and tea in the newly opened foreign trade and the draining of gold from the country by unskillful financial policies. The consequent rise in prices resulted in increased hardship, discontent, and the undermining of financial stability.

As a byplay to the conflict on foreign policy and the defiance of the Bakufu's orders, there were armed clashes between Bakufu forces and Choshu armies. Punitive expeditions were undertaken by the Bakufu but they were indecisive, which also did not add to the prestige of the shogunate. In 1866 the incumbent shogun died, and was succeeded by a man of a lesser branch of the Tokugawa family, Keiki, who already had exercised some influence in the Bakufu. At the same time the emperor died, to be succeeded by the fifteen-year-old youth who reigned under the name of Meiji for forty-five years, through the period of Japan's phenomenal rise to a position as first-rate Power.

All the forces within Japanese society were making for change, and they began to coalesce. The entry of the West and the decline of the shogunate seemed to call for a fresh start and a new order. On the part of all the more alert, open-minded, and vigorous there was recognition that the past had closed. Among them were those intimately associated with the shogunate, including the shogun himself, and before long the handwriting on the wall became legible to all but those unwilling to see. There were negotiations, informal and not openly acknowledged, between Yedo and Kyoto, and in 1867 the new shogun announced his willingness to surrender his powers to the emperor. The imperial court accepted, the shogunate ended, and the emperor assumed full powers, formally announcing the assumption in a restoration rescript early in 1868.

A small group of die-hards in Yedo refused to yield, and there were open clashes between forces of considerable size. The shogun himself, in protest against arbitrary reduction in rank on the emperor's order, rebelled and a punitive expedition had to be sent to put down his followers, he himself being first sentenced to die and then sent into exile. There was one more final flare-up before all resistance ended in 1869. Then Japan was united under the single rule of the imperial dynasty, now substantive instead of symbolical, and the country entered on its remarkable modernization and progress to world eminence, not to be interrupted until the signing of the document of surrender on the U.S.S. "Missouri" on September 2, 1945.

CHAPTER X

China Inert and Immovable

The disastrous defeat of China by Anglo-French forces in the second war with Western Powers (see Chapter VII) resulted in additions to Western privileges. The Chinese appeared to be finally beaten into submission and the foreigners to have won irrevocably a legitimized status in China as states and as persons. China, too, was entering a new era, but one that was not so favored by fortune as Japan's. In fact, a long decline was setting in, one which was not to be arrested for almost a century, if not longer.

By 1860 the first phase of conflict with the West had ended, but internally there was still turmoil. The Taiping Rebellion was still to continue for five years, though it was obviously in its last stages. But there were other internal disturbances of large dimension, especially among the Moslems and non-Chinese peoples of the outer areas who had been brought under Chinese rule in the early vigorous days of the Ching dynasty. In Yunnan, a southwestern province, the Moslems, here mainly Chinese, had risen in 1856 after local clashes with non-Moslem Chinese. In Sinkiang, the western border area which is a meeting ground of various races and adjoins Russian-controlled territory and which, furthermore, has seldom remained peaceful for long, there was rebellion and serious fighting. In the northwest, too, there was conflict with the Moslems.

Not until late in the 1870's was peace completely restored, and then by virtue of the military and organizational genius of two remarkable figures—Chinese, not Manchus. They were Tseng Kuo-fan and Tso Tsung-tang. The former was mainly responsible for the suppression of the Taipings and the latter for the suppression of the Moslems and other rebels in the west and northwest. Tso conducted campaigns lasting for years, moving relentlessly stage by stage from the center of the country to its outermost regions, reducing his enemies as he went. When he had advanced too far from his source of supply and farther than Chinese means of transportation could carry to him, he stopped, set his men to sowing crops and waited until the harvest could provide for another year's campaign. Tseng Kuo-fan, Tso Tsung-tang, and a younger civil official named Li Hung-chang were to be the outstanding Chinese figures of the generation. Had there been more of their like and had they had support of the Manchu reigning house and the Chinese mandarinate, the fate of China for the next fifty years might have been less harsh and less humiliating.

This was not to be, however. The decline of the Chings, which had set in after the death of the Emperor Ch'ien Lung at the end of the eighteenth century, was proceeding with increasing momentum. This was reflected, too, in the Chinese mandarinate, which exercised most of the administrative functions. The Chinese had accepted perforce the inevitability of bowing to the West and admitting the foreigner to the Middle Kingdom, but what this signified in the world they had had to enter and what it portended for China they still did not recognize, let alone understand. Just at this time an event took place at the imperial court that was to be fateful for China. The Emperor Hsien Feng, a dissolute and ineffectual individual, died, leaving as his heir to the throne a fifteen-year-old boy, to be known by the dynastic style T'ung Chih, and bringing to actual power a woman who was to impose her will on the country for almost fifty years.

This was the woman later to be known as the empress dowager or Tzu Hsi, her formal title. She was the second wife or concubine of Hsien Feng, but she had acquired a higher position as the mother of Hsien Feng's only son, the empress being childless. More important, however, she was a woman of strong character—ignorant of the world, superstitious, vain, but of indomitable will and considerable shrewdness. Also she was unscrupulous and relentless in reaching for power and holding it. Those who sought to obstruct her had cause to rue it. After some characteristic palace intrigue, in which she and the dowager empress escaped assassination by those who wanted to exercise the regency for the boy emperor, she became one of three regents, the other two being the dowager empress and Hsien Feng's brother, Prince Kung. But whether joint regent or, as later, exclusive regent, it was she who actually exercised influence and made decisions. By her will and determination she probably arrested the decline of the dynasty and postponed its inevitable downfall. This no doubt was her greatest disservice to China.

Had she been either less unenlightened or of less powerful character China would have come off better. Had she perceived the necessity of compromise with the West, not only with Western power but with Western modernism, as the Japanese were to perceive, then with her force of character and her power she might have set China on a course which would have hastened its adaptation to the time, its acquisition of strength, and its escape from its disastrous descent. Or, had she been a woman of weaker will, then she might not have been able to prevent the earlier collapse of the dynasty, which would have freed the country for a fresh start under able Chinese leaders. At any rate, she would not have been able to restrain or frustrate those who saw the urgency of a larger social and cultural compromise with the West and modern times —who would, in short, have tried to take over from the West those aspects essential to survival in the modern world.

That there were enough men of this outlook is by no means certain, however. There were some, no doubt, and among them men of some influence; but they were few in number and one cannot say with confidence that they would have carried their people with them. Furthermore, judging by what they themselves were to say in the next few decades, one must doubt whether any of them really apprehended the full implication of the advent of the West and the nature of the Western world since the beginning of the nineteenth century. They knew the West was strong. They knew its strength was manifested in its weapons. They wanted China to be strong. Therefore they thought it was enough to acquire the new Western weapons. As they put it in one paraphrase or another from 1860 to as late as 1920—they wanted the material properties of the West and the spirit, customs, and institutions of China: the combination would make China invincible.

They never realized, as did the Japanese very early, that the weapons of the West were an effect of strength, not its cause. They could not grasp that to acquire these weapons it was necessary to have the kind of institutions, the kind of society, in which they were able to be produced. It was necessary to know modern science and to understand it, to apply it in production and communication and transportation, in universal education, in the integration of all the forces of a society. It was necessary, in short, to take over or at least adapt the forms of Western society. This no Chinese of any position ever saw until after the turn of the century. All of them continued to believe that the properties, attributes, and attainments of Chicago, Birmingham, and the Ruhr could be added to sixteenth-century Peking and Hangchow and leave Peking and Hangchow untouched in form and spirit. It was a delusion for which the country was to pay a heavy price.

Here China was to suffer from the defects of its qualities. As already has been said, its culture was old, deeply rooted, and of a high order— through most of history unsurpassed anywhere. It had never had contact with one of a higher order, almost never with any as high. It had been accustomed, not without justification, to look upon itself as giver of light and preceptor. Suddenly, then, to conceive of itself as having to come under tutelage was not easy. Perhaps it was not natural, perhaps not to be expected of any people. The Chinese were inordinately conservative. But conservatism can arise from blind obscurantism and it can also arise from the sense and experience of magnificence and the self-assurance thus bred. The more deeply rooted a culture, the harder it is to change; the more magnificent it is, the greater the inability to see the need to change, the greater the resistance to doing so.

China was in bondage to its past: its achievements in the past were a hostage that bound it for the future. And so it was that, despite the thrust of the West through its ramparts, despite the obvious fissures and revealed weaknesses within, China went on in its accustomed way, as if the world were still the world of the eighteenth century, as if China were still the Middle Kingdom, to which the rest of the planet was a satellite, as if all those beyond its boundaries were still Outer Barbarians. But this was complacency rather than assurance. Conservatism, like obstinacy, can be a sign of weakness rather than of strength.

Still, relations with the West had been established and, however grudgingly, they had to be maintained. For one thing, in the Tientsin treaty the Western Powers had won the right to open legations at Peking, and they did so. The Chinese remained stiff-necked about the kotow, but the issue could be waived, since the emperor was a minor and could not give audiences in any case. At foreign insistence the Chinese government set up a board or ministry called the Tsung Li Yamen to deal with foreign diplomatic representatives, and in the opening years a distant but not uneasy relation was established. On their part the representatives of the four principal Powers—Great Britain, France, Russia, and the United States—consciously strove to be tolerant and friendly and to overcome Chinese hostility.

Their policy was not based on sentiment alone or even mainly. It had a more definite reason. The Western Powers had finally won the right to trade and they wanted to trade. To that end there had to be stability in China. It served no purpose to have succeeded after more than half a century and then to have internal turmoil negate the success. The dislocation and destruction wrought by the Taipings brought that lesson home, and this had something to do with the help the foreign Powers were giving to put the rebellion down. To have won over one ruling group and then to have to repeat the effort with a new one was hardly appealing. Hence the desire to strengthen the government of the Manchus and thus assure a peaceful, normally functioning country. The West, too, helped to prolong the life of the Manchu dynasty—and this was not the only occasion, as we shall see—and in so doing it, too, contributed to China's decline and downfall.

For a few years after 1860 there was harmony in Western-Chinese relations, however. China, it is true, still refused to send diplomatic representatives abroad, but in China itself there was little open friction. For this the farsighted envoys of the Western Powers were to be credited, perhaps an American more than the others. This was Anson Burlingame, the first American minister. Burlingame, a native of Massachusetts, arrived in China in 1861. Though of lesser stature, he was of the same mold as Townsend Harris. He was instructed to bring about friendly, co-operative relations with China and he took his instructions literally. More important, his temperament was sympathetic to his mission. Like Harris, he sought to help the people to whom he was accredited. He would stand on the legal rights of his country and he did, but at the same time he was successful in helping the Chinese. He pressed on the government at Washington the adoption of a policy of preserving China's territorial integrity, of refraining from taking advantage of internal troubles and helping the imperial government to maintain peace and order. Secretary of State Seward was in accord and the American government did on the whole abide by such a policy.

Burlingame succeeded in winning the confidence of the court circles and the higher Chinese officials. He went home on leave in 1866 and the next year returned to Peking and communicated to the Tsung Li Yamen a message from Secretary Seward expressing the wish that China send a diplomatic representative to Washington. At the same time he communicated his own intention of resigning his post and going home after five years of service in China. The Chinese to his surprise drew a connection between his two communications. They proposed that he act as China's diplomatic representative, not only in the United States but in Europe. When Burlingame hesitated the matter was formally pressed. The Chinese said he was manifestly their friend and they trusted him to represent China's interests as faithfully as his own country's. They had particularly in mind that the Tientsin treaties were subject to revision in 1868 and they desired assurances that no more demands would be made of them and that modernization and other drastic changes would not be hastened or forced on them under Western pressure.

Burlingame accepted and in 1868 started across the Pacific at the head of a mission numbering more than thirty. Associated with him were two high officials of the court, one a Manchu and the other a

Chinese. There was also a British secretary and a French secretary, since the mission was to go to Europe as well as America. The rest were staff. They made an imposing procession and their exotic appearance created a minor sensation in the United States, as the unusual did then even more than now. The mission was given a warm welcome but amid the festivities there were also serious negotiations. In July a new agreement, called a supplement to the treaty of 1868, was signed. It provided for reciprocal rights of travel and residence and freedom of religion in both countries, for the opening of Chinese consulates in American ports and for the admission of Chinese immigrants into the United States unless they were brought in as contract laborers. The latter was to be a check on the coolie traffic, which was then subject to scandalous abuses. Also there was an assurance of the maintenance of China's territorial integrity and a significant declaration that in China's internal policies the United States disclaimed any intention to intervene or interfere in order to bring about the construction of railroads or similar enterprises; China was to have the right to decide for itself whether and when such steps in modernization were to be taken. It was this last that concerned the Chinese most. With that won, they were satisfied.

Great Britain gave assurances to the same effect when the mission moved on to Europe. From London it went to other European capitals, but there it obtained less satisfaction. There was less definiteness in the assurances, although not outright refusal. The mission got as far as St. Petersburg in February, 1870, and there Burlingame was stricken with pneumonia and died. It cannot be said to have accomplished much that was concrete, but it did awaken Western consciousness to China and stated China's case for a more sympathetic understanding of its difficulties. In Burlingame's glowing oratory China accepted the world and would henceforth order itself more in conformity with the world of the time; but it asked for patience and forbearance in finding its way and for the right of autonomous decision. Nothing fundamental may have changed, but, for whatever it was worth, China had made its first conciliatory gesture.

There were a few other concessions in these years, enough to signify at least an interest in the West apart from its military power. The opening of the Tsung Li Yamen for the conduct of foreign relations created the need for at least enough knowledge of foreign languages to carry out that function, and there was started in Peking in 1862 a college known as the Tung Wen Kuan to train men for the purpose. A few years later W. A. P. Martin, one of the early American missionaries, was made president of the college. Beginning with the principal European languages, the curriculum was soon expanded to include international law, mathematics, and some of the physical sciences. Out of the Tung Wen Kuan came the corps of interpreters who served in both the Tsung Li Yamen and the Chinese legations abroad for the next generation.

In 1866 a small mission consisting of an official named Pin Ch'un and three students of the Tung Wen Kuan was sent on a tour of Europe, not for diplomatic negotiations but to see what Europe was like. It returned to report mainly on the material and physical wonders of the Western world. A more significant venture was the sending of young men to study in the United States. In all 120 went between 1872 and 1875. They were under the charge of the man responsible for the venture. He was a Cantonese named Yung Wing, who as a boy in the 1840's had learned English at a missionary school in Macao and then been taken to the United States by his teacher. He graduated from Yale in 1854 and returned to China convinced that his country would have to learn about the West by systematic study. He began quietly pressing the idea among officials and succeeded in convincing some of the more progressive, especially Tseng Kuo-fan and Li Hung-chang, and an imperial mandate was issued authorizing boys to be sent in small groups annually. They were to study in high school and college and to live with American families. They made good progress in their schooling and adjusted to American ways, but soon a counteragitation set up at home. The young men were being foreignized, it was said, and in 1881 all of them were ordered home. Yet the venture had its effect. Many of the 120 young men became officials, some of them distinguished, and among them were some who were most eloquent in pressing for modernization, though without much success.

Indirectly another strong influence entered, although without China's intention. This was by way of the Chinese Maritime Customs. As already has been told, the confusion caused at the port of Shanghai by the Taiping Rebellion and the dislocation of trade there led to foreigners being asked to take temporary charge of collecting and safeguarding tariff revenues. This continued throughout the years of the rebellion, having been extended to other ports in 1858 by an Anglo-Chinese agreement. Within a few years it had become a fixed working organization, with men of various nationalities in key posts, though the majority were British. In 1863 the organization was regularized and put on a permanent basis, as the Imperial Maritime Customs, with Robert Hart, a man of remarkable qualities, as Inspector-General. Sir Robert Hart, as he later became, remained at the head of the Customs for fifty years, and for a large part of that time he had more influence on the ruling Chinese than any other foreigner. Under his administrative genius and with the support he was able by sheer personality to win from the Chinese, the Customs became the most efficient and widespread administrative organ of the empire; and, since it was also honestly administered, it provided the revenues that kept the government from foundering. But more than that, by the close association of Chinese and foreign officials which it naturally brought with it, since Chinese also were on the staff at nearly all levels, Chinese gained an insight into Western ideas of government and administration.

Thus regular channels of foreign-Chinese intercourse were being laid and an approach was set to normal international relations. Yet there was no abrupt end to friction. If on a smaller scale than before 1860, incidents still did occur, some of them ugly. One of them had political results of some consequence. This was the Margary affair. Late in the 1860's the British had become interested in the possibility of opening trade routes from India to West China over Burma and had begun sending exploratory expeditions. One such expedition felt the need of an interpreter to deal with the Chinese and asked the British Legation at Peking to assign one. The man chosen was A. R. Margary of the consular service, who started south with a staff of Chinese early in 1875. On the border between Burma and Yunnan Province Margary and his staff were attacked and Margary himself and five of his Chinese were murdered.

The British government decided to make an issue of the affair and presented a series of sweeping demands. Negotiations were protracted and productive of friction and resentment, since the British had expanded the issue beyond the murder of one of their nationals. A settlement was finally reached in September, 1876, in what was known as the Chefoo Convention. It provided payment of an indemnity to the families of the victims and an apology from the government, but this was the least. Four more Chinese ports were opened to foreign trade and six others as ports of call for foreign ships. Civil suits between Chinese and foreigners were to be heard before judges of the defendant's nationality, thus extending extraterritoriality from criminal to civil jurisdiction. And the Chinese tax on internal trade, known as "likin," was to be paid on all imports at the port of entry together with the tariff duty, the goods thereafter being subject to no other imposts of any kind. This was to apply to opium imports too, thus widening the channels for that not very salubrious traffic.

The murder of a British subject was no doubt an outrage, but the penalty therefor can also be said to have been somewhat disproportionate, and the example of Western conceptions of justice thus offered to the Chinese at what was hoped to be the beginning of their tutelage was pedagogically dubious. If later they were to emulate it in application to foreigners when they had the power, that, too, was regrettable, but also understandable.

There were other incidents even more serious, but since they were of a special kind and with distinctive causes they will be dealt with separately.

CHAPTER XI

The Missionary Movement

So large a role has the missionary movement played in modern China, both in its internal development and in its foreign relations, that it must be treated at some length. Indeed, in the whole East-West relationship there has been no stranger phenomenon than the nineteenth-century campaign for proselyting to Christianity. While it had begun three hundred years before with the Catholic missions, first to India and then farther East, it had not taken on proportions of any magnitude until the nineteenth century. Why at that time, it is not easy to explain with certainty.

Perhaps it was part of the dynamism of the time in the Western world, the stirring of new and fresh energy generated by scientific discoveries, the conquest of nature and the industrial revolution. The white race appeared to have achieved or to be achieving the mastery of the universe. Why confine itself, then, to matters of the material world? If mastery over material nature, why not over the things of the spirit too? It was carrying throughout the world its newly produced goods and the new ways of producing goods in prodigious quantity. Why not take, too, its message of man's relation to God and the universe? As we know, the two had been closely related in Western thought since the Reformation. At any rate Western man was thrusting out in all directions. The diplomat, the explorer, the soldier, and the trader were cutting new pathways throughout the planet, and in Asia most of all. Why not also those consecrated to the worship of God? (The one true God, naturally.)

Whatever the reasoning, both Catholic and Protestant missionaries started to the East soon after the beginning of the nineteenth century. In China they waited no less impatiently than the traders for the country to be opened, by persuasion if possible, by force if necessary. In some parts of China, it should be noted, a few Catholic missionaries had remained through the preceding centuries, but they had worked under stringent restrictions and, at times, harsh persecution, but again, less on religious grounds than on political grounds. It was feared they were working for the political interests of European states rather than for the Kingdom of God. After 1842 more missionaries began to enter, both Protestant and Catholic, though even they were confined to Hongkong, Macao, and the five ports opened to trade and their immediate environs.

The treaties of 1860, in which religious proselyting was legalized—together with the importation of opium, it should never be forgotten—opened the gates. In the legalization of Christian proselyting there was something inadvertent. While freedom of religious practice and tutelage was recognized in all the treaties, only in the French treaty was there explicit concession of the right of missionaries to buy land anywhere in the interior and erect buildings thereon for religious purposes, a right which later automatically accrued to missionaries of all nationalities and denominations under the most-favored-nation provision. But there was something in the concession never satisfactorily explained. The clause granting it was in the Chinese text of the Franco-Chinese treaty but not in the French text, which was the official text, and the Chinese have never conceded that it was authoritative. They have always held that it was illegitimately inserted. However, under that dubious franchise missionaries of all creeds began to go into the interior in large numbers to propagate the faith. Within a few years after 1860 they were in practically every province in the empire. In 1865 there were approximately 200 Protestant missionaries in China; by 1890 there were some 1,300. Catholics were about half that number.

Their influence, however, was out of all proportion to their number, and this was the cause of all the difficulties that have arisen from missionary endeavor down to our own day. Given the fundamental elements in the situation—the West impinging by force on the East—and given the nature of human beings as well, the difficulties were inherent and inescapable. Indeed, had it not been for the discrepancy in power between the two races, they would have been greater, would have caused more upheavals and more bloodshed. Allowance must be made, however, for the religious tolerance—perhaps it is only indifference to religion—that has always characterized the Chinese. The meeting of peoples of different color, tradition, and habits is always precarious at the best. When they meet under conditions of duress by one over the other, the precariousness is aggravated. And when the one that imposes himself on the other seeks to force his conception of God and the universe on the other, when he strikes at that which is deepest in the other, the intervention of providence alone can prevent an explosion. Such an imposition the missionaries made or attempted to make in China and wherever else they went. It would have been resented in any circumstances. What made it more resented by the Chinese was that it was carried on under cover of extraterritoriality and thus led to serious abuses.

Missionaries went into small communities in the interior where no white man had ever before been seen. That alone was enough to challenge trouble. Their very difference in appearance, custom, and habits was enough to engender antagonism. Xenophobia is one of the deepest instincts in all men. The Chinese were not likely to be the exception, particularly since over the years they had learned in all except the most remote communities how foreigners had attacked their country, invaded its soil, and twice humbled it in defeat. The missionaries built comfortable dwellings, sometimes large compounds. The Catholics especially were inclined to imposing establishments and opened orphanages into which they took young Chinese children to bring up in the alien faith. As is natural in such circumstances, rumors would circulate that Chinese children were being used by the foreign devils for the practice of black magic, that the foreigners' medicines were made out of the children's eyeballs, etc. It is difficult to conceive of anything that would incense a people more or be more likely to stir up mob violence.

There was a less direct but more constant incitation. Humility could hardly be a trait of those who come to convert others to their own faith. There could be no doubt in their psychological make-up. Conviction of right would inevitably shade into conviction of superiority and the end-product in attitude and action would be intolerance. Intolerance is too mild a word to describe the majority of missionaries who went to China, especially in the earlier years. They were at least as arrogant as the trader. They had come to "save the heathen," to "lead them out of the darkness." Most of them, until after 1900, were men and women of little education and meager background. Some of them, especially those of the small sects that abound in the United States, were barely literate. Except for a few of the more cultivated, of whom there were, it is true, some distinguished examples, they knew nothing of China's history or its religion or its philosophy and they never tried to find out. They were generally unaware that it had a religion or a philosophy, and if they did know it made no difference, for whatever history or philosophy there might be was heathenish, and that was enough.

The missionaries comported themselves accordingly. They publicly ridiculed the most sacred of Chinese beliefs—ancestor worship, the

Confucian precepts, and religious rites in temples, whether the ancestral shrines with simple tablets inscribed with the names of the forebears of the clan, or Buddhist or Taoist shrines, or the simple edifices erected in the memory of Confucius. In many places they were known to charge into temples while Chinese were worshipping and denounce them for bowing to idols. They were publicly and privately insulting to all that meant most to the Chinese. When they made converts they compelled them to break with all the practices of the community, the clan, and the family. They forbade them to pay respect to the family tablets, to enter temples even for semisecular purposes, to take part in the semireligious processions, or to contribute to maintenance of community temples, which were community centers as much as religious edifices. In all essentials they broke the individual convert from his family, and it must be remembered what the family signified in Chinese society.

If there was not more violence, if the Chinese did not more often burst into berserk rages and slaughter the missionaries, who were help-less among them, that was not only because they were tolerant but also because they were coming to know and to fear the cost of yielding to their impulses. The missionaries had the immunity lent by extraterrito-riality. They could not be held to account legally for any of the acts committed by them. At first this may have been only abstract protection, since there was no power nearby to give it effect except near the coastal centers. But as the years passed and the countries of the West showed that they could inflict punishment for transgressions against foreigners, inflict it not only on those guilty but on the whole country, Chinese officials made efforts to protect foreigners from attack, no matter what the provocation. If a missionary made himself unbearably offensive and the wrath of the community mounted, the local mandarin sought to calm it down. If there was a dispute between a local missionary body and a group in the community, the mandarin usually interceded to induce the community to yield or himself ruled in favor of the mission-aries, regardless of the merits of the dispute. He knew that if he did not do so or if harm befell the missionaries or even if they only felt aggrieved, they would protest to the nearest consul, who would com-municate the protest to his minister in Peking, who would take it up with the Tsung Li Yamen and demand redress. (This sort of thing occupied a good deal of the time and attention of the foreign diplomats, who came to resent it but upheld foreign interest on principle.) The Chinese government had to yield. It had learned to its grief the penalty of obduracy. It yielded and then reprimanded the local mandarin for letting the issue arise and thus putting the national government in an awkward position with the foreigners' representatives, who would not be denied and could not be withstood. The local mandarins everywhere soon learned that it was politic for them to find that the local missionary was always right, whatever the cause of the dispute. Thus the missionary got immunity for all of his acts, the kind of immunity that neither he nor any other of his countrymen could enjoy at home.

What was worse, he soon extended his immunity to his Chinese converts. If a convert got into difficulty with the authorities, the missionaries intervened on his behalf, sometimes vigorously. Or if a convert got into trouble with other Chinese (which could easily happen, since his going over to the foreign missionaries was considered a betrayal of his kind), the missionary also intervened. In that case, too, he went to the mandarin and asked for official support for his protégé. And the mandarin usually thought it wise to give it, no matter where right and wrong lay. This was more commonly resorted to by the Catholics than the Protestants, but it was common enough to both. As a result not only foreigners came under the protection of extraterritoriality but Chinese who had missionary protection. In many communities therefore Chinese official authorities could not exercise jurisdiction over all their own people. Another result, of course, was that it put a premium on becoming a convert to one Christian denomination or another and led to an increase in the number of converts, sometimes without much regard to religious conviction. Communities could thus be split, with a small minority enjoying special privileges and immunities, and this in turn produced a great deal of ill-feeling and resentment on the part of the others, especially among the more educated.

An alien irritant had been injected into the Chinese social body and it was bound to fester. Naturally incidents flared up. The most serious occurred in Tientsin in 1870. There the Catholics had erected a cathedral, which after their practice was the most imposing structure in the city. Attached to it was an orphanage. For one reason or another, in a way such episodes begin, reports spread of atrocities committed against the Chinese children in the orphanage. One small event led to another, and a mob arose. It stormed the cathedral and destroyed both the cathedral and the orphanage and the French consulate as well. Eighteen French men and women, including the consul, two priests, and ten nuns, were killed. Three Russians and thirty Chinese servants employed by the French also were murdered. British and American chapels in the city were destroyed or looted but without loss of life. There was intense excitement in the city and neighboring areas in North China; foreign warships began to gather off the coast, and it appeared for a while that another foreign-Chinese conflict was about to break out. Fortunately both sides exercised restraint. The French government presented demands that were not excessive and the Chinese government, with recent lessons fresh in mind, yielded. An official mission proceeded to France to make formal apology. An indemnity of roughly $200,000 was paid, two Tientsin officials were sentenced to exile, and a number of convicted rioters were executed. After that there were no more serious attacks on missionaries until the Boxer uprising between 1898 and 1900.

For the social and cultural historian of the modern era the missionary movement will be a fascinating and tantalizing subject. It calls not only for political and social analysis but for elusive psychological analysis as well. To deal with it objectively and not to yield to comprehensive generalizations that are pat, perhaps too pat, is difficult, if not impossible. It was in the soil and spirit of the time, as has already been said. Even more was it an expression of the humanitarian zeal that also characterized the nineteenth century, when the concept, "Am I my brother's keeper?" for the first time took concrete form in social and political programs. For the first time there was conceived not only the desirability but the practicability of general human betterment and unremitting progress. It this was possible within the confines of one's own country, why not strive for the same ends everywhere? In this sense the missionary movement was inseparable from the development of the time and also beneficent in origin and purpose.

Of the individuals concerned in the movement it must be said that their motives were of the same high order. They went out to confer benefit on their fellow men, as it was given them to see benefit. They sought nothing for themselves, and in that they were almost unique among those who went out to the East. They gave themselves for a cause, asking as their reward only that the cause be served. And to advance that cause they suffered hardships—meager livelihood, loneliness, deprivation of the amenities of Western life, disease, and physical danger. They did confer benefits. Their hospitals and their doctors saved innumerable lives that otherwise would have been sacrificed to the native ignorance of modern medicine, and thus they opened the way to the introduction of modern medicine. Their schools and later their universities gave an opportunity for education to those who would not have had it otherwise. It was they who introduced into the Eastern world the idea of education for all—of its worth and its possibility—and furthermore they brought both the content and the method of modern education. More than all others, they brought to the old world modern science, both in theory and application.

The Christian message itself contributed something of lasting value to China. It gave a fresh impulse to religious thought and feeling where both had been dulled by habitude in old truths that had lost inspiration. The Christian message really carried a new hope, especially to those whose life in this sphere offered few compensations—just as in Europe almost two millenniums before. But it also came to do much to sensitize and galvanize men and women of the cultivated classes who had found something lacking in the austere intellectuality of the Confucian doctrine and the otherworldliness of Buddhism. The element of hope which lies in Christianity more than in other religions carried an appeal and enlivened the spirit. Although the number of converts was not large— probably not more than 1 per cent of the population—it cannot be denied that many Chinese were better and happier men and women for having embraced the new faith.

Yet there was fundamentally something unhealthy and incongruous in the whole missionary idea. If the endeavor had been confined to primitive savages something could have been said for it. But to go out to a race of high culture and long tradition, with philosophical, ethical, and religious systems antedating Christianity, and to go avowedly to save its people from damnation as dwellers in heathen darkness—in that there was something not only spiritually limited but almost grotesque.

Interchange of ideas of man's relation to the universe is healthy and can be conducive to spiritual growth. But only men of inner limitation, both intellectually and spiritually, can gratuitously thrust their beliefs on others on the assumption that they alone have truth—without knowing what truths others hold or even that they hold any. It was out of this innate lack, this poverty of intellect and imagination, that arose the crudity and coarseness and insensitiveness of so much of early missionary practice. Naturally there were exceptions. Even in the earliest days there were missionaries of high intellectual endowment and cultural attainments, and their ways were unexceptionable. Yet they, too, had the subjective commitment. They alone had truth; and all others were blind and lost. And they were in a minority, a small minority. The personality and background of the majority were reflected in their attitudes and their acts. It should be noted, however, that the standard of missionary personnel began to change with the beginning of the twentieth century. Men and women of better educational background were sent out. They did try to learn something of Chinese history and beliefs. They were less given to the raucous crying of "heathen" and "idol-worshippers," more considerate of Chinese sensibilities, at least aware that Chinese had something to offer too.

Essentially the missionary movement rested on power—physical power. It was made possible because the countries from which proselyting came were so much stronger than those to which proselyting was addressed that the missionaries could not be ejected. But that ratio of power no longer obtains. Not only China but the rest of the Eastern world is no longer helpless. The missionary movement, if it survives at all, will be an enterprise of a different order, unrecognizable—and blasphemous—to those who first participated in it. It will not be a gratuitous bearing of light to those who dwell in darkness. It will be an exchange, between equals, of ideas, faith, and experience. Both sides, East and West alike, will be the better therefor. Whatever compensating benefits may have accrued from the century of missionary effort everywhere in the East, the whole missionary conception cannot, on any long perspective, be justified by any mature and civilized standard of judgment.

CHAPTER XII

The Chinese Empire
Breaks Off at the Edges

The decade of the 1870's in Eastern Asia was relatively quiet. It was the last quiet decade Eastern Asia was to know. It was a deceptive lull while the rapidly accumulating power of the West was gathering momentum and the economic development of the industrializing Western countries was building up the necessity of an outward thrust. This thrust was to be aimed at China rather than Japan, mainly because Japan did not seem sufficiently important and tempting. The islands themselves offered little. While China proper was tempting, tantalizingly tempting, to acquire all of it seemed too much to aim for, given the capabilities of even the strongest European countries, but the outer edges of the Chinese Empire, an empire palpably in decline, seemed ripe for the plucking.

At different periods in China's history when it was on the upward movement of a cycle it had taken over in the vast continental territory surrounding it on three sides—not exactly colonies but rather tributaries. In the loose political system of the time and place these were not really governed from the Chinese center. They acknowledged Chinese suzerainty and paid annual tribute delivered at the capital with proper ceremonial humility, but for the rest were left on the whole to their own devices and were, at the least, autonomous. The first part of the Ching dynasty was such a period; between the middle of the seventeenth century and the middle of the eighteenth China had extended widely the range of its power and influence. But as always when China was on the downward swing of the cycle the normally loose attachment of its dependent areas became so tenuous as to be little more than symbolical. The nineteenth century was such a period—unfortunately for China and the peace of Eastern Asia, just at the time when the West was newly endowed with power and conscious of it.

The southernmost part of the Chinese Empire was the goal of the West's next stage in advance, with France taking the lead in what is now called Indo-China. France had had a long-standing interest in that part of the world as the result of its previous position in India, and its eviction from India by the British in the preceding century had enhanced rather than diminished that interest. France's traditional position as defender of the Church everywhere in the East gave it additional incentive and opportunity, for Catholic missionary orders had for some time been working in Indo-China and been subjected to serious persecution, with some loss of life.

Following the murder of a Spanish missionary in Annam in 1857, France and Spain sent a joint punitive expedition. Punishment was duly levied and in 1862 a treaty was signed with the emperor of Annam ceding three provinces of Cochin China (the southernmost part of Indo-China), opening three ports to trade, conceding religious liberty, and providing a small indemnity. Again as in previous similar episodes, the penalty was out of all proportion to the offense. It will already have been noted that missionaries in the East were a valuable negotiable asset in the nineteenth century. Alive, they caused a great deal of difficulty to Western diplomats, who found most of their work arising from missionary activities; but if dead by violence they could be turned to high political profit. Having in mind that the message the missionaries brought to the East included the adjuration to turn the other cheek and forgive those who trespass against one, thoughtful Asians might have detected a discrepancy between creed and act. They no doubt indulged in ironical reflections, which incidentally was the only satisfaction open to them. If missionaries were killed, demands were made—at the rate of half a province per missionary—and demands had to be yielded to.

France had inserted its entering wedge. The next year, following a naval expedition to avenge the murder of yet another Christian, Cambodia, west of the main Indo-China states, became a French protectorate. Four years later another French admiral obtained the cession of all the remaining provinces of Cochin China. It was Tongking in the north, however, that held most attraction for France, since it bordered on China and thus offered a strategic point of entry if claims were to be staked out in that country. In 1873 a French expedition went up the Red River, which flows from west China into the Gulf of Tongking and the South China Sea, and proceeded all the way into Yunnan Province. There was trouble with natives and fighting broke out in which the French commander was killed. This was followed by a treaty in 1874 in which the French recognized Annam's independence (although it was a tributary of China), but Annam conceded to France the right of "protection," with French advisers to train the Annamese army, supervise Annamese finances, etc. In short, Annam became a French protectorate.

That was not all. In 1882 France sent an expedition to Hanoi, a short distance inland from the port of Haiphong in the Gulf of Tongking. In part its purpose was to clear out a body of semi-pirates known as the Black Flags who preyed on French ships. Hanoi was captured, but now China became frightened and protested on the ground of its suzerainty over Tongking and began moving up troops. There was a collision in which the French were defeated. The French now retaliated in force, attacking the port of Foochow and several ports in Formosa. In 1885 hostilities were concluded with a treaty in which China recognized the legitimacy of France's treaties with the emperor of Annam and therefore its position in Indo-China. Thus France obtained all Indo-China—Cochin China as a colony and protectorates over Annam, Tongking, and Cambodia, to which was added later Laos, the land west of Annam. Whatever the legal fiction might be, Indo-China was French.

Much the same happened in Burma, with the British as the active agents. Burma, lying between China and India, had had varied fortunes over the centuries, at times divided and weak, at times of some power and consequence. Its relation to China was of the indeterminate status common to Eastern Asia, but on the whole it, too, acknowledged the position of tributary to China, though this was more a formality than anything else. Its most serious difficulties, however, were with Great Britain after the latter became established in India, and between 1820 and 1885 there were three wars between Great Britain and Burma. Burma was defeated in all three, of course. Each of the first two resulted in some Burmese territory being added to India, and after the third Burma was formally annexed to India. This was expedited by France's advance in Indo-China and Great Britain's fear that the French might come even closer to India. In 1886 a treaty was concluded with China in which China recognized the annexation. It need not be pointed out that China by that time had no option.

In what is now Malaya Great Britain obtained a foothold before the close of the eighteenth century and under one form or another the several native states and principalities of the peninsula fell under British jurisdiction before the nineteenth century was well advanced. The development by the British of Singapore as one of the great seaports of the world, and of the natural resources of the peninsula, mainly rubber and tin, by the system of great plantations made Malaya one of the most valuable colonies of the world. But not until Japan's challenge in 1941 was it the object of international conflict or even of much dispute. Until then Great Britain was too powerful for any rival empire even to hope to deprive it of one of its greatest prizes.

In the northwest, on the hazy boundary between China and Central Asia, Russia had found lodgment in Ili, between Sinkiang and Mongolia. After lengthy negotiations, most of Ili was restored to China in 1881, but a foothold had been retained by Russia.

More important than any part of Southeast Asia, however, was Korea. Korea is a tragic country. It had the unhappy fate of being small, well endowed with natural resources, and situated at a point where neighboring states, all stronger than itself, converge. In consequence the narrow peninsula, 150 miles wide and 600 miles long, has been one of the world's main travelled routes for invasion and counter-invasion, and few places on the planet have seen more bloodshed. It has been prized by the strong not so much for itself as for what it leads to—the Pacific, China, Central Asia, and Russian Siberia. Korea is an old land with an old culture. Its written and verifiable history goes back to the beginning of the Christian Era, not so far as China's but further than Japan's. Its settled and relatively advanced culture is older than Japan's, since it had had contact with China before Japan did. In the main its culture is patterned on China's, and culturally Korea served as a bridge between China and Japan. Its people are believed to have originated in Central Asia and drifted into the peninsula long before the Christian Era.

For some hundreds of years before the seventh century the country was divided into three kingdoms—Koguryo, Silla, and Paekche. Then, as in more recent times, the northern part, which was the Koguryo kingdom, was most subject to attack from without, by troops from Manchuria or Mongolia or China, and perhaps for that reason the North Koreans were and are the most warlike. In the seventh century there was a bitter war with China in which the Chinese were defeated, but soon after Koguryo was overwhelmed by an alliance between China and the kingdom of Silla, and the latter brought the peninsula under its own rule and held it for 300 years. It was in this period, from the seventh to the tenth centuries, that Korea flourished in power, wealth, and culture. Buddhism had come in the fourth century and Chinese art, learning, and technology, then at its fullest flowering under the Tangs, infiltrated and transformed the country's way of life. Like all the rest of Asia except Japan, Korea succumbed to the Mongols at the turn of the thirteenth century and remained under their sway for nearly two hundred years. Incidentally, Korea joined in the abortive Mongol attempt to invade Japan, thus incurring Japan's enmity, for which it was to suffer later.

At the end of the fourteenth century a powerful general named Yi Taejo got control of the whole country and established the dynasty that ruled under the name of Yi, with its capital at Seoul, until the annexation by Japan in 1910. But until the end of the nineteenth century, when Japan defeated China in a war over Korea, Korea was officially a tributary of China. Korea's greatest disaster came with the invasion in 1592 by Hideyoshi, the great Japanese conqueror. Before Hideyoshi was finally repelled at the end of the century, partly as the result of a great Korean naval victory, the country was all but devastated and, in the view of some historians, never really recovered.

Korea had had far less contact with the Western world than China or Japan, naturally being by-passed for the rich continental expanse of the one and the more convenient islands of the other. With Japan there was recurrent trouble, both before and after Hideyoshi, principally on account of raids on Korean shipping by Japanese pirates, but also due to the tribute missions Korea had to send for some time to Yedo, the capital of the shoguns, as well as to China. But by the West, Korea was left alone. Occasional ships from European ports were stranded in Korean waters, but that was all.

The first Catholic missionary, a French priest, came in 1836. He made converts, was followed by other priests, and then persecution began, with periodic bloodshed, thus arousing indignation, especially in France. But the general impetus to Western activity in Eastern Asia was reflected in Korea too in the 1850's and 1860's. In 1866 a Russian ship appeared at a Korean port and formally asked for the right of regular trade. The Koreans replied that they had no right to make such a concession, being tributary to China. At about the same time a French naval expedition sought to enter and was driven off. Also an American vessel, the "General Sherman," attempting to enter one of the rivers, was wrecked and, partly as the result of misunderstanding, was attacked and its crew murdered. As with China and Japan, circumstances called for correction of the situation and the opening of normal relations, and this was soon to come.

As it happened, it was Japan that broke open the way into Korea. In this there was something symbolical and a portent of the future that could not be recognized at that time. Already Japan was assuming for itself, although probably without conscious deliberation, the role of the Eastern state which would act toward the rest of the East as the West was acting toward the East, Japan included. In other words it would capitalize on its prior mastery of the new instrumentalities of power in its relations with its neighbors. The role was one Japan was to fulfill until its downfall in 1945.

When it became clear at the end of the 1860's that the West was going to press in Korea for the same relation it had won in China and Japan, the Japanese began efforts in the same direction. As soon as the overthrow of the shogunate had been accomplished and the emperor given substantive power, the Japanese took the first steps in Korea. They sent formal notification of the change to Seoul, but the Korean government would not even receive the communication. It acted, that is to say, as China and Japan had acted when first pressed to receive the outer world. So, as a matter of fact, did Japan react as the West had reacted before: it became impatient and irritated. Demands began to be voiced for forcible measures to compel the Koreans to open relations. In 1872 a mission was sent to Seoul but it was rebuffed.

In Korea itself there was sharp internal division. In power at Seoul was a regent, the Taiwenkun, a reactionary in the extreme and bitterly antiforeign. He was equally anti-Christian and was responsible for hideous persecution, including some large-scale killings. He was also not much less anti-Japanese than anti-Western, and violent anti-Japanese demonstrations were engineered. Agitation in Japan increased and for a time there was serious danger of what would amount to a Japanese invasion of the peninsula. Not only the Japanese-Korean relation was involved. The Restoration had left rootless elements in Japan, mainly the former samurai, who were in effect becoming technologically unemployed and were therefore discontented and sought an outlet. Matters worsened in 1875, when a Japanese warship appeared at the port of Kanghwa, ostensibly to take on fuel and water, and was fired on by a Korean fort. The Japanese ship responded and the fort was captured and destroyed. The Japanese then firmly demanded that a treaty be negotiated, and when they made clear that they intended to use force if it was not, the Koreans submitted. The Treaty of Kanghwa, signed February 26, 1876, opened the ports of Fusan, Jinsen, and Gensan to trade and provided for the exchange of ministers and consuls and for extraterritoriality for Japanese subjects. Also it explicitly stated that Korea was independent, a statement that China let pass for the moment but that contained the seeds of future conflict.

With the gates opened thus far, the Western Powers began to press more vigorously for right of entry. As in Japan, it was the United States that was first to succeed. It had sent a naval expedition in 1871 in the hope of opening negotiations, but the ships were fired on and in retaliation destroyed a number of Korean forts. A later attempt also proved abortive, and the United States decided to approach China as suzerain. China was not unresponsive, partly because it was already fearful of Japan's success in Korea and wanted a Western counterbalance—for weak Eastern states the standard device of playing one strong Power against another.

Commander R. W. Shufeldt, in command of an American warship sent to negotiate with the Koreans, first sought Japanese mediation. When that failed he approached Li Hung-chang in Tientsin as viceroy of Chihli, the capital province. A draft treaty was drawn up and the Chinese transmitted it to Seoul. Shufeldt followed it there and in May, 1882, it was signed by the Koreans. It provided for the right to trade on a most-favored-nation basis and for the exchange of diplomatic and consular officers. According to precedent, the other Western Powers quickly followed. Great Britain and Germany obtained treaties in 1883 —Germany was already becoming interested in the Far East, too—Italy and Russia in 1884, and France in 1886. In contrast with the Japanese-Korean treaty, each of the Western treaties explicitly affirmed Korea's dependence on China. The Chinese-Japanese rift on Korea had opened, and the maneuvers for paramountcy had begun. At every attempt by any Western Power to deal with Korea as a sovereign state Chinese intrigue was set in motion and pressure was exercised in Seoul.

Thus Korea's relation with the outer world was settled, but not the internal conflict on the same issue, a conflict exacerbated by court intrigue, palace jealousies, and factional rivalries. The Taiwenkun retired in 1873 on the coming of age of the king, but his opinions did not change and his influence did not pass with him. The party favoring accommodation with the West was led by the Min family, the family of the queen, and neither side hesitated to use any stratagem, including incitation to attacks on foreigners, to embarrass the other. The opening of relations with Japan had not ended resentment, and this could be exploited by the antiforeign faction. The situation was not eased by the fact that China was giving full support, if not more, to the antiforeign and reactionary party, not only because it was anti-Japanese but because resistance to change comported with Chinese beliefs.

The most serious incident occurred in the summer of 1882, when a mob consisting of both troops and civilians attacked the Japanese Legation and murdered several officials, the minister himself being forced to flee to the port of Jinsen, where he took refuge on a British ship. This was part of a conspiracy aiming at a coup to dispose of the queen and put power into the hands of the reactionaries. The Japanese, genuinely aroused, sent two warships and a battalion of infantry to escort the minister back to Seoul. This time the Japanese were adamant, and in a treaty the Koreans were forced to sign at Chemulpo in August, 1882, Korea agreed to make formal apology, to pay an indemnity, to punish the guilty and, most important, to permit the permanent stationing of Japanese troops in the capital to protect the legation.

For every step taken by Japan in Korea China took one, generally a longer one. When the Japanese sent troops into Korea after the attack on the legation, the Chinese did too, presumably to help restore order. The Chinese obtained a treaty giving them preferential status in trade and tariffs. Also a permanent Chinese Resident was sent to Seoul. He was Yuan Shih-kai, who was to figure prominently in Chinese history and Chinese-Japanese relations for the next thirty years. Steadily China encroached on Korea to the point where Korea was being converted from a tributary to a protectorate.

In 1884 another coup was executed in Seoul, this time by the progressives, who wanted to do away with conservative leaders and did have some of them assassinated. A cabinet of progressive leaders was formed and at once appealed to the Japanese for protection, the Japanese on the whole having sided with the progressives. The Japanese sent a small detachment to guard the palace. The family of the queen, who had been sidetracked by the progressives, appealed to Yuan Shih-kai for help, and the Chinese, too, sent troops to the palace. There was a clash between Japanese and Chinese troops and a Chinese-Japanese war could easily have broken out, but cooler heads prevailed on both sides and instead negotiations were undertaken in Tientsin between Li Hung-chang and Ito Hirobumi (later Prince Ito and for a time probably Japan's most influential leader). The negotiations led to the Tientsin Convention of 1885, by which China and Japan agreed to withdraw troops from Korea. They agreed also that if disorders took place in Korea in the future, and either side had to send troops, each would notify the other in advance. Thus war was averted, but only for a time.

Korea was not the only scene of gathering conflict between China and Japan. The Ryukyu Islands and Formosa also entered. The Ryukyus had long had a hazy double status. Historically they had paid tribute to China and looked to China for power and influence, but they had for almost four hundred years also sent tribute to Japan, especially since the Japanese Satsumas had conquered part of the islands in the seventeenth century. The question of the status of the Ryukyus came to a head in 1871, when a ship bearing some Ryukyu Islanders was wrecked on Formosa and all on board were murdered by the Formosan aborigines. To the hotheads in Japan, long chafing for action, this gave an excuse. After China disclaimed responsibility Japan sent an expedition to Formosa in 1874 and occupied part of it. The most intransigent of the jingoes demanded war with China, but the matter was settled when

China paid an indemnity, thus by inference acknowledging Japan's right as protector of the Ryukyus. Then in 1879 the Japanese took the king of the Ryukyus to Japan, gave him a title of nobility, and incorporated the islands into the Japanese Empire. China continued to challenge Japan's rights there for a while but in 1881 finally acceded, and Japan's sovereignty over the Ryukus was formally acknowledged.

The most important aspect of this episode was the success of the more far-sighted Japanese leaders in restraining the war party and thus preventing premature adventures that might have led to frustration and punishment by the Great Powers. They not only recognized that Japan was not yet ready to enter into rivalry with the great but they were able to impose their view on those who, while spoiling for action, knew too little of the world to understand the consequences. This self-control they were to enforce on the country until the end of the century, but, unfortunately for Japan, for not much longer.

CHAPTER XIII

Japan Resolves to Modernize

Japan was saved from disastrous adventures, but in the first decade after the Restoration there was laid, too, the foundation of the Japan that was almost foredoomed some day to topple suddenly because the foundation was one that could not support a country in the twentieth century. The medieval Japan died, and died hard; but that which succeeded it, while no longer medieval, was also not modern. The exterior was modern—impressively so; but only the exterior, and for that reason the whole structure was inwardly unsound. It was neither of one age nor of another, neither seventeenth century nor twentieth. It had some of the strength of both but even more of the weaknesses of both. The blend was ultimately fatal.

The shogunate was abolished and the emperor reinstated as the repository of actual power, but that was only a beginning. In 1868, immediately on the accession of the young Emperor Meiji as real ruler, there was issued under his name a sort of Charter Oath, a declaration of fundamentals by which the new state would be guided. It was a statement high in principle, as a set of generalities admirable. It proclaimed the unity of state and people, both state and people consecrating themselves to the common welfare. Old customs and practices were to be discarded in favor of those more suited to the time. Decision on public matters was to be by deliberation of public bodies. All men were to have opportunity to exercise their talents in callings of their own choosing. Knowledge was to be welcomed from all parts of the world for the greater progress of the empire.

The generalities were unexceptionable, but concrete application was to fall far short, as might be expected. First of all, a central government had to be set up. A kind of Council of State was established with ministries to discharge appropriate administrative functions. There was also a legislative body, but it was soon lost sight of; the idea was too alien to

Japanese practice. Significant of the trend to be followed to our own day, the principal executive posts were given to daimyo, court nobles, and some higher ranking samurai. The Tokugawas had been evicted, but the same class still ruled.

The most urgent problem at the outset was the maintenance of public order. This was not easy and was not to be assured for some years. First of all, there was the continuation of peasant discontent, with periodic outbursts of violence. There was no reason for a change in this respect. The passing of the shogunate and later of feudalism brought no amelioration in the lot of the peasants. If anything, it was worse than before. The rice tribute paid to feudal lords became taxes paid to the central government and was probably more onerous under the central government, since the government needed more revenue. One way or another the peasant was lucky if he could keep a third of his crop for his own consumption. Not until 1876 was there any reduction in the peasant's taxes, and between 1868 and that year there were nearly two hundred outbreaks of one dimension or another in different parts of the country, some of them being serious.

More important was the relation of the feudal clans to the central government. They had all, or nearly all, been willing enough to turn out the Tokugawas; but there appears to have been a mental reservation that the strongest and most active of them would succeed to power in their stead under one guise or another. Of the clans the most assertive were the four in the West that had taken the lead in the campaign against the shogunate—Choshu, Satsuma, Hizen, and Tosa. They had been more anti-Tokugawa than pro-Western or pro-Restoration. At the outset each fief was proclaimed a prefecture under the imperial government, with a governor actually chosen by the daimyo of the fief. Nothing was changed, then, except names. The first real break came in 1869, when the daimyo of Choshu, Satsuma, Hizen, and Tosa offered to surrender their fiefs to the imperial government, that is, to turn over to the government their land registers. It is useless to speculate whether their motive was to renounce all power in favor of the new government or whether they believed that in time they would themselves be the central authority functioning as a kind of new but joint shogunate. But they did make the offer and it was accepted, and thus the feudal dyke was broken. Also the four clans offered to put their troops at the disposal of the imperial government, thus giving it the means to make its authority good. Thus emboldened, the government took its next stroke, a historic one. In 1871 an imperial rescript abolished all the feudal clans, giving as its ground that the clans obstructed genuine national government. Thus approximately three hundred daimyo families and their properties came under imperial jurisdiction, at least officially.

This raised the more troublesome question of the status of the samurai. Their position, already difficult long before the passing of the shogunate, now became all but impossible. They were men without means of livelihood. Those attached to daimyo whose fortunes had been waning had long been in straitened circumstances, and some had either drifted into semidignified occupations on the side—handicrafts mainly—or had found some relation with well-to-do merchants. There were also numerous marriages of samurai into rich merchant families, social position being traded for material comfort. The majority, however, remained maladjusted. They had never been trained for anything except fighting and indeed looked down on all other occupations as beneath honorable men. Most of them remained unable to adjust themselves to a new kind of world, poor, idle, and malcontent. They were ripe for adventure, lawful or unlawful, and they could easily be recruited by those who had larger schemes afoot—those who suffered in one way or another under the new regime, those who had counted on something else after the passing of the Tokugawas, and the die-hards who still opposed modernism and the presence of the foreigner. They were the ones who agitated for an expedition to Korea and for war with China, as has already been told, and they were responsible also for the attacks on individual foreigners described in an earlier chapter.

In 1874 a samurai rebellion on a large scale broke out in the territory of the Hizen, some 2,500 participating. It was put down by a punitive expedition despatched from the capital. Another started in Choshu and it, too, was suppressed, as were a few others on a smaller scale. The real center of disaffection, however, was among the Satsuma, in southern Kyushu, where a formidable movement had been organized under the leadership of Saigo Takamori, one of the men most influential in bringing about the Restoration and for the first few years after 1868 one of the most influential men in the imperial government. He was a man of considerable force and strong views, and while neither antiforeign nor opposed to modernism—he had been sent abroad to observe conditions in the West—he was an advocate of an aggressive policy and one of the chauvinistic wing that was already emerging.

In the State Council Saigo pressed vigorously for an invasion of Korea, and when in 1874 he was rebuffed by the majority, he retired to Kyushu. He gathered a group of disciples and started what were called schools. They gave general education but, even more, training in modern military arts. Arms were collected, too, and as the movement spread the central government became worried, especially in view of samurai risings elsewhere. It sent its own men down to Kyushu to survey the situation and to take over actual authority. Among other things, they demanded that arms be turned over to them. This was taken by Saigo's followers as a signal to strike, and they did, although Saigo himself was absent at the time. With an army estimated at 150,000 they set out on the march.

This was the most serious rebellion the new regime was to suffer, and it almost took on the proportions of a civil war. It was crushed but only after severe fighting, with a good deal of slaughter after the Japanese manner on both sides. Saigo himself was killed and thus became a figure in subsequent Japanese legendry. By this victory the new regime proved itself and was never again to be seriously challenged, but the victory had an even greater and more lasting significance. It sounded the death knell of the old feudalism and marked the beginning of a new and more efficient militarism. As will be explained later, military conscription had been introduced a few years before the Satsuma rebellion, and the Saigo rising provided its first test. There it was proved that not only the knight-at-arms, the professional warrior, the chosen few of a nobler breed could fight. The lowly peasant when armed and trained could fight, too, and could even prevail. War as the privilege of the few ended. The monopoly of the noble class was broken. A broader base was found for power, and the beginning of a new militarism laid. Fighting for the Japanese was thenceforth to be not only the privilege but the duty of the many, and in this way the future Japan was to be enabled to fight in broader theaters and for larger ends. In Japan's social history the new element was revolutionary and historic; in the arena of world politics it was to be no less historic.

Something more must be said about the conditions accompanying the disestablishment of feudalism, since they were to leave a permanent impress on the future of Japan. When in 1871 the imperial rescript was issued abolishing the feudal system of land ownership and clan rule, the lands of the daimyo were not expropriated. At first it was provided that the daimyo were to be paid by the government an annual stipend equal to half their normal revenue. The samurai were to receive considerably less than half their annual rice allowance, which brought most of them to a precarious level. For the daimyo this was a highly profitable arrangement, since they were absolved from all risk of crop failure and most of the cost of administering their fiefs; in addition, in some cases their debts were taken over. Since there were some 300 daimyo families and about 400,000 samurai families, there were approximately 2,000,000 persons who for practical purposes had to be supported by the government—about one twelfth of the population of the country—at a time when the government had only meager sources of revenue. It was an untenable situation and the government found itself in desperate financial straits. It sought loans abroad but without success. Therefore in 1876 a new settlement had to be devised and imposed in order to avoid insolvency. By this arrangement the obligation to both daimyo and samurai was to be discharged in a single payment representing a capitalization of their annual stipends, payment being in bonds at a minimum interest rate of 5 per cent and maturing in a varying number of years. The basis of capitalization for daimyo was liberal, but for the samurai it was such that their income would come to about one-sixth of what it had been before 1868. Those who could not find a new niche for themselves faced the prospect of going down, as a large proportion of them did. It was this prospect that had no little to do with the bitterness that flared up in the samurai revolts.

The total cost of the feudal settlement to the government came to 200,000,000 yen (normally $100,000,000), but this was not its most important lasting effect. What it mainly did was to fortify the old Japanese ruling class in its position as the new ruling class, with all the perquisites and privileges of the old under new names. True, the feudal nobility had to share the position with the merchant princes who had slowly gathered economic power over the preceding century, but this, too, only made it stronger. As has been seen, the social and political position of the daimyo and the uppermost ranks of the samurai had been unimpaired by the Restoration. It was out of their class, together with the old court nobility, that the highest officials of the new regime were chosen. Now their economic status was raised. Many of them had long been in economically declining fortunes. Now they were given a fresh lift. By reason of the grants in compensation for their lands the daimyo were able, together with the merchant princes, to get in on the ground floor of the new industrialism and rise as it rose. Japan may have had a revolution, but it was a revolution from the top and by decree, one that left those at the apex of the pyramidal society still at the apex.

The new Japanese government embarked almost at once on a program of laying the foundation of an industrial system. It has been repeatedly pointed out that the Japanese discerned very early that industrialization was the indispensable condition of survival. They proceeded at once to act on their understanding and significantly began with such enterprises as were what we now call strategic—railways and other means of communications, mines, iron and steel works, shipyards, etc. And first of all there had to be banks for purposes of financing, since no facilities existed for mobilizing capital. Given the conception of authority traditional in a country with Japan's past, it was natural that the state—or whatever was the repository of authority—should take the initiative and keep control, and the first modern enterprises and installations were initiated, owned and controlled by the state. There was also a certain practical logic in such a course. It was sound to get certain "pilot enterprises" going to show how modern industry should be conducted and that profits could be reaped. Most of all, there was a need for quick results. Therefore such enterprises as were not actually government controlled received generous state subsidies. Yet the primary need was capital, and to this end the government encouraged, even compelled, the organization of banks, and from these banks investment funds were to come for some years. In this connection this is the point to be emphasized: the bonds that had been given the daimyo in compensation for their lands became, either directly or indirectly through banks, the source from which the first industrial and financial capital came. It is of some importance that, as shown by E. H. Norman in his *Japan's Emergence as a Modern State,* in 1880 out of a total capital of 42,111,100 yen in national banks, 44 per cent was owned by former daimyo and court nobles, 31 per cent by rich former samurai, and 15 per cent by merchant princes. Not only did much of modern industry fall under the control of banks from the beginning, inevitably in the nature of Japanese circumstances, but ownership of the banks and the profits of the early industry fell to the pre-Restoration ruling class.

Whatever the obstacles and whatever the circumstances, however, the new leaders did press forward with the business of making over the country and carried it forward with a vigor, determination, and sweep that were almost dramatic. There was something breath-taking in the first years after 1868, and it is understandable that the Western world has marvelled ever since at what was accomplished. Old customs and habits were legislated out of existence and died. Kuge (the court nobles) and daimyo were given new titles and a new nobility was thus created. Men's hair, which had always been worn long and caught up in a topknot, was ordered to be cut. Women were no longer to blacken their teeth and shave their eyebrows. Samurai were no longer to wear swords, although this practice did not actually die out for years; the old samurai privilege of cutting down a commoner who was disrespectful was expressly outlawed. The eating of beef was not only permitted but encouraged, this being designed to overcome Buddhist prohibition of meat eating. Western clothes began to appear, especially on men. This, though useful for symbolical effect, was not an aesthetic advance. The traditional Japanese costume is beautiful; furthermore, the structural conformation of the Japanese male body hardly lends itself to frock coats and bowler hats. Now that defeat in war and consequent poverty and a simultaneous desire to take the ways of American democracy have led to the adoption of Western dress by Japanese women too, the aesthetic disaster is complete and final, for still less does the structural conformation of the Japanese female body lend itself to Western clothes, especially short skirts.

There were more basic innovations. Among the first was education. The Japanese also discerned very early that literacy was a prerequisite not only to cultural advancement but to proficiency in the most material of activities. An Education Department was set up in 1871 and universal compulsory education decreed. An elementary school system was organized and a teacher training institution opened in 1872. The educational system was highly centralized, on the French model, but in methods and materials it more nearly followed American practices. In fact, a number of American educators were brought in as advisers and Japanese education has borne an American impress since then. Attendance in elementary schools was for eighteen months only in the first few years and only in 1886 was it extended to as much as four years; yet the Japanese were the first Eastern people to recognize that illiteracy was incompatible with progress in a modern society. That they did accounts in some measure for their success at least in industrializing.

At the same time there was a rapid proliferation of translations from foreign languages of major works in all fields of learning: philosophy, economics—perhaps more of economics than anything else—history, international law, literature, and the physical sciences. Unlike the Chinese, the Japanese were not contemptuous of the West's attainment in knowledge. They learned for themselves that it was worthy of respect and they were determined to avail themselves of it for its utility for their own ends. They brought to Japan numerous foreigners to impart their special knowledge, apply it to Japan's needs, and train Japanese to make use of it. They engaged foreign advisers for the army, navy, foreign ministry, and public services such as communications and transportation and factories. Whatever comparative judgments they may have had in their hearts, in practice they had nothing of the blind complacency that held China back until the twentieth century.

Consistent with the underlying philosophy, the building of a defense force was almost at the top of the scale of urgency. Immediately after the Restoration the samurai offered by the first clans to comply with the new order were organized into an army to serve the central government. Soon, however, the conviction was reinforced by the observation of Japanese sent to Europe to study military organization. At first the French army was taken as model, but after its decisive defeat by

Prussia in 1871, it was decided to adopt Prussian military principles and methods. In this decision the main influence was that of Yamagata Aritomo, a young man who had been sent to France and Germany to study their military systems and who had come back won by Prussian military ideas even before the Franco-Prussian war. He became Vice-Minister of Military Affairs and, although at first not listened to by the Council of State, eventually had his way. His influence on Japanese military thought and practice was great from the beginning and was to continue for almost fifty years. For years before he died in 1922 he was the dominant military figure in the country, perhaps even the most powerful individual in the country, the emperor not excepted. The leading generals were his disciples; army opinion reflected his opinion. While he was a militarist, without any shading or inflection, he was also less irresponsible than those who succeeded him in the leadership of the Japanese army and brought the country to reckless adventures and disaster. One of the first results of Yamagata's influence was the adoption of conscription, which went into effect in 1873. For the first time in Japan's history an army representative of the whole population came into being, with revolutionary results as early as the war with the rebellious Satsuma samurai in 1877. At first peasants when called up were resentful and sometimes resisted, but their attitude changed when they began to understand that by being permitted to bear arms their estate in the social scheme, in the race even, was elevated.

The first railroad, seventeen miles long, which connected Tokyo, the capital, with Yokohama, its port, was constructed by the government in 1873. Ten years later more than a hundred miles of railway were in operation. After that private capital entered into railway construction and there was a rapid increase. A national banking system was instituted in 1872 and within two years four large banking houses were in operation. A telegraph system under government ownership and control was established. Then came arsenals, iron works, shipyards and mines—all the requirements of the kind of industry that eventually yields armaments. Only then were light industries started, those that provide consumer goods.

What should be noted above all is the paternalism that was the ruling principle from the beginning. Such enterprises as were not established and controlled by the government received liberal subsidies. The brilliant group of younger men—mainly of the nobility, more vigorous samurai, and merchant princes—who had taken over the direction of the new Japan knew what they wanted and in what priority. They knew that if modern technology was to be learned and its potentiality of large profits demonstrated there had to be central planning, a concept hardly alien to the Japanese. Authority at the top and authoritarianism in philosophy and practice were integral to their traditional system and came naturally to them—and continued to come naturally to them until 1945 despite the outer trappings of parliamentarianism.

Since the state was controlled by a small group at the top and industry and finance were controlled at the top, favorable opportunities were opened from the very beginning to those affiliated with ruling groups. Generous subsidies could be won for new ventures by those in the know or with influence with those who had connections. And later, when the pilot enterprises had served their purposes and there were enough men who had learned how to conduct modern industry, the state began to withdraw from industry and sell its holdings. It sold them at tempting prices and those with connections had the first chance at the bonanza profits that followed. This was the foundation of the system of gigantic holding company trusts owned by a few families and their associates— the Zaibatsu, they are called—that held the whole Japanese economy in an unbreakable oligarchic grip. This was the system, too, that not only provided the power for the Japanese war machine but made it easy for the Japanese militarists to bend the economy to their use.

The beginning of Japan's modernization was a prodigious feat and also a dangerous feat—dangerous, as it turned out, for Japan itself even more than for the rest of the world.

CHAPTER XIV

Constitutionalism, Japanese Style

Besides laying the foundation of an industrialized country, a country modern at least in its material superstructure, Japan was occupied in the two decades after the Restoration with the problem of how to set up a political system more or less consonant with the spirit of a modern state.

Notwithstanding the Western ideal of democracy, by almost unconscious process the small groups that had ruled Japan before 1868 continued to rule it after 1868; yet it was not possible to exclude all Western ideas that were inconvenient. With Western conceptions of the organization and methods of production, Western conceptions of the organization of the state and the relation of state to people had to come in too. Not only were books on Western physical science translated, but books on Western political science and political theory as well. It was impossible to prevent the latter from exercising their appeal too, and there emerged individuals and groups, in a very small minority, it is true, who found Western ideas of representative government as desirable as production by machines. Western political liberalism entered, in short. Its substance was to remain thin and diluted at least until after 1945, but it was there.

The Charter Oath, it will be remembered, contained the emperor's assurance that decision on public questions would be by public discussion, which by any normal construction would imply representative bodies. But in the first years this was given a loose translation, so loose that the original idea, as elsewhere understood, was unrecognizable. A kind of deliberative assembly was set up in 1868, but not only were its members hand-picked but they were given nothing to do and no power to do it with. It was essentially a feudal council. Real power lay in the small Council of State, which was in effect a kind of regency for the young emperor. The nominal deliberative assembly lingered in a kind of desuetude until it passed out of existence entirely in two or three years. However, a few voices already were being heard for broader representation, and in 1875 a second nominal legislative body was convoked, an assembly of local governors. This, too, was representative in a highly restricted sense, since it was confined to governors of the prefectures, all of them appointed officers. It is interesting as a sidelight on Japan's ideas of modern government at that time to quote from the imperial rescript setting up the new body. It read:

"In accordance with the meaning of the Oath taken by Me at the commencement of My reign, and as a gradual development of its policy, I am convening an assembly of representatives of the whole nation, so as by the help of public discussion to ordain laws, thus opening up the way to harmony between the governors and the governed. . . . I have issued this constitution of a Deliberative Assembly . . . as the representative of the people."

The "representatives of the people," who were appointed by the State Council (made up of feudal and court nobility), were to meet once a year. Bills were in the main to be submitted by the assembly's president, who was appointed by the emperor, and if passed were to be sent to the emperor. The emperor would then decide whether the bills were to go into effect. Such bills as originated in the assembly itself were subject to the emperor's veto. This was, of course, a travesty of representation, and some of the more articulate groups in the country, immature as their political development may have been, protested; some protested vigorously, including a few newspapers which had newly found voice and enjoyed its use. In a few years this assembly, too, sank into desuetude for lack of real function and disappeared.

In 1878 still another representative body was born. This was the Fu Ken Kai. It was a system of assemblies in each prefecture to deliberate and act upon matters concerning each locality. The members of the assemblies were to be elected by suffrage, but the property qualifications for voting were so high as to exclude all but a small minority. At the same time a press law was passed, penalizing the kind of criticism that had been directed against the previous assembly. In practice the Fu Ken Kai had little more power than the assembly of local governors, but they did come a step nearer popular representation and could express to a certain extent, even if not to the point of effectiveness in action, popular sentiment on local issues. And to a certain extent, too, they offered a forum for expression of opinions from a wider area than the closely knit oligarchy which presided over the imperial councils in Tokyo. The system was a crude simulacrum of representative government, but a relationship could be traced. And it was a last step before the Constitution of 1889, which at least in name and externals provided for parliamentary government.

It was inevitable that at the same time political parties should be formed, although, again, they were parties with distinctively Japanese inflections. Various motives entered into their formation. Usually there was more than one motive and sometimes these were incompatible one with another. Economic interest entered, of course. So also did ambition for office and to some degree advocacy of wider representation in government. The agrarian interest soon found organized expression, but not so much the interest of the peasant as the interest of the landowner. The peasant was for long to remain mute, humble, and ignored as before.

With the erection of a large and expensive structure of government and priority in interest and support given to industrialization (lavish opportunities were dispensed to the favored few having capital at their disposal), there was little regard for the concerns of the rural population, whether landowner or peasant, and no provision for its representation. The agricultural class was concerned most of all with taxation, the brunt of which had fallen on it from the very beginning and continued to do so until the Allied Occupation. The common interest in taxation acted as a binding force, and in 1881 a party called the Jiyuto was formed, with members from the landed class. To it adhered also some elements concerned with broadening the base of government. In general, the Jiyuto tended to the liberal side, and thus drew to itself some of the underprivileged strata and such as were becoming politically conscious if not politically literate, who also suffered from the inequitable incidence of taxation. In a vague way it stood for more popular rights and a nearer approximation to constitutional government.

The Jiyuto was not the only party. There was the Kaishinto or Progressive party, which had more urban support and can be described—cautiously, since issues were undefined in the first parties—as moderate. Then there was a conservative party known as the Rikken Taiseito, which stood for a powerful centralized state. In themselves, in the issues for which they stood, the methods by which they sought to attain their objects and their actual accomplishments, these parties meant very little. They represented a thin, wavering penetration of modern ideas, so attenuated that they could not survive, and in a few years they did pass. Not until after 1920 did political parties in Japan have the role, the power, or the function of their equivalents in the West. But they were portents. The pioneer groupings in the 1880's did foreshadow the corporate political associations around larger issues inseparable from government in any society not unmixedly absolutist.

In 1881 the government promised a constitution with provision for an elective national assembly by 1889, and though measures were set in motion to that end the agitation for wider representation did not cease. There were demonstrations to emphasize the demands and these sometimes erupted in disorders. The desire for popular representation motivated some of these incidents, and in some cases the desire was exploited for other ends—sometimes relief from high land rents, sometimes relief from high taxes, sometimes pure factional maneuvers by discontented groups seeking a larger share of government jobs. This had something to do with the increasingly repressive actions taken against the political parties and the parties' eventual dissolution. But preparation for a constitutional regime proceeded, and as a first step Ito Hirobumi, who had already risen to eminence in the capital, was sent to Europe and America in 1882 to study Western constitutions and political systems. He returned the following year and began to work on the draft of the constitution.

A Bureau of Investigation of Constitutional Systems was established to work with Ito. It was composed of Ito as chairman and four others, all closely related to the Council of State. The Bureau itself was made a part of the Imperial Household Department and, being a part of the court, was immune to criticism and unanswerable to any other body for its acts and decisions. In 1888 a Privy Council was established—on Ito's initiative—with Ito as president, its function being to pass on the constitution. It was in this spirit and this atmosphere that constitutionalism came to Japan. If it was an answer to popular demand for representation in government, the people can hardly be said to have had much to do with it. It was not a compact of government and people. It was "granted" to the people—a kind of benevolent grant. As a matter of fact it was so administered in the ensuing years. Indeed, it was so designed that under it the Japanese people would have little voice in government.

The point has often been made that the Japanese constitution and the system of government ordained by it reflected German influence on Japan. It is true that of all the governmental systems that Ito observed in Europe the one that impressed him most, that seemed to him best suited to Japanese ways of thought and action, was the German. In that he was probably right, and if the Japanese scheme of government was patterned on the German, that was not the result of the exercise of German influence so much as a conscious Japanese recognition of compatibility. In general political attitudes, in conceptions of the relation of people to state, there was greater similarity between Japan and Germany than between Japan and any other Western country. Authoritarianism was congenial to both. To both the right of the few in the uppermost range in the social scale to rule was in the nature of things.

That both elevated the military arts and military activities to the top of the scale of values also was an expression of an inner community of attitudes and concepts. Neither had—or perhaps has even now—been influenced under the surface by the fundamental values and ideas that were formative for Western peoples in modern times—rights of the individual, subordination of the state to the individual, sovereignty of the people and the supremacy of their judgment over the desires of officials in government, the indispensability of the consent of the governed to the acts of government. To both there has been something messy in democracy, and they have found themselves uncomfortable in attempts to practice it. Order is the highest good, and order comes with unquestioned authority and unquestioning obedience. This, for both, is nature's plan. It was natural, then, that Ito should have found himself most at home with German ideas of government and that his associates should have found the instinct and judgment sound.

The constitution, duly handed down in 1889, served as the foundation of the structure of Japanese government until the Allied Occupation. As can be seen, its aim was a state of which the exterior was to be a parliamentary system while the essentials of oligarchic rule were preserved, and in this aim, as the fifty years that followed proved, it was successful. At the center, the heart from which and to which the blood of the nation flowed, was the emperor. The empire was "to be reigned over and governed by a line of emperors unbroken for ages eternal." Also: "The emperor is sacred and inviolable." Thus was official sanctity conferred on the demonstrably false historical legend of the antiquity of the dynasty and the new myth of the emperor's divinity. The emperor determined the organization of the administration, appointed and dismissed civil and military officers, and fixed their salaries. He was commander-in-chief of the army and navy, concluded treaties, declared war and made peace—all without check. There was a Diet, but "the emperor exercised the legislative power with the consent of the imperial Diet," and he had the right to convoke, prorogue, and dissolve the Diet. More will be said later of how these unlimited imperial powers were manipulated in his name by those who wielded actual control, but here it is necessary only to underline the conceptions of constitutional government prevailing in Japan when it nominally became a modern state.

The Diet was to consist of two houses—a House of Peers, composed of members of the imperial family, a large proportion of the nobility, and a few commoners selected by the emperor for their distinguished records; and a House of Representatives, popularly elected but with a limited franchise. The most significant restriction on the Diet was the limitation put upon it in the area salient to any legislative body and crucial to any representative government—the power of the purse. The annual budget had to be submitted to the Diet, but if the Diet refused to pass it the preceding year's budget held over another year. Thus the control of the government by the Diet was for practical purposes restricted, if not nullified. Furthermore, there were certain fixed expenditures, designated without the Diet's consent, over which the Diet had no control. It could not reject or reduce them without the consent of the cabinet, over which, too, the Diet had no control. These included all military expenditures. Also the emperor had the right to issue imperial ordinances in time of emergency when the Diet was not in session which had the force of law until the next session of the Diet. The imperial ordinances had to be approved by the Privy Council and countersigned by a member of the cabinet, but both these bodies were creatures of the emperor and responsible to him alone. Also the emperor had unrestricted veto power over all acts passed by the Diet.

Of the cabinet little was said in the constitution. There was provision for "Ministers of State" who were to give advice to the emperor. These later formed the cabinet—chosen by the emperor and responsible to him alone. Subsequent ordinances defined the functions of the cabinet in greater detail. In general it had supervision over the administrative organs and determined governmental policies. In all larger matters of state policy, however, it was superseded by the Privy Council. To the Privy Council the emperor submitted such issues as peace or war, treaties, interpretation of the constitution, imperial ordinances, amendments to the constitution. The latter, incidentally, could be initiated only by the emperor. There never was an amendment. The Privy Council was appointed by the emperor and served for life. The practice developed of having nominations to the council made by the prime minister, but this was a highly circumscribed right, not only because the prime minister was chosen by the emperor but because traditionally it was unwise to nominate anyone who was not "safe."

One section of the constitution was devoted to a kind of Bill of Rights —a very diluted Bill of Rights. All the conventional guarantees were there—but with qualifications. Thus, all Japanese subjects were to have liberty of speech, writing, publication, public meetings, and associations —"within the limits of law." Freedom of religious belief was guaranteed "within limits not prejudicial to peace and order and not antagonistic to their duties as subjects." Also, all the provisions on the rights of subjects "shall not affect the exercise of powers appertaining to the emperor in times of war or in cases of national emergency." What these qualifications meant was eloquently illustrated when the various peace preservation laws were enacted before World War II: they were escape clauses from the assurance of individual rights; in effect, they were a denial of individual rights.

Two important sectors of government were left almost entirely out of control. One was the permanent bureaucracy. This was from the out-set almost an autonomous body, self-perpetuating and acting on its own traditions and rules. On the whole an efficient administrative organ-ism, independent of partisan politics, it also conformed to whatever class

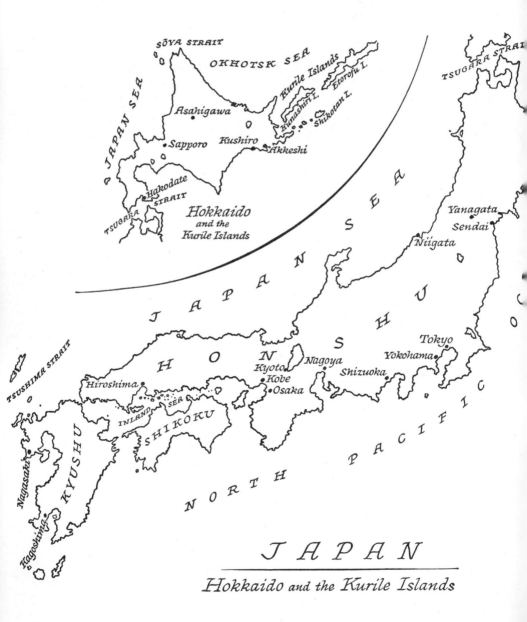

JAPAN

Hokkaido and the Kurile Islands

exercised decisive power. It was a conservative force in both the best and worst sense of the word, but it was in no way responsive to public opinion or even the people's interest.

The other independent sector consisted of the army and navy. The constitution provided almost explicitly that they should be so: "The emperor determines the organization and peace standing of the army and navy." From this it followed, or was made to follow, that the highest ranking officers of the two services, being directly subordinate to the emperor, had direct access to him. And so it came about that they and they alone had such access, and in this way they could bring pressure to bear on him, whereas the civil authorities, even the cabinet, had contact with the emperor at one remove.

There was another development by which the army and navy came to be independent of all control and could wield final power. Although not in the constitution, by subsequent ordinance it was provided that only an active general or lieutenant general could occupy the post of Minister of War and only an admiral or vice-admiral the post of Minister of the Navy. The effect of this was to give the army and navy control of the cabinet and therefore of government policy. If they disapproved of a decision of the cabinet, either the Minister of War or the Minister of the Navy resigned and neither service would permit a successor to be named. The whole cabinet would then have to resign. If a new prime minister tried to form a cabinet, no general or admiral would be permitted by his service to join it until the decision they disapproved was rescinded. Thus government could be paralyzed until the military had their way, and on important matters they always did. This was most conspicuously demonstrated in the decade before Pearl Harbor, when the civilian authorities stood helplessly by while the military plunged on to disaster.

In summary, the Constitution of 1889 was a written regularization of oligarchic rule in Japan, with a slight transformation from landed lords to militarists, sometimes with and sometimes without the support of industrial and financial magnates. With a constitution, a cabinet, a Diet, and all the trappings of nineteenth-century government, Japan remained a feudal oligarchy. Its people were not so much subjects as objects. That it should have followed the course that it did and turned out as it did is not surprising; the reverse would have been surprising. And yet the constitution and the manner of its development were an authentic expression of the traditions, spirit, habits of thought and action of the people. Anything else would have been artificial. That was to be the tragedy of both Eastern Asia and the West. Japan had made an artificial and meretricious leap from one cultural stage to another for which nothing in its history and experience prepared it.

CHAPTER XV

The Climax Begins— Sino-Japanese War

As an arena for critical international politics, Eastern Asia may be said to have entered the decisive phase in 1894—the phase that came to climax in 1941. It was in 1894 that war began between China and Japan, the war that started Japan on its course as a Great Power and China on its decline to the level of a stake in diplomacy and prize in war. The war came over Korea.

In 1885, as we saw in a previous chapter, China and Japan, after a minor clash between their troops in Seoul, had come to an agreement by which each was to withdraw its troops from Korea and notify the other in advance if it had reason to send men to Korea again. Thus war was averted at that time, but the rivalry of the two countries in Korea was unabated. Continuing dissension among the Koreans, with plot and counterplot, one side appealing to Japanese for support and the other to the Chinese, only sharpened the rivalry. Japan and China each came to fear that the other would win outright ascendancy in Korea, and each had ground for its fears. Intrigue was matched by intrigue, and sooner or later the tension had to snap. Japan was in any case bent on asserting itself on the continent or wherever its nascent expansionism and native militancy could find scope, but thus far the more far-sighted among its leaders had been able to curb the headstrong. As for China, it had as yet learned nothing and forgotten nothing. If it was blindly complacent toward the West, it was openly contemptuous toward Japan, whose people it still regarded as primitive (though civilized by China) and negligible. That Japan, too, had acquired new sources of power the Chinese could no more comprehend than they had understood Western force fifty years before.

It was China that forced the pace in Korea, but in extenuation it

must be said that the Chinese had valid reasons for considering preven-
tive measures. Japan's intentions were unmistakable, and Japan was not
alone. There were clear indications that other Powers also were becoming aware of opportunity in Korea and were correspondingly tempted:
the muddied Korean waters made for good fishing. The European rivalries that were to work toward 1914 were already forming, and every
part of the world was soon to be a testing ground and a potential vantage
point. At the time the sharpest conflict of interest was Anglo-Russian,
and Asia was its main setting. Russia was already on the eastward march
across the Asian continent, and if it arrived at its goals not only would
China fall but India would be surrounded and the British Empire be
vulnerable to Russian attack. Korea is contiguous with the Siberian
Maritime Province and was therefore directly in Russia's path.

China was no doubt less concerned with the technical consideration
that Korea was its tributary than with the physical threat of any strong
aggressive Power on its long, undefended borders. Since there were two
such Powers it resorted to the obvious stratagem: play one off against
the other, meanwhile seeking to make Korea its own in reality as in
juridical form. It proceeded to do so. The steady infiltration of Chinese
influence has already been touched on. Li Hung-chang, Viceroy of
Chihli Province, had already taken distant supervision through his Resident, Yuan Shih-kai, a man who combined the mandarin's suppleness
with the dictator's willingness to ride roughshod over opposition. In addition to Yuan, Li had appointed as Inspector-General of Korean Customs first P. G. Möllendorff, a German, and then H. F. Merrill, an
American, both of whom had been in the Chinese Customs. This was
apparently an opening move toward merging the Chinese and Korean
Customs, which could constitute a first step toward formal or informal
annexation. Furthermore, Yuan had openly begun to take a hand in
Korean internal politics. He had for a long time backed the conservative or, rather, reactionary faction led by the Taiwenkun, but soon he
was acting on his own account.

Even before the clash with Japan in 1885 Yuan had had some provocation and pretext for action. At the end of 1884 there were reports that
Russia had entered into the Korean imbroglio by a secret treaty in which
Korea granted it the use of Port Lazareff as a warm water harbor in
exchange for a Russian military mission to train a Korean army. Not
only China and Japan took alarm. The reports could not be confirmed,
but as a matter of insurance and counterbalance Great Britain in 1885
occupied the island of Port Hamilton, off the South Korea coast. This
brought the issue to a head and the so-called treaty was dropped. It was
subsequently revealed that Möllendorff had had a hand in the matter,

and he was dismissed. The episode was closed after China intervened with both Russia and Great Britain, and on Russia's assurance that it would occupy no part of Korea Great Britain agreed to evacuate Port Hamilton. The episode was closed, but it foreshadowed what was to come not only in Korea but everywhere in East Asia—infringement on territory for its own sake or as counterbalance to infringement by another Power.

For China the moral semed to be that to temporize was to lose. The narrow escape from war with Japan in 1885 induced boldness rather than caution. In 1886 China proceeded with the organization of a coup designed to seize the Korean king, queen, and crown prince, deport them to China, and turn over power to the Taiwenkun, whose subservience to China presumably could be counted on. The pretext was an alleged treaty between Russia and Korea giving Russia substantial control over Korea. Such a treaty was produced, but its palpable forgery was exposed, mainly through the efforts of British and American diplomatic representatives, both countries being opposed to China's aggressive policy, if only to prevent the precipitation of a general scramble for Korea. The attempted coup, though frustrated, put Japan on its guard. Likewise the Korean government, which decided in consequence to send its own diplomatic representatives abroad, actually did dispatch a mission to the United States, despite China's vigorous protests.

China next started economic penetration, following much the same course the Western Powers were soon to pursue in China itself. When Japan had obtained from the Korean government the concession to lay a cable line from its islands to Fusan, the principal Korean port, China countered by obtaining the monopolistic right to build a telegraph line from Tientsin across North China and Manchuria to Seoul. Japan then demanded permission to extend its cable over land lines from Fusan to Seoul. On Chinese instigation this was refused, but the Korean government promised to build such a line itself, which it did, though under Chinese supervision. There were similar difficulties over the sale of rice to Japan, the Japanese having become dependent for part of their food supply on Korean rice. The Koreans imposed an embargo. The Japanese first protested and then demanded indemnities. The British and Americans mediated and there was compromise, but tension increased.

The climax was precipitated by the activities of the so-called Tong-Hak Society, an organization of Korean fanatics motivated by a mixture of nationalism, antiforeignism, and a dubious religion. Its strength grew and disorders mounted, culminating in a rebellion of sorts which threatened to overthrow the government if not checked and perhaps also to bring about attacks against foreigners, the majority of whom were Japanese. China, Japan, and the United States all sent warships as a precaution. Yuan Shih-kai proposed to Li Hung-chang that Chinese troops be sent, too, but Li hesitated, aware of the risks of another and more serious clash with Japan. When the Korean king asked Li for help against the Tong-Haks, Li complied, meanwhile notifying Japan in accordance with the treaty of 1885. The Japanese immediately did the same, their troops arriving in Seoul in early June, 1894, before the Chinese.

The Korean government had meanwhile succeeded in putting down the Tong-Hak rebellion, but now the Chinese and Japanese confronted each other in the capital. The Japanese government proposed that China and Japan make joint efforts to effect basic reforms designed to end the chronic disorder in Korea. China arbitrarily refused, saying that it could not interfere in Korea's internal affairs, an extraordinary statement in light of what China had been doing, and one not calculated to mollify the Japanese. It was extraordinary, too, in light of China's frequently expressed contention that Korea was a tributary to China. But Japan's proposal was no less curious in light of its own previous contentions that Korea was independent. Japan decided on direct action nevertheless. By means of pressure reinforced by the presence of its troops it induced the king to declare Korea independent and then laid down a program of reform on its own initiative. China protested and asked the Western Powers to intervene with Japan. They did, but Japan had taken the bit in its teeth and was no longer in a mood to stop. The Korean government, alarmed at the critical turn, asked the Japanese to withdraw their troops while the reforms were being put into effect. This, too, the Japanese sharply refused and demanded instead that the Chinese be made to leave and that all Korea's agreements with China be abrogated. Korea on its part refused, being reluctant to face the Chinese after so drastic an act, and Japan then went into action. On July 23 its troops swept into the capital, seized the palace and the king, installed the Taiwenkun as head of a so-called cabinet (that worthy had now become a pawn for both sides), and forced the issuance of a decree declaring Korea's independence. Four days later it forced the new Korean government, now completely a puppet, to declare war on China and authorize the Japanese to expel Chinese troops. Chinese reinforcements were already on the way from Tientsin. These were intercepted at sea by the Japanese and one ship with nearly a thousand men was sunk by Japanese cruisers. At the same time Chinese troops in Korea were attacked. On August 1 both sides declared war.

The war was, as a war, farcical, but its effects were psychologically startling and politically historic. The world was unprepared for the discovery that China was a hollow shell—a dragon with a paper exterior, empty within. Nor was it prepared for the discovery of how strong Japan had become in twenty years. The two discoveries were to have direct and immediate consequences. The Japanese opened with an offensive on both land and sea, an offensive smartly and efficiently carried out. Chinese resistance was pathetic and humiliating. The Chinese government had gone through the motions of building up a military force, but when the test came it was found that the money appropriated for arms had been diverted either for luxuries for the empress dowager and her court or to the private pockets of her favorites. Guns on ships were without shells or had wooden shells. Soldiers in the field had no ammunition. The most telling illustration, often cited, is the Summer Palace, the lavish pleasure ground outside the city walls of Peking, which had been built for the empress dowager with money appropriated for the navy. The Chinese troops fought bravely but hopelessly, and Japan soon wiped out all opposition on the sea and in three months had landed in Manchuria and was rapidly advancing in the direction of Peking. The Chinese asked one Power after another to mediate. Each did, only to be rebuffed by Japan. Li Hung-chang made direct approaches, offering compromise, and he, too, was rebuffed. The Japanese were in a mood now to dictate, not to compromise. They were determined to humble China and to get tangible rewards as well while they had the opportunity.

When it became clear that nothing could prevent the Japanese from advancing on Peking and taking it, Li Hung-chang himself set out for Japan in March, 1895, to sue for peace. In Shimonoseki he met Ito, then Count Ito and Prime Minister, and Count Mutsu, Minister of Foreign Affairs. At the first session, on March 20, Li asked for an immediate armistice and the Japanese agreed, but on harsh terms—the occupation of the ports of Shanhaikuan, Taku, and Tientsin, all inside the Great Wall, Tientsin being less than eighty miles from Peking. These terms Li could not accept.

Then a dramatic incident supervened to act as solvent. On leaving the third session with the Japanese representatives Li Hung-chang was the victim of an attempt at assassination. He was shot under the eye but not seriously wounded. An unexpected reaction was produced in Japan—a sense of guilt and shame. An attack had been made by a Japanese on a man who, though an enemy, was a guest in the country. The emperor sent a formal apology. Men of all classes sent expressions of sympathy. Negotiations were resumed, at Li's sickbed, in a more conciliatory mood. On April 17 a treaty of peace was signed: the Treaty of Shimonoseki. Its terms were drastic enough. China recognized the independence of Korea. The Liaotung Peninsula, off South Manchuria, containing what are now Port Arthur and Dairen, was ceded to Japan, as were Formosa and the Pescadores. China was to pay an indemnity of 200,000,000 taels, roughly $165,000,000, and Japan was to receive most-favored-nation status for the first time. It was the severest treaty China had yet had to sign with a foreign Power.

With this treaty Eastern Asia was formally incorporated into European politics, never yet to be extricated. The war signified two things: first, that China was ripe for the plucking; and second, that Japan, which had the additional advantage of being within easy reaching distance, would have to be reckoned with as a contender for the fruit. Almost at once the Western Powers began to draw in, with Russia in the lead. Russia had already manifested its interest in Manchuria and Korea and had already started the construction of the Trans-Siberian Railway, which was to extend to Vladivostok on the Pacific. At Russia's instigation, Germany and France joined her at once in a complicated succession of negotiations. Great Britain refused to take part, not only because it had not yet emerged from "splendid isolation" but because it had nothing to gain from the advance of any Western Power in East Asia. Since it was more concerned with trade in East Asia than with territory, any disturbance of the political status there would be to its detriment. With an open field it had enough advantage in industrial and commercial efficiency to get the larger share of economic rewards, but from any region that fell to some other great Power it could expect to be economically excluded precisely because of its competitive advantage. And always there was the transcendent fear of Russia in Asia, the fear of what would happen to India if Russia could extend farther south on the continent. But the other Powers had something in common, if only the need to watch each other. Russia and France had but recently (1893) concluded their military alliance, which by every logical inference was directed against Germany. It was therefore to Germany's interest to give Russia aid and comfort, either to wean it away from France or to direct its attention away from Europe, for Germany's first object in diplomacy was to keep France isolated and its second to keep Russia out of Central and South Europe.

The result was a joint Russo-French-German communication to Japan, presented only six days after the Treaty of Shimonoseki was signed. In identic notes the three Powers informed the Japanese government that the alienation of the Liaotung Peninsula would be a threat to the capital of China, would negate the independence of Korea, and "henceforth be a perpetual obstacle to the peace of the Far East." And to give point to the warning against antisocial conduct in international politics a Russian naval squadron began to steam toward Pacific waters. To an onlooker from another time or planet the not very subtle cynicism displayed by the West might be only amusing, but it injected iron into the soul of the Japanese. From the recent history of larger political events in their part of the world, however, the Japanese had learned to take hints. They yielded and gave up the Liaotung Peninsula in exchange for an additional indemnity of 20,000,000 taels. They yielded, and resolved to bide their time—a time that came ten years later, when they defeated Russia and got the Liaotung Peninsula in the end. Yet that was not the end. Though anticipating, it may be pointed out here that forty years later, after the Japanese surrender, Russia recovered Port Arthur and Dairen. How the names Manchuria, Liaotung Peninsula, Dairen, Port Arthur—how they ring again and again in Far Eastern history, as in a litany or, rather, as in a dirge for devastated countries and young men fallen in war!

China also was soon to learn a lesson in comparative political ethics. While there is no documentary evidence, there were more than indications that Li Hung-chang knew in advance of the intervention on behalf of the Liaotung Peninsula and may even have been secretly negotiating with Russia on it. That he could have done so without recognizing that it carried implications of compensation to Russia is unthinkable. Li was much too wily for that. The compensation was duly exacted, however. First of all there arose the problem of how to pay the indemnity due Japan. To do this out of China's normal revenue was out of the question. The only recourse was foreign loans. This raised no difficulties: on the contrary. There developed at once the classical imperialistic situation. It is one of the apparent paradoxes of the politics of imperialism that Great Powers are not only willing to make loans to weak countries with poor credit; they are eager to do so. This is not out of any passion for self-immolation: but on the contrary. When a strong country has laid a weak one under financial obligation, an obligation that the weak one in the nature of its economic resources is unlikely to be able to discharge, the weak one has gone a long way toward demise as an independent state and the strong one can confidently count on coming into the inheritance.

Russia was the first to proffer the fatal gift. It tendered a loan of 100,000,000 taels, but France desired to share the privilege, and since France would have to be Russia's banker anyway, its claim carried weight. Therefore Russia and France, through a syndicate of banks of the two countries, made a joint loan of some $75,000,000 for a period of thirty-six years at 4 per cent, the loan being guaranteed by the Russian government. But the British were not willing to concede a monopoly of profitable sacrifice and were joined by Germany. The principal German and British banks in the Far East then made two successive joint loans, each for £16,000,000, the first for thirty-six years at 5 per cent and the second for forty-five years at 4½ per cent. All the loans were secured on the Chinese customs revenues. China had begun the hypothecation of its sovereignty.

This, however, was just the beginning. Russia had received only the first installment on its compensation. In 1896 all countries were invited to send representatives to the coronation of Tsar Nicholas II. China chose Li Hung-chang for the mission, not without Russia's urging, since Li had proved himself not unfavorable to Russian advances. Li went, incidentally making a kind of triumphal tour of European capitals on his way out and of the United States on his way back. His formal Chinese costume—the magnificent robes of a high mandarin—his majestic bearing, and the combined charm and dignity of his personality struck the imagination of men in every Western country. But he had more than ceremonial duties to perform.

While in Russia he resumed the negotiations that apparently had begun in China. In all the capitals of the world and most of all in London, rumors had already been circulating that a secret treaty had been contracted by Li and Count Cassini, the Russian Minister in Peking. According to the rumors, this constituted a military alliance. Russia was to support China and send a mission to train its army, and in return three ports on the China coast—Kiaochow, Talienwan (later Dalny and still later Dairen), and Lushunkow (Port Arthur)—were to be put at Russia's disposal in case of need. Also Russia was to have the right to build a railway across north Manchuria to connect the Trans-Siberian line with Vladivostok. This treaty was never confirmed, but while in Europe Li did conclude a convention (the Li-Lobanov treaty) containing some of the same provisions. The most important was the concession for the railway. There were secret clauses as well, but they were never to go into effect.

The provision for the railway resulted in the Chinese Eastern Railway, a thousand miles long, completed in 1904. It was built by a company financed by the Russo-Chinese Bank, chartered in 1895 for that purpose and with full confidence that the purpose would be realized, which is itself significant of what had preceded Li's tour. As usual, most of the money for the bank's capital came from France. The Chinese Eastern Railway Company was to have the right to administer the land on both sides of the railway and to maintain police forces there for the purpose. It would also have the unrestricted right to move its troops on the railway and to enjoy reduced tariff rates on Russian goods carried on it.

Thus Russia had won a foothold on Chinese soil, the most important gained by any Western Power. Also it had laid the mines that were to rock the Far East in periodic explosions for the next fifty years.

Even before this France had won lesser concessions as its compensation. Its interests were to be first consulted if mines were to be developed in the three southern provinces of Kwangtung, Kwangsi, and Yunnan, its engineers and manufacturers having first priority in undertaking such development. Also France was to be permitted to extend its railway from Annam into China. Germany was to withhold its claim but not for long.

Thus the Great Powers were taking their positions for the race that was about to begin, the race to stake claims to the most valuable parts of the Chinese Empire. For already the conviction was forming that China was to go the way Africa was already going—to be cut up and parcelled out, to each according to his greed and the power he could put behind the greed. From the point of view of the end of the nineteenth century the conviction seemed to be sound. From the point of view of the middle of the twentieth century it was the invitation to disaster. Not only the Eastern world was to pay in sacrifice before many decades passed into history.

CHAPTER XVI

Cutting Up the Chinese Melon

The five years that closed the nineteenth century, the years that followed the Sino-Japanese War, seemed also to be the last years of the Chinese Empire. The first steps were being taken toward what seemed to be the certain partitioning of the empire. And with every step there were consultations in the capitals of Europe and the beginnings of the combinations and permutations that were to crystallize in the two camps that came to collision in 1914. Toward that crystallization and the collision that resulted China and its prospective partitioning made a large contribution. In fact, just before 1900 it appeared for a while that a European war might be precipitated over China. Other things were unexpectedly to occur to avert it, and still other issues emerged later that were more urgent than the fate of China and took precedence in the invitation to Armageddon; but among the originating causes of Europe's tragedy China must be counted.

Russia had set the pace. The concession to build the Chinese Eastern Railway, with all the rights appertaining to it—rights that for all practical purposes gave Russia control over North Manchuria and a sword to suspend over the body of China itself—alarmed other European Powers, Great Britain in particular. They feared, Great Britain most of all, that all of East Asia would fall to Russia, with all that meant in the increase of Russian power. If they could not restrain Russia, they wanted a position on the spot from which they might be able at least to counter it.

The opening moves followed quickly. France, which had been working closely with Russia, mainly because its desire for revenge against Germany in Europe was greater than its fear of Russia in Asia, had already received first payment for its part in the joint intervention against Japan on the Liaotung Peninsula. Germany had not, however, and Germany was just entering into its clamant phase. Bismarck had been dismissed by the vainglorious Wilhelm II, and with Bismarck went caution and the resolve to move slowly and only when and where advance was assured. Wilhelm and those of his like in outlook, attitude, and temperament, who were his devoted followers, were adopting the "place in the sun" psychology that was to be Europe's undoing as well as Germany's. Into the still bloodless struggle for the cutting up of Africa Germany had already actively entered. In the mid-Pacific it also had voiced its claims. But the direct object of its ambitions in those years was a big navy, with a chain of bases that went with it. To the China coast therefore its attention had already been directed. With a navy that matched Great Britain's in size it could claim equality with the British in more than politics, always a compelling psychological need for the Germans, perhaps because deep down they have always felt that they were not the equal of the British. Also with a big navy Germany could more successfully contend for desirable colonies and the trade that was to follow from acquisition of colonies. The leading figure in the agitation for the navy was Admiral Alfred von Tirpitz, already exercising influence with the kaiser.

As early as 1896, when Li Hung-chang was in Berlin on his return from the tsar's coronation, the Germans had brought up the question of a base on the China coast, but Li had been evasive. Soon after they began pressing the matter in Peking, but always the Chinese evaded the issue, fearful of precipitating similar demands by other Powers. Since the Russians and French were pressing the Chinese not to yield to the Germans, the Chinese could predict what would happen if they did yield. In 1897 Tirpitz, in command of a squadron, was making a survey of the China coast with a view to choosing the most favorable location for a base, and when he returned to Germany to become minister of the navy he renewed his agitation. Then, in a way not unfamiliar in Far Eastern history, providence intervened on November 1, 1897, when two German Catholic missionaries in Shantung Province were murdered by bandits.

It was Germany's opportunity. A naval squadron proceeded at once to Kiaochow Bay, landed troops on the Shantung coast, and seized the Chinese forts. Before the end of the month demands were made in the usual way, but to the usual ones—apology, indemnity, and dismissal of the highest officials responsible—were added demands more befitting the circumstances of time and place. Germany also asked for a naval base on the Shantung coast and the exclusive right to construct railways and open mines in Shantung Province. The usual demands China accepted without question, but the others were refused. Germany thereupon dispatched reinforcements of ships and men under command of Prince

Heinrich, the kaiser's brother. At a banquet in farewell to Prince Heinrich the kaiser in a characteristically boastful and bumptious speech, which was also prophetic, gave notice that "the German Michael has firmly planted his shield with the device of the German eagle upon the soil of China, in order once for all to give his protection to all who ask for it. . . . Should anyone essay to detract from our just rights or to injure us, then up and at him with your mailed fist." The Germans were to rue that rhetorical fling about the mailed fist before many years passed. It made an excellent motif for Allied propaganda after 1914.

Nevertheless China had to yield. The support it had hoped for from the other Western Powers was not forthcoming. On the contrary, both France and Russia raised no opposition. Russia had earmarked Kiaochow for its own, but the kaiser appears to have won a personal promise from the tsar in August, 1897, not to obstruct the German effort to get it. From this, incidentally, it may be seen how much Germany's humanitarian concern for the fate of the two murdered missionaries had to do with the demand for the naval base. Once again, a murdered missionary, murdered at an opportune time, can be a great convenience to dynamic diplomacy.

On March 6, 1898, China signed a treaty giving Germany a ninety-nine-year lease on both sides of the Kiaochow Bay, including the town of Tsingtao. In addition Germany received the right to construct two railway lines connecting Kiaochow with Tsinanfu, in the center of the province, and a Chinese pledge to look to German bankers, manufacturers, and merchants first when China needed capital or materials for any purpose in Shantung. Thus the rough outline of the "sphere of influence" idea was sketched in.

With this the whole Western advance in China was accelerated and what later became known as the Battle of the Concessions began. A few days after the signing of the treaty giving Germany what it wanted, a Russian fleet arrived in the Gulf of Peichihli to take up winter quarters. Its intention was obvious. There were quick consultations in St. Petersburg, where one influential faction, led by Count Muraviev, Minister of Foreign Affairs, was vigorously advocating a policy of outright aggression in the Far East. Muraviev was opposed by Count Witte, Minister of Finance, who wanted to proceed more cautiously, using economic penetration rather than force. It was Muraviev, however, who won the tsar's approval. Demands were made on China. On March 27, only three weeks after Germany had succeeded, Russia obtained the first of two agreements by which it got Talien-wan (Dalny or Dairen) and Lushunkow (Port Arthur) as naval bases on a lease for twenty-five years, with the right of fortification and maintenance of troops. Also

China agreed to withdraw its troops from a zone of 1,300 square miles which was to be neutralized. Further, Russia obtained the right to construct a branch railway connecting the Chinese Eastern line with Dalny and Port Arthur and with mining concessions on both sides of the railway, all other nations being excluded from any such exploitation. Thus Russia won effective control over south Manchuria as well as north Manchuria.

France came next. It put in its claim immediately. Two weeks after signing a Russian treaty China agreed to give France a ninety-nine-year lease on Kwangchow Bay, in the southeast, as a naval base and pledged itself not to alienate any of its territory on the border of Tongking, another oblique statement of the sphere-of-influence principle. Furthermore, France had the right to build a railway from Tongking to Yunnanfu, the capital of Yunnan Province, in the southwest, and to appoint French advisers to the Chinese Post Office.

The British meanwhile had been inactive but not unconcerned or unobservant. For reasons already explained they wanted to maintain the status quo; only thus would they have the widest and most unimpeded opportunity for trade. From documents not revealed until after World War I, we know that even before the Russians moved to get Port Arthur and Dalny the British had sought to dissuade them. Germany they did not fear particularly yet; Russia they definitely feared.

Lord Salisbury, the British Prime Minister, approached the Russians with a view to accommodation. From their sources of information in Peking (the Chinese were not reluctant to permit leaks when it was to their interest) the British knew before the beginning of the 1898 raids on China's sovereignty that the Russians had been pressing the Chinese government to concede to Russia the right to build and control a system of railroads in north China as well as in Manchuria. The British realized that thereby not only would Manchuria and north China become in practice colonies of Russia but that they themselves would be excluded from both for purposes of trade.

The British government therefore sought an understanding with Russia. In public statements by members of the cabinet designed to let the world in general and Russia in particular know where Great Britain stood on China, it was made clear that Great Britain wanted China preserved as a free field for commercial endeavor for all nations. For that reason it wanted to prevent any infringement of China's territorial integrity. Indeed, it was the British who first enunciated in regard to China the principle that later became official American doctrine. In a resolution adopted by parliament on March 1, 1898, it was declared "that it is of vital importance for British commerce and influence that the independence of Chinese territory should be maintained."

On this basis the British sought to deal with Russia, but without result. Russia clearly had resolved to get a foothold on Liaotung Peninsula after Japan had been excluded from it by the three-Power intervention under Russian leadership. In fact, diplomatic documents subsequently brought to light reveal that Count Witte had frankly told the British ambassador in the discussions undertaken by him that Russia intended to have north China for itself but was not unwilling to leave to Great Britain paramountcy farther south. But the British refused to recede if this meant even indirect alienation of Chinese territory to Russia. As Lord Salisbury said in one dispatch to his ambassador in St. Petersburg: "We aim at no partition of territory but only at partition of preponderance." But preponderance was not enough for Russia, and and on this fundamental divergence the attempt to arrive at an agreement came to nothing. The Russians went ahead and got Dalny and Port Arthur, as they had intended, as the first step of a projected stride over the northern half of the Chinese Empire.

Even before this first step was taken by Russia, Great Britain had moved to protect itself. When the Chinese had rejected the offer of a British loan on the ground that the terms were too onerous and also because the other Powers signified their objection, the British presented formal demands. They asked that certain additional treaty ports be opened to foreign trade, including one in the southeast that lay within what France claimed as its sphere; that China's inland waterways be opened to foreign steamships; and, most important, that China should, as "reasonable security to trade," pledge itself not to alienate any part of the Yangtze Valley to any other Power. China agreed to all except the first. This was in February 1898; about the same time, in a supplemental exchange of communications, China promised that the Inspector General of the Maritime Customs would continue to be a British subject as long as British trade in China exceeded that of any other country.

When Russia proceeded remorselessly toward its goal and obtained the two naval bases and the right to build the railway across south Manchuria to connect with its bases, Great Britain turned to Germany. It made the first of several tenders of what amounted to an alliance. Historians will speculate long but in vain on how the history of the twentieth century would have been changed if these tenders had been successful. The approach was made by Joseph Chamberlain, then Colonial Secretary, to the German ambassador in London the day after China signed the treaty yielding to Russia. Chamberlain left no doubt that the purpose of such an alliance would be common action in the Far East. To that level of importance in international politics had the Far East already come. Significantly, it was on Far Eastern issues that Great Britain was willing to abandon its isolation and contract "entangling alliances."

Plainly expressing the official view, Chamberlain said, in a speech designed not only to prepare the British people for a historic change in national policy but to warn the world how serious a view Great Britain took of what was happening in China:

I am one of those who think that for any country there are worse things than war; there is loss of honour; there is loss of those interests which are so vital to the security of the existence of the nation. . . . It is impossible to overrate the gravity of the issue. It is not a question of a single port in China; that is a very small matter. It is not a question of a single province, it is a question of the whole fate of the Chinese Empire, and our interests in China are so great, our proportion of the trade is so enormous, and the potentialities of that trade so gigantic that I feel no more vital question has ever been presented for the decision of a nation. . . . One thing appears to me to be certain: if the policy of isolation which has hitherto been the policy of this country is to be maintained in the future, then the fate of the Chinese Empire may be, probably will be, hereafter, decided without reference to our wishes and in defiance of our interests.

The British, then, made overtures to Germany. There were numerous interchanges but Germany was unresponsive. No doubt it had its own undeclared purposes in China. There is some evidence that it was reluctant to antagonize Russia. Quite possibly, too, it had already succumbed to egregious vanity and mounted the charger that was to carry it—and not it alone in Europe—to destruction. When the British Empire, on which the sun never set and which was the center of the world's politics, commerce, and finance, came wooing Germany, that was not only Germany's opportunity. It was proof of Germany's importance and thus nourishment to the Germans' all-too-conscious sense of self-importance. Great Britain was rebuffed.

Great Britain then had only one course left. If it could not prevent competitive encroachment on China, it would have to put itself in a position to compete successfully on its own account. Russia had two bases in the Gulf of Peichihli and Germany had one on the coast of Shantung Province. Great Britain asked for a base at Weihaiwei, also in Shantung but opposite Port Arthur. The Chinese demurred, but Britain, too, brought in warships. On British agreement to hold Weihaiwei only as long as Russia held Port Arthur and Dalny the lease was granted on July 1, 1898. At the same time Great Britain gave Germany formal assurances that it would not interfere with prior German rights in the interior of the province. As further compensation, in this case for

France's gains in the south, the British obtained a 99-year lease on the Kowloon Peninsula, on the mainland opposite Hongkong, the tip of which had been ceded to them after China's defeat in 1860. The area involved was more than 375 square miles, and as Hongkong grew in economic power and the foreign trade of south China developed, the Kowloon grant assumed an importance disproportionate to its size.

Something more had happened to China, it can be seen, than the loss of four ports, though that was by no means negligible. The country had been marked off in priorities by the stronger Powers. These were the spheres of influence. About spheres there has always been a great deal of misunderstanding and, even more, of oversimplification. It is often said that south China was a French sphere, central China a British sphere, Shantung a German sphere, Manchuria a Russian sphere, and what little of China was left was a Chinese sphere. This is a falsification. The spheres did not necessarily infringe on China's sovereignty. They consisted of an agreement by China not to alienate any territory in a specified area to a foreign Power. There is something incongruous in this, of course. That a country must be compelled by a show of force not to give away any of its territory hardly seems necessary. The explanation is simple. In each case the Power exacting the promise had a foothold in the area specified and hoped to extend it. But in nearly every case, too, China had to agree to give priority to the country claiming the sphere if there was to be railway construction or development of certain resources. Then the Powers having won such agreements obtained from other Powers recognition of their priority in their own earmarked areas. This was particularly true in the case of railways. What gave the spheres their real importance was that they were a staking out of claims that it was hoped would be commuted in time to outright annexation. They were portents of China's partition and the demarcation of the division among the beneficiaries. But the point is that spheres in themselves did not constitute partition. They did not necessarily always carry the implication of economic monopoly. Thus, Germany continued to compete actively and sometimes successfully with the British for the trade of Shanghai, Nanking, and Hankow in the Yangtze Valley.

Railways were another matter, and here economic penetration was more than economic in its results, and therefore international rivalry over railways was as sharp as for bases. Railways could constitute an oblique but more effective form of bases. At any rate, control of a railway gave to the country exercising it first access to the trade and natural resources of the region thus opened to communication and transportation. The Battle of the Concessions thus became a struggle for railway franchises, with loans to defray costs.

China itself had shown only the barest interest in railways until the 1890's. There was only a hazy idea of their utility, and even that only among a small minority of the higher officials. One small line twelve miles long had been laid in 1876 between Shanghai and Woosung, at the mouth of the Yangtze, but the superstitious fears of the populace were aroused and when one man was accidentally killed by a locomotive the outcry was so great that the railway was abandoned and the tracks were torn up. Another small line was later started in the north to run from the Kaiping coal fields toward the coast, some two hundred miles of track having been completed by 1894; this was soon to become the Peking-Mukden railway. No more was done, partly on the valid ground that China had neither the capital nor the technical capacity to build railways itself and allowing foreigners to do so was politically dangerous.

Then when serious encroachments began after the Sino-Japanese war, China had no choice. The Russians obtained the right to build the Manchurian railway and the Germans to construct a line in Shantung. Thereupon the other Powers entered, simultaneously putting pressure on the Chinese government for their own concessions and seeking to obstruct, on the dog-in-the-manger principle, the granting of concessions to others. Obtaining rights was not difficult, since China was all but helpless, but preventing others from also obtaining concessions was more complicated. First of all Great Britain and Germany, after blocking each other, came to an understanding whereby Great Britain promised not to infringe on German preserves in Shantung and Germany promised not to seek railway concessions in the Yangtze Valley. Thus it was settled that a railway from Shanghai to Tientsin, to which the Chinese had to agree, would be built in part by the British and in part by the Germans.

The Anglo-Russian differences, always the most serious, came to a head when a Belgian syndicate successfully bid for a contract to connect Peking and Hankow, on the Yangtze. This, it was known, was conceived as the first link in a larger system to be spread throughout central and south China, and since the northern terminus was Peking it could connect easily with the south Manchuria railway and thus make a direct route from St. Petersburg to south China. It was known, too, that behind the Belgians stood French and Russian capital. The British responded vehemently. They protested to the Chinese government that the contract infringed on British priority in the Yangtze Valley and at the same time protested to the other Powers concerned against what they called an unfriendly act. The British brought up warships to convince both the Chinese and the other Powers of the seriousness of their position. Again there was a threat of war. The matter was settled when the Chinese agreed to compensate the British by a concession for a whole network of railways extending almost 3,000 miles through central and south China (most of which have never been built) and by a separate agreement between the British and Russians. The British agreed not to seek railway concessions north of the Great Wall and the Russians not to do so in the Yangtze Valley. Each also engaged itself not to obstruct the other in its own sphere. An American banking group also was given a contract to connect central China with Canton, but the line was never built.

Thus the trunk lines in China were constructed by foreigners, with foreign loans and with special privileges on each line for those who made the loans. And thus, incidentally, China was prevented from enjoying the advantage of competitive bidding for all that went into the construction of a railway. Thus also the Chinese railway system, limited as it still is, developed without plan, without any rational or efficient relation of one part to another, without regard to the best interests of the country. Railways were tokens in a larger European struggle for control of East Asia; they were the projections of the intentions of the major contenders.

Thus, too, the ground plan was laid for the breaking up and parcelling out of China. As of 1899 that seemed to be not only certain but imminent.

CHAPTER XVII

China Recoils in Desperation

It was not to be simple, however. Something was happening in China to delay partition, and then something was to come about in the West to prevent it altogether.

The humiliating defeat by Japan had at last jolted China out of its complacency. To be defeated by the West was an act of nature, if not an act of God, for who could resist the supernatural powers of the white man? To be defeated by Japan was another thing, for Japan was of the same environment, even once in China's tutelage. All but the most encrusted reactionaries could perceive that Japan's adaptation of Western-ism had accounted for its success, and in all but the most encrusted there entered first doubt and then panic. They had forebodings of China's extinction, and a period of earnest soul-searching set in.

Like all social movements this was not entirely new-sprung. Even before the war with Japan a few voices had been raised among scholars calling for recognition of China's weakness and the reasons therefor, but these voices were few and little heed was given them. Even among them the basic premise was what Chang Chih-tung, one of the highest officials and a distinguished and progressive scholar, described as *Chung hsueh wei t'i, hsi hsueh wei yung*—"Chinese learning for fundamental principles, Western learning for practical utility." This meant to remain Chinese in all deeper respects and take from the West such material things as would make China strong and efficient—railways, shipyards, factories, arsenals. After the war, however, there developed a school of thought that believed more fundamental reforms were necessary. Its followers held that railways and factories were not enough. They called for application of new ideas, for education that would take account of modern thought, for reorganization of government and administration. In some ways it was education they thought of most. The Confucian classics and the examination system plainly did not prepare men to cope with the problems of the nineteenth century. A considerable body of polemical literature developed. Both liberal and conservative scholars contributed, not all mandarins being opposed to change. In fact, some of the highest officials, such as Tseng Kuo-fan, Li Hung-chang, and Chang Chih-tung, notably the last, were on the side of reform.

Also fifty years of contact with the West had begun to take effect. Whatever might have been the conscious will of even the most determinedly conservative Chinese, the continuous communication with Westerners that the existence of foreign colonies throughout China made unavoidable released influences that slowly penetrated—imperceptibly but steadily. Chinese came to live in the foreign settlements and concessions, where business buildings, residences, furnishings, appliances, conveniences, and manner of living were almost exactly as in Europe and America. It may be observed as an interesting marginal note on the meeting of different cultures and peoples that when men of the West responded to the lure of far, exotic places and went to the East they took with them all the customs, habits, and minor appliances of their native habitat. They were in the East geographically, but in no other way; they did not want to be there in any other way.

This tells less about comparative culture, however, than about the attitude of the West in the nineteenth century. Not only missionaries had the psychology of bringing light to the heathen. The diplomat or businessman may have gone to the East out of curiosity about the heathen or to make money out of the heathen rather than to save him; but he was going to the heathen. The Oriental, of whatever Eastern people, was different. He spoke differently; his habits were different; his customs were different; he managed the affairs of material living differently. Hence he was inferior. And thus came about the air of superiority that the men of the West assumed to the Oriental, the humiliations they put upon him in daily intercourse, the stigma of "lesser breed" they ostentatiously put upon him—and, in consequence, the bitterness engendered in Eastern peoples, manifest now in our time in their intransigence, their oversensitiveness, their occasional unreasonableness, and even their outbursts of hysteria, as in China, in Iran, in Egypt, perhaps in India too.

At any rate the foreign colonies in Peking, Shanghai, Hongkong, Tientsin, Hankow, and Canton were segments of Western civilization and Western society implanted in China. From them radiated Western commodities, Western ways of production and distribution and, most important, Western ideas. Chinese came to live there. Chinese did business with Western businessmen and perforce adopted their ways of doing business. Western trade spread, slowly but unremittingly. Western goods were introduced both for consumption and for production. The use of Western goods formed new habits, new grooves of conduct. Western languages were learned, if only by a minority, and Western books were read, more often in translation than in the original, it is true. Western newspapers were printed in the foreign communities and read not only by foreigners. And most of all, the Western communities stood out as examples of wealth and a life of ease and therefore as a temptation to copy. The West was powerful and successful; these were the ways of the West; therefore Western organization of life was the key to power, to success, to survival.

The beginning of the serious inroads on Chinese sovereignty gave all this emphasis. It also gave a sense of urgency, even of despair. The movement for reform grew and spread. Then, almost by accident, it reached to the highest place in the empire. In 1889 the young emperor known as Kwang Hsu arrived at the age of eighteen, and Tzu Hsi, the empress dowager, then in her second regency, turned over the throne to him. Kwang Hsu, who had only a dubious claim to the succession but was named heir by some unscrupulous manipulations by Tzu Hsi and her court clique, was a weak, ineffectual young man, well meaning and with decent instincts but wholly lacking in the attributes of a ruler, especially in a time of stress. Through an enlightened tutor named Wen Tung-ho he was brought into contact with a small group of reformist scholars, especially a Cantonese named Kang Yu-wei. Kang, one of the most distinguished literati of his time, had become fired with the mission of saving the country by discarding what he thought outworn in the traditional scheme and supplanting it with adaptations from the West. He had read much about the West, though without knowledge of any Western language. He had definite ideas, was a man of strong character, and was among those who believed that China must act at once or be lost.

He gained access to the court and began to work on the suggestible young emperor. In successive night sessions in the Forbidden City, in circumstances more appropriate to pseudo-Oriental melodrama, he began a course of indoctrination of the imperial youth. This was in 1898, while one Western Power after another was paring off slices of the empire; even a young man, with all the limitations of a Manchu brought up in the isolation of the court, could not be unaware that the empire's fate was hanging in the balance. Kang Yu-wei, supported by Liang Chi-chao, also a Cantonese, and one or two others, was persuasive, if not domineering. Kwang Hsu was won over, perhaps not quite realizing the full import of what he was assenting to.

There began the high drama—not without a touch of farce—of the so-called Hundred Days' Reform. Kwang Hsu began issuing imperial mandates, one mandate after another. And mandate by mandate the whole of Chinese civilization and society was made over. A revolution by edict was encompassed overnight—but revolutions are never accomplished by edicts alone. The motive was made clear in one of the earliest of the mandates: not so much the desire to remake Chinese society because of that which was wanting in it as the desire to strengthen it against the onslaught from without then in progress. One of the earliest mandates refers to the "crisis where we are beset on all sides by powerful neighbors who craftily seek advantage from us and who are trying to combine together in overpowering us"; therefore, it continues, the country must take measures to strengthen its defenses. The same motif runs through most of the mandates: danger, throw up the ramparts, hurry. If Chinese society was too weak to meet the danger, make over the society, and since the danger was pressing, make it over at once.

And so it was ordered made over. Almost day by day ancient institutions tightly webbed into the life of the race were abolished and new ones, whose names had barely been heard a few years before, were decreed. The government was reorganized. Countless official posts were abolished, itself a fatal act since it struck at vested bureaucratic interests and made enemies apart from all consideration of the worth of reform. Old ministries were closed, new ones were opened. A new army was established, a navy ordered. The educational system was transformed, the old examination system being abolished. Railways were to be built. Mines were to be opened. Factories were to be started. The land system was to be modified. Agricultural schools were to be opened—to be taught by whom? A new judicial system was set up—with what code of laws? Newspapers were to be started. Segment by segment, Chinese society was discarded, supplanted by something else or drastically renovated.

The capital was stunned. Not only had the eternal verities been annulled; men and vested interests had been extinguished. In the atmosphere of that capital, citadel of Chinese obscurantism, it was hardly to be expected that the revolution would be taken supinely. It was not. The hapless young emperor had nothing but idealism and the advice and high rhetorical style of his counseling literati to buttress him and his plans. The outraged mandarinate banded together and called on its resources of intriguery, which were rich and adept. It called on the empress dowager, herself outraged, vigilant, restless in her compulsory furlough and not unwilling to resume the seat of power. There was a quick coup. The poor young emperor was made to recant. Some of those who were responsible for his conversion were executed; others, including Kang Yu-wei and Liang Chi-chao, escaped from the country. The empress dowager took the throne again as regent and the emperor was imprisoned in an exquisite palace on a tiny island in one of the lakes of the Forbidden City. That island, closely guarded, he never left again until he was carried to his grave ten years later. He died two days before the empress dowager, an occurrence that has always been considered dubiously coincidental. There has always been a suspicion that the process of nature was aided by human hands.

Thus ended the paper revolution, a pathetic but feckless attempt by the more far-seeing Chinese to save their country. Reaction, the darkest of reaction, was in the saddle again. It was to ride the monarchy to its death. But one thing must be observed. Ill-advised and immature the whole reform program may have been. To have attempted the reconstruction of a society by fiat and overnight was proof of lack of understanding, of grasp of the nature of society and government. But the compulsion of haste was not wholly of China's choice or at its discretion. It was at least in part product of the danger that confronted the country. There really was not time for intelligently conceived, planned, and executed change: the enemy was at the door. This was the first but not the last time that China was to take actions dictated not by its considered choice but by external threat over which it had no control and at the time could not repel. From then to our own day its policy and its conduct have been conditioned by the circumstances of foreign politics that in practice meant danger to its national existence. It has time and again acted irrationally and to all appearances impulsively, even foolishly. But also it has seldom, if ever, in recent decades enjoyed the luxury of opportunity for calm deliberation and considered choice. That luxury is one usually denied to a weak country that is coveted by the strong.

An even more dramatic sequel, a more direct product of desperation, was what is called the Boxer Rebellion, though it was hardly a rebellion. The successive inroads on Chinese sovereignty since 1895 and the apparent imminence of subjugation and parcelling out among the Great Powers had repercussions not only in the scholar class. The whole country was becoming aroused in varying degrees of intensity, the degree varying with the level of sophistication. This was manifested, naturally, in antiforeignism, particularly in attacks on isolated foreigners. It also took the form of a gathering resentment against the Manchu dynasty, not only because it was itself alien but because it was unable to protect the country.

Throughout Chinese history there have abounded secret societies of one kind or another, and during the Manchu dynasty many of them had patriotic purposes and in a rather general way were dedicated to the eviction of the Manchus and the restoration of Chinese rulers. In September, 1898, there was formed in the north a sort of amalgamation of such societies under the name of I Ho Chuan, which foreigners translated as

"Boxers" because the members engaged in a kind of ritual dance. This ceremony, incidentally, was supposed to give them immunity against weapons.

The earliest efforts of the Boxers appear to have been directed against the Manchus. Then by skillful manipulation by officials, both Chinese and Manchu, attention was deflected from the dynasty to foreigners. It was not a difficult feat. There had been from the beginning of Western contacts a residual antiforeignism, sometimes subdued and sometimes rising again for one reason or another. The presence of missionaries in the interior had always been resented. And now foreign countries were directly threatening China, a fact of which all but the most ignorant could not help being aware, since the detachments of territory were in all parts of the empire. Before the end of 1898 the propaganda of the Boxers was directed almost exclusively against foreigners; as might be expected, there were antiforeign demonstrations, then antiforeign riots, and then attacks against foreign persons and foreign property. By the middle of 1899 serious violence was in progress and a number of foreign lives had been lost.

This was surreptitiously encouraged in the highest quarters, even by the court and the empress dowager herself. Some of the viceroys and provincial governors recognized that the final outcome would be disastrous for the country and despite orders and incitations from Peking acted to preserve order and protect foreigners. This was true in the provinces in which Shanghai, Canton, and Hankow were situated, where the largest numbers of foreigners resided. It was also true in Shantung where Yuan Shih-kai, who had had experience with foreigners, went so far as to order detachments of Boxers wiped out. Nevertheless as the movement gained in support and grew in violence, foreigners everywhere became alarmed. As the winter of 1899 drew near, the legations at Peking decided to bring in troops from naval vessels in adjacent waters as guards for the foreign colony in the capital. The troops were withdrawn the following spring, but a little later large-scale attacks on foreigners began. Whole mission stations were destroyed, foreign engineers and others working on railways or other projects were driven out. Property was looted and many foreigners were murdered. In Shansi Province, where a fanatic governor named Yu-hsien was inciting the Boxers, 233 missionaries were killed. For this Yu-hsien was subsequently executed on foreign insistence.

Some of the worst excesses occurred in the vicinity of Peking, and in the spring of 1900 the legations decided to bring up guards again, a force of nearly 500 arriving from Tientsin. The Chinese, now not only Boxers being involved, cut the railway and telegraph lines between Tientsin and the capital, and the foreign colony in the capital was isolated. At the same time foreign compounds in the capital itself were being attacked and missionaries and their Chinese converts massacred. On June 10 an international relief expedition started up from Tientsin, but it had to turn back with considerable losses after sharp fighting. Then an official of the Japanese Legation was murdered, and the German Minister, Baron von Ketteler, was assassinated while on his way to the Tsung Li Yamen. All foreign residents in the capital were then brought into the legations for safety. On June 20 formal attacks on the legations began, regular troops as well as Boxers taking part, and on June 21, the Chinese government declared war on the Western Powers and offered a bounty on the heads of all foreigners, men, women, and children. It is noteworthy that, as justification, the declaration of war cited the persistent aggressions of the foreign Powers on China since the middle of the nineteenth century.

The Western Powers, now fully alarmed, organized an international relief expedition. A force of 16,000 men, with contingents from seven countries, landed in Tientsin and started for the capital on August 4. There, meanwhile, the beleaguered foreigners had been desperately resisting siege, thus far successfully and with a minimum of losses. In this instance Chinese military incompetency stood both the foreigners and China in good stead, for if the whole foreign colony had been exterminated a Carthaginian reckoning would later have been taken; moreover, in the struggle for the largest territorial compensation a general war very likely would have ensued. In less than two weeks the expeditionary force was in Peking and the siege was raised. The whole court, led by the empress dowager, ignominiously fled, making a trek of several hundred miles to Sianfu, capital of the northwestern province of Shensi.

What followed was one of the hideous episodes in the history of East-West relations. There began an orgy of looting by foreigners—soldiers and civilians alike, men in uniform, businessmen, diplomats, and missionaries rushed in and out of palaces, in and out of private houses, unashamedly ransacking both and triumphantly carrying off the spoils. It was a dreadful spectacle and a humiliating one. The Chinese had given offense no doubt, and it was an offense of an order to constitute provocation in the extreme; but it must also be said that the manner of requiting was on the same level as the offense. As a demonstration of how the West dealt justice it was hardly calculated to impress on the East the superiority of Western standards. We had come proffering the Christian message, and not only did we not forgive those who trespassed against us, we dealt with them with a vengeful ferocity in the immemorial ways of primitive peoples—rapine and pillage. And yet we went right on thereafter preaching Christianity and urging the emulation of Western civilization.

Unofficial punishment was thus levied, but official punishment was still to come. The court had fled, but a peace treaty and indemnification had still to be negotiated. For this purpose Li Hung-chang, an experienced agent in unpalatable functions, and Prince Ching of the imperial family were deputed to negotiate for China. As there was little room for negotiation, the terms were dictated. Such negotiation as there was lay among the victors, and was more in the nature of political haggling, if not intrigue. They differed as to the degree of punishment to be levied and still more as to the political advantage to be gained out of the situation. The Russians, of course, had special motives; they saw an opportunity to advance toward their goal of complete control of Manchuria and north China. The others, the British in particular, were at least as much concerned with impeding Russia as with punishing China. The Germans, for their part, had special draconian purposes. They had a supreme mandate to that effect. When the German contingent to the international expedition was about to leave under Field Marshal Count von Waldersee, the egregious Wilhelm II speeded their parting with this characteristic adjuration:

"When you meet the foe you will defeat him. No quarter will be given, no prisoners will be taken. Let all who fall into your hands be at your mercy. Just as the Huns a thousand years ago under the leadership of Etzel [Attila] gained a reputation by virtue of which they still live in historical tradition, so may the name of Germany become known in such a manner in China, that no Chinese will ever again even dare to look askance at a German."

The Germans were to rue this rodomontade too, for after 1914 the voluble Wilhelm's words were recalled and used for propaganda purposes. Hence the appellation "Hun" with which the Germans were tagged during World War I and after.

There was considerable jockeying, then, among the victors, some of whom wanted only indemnity and guarantees for the future while others were more interested in making political capital out of the affair. The final terms were punitive enough. An imperial prince had to go to Germany to apologize for Ketteler's assassination, and a memorial arch expressing penitence had to be erected on the scene of the murder. A high imperial official had to go to Tokyo to apologize for the murder of the Japanese Legation official. All examinations were to be suspended for five years in the forty-five cities where excesses against foreigners had been committed. Importation of arms was prohibited for two years. Four of the highest officials were to be put to death and eleven others, including two princes of the imperial family, sentenced to die but with commutation to exile for life. Thirteen others were exiled, and more than fifty were dismissed from office and barred from official service for life.

A money indemnity of 450,000,000 taels (then about $333,000,000) was levied, far in excess of the damage done. Of this sum the Russians got 29 per cent and the Germans 20 per cent, nearly half the total between them. The indemnity was secured on such of the customs revenue as was not already pledged to foreign debts, but it was clear that China could not pay such a sum out of its normal revenue. Therefore it was permitted to raise its tariff rates. It will be remembered that by the first treaties concluded with Western Powers after the Anglo-Chinese war in 1842 China was permitted to change its tariff only by agreement with all the Powers. Naturally such agreement was not forthcoming, since it was to the interest of the foreign Powers to get their goods in as cheaply as possible. By treaty the duty was fixed at 5 per cent ad valorem, with a schedule of prices set for purposes of simplicity. This schedule had not been changed since 1858; because prices all over the world had risen materially since then, however, China was getting in actuality only a rate of 2 per cent. It was now decided to change the schedule of prices so as to yield an effective 5 per cent. With the extra revenue China could pay the idemnity. Comment is superfluous.

Even more serious provisions were included. The quarter in Peking where the legations were situated was put under the exclusive control of the legations, with a permanent guard of troops from each country. Governed and policed exclusively by foreigners, it was entirely withdrawn from Chinese jurisdiction. Thus a portion of the capital of an old empire, a few yards from the palace of the emperor, became a foreign city under a foreign garrison. Furthermore, China had to raze all its forts from Taku, on the sea, to Peking, and foreign troops were to be stationed at different points between the sea and Peking to keep an open route for foreigners in any emergency.

As a postscript it should be added that, recognizing that the idemnity levied was unreasonable, the United States in 1908 remitted the larger part of its share to be used to defray the expense of sending Chinese students to study in American colleges and universities. In the gratitude it earned this was a highly profitable investment. For one thing, it was unique.

Thus ended a mad episode, one that reflected no credit on any of the parties. The Chinese were undoubtedly guilty of inexcusable and unforgivable excesses for which punishment was due. Neither in law nor by the accepted canons of morality could there be extenuation in the fact that their country had been the victim of sustained acts of injustice that would have goaded any people to insensate fury. It can be held against them, too, that they wreaked their vengeance on innocent individuals and not on the states that had treated them with injustice—but this is more nearly the rule than the exception in such situations. If one takes the Boxer uprising in itself, as an isolated episode, the Chinese deserved a terrible penalty. But it may be asked how far it is reasonable to isolate such an episode, to consider it apart from the past and without its antecedents, without all that of which it was a product, in human frailty an inevitable product. And it may be asked, too, whether the punishment inflicted was not tinctured with cupidity and determined as much by desire for gain as by criteria of justice. Whether it was or not, it left still another sore to fester until it ultimately released its pent-up poison in the years from 1925 to the Chinese intervention in Korea in 1950. Once again the conduct of the West had produced in the East a universal conviction of the West's rapacity and cynicism. Justified or not, the conviction has been there, and it has had consequences from which all have suffered.

CHAPTER XVIII

America Asserts Itself in the Pacific

The Boxer Rebellion postponed what had appeared to be the imminent partition of China. What prevented it lay outside China.

First among the external conditions and developments that acted as deterrents was an unprecedented and, as it turned out, historic step by the United States. Second was the steady forward movement of both Japan and Russia in Korea, which had to result in collision unless one of the two receded or something intervened from without. Third was Russia's procrastination in withdrawing from Manchuria after the Boxer uprising, a procrastination obviously calculated and so prolonged as to give clear notification that it did not mean to withdraw at all. This alarmed Great Britain and, in lesser degree, the United States. Taken together with Russia's acts in Korea, it alarmed Japan most of all, for to Japan it constituted a direct and immediate threat to its survival as an independent state. As a result Great Britain and Japan had to make common cause, which was formally registered in the Anglo-Japanese alliance of 1902. And as a result of that the Russo-Japanese War came about not long after. The war changed the whole political face of East Asia. It also gave new content and direction to American foreign policy and left an indelible mark on American history. But above all else was the central fact of world politics in 1900: the prelude to 1914 had begun.

Let us turn first to the development of America's role in East Asia. In the years after the opening of Japan American interest in that part of the world began to recede. Despite a degree of participation in the effort to make Japan live up to its treaties in the 1860's and in the opening of Korea, America was essentially represented rather than active in the politics of East Asia until near the end of the nineteenth century. The reason is fairly obvious. The Civil War, Reconstruction, and most of all internal development dominated the scene.

It was in the decades after 1870 that America came of age economically. It was perhaps in those decades that the Industrial Revolution came of age everywhere. Then the railways in this continent were built, the deposits of natural resources tapped—and in many cases gutted—the great corporations formed. A virgin continent was brought to man's full use. The foundations were laid for that towering economic supremacy which was to be fully recognized after World War II. Naturally all the country's energies were required for internal development, and since this was also prodigiously profitable—in those years the great personal fortunes were built—there was little interest in foreign activities. In fact, there was little or no capital for such activities: the United States was borrowing from abroad to obtain the capital needed for the railway trunk lines, for extracting raw materials and erecting factories to process them. There was neither need nor occasion for political or even economic interest in any other part of the world. Never before or after in American history has there been so little concern with foreign affairs; never before or after so little reason for concern in foreign affairs.

In the last years of the nineteenth century this changed. Then suddenly American interest in foreign affairs reawakened, and the point of highest interest lay in the Pacific and the Far East. Was it coincidence? Coincidences are found in the history of nations, no doubt, as well as in the lives of individuals, but they are rare, and if they are repeated and sustained they are not coincidences but are caused by forces within the nation. In the reawakening of American interest in foreign affairs, more particularly in Far Eastern affairs, domestic forces were important.

They, too, are fairly obvious. The railroads had been built, the mines and other deposits of natural resources opened or claims to them staked out, the giant corporations were in process of formation. The most profitable stage in the higher industrialization had passed or seemed to be passing, for those things that came with the automobile, the radio, and the more recondite technological achievements had not yet been visualized. For the time a stage of diminishing returns seemed to be setting in. No less important, if not more: the United States was ceasing to be an exporter of primary products exclusively—cotton, tobacco, corn, wheat, meat, lumber. It was beginning to export manufactured products or, in other words, it was entering into competition for world markets in goods of which it did not have a monopoly or near monopoly by virtue of nature's bounty. Also free land had passed. In a few words, the United States was no longer a pioneer country. It had come of age, and the strains of that condition were setting in.

It was in keeping with the past that when interest in foreign affairs resumed, it should be in the Pacific and Far East. There the United States had been most active in the first half of the nineteenth century, while turning its back on Europe in obedience to the injunction of the Founding Fathers against participation in European politics. There, too, it turned its attention when energies were free for external activity and internal development had progressed to the point where the profits of foreign enterprise were tempting.

The first centers of interest were Samoa, in the South Pacific, and Hawaii, in the mid-Pacific. American concern with the former was mainly naval, since the harbor of Pago Pago, on the island of Tutuila, had all the requirements of an ideal naval base and since possession of a base in Samoa would provide a screen for the protection of an isthmian canal, a project that had figured in American political and military thinking since the middle of the century. Great Britain and especially Germany, which had both economic interests and colonial hopes, were even more actively concerned in Samoa, however, and a three-cornered rivalry began to form.

As always in such situations, the natives became correspondingly fearful. Of Germany they were most afraid, since Germany was most aggressive. The native rulers therefore sought protection from Great Britain and the United States. In 1872 an American naval officer negotiated a treaty with the native rulers of Tutuila giving the United States an exclusive naval base at Pago Pago, but the Senate failed to approve the treaty. In 1878 another treaty was approved, this one also giving the base but not for exclusive American use. It also conferred extraterritoriality and other privileges and provided as well that the United States would use its good offices in any future dispute between Samoa and another country. Thus the Samoans hoped to get at least some protection. Then the Germans got a base, with additional rights, and the British got one too, together with the assurance that Samoa would grant no country any rights greater than those Great Britain had. Thus all the Powers were even and, parenthetically, the pattern of China and Japan was repeated.

Immediately thereafter the three Powers came to an agreement on what amounted to an unofficial tripartite protectorate over the Samoan Islands, but Germany was unsatisfied and proceeded by one stratagem or another, including a manufactured insurrection, to get exclusive control, actually raising the German flag under the pretext of preserving order. Both Great Britain and the United States protested, the latter more vigorously, and sharp friction developed between the United States and Germany. This could have taken a serious form, since both countries had naval vessels in the island waters. After protracted diplomatic haggling Germany decided not to force the issue, however, and a scheme was worked out by the three Powers in 1889 for an official tripartite condominium. Thus the United States obtained a foothold, its first in the Pacific, though it joined in the scheme reluctantly. Its naval forces are still in Pago Pago.

Hawaii was of greater and more lasting importance. American interest in those islands goes back to the early part of the nineteenth century. Whaling vessels began to put in there for water and supplies, to be followed by traders and missionaries, mostly the latter. From the beginning missionary influence was stronger than any other. In contrast with other nonwhite regions the missionaries' efforts were successful; almost the whole of the native population was Christianized. It should be added that while missionaries brought in the Christian Gospel, sailors and traders brought in liquor and Western diseases, and in less than a hundred years the number of pure Hawaiians decreased by 80 per cent. The first missionaries carried on religious work with success; their descendants devoted themselves to more material enterprise. Mainly they went in for the cultivation of sugar on plantations put together out of lands mortgaged to them by unworldly Hawaiians who squandered the proceeds of the mortgages and saw their lands foreclosed. Before many decades had passed nearly all the tangible wealth of the islands was in the hands of foreigners, the majority of whom were descendants of American missionaries. But in this respect also there is a contrast with missionary endeavor elsewhere. Few missionary families have prospered materially in other lands.

By the middle of the nineteenth century Hawaii was being eyed by the British and French, already imperialistic, as a prize, and the United States, its interest there not only consciously felt but vigorously expressed, was obstructing. That was touched on in the chapter on the opening of Japan. Like the Samoan native rulers, the Hawaiians were fearful, and there were informal proposals of annexation by the United States, but nothing came of them. The United States was still in no mood to depart from the principle of no extracontinental territorial acquisitions. Simultaneously it was still firm on the principle, already being extended from Latin America to the Pacific, that no other strong Power would be permitted to make such acquisitions. The growth of American interests became strong enough to qualify the principle, however, if only unconsciously. A reciprocity treaty was negotiated between the United States and Hawaii in 1875 by which Hawaiian sugar (nearly all American-owned) came into the United States duty-free, while Cuban sugar would still pay a duty. In the same treaty Hawaii pledged itself not to lease or grant any territory to a third Power—the conventional entering wedge for a sphere of influence. In 1884 the reciprocity treaty was renewed, with an additional provision whose historic significance could not have been foreseen. The United States obtained the right to establish a fortified naval base in sheltered waters near Honolulu, subsequently to be known as Pearl Harbor. Reciprocity on sugar and the naval base together gave the United States a special interest in Hawaii which thereafter increased rather than diminished. From then on the danger of European intrusion ended.

A new phase entered in 1890, when a new tariff took the duty off sugar entirely and put a bounty on domestically grown sugar. Thus Hawaii's preference over Cuba was ended and Hawaiian sugar was left at a competitive disadvantage. A heavy blow was struck at American interests in Hawaii. The owners of those interests, which amounted to $25,000,000 in sugar alone, could hardly have been expected to take the blow passively, and they did not. The change in the tariff signalized a change in the destiny of Hawaii. It sounded, in fact, the death knell of Hawaiian independence.

Under the inspired and inspiring, if somewhat dubious, leadership of John F. Stevens, the American Minister, action was not long in coming. Stevens at least had the merit of frankness. By 1892 he was already in his official dispatches to Washington openly advocating annexation. Events, as he immediately thereafter reported, "have moved rapidly," though he did not add that he had some part in accelerating them. In January, 1893, a mass meeting of several hundred prominent foreign residents was held, most of them Americans, and a "Committee of Public Safety" was formed under American leadership. The committee immediately called on the minister for help. The always helpful Mr. Stevens obliged. He asked an American warship to land marines— against whom was not specified. The marines landed. The Committee seized government buildings, declared the Hawaiian monarchy abolished, and set up a provisional government of Hawaii—headed by Americans, of course. The co-operative Mr. Stevens gave the government immediate *de facto* recognition.

The stated motive of these imperious acts naturally was not sugar and profit. It was, of course, law and order and, still more, democracy. The ruling queen—Liliuokalani—had provided a convenient pretext. Liliuokalani had been educated in Europe and there had acquired some modern ideas and European education, and also some of Europe's patronizing attitude toward America, especially American culture. Her feelings were not assuaged when, on assuming the throne, she found that Americans exercised the deciding voice in what mattered most. She appears to have acquired, too, a keen sense of nationalism and something of a delusion of grandeur, a provocative combination. Among her first steps was an enforced revision of the constitution which all but ended representative government and concentrated political power in her own hands. Hence the Americans' concern about democracy and the resolve to act for its preservation for the Hawaiian people, although the Hawaiian people seemed curiously unmoved in the matter. Perhaps if they deplored the passing of democracy, which seems doubtful, they also felt less than enthusiasm for rule by America.

The Americans were not consulting them, however. With the marines to keep the democratic situation in hand in case the Hawaiians seemed dubious about American protection of their democratic rights and acted accordingly, representatives of the provisional government—American, of course—sped to Washington and there presented to the American government a treaty annexing Hawaii to the United States. Incidentally Hawaiian sugar would then be considered domestic sugar and enjoy a bounty and an advantage over the Cuban. Thus the loftiest political philosophy would be combined with the resumption of profits, an appealing combination. President Benjamin Harrison laid the treaty before the Senate on February 15, 1893, just one day short of a month since the marines landed.

Unfortunately for the well-laid plans of American men in Hawaii this was only seventeen days before the Harrison administration went out of office, to be succeeded by Grover Cleveland and a Democratic administration. President Cleveland had old-fashioned ideas about imperialism and about morality in international politics. There was to him something unfragrant about the whole business and he would have none of it. Others in the government also were somewhat sensitive to the aroma, and when a special senatorial commission made a detailed investigation of the whole affair and revealed all those parts that were better left unrevealed, Cleveland became uncompromising and immovable. On the whole he was supported by public opinion. There the matter rested until Cleveland was succeeded by McKinley and a Republican administration in 1897, and a year later, as an incidental accompaniment to the Spanish-American War, Hawaii was annexed. Thus the United States obtained its first territorial possession outside the continental boundaries. The Hawaiian Islands have had just and generous treatment, since they have enjoyed the status of a territory and political autonomy; but the circumstances of their acquisition will never be pleasant to dwell on, even for those who are not squeamish.

CHAPTER XIX

America Enters the China Conflict

Hawaii, however, was for America only a way-station on the road to Asia. Appropriately its acquisition was just an incident in the Spanish-American War of 1898. There were more direct Asiatic consequences of that war. The immediate and avowed cause of the war with Spain, it will be remembered, was American indignation at Spanish cruelties to rebellious Cubans, culminating in a demand that Cuba be emancipated from Spanish rule. It was actually precipitated by the sinking of the U.S.S. "Maine" in a Cuban port, which in the passion of the moment was charged to the Spanish, a charge which never has been proved. Thus a war that began for the liberation of an island in the West Indies ended with American possession of a prized group of islands in the furthermost Pacific, just off the coast of Asia—the Philippines.

The war itself was a contrived war and one that reflects no credit on America. The feeling of outrage at Spanish excesses in Cuba was genuine and justified, but the desire for war was artificially stimulated, partly by demagogues and still more by unscrupulous, sensational newspapers. The war was not desired by the government and was definitely opposed by leaders of industry and finance, which had just recovered from the depression of 1893. Also Spain signified its willingness to yield to American conditions on Cuba. But the hysteria had mounted beyond control, especially after the sinking of the "Maine," and the government's hand was forced.

The war was almost farcical. Spain was unable to make real resistance and in a few weeks hostilities ended. The decisive battle was the naval engagement in Manila Bay on May 1, 1898. It was decisive not in a military sense, since the result was a foregone conclusion, but for its political consequences. With that victory leaders of industry, commerce, and finance, until then cool to the war if not hostile, made a complete reversal. They now saw in it objects worth attaining. These were the objects Commodore Perry had in mind, the objects President Fillmore alluded to in the message to Congress already quoted: the prospects of trade with the Eastern coast of Asia and with China in particular. Perry had written about the usefulness of a base from which to operate for the China trade. Members of Congress, bankers, and manufacturers now echoed his opinions, now with the greater urgency of immediate opportunity, recent events in China having made the whole world conscious of that country. They called for retention of the Philippines. The demand became insistent, and the peace negotiations at Paris ended with a treaty giving the United States the Philippines in return for a payment of $20,000,000 to Spain.

When the time came for Senate approval of the treaty there was a sharp, almost bitter debate, the point at issue being retention of the Philippines. There were warning voices. America was abandoning its traditions. It was gaining territory outside the continental confines by conquest, territory inhabited by people of different race, culture, and beliefs. It was going the way of imperialism and would suffer the fate of all empires. The principles on which the republic was founded were being violated. The original American idea, dream even, was a nation of free men associated of their free will; now it would become a nation of rulers and subjects, subjects brought in against their will, never to be assimilated, always to be subjects. The debate was impressive. The issues were unmistakably stated and squarely met. But the tide was too strong. The treaty was approved, though with only two votes to spare. America had its first colony. The warning of 1899 may not have been remembered in 1942, in the days of the siege of Bataan, but it could have been.

About the origins of the Philippines episode there has been much dispute among historians and considerable misunderstanding. There entered into it accident, caprice, frivolity, irresponsibility, diplomatic adolescence, and some sharp practice. Few Americans, including the President, could have said with precision a few months before the war what and where the Philippines were. Certainly there was no conscious long-cherished design. There was, it is true, a small, vigorous, and highly articulate group in Washington that had contrived great schemes by which America would throw its weight about. Its leaders were Theodore Roosevelt, then Assistant Secretary of the Navy, Senator Henry Cabot Lodge, Captain Alfred Mahan, the Navy's strategist, historian, and philosopher, and a few others. They and not a few like them were chafing restlessly at America's inactivity while other Great Powers were sweeping all over the world and carving up the continents. The lure of the white man's burden was captivating just then, and in that atmosphere the Roosevelts, Lodges, and their like fancied themselves as conquerors and proconsuls. To Theodore Roosevelt, most active and most vocal of them all, playing soldier boy exercised a lifelong appeal. Yet he came to rue his adventure later. As President, only a few years after 1898, he remarked once that the Philippines were the Achilles' heel of America.

All this may be true, and it might have accounted for the extension of the war from Cuba and Puerto Rico in the Atlantic to the Philippines in the far Pacific; but it does not account for the retention of the islands. It does not account for the sudden enthusiasm for the war among the economically influential when it drew near the coast of Asia. Caprice and adolescent irresponsibility may have initiated the adventure, but something else gave it historic permanence. The flood of petitions and memorials from chambers of commerce, business organizations, and individuals urging that the Philippines be kept bear witness that something more tangible was at play. As Lodge wrote in an unromantic moment, Manila was the great prize, "the thing which will give us the Eastern trade."

The direct application came soon. The events in China in the last three years of the century have already been told: the carving out of spheres of influence and territorial leaseholds, the preliminaries of formal partition, and the Boxer uprising, a mixture of ignorant, superstitious fanaticism and desperation at the fate that hung over the country. When the Allied expedition fought its way through to Peking and the court fled, the first unofficial negotiations began on the punishment and indemnification to be meted out to the Chinese. The intimation of the intentions of the Powers was ominous. Russia was most suspect. The remorselessness of its advance toward the Pacific in the preceding years was ample ground for fear and suspicion. Also it was clear that if Russia took advantage of China's weakness to detach more of its soil, the other Powers would make compensating acquisitions and the break-up of China would begin, peaceably at first perhaps, but inevitably leading to eventual collision of the Powers and a Balkanization of China.

Of this Great Britain and Japan were most fearful, at first Great Britain more than Japan. The reasons for Great Britain's fears have already been explained. Its main desire was trade, not territory. From such parts of China as came under the sway of other Powers it would be excluded commercially, since its higher efficiency gave it insuperable competitive advantages. In a scramble for territory it would be at a disadvantage, since Russia was closer to China and would have French support, while Germany had already adopted the strategy of playing Great Britain and Russia off against each other and exacting compensation from both. For Britain there was only one satisfactory way out. This was to prevent partition if possible and, if not possible, to work for a regime of free and fair economic competition in all parts of China, no matter under whose sovereignty, control, or "influence" each part came. This meant guarantees against discrimination in the form of tariffs, special taxes, or other legal provisions. The "Open Door" this came to be called. It was the principle and doctrine to be formally adopted by the United States, steadfastly maintained, and finally acted upon when compromise or evasion was no longer possible—in December, 1941.

The origins of the American policy of the Open Door in China have been clouded with controversy and misunderstanding. It has been irrefutably demonstrated that it was first conceived, considered, and formulated by the British, urged on the American government, then by Secretary of State Hay officially proposed to the other Powers. The matter had been gently but persuasively pressed on Mr. Hay while he was in London as ambassador before he became Secretary.

It is clear that Great Britain had the largest economic stake in China. Some two-thirds of China's foreign trade was with Great Britain, and of the ships that carried the trade four-fifths were British. To repeat once again, Great Britain was correspondingly alert to the consequences of partition and equally resolved to forestall it or mitigate its consequences. The overtures to Germany for concerted measures to check Russia in China have already been told. Also as early as February, 1898, Joseph Chamberlain, who appears to have taken the lead in advocating positive action in the Far East, proposed to Arthur J. Balfour, then acting Foreign Secretary, to make similar overtures to the United States. In the memorandum containing the proposal he made the concrete suggestion that any Chinese port taken by a foreign Power should be declared "open to all on precisely similar conditions." Such an approach was made to the American government later by Lord Pauncefote, British Ambassador in Washington, and summarily rejected.

Then came the Battle of the Concessions in China, during which American vigilance on China was sharpened, but again British proposals for common action were rejected. Meanwhile Hay in London was becoming an advocate of the British view. Also the American public became increasingly conscious of the wider prospects available following the inroads of Western Powers into an ever larger part of China. Thus aware, American commercial interests became concerned at the danger of exclusion and the government itself was not unmoved, the more so since its own Bureau of Foreign and Domestic Commerce had just issued a report dwelling glowingly on the opportunities for

American exports to China if not excluded by arbitrary actions of other Powers. The government addressed itself to the Russian and German governments, asking their intentions toward the trade of other countries in the leaseholds they had just acquired. Germany and Russia responded in soothing but general and meaningless terms.

John Hay then left the London embassy to become Secretary of State, and the atmosphere in Washington subtly changed; perhaps he had brought something of the air of London with him. While it is too much to say that gentle British persuasions in London had already converted him to the idea of diplomatic intervention in China to secure guarantees of free competition in all alienated territories, they had at least prepared him for conversion. Closely associated with Hay was a veteran of the Foreign Service of considerable distinction, William W. Rockhill. He had been stationed in China, had travelled extensively there and in Mongolia and Tibet, and was a serious student of the Far East, though in the years before Hay became Secretary of State he had been in diplomatic posts in the Balkans. Rockhill became Hay's close adviser on Chinese affairs, but Rockhill himself had an adviser, an unofficial, unacknowledged one. This was an Englishman named Alfred E. Hippisley.

Hippisley was a long-time resident of China, where he had known Rockhill intimately, and had been an official in the Chinese Maritime Customs. A thoughtful man and a student of Chinese affairs, he had developed ideas of his own on those affairs and had also imbibed some of the ideas current in official circles while on leave in England. He then came to the United States in 1899 to visit the relatives of his wife, a Baltimore woman whom he had met in Peking while she was visiting the Rockhills. He renewed his association with Rockhill and naturally the parlous events then taking place in China occupied them. Hippisley's ideas on what to do about China coincided, not accidentally, with those held by British officials. There began a series of conversations on China between Rockhill and Hippisley and, more important, an exchange of written communications which propounded concrete measures to be taken in China. In short, Rockhill wrote a memorandum for Secretary Hay which followed very closely a memorandum written for Rockhill by Hippisley, and the State Department on September 6, 1899, sent to Great Britain, Germany, and Russia (and later to other Powers) the communications subsequently famous as the Open Door notes. A textual comparison of the three—Hippisley, Rockhill, Hay—is conclusive and startling. The paternity of the Open Door policy as officially expressed is clear. It is British.

Yet it is sound to avoid drawing obvious but fallacious deductions from this fact. The inception of the Open Door was British; that is true. The initiative in propounding it as international policy and even in formulating it was British; that, too, is true. From that it does not follow, however, that it was only and wholly a British policy and that the United States was innocently trapped or seduced into serving Great Britain's interest, as has been said by so many American writers on the Far East. As in so many instances in American history, the government took action that accrued to Great Britain's advantage, but Great Britain's advantage was coincidental. It happened to coincide with what was America's advantage too. Sooner or later, if not just then, America would have acted as it did even if British interest was not involved. The Open Door may have been a British policy, but it was also an American policy, and for the latter reason America enunciated it. America may have pulled British chestnuts out of the fire, as it did before (and after) but if it did, it did so by inadvertence and without intention. It had put its hand into the fire to pull out its own chestnuts; if it drew out British chestnuts too that was by accident. The same may be said for other important decisions and acts in American foreign relations, World Wars I and II included.

What did the Open Door pronouncement ask and what did it accomplish? On this, too, there has been a great deal of misconception. It is almost a legend of American history that the Open Door declaration saved China from partition. Like most folk legend this is warming but contrary to sober fact. If China was not partitioned, that was not because of the Open Door notes or anything else that the United States did or could do. The United States was not of sufficient consequence at that time to prevent anything the European Powers decided to do. The Spanish-American War notwithstanding, the United States was in 1899 a second-class Power. If Great Britain, Russia, Germany, and France had decided to cut up China and had found a formula for division acceptable to all of them, they could have ignored the United States. This country would not have used force to deter them and if it tried it would have failed ignominiously.

If China survived as a country, that was because no one European Power dared to take the whole of it, since that would have arrayed all the other great Powers against it, and they could not agree on any principle of division that would leave each one satisfied. For that European rivalries and jealousies had already become too rancorous: Great Britain against Russia mainly, Great Britain against Germany already, France against Germany always. The only recourse left was the dog-in-the-manger principle. No one got anything. Therefore China survived, its life owed to Europe's ancient blood-feud. Whatever America did was coincidental. Any other interpretation is myth, however widely held and cherished.

The Open Door notes did not enjoin the breaking up of China. They scarcely mentioned it. On the contrary, they acknowledged and by inference accepted the alienation of ports, leaseholds, and spheres already made. They only asked the Great Powers concerned to pledge themselves not to discriminate in their respective spheres and leaseholds against other countries in matters of trade. Specifically, in those areas they were to apply only the regular Chinese tariff to all imports, no matter from what country; not to levy higher harbor duties on ships of other nations than were paid by their own; and on the railways they controlled, not to charge higher freight rates on goods of other nations than on their own. In short, no country was to derive any special economic advantage in Chinese territory it controlled. There was thus to be complete equality for trade everywhere in China no matter what country had usurped power within it.

Obviously there was in this nothing new. It was formal official expression for the first time of a position that the United States had taken in the Far East since relations had been opened with China. It was a position felt, if not reasoned, and firmly held, even if not officially avowed. Right or wrong—and which it was has never been determined and probably never can be—this was the role America had taken for itself in that part of the world. Save only the principle of nonintervention in European politics and the Monroe Doctrine, no other position has been so definitely and resolutely adopted. Whatever the immediate origin or motive of the Open Door notes may have been, they were in full consistency with American foreign policy. Indeed, they were one of the few points of American relations with the outer world in which there can be said to have been anything as definite as a policy.

Nor was it without rational basis. This was a trading nation. From its earliest beginnings it had plied the high seas of the whole globe for commerce, had exchanged goods with almost every inhabited part, however firmly it was resolved to have no political traffic with any other part. Still less than Great Britain did it have any need or desire for territory. It had an open continental expanse for habitation and exploitation of nature's bounty. But since that bounty was high it wanted to exchange its riches for luxuries or special necessities from without. From the very beginning the American economy was founded on the exchange of its raw materials and agricultural produce for finished products. At first it could not have been self-sufficient. Later it could have been, but self-sufficiency was not so profitable as the exchange of goods with the outer world. And with a kind of inner compulsion hard to explain, it had very early come to look upon the other shore of the Pacific as an area marked out for its enterprise. In this it was not unique. The lure of the Indies, the wealth of the East, had tempted men of the West for time immemorial. Translated into action, this meant for America abstention from efforts and opportunities to acquire territory in China, but insistence on equality of opportunity for trade. So it had been in the 1840's; so it had been when the fate of Hawaii was in question in the middle of the nineteenth century; so it was when China appeared about to be cut up and ingress for American trade denied.

Therefore the formal effort was made to ensure the Open Door. The results were disappointing, the legend to the contrary notwithstanding. Each Power replied affirmatively in generalities, with reservations that cancelled out assent. In sum, each said it would observe equality of opportunity where it had power if others did so, meaning that everything would be as it had been, a dubious prospect. Then the issue moved one step further with the Boxer Rebellion and what seemed to be not only the probability but certainty of the partition of China. Russian troops were already ensconced in Manchuria and apparently in no mood to leave. Hay then made another pronouncement.

In July, 1900, when the armies of the Allied Powers, America included, were gathering for the assault on Peking, Hay addressed himself to the Great Powers. In a circular note dispatched July 3 he took cognizance of what was happening in China and, by inference, what he feared was about to happen. Then he declared American policy. This time he went beyond equality of opportunity for trade. America desired, in his words, to "safeguard for the world the principle of equal and impartial trade with all parts of the Chinese empire," but still more it sought "a solution which may bring about permanent safety and peace to China, and *preserve Chinese territorial and administrative integrity.*" For the first time the United States had broadened its position from the economic to the political and taken its stand: China must survive as an independent country. For the first time, but not the last, the country had made a historic commitment.

The commitment was, however, implicit in the position previously taken. Clearly, as has already been said, equality of trade in China for all countries could be ensured on one condition only: the inviolability of Chinese territory. Great Powers would not go to the risk, trouble, and expense of seizing parts of China only to allow the economic perquisites thereof to go to another country. Unless, like Great Britain, they could be confident of success in open competition they would use one means or other to keep a monopoly of trade wherever they had power.

The integrity of China thus was not an end in itself for the United States. It was a means, a means to an end already desired—equality of opportunity for American trade. But whatever the purpose and sound or not, a hostage had been given. It was to grow in value and risk almost year by year thereafter, until in 1941 it had to be redeemed. Casual the pronouncements of 1899 and 1900 may have been and never fully weighed for their consequences; but they were to influence the course of the history of the republic and of Eastern Asia as well.

CHAPTER XX

Russo-Japanese War

To a degree, then, America's active intervention in the Far East for the first time contributed to preventing the partitioning of China, but only insofar as it had become one more party to an international struggle over China. More important than any act or policy of America's was the steady movement of Japan and Russia toward collision in Korea.

The Japan that confronted Russia after 1895 was, if not a new Japan, a Japan with a new inner energy and magnified inner resource. Industrialization, modernization generally, may be hard to institute and get going. Once got going, it moves by geometric progression. This is as true of not yet industrialized countries as it is of new armament factories at the outset of a war. The hardest and longest stage is the establishment of plant and tooling up. Once that is accomplished, production comes with steadily increasing speed. Japan was already past its first stage. It had an effectively functioning administration of government. It had railways, a merchant marine, telegraph lines, and roads. It had a sound currency and banking system, sounder by virtue of the underpinning of gold from the war indemnity imposed on China in 1895. Factories were in operation producing basic commodities, armament not least. Foreign trade had increased from 48,000,000 yen in 1875 to 265,000,000 yen in 1895. Exports alone had increased from 18,600,000 yen in 1875 to 136,000,000 yen in 1895, more then sevenfold. Most of all, it had an army and navy of mettle and high efficiency by the most exacting standards of the time. Further, it had a professional military class, in both the army and navy, which, though politically unenlightened, even anachronistic, was as competent as its kind anywhere else in the world—as the world was painfully to realize in the 1930's. Of all the ways of the modern world, it was in the military art that the Japanese found themselves most easily at home. Given their history, this was understandable, if not inevitable. Japan, then, was not yet a modern country or a first-class Power, but quite definitely it was no longer medieval and materially undeveloped or negligible.

The Japanese had defeated China and eliminated it from Korea. But this left them far from supreme or unchallenged. Korea itself scarcely had to be considered. It was helpless and demoralized, then as before —and also after—more concerned with its internecine feuds than with the danger from without. The Koreans have had, and still have, a peculiar genius for fratricide, an incontinent and fateful inclination for inviting self-destruction. Korea itself was negligible; but Russia was left, watchful, looming, relentless as a force of nature. Also it was blinded by self-assurance, an assurance born of underestimation of Japan. Like all the Western world, it persisted in thinking of Japan as a trifling inconvenience, to be brushed aside at will.

Clearly the fate of Korea hung on the interests and ambitions, aims and purposes of Russia and Japan. It was therefore not a very auspicious fate. The prospect of peaceful accord or harmonious adjustment was slim. The prospect of an accord that did not leave Korea amputated or extinct was almost nonexistent. On the one hand, Russia was in its most dynamic phase. In St. Petersburg there was unanimous agreement on the desirability and feasibility of expansion to the Pacific coast through Manchuria, Korea, and North China, an agreement that had the tsar's assent. The only difference of opinion was as to method. One group favored direct military measures, the other a more subtle encroachment through economic penetration. On the other hand, Japan was in a mood of elation by reason of its easy triumph over China and at the same time embittered at being deprived of the fruits of victory in Manchuria by the European intervention under Russian leadership. The atmosphere was hardly propitious for amicable compromise or for compromise of any kind.

Japan had been victorious and had exacted from China acknowledgment of Korea's independence. But that did not make Korea independent or Japan supreme. When the confusion and excitement of the war had settled, Japan resumed the efforts it was engaged in before. Japanese advisers were forced on the Korean government, "advisers" in the connotation of the imperial-colonial relationship: they give advice, and the advice is refused or ignored by the nominal officials of the government at their peril; needless to say, it seldom is refused or ignored. At the same time Japan resumed its pressure for reforms—reforms that in themselves were desirable, even necessary. But the Koreans resisted or tried to sabotage the reforms, partly because they resented alien dictation and partly because they resented change. The Korean ruling class had learned nothing from its recent experience. The small group that composed it was still ostrich-like about the world and, what counted more, was reluctant to see any change that would deprive it of the perquisites of corrupt government. Also the feuds around the court had not been assuaged, and furthermore the Russians were intriguing against the reform party and inciting the reactionaries. Partly as the result of these feuds and partly at Japanese instigation there was a coup on October 8, 1895, in which the palace was seized and Queen Min, still opposed to reform, was brutally murdered. The crime was committed by Koreans but the guilt was clearly Japanese, and thereby the hatred of Japan was deepened, not only among the corrupt and reactionary.

Much the same condition prevailed as before 1894, a fact of which Russia soon took advantage. Early in 1896 Russian guards arrived in Seoul, presumably to protect the legation, and immediately thereafter the king escaped from his palace—and the Japanese—and took refuge in the Russian Legation. The Japanese were chagrined, and with reason. The Russians capitalized on their possession of the king's person. They proceeded toward possession of the king's country. They had Japanese advisers dismissed, especially from the Korean army, and many of the reforms were cancelled. They obtained timber and mining concessions in the north, concessions that were to play a large part in bringing about collision with Japan.

At this stage the Japanese sought compromise. An occasion was provided by the coronation ceremonies at Moscow, to which diplomats came from all over the world. It was then, it will be remembered, that the Russians got from Li Hung-chang, the Chinese representative, the concession for the Manchurian railway. Aritomo Yamagata, the dominant figure in the Japanese army, was sent as Japan's representative, charged incidentally with the mission of seeing what kind of agreement could be struck with the Russians. He proposed that Korea be divided into spheres, the Russians having the north and the Japanese the south. The dividing line was to be, as it happened, the thirty-eighth parallel. The Russians refused. No doubt they were confident that in time no division would be necessary. Instead a more general agreement was made, to be known as the Yamagata-Lobanov Protocol, which consisted mainly of generalities. The two countries would be on an equal footing in Korea. Both would withdraw their troops. Both would advise the king to introduce reforms to strengthen the country. This agreement the Russians were soon violating, especially in the matter of advisers, and new negotiations were entered into. In April, 1898, the Rosen-Nishi Convention was signed. The Russians were now more conciliatory. Both bound themselves to preserve the independence and integrity of Korea

—an ominous sign for any country that is weak and prized by the strong—and to refrain from interference in Korean internal affairs. Neither would send advisers without the other's consent. But Russia also bound itself not to obstruct Japan in obtaining and developing economic interests in Korea, an important concession. By that time Russia was doubtless more concerned with its plans for Manchuria. Korea was thus laid away in escrow, to await a more propitious time for its truncation or demise. Nevertheless the maneuvers and intrigues by both Russia and Japan for paramount position continued unabated.

The Russians were indeed concerned with Manchuria. The building of the railway had given them their start. They were seeking opportunity to make the most of it and the Boxer uprising provided it. The Boxers had begun marauding in Manchuria too and parts of the railway were being torn up. The Russians found their pretext. Count Witte, the Russian Minister of Finance, who figured so prominently in Russian expansion in the Far East though an advocate of economic penetration as a stage to absorption, writes in his memoirs that as soon as the Boxer raids had become serious, General Kuropatkin, the Minister of War, had told him "this will give us our excuse for seizing Manchuria."

Kuropatkin was as good as his word. Early in July, 1900, Russian troops drove into north Manchuria, ostensibly to protect the railway, and soon city after city was falling to them. Before many weeks Mukden, in the south, the main city of the Manchurian provinces, was in their hands. Thus the Russians were participating in the Allied expedition to rescue the legations in Peking and at the same time conducting their private war in Manchuria with none to keep a check on them. After the capture of Peking by the Allied forces and the cessation of fighting in China, the Chinese requested the Russians to cease their advance in Manchuria and withdraw their troops. The Russians replied that the troops had to remain to preserve order, which incidentally was no longer being disturbed except by them.

Two sets of negotiations then began, one relatively open between the representatives of the Allied Powers and the Chinese for a general settlement of the Boxer adventure and the other, altogether secret, between the Russians and Chinese first in Manchuria and then in St. Petersburg. In Manchuria there was concluded in November, 1900, the Alexeieff-Tseng Agreement, Alexeieff being the Russian governor of the Russian leasehold in Port Arthur and Dalny and Tseng Chi the highest ranking Chinese official in Manchuria. The agreement bore Tseng Chi's name but actually it was made by a minor official of dubious repute named Chou Mien. The agreement permitted Russia to maintain troops in Manchuria and appoint a Resident with a seat in Mukden. Also the

Chinese military commander in the region was to be appointed subject to Russian approval. For practical purposes this meant a Russian protectorate over Manchuria.

The agreement was reported to the Chinese government but otherwise kept secret. The government balked and the negotiations were transferred to St. Petersburg, where the Russians began the application of ruthless pressure on the Chinese minister, combining blandishments with threats to compel him to sign. He refused to sign without the authorization of his government and in Peking the government, torn between resentment and fear, could not bring itself to a decision. One group held that to refuse meant the loss to Russia of the whole of Manchuria, another group that to sign would have the same effect at once and it was better to refuse and let the Russians bear the onus of aggression. As a matter of fact Witte did inform the Chinese minister that unless China would accept the compromise status for Manchuria, Russia would annex it outright. The Chinese resorted to a stratagem since then become familiar. They allowed the Alexeieff-Tseng Agreement to leak out to foreigners, and it was reported almost in its entirety in the London *Times* in January, 1901.

There was a flurry of excitement in all Western capitals, and consultations began to take place among the governments of the Great Powers. The most wrought up was Japan, which of course had most to fear next to China. The Japanese on their part brought pressure on the Chinese government not to submit. At the same time they approached the other Powers, asking specifically what support they would get if Russia seized Manchuria and Japan resisted with force. Germany and France were unresponsive, if not unsympathetic. Great Britain was noncommittal, which itself was encouraging to the Japanese. Great Britain also inquired of Germany as to its intentions if Russia acted, and the Germans were coy, although they were willing to sign an accord by which the two Powers would seek to maintain China's territorial integrity; but a more definite commitment they would not make. The representatives of the Powers in Peking did, however, formally ask that the Manchuria issue be settled in general negotiations among all of them and showed an intention to be firm. This in turn stiffened China. In St. Petersburg the Russians haggled over variations in the terms of the agreement and alternately coaxed and threatened, but when it became apparent that they could not proceed with their plans for Manchuria without antagonizing all the Powers they suddenly retreated. The Alexeieff-Tseng Agreement was withdrawn. But Russian troops were not. Russia would merely bide its time and await another opportunity.

After the signing of the protocol in Peking between China and the

Powers on September 7, 1901, finally settling the Boxer episode, the question of Russian troops in Manchuria arose again. Russia now proposed to China to withdraw its troops in three years if China would agree not to permit nationals of any other country but Russia to build railways in south Manchuria without Russian consent. China objected and communicated the proposal to the American minister in Peking. China asked withdrawal of the troops in one year and Russia countered with an offer to withdraw in two years, again on a condition, this time that Russians should get priority in loans for development of Manchurian industries—Manchuria being the richest source of raw materials in the empire. Now the British, French, and American governments protested vigorously and the matter was deadlocked. But Great Britain and Japan did more than protest.

The initiative was taken by Japan, which had a special stimulus. Japan had watched the glacial movement of the Russians, slow but unrelenting, toward the shore of Asia opposite their islands. It was clear that either Russia would have all Manchuria and Korea or it would have to be stopped by force. It was evident, too, that the race for paramountcy in China was on among all the Powers and that one or more would presumably be established in striking distance of Japan. The Japanese did not need much stimulation. Militant and militaristic in their own nature, in their own designs on the continent, as they had shown in the 1870's, and heady with the wine of victory over China, they came almost by reflex to the conclusion that they themselves might better enter the race. There was some justification apart from their own inner aggressiveness. It was not illogical to reason that clearly China's end was impending and that if China had to fall to Great Powers it was both safer and more desirable that it fall to Japan. But the cautiousness that had restrained them in the 1870's from premature adventuring without the power to sustain adventure had not been lost. The young leaders who had so skillfully piloted the transition to modernism after the Restoration were now in the full vigor of middle age and had kept their balance and insight; they were by no means pacific but under self-control. They were still aware that they could not challenge all the Western Powers. They had to strike a bargain with one or more among them to be free to face the others.

There were anxious searchings of heart and warm debates among the ruling group in Tokyo. One faction wanted to come to accord with Russia looking toward a division of the spoils. Another wanted an alliance with Great Britain as the country with which Japan most nearly had common cause. At that time Japan could come to reckoning with Russia. Ito went to St. Petersburg and Baron Hayashi, the Minister in

London, sounded out the British government. Ito was prepared to concede a free hand to Russia in Manchuria if Japan could have the same in Korea. But Russia was always intractable. It wanted both. The British were not intractable.

The British were in fact hospitable to suggestions. It has already been seen that by the end of the nineteenth century they were coming to realize that isolation was no longer feasible. Menaced by Russia on one side and by a now ebullient and importunate Germany on the other, Great Britain could no longer remain aloof, confident that it could still go it alone, no matter what came. It had to have friends it could count on. With Russia it had no more success in coming to an understanding than had Japan. Russia was evasive and elusive. Plainly it wanted everything. Germany was unresponsive, as Joseph Chamberlain had found. Japan was willing and could be useful. It could act as a check on Russia in Asia.

Negotiations at London went smoothly, so smoothly that an Imperial Council in Tokyo in December, 1901, decided that it was hopeless to strike a bargain with Russia and therefore it was better to conclude an arrangement with Great Britain. On these instructions Hayashi did so, and on January 30, 1902, papers were signed contracting a five-year alliance between Great Britain and Japan. The treaty provided that if either party became involved in war the other would remain neutral, but if a third country entered the other party would come to the assistance of its ally. What this meant was that in a war between Japan and Russia, Germany and France could not intervene without bringing in Great Britain on Japan's side. For practical purposes this was to make sure that neither of them would, and thus Japan could act with less anxiety. Great Britain and Japan also expressed their recognition of the independence of China and Korea, but Japan conceded Britain's special interest in China and Great Britain Japan's special interest in Korea. Thus Japan won a partial diplomatic victory. For the first time a Western Power granted it special position in Korea. Its own concession to Great Britain about China meant little, for Great Britain had numerous rivals in China that could keep it in check.

Thereby, however, a Russo-Japanese war, already probable, became certain.

It did not take long for the war to develop. Russia was given some pause by the Anglo-Japanese alliance, but only pause. The troops remained in Manchuria, the onward thrust in Korea was unrelaxed. The Chinese still pressed for evacuation. Only in April, 1902, did Russia seem to relent. Then it agreed to evacuate in three stages within eighteen months. Agreement was one thing, fulfillment another. At the end of the first six months' period troops were merely moved from one part of Manchuria to another. At the end of the next period Russia agreed to move in exchange for concessions that would have given it substantial control over both Manchuria and Mongolia. The Chinese were obdurate. America protested on the grounds of the Open Door. Nothing was changed, however.

For Japan the time had come for decision. It proposed to Russia the opening of formal negotiations for a comprehensive settlement of the differences between them on the whole Far East. In July, 1903, the Japanese minister in St. Petersburg submitted concrete terms to Lamsdorff, the Russian Foreign Minister. These included the recognition of the independence and territorial integrity of Korea and at the same time (reflecting the elastic definitions of terms used in the earlier diplomacy) what amounted to a division of spheres in Korea, Russia to be unimpeded in the north and Japan in the south. This was not very different from what Japan had suggested before, and the effect was the same as before. There followed months of haggling after the fashion of an Oriental bazaar. Whenever an agreement seemed in sight Russia injected new terms, generally asking something more. Parenthetically, it will be evident to men of a later era that Russian principles and methods of international political discourse do not vary with time or the color of Russian ideology. White, red, or any shade in between, it deals, moves, and acts the same in transactions with other countries. Months passed, and there was no prospect of settlement. The Russians evaded, temporized, conceded, demanded. The Japanese concluded that the Russians were not negotiating in good faith, and they were not far wrong. They lost patience and decided to act. On February 6, 1904, Japan broke off diplomatic relations. On February 8, without an ultimatum or declaration of war, Japanese ships attacked Port Arthur. The war was on. Plainly, the Japanese, too, do not vary their methods of diplomatic intercourse with time, as December 7, 1941, showed.

Both Russia and Japan had motives that were hardly conducive to peace in Eastern Asia; yet on the whole the right was more nearly on Japan's side. On the whole, it was for Japan a defensive war. Had it not acted, first Manchuria, then Korea, then north China, and then it itself would have fallen to an aggressive, unappeasable Russian imperialism. For Japan it was a war for survival and to that extent justified. In general this was the world's verdict. The course of the war astounded the world as had few political events in the preceding century. It also injected into the Eastern world a galvanizing element the effect of which was still being felt fifty years later, perhaps being felt most then.

Only ten years before Japan had seemed negligible as a Power. Then it had surprised the world by its easy victory over China, for which, if only because of its size, there had been some respect. In the ensuing decade it had been generally recognized that Japan had been gathering strength; but yet it was a minor island Power with slender resources, newly arrived in the modern world and never yet tried against a state of any consequence. Now it was pitting itself against the Russian colossus that had struck fear into the greatest of the great, even into Great Britain at the pinnacle of its might. To the world's astonishment the Japanese won victory after victory, on land and on sea, bloody and costly victories but also decisive. The Russian forces were sent reeling from the coast across Manchuria, with little hope of recovery and recapture of the lost territory. Their navy was destroyed and their army demoralized. Worse yet, the Russian people, who knew little of the origins and purposes of the war and never had their heart in it, became dangerously disgruntled and there were rumblings of revolt. Before the war was eighteen months old, Russia was forced to acknowledge that it was ready for peace.

So as a matter of fact was Japan. Japan was victorious but spent. Coolly and objectively analyzed, the Japanese victory was politically an optical illusion. It is not uncommon in history that deceptive appearances have as much effect on the course of human events as reality. So it was with the Russo-Japanese war. Japan did not really defeat Russia; Russia defeated Russia. It was fighting several thousand miles from its center, with a single-track railway the only means of communication between the home base and the scene of military operations. Its armies were badly led and inefficiently supplied. There was as much corruption as inefficiency. Both political and military intelligence was deficient, if it existed at all. Troops had poor morale; again, they did not know why they had been conscripted and sent across a continent to fight when they had no desire to fight. Oppression and misrule had made them men of doubtful loyalty in any circumstances. The Japanese on the other hand had a cause. They were fighting for survival and knew it. Japan fought with all its being, Russia with only part of its being. Naturally, Japan won or, rather, Russia lost. The effect on the outcome was the same nevertheless. By midsummer of 1905 Japan clearly had military ascendancy. It had only military ascendancy, however, for Japan was actually at the end of its resources. It had been sustained until then in considerable part by British and American financial support, but there was a visible limit to that support if the war was to be protracted. Both sides therefore, while professing a resolve to go on to the bitter end, were open to offers of mediation.

President Theodore Roosevelt made such an offer. He had watched the prelude to war and the war itself with close attention, as had his administration. Both he and his government and almost all Americans with political knowledge were pro-Japanese. There had been something more than irritation in Washington at Russia's brazen aggression in Manchuria, the more so since it was clear that Russian success meant exclusion of all others for any purpose whatever and therefore the negation of the Open Door policy. The American government had repeatedly inquired, proposed, protested, but in vain. The Russians replied either disingenuously or in words that cancelled each other out. If they were less abusive in words than the Communist Russians that succeeded them, their purposes and their methods were similar. There was intercourse but no communication. The American government, like the British, became impatient, distrustful and fearful, then definitely hostile. Both the British and Americans supported Japan. They saw in it a means of interposing a check on Russia's manifest intention to establish hegemony over all Eastern Asia.

Both Russia and Japan accepted Roosevelt's mediation. There was a prolonged period of haggling, both sides threatening at intervals to break off negotiations and resume fighting; but they did not, since each knew that resumption of war would hurt itself as much as the enemy. The final stumbling-block was Japan's insistence on a large indemnity and cession of the whole island of Sakhalin, the island off the Siberian shore. On Roosevelt's pressure Japan agreed to compromise, yielding entirely on the indemnity and getting only the southern half of Sakhalin. The Treaty of Portsmouth, then quickly concluded, was an acknowledgment of Japan's victory. Both sides agreed to withdraw their armies from Manchuria, but Japan succeeded to all Russian rights in south Manchuria, including the leasehold on Port Arthur, Dalny, and the whole of the Liaotung Peninsula—the fruit of victory of which Russia had deprived it ten years before. In addition, Japan obtained the southern half of the Chinese Eastern Railway running from Changchun to the coast, together with coal mines on both sides. Under Japanese control this line became the South Manchuria Railway, destined to play a historic part in subsequent Far Eastern relations. Also Russia conceded to Japan political, military, and economic paramountcy in Korea, thus signing Korea's death warrant.

The war made Japan a world Power but it had an even greater significance. It lighted a spark in all Asia. It demonstrated to all the peoples of that continent that it was not God's dispensation that Asian peoples must be ruled by the white. It demonstrated that white empires were not irresistible or invulnerable, as till then had been accepted with fatalistic resignation. One of the smallest of the Asian peoples had stood up to one of the mightiest of the white empires and overcome it. Plainly there was hope for others, if only they were resolved and prepared themselves. A thrill of hope ran through the nonwhite peoples. From Turkey at one end of Asia to China at the other nationalistic movements burgeoned, and from the Young Turk revolution in 1908, only three years after the war, to the risings in French Indo-China, Dutch Indonesia, and British Malaya after World War II—and including the Indian and Chinese emancipation—the flame lit by the Japanese victory was burning its course. On the day the Treaty of Portsmouth was signed the historically minded could have predicted with confidence that the twilight of Western rule in Asia had set in. Had such prophets been more numerous and their influence greater, the world would have been spared much sacrifice and suffering. But in any event in Eastern Asia a new era was inaugurated with Japan's emergence as one of the great states of the world and a dominating power in its own region.

CHAPTER XXI

China's Belated Conversion

Nowhere was the unhinging of the Japanese victory more stirringly felt than in China. There it reinforced the shock of the humiliating punishment inflicted by the Great Powers after the Boxer Rebellion only five years before.

The Boxer episode had left the die-hard Manchu-mandarin spirit crushed at last. The defeat by Japan, the ignominious flight of the imperial court to the barren northwest, and the subsequent penalties paid for the Boxer madness had irrefutably demonstrated that there was something inherently wrong, that the reform movement of 1898 had some basis, and that China would have to take some account of the time and make some compromise with the modern spirit as represented by the West. Japan's success was an example and a lesson. If Japan by adaptation to the West could accomplish what it had and make its way not only to independence and safety but to a place among the great, so presumably could China. The imperial court and its supporters among the conservative Chinese were chastened, repentant, and prepared to learn.

It would be too much to say that they had entirely recanted, that they had entirely abandoned the comforting belief that it was enough to take over the barbarians' mechanical and material devices in order to be strong, while preserving everything fundamental that was Chinese in order to remain spiritually superior; but there was at least a tendency to a kind of revisionism, to an admission that there was something in the West that yielded benefits in the lives of countries and individuals. The belief did not strike very deep but it had gone below the surface. At least the small minority who knew something about the West and agitated for change in that direction could no longer be altogether denied.

Some of the appurtenances of the West had already been taken over.

Arsenals had been built, the first as far back as the 1860's; even then it was clear that the new weapons were essential to survival. Dockyards had been constructed, with facilities, though meager, for building steamships. A telegraph line had been strung along the coast from Shanghai to Tientsin in 1881 and then extended. An imperial Post Office was established in 1886, replacing the private companies that had carried mail until then. The China Merchants' Steamship Company was founded with government subsidy for coast and river traffic. In the early 1880's a railway was built to connect Tientsin with the nearby Kaiping coal fields and later extended to Peking. Also a small number of modern industrial enterprises using simple machinery had been started—iron and steel works, silk and cotton mills. All these, however, were but excrescences; the surface itself was barely scratched. Even those who advocated such activities, men like Li Hung-chang, Tseng Kuo-fan, and Chang Chih-tung, the more enlightened of the ranking mandarins, continued to think that the West had nothing to teach but the material, that China could still remain the China of the ages—the Middle Kingdom, center of light, wisdom, and culture.

This attitude, which was to change by 1906, began to pass in 1901, even before the empress dowager and the court left their compulsory exile in Sianfu. Penitence and enlightenment were formally proclaimed in an edict issued by the empress dowager in which she said she had "now decided that we should correct our shortcomings by adopting the best methods and systems which obtain in foreign countries." Whether she really understood what she was saying or, understanding, had her tongue in her cheek, is difficult to decide. The latter is the more plausible. In either case her words, pronounced with the sanction of the head of the imperial court and the leader of the obstructionists, gave weight to those of lesser position who either had been openly agitating for reform or had become, however regretfully, convinced of its necessity. Thus put in motion, the movement for change inevitably gathered momentum. In the next few years a succession of decrees ordering change in the Chinese system were proclaimed. They were set going at least on paper.

Education was declared to be the first imperative. As a beginning the examination system by which government officials were chosen was to be broadened to cover subjects besides history, philosophy, literature, and essays, all based on the Confucian classics. More schools were ordered. An educational system in the modern sense had been non-existent before. Peiyang University, the first modern institution of higher learning, had been started in Tientsin in 1895 on the initiative of Li Hung-chang. Peking University, which was to become in twenty years one of the most vital intellectual centers of Eastern Asia, was founded soon after, as was Nanyang University, in Nanking, an institution for technical education. But these were all. Otherwise education continued to be concentrated on the old classical books and commentaries and conducted in private schools, which were few and mainly restricted to the wealthy classes. Of public schools there were none. These were now ordered and a few actually established. In 1904 a national system of public schools, from elementary to universities, was decreed. At the same time young men were encouraged to go abroad for education. They did so, the first of them, significantly, to Japan. In a few years there were several thousand Chinese students in that country. A few hundred chose Europe and America, more of them America than Europe. The most drastic step was taken in 1905, when the examination system was abolished entirely, culturally a truly revolutionary measure. More than anything else this was abandonment of the historic tradition and perhaps a confession of cultural defeat.

At the same time and more important in the eyes of those who advocated change were political reforms. For them the time had gone for a monarchical system even in name absolute. Representation in government had become the rule the world over; even Japan had a constitution and a parliament. The empress dowager and her retinue went through at least the forms of concession. In 1905 a commission was sent abroad to study systems of government in Europe and America, as the Japanese had done. The commission reported, as might have been expected, that parliaments and popular representation were the rule almost everywhere in the world, and the court, as might have been expected, conformed at least verbally. It did so, but without a modicum of the perception of the Japanese that this was inherent in Westernism and inseparable from it, and that the institutions of the West went with the power of the West. In 1906 an imperial edict promised the introduction of constitutional government after the preparatory steps had been taken, the indications being that this meant after sufficiently widespread education. As a first step the central government was reorganized, with provisions for ten ministries at the head of administrative departments, at least a semblance of a cabinet, although decision would still rest with the empress dowager and her successors. Also the convocation of provincial assemblies and later of a national assembly was promised. In 1908 definite measures were taken to convoke the provincial bodies immediately and the principles of the future constitution were proclaimed. A national parliament was to come into being in 1917.

The constitutional provisions were a long way from representative government. The object was to preserve the power of the throne behind the shadow-play of elected representatives. In the words of an official pronouncement: "The Constitution is designed to conserve the power of the Sovereign and protect the officials and people." In 1908 Tzu Hsi, the empress dowager, died. Two days before Kwang Hsu, the titular Emperor, had died in his palace prison in the Forbidden City. Whether his death came by coincidence or was assisted was a subject of speculation in Peking then and later. Since the dowager had already designated the successor to the throne, the two-year-old Pu-yi, and appointed Prince Chun as Regent, Kwang Hsu's survival might have become embarrassing to the dowager's court clique. The dowager's death, however, did give both encouragement and impetus to the reform advocates but this served only to expedite the reforms that had been decreed rather than to change their spirit.

The first provincial assemblies met in 1909. According to plan, they were to be merely sounding boards, if not rubber stamps. The members were elected by a narrowly restricted list, in effect composed of the wealthy classes. By official order their function was limited to debate and in practice it turned out that even debate was limited to questions submitted by the government. Thus was the official order and expectation, but the times had been too unhinged for easy compliance. Appetite had been whetted. The dynasty had admitted too much and, besides, the fiasco of the war with Japan, the heedless folly of the Boxer Rebellion, the demonstrated incompetence of the monarchical government, and the unenlightened domineering of the empress dowager had produced irritation, if not a nascent rebelliousness. Increasing numbers of the educated class were in no mood for supine obedience. They had had the promise of representative government and they wanted it. The assemblies were recalcitrant and demanding. They insisted that the proposed reforms be accelerated and that a national assembly be called at once. The government tried threats but they had no effect. It had to yield. It promised a national consultative assembly the following year.

The national assembly met in October, 1910. Its membership consisted of one hundred chosen by the throne and one hundred chosen by the provincial assemblies. Theoretically this body, at least half of it hand-picked, should have been docile. It was not. It was even more recalcitrant than the provincial assemblies and equally unamenable to discipline. It demanded the early grant of a constitution and an earlier elected national parliament. Again the government yielded and announced that a parliament would be summoned in 1913. The assembly then demanded a responsible cabinet and on its becoming too obstreperous was dissolved in January, 1911. But matters had gone too far. The movement against the Manchu rulers had become too strong and as a concession the assembly was reconvened in October. That was too late. The dynasty could no longer be saved.

One more historic measure must be recorded. This was the beginning of the prohibition of opium. The drug had become the country's curse. Rich and poor alike were being impoverished, enervated, and poisoned. Educational reforms, political reforms, economic development, all alike were futile as long as opium continued to besot the race. Opium and progress could not coexist, however resolute the demand for progress. In the decades since opium had been legalized by the treaties of 1858 that ended the war with Great Britain and France, the imports of the drug, principally from India, had grown by leaps. So had the cultivation of native opium, whole regions being given up to it since it brought so high a price compared to food crops. The production of food was correspondingly reduced, with catastrophic results if there was drought or flood and resulting famine. By 1888 opium imports from India amounted to more than £10,000,000 a year. The British raj in India had a vested interest in the opium trade, since opium was a government monopoly and the profits kept taxes low, a satisfying condition to British economic interests in the colony. After 1888 imports dropped, since the Chinese product increased so heavily and, being cheaper, won much of the market. By 1906 only £7,000,000 worth were coming in from India, but native production was three times as large.

In the new spirit of the early years of the century the movement for modernization and reform was extended to the problem of opium. To this there was much less opposition than to the rest of the program. The feeling was widespread in all classes that opium was the country's greatest danger. At first it was decided to work for suppression by exorbitant taxation on opium lands. A decree to that effect was issued in September, 1906, with the aim of wiping out production in ten years, and to this the empress dowager gave genuine support. It was of little use, however, to stop the cultivation of opium in China if it could still be brought in from without; on the contrary, it would only drain the country financially. Here foreign relations entered and appeal was made to Great Britain in particular. The appeal commended itself to British public opinion and pressure was put on the India government. In 1908 an agreement was signed by which India was to reduce its opium exports to China by one-tenth every year, at first for three years and, if the results were satisfactory, for the remaining seven years. In 1911 a British investigating commission found that progress had been made in curbing the use of the drug and recommended continuance of the agreement until exports ceased altogether. Indeed, if turmoil had not set in after 1911 opium would have disappeared in China or at least become no more common than in Europe or America. But the years of internal disturbance brought about retrogression, although even so it has never again had the hold on the people that it had before 1900.

Without deliberation, without plan, perhaps even without consciousness, other new forces had been working in the body of China—economic forces. Imperceptibly, subtly, the direction and content of the economy were changing. There might be conscious resolve to keep the West out as inferior, but the West was entering in irresistible ways. Trade always has broken across ideational barriers; it did in China too. Western goods were coming in. Western goods meant new things of use, and new things of use meant new habits, and new habits work changes in those that contract them. Before 1900 the main import into China was opium. After 1900 other things entered. In 1900 textiles accounted for most of China's imports. Bringing in wearing apparel meant that home industries were passing, since they could not compete in price with the foreign machine product. Textiles have a symbolical value in the relation of the old world and the new. They are the spear point of the new. When an old people have begun to use machine-made textiles brought from without they have taken the first step in subjection to the outer world. When the first machine-made textiles enter a country which has not known them, the cultural subjection of that country has begun. It must learn to produce by machine one of the three essentials to survival—food, clothing, and shelter—or it cannot survive. Yet even textile imports were declining in the years after 1900. The importation of metals and machinery was beginning. That signified that China's way of production was changing and therefore the way of living of the Chinese people. They were bringing in and making use not only of consumer goods but of those articles that changed their economic activities and their customs. They might consciously reject Western ideas, but they were taking Western things that later would give form to ideas. An illustration is kerosene, used for illumination. By 1910 kerosene constituted 5 per cent of Chinese imports. Better illumination created new leisure habits and working habits—incidentally it also made for better health. Foreign goods, by creating their own demand, made the Chinese more dependent on foreign trade. Not only were the movement and direction of the Chinese economy changing, but thus the impenetrable walls of China were being cut through much more effectively and permanently than ever they were by the British gunboats in 1840. Mandarins might argue philosophically in their yamens, but the forces of the time were overrunning them while they made Confucian aphorisms.

CHAPTER XXII

Revolution in China: The Republic

The collapse came suddenly and unexpectedly—unexpectedly as to time and circumstance but not as to outcome. The Manchu dynasty had run its course. In the thought and expression of Chinese philosophy, the Confucian-Mencian scheme, it had forfeited the mandate of Heaven. By its ineffectiveness and misrule it had shown that it was no longer trustee for the benevolent spirit of nature: the Son of Heaven was therefore a usurper. There was a moral right to dethrone him.

The feeling against the Manchus had long been gathering, too slowly perhaps for it was still too inarticulate to be recognizable or acknowledged. The Chinese have never been easily reconciled to alien rulers, despite the common myth about their complaisance. Until the death in 1797 of Ch'ien Lung, the second of the two great Manchu emperors who together reigned for 120 years with a short interval between them, there was little disaffection. A few secret societies of the kind to which the Chinese are prone did aspire to bring back a Chinese dynasty, but on the whole life for the Chinese people under the two rulers, K'ang Hsi and Ch'ien Lung, was orderly and beneficent. With the death of Ch'ien Lung deterioration set in. Ch'ien Lung's successors were ineffectual and the Chinese mandarinate that served them were not much better and, besides, were increasingly hide-bound in their conservatism. Administrative slackness, inefficiency, and corruption grew ever worse. Misrule was reflected directly in hardship for the masses of the people, as always in China. The Taiping Rebellion was a portent. The omens were to be more clear as the end of the nineteenth century approached.

The Manchus had conspicuously failed in the one obligation laid against any government anywhere, whatever the system—the ability to defend the country. As the failure was cumulative, so was the effect. At first foreigners established their settlements in Chinese ports, independent of Chinese control. Missionaries were spread over the land, ostentatiously flouting local authority. Strips of territory were shorn off the empire. Formidable foreign islands lay in the populous regions of the country. Japan, never held in respect, inflicted a humiliating defeat. Then at the end of the century came the series of foreign leaseholds and the marking out of spheres which seemed to presage the passing of the empire. There followed the humiliating spectacle of the Boxers, the wretched scuttling of the empress dowager and her court, and the drastic penalties levied by the foreign powers. Finally, as an astringent lesson there was the demonstration of what Japan, a lesser neighbor, could do by contrast. Plainly the Manchus could only live in parasitic ease off the country's substance. They could not govern it properly. They could not protect it from a host of enemies. They could not even preserve its dignity.

The antidynastic movement, still inchoate in the latter part of the nineteenth century, began to take form after 1900. It gathered around a remarkable man, one of the most remarkable men of his time: Sun Yat-sen. The Manchus would have been overthrown and a republic established if Sun Yat-sen had never been born. But the early date and the method of the Manchus' overthrow and the nature of the new republic are attributable to Sun Yat-sen more than to any other man or force. He organized the movement for the overthrow, inspired the men who joined it, gave it and them faith and courage and spirit, and kept their faith unflagging until the effort succeeded. More will be said later of his personality and the influence he exercised after the republic was instituted, but first it is necessary to tell something of his own history, so inseparable is it from a chapter in the history of his country.

Sun was born in 1866 of a poor peasant family in a village near Canton, the district from which most Chinese emigrants have gone to all parts of the world since the latter part of the nineteenth century. His father had come under missionary influence and professed Christianity. Canton was itself the center of all Western influences at that time. At the age of thirteen he went to Honolulu to join an older brother who had emigrated there some years before. There he went to a school conducted by the Anglican church for Hawaiian boys and studied English and other Western subjects, his first introduction to the world of new ideas. In his seventeenth year he returned to his native village, but he was no longer contented with the restricted life of a peasant in a backward area. His ideas soon manifested themselves in a destructive form that made him an apostate to his parents' neighbors. He mocked at the idols in the village temple and openly scorned the religious beliefs and superstitions they embodied. He outraged the village to such a degree that his parents decided to send him away. He went to Hongkong and later entered

Queens College, a British institution. At the age of eighteen he was baptized a Christian.

The Hongkong experience definitely committed Sun to the modern world. He made a short visit to Hawaii again and then returned to China to study medicine. In this way he could best serve his people. For five years from 1887 to 1892 he prepared himself for the medical profession under James Cantlie, later Sir James Cantlie, who was to play an important part in his life and also became his biographer. He finished his medical course, but soon forswore medicine for political agitation. He dedicated himself to the rebirth of his country into the modern world as master of its own destiny. In 1894 he began his political career with the formation of a secret society with the object of uplifting the Chinese people by education, better cultivation of the soil, and more efficient production of other goods. Branches of the society were organized at various points, always in secret, and then a year later, with a weakness for premature coups which was to lead him into one disaster after another throughout his life, he launched an attempt to seize the Kwangtung provincial headquarters in Canton. It failed, of course, since it had not even meager support. A number of the men involved were caught and executed but Sun himself escaped. He took refuge in Japan, where he appealed for help to influential Japanese, including some of the worst reactionaries who already had designs on China. This, be it remembered, was just when China was being defeated by Japan. The Japanese promised and did give him material help, many no doubt with mental reservations. It was to their advantage that China should be crippled by internal dissension. But credulity was one of Sun's unfortunate weaknesses and as much as any other quality it was responsible for some of his farcical adventures. Vague and general promises of support were always construed by him as guarantees and he acted as if they were, with unfortunate consequences for himself and his followers.

From Japan Sun Yat-sen went to London in 1895. A price had already been put on his head by the Manchu government, and while in London he allowed himself to be trapped in the Chinese Legation. Arrangements were being made to smuggle him on board a ship bound for China, where he undoubtedly would have met death by torture, but he managed to slip a note out of the legation which got to Cantlie, his old teacher, who was then in London. Cantlie notified Scotland Yard and the press. There was a storm of public protest and the legation was forced to release Sun. The incident made him known throughout the world. Then began a career of the kind that can be found only in E. Phillips Oppenheim thrillers and ordinarily can be believed only in such thrillers. He went all over the world, recruiting followers from the Chinese colonies to be found everywhere and raising money to finance the movement. Since most of the Chinese who had emigrated were Cantonese, his own people, the task was eased. He returned to East Asia at intervals. He slipped into Asian ports to attend secret meetings of his followers, then organized in branches at various points. Every such meeting was a gamble with death, for the Manchus were not without spies and secret agents. Newspapers were started and secretly circulated. Sun himself wrote manifestoes and pamphlets stating the philosophy and program for the future China and they came to be fairly widely circulated. Thus nuclei of revolution were forming and grew, the more rapidly as a spirit of restlessness was being stirred throughout the country anyway by the reform movement that began after 1900. Students who had had some contact with the Western world or, in the new Chinese universities, with Western ideas responded most of all. In 1905 Sun organized the Tung Meng Hui, a society rather than a party, and to it adhered a number of other groups with the same objects, mainly the overthrow of the Manchus. Japan was the main center of such groups and a radiating point for revolutionary literature.

The movement spread and a number of minor coups were attempted, all of them premature and easily crushed. But with every year it gathered force and the government's policy of giving with one hand and taking away with the other in political reforms added followers and increased determination. Conditions were ripening for something more drastic than reform. The climax was precipitated by an issue only partly political. In the spirit of adaptation to the West that prevailed after 1901 there was a sudden interest in railway construction. This was not illogical. If China was to be made over there had to be better communications throughout the land; the vast expanse of the country had to be linked as a national entity. Since the Western Powers had not only shown interest in financing railroads in China but had used threats to get the privilege of doing so, and since China lacked the necessary capital, the government now was receptive to offers. West China was as yet untouched by rail communication and as it contained some of the most fertile areas in the country opportunity beckoned there.

As early as 1903 British and American interests offered to make loans for a line between Hankow, the river port in the Central Yangtze Valley where some of the new industries were being started, and Szechuan, the westernmost province. The government agreed to give them first consideration. Then an Anglo-French syndicate offered to build a line from Hankow south through Hunan Province to meet a projected line coming north from Canton. Thus there would be direct rail communication from Peking to the southernmost point in the empire. The Germans then made a bid for the same lines and were admitted into the Anglo-French syndicate. The Americans meanwhile had dropped out. But when in 1909 it appeared that there was a serious prospect of construction President Taft, who had already embarked on the policy of dollar diplomacy, insisted on the right of readmission. When the European Powers objected, Taft addressed himself directly to Prince Chun, the regent. Chun agreed and American banks were promised a share of a four-Power loan of $19,000,000, the final agreement being signed in May, 1911.

By this time, however, internal complications had entered. The provinces had become suspicious of the central government's plans, partly because of the general anti-Manchu sentiment and the recognition that the central government would acquire more power through railroads and partly because of the traditionally jealous guarding of provincial autonomy. Szechuan Province, which has always had an especially strong local loyalty, almost a sense of separatism, had already decided to build a railway under its own auspices. A company had been formed and shares subscribed, but little progress was made. When the international agreement was concluded in May, there was a sharp protest in Chengtu, the provincial capital. The shareholders of the provincial company demanded reimbursement by the central government. When the central government showed its reluctance, riots broke out in Chengtu. Troops were sent to put down the riots but had only partial success. On September 9 a demonstration gathered outside the city gates of Chengtu and demanded admission to see the viceroy. Many of the demonstrators were armed and the guards at the city gate offered to admit them if they would surrender their arms. The arms were surrendered and then the guards fired, killing and wounding a large number. At this the whole province flared up. Violence broke out at several points. Government troops were attacked and official buildings seized or destroyed. The government ordered a detachment of troops from Hankow to suppress the disorders, but while the troops were on the way more serious events were taking place in Hankow itself. On the merits of the issue in Szechuan the government was in the right. A system of individual provincial railways, each planned and built and conducted independently of the others, could not possibly function. But the point had passed where political issues could be determined on their merits.

News of the Szechuan disturbances and their cause had spread and the revolutionary societies and less organized groups everywhere sensed opportunity. In Canton there had been a rising in the spring, with some serious fighting, and seventy-two of the participants were captured and executed. More disturbances followed, increasing in tempo and intensity with the outbreaks in Szechuan. One of the more active revolutionary groups had long been plotting in Hankow. It had set up a workshop for making bombs in one of the foreign concessions there and on the night of October 9 one of the bombs accidentally exploded. There was an immediate investigation, the identity of the plotters was discovered, and several of them were rounded up and executed.

This acted as a spark. The next day a regiment guarding the viceroy's yamen in Wuchang, across the river from Hankow, mutinied. The mutineers forced their colonel, Li Yuan-hung, to take command. According to the story told at the time and not denied, they found him hiding under a bed and gave him a choice between acting as their leader or being shot forthwith. He chose to lead—and a few years later was president of the republic. There was now open revolt and it spread rapidly. Hankow, Wuchang, and the neighboring city of Hanyang, where the steel mills were, soon were in rebel hands. Four of the southwestern provinces declared their independence of the imperial government and were followed by nine other provinces. A provisional government was set up in Hankow under Li Yuan-hung, but the center soon passed to Shanghai, where revolutionary leaders were gathering under the asylum offered by the International Settlement. Shanghai became the seat of the new government under the leadership of Wu Ting-fang, a Cantonese who had been minister to the United States and was later to be minister of foreign affairs of the republic.

Peking at first was disturbed but not unduly frightened. With their usual lack of perception the Manchus did not recognize the full import of what was in the making. At the time of the outbreak in Hankow the National Assembly, which had been reconvened, was still sitting. It used the risings as a lever to pry more liberal concessions from the court. A constitution was quickly drafted and promulgated. It provided for a parliament, a cabinet responsible to the parliament, and compulsory promulgation of all laws passed by the parliament. The government then bestirred itself to put down the fast-growing rebellion. As a first step it sought to recall Yuan Shih-kai from his compulsory exile in his native place. Yuan, the "strong man" of the last years of the empress dowager's rule, had organized the nearest thing to a modern army but he had incurred the enmity of Prince Chun and was fortunate to get off with exile when Chun became regent. Prince Chun turned over the regency to Lung Yu, widow of the Emperor Kwang Hsu, and Yuan was asked to return and take command of a punitive expedition against the rebels, but he refused. On being urged he made conditions. He stipulated that he be given complete control of all the armed forces, free of any inter-ference from Peking. The court yielded and in mid-November Yuan became not only supreme commander but premier.

Yuan started south against the rebels and at first had little difficulty. The rebels were little more than an armed mob rather than an army and Yuan quickly recovered Hankow and Hanyang, but Wuchang re-mained in the rebels' hands, since the imperial forces lacked the ships to take them across the river. Nevertheless Yuan had the power to crush the rebels but for reasons then known only to himself hesitated to press for a decision. There was nothing mystical in his hesitation. He saw an opportunity to play the Manchus and the rebels against each other for purposes of his own. Neither side was strong enough to defeat the other decisively and Yuan could make capital of his position. While he pro-crastinated the rebels became stronger and in the artificially created stalemate Yuan himself suggested to the court that it start negotiations for a compromise.

The negotiations opened in Shanghai on December 17. The rebels were represented by Wu Ting-fang and Peking by Tang Shao-yi, another Cantonese who was a long-time subordinate and henchman of Yuan Shih-kai, though himself a man of distinctly progressive convictions. As a matter of fact, Tang's appointment as representative was suggested by Yuan. It was a strange proceeding for negotiations between enemies. The two Cantonese quickly came to the conviction that the Manchus would have to go and a republic succeed. Tang so reported to Peking. Yuan remained strangely (and disingenuously) silent. Sun Yat-sen, who had himself been in the United States raising funds when the rebellion broke out, returned to Shanghai at the end of December. He was im-mediately elected president of the provisional republican government, which was formally established in Nanking, one-time capital of the Ming emperors. Negotiations with Peking dragged on, but it was clear which way events were moving. A group of generals of the imperial army, undoubtedly not without intimations from Yuan Shih-kai, sent a memorial to Peking urging adoption of the republicans' terms. It was plain to Peking that it had no choice, and, although the accusation was not openly made, that Yuan was disloyal. The court submitted.

On February 12, Lung Yu, the regent, issued an edict of abdication, a pathetic document. "It is evident that the hearts of the majority of the people are in favor of a republican form of government," she said. The Manchus would cease to rule, but the imperial family would con-tinue to reside in its palaces in one part of the Forbidden City and re-ceive an annual grant of the equivalent of $2,000,000 for its mainte-nance. So it was agreed and the imperial family did remain in its palaces in the heart of the capital of the republic for some twenty years. It was another bizarre touch in a bizarre revolution. As a marginal note, however, it must be recorded that in the early days of the rising Manchu residents in several cities were mercilessly slaughtered by Chinese mobs.

Thus the republic was ushered in, beginning as inauspiciously and paradoxically as later it was to end. For Yuan Shih-kai's purposes had yet to be served. The republic had all the paraphernalia of republican government, but Yuan had the military power. By various manipulations to demonstrate his power, including a manufactured mutiny and a night of looting in Peking when a group of delegates of the republican government had come from Nanking to invite Yuan to go down there, he convinced the southern leaders that he could not and would not leave Peking and that against his opposition they and the republic could not long survive. Like the Manchus, the republican leaders read the signs accurately, and after another set of negotiations, which incidentally were as strange a proceeding as the first, Sun Yat-sen agreed to step down as president. On March 10, 1912, Yuan Shih-kai became provisional president of the republic and the capital was re-established in Peking. That, too, was a bizarre touch to a unique revolution.

Yuan Shih-kai had had his way, as he had planned, but not in all its fullness, as was to be revealed three years later.

CHAPTER XXIII

Japan Takes the Road to Empire

While China was entering on a new phase in its history, so in a less obviously dramatic way was Japan. Japan had defeated a great white Power, had won a foothold on the Asiatic continent, and had itself become a Great Power. How would it conceive its new role? How would it act in world affairs? The history of the Eastern Hemisphere would turn on that.

Its decision was not long in coming and soon after was evident to the whole world. There were two paths Japan could take into the future. The first was to do in East Asia what all the Great Powers had done as soon as they commanded the means—try to get possession or control over all the countries and principalities that were too weak to resist. Then it would enter the imperialistic race for mastery over the Asiatic continent, China in particular, hoping to win over the other contenders because it was nearer the goal. The other path Japan could choose was the direct opposite. It had itself barely escaped subjugation to the West, had done so by foresight, intelligent preparation, and high resolve. In doing so it had set an example to its still weak neighbors and, furthermore, having proved that an Eastern nation could save itself by its own efforts, it could take the lead in showing its neighbors how to do so. It could, in short, set itself up as protector of its part of the world against the aggressive West. It could, without formal verbal pronouncement, institute a kind of Monroe Doctrine for Asia—not interfering with such territorial possessions and political and economic privileges as the West already had but enjoining any more. At the same time it could help its neighbors. China above all, to follow its example. It had the technical ability, the experience, and in some measure the means to do so. It could take its compensation in political friendship and acceleration of the potentialities for trade with the continent. It could, in a word, make itself the leader of Eastern Asia, which would have proved an invaluable asset in the years to come.

Japan chose the first. There were unmistakable intimations as early as the Portsmouth Peace Conference, at which it insisted on taking over Russia's leasehold on the Liaotung Peninsula and the southern half of the Manchurian railway. Thereby it acquired Port Arthur and Dalny (then renamed Dairen) and a foothold on Chinese soil. Thus, too, it supplanted Russia as one of the Powers encroaching on Chinese territory and presumably having further designs on its independence. China, of course, was forced in a formal agreement to concede the transfer of Russian rights to Japan, with some additional rights that Russia had not had. To China therefore it made little difference whether it was Russia or Japan that it had to fear, and to future international relations, to the question whether there would be peace or war for supremacy over China, it also made little difference. It became evident, too, that Japan had supplanted Russia in the intention to close its part of Manchuria to the economic enterprise of other countries. Japan, then, had crossed a bridge over which there would be no returning until its representative signed the treaty of surrender in the presence of General Douglas MacArthur and other Allied commanders.

The treatment of Korea was even more indicative than Manchuria. The Treaty of Shimonoseki, which ended the China-Japan war in 1895, contained a formal pronouncement of Korea's independence. This was reaffirmed in the Nishi-Rosen Convention of 1898, in which Russia and Japan bound themselves not to infringe on Korea's political and territorial integrity. The treaty of Portsmouth, it will be remembered, included Russian recognition of Japan's paramount interests in Korea, and Japan at once made clear its construction of that provision. Even before the end of the war, however, it had left no doubt as to what it would do if it had a free hand in Korea. Simultaneously with the attack on Port Arthur it landed a military force in the port of Chemulpo and occupied Seoul. On February 23, 1904, before the war was a month old, a protocol was signed between Korea and Japan, under Japanese guns, of course, which laid the foundation for a protectorate. Although Japan once again affirmed Korean independence, it received the right to station troops at strategic points in the country in case of danger from a third Power and to give the Korean government "advice" on the proper conduct of its administration. In August this was expanded into an agreement by which Korea was to engage a Japanese subject as financial adviser and a national of another country (American, as it turned out) as diplomatic adviser. Also Japan was to be consulted before Korea concluded treaties or agreements with any other Power. Furthermore, the Anglo-Japanese alliance was revised in August, 1905, before the conclusion of peace. The most conspicuous change was in the omission of the reference in the earlier treaty to the independence of Korea.

The way being cleared, Japan proceeded to its goal. On November 17, two months after peace with Russia was concluded, Japan wrung from the helpless court at Seoul a convention by which it obtained control of Korea's foreign relations and the right to maintain a Resident in Seoul. The Koreans sought help from without, but in vain. The first treaty with the United States provided that the United States would extend its good offices if Korea had difficulties with another Power, but the Roosevelt administration did not construe the current situation as applicable, since the Korean government had itself acceded to the convention. The Resident, the same Marquis Ito who had negotiated the convention, took over in February, 1906, together with a large staff.

There was thus a dual government in Korea, one being Japanese. It was naturally the more important. Ito laid out a comprehensive scheme of governmental reforms, most of them necessary and beneficial to Korea, but the Koreans were resentful and therefore obstructive, and little progress was made. The unavowed deadlock that ensued, which could not have lasted long in any case, was broken by an incident in 1907. A mission of three Koreans, with the undoubted though unacknowledged sanction of the emperor, departed secretly for The Hague to lay before the International Court a protest against Japanese highhandedness. The Japanese retaliated sharply and quickly. The emperor was forced to step down in favor of his son and still another agreement was signed, this one in July, 1907, by which the Japanese Resident took substantive authority. His approval was to be necessary for all laws and important administrative measures, as well as the appointment of higher officers. He became the real ruler of Korea.

What was clearly foreshadowed then came to pass. In October, 1909, Marquis Ito was assassinated by a Korean in Harbin, in north Manchuria, where he had gone for a conference with a Russian representative. Japanese opinion was inflamed and after a due interval for the sake of appearances Japan made an end of the situation and of Korea. On August 22, 1910, Korea was annexed. What the Japanese had set as their end thirty years before they now obtained. And Japan became formally an imperialistic Power, imperialistic and on the march.

It was in Manchuria that Japan most clearly committed itself to imperialistic orthodoxy, participating in the purest imperialistic rites— division of prospective spoils by rivals both desiring the whole, suspicious of each other, but not yet ready to try conclusions. After some preliminary maneuvers, with France, Russia's ally, as go-between, Russia and Japan contracted a new agreement on July 30, 1907, which sought to make precise the future relations between them in East Asia.

There was a public agreement and another, kept secret, which really counted. Publicly they engaged themselves to respect the independence and integrity of China, which in the diplomatic lexicon of the time boded ill for China, as the fate of Korea testified. They also pledged themselves to join in maintaining the status quo in Eastern Asia, the status quo being left conveniently undefined. The secret agreement contained what really interested the two parties and brought them together. A line was drawn in Manchuria marking two spheres, Russia having the north and Japan the south. Neither would interfere in the sphere of the other in political and economic matters. Russia again recognized Japan's "special interests" in Korea, while Japan—this was new and significant—recognized Russia's special interests in Mongolia, thereby confirming the death sentence for both Korea and Mongolia and laying out a surgeon's plan for the further truncation of China. How completely Japan had adapted Western diplomacy!

The not quite acknowledged partnership of the two former enemies was reinforced in the next few years. One reason was China's evident concern that Manchuria was about to go the way of other territories at the extremities of the empire and to be permanently cut away. The new *rapprochement* between Russia and Japan—and nobody had any illusion that the public version of the treaty between them was the whole of it—raised the sound fear that the two main contenders for Manchuria were now working together instead of checking each other as before, from which it might be assumed that Manchuria was close to being lost to China. The Chinese therefore decided to push their own influence there by building railroads themselves, preferably with foreign capital, which would give other Powers a stake in maintaining the status quo. Other Powers, too, began to interest themselves in the development of Manchuria, mainly through railway construction. The British obtained from the Chinese a concession to build one line, although the contract was never fulfilled, partly because of Japanese objection. Also the United States intervened in Manchurian politics for the first time.

E. H. Harriman, the American railway magnate who had already built a rail empire in his own country, conceived the dream of a railway belt encircling the globe. After the Russo-Japanese war he made tenders for the purchase of the South Manchuria Railway. He was rebuffed, of course, but his interest had not faded. With Taft in the White House and Philander C. Knox as Secretary of State, dollar diplomacy became the guiding principle: the government shared Harriman's interest and actively engaged itself in Manchurian politics. From this time forward the international politics of Manchuria was railway politics. At least, railways became the tokens in the international struggle. With Willard

Straight, an American consul, as agent, an American banking group obtained a contract for a rail line from Chinchow in south Manchuria north to Aigun on the Siberian border, running through both Russian and Japanese spheres. In this contract a British company had a share.

This alone was enough to arouse the apprehensions of both Russia and Japan, but there was more. Secretary Knox conceived the idea of cutting through the whole net of rivalries in Manchuria by internationalizing and neutralizing the entire railway system of the area, with ownership vested in China but the capital and administration international. With an impetuosity that did more credit to his temperamental qualities than to his diplomatic acumen Secretary Knox communicated his scheme to the British government in November, 1909, without first sounding out all the interested parties. Sir Edward Grey, the Foreign Secretary, with a fine British instinct for diplomatic generalities, endorsed the principle but was lukewarm as to action. Interpreting approval in the abstract as assent in the concrete, Knox then formally sent the proposal to the Russian, Japanese, German, French, and Chinese governments. After consultations with each other the Russians and Japanese rejected it brusquely and with finality, simultaneously refusing to concede the right of the Anglo-American group to construct the Chinchow-Aigun line. Great Britain remained neutral, the others were noncommittal and Knox, left in unsplendid isolation, dropped his project. Considered in itself, it was a good idea. It might have led to the development of Manchuria without the rancors of international rivalry, for the benefit of all, and with China's position protected, since under a kind of international trusteeship Manchuria would be safe from alienation.

Russia and Japan now decided to close ranks against all interlopers in their private preserve. They moved to make their quasi alliance more explicit. There were more negotiations and in 1910 another treaty was concluded, also part of it public and the more important part secret. This agreement reaffirmed the division of spheres made in 1907 but went further than the pledge not to interfere with rights in the other's sphere. Now both declared, but in the secret treaty (which like other Russian secret treaties was exposed by the Communists after they took power), that if the interests of either in its sphere should be threatened (as for example by the Knox neutralization scheme, though that was not mentioned) the other would come to its support. If not an outright alliance, this at least was an alliance for specific purposes.

Still another agreement was concluded in 1912 which broadened the scope of the limited alliance by extending the spheres of influence. Inner Mongolia was now included in the area allocated to the "special interests" of the two parties, Russia getting a free hand in western Inner

Mongolia and Japan in eastern Inner Mongolia. Outer Mongolia, incidentally, had before been marked out by Russia for its exclusive purposes. Korea having been settled, Manchuria being in process of settlement, Mongolia was now designated for transactions of the same order. This was to be confirmed soon enough, though international events moved too rapidly for consummation in Mongolia. World War I intervened and interrupted the process—interrupted it, but did not put an end to it.

Seven short years had, at least to all appearances, worked a transmutation in the relations of the two countries. They had fought one of the most terrible wars since Waterloo, and in less than a decade had become partners. But since they were partners in the acquisition and distribution of loot, in hand and in prospect, the change in relation may have been external and temporary rather than genuine and lasting. And so it came to be revealed in a few more years. But Japan's role in the politics of East Asia was now unmistakable. The island Power was to shape forces and events in East Asia for a generation and ultimately to spread ruin there.

CHAPTER XXIV

Japanese Constitutionalism as a Façade

Japan, then, had entered on the path of empire. What, if anything, was there in its development in the preceding years to bring it to that decision?

The first thing to be said is that anything else would have been surprising, in light of Japan's history, institutions, spirit, and scheme of collective morality (its conception of public right and wrong). Given the past, it could hardly have been expected to weigh the two courses open to it in an even balance and then plight itself to the course inclined toward its future good. What it decided to do and did was in its blood, in its habit of thought and feeling. Nothing in the years between the war with China and the annexation of Korea was required to give it the direction it took.

As has already been explained, the Japanese always had been a militaristic people, a warrior people, revering the art of war as the highest and noblest of man's activities. Violence was the most natural and logical means to attain an end. A latent expansionism had also manifested itself periodically—notably with the invasion of Korea at the end of the sixteenth century and immediately after the Restoration with the cry to take Korea and Formosa. Also authoritarianism, a feudal, military authoritarianism, was the only mode of existence experienced by it, familiar to it, and respected. One more thing entered, of more recent origin. That was the success that efforts at expansion had already enjoyed. The war with China had been won with ease, with little sacrifice of blood and with considerable material gain in the form of territory and a money indemnity. The war with Russia had entailed great sacrifice, of both blood and treasure, but yielded an even higher reward, territorially, politically, and psychologically. Surely there was every reason to believe that the way of conquest was not hard but satisfying. Finally, there was the stimulus of both example and fear. Every other Power was expanding by aggression everywhere, especially in Asia. As long as there was expansion in Asia Japan lay under threat. Offense was the best defense. Japan could most surely come through if it forestalled other Powers in the part of Asia nearest it. That it set out to do.

Meanwhile what had been happening in Japan's internal affairs? What had been the development in its political and social structure? As we have seen, industrialization was well under way. The foundation of the social structure of an industrial system had been laid by the 1890's and the physical attributes of an industrial society were being acquired. A constitution had been promulgated—handed down, rather—by the emperor in 1889, providing at least the externals of a parliamentary system. How had it worked in twenty years? What had it accomplished, what changes brought about in the Japanese scheme of relations?

In accordance with the constitution the first national elections were held in July, 1890, to choose 300 members of the House of Representatives of the Diet. The House of Peers, with 250 members, was composed of members of the nobility, with a small group of men appointed by the emperor for distinguished service or as being among the highest taxpayers. The election was a momentous departure in the history of the Japanese people and aroused considerable enthusiasm. As everywhere when the right of suffrage is first granted, the initial response was high and fell off later. In the first election 95 per cent of those eligible voted. This does not signify as much as appears, since the right of suffrage was sharply restricted. One of the qualifications was the payment of at least 15 yen ($7.50) in direct national tax, which, small as it seems, excluded most of the population. Out of 40,000,000 only 450,000 had the right to vote—one in 90. If this was representative government it was limited representation—representation of the wealthy.

The first Prime Minister was Aritomo Yamagata, who, as already has been told, was the dominant military figure for the generation after the Restoration and who was now one of the most powerful figures in the nation. Powerful as he was and carrying all the prestige he did, he nevertheless found himself impeded by obstructions that were not anticipated when the constitution was written and for which he and others of his stamp were not prepared. The Diet may not have had much power and its functions were purposely limited by the makers of the constitution; but it could do one thing: it could make trouble and it did. Those in the small ruling caste who had believed they could rule with the imperious arbitrariness to which they were accustomed were quickly disillusioned. The elected lower house was clamorous and obstreperous, obstructing something to prove that it could and enjoying the prerogative. It was also hostile to the government. It could not exercise decision but it could act as a sounding board and stir up public opinion, such public opinion as there was. It had a certain nuisance value. And this must be said: for all the limitations on representative government that obtained, notwithstanding the preservation of power of decision in the small oligarchy of the uppermost classes, the oligarchy was never again to have the smooth sailing it traditionally had had in Japanese history.

The political parties were the vehicle of opposition. Perhaps it is better to say the so-called political parties, since they had small relation to the party system developed in the West. They were rather associations of a few important personages and their henchmen banded together to preserve or make official careers or forward some concrete material interest. Political conviction, principles of government, divided them to a certain extent, but these were highly malleable. There were certain lines of division in the country, lines of interest which the parties reflected in a general way but only in a general way and with strange shiftings and permutations. There were the two major clans, the Choshu and Satsuma, with whom the old Kyoto court nobility were usually allied. They had brought about the Restoration and meant to keep power in their own hands. There were two other great clans—the Hizen and Tosa—smaller than the Choshu and Satsuma and inclined to challenge their dominion. There was also a number of minor clans, jealous of the large ones and desirous of a share in the perquisites of public office. Many of the less important samurai of these clans went into minor posts in the government service after the Restoration and later played a large role in the permanent bureaucracy. To these must be added two groups—the owners of land holdings who were not of the daimyo but had grown wealthy in the declining years of the Tokugawa shogunate and the heads of the larger mercantile houses that had developed at the same time. Later were to come the new industrial plutocrats, those who had got in on the ground floor of the first manufacturing enterprises. All of these groups, except the four major clans, sought to have their interests represented in parties, though the connection was sometimes hard to trace.

The parties, such as they were, had been formed some years before the constitution went into effect. There was the Jiyuto, which could roughly be called liberal, though in a somewhat loose construction of that adjective. There was the Kaishinto, meaning, again roughly, constitutional progressive party. Later came the Teiseito or constitutional imperialist party, standing for a strong central government. All these parties were active in the first Diet, the liberals most vociferously.

Yamagata was in no mood for what he could only consider antics and while not unwilling to let the parties indulge in them, he had no intention of letting them interfere with the process of government. Policy and administration were reserved to the elite. He instructed prefectural governors and other ranking administrative officers to exercise their functions in accordance with precedent, rules, and their own judgment, always checked by the central government in Tokyo. The parties and their spokesmen and activities were to be ignored. It was more easily said than done, in spite of the stringent legislation designed to keep the irreverent in bounds—the press law, the law restricting public meetings and similar enactments in restraint. Both in the Diet and in the localities the organized opposition carried on its obstructive tactics and its public protests. The focal point was the budget, the one subject on which the Diet had some voice, for the lower house had to approve a new budget. Yet, as has been previously mentioned, approval was not indispensable, since if it was not granted the budget of the preceding year continued in effect for another year, enabling the government to carry on.

The budget, then, became a symbol, and the Diet made itself so objectionable that Yamagata, unaccustomed to such proceedings, resigned in disgust. He was succeeded by Marquis Matsukata, also one of the early makers of the Restoration. Thus was established a precedent that was to hold for years. Yamagata was of the Choshu, which had its stronghold in the army. Matsukata was of the Satsuma, which had its stronghold in the navy. For years the Choshu and Satsuma were to alternate at the helm of the government. It was an unofficial allotment of power challenged by lesser clans, by some of the bureaucracy, and later by certain commercial and financial groups, but it held nevertheless. Matsukata came off little better than Yamagata. The lower house was no less obstreperous, again nominally over the budget, and in a burst of impatience Matsukata dissolved the Diet, an unfortunate precedent which was subsequently followed.

Another election was called for in 1892 and now the clan leaders set out to build their political fences. They had already in the first sessions resorted to a stratagem that was to become standard practice in Japanese politics. This was the liberal use of a slush fund. Many of the recalcitrants in the lower house could be mollified by generous bribes, but not enough to be effective in the major disputes between the lower house and the cabinet and thus relieve the latter of its perplexities. The strategy was widely employed in the election of 1892, voters now being the beneficiaries. Violence was even more extensively employed. Orders went out from the government in Tokyo to prefectural governors and to the police, then as later under direct control from the capital, to obstruct the parties and to bring about the defeat of their candidates. The orders were carried out. Voters were intimidated. Police broke up political meetings and tried to prevent voters from going to the polls. Police and mobs clashed and serious riots broke out in various places. Nevertheless the opposition parties won a majority of the seats. The new Diet met and the same old wrangling set in, with the budget as symbol, and Matsukata gave up, being succeeded by Ito. The atmosphere remained unchanged and the Diet again was dissolved. Yet government went on, since the essence of authority was in the executive, a closely bound, compact group that knew its own mind, was sure of what it wanted and got it, though with annoyance.

The war with China called a truce in the internal political struggle— that may have had something to do with unleashing it—but afterward the same process was resumed. Then a new progressive party was formed under the leadership of Count Shigenobu Okuma, one of the forward-looking younger samurai in 1868 who even later in life actually did have some progressive ideas, certainly some understanding of what representative government meant. Party organization then became a little more regularized, as did relations between the executive and the parties. The men who generally controlled the executive resigned themselves to deferring in a measure to the parties, especially in the matter of appointments, which naturally tamed the parties more than concession on principles. Also in the rivalry among those in the upper strata, party support had now become something of an asset, which gave the various parties bargaining power. The more liberal and progressive groups tended to coalesce, at first into what was called the Kenseito, while a more conservative group formed the Seiyukai under the leadership of Ito.

In 1898 there was a mild attempt at party government when a cabinet was installed with Ito and Itagaki of the Kenseito as its heads, but it was short-lived. Later something approximating a two-party system began to form, the Seiyukai, nominally more conservative, and the Kenseikai, nominally more liberal, being the two parties. The designations are somewhat forced. Neither was definitely liberal or conservative. (Here one writing for publication in the United States must be careful lest he be patronizing and pharisaical; what has just been said about Japanese parties in 1900 might be said by a Japanese about American parties in 1950.) The Seiyukai spoke on the whole for the large landholding interests, the Kenseikai for the industrialists and financiers. It is revealing that the voice of big business should be described as liberal, but in the Japanese setting this is not wholly out of place. Those who had to do with large-scale modern enterprise, who perforce had more contact and association with the outer world, knew that the old feudal authoritarianism hardly comported with the time and spirit of that world. They were not democratic and they were not liberal; on the contrary, in the traditional political lexicon they were conservative—conservative with a plutocratic tinge. But they did understand that the institutions of the time had to be compromised with in more than name.

Outside the party system stood the permanent bureaucracy and, more important, the military. Those two, however, were often closely allied and at some periods indistinguishable from each other. But over the years the bureaucracy developed as a solid core of civil servants, who administered, no matter what groups exercised the highest titular functions, and as administrators had an enormous influence on government. They were devoted and efficient—some of them open to corruption, most of them not. But in the nature of politics everywhere they served things as they were, complied with the aims of those who desired things as they were. Essentially they buttressed the established order.

The army and navy constituted an organ outside the body politic. That was their prerogative. The constitution decreed that it should be so and it remained so until after 1945. The ways by which this was assured have already been discussed. It will be recalled that since the emperor was commander-in-chief and theoretically had direct control of the armed forces, the ministers of war and navy had to have direct access to him and therefore could go over the heads of the cabinet and Diet. Also by an imperial ordinance on May, 1900, it was decreed that only a general or lieutenant-general on the active list could be Minister of War and only an admiral or vice-admiral on the active list could be Minister of the Navy. For a time officers of the same rank on the retired list could serve in cabinets but only for a time. The effect of this is obvious. Whenever the two armed services were displeased at government policy they could overthrow a cabinet by resigning, since discipline within the services was so tight that no officer would accept civil office unless sanctioned by the highest officers of his service. In the same way no new premier charged with forming a cabinet could do so unless he submitted in advance to the armed services, since otherwise nobody would accept the portfolio of war or navy. Therefore the army and navy could normally get all the appropriations they wanted, regardless of the state of the country's finances, for otherwise they would bring about the existing cabinet's downfall. So also they could lay down foreign policies, as was proved in 1931, when they embarked on the conquest of Manchuria in spite of the reluctance, if not active opposition, of the cabinet, and again in 1937, when they launched the invasion of China, also despite the reluctance, if not the active opposition, of the cabinet. The army and navy in this way constituted a government within a government, independent of all control save by the emperor, who almost never intervened, since he always deemed it politic to take their "advice." The historic exception came in 1945, when the emperor pronounced the decision to surrender, though the army—but not the navy—wanted to go on fighting, however hopeless was further resistance to the American forces.

One other extraconstitutional organ must be taken into account. This was the Genro or body of Elder Statesmen. Since the cabinet was responsible to the emperor and not to the Diet the frequent cabinet changes raised difficult problems. How would the new premier be chosen? The emperor was supposed to be above the battle and, being kept in seclusion from the life of his people, usually was outside if not above it. There had to be some device to help him to decide. This was provided by the Genro, a group of men chosen without fixed procedure or any rules at all. They were usually distinguished elderly men who had held high position —as prime minister, cabinet member, in the armed services, or in diplomacy. Usually they became members of the Genro only after they were no longer in active public life. If a cabinet resigned the Genro met to decide who should be the next prime minister. Naturally they chose one of their own sort, one whose outlook, attitude, and convictions they approved. They made their recommendation to the emperor, who seldom rejected it. This procedure continued until World War II, when Prince Saionji, the only surviving Genro—the more recent statesmen were not deemed qualified for the status or the usage was fading—was always consulted on cabinet changes, although he was more than ninety years old. Since he was too feeble to move about easily his secretary would travel between Tokyo and his country place to confer. He would send back his suggestions. They were not always followed as rigidly as the Genro's recommendations had been before, but they still exercised great influence. It need hardly be said that the Genro were beyond the reach of the official government structure or public opinion. If not, too, a government within a government, they were an organ of government outside the government.

The new big business has been referred to. This had made long strides between 1890 and 1910, in part because of the two wars. The indemnity levied on China had given the country something to work on. War orders had been a stimulus to the growth of manufacturing and trade as always. As everywhere, industrialization, once established, advanced by geometric progression. The beginning of railroads, telegraphs, modern banks, and key industries, with government subsidies to accelerate their establishment and growth, has already been told. By the end of the nineteenth century the results could be seen. As in all newly industrializing countries production of textiles came first. The making of clothing by the machine is the easiest to learn and it satisfies the demand for one of man's elemental needs. In 1895 there were 600,000 spindles in operation; ten years later there were 1,400,000. Production of cotton yarn increased proportionately. Between 1890 and 1900 the production of raw silk doubled. In 1887 there were 642 miles of railway in operation; twenty years later there were seven times as many. In 1890, 30 steamships with a tonnage of 4,291 had been built and in 1910 construction had risen to 93 with a tonnage of 72,000.

Manufacturing centers were springing up in different parts of the country, smaller in scale but not different in kind from those to be found in the West. The main lines of activity were textiles, metallurgy, machinery and tools, ceramics and glassware, chemicals, lumber and woodworking, printing, food and drink. Industrial growth was reflected in foreign trade. In 1890 the total value of imports and exports was 137,000,000 yen; in 1900 it was 490,000,000 yen; in 1910 it was 922,000,000—a sevenfold increase in twenty years. Japan was still in an economy of light industry, producing mainly consumer goods, and was to remain so until World War I; but it was an industrial country nevertheless, in process of full incorporation into the twentieth-century world economy. The social results were not fully visible until after World War I, but they could already be detected. Perhaps since it reflected all the characteristics of the early nineteenth-century industrial economy rather than the twentieth, the social effects were to become more easily recognizable. For it still had all the evils of early industrialism, those which disfigured, if not debased, early nineteenth-century England, Germany, and the United States until ameliorated by the newly awakened social consciousness in the middle of the nineteenth century. At any rate Japan was more fully incorporated into the twentieth-century economy than into the twentieth-century political system and social and political thought.

One effect of industrialization was not only clear but conspicuous. As in every newly industrializing country the population increased with production, in Japan probably more rapidly than production because of improved medical care. Between 1880 and 1890 the population of Japan increased from 36,649,000 to 39,902,000; by 1900 it had soared to 43,847,000; by 1910 it had reached 49,184,000. Thus the population had grown by more than a third in thirty years in a tiny country of which only one-fifth was arable. This was later to have political consequences, internal and international. For Japan was to use population pressure to justify its expansion, whatever the method, even if accomplished by military invasion. The validity of this argument as a justification will be examined later.

Japan had acquired one other attribute of a country which has both won international status and entered into modernity. It had achieved juridical equality. The treaties by which Japan was opened, like the treaties by which China was opened, put definite limitations on Japan's sovereignty. The tariff was fixed by convention and could be changed only by new treaties with all the Powers. Also foreign residents in Japan had extraterritorial rights and could be tried only in their own courts under their own laws. Galling to any people in any circumstances, this rankled the more bitterly in the Japanese as their country became stronger. As early as the 1870's they began strenuous efforts to free themselves of the encumbrances, pointing out for one thing that the limitations on the tariff imposed handicaps on their economic development. They received short shrift from the principal Powers, in part because the compulsory tariff rates—5 per cent ad valorem—worked to the advantage of countries that wanted to increase their exports to Japan. The United States alone was sympathetic and agreed to give Japan tariff autonomy if the other Powers acceded. The other Powers did not. On extraterritoriality there was no offer of concessions. It was said that Japan's administration of justice would first have to come up to the standards observed in the West. This argument had some merit.

The Japanese pressed on with determination and feelings ran high after repeated rebuffs. Negotiations with the Powers were almost continuous through the 1880's but without success. Not until 1897—significantly, not until after Japan had shown that it had military power— were the treaties ratified by which foreign restrictions were annulled. Extraterritoriality was to end in 1899, but full control by Japan of its tariffs did not go into effect until 1911.

Japan was a great state and a modern one. Its mode of life was undergoing transformation. But the distribution of power within, the motive force that propelled it, and the spirit that gave form to its actions had changed but little. It was Western on the surface, but on the surface only. Deep within it was martial and authoritarian.

CHAPTER XXV

Fiasco of the Chinese Republic

It was a fateful combination of circumstances, one destined to change the face of the Eastern world and the direction of its development, that just as Japan set out on the path of conquest China began sliding into its lowest depths for centuries. It was a sardonic paradox that this should befall China when it had resolved that it, too, would make for itself a place in the new world with the strength, dignity, and status that it had had in the old. For the republic, symbol of its resolve, marked the last stage in its descent. The republic began inauspiciously, as has been seen, continued farcically, and ended ignominiously.

Yuan Shih-kai's accession to the presidency might alone have been taken as the death knell of the republic. Yuan may have had some modern ideas. Certainly he had no more tolerance for continued Manchu rule than most educated Chinese and he knew that China could no longer continue its old institutions and practices. But he had little understanding of what a republic meant and no patience with what he did understand. Western military knowledge, Western military skill, Western administrative methods—these were desirable enough; but voice of the people in government, choice of the head of the state periodically by ballot, a check on the executive by an elected body made up of men with no direct responsibility—to his mind that made no sense for China and also was not to his taste. Most of all, it did not comport with his personal ambitions. And with his extraordinary skill in manipulation and intrigue he set about to circumvent it.

The issue was drawn quickly. The National Council, sitting in Nanking since the republic was initiated and dominated by Southerners and republican advocates, drew up a provisional constitution in March, 1912, before moving to Peking. By the constitution the president was subordinated to the legislative body in all important functions. This was in accordance with the political theory of the members and followed from their recognition of Yuan Shih-kai's ambition and their determination to curb it. A parliament was to be elected under laws to be drafted by the council, but before it was elected a temporary council, composed of five representatives of each province, would sit. The cabinet was to be appointed by the president, subject to the council's approval. The council also had to give its assent to all important executive acts such as treaties, finance, and major administrative changes. This left little independent power to the president, and it could have been expected that Yuan would chafe under the restrictions.

The issue was joined with little delay. In April, 1913, a parliament elected under the law drafted by the National Council assembled. Having been returned under the auspices of the Nanking group, this was a fairly homogeneous body. The majority was of the Southern, radical, ardently republican wing, now under the banner of the Kuomintang (Nationalist party), an amalgamation of a number of like-minded factions around the core of the Tung Meng Hui, Sun Yat-sen's original revolutionary party. In name, though not in principles or ideals, the Kuomintang survived until after the Communists came to power in 1949. The Kuomintang was in 1913 homogeneous in conviction as well as allegiance. It was bent on keeping Yuan in his place. Yuan was equally bent on subduing the parliament or putting it where it could do no harm.

The first break came on finances. The revolution and the civil war had left the government disorganized in both administration and revenue. Raising additional troops and fighting had increased expenditures, while receipts had decreased because of the fighting and administrative confusion. It was necessary first of all to pay the troops or at least feed them. They were getting restive and some already were out of hand. Tang Shao-yi, Yuan's first prime minister, who had negotiated with the Southern rebels in 1911 and settled on the republic, made the rounds of the legations asking for emergency financial help to avert disaster. He was successful in getting small sums from time to time to tide the government over but this was a stop-gap arrangement, satisfying neither China nor the foreign governments nor the foreign banks which had to make the advances. The question then arose of a large loan to see the new regime through what was believed to be a transitional stage. This brought up the old question of international finance in China, accompanied by all the international political rivalries. It also sharpened the conflict between Yuan Shih-kai and parliament.

The four banking syndicates—British, German, French, and American —which had joined in the proposed loans for railway construction (the projects that precipitated the Hankow uprising and the downfall of the Manchus) had since then made formal arrangements for collective action. They founded what became known as the consortium, the object being to make all loans to China jointly, thus eliminating international financial competition and the political conflict that such competition was sure to generate. Insofar as that object could be advanced, the consortium was a healthy and constructive departure from the traditional ways of diplomacy in the Far East, but for China it carried certain dangers. It meant that China would have to deal with a monopoly; no longer would it have the advantage of stimulating competitive bidding for its financial favors to enable it to drive a better bargain. It would thus be at the mercy of combined international finance and diplomacy, especially after the Russians and Japanese had been admitted into the consortium. But the Chinese had no choice and therefore approached the Six-Power group for a large loan for purposes of reorganization. They had first tried to circumvent the consortium by signing a contract for a separate loan of £10,000,000 from an independent Anglo-Belgian syndicate, but this was frustrated, partly by the British, through their influence in the world's money markets, and partly by the consortium itself, which informed the Chinese government that it would get no money from it unless the other loan was cancelled. The Chinese government was forced to yield.

Yuan Shih-kai then opened negotiations with representatives of the consortium. The negotiations were stubbornly fought, since the consortium's members had already agreed that no loans were to be made to China without supervision of the branches of the government whose revenues were pledged as security. To this supervision the Chinese strenuously objected, especially now when the men who had overthrown Manchu rule were conscious of the prerogatives of sovereignty and the foreign encroachments on it. There was justice in both positions. Without a measure of supervision it was highly doubtful whether the security for loans would be sound, whether the revenues pledged would not be wasted in inefficiency or diverted for domestic political ends or trickled away in corruption. As a matter of fact foreign control of the Maritime Customs had not only assured the service of China's foreign loans but a surplus for general administrative expenses. On the other hand, foreign supervision, even with good results, not only infringed on China's sovereignty but laid the country at the mercy of the Powers if they on their part had ulterior motives—a contingency not unlikely, as experience had shown. The Powers were adamant, however, and China submitted. A loan was contracted for £25,000,000, secured by the revenue of the Salt Gabelle, a government monopoly, which was put under foreign supervision with a Briton as inspector-general. The agreement was signed in April, 1913. Before its signature there was a sensational

American repercussion. President Woodrow Wilson, who had just assumed office, announced that the American government would no longer
support the American banking group in the consortium. He gave as
his reason that the consortium's conditions were an unwarranted interference in China's administrative independence and therefore contravened American policy in China. The American bankers then withdrew from the consortium and had no part in the Reorganization Loan,
as it was called.

The repercussion in Chinese politics was even greater. The loan in-
furiated the Kuomintang, which saw clearly—more clearly than the
foreigners—that the loan proceeds would go to strengthening Yuan's
hold on the government as well as to reorganizing government. Yuan's
objects were only too obvious, and the Kuomintang was later proved right
when Yuan so used the proceeds. With them he built up a military force
that was at his bidding for his purposes. It was with this foreboding
that representatives of the Kuomintang in the parliament called on the
legations and pleaded with them not to sanction the loan. They also
warned that it violated the provisional constitution unless it was approved
by the parliament, and since it never would be approved by the parliament it would not be legally binding.

The loan was made nevertheless, and Yuan was enabled to consolidate his hold. This was wholly in keeping with the form and spirit
of relations between Great Powers and China or, for that matter, between Great Powers and all weak and undeveloped countries. The fact
is the Great Powers have always supported reactionary elements in such
countries, especially when those elements gave promise of being strong
enough to ensure stability. The desire for stability anywhere is unexceptionable, but something more was usually sought—stability plus
pliancy. The reactionary elements are able to maintain order and keep
down dissidence. They are also willing to give the foreign Powers what
they want politically as states and what their nationals want economically
as individuals. They are strong enough to prevent internal challenge but
not so strong as to be able to resist foreign pressure. Essentially they are
proconsuls or Residents General for one or more foreign Powers, taking the profits from unchallenged rule over their own people as compensation for subjecting their country to foreign exploitation.

Here again is the note of pharisaism that makes the whole history of
the relations of East and West, of the weak and strong, in the nineteenth century so hard on the squeamish stomach. Always the West,
when taking over by superior force a weak country, whether in Asia
or Africa or anywhere else, has said with high rhetorical piety that it
was doing so only temporarily and for the good of the people taken

over. It has said that whenever the country would awaken, start on the path of progress, and set its house in order, the West would withdraw and leave the country in full exercise of its independence. But whenever a modern-minded group in such a country did resolve to do just what the West said it wanted and did make an effort to take control in the country for that purpose, the Western states in power have almost by reflex sprung to the support of reactionaries bent on keeping things as they were. The Western Powers' desire to maintain easy access to profitable pickings among the helpless was not the only explanation for the action. It followed from an obscurantism about nonwhite countries as blind and bigoted as the obscurantism of the most unenlightened among any nonwhite people.

As between Chinese mandarins and Western officials dealing with China there was little to choose in point of lack of perception and backward outlook. For any nonwhite people, leaders of the West had one universal remedy, the only remedy: the "strong man." We preached democracy for all, but for weak countries—weak countries we wanted to dominate—we had only one political theory: one strong man must rule. It was starkly visible at the end of the nineteenth century and later that strong men were losing their grip everywhere and that wherever they ruled, instability and disorder were increasing; yet we could see no solution except another strong man, and the strong man we backed, against all the evidence, against all the pleas of the enlightened among the native people, against common sense, if not moral sense. And everywhere, incidentally, as time proved, we failed. The strong men we set up crumbled and were swept away, and the people over whom we set them turned against us. So almost instinctively in China the West supported Yuan Shih-kai, with moral support or financial support or both. It had done the same with the empress dowager in 1901, when it could have thrown its weight to the side of the kind of men who had advocated the reforms of 1898, but instead the West had only patronizing scorn for "new-fangled notions" and let the dowager and her politically and intellectually primitive court clique return to power.

Yuan Shih-kai, then, was backed with money and more than money, in consonance with the West's misguided policy, and the results, as we shall see, were as might have been expected.

The loan exacerbated the already rancorous relations between Yuan Shih-kai and the Kuomintang opposition. Yuan was steadily consolidating his power, putting his trusted henchmen in civil offices and shifting the command of troops so that generals of doubtful loyalty to himself were replaced by men who would do his bidding. Unable to resist him in these maneuvers, the Kuomintang fought back on every question that arose in parliament, sometimes on matters of little weight, sometimes on unimportant questions of procedure and constitutional forms and phrases. The Kuomintang's opposition, it should be said, was feckless and fiddling. It obstructed for the sake of obstruction, raised trivial issues, made no constructive proposals and apparently had none to make. It was doctrinaire and unreal and, besides, driven to desperation by its admitted helplessness. In part this was justified, but the result was to paralyze government, and not only supporters of Yuan Shih-kai became impatient. The Reorganization Loan drew the Kuomintang's bitterest attacks. It called the loan illegal and openly threatened to repudiate it. Even if the threat was idle, it sharpened antagonism. Another issue was the new permanent constitution that was being drafted. The Kuomintang majority in the drafting body was determinedly writing in provisions to tie the president's hands and doing so, it should be said, in deference to abstract political formulas that were remote from Chinese social and political conditions. But this was enough to put Yuan Shih-kai on his guard and to make him conclude that there could be no compromise or truce. Either he or the extreme republican and liberal faction would have to go.

Yuan, never squeamish in his methods, resorted to direct action to rid himself of his opponents. In March, 1913, Sung Chiao-jen, one of the Kuomintang leaders and one of the ablest and highest-minded of them, was assassinated in Shanghai on his way south from Peking. There was little doubt that Yuan had instigated the assassination. This inflamed the Kuomintang and many others who were not its partisans. The Kuomintang, too, decided on direct action and in midsummer of 1913 an armed rising broke out, again on the call of Sun Yat-sen. A number of provinces rallied to it, declaring their independence of the Peking regime, but it was an ill-advised move nevertheless, premature and hopeless, like so many of Sun Yat-sen's impulsive adventures. The rebels may have had popular support in the educated class, but Yuan had the troops and the arms. The revolt was put down with ease. Sun Yat-sen and many of his principal followers fled to Japan, Singapore, or other foreign parts, but a much larger number were caught and punished with draconian ferocity. Life meant little to Yuan where his enemies were concerned, even Chinese enemies.

This broke the back of resistance in the parliament, which carried on in desultory fashion. Yuan decided to have himself elected permanent president and on October 10, 1913, anniversary of the Hankow rising, was duly elected, with Li Yuan-hung, commander of the first rebel troops in Hankow, as vice-president. Threats, coercion, and bribes procured enough votes for Yuan. Having thus obtained a free hand, he proceeded to clear himself of even the weak shackles that had restrained him. A few weeks after the election he ordered the Kuomintang dissolved on grounds of seditious acts and a few weeks after that dissolved the parliament itself. The permanent constitution meanwhile had been drafted but he soon emasculated that. Now he really was free.

Now, too, he could proceed to fulfill the purposes that he had had in mind since the revolution broke out and that had guided him in the first fighting as the Manchus' commander, in his curious reluctance to press for a decisive victory, in the negotiations that led to the Manchus' abdication, in the manufactured mutiny that brought the capital of the republic to his stronghold in Peking, and in his election as provisional president in place of Sun Yat-sen. But he acted cautiously, patiently, and with careful preparation, as was his custom. For a while he ruled according to his will but under the semblance of republican government. There was public order, since the opposition had been crushed, and outwardly normal conditions had returned. The few who were deemed to be potentially dangerous, who might serve as nuclei of a new opposition, were suppressed, some by threat and some by more violent methods. The expression of critical opinions was fraught with danger and seldom attempted except in the asylum of foreign concessions and settlements. It was a dictatorship under a republican guise, though a dictatorship of an older order, without the barbarous recidivism of later years.

Then toward the end of 1915 Yuan concluded that his hour had struck. Professor Frank J. Goodnow, a distinguished American scholar and authority on constitutional law who had been engaged as adviser to the Chinese government, was asked to write a memorandum on long-range, fundamental problems of government, especially those applicable to the Chinese state. Innocent in Chinese politics and not knowing what was afoot, he complied. In an abstract and theoretical discussion of forms of government and without any thought of application to contemporaneous China he wrote that for countries with a past such as China's a constitutional monarchy might be better than a republic. Yuan seized his opportunity. Here was a distinguished American scholar, neutral in Chinese political affairs, and these were his objective conclusions. What more respectable in a country which had always exalted political philosophy, and what auspices could be more respectable for Yuan's earthy and concrete ends?

On this happy conjuncture there was formed and publicly announced an organization with the innocent name of the Chou An Hui—the Society for the Preservation of Peace. By an equally happy coincidence the Chou An Hui on serious deliberation concluded that only a monarchy could preserve peace and that only Yuan Shih-kai could lead such a monarchy. With a spontaneity not surprising telegrams then began pouring in to Peking urging Yuan to fulfill his duty to his country and become emperor. This was toward the close of 1915. Like Caesar, Yuan spurned the blandishments and refused to accept the Crown, for was not China a republic and he its first president? The urging turned to pleading in still more telegrams, and still Yuan was firm. But while he was sternly refusing, everybody in Peking knew that the Throne Room, where the emperors took the seat of the Son of Heaven, was being hastily redecorated and made ready for another ascension. At length Yuan yielded to the country-wide supplications and, unlike Caesar, announced that he would become emperor—as everybody already knew he would. The Chinese may not yet have become politically modern, but in the devices of lobbying, as in all political stratagems, they were adept and always had been. New political institutions we might be able to teach them but not the tricks of politics.

It was all settled. The monarchy was to be resumed. Yuan Shih-kai was to found a new dynasty. But there was a profound miscalculation, one for which neither Yuan nor anyone else was prepared. Yuan believed that as from time immemorial an edict had only to be issued and that was all. The people would obey. The foreign residents, whether ministers in legations or bankers or traders or correspondents, would also accept all that passed; as was usual in Eastern countries, they would be unable to perceive anything not on the surface, since they got their opinions from each other and did not trouble to ask the Chinese. What did the Chinese people care who ruled them? So they said in their dispatches to their governments, their home offices, and their newspapers. Besides, it was all for the best. There would be law and order and a strong man, the first desideratum of foreigners in Eastern countries —in fact their only political theory for such countries. But time immemorial was no more. Too many strange new winds had blown from the unknown quarter of the West, and too much without precedent had happened. Liang Chi-chao, the philosopher, one of the two leaders of the unsuccessful reform movement of 1898 and himself a monarchist and more conservative than liberal, wrote at this time:

"We carve wood or mold clay in the image of a person and call it a god. Place it in a beautiful temple, and seat it in a glorious shrine and the people will worship it and find it mysteriously potent. But suppose some insane person should pull it down, tread it under foot and throw it into a dirty pond and suppose someone should discover it and carry it back to its original sacred abode, you will find the charm has gone from it." Therefore Liang, though a monarchist, was opposed to the restoration.

It turned out as he said. There was no articulate protest, if only because of the suppression that lay over the few newspapers of any consequence. But the intelligentsia were shocked and in no mood to be supine. The Kuomintang, despite its shortcomings and its penchant for phrases and its irresponsibility in action, did include the more enlightened younger men in the country. That class had worked too hard for a complete break from the autocracy and its dead forms and cared too deeply about what it had worked for to accept meekly the nullification of all it had already won. There was a revulsion from the cynicism of Yuan Shih-kai's maneuvers. Leaders in various parts of the country began to communicate and there was a call for action, silent but compelling.

The first response in action came from the Southwest, where Tsai Ao, a young military commander in Yunnan Province, issued a circular telegram to all the provinces protesting against the restoration of the monarchy and declaring Yunnan's secession from the Peking government. There was widespread and overwhelming approval, now publicly expressed. Chinese public opinion has always been inarticulate, though less so since World War I, and therefore foreign observers have always assumed that it did not exist. It manifests itself among the educated and politically conscious and then radiates outward from them to the mass of the people. Public opinion was now registered, unmistakably and vigorously. Yuan Shih-kai had outraged the country. The people may not have had a positive desire for a republic but they did not want a monarchy. Mainly they did not want one brought about as this one was. Yuan still may have had the troops, but it was all he had, and now that was not enough. Province after province followed the lead of Yunnan and broke with Peking. Yuan did not dare to use force. In a few weeks he yielded without even a show of resistance. In March he issued a mandate cancelling the monarchy, expressing his penitence and promising to recall the parliament and to establish a government responsible to it. And in June he died, humiliated and embittered. A dictator had been swept away without the firing of a shot, simply by the sheer force of unorganized and inchoate public opinion in a country where there never had been a system of government in which public opinion played a part. It was a dramatic coup in reverse and a historic one. The Chinese people had felt their power. They were not again to lose the sense of it.

Yuan Shih-kai was dead and so was his monarchy, but the harm that he did lived after him. He was succeeded in the presidency by Li Yuan-hung, the vice-president, an upright man of honorable intentions but irresolute and of little understanding. Though elevated in title, he was still the weak individual who had to be dragged from under a bed in Hankow on the night of October 9, 1911, to lead the revolution. But power had to be exercised and there was none to succeed Yuan in that function. That is the penalty always paid by a country after a dictatorship, an excessive price for a momentary maintenance of order. The succession is always disputed by the dictator's underlings, but none has the force or the stature to take his place. This does not, however, prevent a squabble for the privilege, and so it was in China after 1916.

Yuan had steadily built up his military power to buttress his ambition. There was a large army, fairly well armed, under commanders of his own choosing and loyal to him alone. Much of this he owed to the £25,000,000 foreign loan of 1913, part of which did go to building up his army, as the Kuomintang warned it would. There the army was, then, with its generals, each large in his ambitions and small in his ability, and each began to strive for personal ascendancy. Li Yuan-hung had recalled the parliament Yuan had dismissed and named as his premier Tuan Chi-jui, an ignorant and dull-witted general who was one of Yuan's principal lieutenants. The parliament was as ineffectual as before. It started to draft a permanent constitution and spent its time indulging in disputations on minute constitutional forms, wrangling and dissipating time and energy in irrelevant words.

The generals meanwhile were making their dispositions, each planning to eliminate the others and all flouting civil authority. The issue of control over the military was thus posed and the parliament pressed hard for it, supported, it should be said, by most of the educated class. Li Yuan-hung was forced to decision and in 1917 dismissed General Tuan Chi-jui from the premiership. This aroused the generals. The first to act was Chang Hsun, who had been stationed with a sort of private army astride the Tientsin-Pukow railway between Shanghai and Peking. Chang, an illiterate one-time stableboy, was an unreconstructed monarchist who had kept his own hair queue and made his troops wear them. (Here it should be pointed out that one of the first acts of the republic was to order all Chinese men to cut off their queues, since queues had been imposed on the Chinese by the conquering Manchus and were thus a badge of servitude. Probably nothing the republican leaders first did outraged the conservatives more than this: not even the passing of the Son of Heaven, not even the republican form of government as such, with its uncouth debatings by men chosen by ballot instead of examination in the classics. The queue had been imposed by a conqueror, but it had been worn for nearly three hundred years, and so it was sacred and the sanctities of the past were being violated. It was old; so it was inviolable, notwithstanding its origin.

From this some deductions might be drawn about the nature of all conservatism but this is not the place for them.)

Chang Hsun and his pig-tailed army journeyed to Peking in July, and a few days later after a convivial evening Chang decided to reinstate the monarchy. In the middle of the night he dragged the displaced boy Emperor Pu Yi out of his bed, frightened and whimpering, and set him on the throne still whimpering. In the morning Peking discovered that China was a monarchy again but was more amused than indignant. The episode was too farcical to be taken seriously. In a few hours military leaders in the neighborhood of Peking began moving their troops on the capital. It was not that they cared about the republic. As a matter of fact, they did not. But they did not want Chang Hsun or any other individual among them to have primacy. In a few days the poor, bewildered, pig-tailed ex-hostler, wondering why nobody understood him, declared the monarchy abolished. The little boy Pu Yi was taken back to his own courtyard in the rear of the Forbidden City to pick up his toys again and play in peace. A few years afterward another victorious general who seized Peking turned him out of the Forbidden City and packed him off to Tientsin, where he dwelt in obscurity and genteel poverty until 1937, when he was picked up again, this time by the Japanese, and carried off to Manchuria and made emperor of the bogus state of Manchukuo, issuing imperial mandates that the Japanese wrote for him: a pathetic, unmajestic finish for a Son of Heaven descended from K'ang Hsl and Ch'ien Lung. Chang Hsun himself escaped and took refuge in the Dutch Legation, where he stayed for the rest of his life, tranquilly sunning himself in a back garden, meditating on what he had done wrong by the lights of all the old dramas and storytellers' tales of the great ancient days. The Chinese revolution, from its beginning in the Hankow bomb explosion to the accession of Mao Tse-tung and the Communists, has been on the whole a tragedy; but it also has had its comic passages.

The generals now felt their power. President Li was forced to dismiss the parliament once more and he himself resigned in favor of Feng Kuo-chang, who had been elected vice-president. Feng was a commonplace figure of no particular consequence and the rout was on. The republican regime degenerated into a number of quasi-military satrapies, each under a military man, independent for all important purposes. These military men were the so-called warlords—so-called because few of them were competent to lead a battalion. Most of them were crude, ignorant men and nearly all were conscienceless. They did less fighting than looting, and victory in their successive wars was more often than not decided by bribery rather than test at arms. But the country was in constant turmoil and much of it was despoiled, ravaged as by locusts. Special taxes were levied, collected, and immediately levied anew. Some districts were forced to pay taxes years in advance, and then the local warlord would be driven out and the one who took over levied another year's tax in advance. Men were put to death or held to a ransom that was called a fine without any cause and on some officer's caprice. Farm workers, cattle, carts, feed, and fuel were requisitioned at will and without compensation. Communications were periodically severed and trade was crippled. A blight settled on the land. It was one of the worst periods in Chinese history.

The republic sank wretchedly to its end, a squalid failure. Yet it was not a republic that failed. There really had been no republic. Of the kind that was attempted there could not have been. The whole experiment was the first manifestation of a weakness that has handicapped China ever since. This was a tendency to take on veneers, a tendency growing out of glib superficiality. It must be said that the circumstances in which China entered the modern world were almost diametrically opposite those attending Japan's emergence. Japan began under the leadership and direction of a group of extraordinarily able younger men who read the world and the time aright, who had not only insight but intellect and force. China began with men of lower stature than it had before, men of little understanding, no intellectual depth, and almost no quality of leadership. Mainly they were superficial and given to pattering phrases they had quickly picked up and did not comprehend.

Their fault lay not in making the revolution. That was genuine. Sooner or later it had to come. The Manchus had to be evicted: they were a drag on the country and a danger to its future. Nor did it lie in their advocacy of a republic. A limited monarchy would have been less sharp a break with the past, but it would not have been much easier to make function. The necessary feature was representation or a system of legally prescribed restraints on absolute authority. In other words, if a constitutional monarchy could work, so could a republic. There was nothing particularly fallacious, then, in adopting a republican form of government as such. What was wrong, absurd even, was to import a full-scale, exact model of a foreign republic—the American, as it happened. It was absurd to set up in China in 1911 an imitation of the American republic, set it up overnight as it stood in its own habitat and make the forms of that republic ends in themselves for the China of that day. The republic, that kind of republic, was a fiasco because it had no roots in Chinese history, traditions, political experience, institutions, instincts, beliefs, attitudes, or habits. It was alien and empty. It was superimposed on China. It washed off with time, a very short time. It did not represent political thought but a caricature of political thought, a crude, callow, schoolboy caricature.

To a degree American influence and education was to blame. The years preceding 1911 were those in which young Chinese went to America to study. Many of these young men were the leaders in the first years of the republic. Conforming to their own philosophy of education, they studied the subject most proper to educated men—political science. Conforming to the pedagogical method of the Confucian system of education, they learned by memorization. They memorized the parts of the structure of American government and the words in which it was described. They learned constitutional provisions and formulas—checks and balances and the like. That American constitutionalism had roots in old Anglo-Saxon soil, had developed slowly and naturally out of Anglo-Saxon thought and experience they did not understand. Of the real working forces of American government and politics they had no conception at all. They had learned little, if anything, of the modifications, the tacit reservations, attached to constitutional theory and practice by American usage and the sanction of American tradition. They learned only phrases. They memorized them and came home with their advanced degrees and prepared a fair copy of American constitutionalism.

The republican government they set up may have been creditable in examination bluebooks, but it had one major flaw: it had no meaning for the Chinese people and there was no reason why it should or could have. American constitutionalism became to the young republican leaders an end in itself. They made a fetish of constitutional forms, and details of constitutional practices became sacred causes, to be argued with American documentation. There was no attempt to make a selection and adaptation to the institutions, traditions, and genius of the Chinese people, the kind that the Japanese had so skillfully made for themselves a generation earlier. It was intellectually immature, adolescent. It was comic in itself but tragic in its results. And the republic failed, as it had to. But the failure did something to the Chinese people. What they believed to be a new dispensation had lifted their hopes. The fiasco left them dispirited, disheartened, disillusioned. That was almost its worst effect, worse perhaps than the disintegration and destruction that followed in the turbulence of sordid warlord squabbles. But it was not a form of government that failed; it was a generation.

CHAPTER XXVI

World War I:
Japan Becomes Aggressive

A still greater transformation was now about to set in for East Asia, precipitated by events outside of Asia that were to shake all the continents. The European war broke out. That large proportion of the human race that inhabited Asia was not even dimly aware of why the war came and what brought it about and was even less concerned; but it was destined to be only a little less affected than the part of the world directly involved. In fact, the modern history of the East can be divided into two parts: one from about 1800 to 1914 and the other from 1914 on. But all the cumulative effects of forces in East Asia for the preceding five centuries were not so great as those that shook it in the generation after World War I. It is true that the war created nothing new in East Asia. Wars never do; they only accelerate what is already taking place even if not yet perceived. Everything that has happened in East Asia in recent years would have happened even if there had been no world war, but it would not have come so swiftly—and therefore so disastrously; without war gradual change might have been assimilated stage by stage.

The first effect of the war was to make international relations the focal point of politics in East Asia again. In China especially these had been on the whole subordinated to internal forces and events for a time. This was not entirely true, for even before 1914 there had been some activity with the usual purpose of slicing off some of the peripheries. This was notably true in Tibet and Mongolia, with Great Britain and Russia primarily concerned. Great Britain's interest in Tibet came by extension from its position in India and Burma, Russia's from its general aspiration in Asia.

Tibet, like so many other countries in East Asia, was a tributary of

China, although on the whole autonomous, like nearly all of China's tributary states. But as British influence sought to percolate into Tibet, China, knowing from experience what to expect, tried to tighten its hold on the country. The Tibetans were as fearful of one as of the other. At the turn of the century, when all Powers were getting into position for the final raid, or what was thought to be the final raid, on Chinese territory, the Russians made their usual preliminary advances in the direction of Tibet. With their usual reflex the British got ready to obstruct. In 1903 a British expedition under the well-known Major Sir Francis Younghusband entered Tibet. There were the customary skirmishes, with the customary result when native troops confronted well-armed foreign forces, and there was the usual treaty. Tibet pledged itself not to cede or lease any part of its territory to any other Power, to admit no agent or representative of any other Power, and to give no railway, mining or similar rights to any other Power—the classical entering wedge. China was perturbed and in 1906 began negotiations with Great Britain that led to an agreement binding both not to take any part of Tibet or interfere in its internal affairs. In this way Great Britain did recognize China's suzerainty but on the other hand China recognized Britain's agreement with Tibet, with the sole change that China was exempted from the prohibition against economic concessions to other Powers. In 1907, when Great Britain and Russia made the historic agreement that brought Russia into the Anglo-French entente against Germany, one of the issues settled between them was Tibet. Both parties pledged themselves not to interfere in that country, but the agreement contained an implicit acknowledgment of Britain's prior interest there.

The advent of the republic in China put the status of Tibet in question. The ambitious young leaders of the republic wanted to incorporate all the minority peoples into the new regime or at least give them representation in parliament, a laudable enough object. But the Tibetans feared closer connections with China and refused to send representatives. There was trouble, and China threatened to send troops. Britain then intervened and China had to back down. Then in 1913 tripartite negotiations took place and a convention was drafted by which Outer Tibet was to be autonomous under Chinese suzerainty but neither China nor Great Britain would interfere in its internal administration. China was to maintain a Resident in Lhasa, the capital, with a small guard, but Tibet would not have to send representatives to the Chinese parliament. Also Britain was entitled to send an agent to Tibet when it desired, accompanied by an escort, and any dispute that arose between China and Tibet was to be referred to Britain for adjustment. China then refused to ratify the convention but Tibet did, strengthening Britain's position. This was the status of Tibet when the European war began.

Mongolia was Russia's arena of activity, and the Russians, as usual in the Far East, were less hampered by restraint than the British. By secret treaty with Japan Russia already had obtained a sphere of influence in Outer Mongolia, with or without the consent of the Mongols and Chinese. It must be pointed out, however, that the Mongols were almost as suspicious of China as they were of Russia and probably more resentful. There had been an influx of Chinese into Mongolia over the years and since they were more efficient than the natives both as farmers and traders they were taking over the land and crowding out the natives. China pressed increasingly and in the summer of 1911 a group of Mongol princes sent a delegation to St. Petersburg to ask Russian help, a degree of political innocence of which only nomad tribal chieftains could be capable. Russia, of course, was only too obliging and complied happily. It sent officials and traders and prepared to send more. Then came the Chinese revolution, and simultaneously Mongolia saw an opportunity to loosen the tie to China and Russia saw an opportunity to strangle Mongolia in ties of its own. Through its representatives there it was quietly but relentlessly obtaining a kind of psychological ascendancy. Outer Mongolia declared its independence of China, not without Russian encouragement, and Russia officially promised to help it. In return Russia got the right to own land and to trade. In 1913 in a treaty with China Russia recognized Chinese sovereignty over Outer Mongolia, but by the time of the European war Outer Mongolia was nevertheless well on the way to becoming a Russian protectorate. From that aim Russia never thereafter deviated, whether under the tsar or Lenin or Stalin or Malenkov or Khrushchev.

The European war put the whole Far East in flux. The first and perhaps most important thing it did was to give Japan a free hand in that part of the world. Europe was engaged in its own death grapple and had neither time nor strength for remote parts. America, at first unengaged, was partially involved, both through its emotions and its desire to maintain freedom of the seas. America therefore could give only half of its attention to the Far East until 1917 and after that no attention at all. Now for the first time in the relations of East and West one Power had a free hand in East Asia. Japan made the most of it.

The Anglo-Japanese alliance was brought into force soon after the outbreak of the war, though in a way that must have been furthest from the minds of the British statesmen who contracted it in 1902 and probably even of those who renewed it in 1911. There was some evidence, though not explicit or acknowledged, that its application was not altogether to the liking of the British in 1914. Indeed, when two days after the war began China officially proposed to the warring Powers that they refrain from hostilities on Chinese territory and in adjacent waters and the proposal was seconded by the United States, both the British and German governments agreed. But the Japanese were not to be deflected from their plighted loyalty to an ally, especially when there was territory to be gained. (As a matter of fact it was generally known in the Far East during the war that the Japanese army's sympathies were on the side of Germany.) On August 15, Japan gave Germany an ultimatum demanding that it withdraw all its armed ships from Chinese and Japanese waters and furthermore turn over to Japan, *not China,* its leased territory in the Kiaochow Peninsula "with a view to eventual restoration to China." Why the territory could not be turned over to China directly and at once was not made clear by Japan, but the reason was not difficult to discern.

Japan declared war on Germany on August 23 and prepared to drive the Germans out of Tsingtao and the surrounding area. The British sent token forces in the hope that they would have a voice in the final settlement of the German leasehold. The Japanese had an easy time, since the Germans had too few troops and ships to make resistance. The Germans surrendered on November 7. Easy as the military task was, the Japanese found it necessary to extend their activities beyond the bounds of the German leasehold. They occupied a Chinese area of considerable size and continued to occupy it after the Germans surrendered, incidentally starting to build another railway outside the leasehold, posting garrisons that seemed far from temporary and mistreating Chinese inhabitants. The Chinese government protested and the Japanese replied sharply and in a tone of injured feelings, speaking sadly of China's apparent want of confidence in Japan's friendship and good faith. The accusation was just. The Chinese had no such faith— and rightly so.

How right they were was soon demonstrated. There followed the historic episode of the Twenty-one Demands. With this episode Japan's role for the next generation was proclaimed for the whole world to see. The spectacle was not reassuring. The Chinese-Japanese diplomatic debate on China's technical rights as a neutral and the propriety of Japan's conduct as a belligerent was broken through by an act, a startling act. On January 18, 1915, the Japanese representative in Peking, Eki Hioki, asked for a private and confidential audience with President Yuan Shih-kai. To Yuan he presented a series of demands—demands revolutionary in their scope and content. Furthermore, he forbade Yuan to reveal them to anybody. Yuan did not keep them secret, of course.

He did not publish them or officially communicate them. In conformity with Chinese practice he let them leak out. So sensational were the demands as to be incredible to the outside world. Frederick Moore, the correspondent of the Associated Press, who was among the first to be apprized of the demands, cabled them to his home office as a matter of newspaper routine. The Associated Press asked the Japanese Embassy in Washington for confirmation, and the Embassy vigorously denied the report. The Associated Press suppressed it and reprimanded Moore. Moore resigned, his pride offended. The report continued to circulate and continued to be denied; the world continued to disbelieve. No responsible person would credit that Japan would be guilty of such a step. A few weeks later confirmation was beyond dispute. The full text of the Twenty-one Demands was on the desk of the foreign minister of every state in the world. They were indeed calculated to defy credence.

Their import was to make China a Japanese protectorate at a single stroke. They were in five groups. The first constrained China to agree to any arrangement Japan made with Germany after the war for the German territorial holdings and rights in Shantung Province—this despite the statement about eventual "restoration to China" in the ultimatum to Germany. In addition Japan demanded rights in Shantung that Germany never enjoyed. Still more important was the second group, which dealt with Manchuria. By this China would be compelled to extend to ninety-nine years the lease on Port Arthur and Dairen, which by the original Russo-Chinese agreement was to expire in 1923. The Japanese also broadened the scope of that agreement to include Eastern Inner Mongolia. Japanese were to be permitted to own land and trade in both South Manchuria and Eastern Inner Mongolia and to have the right to work mines there. China was not to contract a loan from any other Power or concede to other foreigners the right to build a railway in either region without Japan's consent, and only Japanese advisers were to be engaged for political, military, or economic functions there. Also the railway between Changchun and Kirin was to be handed over to the Japanese. By the third group the Hanyehping iron and steel works in the central Yangtze Valley, the largest in the country, were to be under joint Chinese-Japanese control. By the fourth group China pledged itself not to cede or lease to any Power any harbor along its coast.

The nub of the matter lay in the fifth group. By it China's survival was put in jeopardy. It would have compelled China to accept Japanese political, military, and financial advisers for the whole country, to put its police under joint Chinese-Japanese supervision, and to set up an arsenal under joint control. Japanese schools, hospitals, and temples would have the right to own land in the Chinese interior and "Japanese subjects" would have the right to preach in China. Plainly those subjects could be Buddhist missionaries, although there already was a Buddhist temple in practically every Chinese community, or they could be Japanese agents in ecclesiastical garb but with far from ecclesiastical purposes. Japan also would have the right to build several railways in central and southern China.

The Chinese were stunned when the demands were made public. The whole country was aroused. Probably China's virulent anti-Japanese feeling dates from that time. The Japanese representatives in Peking worked on Yuan Shih-kai with threats and blandishments but he was obdurate, as he knew he had to be in order to preserve his own position. There were four months of acrimonious negotiations and at length Japan became impatient and on May 7 delivered a 48-hour ultimatum, simultaneously beginning to move up troops in Manchuria. But even in the face of the ultimatum China yielded only partly. It accepted the first four groups with only minor changes but Group V was "reserved for further discussion," which both sides knew would never come. Although Group V contained what Japan really wanted—the first stage in a protectorate over China—it still did not dare go to the extreme of war to have its way. To defy the world to this extent it was not yet ready, and in a measure it accepted partial defeat, but South Manchuria and Eastern Inner Mongolia it had.

As the price therefore, however, Japan incurred the definite, open suspicion of the rest of the world, which it was never to lose until brought to defeat in 1945. The United States spoke out at once. On May 13, a week after the presentation of the ultimatum, the government sent to both China and Japan notes declaring that it would recognize as valid no agreements between them that contravened American rights under treaties guaranteeing China's integrity and the Open Door. It was a reservation of rights rather than action, but it laid a foundation for future action.

Japan, too, had laid a foundation—a foundation for an Asiatic empire, with China as the colonial center. It proceeded to build on it without cease until twenty years later the actual invasion of China became necessary for the consummation of its ambition.

The direct thrust having failed of complete success, Japan now took to the oblique approach. It adopted a strategy time-honored in the relations of strong and weak nations. It would attempt to conquer a country through some of that country's own nationals. It would look for a political faction that wanted support against its rivals and give it that support in return for doing Japan's bidding, in other words the technique of finding, establishing, and working through puppets. In the atmosphere of warlord contention that prevailed in China then this was easy.

With some skillful manipulation, both Chinese and Japanese, there coalesced a group of the more unscrupulous in North China, so-called warlords and their associates in civil office. This group became known as the Anfu Club. It gathered to itself considerable strength, both civil and military, with a Japanese slush fund as its cement. By the end of 1917 it had its members in enough key positions in what passed for a cabinet in Peking to begin delivering the goods to Japan as per order. The mechanism was found in Japanese loans—the Nishihara loans, they were called. Their total amount and their exact purpose were never accurately known, but they were estimated at $150,000,000. Nominally they were to enable the Peking government to function or to start needed projects, but in actuality a large proportion lined the pockets of favored officials or went to build up a political and military machine to strengthen the Anfu clique. What was more serious was that as security for the loans Japan was beginning to get a mortgage on China's communications and natural resources and would have succeeded in getting into a position to foreclose them if events had not supervened outside the Far East to impose a check. For a year or two, however, the deciding voice in China's internal political affairs was Japanese, not Chinese. Since the whole process had the color of legality the other Powers could not intervene, even if the war had not inhibited them, while the Chinese people themselves were helpless, though not unaware of what was transpiring.

In April, 1917, the United States went to war with Germany. One of its first acts was to begin pressure on China also to join the Allies. Just why has never been completely understood. It may have been natural American exuberance or it may have been the belief that there was an advantage in having China represented at the peace table, where the issue between itself and Japan growing out of Japan's wartime acts could be brought to judgment. At any rate, Americans in Peking, both diplomatic and unofficial, began a whirlwind campaign of persuasion in the best manner of Washington, D.C., lobbying. Nor can it be said with confidence whether those in the Chinese government—none too astute at the best, for at that time they did not rise to power by their astuteness —were swept off their feet or whether they thought it impolitic to offend the United States or whether they, too, thought it best to be at the peace table and plead their case with American support. China acceded nevertheless and on August 14, 1917, declared war on Germany, though the heart of Chinese officialdom was by no means in it and the Chinese people were not in the least concerned. China's part in the war was only formal and nominal anyway. Some Chinese labor battalions were sent to France as hewers of wood and drawers of water for the Allied armies and in China itself German business was taken over and German nationals were suppressed. The latter inured to the material profit of the Allied nationals in China, the British in particular, and may have had some part in the decision to make China a belligerent, though it is true the British had been lukewarm in the matter and mainly deemed it expedient to indulge the Americans, always notoriously sentimental about China.

China entered the war but did so in ignorance of the most vital consideration affecting its decision—its position at the peace conference. It did not know that victory for the side it joined would make little difference to its fortunes. Not until after the war did it learn that any expectation of benefit as a belligerent had been made illusory long before it became one, before America began pressing it to become one, even before America itself had entered the war. For in March, 1917, Japan had made secret agreements with Great Britain and France by which the Allied Powers promised to support at the peace conference Japan's claims to the German leasehold in Shantung Province and the German islands in the Pacific north of the Equator.

It was far from a willing grant by the Allied Powers. It was wrung from their fear of defeat. The early months of 1917 were the dark period of the war for the Allies. Russia was recognizably at the point of exhaustion. France was becoming spent. Just then Japan gave intimations of intending to change sides or at least desert the Allied cause, if only because the Japanese army was confident Germany would win. The prospect of Japanese naval strength being added to the German fleet was frightening, especially as America was not yet in the war. Whether or not Japan really would have changed sides is conjectural, but even the danger thereof was frightening. Japan stated its price and got it. The consequence was to plague American relations with Britain and France for some years, to fester in China's relations with the West, and to be felt poignantly in the bloody campaigns in the Pacific islands between 1943 and 1945. In fact, it made a war in the Pacific and Far East more nearly inescapable.

Japan moved to wrest the same kind of concessions from the United States after it had entered the war but thought it unwise to be as specific as with the other Powers. It sent to the United States as special ambassador, ostensibly for a general discussion of American-Japanese relations, Viscount Ishii, one of its most experienced diplomats. Delicately and in generalities Viscount Ishii raised with Secretary of State Lansing the subject of Japan's relation to China. Still dealing in generalities, he asked Secretary Lansing to join in a declaration of their common conception of that relation. The result was an exchange of letters on November 2, 1917, known as the Lansing-Ishii Agreement, which caused a sensation far beyond its intrinsic content. Secretary Lansing acknowledged that territorial propinquity created special relations between countries and that therefore Japan had special interests in China (those not being defined), especially in those parts of China contiguous to Japanese possessions. Lest this abstraction be given the wrong concrete content Secretary Lansing added that it was nevertheless the firm conception of the United States that the territorial integrity of China was unimpaired and that while geography did give Japan special interests, the United States accepted Japan's assurances that it would not infringe on that integrity or violate the Open Door principle already stated in numerous treaties. Japan for its part renewed its assurances to this effect.

While the agreement appeared to have two parts which cancelled each other or to take away by definition what was given by assertion, it caused consternation, especially in China. For one thing, the first news of it came to China from Japanese sources. This news was framed in such a way as to convey to the Chinese that the United States had acknowledged Japan's unique rights in China and by derivation therefore a free hand. The Chinese were dismayed, especially in light of their expectations from having joined the war under American patronage. By the time fuller and more accurate explanation came from the United States, the first impression had already registered and the corrective effect was diminished. What no doubt appeared to the American government to be a harmless statement of the obvious and perhaps another effort to bind Japan to restraint, besides being called for by Japan's vacillation as an ally, turned out to be a diplomatic indiscretion or, at the best, an unfortunate incident. But the Lansing-Ishii Agreement was destined to be short-lived. Since it was subject to such controversial interpretation, the United States asked for its abrogation at the Washington Conference in 1922 and the Japanese had to consent.

The Russian revolution also had repercussions, though these were not fully felt until after the war. Russia's hold on Outer Mongolia was relaxed and by so much the prospect of Japan's hold on it increased. Still more, the Chinese Eastern Railway in North Manchuria, which had remained under Russian control since the war with Japan, was now left without any effective administration. An emergency international administration was improvised on American initiative with Colonel John F. Stevens, an American engineer, as director. It kept the railway going but raised diplomatic questions and intensified friction, since Japan had other purposes in North Manchuria and, at the least, sought to frustrate the international administration of the railway. The friction was intensified by the inter-Allied expedition to Siberia in 1918, when a minor ancillary war began in the Far East among the Allies in the European war. This will be dealt with later.

Unrealized at the time, perhaps, World War I had closed a relatively simple chapter in Far Eastern international relations and opened a more complex and deadly one. Also it had brought the beginning of the end of the China that had existed for three thousand years.

CHAPTER XXVII

Aftermath of World War I

Before proceeding to the most lasting consequences of the war in East Asia, those which affected the relations between Asian peoples and the Western states which had ruled or controlled them, it is better to complete the record of the dealings among the belligerent Powers concerning East Asia. They were of no small importance in themselves.

The sudden collapse of Germany and the surrender on November 11, 1918, came as a shock to the Japanese. Despite all the conclusive evidence visible everywhere else that Germany was nearing its end, the Japanese were thinking and preparing to act on the assumption that they could continue with impunity their advance on the continent for a long time. On the morning of November 11, a few hours before the signature of the armistice was to be formally announced to the world, a Japanese army officer was scheduled to deliver a lecture on why it was certain that Germany would be victorious. But now the Japanese knew the hour would soon come when they were called to a reckoning and they hastened to make the most of the interval. New loans were contracted with the Chinese government through the Anfu clique. Moves were made, without pretense, to fasten a permanent hold on Eastern Shantung and to close a grip on Eastern Inner Mongolia. Still more, there was Siberia, where a golden opportunity had opened up for Japan, an opportunity to evict Russia from northeast Asia as far west as Lake Baikal, to plant the Japanese flag there and, with eventual success in China, to make a solid Japanese territorial bloc from the Eastern Arctic down to the waters of the South China Sea north of the Philippines. In this ambitious design it was the Siberian situation that raised the most serious immediate consequences in international politics.

Just before and immediately after the end of the war North Manchuria, Mongolia, and Siberia became not so much a vacuum as a chaos. Dissidents, conspirators, agents of various Powers, ideological partisans, adventurers, brigands, and sadists driven to blood-letting for its own sake organized, plotted, and clashed in fluctuating combinations or no combination at all, killing, looting, and laying waste. The aftermath of a great war is always a time of turbulence and human suffering. In northeast Asia after 1918 there were especially severe torments for the inhabitants.

The Chinese had been, quite justifiably, resentful of Russian encroachment in Outer Mongolia, an encroachment no less cynical because the Mongolians were in part innocent of what was happening and in part so bitter at the Chinese that they condoned Russia's assumption of rights. With the downfall of the Tsarist government China seized the opportunity to reassert itself in Outer Mongolia. Legally it may have been within its rights, but the manner in which it exercised them only alienated the Mongols still further. It sent to Urga, the capital, troops under command of General Hsu Shu-tseng. Hsu, one of the Anfu leaders, was a man wholly without scruple, the quintessence of the worst sort of warlord. Hsu's troops acted as a primitive, conquering horde. Outer Mongolia had to rescind its declaration of independence. This was not the worst, however. Hsu's officials and his troops let loose a wave of terrorism, of loot and rapine that not only outraged the Mongols but disposed them to welcome any alternative, whatever it might be.

The alternative presented itself in one Baron von Ungern-Sternberg, a mad, literally mad, White Russian nobleman, a bizarre, macabre figure with a pronounced streak of sadism. He conceived himself a modern Genghis Khan with the sacred mission of extirpating Bolshevism and at the same time establishing a new Mongol Empire. Ungern had Genghis Khan's talent for slaughter, preferably following torture, without his military genius, administrative ability, and intelligence. The Russian seized Urga as his base after a successful attack on the Chinese. In this he had the support of the Mongols, who, not yet knowing Ungern, preferred him to the Chinese. Ungern initiated his rule, and periodically punctuated it, with indiscriminate killings. He himself was subsequently captured by Bolshevik forces and executed. But it was not the Chinese who returned. They had antagonized the Mongols too much to be acceptable. It was the Bolsheviki, under Russian aegis, who succeeded and have remained ever since, a fact attributable as much to China's failure as to Russia's success.

The real center of international intrigue and indiscriminate bloodletting lay in Siberia. Soon after the Russian revolution, left or leftist parties set themselves up in parts of Siberia, most of them socialist or democratic or perhaps Menshevists and only a small proportion Bolshevist. Partisans of the old regime, even more numerous, set themselves up at the same time, and coalesced under Admiral Kolchak, an upright but politically not very intelligent naval officer who came to style himself Supreme Ruler. Under him were a number of White Russians, former bureaucrats and officers, some of high character who, besides being anti-Communist, sought to preserve the Russian patrimony. Also there were some mercenaries notable for butchery more than for anything else, foremost among them one General Semenoff, first a mercenary under Kolchak and later a mercenary for the Japanese, in both roles conspicuous for plunder and murder. Wherever he set foot, scourge fell. Years later he was caught by Communists and dispatched, probably not too gently.

During the years 1918 and 1919 the British and French intervened in various parts of Russia with the object of overthrowing the Communist government. In furtherance of that object the Allies supported Kolchak, doubtless unaware that the excesses of the men under him, for which, it is true, he was not responsible, doomed his regime. It was doomed not because the peasants of Siberia were pro-Communist, as they were not, but because the depredations and bestialities of many of Kolchak's underlings would have antagonized any people, regardless of philosophical affiliations. In addition it was plain that Kolchak's permanent success would perpetuate the worst evils of the Tsarist land system. Many Russian conservatives and nearly all liberals, it should be observed, were embarrassed by the same gentry but could do nothing to curb them. Kolchak was either ignorant of what was taking place or helpless, probably both. Support of Kolchak was not deemed sufficiently effective by the Allied leaders, and in 1918 sentiment began to develop for an inter-Allied intervention in Siberia. Various reasons were urged for this action, some genuinely held and some just pretexts.

Soon after the Communists took control in Russia the problem arose of what to do with about 50,000 Czech troops who had deserted from the Austrian army and joined Russian forces. When the Treaty of Brest-Litovsk was made and the Russian army disintegrated, the Czechs were left intact and on orders from the provisional Czech government, with headquarters in Paris, started to move eastward across Siberia. It was the intention to evacuate them from Siberia and bring them to Europe to be incorporated in the French army, and to this Moscow agreed. As they made their way across Siberia through the prevailing turbulence, they had to fight their way periodically through one band or another and they found themselves most often being attacked by Bolshevik detachments. This led to a demand in Europe that they be rescued from the Communists.

There were simultaneously hundreds of thousands of Austrian and

German prisoners in Russian prison camps, both in European Russia and in Siberia. It was rumored among the Allies that they had been let out of the prison camps, which was true, and that they were being armed by the Bolsheviks, which was later proved to be untrue. This was offered as another reason for intervening in Siberia, though whether it was really believed by the British and French has always been open to doubt. A third reason was that in Vladivostok was held a quantity of arms and military supplies that had been sent by the Allies when it was still thought the Russians would and could resist Germany. It was urged that these supplies must be kept from falling into the hands of the Bolsheviks and later, perhaps, the Germans.

These were the avowed reasons. The real one was the desire to get into a position to crush the Communists at the start and expunge the regime of Lenin and his followers, the same reason that led to British and French intervention on the European borders of Russia. This was held more strongly by the French than the British, but the difference was only one of degree. (Later it was of no small influence that the Briton who shared the French opinion with peculiar ardor was a man named Winston Churchill. Others may have forgotten that fact over the years. A Russian who had not was named Josef Stalin.) The Japanese, of course, needed no special reason. They just wanted Siberia.

The position of the United States was wholly different. It was definitely reluctant, for one thing because there was general recognition that the reasons avowed for intervention were specious, the real motive being interference in Russian internal affairs to overthrow a government not to Anglo-French liking. This went against the grain for Woodrow Wilson. It violated both his instincts and his political principles, and, besides, there was more concern in Washington about Japanese aggression than there was in London and Paris. Without American participation the British and French hesitated to undertake the Siberian venture, and Wilson held out for months. Finally his hand was forced by two developments. First, it became certain that the Allies were resolved to go ahead anyway. Second, it became alarmingly clear that the Japanese would intervene by themselves even if the Allies did not. This was underlined when, early in 1918, after two Japanese had been killed in Vladivostok, Japan landed troops in the port. It was not long before the Japanese according to their custom in such situations, gave evidence that although the landing was occasioned by an emergency it would probably be permanent.

The American government then could do one of two things. It could remain consistent with its principles and refuse to interfere with any country in order to dictate its form of government. Or it could resign itself to the fact that intervention in Siberia was inevitable and that if it had to come there was an advantage in being in a position to watch what was occurring and to try to obstruct acts it considered unwise or politically dangerous. It chose the second, though reluctantly, and on July 17, 1918, notified the Allied governments it would take part but only to help the Czechs save themselves and to preserve military stores which might "subsequently be needed by the Russians for their own defense." Naturally the Allied governments entered no objections to this, whatever tacit reservations they may have had. In the next few months British, French, American, Italian, and Japanese troops landed in Vladivostok and moved inland. The British, French, and American contingents numbered between 7,000 and 9,000 each; the Japanese sent 72,000. They had their own private objects.

The Siberian intervention created more problems than it solved—if it solved any at all. So far from leading to any accord it only created ill-will, among the Allies and between the Allies and the inhabitants. It was, in fact, one of the ugliest episodes of the war. And despite the hopes and intentions of the British and French its effect was not to consolidate a force for the overthrow of the Communist regime but to throw the Siberians into the arms of the Communists. Whether Communist or not—and nearly all of them at that time were not—they preferred their own people, though Communist, to alien invaders who subsidized and protected the most vicious elements among them— mercenaries like Semenoff—and condoned their barbarities. They were particularly embittered by the Japanese, who not only abetted the most outrageous of the mercenaries but themselves were guilty of atrocities.

Conflict arose at once between the Americans and the others, the sharpest being between the Americans and the Japanese, with the British and French most often throwing their weight on the Japanese side. The commander of the American expedition, General William S. Graves, was a God-fearing, tough-minded Texan who took his democracy seriously. He had received from Secretary of War Newton D. Baker instructions that were to govern him in his mission. In a finely worded state paper combining high statesmanship with lofty human values Secretary Baker told him his mission was to see that the Czechs came through safely and to safeguard the military stores in Vladivostok, but he was not to interfere in those matters that concerned the Russians alone. The Russians were to be left free to choose for themselves their own form of government.

To these instructions Graves held with stubborn immovability. He would not lend American strength to set up brigands whose only claim to recognition and support was that they called themselves anti-Bolshevik, nor would he underpin puppet regimes, nor even help unexceptionable groups who had not yet won popular support. He was simply not intervening, as he had been told not to do. In so doing he incurred the hostility not only of the Japanese but of the British and French, whose commanders, Generals Knox and Janin, sought first to persuade him and then to undermine him. When blandishment and persuasion were not enough an attempt was made to have him removed by accusations that were nothing less than indecent. Whispering campaigns were set going at the peace conference in Paris, already in session, to the effect that Graves was a radical, that he was being bribed, that he was under the hypnotic influence of Russian mistresses, etc. They were designed to get Wilson's ear and convince him that he was being betrayed by his commander in Siberia. Wilson and Baker were unmoved. The British and French continued to work on Graves to get him to use his forces to back Kolchak or somebody like Kolchak, to set up regimes composed of the most reactionary, retrogressive Tsarist elements, so long as they were anti-Bolshevik. They distrusted the Japanese but they disliked Lenin and his followers even more. Graves was adamant. He had been ordered not to engage in a Russian civil war and he continued to obey his orders. Wilson continued to support him.

To carry out his orders Graves on occasion had to frustrate the Japanese, and at times his troops and the Japanese came to the verge of combat. While nothing came of them but minor skirmishes, feelings were rasped and there was enough timber lying about to threaten conflagration. There was bitterness and stalemate, but nothing conclusive came of the intervention. No base was set up for an attack on the Communist regime in European Russia. No puppet regime was established, principally because none could be found that could win native support. The combination of bandits, sadists, and foreign invaders gathered under Kolchak's banner and sanctioning not only reaction but terrorism was enough to doom any regime so supported. That was the price the Western world paid for choosing as its exemplars, as its alternative to communism, what was worst in the old regime. The question may be ventured whether the West has not repeated the same mistake in other parts of the world after World War II, but that question does not concern us at this stage. Interventions are seldom successful enterprises, even when their motives are purest and they are undertaken on the side of justice. It is a deeply embedded human instinct to resent the alien intruder, whatever his purposes, and to prefer the evils that emanate from one's own kind. The Siberian intervention remained in a state of suspense throughout the peace conference and until brought to review at the Washington Conference in 1922. Kolchak's government fell apart and he himself was captured and executed, a fate which he did not deserve. Whatever his failings and his mistakes, his intentions were good.

This brings us to the peace conference. The Far East was the subject of some of the most acrimonious controversies in that far from harmonious conclave. Japan presented its claims to the German holdings in Shantung and the islands in the Pacific. The British, French, and Italian delegations informed Wilson that by their treaty obligations they had to support the claims. China vigorously protested, asking instead that the German leasehold be restored to it as its own territory, and the United States as vigorously supported China. There was a deadlock lasting for weeks, but the United States, with all the principal Powers arrayed against it and uncompromising, had to yield. The Treaty of Versailles gave both the Kiaochow Peninsula and the German islands north of the Equator to Japan, but that was far from the end of the matter. China was embittered at what it considered a betrayal. It had gone into the war on the side of the Allies on the urging of one of them and had been encouraged, like the small and weak states, by the promise of the Fourteen Points. And after the victory it found that part of its territory had been bartered away by most of its allies to another ally. Had it been on the defeated side it could hardly have fared worse. China refused to sign the Treaty of Versailles, but it was to show its feelings in more positive ways and with more serious consequences, as we shall see. In the United States, too, the provisions relating to Shantung had a profound and lasting effect. They were used by Wilson's opponents as one of the main arguments against ratification of the Treaty of Versailles and entrance into the League. Probably, more than any other single consideration they accounted for the final refusal to have anything to do with either. Whether or not Wilson's opponents sincerely felt so strongly about Shantung, they used it as their main talking point, and it proved effective.

Japan had a third demand, but on this it suffered defeat. It had asked, as part of the new order of relations between states then being promulgated, a declaration of equality between the races regardless of color. This did not arise out of any concern for abstract idealism. It had a concrete motive, and for that reason it was opposed even more vigorously than the Shantung provision. For more than ten years the question of Japanese immigration into the United States had been a sore point between the two countries, at times taking on a threatening aspect. Alarmed at the swarming of Japanese peasants into the states on the Pacific seaboard, those states began to clamor for exclusion of Japanese, as earlier they had clamored, successfully, for Chinese exclusion. Furthermore, they had passed and were enforcing legislation imposing stringent restrictions on Japanese, especially in schools and ownership of land. The Japanese protested and the federal government tried to persuade the states to moderate the provisions of the statutes but was only partly successful. A compromise was arrived at between the two countries in the form of a "gentlemen's agreement," under which Japan promised voluntarily to limit the number of passports to be issued for emigration to the United States. The Japanese lived up to the agreement, but it rankled nonetheless.

There was right and wrong on both sides. If the United States had permitted unrestricted Japanese immigration to the United States, as it then did immigration from European countries, there can be little doubt that before long large parts of California, Oregon, and Washington would have become in fact, if not in name, Japanese colonies or at least Japanese islands. The long working hours and low living standards of Japanese peasants would have set up competition, both in farming and in small trade, that the other inhabitants could not meet without lowering their own standards to a level Americans would not accept. The differences of customs and habits, trying at best when peoples of different origin meet, were so extreme as to produce a maximum of irritation. There would have been yet another race problem to fester in the United States, and in time there would have been a pathological social situation on the Pacific Coast. On the other hand, the restriction on immigration and, still more, the discriminatory legislation, though justified in the American view, did doubtless put a stigma of inferiority on the Japanese and the treatment of their people in daily intercourse rubbed it in. There was an unofficial Jim Crowism, in fact. This stigma was one that no race willingly endures, least of all when it has the physical power to seek satisfaction for the offense to its self-respect.

The Japanese maintained that they wanted only a declaration of principle in vindication of their honor and disclaimed any intention of asking concrete application of the principle. But the Americans and even more the Australians feared that the Japanese would later use the principle as the basis for equal rights of immigration anywhere, a claim it would be difficult to deny without inconsistency. This issue, too, was disputed with acrimony, but the Americans were firm and the Australians intransigent, in conformity with rigid "White Australia" policy. The Japanese were rebuffed. They, too, went home disgruntled despite the spoils they had won in a war in which they did very little.

It would have been better for the future of both East and West if the United States had been more uncompromising on Shantung and more conciliatory on racial equality. Both China and Japan now had grievances. The Japanese were to make skillful use of theirs. They were to justify their expansion on the Asian continent by the refusal of other lands to admit their immigrants. Since they had said the declaration of racial equality was only a matter of principle, this was disingenuous. Japan's whole argument of "outlet for population" as excuse for expansion was somewhat fraudulent. For one thing, China, which they insisted on having, was as overpopulated as Japan, and, besides, the military masters of Japan, who decreed aggressive expansion, cared very little whether Japanese peasants did or did not find a home in the United States. On the contrary, if the United States had thrown its doors open to the millions of Japanese who wanted to come, the Japanese militarists might have refused to let them leave. For peasants made the best soldiers and the militarists needed soldiers to realize their ambitions. By the criterion of supranational and abstract morality—if there is such a thing—America was in the wrong, certainly at fault in its manners; but so far as Japan's international policy and action were concerned, the immigration question was only an instrument of propaganda to be wielded among its own people. It was so wielded, and wielded successfully. It helped convince a large part of the Japanese people that expansion by force was justified.

The peace conference was an interlude for the Far East, a postponement of thorny issues, if not an evasion. The content and spirit of the settlement for that part of the world rankled on all sides, and between Japan and the United States relations became increasingly strained, at times so much so that war was not out of the question. In the two years after the peace treaty was signed Japan pressed forward to close its grip on China, using the Anfu mercenaries as talons. In Siberia it was giving every sign of a resolve to stay permanently. The garrisons for its troops were plainly built to endure and it was buying puppets of all nationalities to do its work for it, always obstructed, however, by the United States. Both sides were building fighting ships and a naval race had begun, with Great Britain caught in the middle. Britain's position was anomalous. On the one hand it was an ally of Japan; on the other, in all that counted it had to stand with America, not only because of its own tradition but because of the Dominions, which it knew would not stand by Great Britain against America in a Japanese-American war.

Some way had to be found out of the impasse, and the naval race seemed to offer the best avenue of approach. The prevailing peace sentiment in the United States, if only the product of disillusionment with the late venture in European wars, gave rise to a call for a halt to the armament race. On the initiative of Senator William E. Borah, who was as much opposed to war as he was isolationist, the demand arose for a disarmament conference. Great Britain responded with alacrity, perceiving a way out of its dilemma. The dilemma was peculiarly painful, since the Anglo-Japanese alliance came up for renewal in 1921. Renewal would have antagonized America irrecoverably. Denunciation would have antagonized Japan. The British therefore warmly seconded the proposal for a conference and suggested that it take up political as well as military matters. In this there was political logic as well as British self-interest, since it was useless to seek military adjustments if the political conflicts that brought on armaments were untouched. Japan was wary but could not decline without both isolating and incriminating itself. Accordingly, in November, 1921, there opened in Washington a conference of the nine Powers with interests in the Far East to discuss naval reduction and unsettled disputes in the area. Russia was conspicuously left out—inevitably, since its government was recognized by none of the major states, but regrettably, since no Far Eastern settlement was very solid in which it did not have a part.

The conference opened with a sensation, when Secretary of State Charles E. Hughes in a calm, almost uninflected voice made one of the most startling proposals ever laid before an international body. The way to disarm, he said, was to disarm: not only to stop making armament but to destroy much of what already had been made. Therefore there should be no more construction of capital ships for ten years; those then under construction should be scrapped; the maximum tonnage of capital ships should not exceed 500,000 for the ensuing ten years, and the tonnage for each Power was to be on the ratio: 500,000 tons each for Great Britain and the United States, 300,000 for Japan, 175,000 each for France and Italy, with a corresponding ratio for aircraft carriers, cruisers, destroyers, and submarines. Because the proposals were so concrete as well as so sweeping, the effect was to stun the distinguished official assemblage and to thrill the whole of the Western world, still bleeding from the wounds of one terrible war and prayerfully hoping that it would be the last. It was indeed an imposing assemblage, with Secretary Hughes, Elihu Root, and Henry Cabot Lodge in the American delegation, Arthur James Balfour heading the British, Aristide Briand and René Viviani in the French, and Admiral Baron Kato as head of the Japanese.

It took time for the governments of the great Powers to get their bearings. British and American public sentiment was overwhelmingly favorable, French and Italian not much less so, although France smarted somewhat at being put on the same plane as Italy. It need hardly be said that while public sentiment was enthusiastic the navy men of all the countries were united in displeasure, but in the prevailing attitude toward war and all associated with it they had to be discreet, if not silent. Also it need hardly be said that the Japanese were opposed. Presumably it was the inferior status they objected to rather than reduction, since they could not help being aware that in a naval race the United States would so far outbuild them as to leave them in peril. They fought hard to get their allotment raised, pleading both pride and equity, but they were unsuccessful. They had to accept. Not to have done so would have made their world position incomparably worse. The Hughes proposals were adopted with revision only in detail and a ten-year treaty was concluded. It was an act without precedent in international relations and it lifted the hopes and hearts of millions the world over.

Ships and guns, however, are not the only means of making war. Japan brought up another category—bases and fortifications—and asked that they be eliminated or reduced in the vicinity of its waters. As this seemed logical the other Powers agreed, not unaware that it was to their disadvantage. The United States promised not to add to its bases in the Aleutians, Guam, Samoa, and the Philippines; Hawaii was exempted. Great Britain promised not to do so in its possessions east of 110 degrees east longitude, thus exempting Singapore, or on the islands adjacent to Canada, Australia, and New Zealand. The exemption of Singapore was not to Japan's liking, but on that it had to make a concession; America agreed to the exemption, assuming that if there should be war in the Pacific it would be on the same side as Great Britain and have the use of Singapore. As it turned out, Singapore fell to the Japanese less than three months after the Pacific war began. The Japanese for their part promised not to add to fortifications in the Kuriles, Bonins, Ryukyus, Pescadores, and Formosa.

From the larger point of view the naval agreements advanced the cause of peace. Certainly they stopped a naval race, with all the potentialities for disaster such a race holds. They brought about a relaxation of tension at least for a period, which is beneficial in itself, since it provides an interval in which to work out a basis for conciliation. But also it should be pointed out that on balance the treaties operated to Japan's advantage. Despite its lower ratio in capital ships it was left in a strong position. With all the mathematical superiority the British and Americans combined had, the reduction in absolute figures left them unable to stop Japan in its own part of the world, especially as they had renounced the right to develop strong bases near Japan's waters. Japan was therefore invulnerable and supreme in East Asia, the area in which it had ambitious designs. The Japanese felt themselves wronged, but their apparent concessions left them freedom of action.

Also at the conference a Four-Power treaty was signed by Great Britain, France, the United States, and Japan, by which all the signatories promised to "respect" the rights of the others in the Pacific insular possessions and to consult in case of any controversy in the Pacific. This meant little or nothing. Its significance was that it provided for Great Britain a graceful exit from the Anglo-Japanese Alliance and for Japan escape from loss of prestige because of British withdrawal from the alliance.

The naval question was relatively simple; the political was more difficult. There was among the parties to the conference no common purpose, no common conception of how issues in the Far East should be dealt with or even what they were. For the United States and China the object was to call Japan to account. China had the additional object of getting fundamental redress of its position as a state in international relations. For Great Britain and France the main object was to disturb the existing status as little as possible. For Japan the object was to go home with as little done as possible, in any case not to be deprived of any of its spoils.

The most difficult issue, leading to the most protracted negotiations, was Shantung. This was not dealt with by the conference at all, since Japan could not admit that it was up for trial and insisted that the matter lay between itself and China alone. The Chinese and Japanese delegations took up the question separately, with Great Britain and the United States mediating when necessary. Mediation was repeatedly necessary and there were periodic deadlocks, but finally agreement was reached. In large measure because of American pressure Japan agreed to retrocede to China the former German territory. It did so in 1923 after China had made financial arrangements to compensate it for the former German railway in Shantung. In this instance China won a distinct victory. On Manchuria, however, Japan was adamant. Nor would it discuss any of the other provisions of the Twenty-one Demands treaties, which it insisted were accomplished facts and not subject to discussion. On this, too, it was immovable.

On Siberia Japan made a marked concession. The British, French, and American expeditions had withdrawn long before the conference began, recognizing the hopelessness of the venture and the fallacy of having undertaken it. There had been organized in Siberia by that time a fairly united regime called the Far Eastern Republic, theoretically independent but, it was already evident, sooner or later to be incorporated into the Soviet Union. The Japanese therefore for an interval had Siberia to themselves, but to their chagrin they found their difficulties steadily mounting, the rewards meager, and the prospects ominous. Siberian resistance was stiffening. Japan's mercenaries were being overcome and the Japanese themselves were having to face guerilla attacks.

It was proving a costly enterprise. The climatic conditions were hard on Japanese troops. The hatred of the Japanese among all classes in Siberia was virulent and threatening. The whole affair was unpopular at home and mutterings of discontent had arisen. It was not only American pressure that induced Japan to write off the whole enterprise as a mistake. In any case it agreed to evacuate Siberia and before 1922 was out actually did so.

Beyond these concrete questions China presented to the conference a statement embodying its ideas of what its position should be in the future. The nub of the statement lay in the request that "immediately or as soon as circumstances would permit, existing limitations on China's political, jurisdictional, and administrative freedom of action should be removed." What came under this category was, though without specific designation, extraterritoriality, foreign control of the tariff, leaseholds, foreign residential concessions and settlements—Hankow, Tientsin, Shanghai, for example—the spheres of influence, foreign control of the Customs and Salt Gabelle, the whole body of territorial acquisitions, and political and economic special rights accumulated since 1842.

On this China got little satisfaction. The conference drafted and adopted a Nine-Power Treaty. This was hailed as a Magna Carta for China and a great act of constructive statesmanship and (in the American view) an instructive contrast with the Treaty of Versailles. The conference had a magnificent press in the United States, and Europe echoed with tongue in cheek. Even those not wholly ignorant of the diplomatic history of the Far East let themselves go injudiciously, if not sentimentally. It was a kind of silly season in diplomacy.

In sober fact all the Nine-Power Treaty did was to reaffirm respect for China's sovereignty and independence and pledge observance of the Open Door. No concrete applications were made, no definitions stated. Nothing was said about those infringements on China's sovereignty already existing. There was a separate promise to hold an international conference to prepare the way for granting China tariff autonomy. Meanwhile it was agreed to revise the schedule of prices on which the existing tariff was based so that there could be an effective 5 per cent levy as provided by treaty. Also there was a promise to convene in Peking at a later date an international conference to examine whether, when, and how far extraterritoriality should be given up. It should be observed that there was no pledge or promise to abolish tariff control and extraterritoriality; the projected conferences were only to consider whether to do so. As a matter of fact such conferences did take place later and came to nothing, partly, it must be admitted, because of the civil strife then prevailing in China. One beneficent grant the Washington Conference did make. The foreign Powers maintaining their own post offices in China agreed to withdraw them. For this great deliverance China was expected to render appropriate thanks.

Viewed in historical perspective, in the logic of world politics and in the light of the preceding decade, the Washington Conference can be described, except in the naval provisions, as a shabby farce, a parade of hollow pretense, and all the stimulated public jubilation over its transactions was a mockery of the world's hope. If the international atmosphere in the Far East was so threatening as to make such a conference imperative, then nothing was done in Washington to change that atmosphere or the conditions that produced it. What had been done? In what way had rivalries been eliminated or conflict assuaged? Shantung and Siberia had been settled, true; and China had been liberated of a few post offices. What else? The Nine-Power Treaty; but there was nothing in that treaty that had not been pledged, promised, and said time and again by all the Powers that now said it once more so ceremoniously. But if saying it before had not served to prevent conflict and war, why should saying it again do so, even if said with high panoply?

The world had just seen how cumulative conflict over rival ambitions can devastate a continent and blot out hope and happiness for a race. It required no special prescience or knowledge of East Asia to know that it then stood where Europe had stood thirty or forty years before, and the same causes would have the same effects. If the conditions that already produced diplomatic tensions and minor clashes were to be allowed to continue, they would evolve into major conflicts and continental war, just as in Europe. If there was any real intention to bring about assurance of peace in East Asia, it was necessary to eliminate those conditions or set in train the process of their elimination.

What were they? For years every Power that was strong enough to do so had been staking out claims for paramountcy in China with a view to eventual exclusive hegemony over all or part of it—or, if not hegemony, then a degree of control that would assure exclusive political advantage and economic profit. No one of them had had enough strength to succeed. But, their ambition greater than their strength, they strove against each other. In proportion to the bitterness of their striving the danger of large-scale war mounted. There could be no other result. If the striving continued, sooner or later crisis would come, then the point from which there was no receding, then war, even if none of the contenders wanted war. And with Japan forcing the pace, the crisis was approaching.

These were the conditions, the conditions that inevitably made for war. They could be removed only if China was taken out of the arena of international struggle, if it ceased to be a prize of aggressive expansion. No single Power would voluntarily and unilaterally withdraw itself. There was only one way out. All Powers had to renounce the hope of making China or any part of it their own, and in token thereof they had to retrocede those positions from which they hoped to spring to success.

It is true that that would have left Japan momentarily in the ascendant. But it would also have left Japan isolated. It would have deprived Japan of the excuse that if it did not conquer China others would do so, thereby imperilling Japan itself. And the act of renunciation by other Powers would by so much have strengthened China, and simultaneously the rest of the world could have formally declared that China was out of bounds for aggression or penetration, a declaration that in those circumstances Japan probably would have hesitated to defy. Then China might no longer be a prize for successful aggression, and war might have been avoided. There is no guarantee for this; but it might have been, and at any rate the attempt to prevent it would have been made. As things went, the struggle was not assuaged, and only nineteen years later the war came. Given the same situation, the same causes will always have the same effects. What had happened in Europe, the sacrifice, the devastation, the devitalization of the race, had taught us nothing to apply to Asia.

That was the tragedy of the Washington Conference—tragic in its results, if farcical in its acts. It might not be unjust to say that the last chance to prevent the war that broke out on December 7, 1941, was in Washington in 1922.

CHAPTER XXVIII

Nationalism Rises in China

It was said in the last chapter that World War I ended one epoch in the history of East Asia and began another. Yet it will have been observed that nothing recounted in that chapter denoted any fundamental change either in content or spirit. The events narrated were all on a familiar pattern. What ushered in the new was that after the war East Asia ceased to be a passive factor. More precisely, China ceased to be a passive factor, and as has been pointed out before, China is the pivotal point of East Asia and as China moves so does the rest of East Asia.

The agent of change was the advent of nationalism. It was to work a revolution deeper than anything East Asia had known in its history. This was to be not only a revolution in its relations with the West but an internal revolution, a revolution not only political but social and cultural as well. Whether or not what it wrought was a new East Asia —that is still too early to tell—there would certainly be a different East Asia from what had been; that is already clear.

Once more it must be emphasized that wars do not create anything but only force the growth of what is already rooted in a society. So, too, World War I did not create East Asian nationalism. That was already present, latent but ineradicable. The war brought it to the surface and fertilized the soil around it to make it bear fruit earlier than in the natural process. Indeed, it may be said that no power on earth could have prevented the coming of nationalism to the East and its development into a potent force. It was in the time, inseparable from the forces that gave the time its form. Industrialism, nationalism, and democracy—these had been the prime movers in Western society since the Napoleonic wars, and of these three nationalism had the most nearly universal appeal and was the easiest to transplant and to cultivate in a new soil.

How could it have been kept from making its way to the East even if the danger of its transmission had been recognized and a conscious effort made to check its passage? Whatever may be the precise definition of nationalism, whether it is blood kinship, common traditions, common customs, or a common language that links men in consciousness of kind, there is such a consciousness among all sorts and conditions of men and at every stage in the scale of civilization. It may not always express itself in the sort of patriotism that has been characteristic of Western nations since the end of the eighteenth century—and in its fullness only since then—but it is and always has been present everywhere. The sense of the distinctiveness of one's own group and one's loyalty to it as against others, if not actual resentment of others, is among the deepest human instincts.

By the West this was institutionalized in a virulent form in the nineteenth century and given expression in action. To all the motives for acquisition and conquest that had impelled men since the beginning of time there was added now the motive of glory for the national group. While this may not have been the only motive for the kind of conquest that was called imperialism in the nineteenth century, the result in any case was the subjection to the West of the whole nonwhite world (with the exception of a few independent enclaves such as Japan and perhaps Ethiopia and Siam).

Now if consciousness of kind and its preservation inviolate had any meaning to the conquered, even if not felt in the same way as nineteenth-century patriotism, they were bound to react instinctively in feeling even if they had not the power to act. Until the instinct of kind took the form of Western nationalism, it was restricted to a sense of frustration and suppressed bitterness. But it was only a question of time before it would be expressed as patriotism in the Western mold. And we ourselves shortened the time. We could not help it.

The new and easy means of communication of the industrial age could not be confined to the movement of textiles, tools and trinkets, of guns and liquor, and troops and weapons to subdue those to whom we sold. Ideas are carried, too, whether deliberately or not. Inevitably, therefore, the idea of nationalism was carried to the East. So, too, was the idea of democracy, of the equality of all men before the law. And so was Christianity, with the equality of all men under the fatherhood of God, each having the same dignity in His eyes as every other. All of them were ideas irreconcilable with the dispensation under which one small group of white men ruled for their own profit over all others, treating those others as a species of a lower order. The irreconcilable ideas in time inevitably destroyed that dispensation.

Not only did these ideas come to the East in the natural course but we ourselves brought them there, though many of them unwittingly. We established Western communities everywhere in our colonial possessions because we wanted to live in our accustomed way, and each such community reproduced as far as possible the properties and characteristics of similar communities in the West. There were foreign administrative and business methods, foreign shops, foreign schools, foreign places of relaxation and entertainment, newspapers in Western languages expressing Western opinions and outlooks on political and social questions. Such communities inevitably radiated Western ideas, principally national glory and patriotism. The wealth conspicuous where foreigners lived and the demonstration of how easily it could be produced if one adopted Western ways made those ideas infectious. So also did the conveniences of daily living, the saving of labor, visible wherever foreigners resided.

We ourselves made the transmission even easier. We brought young men from all over Asia to our own countries to study in our universities or at least encouraged them to go there. We also established colleges and schools for native young men in all Eastern lands and gave them Western education in Western languages. The stuff of this education was not only the knowledge accumulated in the West but the ideas held in the West. Since there were more British colonies than any other and American missionary schools and colleges were conducted even in the territorial possessions of other countries, most of these ideas were Anglo-Saxon and peculiarly subversive of the imperialistic order or any other order based on absolute authority.

The British taught Indian young men of the upper and middle classes about Magna Carta, the head of Charles I, the suppression of Charles II, and the rising ascendancy of Parliament over the Crown. Americans taught boys and girls of all Eastern peoples about the Declaration of Independence and the Revolution, about all men being created equal and the glory of "Give me liberty or give me death." The young are impressionable everywhere, peculiarly so in conquered countries. The concepts behind Magna Carta and the execution of Charles I and the Declaration of Independence found welcome lodgment in the young, who saw their own people under the heel of alien conquerors. How reconcile Magna Carta and the execution of Charles I and "Give me liberty or give me death" with willing submission to the British raj in India or the rule of a General Wood in the Philippines? We boasted in our schools and in our newspapers that our greatness was that we had fought and bled and died for liberty. Why should not those to whom liberty was denied also seek such greatness, why they, too, not resolve to fight and bleed and die for their liberty? . . . As in time they did.

Now, it must be understood that this indiscretion, if it was that, did not grow out of innocence or naïveté or miscalculation. On the contrary, both in the colonies and in the home capitals there were many who pointed out the unwisdom of such indulgences. Why put notions in the heads of natives? they asked, just as the same classes opposed universal schooling at home because it would put notions in the heads of the working classes and make them discontented. They were right. Indians and Chinese and Filipinos—and later Indo-Chinese, Burmese, Javanese, Moroccans, Tunisians, Egyptians, and Nigerians—did get notions, disruptive notions. And at home the British and American working classes got notions, too, and out of them came the British Labour Party and the American C.I.O.

The practical men who sounded the warnings were right, but they could not help themselves. In our rampage of conquest over the whole world, sometimes with the cruelties and trickeries that are not pleasant to remember, we had to have some self-justification. We were conquering for the good of the conquered: it was the white man's burden and we had the moral duty to bear it. (Curiously, whenever any other country tried to relieve us of the burden, we fought back with ferocity so we could continue making the sacrifice, but that is another matter.) The nineteenth century was a time of liberalism, of humanitarianism, of awakened social consciousness, as we have seen, and there were men and women in all Western countries to whom those values meant much. Such men and women could reconcile themselves to the unjust and cruel accompaniments of conquest—opium in China, forced labor in Africa, punitive expeditions dealing death mercilessly when natives rose in resistance —only by the thought that we were bringing with us the benefits of Western civilization—education, the message of Christianity, sanitation and health, efficient government, the rule of law. Therefore the practical men who wanted to go on enjoying the profits of empire could not ignore the "visionary idealists" at home; while they ruled with an iron hand and grew fabulously rich in doing so, they could not at the same time forbid the establishment of schools and hospitals to educate and cure the natives. A ransom had to be paid to the new conscience of the Western world, and the price was the kind of education, in schools and other media, that taught native peoples everywhere the things that would inevitably generate a passion for their own independence.

Nationalism was the consequence, appearing first in those peoples of a longer tradition and more highly developed culture and a history of past greatness—the Indians, the Chinese, the Arabs. It had emerged already before the war. The Indian National Congress did not start with Gandhi. It was founded in the 1880's. In China, as we have seen, the Boxer Rebellion was not only an outburst of mob hysteria but a last despairing effort to save the country. The Filipinos had rebelled several times against the Spanish and resisted the imposition of American rule with three years of guerilla fighting. It was only after 1919, however, that nationalism in Asia became virulent and acquired enough power to be reckoned with by the Western empires. This was most true in China and India and, as it happened, came first to climax in China.

There were less abstract reasons for the reaction in the East. One was touched on in an earlier chapter. The Japanese victory over Russia had pointed a way. Certainly it had raised doubts about fate's decrees. If Japan could humble a great white Power, no white Power was endowed with omnipotence. Thereby that curious but almost miracle-working intangible known as the white man's prestige was put into question. What was the white man's prestige? It is hard to define but in general it was the common acceptance of the superiority, the invincibility, of the Occidental. It did not denote the entire rejection of the belief that he was a barbarian. He was a barbarian who could not be resisted, who somewhat had been touched by Divine fire and acquired powers beyond the range of mortal men. He could travel at a speed unknown to ordinary men by merely attaching a receptacle containing fire to a string of carts or putting a stove into ships. He had weapons that could kill men and raze cities further than the eye could reach. He could speak into a box and converse over a distance of miles. He could send written messages along wires across a continent. He could sit before metal contraptions and make as many objects in an hour as ordinary men did in two days with their hands. He could take dying people, cut them open, sew them together, and they were cured. Perhaps most of all, he had the touch of Midas, and he could punish disobedience or disrespect with the vengeance of the gods.

This had been accepted with a kind of fatalism. Thus it had come about that a few thousand British troops could keep 300,000,000 in India orderly and obedient, however resentful they might be, and in Shanghai, a city of some three million, a few hundred white police were enough to do the same. Measured by sheer power, the native people of either place could have exterminated all the white persons among them with ease, but they knew better than to try. They knew that those few hundred or thousand white men were a symbol—a symbol of irresistible might that could be summoned to take terrible retribution. This might, visible or invisible, and his command over nature, a command never before given to mankind, imparted to the white man prestige.

The Japanese victory over Russia had raised doubts about that prestige. World War I shook it. The war was a revealing, disillusioning spectacle to those who had thought the white race had found the key to a superior order of life. Yet here white men were slaughtering each other and devastating each other's lands much as the people of Asia had themselves done even in olden times. What difference was there, and where the superiority?

World War I was uncomplex compared to World War II, but already we were in the first stage of total war. All the resources of the whole world were needed by a country for combat or preparation for combat, and conversely as much of the world's resources as possible had to be shut off from the enemy. Therefore every area, every nation, every tribe, had to be won over to one's own side and, therefore in turn, propaganda was an essential weapon. The Allies and the Central Powers both employed propaganda throughout the globe. What was self-evident—the abuses to which the British had subjected their colonial peoples—these were numerous and impressive, and their recapitulation, not without underlining by the Germans, was persuasive. Naturally, Chinese, Indians, and others, who never had forgotten, now had their memories sensitized afresh. The British for their part also had material to work with. The Germans had perpetrated some of the worst atrocities in Africa, and the British spread the account in detail and with considerable skill throughout Asia. Both sides were convincing and, as might have been foreseen, the result was only to prove to the people of Asia that both sides were evil, all white nations were beastly, and they themselves had suffered injury and injustice from both and had a score to pay.

American propaganda was even more disruptive. It was nothing less than subversive. Until 1917 the Allies had stated their war aims in quite general and harmless terms—to punish the breach of treaties, put down militarism, suppress the Kaiser, etc. It was Woodrow Wilson who gave the Allies' war aims dramatic, even revolutionary force and produced effects which have been felt ever since. The Allied Powers, of which Great Britain and France were the strongest empires, owed an immeasurable debt to America for its entrance into the war. It probably delivered them from defeat. But they also paid heavily for it, for while delivering them from the Germans it also undermined them in their imperial possessions. America proclaimed as its purpose to make the world safe for democracy. Worse still from the point of view of the existing order were the Fourteen Points. It may not be an exaggeration to say that in modern times only the Communist Manifesto of Karl Marx was more subversive. Indeed, in the relations of empires and colonies Marx was probably less subversive than Wilson. Since World War II there has been a general belief in the West that it is Russia that has stirred rebellion in Asia. In a measure this is true, but it is also true that Woodrow Wilson did more to bring that about than Nikolai Lenin and Josef Stalin. Certainly he prepared the ground for Lenin and Stalin.

What was the Wilsonian message? What did he set forth as the basis of the peace and the postwar world? The rights of small and weak nations; justice for all, whether large or small, strong or weak; self-determination for all people, regardless of race, color, or military power; adjustment of colonial claims with concern for the wishes and interests of the inhabitants. And this message was carried to the remotest parts of the earth, disseminated with the most adept mechanisms of propaganda that American ingenuity had devised, and made known to the humblest and most unlettered of men, and by them accepted as the purposes for which the Allies fought. How would that message be received by those who had been denied the privileges of democracy, the status of equality and the claims of justice precisely because they were small and weak and helpless? What would it mean to Indians and Chinese and Filipinos and Egyptians and Persians? To whom would it carry a more compelling appeal? It gave them a hope—a hope for emancipation, a fairer status in the world and dignity; and hope can be the stimulus to resolve. And so it was, as we now know. In fact, it may be said that it was only the people in subjection, colonial people accustomed to being done by without their consent, who were convinced by the Wilsonian message and took it as their cause. The transactions of the peace conference surely showed only the barest trace of its influence.

It did strike home in Asia, however, where there was tinder from which to draw fire. It may be that what made the nonwhite peoples rebel was not only nationalism, not the loss of independence, not revulsion from alien rule, not the objection to economic exploitation but, more than these, the affront to pride, if not self-respect. Sovereignty, tariff control, extraterritoriality, even economic exploitation through control of natural resources are all abstract, indirect in their impact on the mass of the people and by them felt little, if at all. But the offense to pride strikes universally. And this, the worst offense we committed against those we conquered, generated the most acrid bitterness against us. One may almost state a general law in the psychology of the relations among nations: one nation may conquer another, govern it harshly and exploit it ruthlessly, but if the people are treated in ordinary human intercourse in such a way as to save their pride, the conquering nation may escape retribution; whereas if a nation justly governs a conquered nation and in all economic matters deals with it in full equity, but in ordinary human intercourse humiliates its people, they will nurse their bitterness and some day exact revenge. For even in the most material age the things of the spirit override all others in time.

We of the West did treat the nonwhite peoples we governed in such a way as to outrage pride and self-respect. We put on them the stigma of inferiority not only in political status but in day-to-day human relations, which was worse. The white man's burden, "the lesser breed" in Kipling's phrase, the "native," meaning every inhabitant of a colony, if nonwhite, whether he was a begrimed, illiterate peasant or a cultivated man of long and distinguished lineage—this reflected our attitude. And we acted accordingly. We maintained a kind of Jim Crow regime. The native, whether aristocrat or plebeian, was barred in his own land. He could not enter a club except as a servant. He was not admitted into a hotel dining room in the costume of his own country and sometimes not even in Western clothes. He could come in by a side door and eat in a back room. There were public parks which he could not enter except as a ground sweeper or nursemaid to a white child. Gandhi was educated in England in the law but while in South Africa was ordered out of a first-class railway carriage because he was not white, and when he refused to go he was put off the train. He was also forbidden to ride in an elevator and had to walk up flights of stairs in the heat if he went to an office building to see a client. For a newly arrived Briton or American in Calcutta or Shanghai to invite to the boarding house in which he was staying a Hindu or Chinese friend he had known in London or New York was a *faux pas* which would be forgiven him only because, being a newcomer, he did not know better. And if a young white man, though himself ignorant, vulgar, uncouth, and of the lower classes, married a native woman, though a patrician and well bred, he was thereafter ostracized by other white men and women. It was *infra dig* to have any association with the inhabitants except in business relations or the relation of master and servant, and to show a serious interest in the life and culture of the country was to "go native," an infraction of the social law. Also if one became impatient at the slow pace of pedestrians in a crowded street one shoved them into the gutter. And if a shop clerk was not quite brisk enough in his attention one leaned across the counter and boxed his ears. In sum, the inhabitants of our colonial possessions, because they were not white, were put beyond a pale and made to feel their station every moment of their lives. We not only considered them inferior and acted as if they were of a lower human order but told them they were. They were not even credited with feelings.

In the years following World War II, in all the disturbances in colonies and other countries under effective foreign control, there was one common phenomenon: not only intransigence, unwillingness even to consider compromise; not only unreasonableness; but irrationality, sometimes hysteria. It has been trying and has provoked irritation even in those Westerners who may be called anti-imperialist. The Iranians in their actions on the oil controversy, the Egyptians on the Suez Canal and the Sudan, the Tunisians on graduated reforms proposed by the French, the Indonesians on New Guinea—judged by the criterion of logic, all have been wrong more often than right, surely refractory, like ill-tempered children. Their attitudes have made fair and reasonable settlement difficult, if not impossible. Even from their own point of view, they have been short-sighted, and the most impartial, dispassionate men became impatient and at times felt that what they needed was the chastisement given fractious children.

Yet, was it fair to judge them by the criterion of logic? They were not acting on intellectual processes or impelled by conclusions arrived at after calm deliberation. Emotions long pent were welling up in them. Memories deeply graven were now come fresh. Grudges neither dead nor buried sought satisfaction. A long past of outraged pride, of humiliation, of injury to the spirit, of offense against human dignity called for expiation. By all that lies in the human make-up there could be no rational approach, no decisions based on the merits of an issue. We who had trespassed against them had forgotten our trespass; it is always so. They who had been trespassed against did not forget and could not; that, too, is always so. A Persian could hardly forget what the British, together with the Russians, had done in his country between 1900 and 1914. Men in power in Teheran in 1950 were already alive at that time and their memory was green. They sought retribution and enjoyed it, preferred it even if it was ultimately to their country's detriment. Men ought to turn the other cheek, no doubt, but is it fair to ask a Persian or an Egyptian—or a Chinese Communist—to be the first of the species to do so?

It was after World War I that the account came up for reckoning, first and most insistently in China. A Chinese delegation had gone to the Paris Peace Conference. Not knowing of the secret treaties between the Allies and Japan on Shantung, believing only that a new order of affairs in the relations of nations was about to be fashioned, they came asking not only restitution of what Germany, the enemy state, had taken from them but a reconsideration of their position in terms of Allied war aims as stated by Wilson. What happened to Shantung we know. On their more general wishes they were given short shrift. There was not even courteous consideration.

They went home frustrated in general and on Shantung smouldering. But news of what happened to Shantung preceded them, and when it was made public there was an explosion. There may be no public opinion in China, as is commonly said, and the Chinese may not care anything about their country but only about their clan and family, etc., etc., but when the news about Shantung became generally known, something of almost elemental force was released. It began with a demonstration by university students in Peking. They paraded through the streets of the capital and without direction but with a kind of intuition made their way to the residence of one of the Anfu cabinet leaders, one most closely identified with the Japanese. They burned his house down and then went seeking after others of the same ilk. Some had their houses smashed, some were caught and beaten up. The police tried to suppress them and finally fired, killing some and wounding others. News of the Peking demonstration spread quickly to other cities and caused a wave of indignation. Students protesting the betrayal of their country had been punished for their patriotism: similar demonstrations broke out elsewhere. When police tried to suppress the students there too, merchants came to the support of the students and guilds gave formal approval. Shops were closed, shutters were run down, public services were suspended: there was a general strike. The strike ended but out of it came a country-wide boycott of Japanese goods. There was something impressive in the spectacle. It was spontaneous and genuine. This has since become known in Chinese history as the May 4 Incident. It gave birth to the student movement, which was to become a force in Chinese politics. It also gave birth to something larger in its result—Chinese nationalism.

At the Washington Conference, as we have seen, China again asked for a reconsideration of its status in the expectation of restoration of national equality. There it was not casually dismissed, as in Paris, but it got little more satisfaction. It was told to go home and set its house in order and in time the West might take up the matter. It went home but no longer in a supplicant mood, no longer willing to appeal with sweet reasonableness to generosity. The iron had entered its soul and was to stiffen the spirit.

China was not alone in the Far East in its demonstrations. It was followed by Korea in the midsummer of 1919. A Korean delegation composed of exiles living in Europe or America also had gone to the Paris Peace Conference to ask for a place in the new day. It did not even get a hearing. Outwardly the Koreans had been submissive since annexation to Japan in 1910. So unrelenting was Japanese vigilance and so unsparing of harsh repression at any sign of dissidence that the Koreans had no choice. Inwardly they seethed nevertheless. The Japanese gave ample provocation therefor. They had not only applied repression, but ruled with an iron hand and with full intent to stamp out everything authentically Korean. They used the Koreans as serfs without rendering the stewardship and protection that is the obligation of feudalism. Korean history and legendry were proscribed. Expression of opinion was savagely suppressed. Education was forbidden beyond the elementary schools, and in the schools Japanese teachers came to their desks in uniform and wearing swords. Economic opportunity was denied to Koreans. They might rise to the level of foreman but no higher. Business was a Japanese monopoly. There was no more oppressive colonial regime anywhere in modern times.

The Koreans had borne their lot with apparent resignation, but in 1919 they, too, rose. It was a nonviolent rising. Men and women, boys and girls paraded silently through cities carrying banners but nothing else —nothing with which to defend themselves. Japanese police charged into the processions with their batons, swinging wildly and mercilessly. The first rows would go down under the attack. Those who followed marched on over them, silently or crying "Long live Korea," until they, too, were struck down. It was a Korean version of the Gandhi doctrine and method. It was moving, pitiful, cruel to watch, and futile. Gandhian nonresistance might work in India, where British public opinion imposed restrictions on the kind of punishment that could be levied, but no restrictions were imposed in Korea. The Japanese army was free to use any and all methods, to know no mercy. The movement was broken. The jails were filled with young and old, young more than old. Some of the leaders were caught and dealt with as might be expected. Others escaped. Of these last many made their way through the North Korea mountains and over the border into Siberia, where they became Communists. Some of them were heard from later, when they led the North Korean Communist government and armies that so long and so bitterly fought the American and United Nations forces. Korean communism was made in Japan, not in Russia.

CHAPTER XXIX

Russia Enters Again

Simultaneously with the rise of nationalism in China and the demand for a status of equality with other nations there was, paradoxically, a steady degeneration in the public life of the country almost to the point where China could be called a state only by courtesy. The central government exercised few of the functions of a government and exercised those clumsily and venally. Its authority ran only a short distance from the capital, elsewhere being subject to approval according to the interest or caprice of whatever military man happened to be in control. Purely local administration went on, as it always did in China, by force of tradition or momentum, again except when it interfered with the political or monetary profit of the local military commander. In the larger urban centers manufacturing and trade went on and even progressed, for they were less obstructed there, and advances in modern production enlarged local markets. Ironically, this was especially true in the foreign settlements and concessions. There the local satraps could not intrude. Order was maintained. There was no pillaging. Property was safe and both property and persons were assured of freedom from confiscatory taxation to line the pockets of a voracious general and his corrupt civil associates. On the whole the Chinese people were demoralized. They were apathetic or despairing, according to temperament, and no hope seemed to be in sight.

Civil strife between the so-called warlords continued, breaking out now and then with or without discernible reason but usually because some military satrap thought he could move toward exclusive national control or merely sought richer fields for loot. In addition to these separate squabblings there was a broader regional division, brought about again by Dr. Sun Yat-sen. Sun had been living quietly in Shanghai during the war years, receiving his disciples and making plans, safe under the foreign flags of the International Settlement. After the war he went down to Canton, taking advantage of temporary local weakness and the fact that in his own province he was most likely to find followers. There he decided to set up an independent government, proclaiming the Peking government to be illegitimate, since it did not have the sanction of the parliament and the constitution.

Sun summoned to Canton the members of the parliament elected in 1913 and evicted from Peking by Yuan Shih-kai. Of the 580 members originally elected 222 obeyed the call and reassembled in Canton. It was a rump parliament but it proclaimed its legitimacy as the lawgiver of the land. On Sun's urging it proceeded to elect him president of China on April 17, 1921, although according to the constitution drafted by the group the votes of three-quarters of the whole membership were required for the election of a president. For one who was a stickler for constitutional correctness this was an extraordinarily broad-minded construction, but consistency never troubled Sun Yat-sen overmuch.

Dr. Sun had the support of some of the local armies in adjoining provinces, but these were of limited number and doubtful use. Nevertheless he ordered a military expedition to march north and evict the Peking government, with the incidental mission of crushing all the armies that lay in the intervening thousand or more miles. With what he expected to accomplish this feat he did not trouble to explain, probably not even to himself. It was his usual practice, one more example of the heedlessness with which he had launched so many hopeless adventures, all coming to grief and costing the lives of devoted followers. But money, time, and energy were squandered in preparations and meanwhile he began a kind of diplomatic parleying with northern warlords, seeking a military alliance with one against the others—also an incongruous procedure for a constitutional legitimist.

Something must be said at this juncture about the higher politics of warlordism in the early 1920's in order to comprehend the setting in which subsequent events arose to transform the country. At that time the most powerful individual in central China was General Wu Pei-fu. He was a somewhat exceptional figure, of an incomparably higher type than the other military men of the time. He had had some education, was endowed with some scruples, was honest in the main, had some conception of the country's welfare and, wherever he was in power, held his troops in check and maintained public order by ruthless discipline. But he was also self-willed, bent on having his way and determined to win mastery over the country. Almost equal to him in power was General Chang Tso-lin, who held sway in Manchuria, though by leave of the Japanese, whom he did not exactly serve but also did not dare to offend. He was a former bandit chieftain, had helped the Japanese in the war with Russia as a kind of mercenary, and was wholly without conscience or scruple; but he knew how to rule men. The president of the country then was Hsu Shih-chang, a scholar-mandarin of the old school. He was a cultivated man but a weak one, more adept in intrigue than in any of the other arts of government.

Between Wu Pei-fu and Chang Tso-lin there was an unappeasable feud, of course, and although they were not always fighting they were always preparing to fight. Sun therefore sent emissaries to Chang Tso-lin to propose that they join hands against Wu and drive him out of central China. How Sun could reconcile his declared convictions and consorting with one of Chang's like he never confided to his associates. Nor did he appear to ask himself what good it would do him to help Chang eliminate Wu Pei-fu, and how he would manage to make himself the head of the national government when Chang, with his huge army, had no powerful rival to check him. Details also did not trouble Sun overmuch. Chang's answer to Sun's proposal was inconclusive, doubtless because he did not take Sun seriously. War broke out in spring, 1922, when Chang advanced on Peking from the north. He was badly defeated by Wu's armies and driven back to Manchuria. Sun, of course, did nothing to help him. He had no force with which to help, as Chang knew in advance.

Wu Pei-fu now substantially held control in Peking, though he did not take titular office. Since he was not wholly of the warlord breed, he announced that he wanted the Peking government under his influence to have the color of constitutionalism. Therefore he invited the original parliament, the rump of which was sitting in Canton, to return to Peking and resume its proper function. He also asked Li Yuan-hung to resume the presidency, which he had had to abandon in 1917. Hsu Shih-chang had himself given up the office after Chang Tso-lin's defeat. Wu was apparently attempting to conciliate Sun Yat-sen and bridge that break in the country, but Sun refused. He tried to prevent both Li Yuan-hung and the parliamentarians from accepting Wu's invitation. Then something happened to change Sun's fortunes once more.

Chen Chiung-ming, the local military commander in Canton, who was not one of Sun's disciples but had agreed to support him, was becoming increasingly impatient with Sun's grandiose and baseless designs. Like many others in Canton, including some who were Sun's disciples, he believed it was useless and a waste of money and effort to go on planning futile campaigns of national conquest. Instead he favored a program of good provincial government and internal provincial reforms. Kwangtung, being one of the richest provinces in the country and one of the most progressive, lent itself to such a program, the more so since its situation in the southeast corner made it relatively secure from attack.

Then by the contrast of its example Kwangtung could exercise a power of attraction on other provinces, weary of misgovernment and spoliation, and in a slower process win over the country. This was, incidentally, classical Confucian political reasoning. Sun was beyond persuasion, however. He was going to fulfill his mission. The Chinese people were waiting to flock to his banner and he would lead them to Peking and victory. Chen Chiung-ming could no longer restrain his impatience. He struck, and in June, 1922, Sun Yat-sen was driven out of Canton, once more to take refuge under a foreign flag.

Li Yuan-hung did resume the presidency on Wu Pei-fu's invitation, although with the understanding that he would hold office only until a regular election could take place. He did so against Sun's opposition and to his chagrin. In October, 1923, the parliament, which had reassembled in Peking, elected as president one Tsao Kun, an ignorant man of unsavory career. Tsao Kun then proclaimed the constitution drafted in 1913 as the law of the land. Sun Yat-sen was by that time back again in Canton and it was hoped that since this was the constitution sponsored by him, and the parliament he considered legitimate was functioning in the capital, he would be willing to come to some agreement with Peking and heal the breach between North and South; but he was uncompromising. He had thrown out Chen Chiung-ming with the aid of troops from a neighboring province and he was making plans of conquest again. But the lawless conduct of his troops began to cause disaffection even among Cantonese, traditionally loyal to him.

Even among Sun's most devoted followers there was growing skepticism of his obsession and his chronic revolutionism. For one thing, the country was weary of civil wars. But Sun was not dismayed. His regime and his alone was the legitimate government of China, wherever he might be and no matter how few supported him. He therefore demanded that the other governments of the world recognize him and drew up flamboyant plans for remaking the country at the cost of billions, which he asked foreign governments, especially the American, to lend him. On what grounds, either in legal precedent or political logic, they should do so he did not explain. The Peking regime was discredited, it is true, but why Sun should be recognized more than any other contender when he had a precarious hold only on one corner of one province in one corner of the country did not trouble Sun. He was dedicated to his mission and it had to be fulfilled, and it was the moral duty of the rest of the world to help him do so. Only one part of the world saw its duty. That was Russia. Russia saw its duty only too gladly. As a matter of fact Russia had been eyeing China vigilantly since Lenin's rule had become secure—vigilantly and hopefully.

Almost as soon as the Communists had become established in Moscow the Russians began to lay their lines to China. As early as 1920 they began sending unofficial emissaries to China to sound out the possibilities of recognition and formal diplomatic relations. Each had to walk cautiously, his approaches necessarily oblique, since the great Powers were antagonistic and China hesitated to give them too direct affront. Russia, however, put temptation in the way of the Chinese. It played on contrasts with considerable skill. While the Western Powers, despite their professions of democracy, refused to remit the faintest trace of their imperialistic privileges in China, the Russians ostentatiously announced the waiving of all treaties by which Russia had obtained territory and special privileges in China. There were some tacit reservations, but their import did not come to light until later. When on July 21, 1919, Leo Karakhan, the Russian Deputy Commissioner of Foreign Affairs, formally proclaimed the unilateral denunciation of the treaties with China and the secret treaties with other Powers concerning China, the Chinese were impressed and gratified. It was for China a unique experience. Never before had a Western Power given up anything it had taken from China or shown the slightest disposition to do so. And after the rebuff at the Paris Peace Conference the experience was calculated to strike home.

The Russian emissaries who arrived in China proceeded adroitly. With Chinese officials they drew attention to the promises they came bearing. With the intellectual class and, more especially, with university students, emotionally aroused by what had happened in Paris and later in the Washington Conference, they came bearing sympathy and encouragement in their national aspirations. That, too, no other foreigners had ever done before and conspicuously were not doing then. On the contrary, foreigners in China, both official and unofficial, were paternally lecturing the students on their unwisdom or sternly scolding them for their presumptuousness.

Chinese students were grateful to the Russians, but Chinese officials were hard-bitten. When the Russian emissaries proposed negotiations for a new treaty, which by inference carried recognition, the officials went into details. Extraterritoriality, control of the tariff, and Russian residential concessions in places such as Tientsin and Hankow—the remission of these was gratefully received; but what about Outer Mongolia and, also, what about the Chinese Eastern Railway in north Manchuria? These were incomparably more important. From the Chinese point of view they constituted Russia's most serious encroachments on China's sovereignty; from Russia's point of view they were the most valuable inroads it had made on China. And on those two the Russian emissaries were less than frank and much less than clear. They had acknowledged China's sovereignty over Outer Mongolia, had they not? Then what did it matter if Russia did occupy a certain position there? As to the Chinese Eastern Railway, Russia was carrying water on both shoulders. One official pronouncement said or seemed to say that the retrocession of the railway was included in the basis of the new relation to be set up between the two countries. Subsequent statements exempted the railway from the rights to be given up. Pressed for precise definition, the Russian emissaries evaded in generalities. Russia had a special interest in the area and in the railway and that interest would have to be taken into consideration, etc., etc. Plainly what was meant was that Russia would give up everything it had in China except what was worth most to it, in fact, the only thing that was worth much. The Chinese were not taken in, however, and the emissaries went home one by one, empty-handed.

With the intellectuals, especially the young, the Russians had more success. In the mood of disenchantment that prevailed in this class— disenchantment with China as it was and with the West for the way it had acted—the Russian revolution appeared as the harbinger of a new and better world. Groups of students and young men newly out of the university began to study Marx and found him good. Not all of them accepted the whole of the doctrine but they did accord with enough to convince them that the existing order in the world was unjust and Marxism promised a better order. The first actual conversions to communism and the formation of communist groups came in 1920 and gains were made in the next two years. This will be told in greater detail at a later point. But enough favor had been aroused both for the Russian revolution and for Marxism as a philosophy and a program to give Russia a base from which to proceed toward more definite ends. The state of mind of Sun Yat-sen pointed the direction in which to move.

As was told earlier in this chapter, Sun Yat-sen had asked, and somewhat imperiously, that his provisional government in Canton be recognized by the other Powers as the legitimate government of all China and the Powers had refused. In fact, they had not even taken much cognizance of the request, and there was no reason why they should have. As it happened, soon after Sun made his first request he was summarily turned out of Canton by his local opponents. Nevertheless he came to the conclusion—an interesting reflection on the working of his mind, especially when frustrated—that if the Western Powers, America above all, would not see the light, recognize their duty and do it, he would go to others who would. There were several logical lapses in his reasoning, of course. If he had a right to demand recognition because he had set himself up in Canton by his own mandate, then so did any other local military leader who decided to call himself the head of the national government, no matter where he was, how little power he had, and how little support he commanded outside his own circle. In that case every Great Power could choose for itself where the Chinese government would be and who would be its head, an arrangement which would delight the Japanese above all, for that was exactly what they were trying to bring about for their own purposes. Sun therefore decided to turn to others, and who could have been more hospitable than the Russians? That was more than they hoped for. And thereafter Sun's intimate circle blamed the United States for having thrown China into Russia's arms by not recognizing Sun as the legitimate ruler of the country and underwriting him financially. Why it should have chosen him from the many contenders and what effect the example would have had on other Powers—and therefore ultimately on China —were apparently irrelevant questions.

Russia was ready and willing. In the summer of 1922 it had sent to China as another emissary the highest-ranking man it had yet designated, perhaps because it had sensed opportunity. He was Adolf Joffe, who subsequently committed suicide while ambassador to Berlin after Stalin's methods had become clear. (By committing suicide he undoubtedly anticipated being gathered to his forefathers by only a short period.) Joffe had gone to Peking to renew efforts for a treaty and recognition of the Soviet government. The Chinese officials were not unwilling but demanded that first as a token of Russia's good faith in its anti-imperialist professions Russian troops evacuate Outer Mongolia, where they had been since the fall of Ungern-Sternberg. Joffe could not meet that condition, of course, and the Chinese refused even to negotiate. Joffe sought more fruitful fields. He went to Shanghai, where Sun was living in one of his periods of compulsory exile. There he found a bountiful crop.

Dr. Sun did negotiate. For here was the representative of a foreign Power which did discern his importance and understand his mission. He and Joffe came to what is better called an understanding rather than an agreement, and it was made public. In light of what had gone before and what was to come later the joint statement warrants giving in some detail. In the first paragraph it said: "Dr. Sun Yat-sen holds that the Communist order or even the Soviet system cannot actually be introduced into China, because there do not exist here the conditions for the successful establishment of either Communism or Sovietism. This view is entirely shared by Mr. Joffe." . . . (It was apparently not shared later by Mr. Molotov.)

Then Mr. Joffe acknowledged that China's paramount problem was to achieve national unification and full national independence and "assured Dr. Sun Yat-sen that China has the warmest sympathy of the Russian people and can count on the support of Russia." Few realized how expansive an interpretation was to be given these last few words in a year or two, perhaps not even Dr. Sun.

Then further on more concrete questions: on Sun's request Mr. Joffe categorically stated that Russia was still willing to renounce "all the treaties and exactions which the Tsardom imposed on China, including the treaty or treaties and agreements relating to the Chinese Eastern Railway." On this, however, some weasel words were entered, to which Sun gave assent. "Dr. Sun is of the opinion that the realities of the situation point to the desirability of a modus vivendi in the matter of the present management of the Railway." In plainer words, the Russians could go on controlling the railway. As to Outer Mongolia, Joffe "categorically declared" and Dr. Sun was "fully satisfied" that the present [i.e., Soviet] Russian government had no intention to pursue an imperialistic policy in Outer Mongolia and therefore Dr. Sun "does not view an immediate evacuation of Russian troops from Outer Mongolia as either imperative or in the real interest of China."

In other words, what the militarists of the Peking government refused to concede to Russia as being contrary to the national interest Sun Yat-sen, the original Chinese nationalist, first knight of anti-imperialism and libertarian, willingly conceded. Now, it should be explained that Sun was neither venal nor stupid nor willing to barter his country's birthright for foreign support. He was in some ways naïve, especially where his ego was engaged, but not so naïve as not to recognize the peril to his country or so overweening in personal ambition as to sacrifice his country for his own power or glory. He was psychologically more complicated. He was just so sure of himself and his mission, so confident that his personality could overcome all opposition and obstacles, even the opposition dictated by a more powerful country's national interest, that all, Lenin included, would see the light and yield to him. It was folly, childish folly, tragic folly; but there was in it neither meanness of spirit nor moral dereliction.

The bargain had been struck, however, and thus it came about that the Russian camel had got his nose under the Chinese tent. All the rest of him was eventually to make his way in, and even thirty years later none could venture to say when, if ever, he would be expelled or deem it expedient voluntarily to leave.

CHAPTER XXX

Russia's Part
in the Chinese Nationalist Movement

This is a logical point at which to take up the larger question of communist Russia's whole relation to the nationalist movements in Asia, the movements for independence that have shaken that continent since 1919 as it had not been shaken in the preceding 2500 years, not even by the seismic upheavals that accompanied the incursions of the great conquerors—Alexander, Timurlane, Genghis Khan. It is a question that grew steadily in importance after 1919 and became crucial for the world after 1945. It showed itself most exigently in China from the beginning, but its scope was wider than China. It was only more highlighted in China and first came to climax there. But it cannot be understood unless Russia's role is seen in its proper proportion and without the emotional overlayers taken on with the friction between Russia and the West.

In the Chinese the invitation to Russia may have been adventitious, impulsive, even capricious; in the Russians the entry into China was calculated, the result of a conscious strategy, almost of a philosophy of history. Like so much in Russia after 1917, it was less a projection and expression of Marx than a principle and stratagem of Lenin. Lenin had shown little knowledge of or interest in China before 1914, but his mind had dwelt long on the relations of Western empires to Eastern colonies, as his famous book, *Imperialism,* published in 1917, showed. The central thesis of this book is that imperialism is the highest stage of capitalism, that the two are interdependent: imperialism is the inevitable product of capitalism and capitalism rests on a foundation of imperialism and is incapable of surviving except on that foundation. This theory was further developed and given concrete application in his "theses" expounded at the second congress of the Communist International in midsummer, 1920.

Whatever else may be said of Lenin, he was capable of straight-forward, honest revision of his views. For one of his dictatorial position and his doctrinaire, dogmatic cast of mind, he was singularly free from intellectual rigidity: he could re-examine his opinions and certainly his political methods when the evidence before him called for re-examination and change. By all the logical development of his tenets the Western world should have become communist after 1919. A war as destructive as that which had just closed, as destructive of the welfare of the common man, should have undermined the capitalist system and released a surge of proletarians in triumphant communist revolution. There is evidence that he even had confident expectation of an imminent revolution in the United States. But capitalism did not collapse. The revolution scarcely raised its head. A few feeble putsches in Europe were disposed of with ease. The Western social system was tougher than he had supposed. It had been maimed, but it still had the capacity as well as the will to survive. Lenin had to re-examine his premises; he worked out a new theory and program of revolution, a new analysis of the motive forces of modern society, which he then expounded to the faithful at the second congress. He returned to imperialism as the key to the evolution of history in our time.

A new attack had to be directed against capitalism. Since imperialism was its foundation, it was most vulnerable in the colonies. And conditions in the colonies, Lenin held, lent themselves to action. Two movements were already in being among the colonial peoples, he said. One aimed at emancipation from foreign rule, the other at social revolution for the benefit of the downtrodden masses. On the first, he was undoubtedly right, as China and India clearly testified; on the second he was indulging in the same doctrinaire, closet-philosopher logic that had made him believe revolution to be imminent in Europe two years before. In any case, for the furtherance of the world revolution it was sound strategy to attack the capitalist countries at their weakest point, which was in the colonies, and there attack them by encouraging and assisting the movements already under way. The most favorable of these was the nationalist movement, since that had the support of all classes, the wealthy landowners and *bourgeoisie* as well as peasants and proletarians.

Lenin also sketched out his plan of campaign in some detail, a plan that in some of its aspects has been recognizable in the course of events in Asia since he spoke in 1920. It was to be the duty of communists everywhere in the world to give active assistance to dissident groups in the colonies, whatever the grounds of dissidence. Compact communist groups were to be formed in the colonies, but they were not to function in isolation. They were to ally themselves and work with the discontented, playing particularly on the aspiration for national independence. While keeping themselves intact as a separate corps, they were to join whatever parties or groups gave promise of being effective. While stimulating nationalism, since that would be a direct blow at the capitalist, imperialist Powers, they were also to foment social discontent, which Lenin said was already actively stirring, especially among the peasants. They were not, however, to work for a revolution and a communist system at once. They were to visualize a transitional stage in which a bourgeois democratic system would function but would nevertheless move through stages of increasingly drastic land reforms in the interests of poor peasants until a country finally was ready for a fully Marxist society. At that point the communist core would take over in full by force, suppress those groups that did not accept the whole communist program, and institute a dictatorship of the proletariat. As a matter of fact communist action in Asia from 1920 on conformed fairly closely to the essentials of Lenin's strategy.

While Lenin was not explicit on the point and was even discreetly silent, it followed from the logic of his position that the most promising scene of action would be in the British Empire. Great Britain was still in the forefront of both capitalism and imperialism; strike it and, if successful, the whole system, capitalist and imperialist, would topple. And it was on the peripheries of the empire that Great Britain would be the most vulnerable. To strike in India was too risky, however. India was the most precious jewel in the British crown and for it Britain would surely fight. To challenge Britain there would invite retaliation and for that Russia was hardly prepared in the 1920's. China offered more promise. There Great Britain did not have exclusive control, although its economic interests were greater than any other single Power's. Furthermore, its interests there were not vital to it, as they were in India. Britain might oppose Russian incursion in China, but it would not fight. Russia could move with impunity in China when the occasion arose, and Sun Yat-sen's impetuosity and gullibility provided the occasion.

There was one other fact on which Lenin was discreetly silent. This was the fact that the strategy for world revolution coincided point for point with the historic strategy of old Russia. It worked to the interest of world revolution to strike at Great Britain in Asia; but it had also worked to the interest of Tsarist expansion to strike at Great Britain in Asia. And the places chosen by communist Russia for attack were those which Nicholas II and his supporters had chosen for attack. Nicholas II, Muraviev, Bezobrazov, Witte, and other exponents of Russian expansion in the Far East in the preceding fifty years might gleefully have burned Lenin at the stake, but they would also have applauded his foreign policy. Thirty years after Lenin's death this was still true. What Stalin was doing in China, Korea, and Indo-China and trying to do in India, the court of the tsar for the preceding century had wanted to do. Was it coincidence only? Was Russia in Asia after World War II Marx on the march or Peter the Great and Nicholas II on the march? Was Marx an intellectual outer skin put on by the traditional Russian bear, even if instinctively, perhaps unconsciously put on? The question is of the kind that history can never answer and also never ignore.

In either case Sun Yat-sen had been the beneficent angel giving invocation. In the agreement signed by Sun and Joffe, it will be remembered, Joffe had said that in its aspirations for full national independence China had "the warmest sympathy of the Russian people and can count on the support of Russia." Before the year 1923, the year in which the agreement had been signed, the word "support" got concrete definition. Russian military and civilian advisers began to arrive in Canton. One General Galen, also known as Bluecher, a mysterious figure who in the purges of 1936–38 went the way of so much official Russian flesh, took on the training of a new modern Chinese army. Among the first steps was the establishment of the Whampoa Military Academy, soon to come under the direction of a young officer named Chiang Kai-shek, who was first sent to Moscow to imbibe both military and civil inspiration, a mission the end of which neither Chiang Kai-shek nor the Russians could foresee. Still more influential was one Michael Borodin, attached to Sun Yat-sen and the Kuomintang as civilian adviser. Borodin, a youngish communist who for a time had, like Trotsky, lived in the United States under another name, became for a few years almost the most influential man in China, indeed second only to Sun Yat-sen. At some stages he was even more influential than Sun, since Sun was pliable to Borodin's wishes, and Borodin was plausible, sincere, probably genuinely devoted to China's welfare and adept at flattery, always effective with Sun Yat-sen.

By the time the Russian advisers arrived in Canton there was already a nucleus of Chinese Communists with whom they could work, though cautiously and indirectly. It was a small nucleus, politically not very influential, ideologically not very substantial, but already dedicated. In China, as everywhere else, it was among the disenchanted intellectuals that communism was first successful. It may be said that it was out of despair rather than philosophic conviction that the first Chinese became converted to it. The republic was a dismal, humiliating failure.

The country was being despoiled by scoundrelly warlords and visibly falling apart. The West had failed it, both socially and politically. What had been hoped for from the adoption of Western ideas had not been realized. Even worse, the West had shown no disposition to make the slightest concession to Chinese aspirations for recovery of national dignity. Moreover, even to Chinese without radical inclinations, there was something impressive in the success with which a vigorous and determined minority had carried out the Russian Revolution, had first overthrown autocracy and then victoriously defended the revolution against foreign intervention. To all appearances the victorious Russian party had established a new social order promising strength and stability for the country and a more satisfying life for the Russian people than they had ever known before. In the state of mind in which all Chinese found themselves the Russian example was infectious.

The sequel to the Paris Peace Conference, the student risings of 1919, and the outburst of nationalistic feeling that developed had stimulated the heart-searching that even before had begun among young Chinese intellectuals. They had set upon a quest for new truths by which their country might be saved. They read widely, voraciously but not always discriminately, taking all the ideas in the world for their province. They invited distinguished scholars from the West to come and lecture in their universities, foremost among them John Dewey and Bertrand Russell. In the Peking National University, the country's leading educational institution and the center of the new intellectual ferment, a group of younger faculty members had begun to read Marx and had formed study groups in his doctrine. Two men emerged as leaders in the new thought, two younger professors named Chen Tu-hsiu and Li Ta-chao. After some wandering among social philosophies they espoused Marxism and drew a few still younger men to themselves, among them Mao Tse-tung, of subsequent fame. By the middle of 1921 there were avowed communist groups in the principal academic and urban centers, especially Peking and Shanghai.

Something must be said about these communist beginnings, since they reflect China's past and indicate the future. They conformed in general to the atmosphere and spirit of the founding and first years of the republic. Now as in 1911 the need and desire for change, for something new, for a break with what existed, were genuine. What was chosen was not. The young men who initiated the communist movement were not very different from those who snatched at American constitutionalism a few years before. Both had snatched at ideas with little understanding, attracted mainly by their novelty and glitter. Chen Tu-hsiu, for example, who was for long the leader of the communists, had in a few years moved in broad leaps along the whole span of philosophical beliefs, taking each of them up quickly and discarding them just as quickly. He went from mild modernist reformism to complete adaptation of Western science and technology to Anglo-Saxon democracy to socialism to communism, taking the phrases of one and quickly dropping them for the phrases of the next. This was even more true of his followers, who made the transition from position to position even more abruptly, who indeed in many cases leaped the whole span at once. All were swept on one gust of doctrine after another, wafted on each in turn, with little sense of whence it had arisen and whither it was bearing them. Whatever may have been the truth about Chinese communism later, in its origin it was meretricious and synthetic.

Just as the young men of 1911 had taken over American constitutionalism in all its external forms and set up a replica of the American republican system, so the young men of 1923 and their followers took over the external forms of the Russian communist system and made of the Kuomintang a replica of the Russian monolithic Communist party. Under Borodin's inspiration and guidance and with Yat-sen's approval, the Kuomintang underwent a kind of transmogrification, as did the government of south China and later, after the national victory of the Kuomintang, the government of all China. The model of the Russian political "apparatus" with all its appurtenances was reproduced: there was a party congress, a central executive committee, a standing committee, a pyramidal hierarchy and a parallelism of party and government at every administrative level, with the party always supreme. It was a detailed tracing from a Moscow blueprint.

It was a mongrel monolithism nevertheless. The whole theory and practice of dictatorship by a monopoly party was an alien veneer thinly laid over the body of China just as American constitutionalism had been. There was nothing in China that could have absorbed it. In Russia there might have been a place for a party dictatorship and there it might work. Autocracy was innate in the Russian scheme, accepted by the people as part of nature. They had experienced nothing else and all except the tiny minority of the educated who had travelled in Europe had never seen anything else. Furthermore, the Russian communist leaders in their years of exile in Western Europe, when they sat in the libraries and coffee houses of one capital or another, had had time to think out a theory of party dictatorship and to work out a method of procedure when they came to power. They knew why they wanted a party dictatorship and had planned its operation. Also they had a mechanism with which to operate it. The Russian Communist party was old and closely organized. It had a tested, disciplined, indoctrinated membership on which it could count, held together by long association and a common consciousness. It had a closely reasoned philosophy, evolved in study and debate over the years. Russian Communist authoritarianism was at least founded on reality.

Almost the exact opposite was true of the Kuomintang. It had never been a party in the accepted political sense. It was little more than an expression of community of general belief—belief in republicanism and modernism, both without precise definition. It was the vehicle of an idea rather than a political organization. It had never had a fixed membership; the discordant elements associated with it were sometimes in the party, sometimes out of it, and sometimes not quite sure whether in or out. It was inchoate, lacking in cohesion, nebulous in doctrine, indefinite in program, and unstable as to both theory and practice, shifting from point to point as often without reason as with reason. In short, it had little or no reality. Then suddenly it was transformed into a dictatorial party, a mechanism of omnipresent government. But it never became a monolithic party. It was only the caricature of one. And the system of government it instituted was not authoritarian rule but the caricature of it. The interlocking committees and councils and the interminable meetings got nothing done. There was dissipation of energy in phrases and forms, precisely as in the first parliament.

There was the parallel system in government, with appointed administrative officers and, beside them, the party functionaries, as in Russia. And as in Russia, it was usually the party functionaries who exercised power. But whereas in Russia these were tried and true Communists, disciplined and, however dogmatic and fanatic and cruel, dedicated to an idea, in China they were generally political placemen, many of them having swarmed into the party after it became successful to use it to enrich themselves. The overwhelming majority had no training, no knowledge of government, no ideas. They had no qualifications except party membership and a knowledge of phrases that could be pattered. Even where intentions were good, the whole system was so confusing and so unreal that men floundered ineffectually despite their good intentions. To seek the satisfaction of political advancement and profit was almost the line of least resistance. That at least had reality. The result was that the country was to an ever increasing extent ruled by little local dictators, acting on whim and for self-interest. They enjoyed all the powers of the warlords and in the main despoiled the country about as much. At the best it was farcical; at the worst—and it was more often closer to the worst than the best—it had all the nastiness of a dictatorship without a dictatorship's efficiency. If it was as much of a veneer as the republic it was an uglier one and did more harm.

Nevertheless communism *à la russe* had found lodgment in China. The consequences were felt at once and were to be epochal. The groundlessness and superficiality of the modern Chinese, cut off from the old and not yet finding themselves in the new, was to take a terrible toll of the race. The kind of cultural transition the Chinese had to make— maybe it was cultural rebirth rather than transition—cannot in any circumstances be made without suffering for human beings; but the defects and weaknesses of the Chinese since 1900 added to the sufferings of the race beyond the necessities of the time and environment. In a sense it may have been inevitable. It may be that no people of a long and distinguished lineage can cut themselves off from their past without floundering in a kind of vacuum before they find themselves in the present and lay a foundation for the future.

So the Chinese had done. Their own scheme of education had been discarded, and it had to be, since it was no longer adequate to the survival of the nation and its culture; but they could not yet find another scheme of education that would provide them with criteria, sure, intuitive, almost reflex criteria, by which to judge what was sound and what was unsound, what was good and what was not good. The system of values that had sustained them for two millennia was lost. They could not quickly improvise another for themselves or adjust themselves to one that had guided other peoples. It may all have been inevitable; or it may have followed from intellectual overdevelopment in the Chinese, which makes for too great mental agility, for too easy adaptiveness, for glibness, for assimilating new ideas without perceiving what lies in and behind them. Intellectual overdevelopment, an advantage in certain situations, can also make for instability. Whatever the truth may be, the consequences of the affiliation with Russia and Russian communism were historic and on the whole tragic.

The Russians had gained a foothold in China, however. The first goal of Lenin's strategy had been attained. They proceeded to make the most of it. With the prestige that accrued from the arrival of the Russian advisers and their influence in Canton the number of Chinese Communists increased. While their own direct influence did not increase in proportion—the Russians were shrewd enough to see that that was inadvisable—the influence of the Russians themselves did increase out of proportion to their numbers, principally because they were close to Sun Yat-sen and his leading disciples. The effects were soon visible. The first and most important was the momentum given the nationalist movement. This took a negative form at the beginning with the slogan "Down with Imperialism" and later a more positive form with attacks directly aimed at the British. Anti-imperialism, with a concomitant antiforeignism, swept the country, whipped up by adept propaganda. Before long it was to reach the point of hysteria and violence against foreign individuals. The second effect, though not so visible at first and never gaining the same momentum or power, was stimulation of social discontent. Both Russian and Chinese Communists were not losing sight of Lenin's counsels. Labor unions were formed and strikes became general. Peasant unions were formed and in many localities, where abuses by rich landowners and town merchants had been most flagrant, there was direct action, stores of grain being looted and persons attacked. A kind of spiral of emotional intensity was rising.

The Russians contributed to this, even accentuated it, no doubt. But their part must be correctly measured if modern China is to be understood at all. The Russians did not create what came about in China in the next few years. They only took advantage of it and exploited it. They gave the Kuomintang a scheme of organization and a technique of propaganda. They instilled both into the Kuomintang and the politically conscious of the whole country an *élan* and renewed hope. They set the direction and subtly guided the course of the aroused nation. But there was nothing that came about in China in those years that would not have come about anyway, though probably somewhat later. Nationalism was a product of history, as we have seen. Resentment of foreign rule was working deep in the Chinese people even before the Russian Revolution and World War I, and especially the Paris Peace Conference, had brought it to the surface. The Russians made capital of what they found in China—and after World War II everywhere else in Asia—and did it on a conscious plan set by Lenin. But they are not responsible for what was there and are not to be blamed for it—or credited with it, according to the point of view.

Sooner or later there would have been a nationalist, anti-imperialist, antiforeign movement in China if there never had been a Karl Marx or Lenin, if there never had been a Russian revolution, and if Nicholas II and the Tsarina and Rasputin had continued to conduct their strange ceremonies in St. Petersburg for another hundred years. To attribute what happened in China—and later in Indo-China, Burma, Indonesia, Malaya, Iran, and elsewhere in Asia—to the Russians or to communism is hopelessly to misunderstand Asia and the forces of the twentieth century. It may perhaps be enough to cite the fact that in Egypt, Syria, Iran, Tunisia, and India when there were no communists and no alliances with Russia, much the same happened as in China. Russia made use of the forces of the twentieth century in the nonwhite parts of the world. It did not create them. But this, too, must be said: the Western world played into Russia's hands. By its own obscurantism, its own blindness to what was moving in Asia, its own inability to see that conditions had changed or, when it did see, its unwillingness to make the concessions that change imperatively called for, the West left Asia to go to Russia by default. It almost drove Asia into Russian arms. It did so just when Russia, by its revolutionary doctrine, was more feared than ever it had been before.

CHAPTER XXXI

Revolution Begins in China

For years men in the West had talked, sentimentally and on the whole superficially, about "new China." Now if there was not a new China, at least the old one was ending. In all the fundamentals that count in a people and a society, by the end of 1928 (five years after the alliance with Russia, the reorganization of the Kuomintang, and the serious onset of nationalism) the old China, the form of life Chinese had lived for two thousand years, had begun consciously and visibly to pass. In the course of its passing China was to experience national emancipation, violent revolution, consolidation and internal disruption, civil war and war against an invader, and adoption of communism as a scheme of state and society—but, above all, suffering such as few nations have endured in the history of mankind.

The years 1923 and 1924 set the direction that events were to take. All that came after, even to the accession of the Communists in 1949, followed from the events of those two years. The Kuomintang was reorganized as a powerful, centralized party. The Communists were admitted into the Kuomintang. The nationalist movement was rising, demands on foreign Powers were more insistent, and open clashes with foreign authority and foreign persons were more frequent. Sun Yat-sen made the pronunciamentos that at least nominally became the program, almost the sacred books, first of the Kuomintang and then of the whole country. Also the first cracks of fissure opened within the country and the Kuomintang, the fissure between left and right, never to be closed.

In January, 1924, the first National Party Congress of the Kuomintang was held—just like the Communist party in Russia, of course. It was then the Communists were admitted into the Kuomintang. They were admitted only as individuals rather than as a party or bloc and they were required to take the oath of obedience to the Kuomintang, although they could remain Communists. How the two obligations were to be reconciled when they were in conflict and whether they would not inevitably be in conflict were questions conveniently elided. The characteristic vagueness of the Kuomintang and of Sun Yat-sen had not been dissipated in the systematic reorganization. There were those who were not unaware of the questions and called attention to them. Many actually and vigorously opposed taking in the Communists on any condition. But Borodin was deft and persuasive, and Sun Yat-sen was credulous as always. Borodin had said the Communists would be loyal, and Borodin had pledged himself to help Sun save China; for Sun that was enough. Not only Sun Yat-sen was won over by Borodin. He was equally successful with many of Sun's younger lieutenants and disciples. They were meet for persuasion. Their desperation simultaneous with their newly generated enthusiasm prompted them to lend themselves to anything that promised success.

Theoretically the Communists were in the Kuomintang as so many individuals, but as individuals also they were united by a separate common belief, steadily growing in intensity of conviction and subject to the discipline of a tight organization. They were an organ within a body but not articulated in that body, and that made for ill health, no matter what Borodin promised. The Communists, outwardly faithful to their pledge, went on organizing in their own way and for their own purposes. They carried their message to the intellectuals, especially the young, and because their promises were radiant, more than they could ever have been in fulfillment, they made converts, especially among the young. With the peasants and urban laborers they were equally lavish in their promises, and for that reason had some success among them too, especially among the peasants. Their boldness increased in proportion to their success, and the more conservative Kuomintang leaders chafed correspondingly. There were some clashes in Canton, verbal more often than physical, but the influence of Sun Yat-sen prevented an open break.

In 1924 Sun Yat-sen gave a series of lectures in Canton. Seldom, if ever, in Chinese history had public discourse had an influence so widespread and so pronounced, even if not deep or lasting. These lectures were collected and published under the title, *San Min Chu I* ("The Three Principles of the People"). They were a kind of summary and recapitulation of his philosophy, some of it developed over the years and some newly caught and not yet assimilated. Their significance lay more in their political effect, which was great, than in their content, which was slight.

Sun Yat-sen's thoughts about China—and about the world, for that matter—are embodied in three works which he himself chose later in his will: *Plans for National Reconstruction, Fundamentals of National Reconstruction,* and *The Three Principles of the People.* To these should be added a book published in 1921—*The International Development of China.* In the *Plans* and the *Fundamentals* are worked out most of his basic ideas. Most of those in the "Plans" had been thought out and expressed at intervals over the preceding twenty years.

The most important parts of the books have to do with democracy and education, the latter as the foundation of the former. Here he emphasized one of the aphorisms that he appeared to take as the cornerstone of his philosophy: to do is easy, to know is difficult. From this he reasoned that the Chinese people needed only to be taught the meaning of democracy and to understand it in all its implications; there would then be no serious obstacle to its proper functioning. Therefore, since a genuine democracy for China was his object, the prime requisite was widespread and proper education. But not all were equally qualified to perform the tasks of government. There were three classes: the leaders, men of vision and wisdom who recognized the needs of a society and could fulfill them; a larger number who, without the same degree of vision and wisdom, could understand the motives and actions of the first class and follow that class intelligently; and the mass, who without real understanding, would yet see the advantage of doing as the leaders wished. So far there is no great departure from the essentials of Confucian thought, but so far as there is an attempt to adapt it to modern society and democratic forms, it is schematically oversimplified and somewhat naïve, if not actually challengeable as to validity.

On this reasoning Sun based a plan of progression to modern democratic government in three stages. The first stage was to be one of conquest of the country by a modern republican party and of military rule until control of the country was consolidated. The second stage was to be one of tutelage, in which the people were to be prepared for self-government, beginning with local units. When enough local units in a province—the *hsiens* or counties—were certified as fit for self-government the whole province would become autonomous and self-governing. When enough provinces were self-governing, then the final stage of constitutional government would begin and China would have a full-fledged democratic system. While this had some of the misleading simplicity of an elementary textbook, there was something to be said for it. It at least recognized that China could not take republican and democratic institutions at a gulp and that some period of preparation was necessary, a recognition that was forgotten in 1911. But there was an airy indifference to subtle considerations of power: how to make sure that those who had the prestige, privileges, and emoluments of rule in the period of tutelage would admit that the tutelary stage had passed and that they themselves could be dispensed with.

The constitutional government to be established was to be one of five powers—the so-called five-*yuan* system, a *yuan* being the equivalent of a ministry or department. There were the usual functions, executive, legislative, and judicial, and, in addition, examination and control. The examination *yuan* was to administer civil service examinations. The control *yuan* was an adaptation of the ancient system of censors. Under the monarchy, while the emperors were supreme and absolute, there were official censors who were authorized to investigate any department or official of government, and to report any malfeasance, dereliction, or inefficiency found and recommend any change or reforms deemed necessary. They had theoretically free rein and theoretically no one was immune from their criticism, not even the emperor. In actuality they had to be almost preternaturally discreet. Too many remonstrances to a headstrong emperor or against his court favorites might cost a censor his head and on numerous occasions did.

Notwithstanding all the lush, almost lyric propaganda played on this scheme of government in the subsequent Nationalist regime, when it was hailed as something new and more than Aristotelian in political theory, there was nothing particularly original in it. The division of governmental functions into executive, legislative, and judicial and the idea of the separation of powers, which is only loosely worked out in Sun's writings, was hundreds of years old. The examination and control powers were taken from the traditional Chinese system. Putting them together was not a particularly original or creative accomplishment. That the celebrants of the Kuomintang hailed it with the purple passages that flourished in all the public prints of the country for years was not only disingenuousness for propaganda purposes, though it was partly that; it also testified to the political ignorance of so many of the leaders of the time. In them, too, was much intellectual chop suey: a mixture of intellectual materials taken indiscriminately from everywhere and thrown together with little regard for fitness and proportion. The product did not set well in the Chinese body politic and was soon regurgitated.

In the *International Development of China,* a book that appeared in the spring of 1921 but contained material dealt with in general before, Sun Yat-sen outlined a grandiose, gigantic plan for the material remaking of China. It was on a scale that surpassed anything proposed in the Point Four plans of later years. The country was to be physically modernized at a breathless pace. Networks of railroads were to be built throughout the country. Highways were to be laid out everywhere. All other means of communication and transportation were to be provided.

Land was to be reclaimed. Irrigation systems were to be completed. The country was to be reforested. All existing sources of raw materials were to be exploited by modern methods and new ones discovered and worked. Industries were to be established everywhere. The whole scheme, neatly laid out chapter by chapter, would have required billions in money and called for technical skill of the degree and kind to be found in only two or three countries in the world.

Where were these to come from? From foreign countries in the form of loans, Dr. Sun blandly explained. How loans in such amounts could be obtained from foreign countries just then, after an economically ruinous war, and without submitting to a good deal of foreign control, and how this was to be reconciled with the resolve to free China from all foreign restrictions on its sovereignty—this question, too, Dr. Sun blandly passed over after his fashion. Nothing, of course, came of the Olympian scheme and nothing could have. But it should be observed that two years after the publication of the book laying it before the world Dr. Sun was renouncing capitalism, capitalistic countries, and all their works.

The most important of Dr. Sun's pronouncements, however, and that which had the greatest effect was *The Three Principles of the People*. There was, as has been said, little in the lectures constituting the book that had not been written or publicly declared by Sun before. They were a recapitulation and, most of all, a popularization of his ideas, and in the receptive, eager atmosphere of the time they had an electrifying effect. The effect was intensified by the propaganda that followed. The three principles are nationalism, democracy, and people's livelihood.

The first two are self-explanatory. By nationalism Sun meant something familiar to men of the West, a principle that had governed them since the end of the eighteenth century. He wanted the Chinese to be bound by the kind of patriotism that binds Western nations—a sense of unity and homogeneity within the boundaries that constituted the Chinese state instead of the local and parochial loyalty that had characterized the Chinese until then. He wanted, in other words, a country impelled by the same motives to action as Western countries. By democracy he meant what is generally meant, subject to the qualifications just explained, those stated in the *Plans for Social Reconstruction*.

It was in the third series of lectures, those dealing with general economic welfare, that some of the most interesting and original observations are to be found. What he proposes is in general a welfare state, although he does not go into particulars. He advocates state control of some industries and governmental regulation of others, with private ownership and control for the rest. The most detailed proposals have to do with the agrarian question. There is an eloquent plea for alleviation of the peasants' lot through lower crop rents and other measures. Most important is a plan for returning to the state, for use toward general welfare, the unearned increment from large landholdings through a modification of the single tax of Henry George, whose works Sun read. Since this series of lectures was never completed, it is not known how much he would have gone into detail in the program of social and economic reorganization; but what is most interesting in his discussion of the economic question is his attitude or change of attitude on fundamental social and economic principles.

The lectures that make up *The Three Principles* began in January, 1924, and ended in August. The earliest ones showed a distinct inclination toward communist thought. If they did not accept all of Marx, they accepted most. He was then in the phase of complete rapport with Borodin and the Moscow Gospel. In the ensuing months, however, he had come upon an almost unknown book by a New York dentist named Maurice William under the title, *The Social Interpretation of History*. Dr. William, once sympathetic to Marxian socialism, had after considerable study come to be repelled by its rigidity and its doctrine of class hate, and had written the book in revolt, stating, incidentally a powerful case. Dr. William convinced Sun on one reading, and in the interval of the few months in which he was giving his lectures he changed his fundamental philosophy. He, too, repudiates dialectical materialism, the class war, and the dictatorship of the proletariat. In fact, in lengthy passages he takes over almost verbatim, but without quotation marks, Dr. William's arguments and illustrations. It is characteristic of the man that two years after writing a book advocating the loan of billions from capitalistic and presumably imperialistic countries he becomes, if not a communist believer at least a convinced Marxist, and then, on reading one book by an author so unknown to him that he misstates his name, he changes back again and repudiates Marxian thought. Again he had caught ideas on the fly—two contradictory ones in two years—and swallowed both, one after another.

The Three Principles of the People, objectively examined, is a book of strange contrasts. Some of it is imaginative and penetrating as social thought. More of it is callow, so erroneous in pure point of fact that a sophomore who wrote it in an examination paper would be failed. Judged as a document, it cannot be taken seriously. It is a caricature of political and social thought. But it had a prodigious influence in China. It was elevated to the position of Gospel. It was used in Kuomintang party polemics as Holy Writ. It was a compulsory text in schools and colleges, serving as the principal material in social studies and immune from criticism. The sayings and the commentaries were to be accepted as implicitly as the Confucian teachings and treated as reverently. For years Chinese young men and women got their ideas of history, economics, and political theory out of a hodge-podge of superficial notions, logical fallacies, and factual errors, with a lacing of sound observations. The best of them no doubt silently rejected it, but they had to pretend they accepted it, as did their teachers. It did something to the minds of a generation. Even making allowance for the fact that its dignification was a feat of Communist propaganda of the kind in which Moscow and its disciples are so deft, its elevation almost to sanctification is a reflection of the intellectual decline, if only temporary, of a people for whom intellectual excellence had once been the highest criterion. Perhaps it reflected more the quality of the Kuomintang elite than the perception of the Chinese people, who perforce accepted and were silent. They cried the *San Min Chu I* slogans, but it may have been their voice, not their judgment, that was heard. The fact is that both under the rule of the Kuomintang, with Chiang Kai-shek as leader, then later under the rule of the Communists the *San Min Chu I* was given only lip service. It was lavishly proclaimed in words and studiously ignored in act.

Even while Sun Yat-sen was giving his *San Min Chu I* lectures and propaganda was building up for a national revolution under the auspices of the invigorated Kuomintang, the friction within the party was becoming more abrasive and the internal division was deepening and widening. In proportion as the Communists were becoming more assertive and more successful in arousing mass discontent the more conservative members of the party, those more concerned with national independence than with social reform, became more fearful and antagonistic. The Kuomintang was becoming an uneasy temporary partnership of hostile elements rather than a coalition. There were plots of one faction against another and plots within plots. Personal allegiances shifted from one group to another according to temporary expediency and for the advantage of winning Sun's favor, especially his sponsorship for official position.

Over this shifting intriguery within an ostensible union Sun Yat-sen presided or, rather, balanced, he and he alone preventing it from dissolving into warring factions. By his side always was Borodin in a dual role, on the one hand advising him on how to keep the party united toward the end of national unification under his control and on the other hand advising the Communists on how to win for themselves control of the country and then of the party, even if it meant suppressing all opposing groups in the party. Sun's task as stabilizer and guardian of inner peace became ever harder. There were arrests, first on one side and then on another, banishments, attacks on individuals and some assassinations, even among the prominent.

Toward the end of 1924 there was a serious clash in Canton, with two days of sharp fighting. In growing impatience with the intriguery, confusion, misrule, and undiminished corruption that plagued all commercial activity, the merchants of Canton organized to protect their interests and formed a Merchants Volunteer Corps. They were also fearful of the growing radicalism which menaced their interests. On either ground they believed only force would give their protestations effectiveness. At first Sun Yat-sen sanctioned their action and consented to their bringing in a large consignment of guns and bullets from abroad. Thus fortified, the merchants began to play politics on their own account. With or without justification in the hectic conditions that prevailed, they allied themselves with those who wanted to get rid of both Sun Yat-sen and the Communists. Sun Yat-sen then reproved them for bringing in as large a store of armament as they had and ordered the ship carrying it to be held up in the port. The merchants refused to obey. In August the Volunteer Corps took possession of the guns and decided to use them. The merchants ordered a general strike in Canton, threw up barricades, and moved to take over the city. A battle was imminent but peace was preserved, in large part because the British notified they would intervene if Sun carried out his threat to bombard the city. In October, however, formal fighting did break out and the Volunteer Corps was crushed. The Kuomintang regime was saved but only at the cost of formal collision, with a considerable number killed and wounded, a poor augury for the unification that was hoped for.

Before this last skirmish took place Sun Yat-sen had already left Canton for north China. The reasons, never ascertained exactly, were probably mixed. There were indications that he was becoming restive again. Results were not materializing as fast as his temperament called for. It was a year and a half since he had made his agreement with the Russians; the Kuomintang had been organized and its campaign was under way, and he was still in Canton. All China was not yet conquered and under his sway. He had never waited. When impeded by delay, no matter from what cause, he chafed at the bit and wanted to be off, no matter what the real prospect of success. Something of this was probably present now, especially as growing internal dissension threatened further postponement. He was restless. He wanted to do something quickly, as often before in his career. As it happened, events elsewhere gave him what seemed to be an opportunity.

In the north another war had broken out between factions led by rival warlords. While it was in progress, Feng Yu-hsiang, known as the Christian General, changed sides and thus gave victory to Chang Tso-lin, the ex-bandit ruler of Manchuria, over Wu Pei-fu, who had been Feng's chief. Tuan Chi-jui, who had been the figurehead of the Anfu or pro-Japanese clique, was made president of China. Tuan invited Sun to come north to discuss common action for national unification. One would have to know more of the innermost processes of Sun's mind than one can know to fathom how he could reconcile affiliation with gentry of that ilk with the purpose and preachments of the Kuomintang and his own cherished aspirations. He had just been expounding democracy

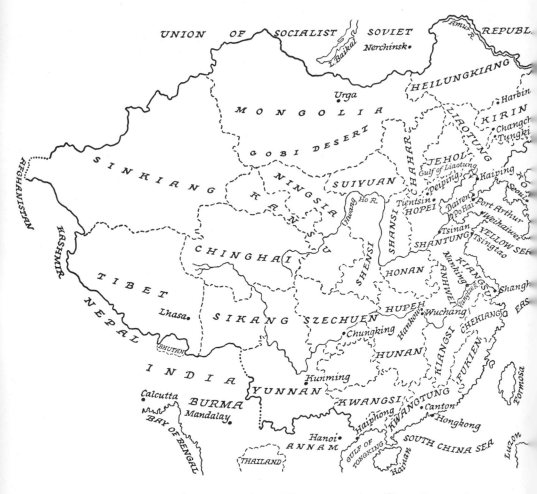

China before the Japanese Onslaught

and reconstruction of a welfare state. He was now prepared to discuss common action with warlords like Chang Tso-lin and figureheads of Japanese puppets like Tuan Chi-jui. In what would a compact with such men ensue? They had troops and power; he had few of the first and only a trace, at the most, of the second. Would they submit to his leadership or swallow him up? The answer is self-evident; but Sun doubtless believed he would convert them. No doubt they would have professed conversion and he would have believed them. At any rate he was willing to treat with them and, if possible, come to an agreement. This little but significant episode, incidentally, is tactfully glided over in Kuomintang propaganda paeans to Sun Yat-sen as father of both the republic and Nationalist China. The historic fact is nevertheless that Sun was willing to compromise the new-born nationalist regime in partnership with the warlord dispensation.

Fate intervened to prevent the issue from being put to the test. Sun had been indisposed before he left Canton and in November became seriously ill in the north. He went to Peking and entered the American Rockefeller hospital there. His malady was diagnosed as cancer and on March 12, 1925, he died.

Thus ended one of the most remarkable careers in modern Asian history, one that left its stamp on that part of the world as have few others in our era—no others in fact except Gandhi and Kemal of Turkey. Sun was a man of so many contradictory traits that it is all but impossible to assess him properly. He was one man one day, but could be a different man in the same day. As the episodes in his career unroll before one, one can only conclude that he was a fool, rattle-brained and irresponsible. His adventurism, his comic-opera coups, his gallopings off in two opposite directions one right after another—all these made him a ludicrous figure. His espousal of various philosophies one after another and in contradiction of each other makes him seem light-witted. Yet he was not; or, if he was irresponsible, ludicrous, light-witted in some measure, these were counterbalanced by opposite traits.

Undoubtedly he was intellectually unstable. Undoubtedly, too, he was undereducated and superficial. The combination accounted for the thinness and impracticability of his policies and programs, for his being easily beguiled by ideologies with an attractive surface, for his bad judgment of men and ideas, and for his flamboyant gesturings in intellectual space. His standards were poor, shifting, and shaky. Most unfortunate of all was his credulity. He could believe what he wanted to believe to a degree beyond the generality of men. This, combined with a pronounced vanity that grew as he became older, made him prey to the flattery of self-seekers, fools, charlatans, and rogues. Whoever laid unction to his ego had his ear, and whoever had his ear with something externally plausible and promising quick success for whatever end Sun desired at the time had his consent and approval, no matter how specious the proposal might be. Borodin's feat was not so extraordinary; lesser men with less to offer had captured Sun as completely. Hence so much in his career that was futile, so much that was farcical, and so much that had tragic consequences for China. Successive failures of preposterous enterprises may have left his spirit undimmed, since he had measureless inner emotional resources, but the disillusionment that followed the collapse of one bizarre episode after another did something to the spirit of the best elements of the Chinese people, so many of whom gave him their loyalty and looked to him for the regeneration of their country.

A man of only these traits, however, could never have commanded for long the respect he undoubtedly had and impressed himself so deeply on his countrymen. There had to be something else, and there was. For all Sun Yat-sen's vanity he was also selfless. It was his people's good and not his own personal aggrandizement that he strove for. To that he dedicated himself when young and to that he was faithful in his fashion to the end, however erroneous his judgment and ill-considered his acts. This the Chinese sensed and for it they held him in esteem even when they were critical of him, for the contrast in this respect between him and nearly all other officials was eloquent and persuasive. He was a genuine patriot, and even his political enemies knew it. They knew, too, that he was of unimpeachable integrity. No one who knew him could ever have doubted that. Nor could one talk with him and not be moved by his patent sincerity, no matter how much one might disagree with what he was saying. He had personal magnetism. He had that which is given to few men: the power to move men singly or in large numbers, move them to follow him loyally and blindly. It is a power that in a Hitler or Napoleon can lead, out of mad ambition or psychopathic malevolence, to death and destruction. In Sun Yat-sen it was mingled with compassion, with zeal for the welfare of his people.

For all of Sun Yat-sen's failings, weaknesses, and mistakes there was in him grandeur—grandeur of the sort that makes history and makes men live in history. Much that he did was to his country's good: he stirred it to resolve, gave it confidence, set it on the way to recovering its dignity and its place in the world. Much that he did was to his country's harm: the reckless adventurism he instilled in it, the callow flights into half-understood philosophies, the disestablishment of critical judgment and the premium on superficiality, the impatience that gave it the habit of trying to build without foundations. Unfortunately the harm probably outweighed the good.

CHAPTER XXXII

The Nationalists Take the Offensive: Fighting Begins

The death of Sun Yat-sen lifted the only effective restraint on the internal friction in Canton and the Kuomintang. As long as he lived his personality and prestige and his unchallengeable leadership kept both sides under control and prevented a serious open break. It also acted as a check on the aggressiveness of the Communists. With his death both the Communists and the conservatives, who were becoming increasingly more incensed by the Communists' boldness, had a free hand and each was determined to suppress the other. The issue was now nationalist revolution or social revolution, and as matters stood in mid-1925 the Communists were gaining rapidly, both in Canton and throughout south China. At the same time the influence of Borodin and, through him, of the Russians was gaining correspondingly, which also outraged the conservatives. The conservatives were generally middle-aged or older, and older Chinese had not lost the memory of Russia's aggressions on China.

It was outside Canton, however, that something occurred to overshadow the conflict in Canton, change the course of the nationalist revolution, and give a new and more serious turn both to the politics of China itself and the relations of China with the outer world. This has since been known as the May 30 Incident. Strikes had become almost chronic in all the urban centers since the latter part of 1924. Wages, hours, and working conditions warranted strikes, to be sure, but these were strikes for political purposes more than for anything else. Some of the wage demands were fantastic and plainly were not made in any hope of settlement. The strikes were incited and in some cases directed by Communists, and they had no desire for settlement. They wanted pretext for agitation and propaganda, and amicable settlement, even one with concessions to the workers, would impede them. Late in the spring of 1925 a strike had broken out in one of the Japanese-owned textile mills in Shanghai. Efforts to end it were vain, and there were the usual minor disorders. Then a call was issued for a large demonstration on May 30 by strikers, labor sympathizers, and students within the boundaries of the International Settlement. In one way or another the large and noisy crowd converged on one of the Settlement police stations, and there appeared to be signs of intention to force an entrance. The British police officer in charge ordered the mob to retire and disperse. They did not, probably more because of confusion than of unwillingness. Without warning the police officer ordered his men to fire—not even over the heads of the demonstrators to point a warning but directly into the seething mass in the first volley. Some thirty fell, twenty of them dead, many of whom were students.

The thoughtlessness of one British police officer ignited a spark throughout the country. Not only Communists and Communist sympathizers, not only students were aroused. Even conservatives were outraged at what they believed to be foreign callousness or, rather, British callousness, for Great Britain was already the target of the anti-imperialist propaganda. The Russians had more to do with giving it that direction than the Chinese. No single incident in those years contributed as much as the shooting on May 30 to the strength of the Kuomintang, the Communists, and the nationalist movement. The line was drawn sharply for all Chinese—for or against the foreigner. Demonstrations and strikes took place throughout the country. Among students recruits to the extreme left were made by the thousands. The May 30 Incident may be said to have marked the turning of the tide in China; the ebb of foreign power and influence then set in.

In Canton naturally there were some of the most boisterous demonstrations. One of them was called for June 23. The route was laid along the narrow creek that divides the city from the small island of Shameen, where the foreign concession was situated. Quite likely this was deliberately designed as a provocation of foreign attack, which could be turned to as good account by the Communists as that which happened on May 30. If so, the foreigners fell into the trap. When the demonstrators seemed to threaten to rush on to the bridge leading to the island the British and French fired. Between forty and fifty were killed or wounded, again many of them students, including students at the Whampoa military academy, where the headiest antiforeign indoctrination was being given. This was fresh fuel on the fire.

The first and most serious effect was felt in Hongkong. There a general strike was called. Within a few weeks activity in the colony, one of the busiest and most prosperous in the British Empire, was suspended. The harbor was deserted. Ships could not be loaded or unloaded. Factories were still. Shops closed. Means of transportation ceased to function. Even household servants left, and in the system of life for foreigners in an Eastern community that meant that households were paralyzed. Hongkong had an air of death in life. The losses to foreigners and foreign enterprises were prodigious. The British were helpless. There were no strikebreakers. Only the foolhardiest Chinese would dare to violate the stoppage. Not for more than a year did life become normal in Hongkong again. The Chinese had demonstrated their power. The little foreign islands in the vast empire, hitherto invulnerable, if not sacrosanct, were now exposed in their innate weakness. The lesson sank in.

Simultaneously the tempo of action in Canton speeded up. The occasion beckoned to direct measures, but what had not been settled yet was measures by whom and for what end. Neither faction in the Kuomintang felt strong enough to attempt an actual coup, but the preliminary intriguing was intensified both in ferocity and deviousness. Some of the older of Sun Yat-sen's disciples sought to maintain control and assure some adherence to his principles—men like Wang Ching-wei, later to be in noxious disrepute because of his desertion to the Japanese during the war; Sun Yat-sen's widow; Liao Chung-kai; T. V. Soong, brother of Mrs. Sun Yat-sen and already a rising figure because of his skill in finance. There were others who sided with the conservatives but still tried to remain faithful to Sun's principles—men like Wang Chung-hui, the jurist, and Hu Han-min, who at times also arrayed himself with the leftists, however. In addition to them there was coming to the fore a young man who was destined to play a larger role than any of the others, as large perhaps as the role of Sun Yat-sen. He was Chiang Kai-shek. Chiang was one of a large number who had attached themselves to Sun while he was in Japan. After the revolution of 1911 and its farcical aftermath he had sunk to obscurity in Shanghai, making his living by his wits, and then had followed Sun to Canton after World War I. After the alliance with Russia he was sent to Moscow for indoctrination and training both as a revolutionary and as a soldier and then brought back to Canton as head of the Whampoa Military Academy, with General Galen, the Russian, as supervisor and general mentor. Neither the philosophical nor the military tutelage of Moscow seems to have gone very deep in Chiang. The philosophical he shook off very soon; in the military he was more resolute than skillful, as subsequent years were to prove. But he was ambitious and iron-willed, adroit in political maneuvering, and not too delicate in the methods he chose to dispose of his political enemies. His position as head of the Whampoa Academy gave him the makings of a loyal political and military machine that he was to have at his service for twenty-five years. He was coming to the fore, but few discerned then how far he was to go.

The personal struggle for mastery was beyond appeasement or compromise. In June there was another minor battle in Canton when a new force officered by Chiang Kai-shek's pupils turned on Yunnan provincial troops and drove them from the city. In this both factions joined, not only because the Yunnanese were more or less a mercenary body but because each faction feared that in time they would be used by the other against itself. This was only a pause, however. Later Hu Han-min, accused of plotting, went into hiding, fearing assassination—justly. He was found and arrested but escaped with banishment. Liao Chung-kai was assassinated, which whipped up the fury of the left wing. Borodin tried to bring about and maintain unification, taking over Sun Yat-sen's role as pacificator, the just judge holding both sides to arbitrament and concord. There is reason to believe that he had by then become interested in China's welfare for its own sake and was not only seeking to maintain unity as a more effective means to Russia's ends. He won assent to a scheme of reorganization of government under a kind of triumvirate consisting of Chiang Kai-shek, Wang Ching-wei and Hsu Chung-tze, the latter being a man of lesser consequence. There was provided later a scheme under which there were to be a Political Council, deciding matters of high policy, and an Administrative Council consisting of heads of administrative departments. While this was supposed to be the system of government for the whole country, it really obtained only in Canton and its immediate environs. Even there its principal result was that the Political Council became the arena for the struggle between the rival factions in the Kuomintang—the conservatives and the leftists, the latter steadily drifting closer to the Communists.

The first formal break came in November, 1925, when a group of conservatives in the Kuomintang left Canton for Peking, where they convened a meeting in the Western Hills, outside the walls of the capital. The meeting made a formal protest against the trend of events in Canton and called for a break with the Communists and the Russians. An appeal was also addressed to the Chinese people for support in saving the Kuomintang and restoring it to its original purposes. The effort came to nothing. The tide had set in south China and was too strong to be reversed.

Early in 1926 there was a more forcible and successful effort. In March Chiang Kai-shek suddenly swooped down on the left-wing leaders and arrested a large number, while several, including Wang Ching-wei and Hu Han-min, were compelled to flee. An uneasy compromise was arrived at, Borodin being permitted to remain as adviser and Chiang Kai-shek taking the post of Chairman of the Standing Committee of the Central Executive Committee of the Kuomintang, the most powerful position in the party. The coup had two results. It demonstrated that Chiang had dominance in Canton and it revealed that the Communists were the only formidable opposition in the struggle for control. A few weeks later Chiang set out to prove that he was brooking no challenge from any group by evicting a number of conservative leaders. There was to be no doubt now who was master in Canton.

All sides in Canton were becoming impatient for broader fields in which to operate. Chiang Kai-shek's new military force had been blooded and appeared to be ready for something more than local coups. A general military advance from Canton might also have the effect of overriding internecine warfare by providing a common enemy. The private feud might be temporarily adjourned, and from that neither side seemed particularly averse. At the same time the progressive deterioration in the North seemed to present opportunity. There not only were the rival warlords chewing each other up but the nominal central government was falling apart. Economic conditions were all but intolerable. The people were demoralized. They were psychologically prepared for anything except what they had. The North could almost be called a vacuum. Chiang and his associates decided to fill it. It should be noted that Borodin counselled against the decision. He thought the Kuomintang forces should be held in reserve until they had built up greater strength, until Kwangtung Province itself had a solider government and the ground in the North was better prepared by intensive propaganda and organization of the masses. He had no doubt read and drawn deductions from Sun Yat-sen's record of premature flights. But he was overruled. Perhaps that aspect of Sun's spirit had been transmitted to Chiang and his followers.

The northern expedition was decided on and was formally launched in July, 1926. As it proved, Chiang's confidence was vindicated. From the outset province after province fell like overripe fruit. It was almost unnecessary to fight. In places there was only token resistance. The whole of Kwangtung Province was quickly consolidated, as was the adjoining province of Kwangsi. Hunan, on the way to the Yangtze, went equally quickly. The local commanders there had been won over to the Nationalists before and the peasants had been well indoctrinated and won over by promises of utopia to come. The provincial commanders who remained loyal to the North were cut off in the rear by popular action. Here the first signs of mass violence appeared. The peasants, convinced that their time had come—and in Hunan agrarian abuses had been flagrant—seized land and stores of grain and in some parts killed large landowners as well. Since the peasants had been dependent on surplus stores on large estates for seed grain, though on loan and at usurious interest, they were to suffer later, when much of the rice had been eaten and there was little to plant.

By the end of the year the Nationalist armies were on the Yangtze, at the strategical and economic centers of Hankow and Wuchang. In the east, near the mouth of the river, they were also advancing on Shanghai and Nanking. It was an astonishing exploit, though more a political and moral victory than a military victory. The fact was astonishing nonetheless, to the Chinese people almost as much as to the representatives of foreign Powers. At the end of 1926 the Nationalist armies swept across the Yangtze into Hankow with its foreign concessions, aiming especially at the British Concession. There the large population arose, stormed the British area, and took it over. Mob violence whipped up and it appeared that anything might happen, including a repetition of the Boxer massacres. The British were confronted with a difficult choice. They had gunboats in the river and could have held at bay the Nationalist armies and dealt dire punishment to the Chinese mobs. But they could not have done so without the slaughter of civilians and that would have released a volcanic eruption throughout the country and terrible revenge against foreign residents everywhere. They elected wisely to let the Chinese take over. Later the retrocession of the British Concession in Hankow was formally negotiated between British and Chinese Nationalist official representatives. The same thing happened at Kiukiang farther down the river, where there also was a British concession.

Thus for the first time since 1842 the Chinese had recovered something of their own from foreign Powers. They had won it back not by pleas, by appeals to justice or reason, but by sheer force. They had seized, and the foreigner had submitted. Instead of the punitive measures conventionally taken on those of lesser power and darker color who committed such infractions of the foreigner's law, Sir Austen Chamberlain, British Foreign Secretary, made a formal declaration to the effect that China's "legitimate aspirations" must be met and a new policy of conciliation adopted. He also proposed further compromise, including restoration of China's tariff autonomy. China's aspirations, it appeared, were legitimate, not when presented in rational, peaceful discussion but when the Chinese acted with violence. Force, it appeared, conferred legitimacy: a moral law in international relations—or in the relations between strong white Powers and weak nonwhite countries—that the Chinese proceeded to act on.

Another almost universal law had also been invoked, however unwittingly: Time is the principal determinant of the success or failure of any action between the strong and the weak. The effectiveness of any compromise depends on when it is made. What serves in one year may be useless the next. Put otherwise, voluntary appeasement from strength earns gratitude; involuntary appeasement from weakness begets more demands and defiance if they are not granted. If the foreign Powers had been willing to offer as much in 1919 as they were compelled to concede in 1927 they would have retained the other half much longer than 1927 and the Chinese would have been grateful for something given in generosity. In 1927 that which they had wrested by force spurred them to insist on still more, for they perceived, as it was not difficult to perceive, that it had been given them out of necessity, the necessity born of weakness. After 1919 the choice in China for the Western Powers was either to meet Chinese nationalism half way and do so before it became virulent or to crush it at the outset by a military expedition. The latter was out of the question, of course, after four years of war. But they did not therefore take the alternative of prompt concessions. They did nothing. The result was that in a few years they lost everything they had held in China and did not have the good will of the Chinese.

After their success the Chinese were riding high. They pressed their advantage both against their enemies of the North and against the foreigners. By the spring of 1927 only two northern provinces held out against them. But before then two events had occurred that again shook the country and affected its relations with the outer world. Nanking and Shanghai fell, but there was more in their falling than transfer of control over two cities.

After the Nationalists' occupation of Hankow the split between the two camps in the Kuomintang became open and unbridgeable. It was now a chasm. The capital of Nationalist China was moved from Canton to Hankow and there the leftist and Communist wings won the ascendancy. Chiang Kai-shek, who was with the armies, had established headquarters in Nanchang, in Kiangsi Province, nearer the coast, and was worried. Then he saw the same menace nearer at hand. Shanghai was about to be lost by its northern defenders, and it was clear that it would be taken by the Communists and their adherents among the Nationalists unless prevented by vigorous countermeasures from within the Kuomintang. The city was in turmoil, the International Settlement no less than the Chinese city. Strikes had been called. Demonstrations were in progress. Agitators and Communist agents had infiltrated and all preparations had been made for a coup that would make Shanghai a Communist city.

Chiang Kai-shek struck first. His troops took the city on March 22. With the aid of his own agents and some of the most unsavory elements in Shanghai, including the members of a secret society who really were gangsters of the most pernicious order, he made a lightning attack, caught the leftists by surprise, and seized the Chinese city, the part outside the International Settlement. Then followed an unforgettable dreadful night. The Communists had all been marked down in advance by Chiang's agents. They were hunted out and those who could not escape were either tortured to extract information or summarily killed. Among those killed were many against whom the evidence was doubtful or who were only generally sympathetic, including students and other youngsters who were only carried on the new wave of patriotism.

There was, in short, a period of terror, of white terror, with all the accompaniments of terror everywhere. It has never been forgotten. Chiang had executed a successful coup and won his victory. He was master of the country's largest city and he had purged his opponents there. But he was to pay a price the exorbitance of which he could not guess. For there was laid up a store of hatred, an implacable enmity, a feudists' vendetta, that made internal peace thereafter impossible. Either Chiang and his supporters had to be eliminated or the Communists had to be exterminated. No strife is ever as deadly as civil strife, and no civil strife has ever been more ferocious than that in China after 1927. It had to be death to one or the other. That was shown, incidentally, in the failure to make a compromise after Japan's surrender, despite American pressure. There was more than conflict over forms of government and society. There was a score to be paid, blood vengeance to be exacted. But for the time Chiang Kai-shek and his conservative allies had Shanghai.

Two days after the Nationalists' conquest of Shanghai they swarmed into Nanking. In that city there was a bloody episode of another order and with other victims. The conquering forces got out of hand and started to attack foreigners of all nationalities. Houses were looted and a number of foreigners were killed. There was terror, too, but of a different kind. How it came about was never known. Whether it was only the doing of troops, undisciplined at best, who had gone amok in victory or whether it was instigated by the Communists in order to embroil Chiang

Kai-shek with the foreign Powers could never be decided. There was some evidence for both explanations. But when the massacre of all the foreigners in the city appeared to be in prospect British and American ships lying in the Yangtze off the harbor laid down a bombardment to keep the soldiers and mobs at bay until all foreigners could make their way to the harbor and be brought off in small boats, to be taken down to Shanghai. Thus nearly all of them were saved. The governments of the foreign Powers protested vigorously, but short of a punitive military expedition, which meant a full-scale war, they could do nothing. They chose the part of discretion, an even more conclusive confession than any yet made that the Chinese could act with impunity. There would be no restraint on them except that which was self-imposed.

CHAPTER XXXIII

1927-28: Years of Crisis

The crisis in China was to come, however, not between the Chinese and the foreigners but between Chinese Communists and anti-Communists. With the establishment of the new Nationalist capital in Wuhan (the three cities of Wuchang, Nanyang, and Hankow on the Yangtze) and Chiang Kai-shek and his closest associates conducting the military campaign in the eastern part of the country, the inner conflict could no longer be evaded or its climax long postponed. With Chiang away, the left wing of the Kuomintang and the Communists were in the saddle in Wuhan. In effect this meant the Communists, since they are trained everywhere in the art of seizing the initiative and, because they always know what they want, succeed in having their way even if in a minority.

It was the Communists who now took over the direction of agitation and propaganda and the mobilizing of peasant and worker discontent. The conservative wing of the Kuomintang looked on in frustrated wrath, the left wing in ineffectual uneasiness. The result was still more strikes in cities than before, with still more demands impossible to meet under existing conditions and still more violence and disorder in rural areas. In cities manufacturers and merchants almost ceased to function. Enterprises of any size were closed either by strikes incited for political purposes or by employers' lockouts by way of retaliation. Thousands were out of work and prices rose, increasing confusion, unrest, and rioting. The countryside was in turmoil. Not only landlords but those peasants who did not themselves take part in despoiling property owners were beginning to suffer. That part of the country which was under Nationalist control was increasingly getting out of hand.

This inevitably aggravated the doctrinal antagonism between the two factions in the Kuomintang and also inevitably had political consequences. The leftist-Communist coalition in Wuhan decided that the time had come to rid itself of Chiang Kai-shek once and for all and thus remove the principal obstruction to gaining its ends—the leftists had not yet considered how far their own ends coincided with the Communists'. The Central Executive Committee met in Hankow, with a comfortable majority of leftists and Communists, and dismissed Chiang Kai-shek from the chairmanship of the Standing Committee of the Central Executive Committee, which was in effect to nullify him as a force in the Kuomintang. It was not in Chiang Kai-shek's character to take this submissively, and he did not. Two weeks after the decision in Hankow he set up the central government of Nationalist China in Nanking, thus declaring the Hankow regime illegitimate. Then began a succession of combinations and countercombinations, plots and counterplots, of rapidly shifting alliances, of intrigues and even of clashes between large army units, that can be followed only with the aid of a map. The northern militarists took advantage of this and won a number of military successes while the two rival capitals were trying to eliminate each other. For a time it seemed that the Nationalist cause was lost, defeated from within, and Chiang Kai-shek at one time went into retirement. Then the issue was forced by a sudden development from without and the question whether Communists or non-Communists would rule in China came to a head.

The decision to force the issue was made in Moscow, not China. By 1927 an internal conflict was also seething in Russia. This was the feud between Trotsky and Stalin. The one held that communism could become the law and the mode of the world by world revolution at once and the other that the world revolution would be ultimately consummated only if communism became impregnably established in one country, which at the time meant Russia. China became the test case. Trotsky wanted to push at once and to the full an effort to make China a completely communist state under a dictatorship of the proletariat. He thought that conditions in China were ripe for such a stroke or could be quickly ripened under Russia's light. Stalin was more cautious. He thought that China was not yet ready for revolution (as Joffe had admitted in his agreement with Sun Yat-sen in 1923) and that conditions would first have to be carefully prepared. On this issue the polemics became fierce and uncompromising in the highest circles of the Kremlin, and the feud between Stalin and Trotsky passed beyond compromise. Officially at least it was on this that Stalin and Trotsky came to the struggle to the death. It may also be that by the inner drive of both, each was compelled to seek to eliminate the other and China was a convenient pretext. With philosophical difference to sharpen the edge of personal hate each could proceed with special gusto to the dispatch of the other.

What happened in the innermost circles in the Kremlin no one will ever know unless the Communist regime collapses or is overthrown from without and the secret documents are revealed to the world—if, that is, important transactions were recorded in writing. At any rate Moscow showed its hand in China in June, 1927. The official representative of the Russian Communist party and the Communist International was Borodin but, as is Russia's custom, there was another representative to watch the official representative. He was M. N. Roy, a Hindu Communist. On June 1, Roy met Wang Ching-wei, leader of the Kuomintang and then the leading non-Communist figure in Wuhan, and told him that Stalin had sent a telegram dealing with China that Borodin had not yet shown to any Chinese. What he did not explain but from later evidence seems to be true is that Borodin considered it unwise to reveal the message. Borodin, being in China and knowing Chinese persons and conditions, realized that the message would either frighten or anger the Chinese. Communists in Moscow after their fashion knew all about China without being there. "Scientific Socialism" always told them; it was necessary only to consult the diagram.

Roy did show the telegram to Wan Ching-wei, who, despite his leaning toward the Communists at the time, was as stunned as Borodin feared. The telegram, though signed by Stalin, put a series of demands only slightly less stringent than Trotsky's position, an interesting reflection on the relation between the personal and impersonal in Kremlin politics. Stalin told the Chinese Communists to insist on a reorganization of the Kuomintang which would give them a larger representation in its principal organs, especially the Central Executive Committee. Also a separate Communist army was to be formed, together with an additional force of 50,000 peasants and workers to be used against Kuomintang forces that remained "recalcitrant." Further, revolutionary courts were to be set up to deal with anti-Communist officers in the Kuomintang armies. Obviously this meant that the Communists and their Russian advisers would rule the Kuomintang and, if the Nationalists were successful, all of China. And this in turn meant that China would be ruled from Moscow.

Thus Wang Ching-wei construed the message and he protested vigorously to Roy. Borodin also protested to Roy when he heard of his indiscretion, but by then it was too late. Wang immediately consulted his colleagues in the government and party, who were not only indignant but frightened. They ordered the known Communists in the armies to be put under surveillance in order to prevent a coup. Actually some clashes did take place but the Communists did not prove strong enough to succeed. There was almost unanimous recognition that with or without intention Stalin's demands constituted an ultimatum and that the time for choice had come. The Communists and the Kuomintang could not co-exist. Either the Communists would have to be disbanded and the Russians forced to leave or the Kuomintang would pass out of existence in favor of Communist and Russian rule. For even the most ardent leftists, with a few exceptions, the decision was clear. The Communists would have to go. Borodin, sure of the outcome, resigned his advisership. On July 15 the decision was taken and officially pronounced. Borodin had to go. Communists were dismissed from their posts in the government and the army. The break had come. Some skirmishes followed but the Communists had overestimated their strength and were suppressed. The first Communist effort to take over the country resulted in dismal failure.

Unity within the Kuomintang did not follow, however. The rival claims of Wuhan and Nanking could not be reconciled, if only because Chiang Kai-shek's ambition stood in the way of compromise. The Wuhan faction did not want Chiang domineering them and Chiang would not play second fiddle to any group or individual. There were months of the usual maneuvering, with all the intriguery of which revolutionary Chinese were capable and at which they were so adept, but by the end of the year Nanking had proved it could not be withstood, principally because it had the preponderance of military force. The Wuhan government voluntarily dissolved and a new Central Government was established in Nanking with the leftist factions incorporated but in a minor role. The conservatives had won, and of them a large number, if not most, were more reactionary than conservative. Radicalism was suppressed in the cities and on the land. *The Three Principles of the People* was still the official philosophy and program but it was never again to receive anything but lip service—if it had ever had anything else.

Yet it is not accurate to say, as has been widely said since, that the victory of Chiang Kai-shek and his supporters was a betrayal of the revolutionary faith inspired by Sun Yat-sen and that Chiang and his supporters broke with the Communists only in order to save their interests as rich landlords and merchants. It is a mistake to construe the whole episode as a betrayal at all. The motives were mixed, as in any political situation anywhere. To a certain extent there was undoubtedly a desire to protect the vested interests of the wealthy minority. But another consideration had entered even before this motive could come into play. That was the question whether China should be ruled by Chinese or Russians. This was after all a nationalist revolution. Even in Sun Yat-sen's mind it was more political than social, its primary purpose being to cancel foreign special privileges and recover national independence. It was in this cause that he won his first disciples and then later the thousands of the young and the intellectuals who flocked to his banner.

What would it have gained China to shake off all the great Powers except one and leave that one more powerful than any or all of them had been before? If it had to submit to mastery it was better to have many masters than one, for then they might check one another and China could play one off against another. With Russia alone left in China with special position and privileges—and its military power—the time would be short before China finally became a colony, and for that the Chinese revolutionaries, especially the original ones, had not striven all these years. Even the more radical among the Kuomintang leaders turned against the Communists, and even from the point of view of social change and the aspiration to modulate the injustices of Chinese society they were right. To reform Chinese society but to lose China was no advance for the Chinese, however socially enlightened they might be.

With the Nationalists at least outwardly united the next step was to resume the expedition to the north and bring the whole country under their sway. Some of the Kuomintang forces defected—they became the nucleus of the army that expanded in the next twenty years until it overran the whole country and established the Communist regime—but almost all of the Nationalist armies came under the command of Chiang Kai-shek. A united force could now advance to complete the conquest of the country. The official enemy was the loose combination of warlords, especially Chang Tso-lin, who was then in Peking and controlled Chihli Province and environs as well as Manchuria. But opposition was to emerge from another quarter. This was Japan. Another phase was to begin both in China's internal politics and its external relations.

In the first years of the Chinese Nationalist movement Japan played a negative role. This was indeed its role in all its relations with the outer world in that period for reasons to be discussed later. While the Japanese suffered less from the Nationalists' acts than the British they, too, suffered, but they took no reprisals. They were on the contrary conspicuously correct. Perhaps restraint was mixed with shrewdness. While they could not help perceive that an aroused and ultimately united China boded no good to their own ambitions, they also could not have felt excessive regret at the prospect of the eviction of the Western Powers. That would at least leave them greater freedom for whatever action they might in time take there. But no matter in what proportion the new antimilitarism, or rather, nonmilitarism, was mixed with shrewd foresight, the Japanese showed more forbearance to China in those years than for years past and less hostility to its aspirations than other Powers.

The unexpected successes of the Chinese, their apparent strides toward unity, and their unmistakable determination to make an end of all foreign encroachment seem to have taken the Japanese by surprise and made them uncomfortable in their restraint. Also the unwonted exercise of moderation seems to have chafed their most influential leaders. Repression did not come easily to the overenergetic among them, least easily when self-imposed. The military began to feel the need of self-expression in the traditional mode and there were premonitions of a return to the old, familiar ways. The first signs appeared as early as spring, 1927, when the "weak," that is, nonaggressive, government of Baron Wakatsuki and his Foreign Minister, Baron Shidehara, was overthrown. Shidehara was the best-known advocate of moderation toward China. He believed in confining Japan's policy to winning economic paramountcy in China. Men of his stamp seemed to have their way in the period of Japan's moratorium on expansion. The Wakatsuki government was succeeded by one headed by Baron Giichi Tanaka, a general and the favorite of Prince Yamagata. Tanaka became Foreign Minister as well as premier. Tanaka took from his master all his military cast of mind, his ambition for himself and his country, his determination to make Japan safe and strong, even at the expense of others; but unfortunately he was a Yamagata in a smaller mold. He had not had inculcated in him his master's knowledge of the world, his insight, self-control, and general intelligence. It was he who conceived the so-called "positive policy" in China, the policy that in eighteen years was to negate Japan as a world Power.

The first evidence of positiveness came as early as May, 1927, soon after Tanaka came into power. Before the more serious split in the Kuomintang was recognized and all opposition seemed to be falling before it, Japanese troops were sent into Shantung Province. Their ostensible object was to protect Japanese lives and property in the path of the Nationalists' advance. The actual purpose was to block that advance. The test did not come, since the dissension within the Kuomintang postponed military activity. But it came a year later when the Nationalists' northern advance was resumed. As the Nationalist forces entered Shantung more Japanese troops were sent in. They took up positions at Tsinanfu astride the Tientsin-Pukow Railway, along which the Nationalists would have to move if they were to get to Tientsin and Peking. The Nationalists pressed on nevertheless and early in May, 1928, there was a collision between Japanese and Chinese troops, with casualties on both sides. The Japanese immediately dispatched reinforcements and gave the Nationalists an ultimatum to withdraw from Tsinanfu and the railway, which meant they would have to give up the campaign in that part of the country. It was clear the Japanese meant business and the Chinese had to submit, though with a protest to the League of Nations. With that Chinese-Japanese relations entered on another phase or, perhaps, returned to the normal phase.

The Nationalists abandoned the campaign in East China under Chiang Kai-shek's direct command but ordered it to be taken up further west, where another Nationalist army started northward along the railway from Hankow to Peking. It met little opposition. Northern troops faded away before the Nationalists and by the end of May the latter were approaching Peking. A few days later Chang Tso-lin and his bodyguard unceremoniously fled from Peking, boarding commandeered trains to take them back to Manchuria. On June 8 the Nationalists entered the capital. For practical purposes they held all of China, though there were still some local pockets of resistance. The name of the capital was changed to Peiping, meaning northern peace, and Nanking was made the capital of the country. On July 3 Chiang Kai-shek made his official entry into Peking and three days later repaired to the Buddhist temple in the Western Hills, where Sun Yat-sen's body was lying in temporary burial, to report to the founder of the revolution that his mission had been consummated; the revolution to which he had dedicated his life had been completed. It had indeed; but that it was the kind of revolution Sun Yat-sen had conceived was already open to question.

Before then, however, another event had occurred, less important in itself than for what it portended. As has been told, Chang Tso-lin left Peking for Mukden, but just before his train arrived there was an explosion on the track over which it was passing and Chang and some of his retinue were instantly killed. There was never any doubt about what had happened. A bomb had been placed on the track for the purpose of killing him and it was placed there by Japanese soldiers. This was admitted almost openly in Tokyo and when investigations were pressed there and a demand made in the Diet that the findings be made public, Tanaka was forced to resign. Thus the "positive policy" in China, which had been designed as a corrective of the "weak" policy of the preceding liberal governments, was discarded, at least temporarily. But another force had emerged that was not to be arrested until Tokyo lay in ruins. This was the "dynamism" of the "Young Officer" class. Year by year this class was to grow stronger. As new recruits from the lower commissioned ranks were added to it, it was to become more daring, more defiant, more irresponsible, and more violent until it was a law unto itself. If not quite able to determine Japan's foreign policy, it could at least force the government's hand by direct action. By 1940 one could not tell whether Japan was ruled by an emperor and a civil government or by a camarilla of younger military men who by threats, coups, and assassinations exercised a kind of government by terror.

In Nanking a government was set up with at least nominal jurisdiction over the whole country. Such recalcitrant warlords as there were lacked the strength to offer a real challenge. There were others who were not actually recalcitrant but whose loyalty was doubtful. They disliked Chiang Kai-shek only slightly less than the Communists and were jealous of his ascendancy. Much of Chiang's effort in the ensuing years had to be directed toward eliminating or neutralizing them. They did not quite dare to come out in opposition, however, and in law and, on the whole, in fact the authority of government resided in Nanking. Then the period of tutelage was formally proclaimed. This was the stage after military conquest and unification as planned by Sun Yat-sen. An Organic Law was drafted and adopted and the five-power system of government was instituted.

Since this was the period of tutelage, sovereignty rested not in the people but in the Kuomintang. The heritage of Russian communist political theory had not been shaken off entirely. By the party all officials were appointed and to it all officials were responsible. Theoretically the supreme organ of the Kuomintang was the national party congress— again the Russian model—which was to meet every two years (but did not always do so, again the Russian touch) and which when it did meet had little to say. The actual executive body was the Central Executive Committee, composed of thirty-six members, which exercised power when the party congress was not in session, which is to say always. There was also a Central Supervisory Committee with loosely defined powers—theoretically a kind of watchdog body. In addition there was a Central Political Council that had direct control of administration, appointing the heads of the five *yuan* or departments and in general supervising their activities. But real power centered in the small Standing Committee of the Central Executive Committee, which met when the Central Executive Committee was not in session: the Chairman of the Standing Committee was the president of the country and commander-in-chief of the armed forces.

That post was held, of course, by Chiang Kai-shek. Thus, while there was a nominal structure of government, the country was ruled by a monopoly party, and that party was ruled by a large committee, and that committee by a small committee, and that committee by a small group, within which real power of decision rested with Chiang Kai-shek and his closest associates—again, the Russian touch. Throughout the country there was the same dual machinery of government and party—a locus of nominal power and a center of real power not really responsible to anyone. It would be difficult to devise a system more surely designed to produce confusion, inefficiency, waste of energy and resources, and opportunity for both evasion of responsibility and corruption. That the system did not break down earlier than it did is attributable to the fact that China was used to carrying on by momentum, to proceeding almost automatically in the conduct of affairs that did not lie in the private sphere. But all the potentialities of inefficiency, waste, and corruption were realized to the full, though it was at times difficult to tell which was the greater—inefficiency or corruption. Certainly it was an inauspicious beginning for a new order.

CHAPTER XXXIV

The Passing of the Old Order in China

It is appropriate at this time to recapitulate the eventful years in China since 1900, the years in which the old China, the China of history, which had been at some stages one of the world's great empires and at all times one of its most elevated cultures, ever more rapidly approached its end. It is always artificial to mark off historical epochs with precise dates, but it is not far wrong to say that in 1928 the collapse of the old China—both state and civilization—was on the way, well on the way to completion, in fact. The old China was gone; that was certain; what would be was not even dimly discernible. Even twenty years later that was still true. All that could be said with assurance was that to a Chinese of the eighteenth century now resurrected, the landscape, the flora and fauna, place names, language, and the appearance of his people would seem familiar; but he would feel alien nevertheless and adjust himself to the way of life slowly and with difficulty.

This was the real revolution, this and not the outwardly more dramatic overturn by the Communists in 1949. It was one of the most world-shaking revolutions of our era, unrecognized as it may have been at the time. By it that half of the human race which inhabits Asia was irrevocably changed, with consequences that could hardly be assessed even in the middle of the twentieth century. Yet it was not a revolution made by men. It was made by the forces of the time and therefore inevitable. In the later stages of China's breakdown men everywhere used to talk magisterially and in accents mingling patronage with reproof about "chaos" in China, and the words chaos and China became almost synonymous in the West. What was inferred therefrom was that the Chinese were congenitally incapable of governing themselves. From this it was only one step in logic to the conclusion that it were better if they were governed by others, better even for themselves. And in all Western countries with interests in China there was much eloquent but loose talk about international intervention to "put China's house in order." Just what countries would do it and how they would manage to have their own way over the whole of China when they could not be sure of maintaining their small concessions there appeared to be a matter of detail. It would have been just as logical to talk about appointing an international commission of traffic policement to direct the movements of an earthquake.

Apart from the question of practicability the whole idea was empty because based on a superficial understanding of what was taking place in China. What was called chaos was not the cause of China's difficulties —the confusion, ineffectiveness, turbulence, civil wars, and slow disintegration. It was a symptom—a symptom of a disease organic, ineradicable, and incurable. China had been attacked by modern civilization and the attack was fatal. The disease had been eating away slowly, and now the cumulative effect was telling. There was no resistance left in the social body, and China was passing away. These were its last throes, and we described what we saw as chaos. It was an unthinking, foolish description. For China had no control of what was happening to it, and could not have had.

The authentic Chinese system had failed to fulfill the needs of the Chinese people. It had failed in the first, almost elemental need, which was to preserve their existence as a nation. By the new nationalistic drive they had succeeded in recovering part of their lost sovereignty, but Japan had proved that it could frustrate unification. The system had failed, too, in that it was unsuited to the world: it left China a second-class state and society, a kind of permanent proletarian state, permanent dweller in the world's slums. This was no less true under the republic than under the monarchy, which signified that the truth lay deeper than form of government.

It can be stated almost as a rule of history that whenever in any community, whether primitive tribe or highly organized society, the organism which rules has lost moral authority, whether it be a tribal chieftain or an absolute monarchy or a parliament, that organism is on the way out and there will be a period of confusion and even violence in the community over which it has ruled. This was true in China. It had been true since the latter part of the nineteenth century and the truth could not be concealed from the Chinese people, since the evidence was visible, even palpable.

Foreign military forces had successfully invaded the country more than once. Large segments of territory had been cut away on the outer borders of the empire—Burma, Indo-China, Outer Mongolia. Leaseholds had been carved out of the inner boundaries and occupied by foreign Powers—Port Arthur and Dairen on the Manchurian coast, first by Russia and then by Japan; Weihaiwei on the north China coast by Great Britain; Tsingtao, further south on the coast, first by Germany and then by Japan; Kwangchaowan, in the south, by France. In the south there was a French sphere, in the center a British sphere, in the northeast a German sphere that later became Japanese, further north a Russian and a Japanese sphere—Manchuria and Mongolia. In six of the most important ports there were foreign settlements and residential concessions, governed exclusively by the Powers, singly or in combination. In several other ports and inland cities there were similar foreign residential concessions either by grant or prescriptive right. Foreigners were immune from Chinese legal jurisdiction and not subject to Chinese taxation. The Chinese tariff was fixed by foreign governments. The customs, railways, telegraphs, post office, and salt monopoly were under foreign control. Most of the country's revenue was pledged to the service of foreign loans nearly all of which had been forced on the Chinese government. The most profitable manufacturing and commercial enterprises were in foreign hands and in the economy of the country the small foreign minority enjoyed a kind of priority.

Not only in such official ways was the Chinese government shown to be impotent. Its authority was even more ostentatiously and contemptuously flouted by foreign individuals. Missionaries demonstrated in the smallest communities throughout the country that they could not only ignore officials but force them to submit to their demands, whether legitimate or capricious. In the ports foreign businessmen could go their way without even acknowledging the existence of Chinese officials. It was small wonder that Chinese government authority fell into disrepute among its own people. The Son of Heaven had scant respect in his own earthly realm, the republic even less. Neither could exercise command by its writ. The principle of authority was weakened and then broke, and that is fatal to any system of government at any place or time. It is especially so in a system such as the Chinese in which government ruled by symbol, by the respect attached to it rather than by force.

Simultaneously and even more serious, there was the erosion of the Chinese way of life—institutions, customs, and beliefs—by Western ideas and Western forms, which with increasing force over the years had been wearing away first the surface of China and then the sublayer. It was said in an earlier chapter that under the symbolical reign of the Throne, emblem of the race and culture and the cement that bound them, the actual administration of the affairs of Chinese society was carried out by the guild and the family. Both were undermined by the sapping of what radiated from railroads, factories, machine production, and modern banks.

The guild could function as director and arbiter of the economy as long as all transactions, whether of production or distribution, came under its purview. It could set standards of weights and measures, apprenticeship, and labor conditions. It could fix prices—minimum, not maximum, it must be remembered—regulate credit conditions and trade practices, and arbitrate business disputes. All the commodities and services supplied in the community were locally produced and under the observation and supervision of guild members and officers. Infractions of rules could be detected and punished. But when factories made cotton yarn or cotton cloth or flour or cement or cigarettes or cheap toilet articles by machinery and, on telegraphic order, shipped these goods via railway freight to markets two hundred miles away, the transactions could not be checked. Price restrictions, discounts, and credit conditions could not be enforced. Disputes between companies two hundred miles apart, each unknown in the locality of the other, could hardly be adjudicated by the two guilds concerned. Furthermore, modern production crosses numerous trade lines. No one trade guild can exercise effective jurisdiction. Under the conditions of industrialism the guild has no real function. Therefore chambers of commerce began to form, at least in the cities, taking in all lines of activity, but they never were endowed with the powers the guilds had possessed. For practical purposes the economy of China, as soon as it began the transition to factory production, was left ungoverned. In the most crucial sector of a society there had to be a vacuum until there was a political government that could exercise control of the economy or at least prescribe the basic laws under which it operated, as in the West.

The economy was disorganized in other ways. It was an economy organized in small local units, but yet even such an economy has its equilibrium and is stable only when all the parts are in balance. In China the balance was thrown off by the intrusion of foreign manufacturing and trading centers in the coastal ports. These had become by 1910 the most active and vital points in the Chinese economy, the arterial centers to which the blood of the whole system was drawn. Surplus capital, of which there is little enough in an unindustrialized country, flowed irresistibly to the foreign cities. There large profits were being made in the new factories and the merchant houses that sold their wares throughout the country. There opportunity could be found, and since the Chinese are second to none in native skill at any kind of business they soon made their way into modern enterprise, establishing small factories for textile

spinning and weaving, flour milling, cigarette making, and similar activities. They also established themselves as merchants, middlemen, and
brokers, dealing in both imported and domestic products. Many of these
firms became rich and powerful and attracted more capital from the interior.

Not only opportunity beckoned to Chinese but security. In the foreign concessions and settlements there was order and freedom from civil
wars and from irregular, capricious taxation to pay for civil wars or
enrich warlords. In such areas politics was not the greatest hazard of
business, as in China proper. Also there Chinese business interests could
enjoy, by a kind of percolation downward, the advantages of the special
position of the foreigners, especially freedom from Chinese legal restrictions or governmental regulation of any kind.

The magnetic pull on Chinese capital is easily understood. So, too, are
its unfortunate results. The country's economy became lopsided. Its
strength lay on the rim almost separated from the main mass. There
vested interest was concentrating, there the country's modern development was determined, and there flowed the profits from the early stages
of such development. In a sense China became economically colonial to
a fringe of its own land. Inevitably development took the course that
worked most advantageously to the foreigners and the Chinese gathered
under their protective shadow, who themselves had their part shaped
and limited by the foreigners. For the country's future welfare the whole
of it should have been set on the path to industrialization. Instead an
industrial belt was being girded around a handicraft-peasant country.
The money, energy, and men of ability who should have been engaged
in materially transforming the whole country were being drawn to the
foreign periphery.

Something must be said, too, of the displacement of native handicraft
products by cheaper machine-made products. While the effect of this
was not so serious as in India it was felt nevertheless. As everywhere,
the greatest inroads were in textiles. In transportation the dislocation was
almost as great. The railway and steamship and later the motor vehicle
displaced the small boatmen, carters, wheelbarrowmen and carriers,
those who transported goods suspended from the two ends of a pole. A
large proportion of Chinese had always been engaged in the carrying
trade and no one knows how many hundreds of thousands were left
without means of livelihood in this way alone. The dislocations produced by technological obsolescence are not easily adjusted in an industrial system. They are as disastrous in an unindustrialized system, perhaps more so, since more individuals are thrown out of work. In addition the increased use of imported goods, which penetrated along the

new channels of transportation, drained capital out of the interior, thus adding to the flow to foreign ports that deprived most of the country of the resources for new enterprise.

The family, the other arm of effective government, was no less undermined than the guild. It, too, could not maintain jurisdiction and authority in the conditions that prevailed when once the new forms entered. The family or clan could regulate the conduct of its members and enforce obedience only so long as they came under the purview of the elders, whether as peasants they all worked the land together, or as merchants and artisans they all worked together in the shop, or as gentry they all inhabited the larger houses, a kind of manor. But when factories in the new cities drew labor from the neighboring small towns and then from the countryside, the young who went to the cities were free from parental control. If unmarried, they lived in lodgings, generally mean and squalid ones; if married, they lived with their wives and children in crowded tenements that made up the new industrial slums. They did not add their earnings to the pooled family income. They could not be told when and how to live. After a time they could not be made to marry by family arrangements and without acquaintance with the future marital partner. The sanctions of usage according to the Confucian canon of manners and conduct were weakening. The conditions for the discipline indispensable to maintaining the family as the integral unit of the society were passing. There was emerging the individualism characteristic of the industrialized West, but it was an individualism without the sanctions developed in the West as part of the moral system. Instead a kind of moral anarchy or at least nihilism was forming.

It was this incipient anarchy that signified the real collapse of China. The visible inadequacy of the traditional system to meet the needs of the race and the visible superiority of the Western system for purposes of national survival and material fulfillment combined to throw into disrepute all that the Chinese had esteemed as their own. Education was perhaps the most telling example. As has been said, this was for the Chinese the highest value. Learning was the highest goal, the highest achievement. Nowhere did learning give men as lofty a nobility as in China. This was what the conservatives of not so many years before had meant by culture—the superior culture they wanted to preserve while taking from the culturally lower West the mechanical devices that gave physical power. Already twenty years before the Nationalists came to power the abolition of the examination system as the exclusive means of choosing government officials was partial confession that the Confucian body of thought was not sufficient as a guide to the conduct of the state. By the time that nationalism had found its stride there was a movement for abolishing the old education altogether.

This movement took form in what came to be called the Chinese Renaissance—a name more convenient than accurate, for it denoted more than was contained in the movement. All that it itself aimed at was the disestablishment of the classical language as the vehicle for written Chinese and the substitution of the vulgate, as Latin was supplanted in Europe. In China, too, there had been a separation between the written language and the spoken tongue. This had its uses in a country with a good deal of dialectical variation. It meant that while Chinese in different parts might give a different pronunciation to a character or word, they all understood exactly the same thing by it. And this made Chinese thought equally accessible to all who could read, thus giving the whole race a unity of thought. But the classical language remained unchanged and became increasingly recondite, increasingly difficult to learn for all except those of really advanced education. It was a medium for the elite alone, and since all serious written discourse was expressed in it, education was closed to all but an infinitesimal minority.

The Renaissance started as a movement to abolish the distinction between the written and spoken language and to make *pai hua,* the spoken language, the vehicle of literature and all forms of serious thought. Its proponents and most persuasive advocates were a small group in the Peking National University led by Dr. Hu Shih, a graduate of Cornell and Columbia universities, later to become one of China's best-known living philosophers and eventually ambassador to the United States. They pressed their cause in trenchant periodicals published at the university and widely circulated among young intellectuals throughout the country. To those whose allegiance was still to the old order, what these young men proposed was really revolutionary, more subversive than the overthrow of the monarchy, more subversive than anything done or proposed since the dictator Emperor Chin Shih burned the Books (the Confucian classics) more than two thousand years before. Even in the times of alien conquest, whether by Tartars, Mongols, or Manchus, nothing so destructive of Chinese sanctity had been attempted. The men of this class were not being hysterical. The classical language was indeed a symbol of traditional China. It was the repository of Chinese thought, the quintessence of its culture, the material of its education; and education was the medium for the transmission of what was uniquely, truly Chinese. To strike at that was indeed to strike at the foundations of China. Where they erred, where they had erred for nearly fifty years, was that they did not perceive that the foundations had already been sapped and that the attack against the classical language was only one of the results of that tragic but inescapable fact.

The adoption of *pai hua* had become the focal point, if not the symbol, of the embittered controversy between the adherents of the old order and the brilliant, iconoclastic young men. It became the issue on which they divided, but on each side there lay more than the issue itself. The conflict was one of the old versus the new or, rather, whether to preserve or to disestablish the old China. Among the advocates of the vulgate—*pai hua*—there emerged an extreme wing that broadened the attack to strike at everything old. For the men of this faction not only the language of the classics but their content was no longer of use for education. As philosophy they were held to be backward, as education no longer capable of fitting men to cope with the problems of life either as individuals or as a group in the state. The iconoclastic young men were too sweeping perhaps, but in large measure they were right. They were only calling for recognition of what already existed and for action in accordance. On the whole, too, they were successful, but successful mainly in their negative objects.

The old education actually was abandoned except in the minority of conservative families. The classics were taught as Latin and Greek are taught in American schools—as sources of culture only. What succeeded in the name of education was not the source of anything for the Chinese, however, nor was it a body of knowledge and ideas to guide them. It was only doubtfully education at all. There were "subjects" taken from Western educational systems, especially American, and combined haphazardly in curricula on no definite, thought-out principle or logic. So "given," it may have been modern, but it was as sterile as the old and no more calculated to equip Chinese to meet the problems of Chinese life in a changing civilization. It was rather a kind of intellectual chop suey. And when the *Three Principles of the People* was elevated to the status of a classic and used as the compendium of history, philosophy, and the social sciences, it became ludicrous. The old education was at least a body of ideas and precepts from which to draw guidance. It had substance, depth, and coherence. It did prepare men to deal successfully with the environment in which they then found themselves. That which succeeded it had nothing—neither knowledge nor philosophy nor ideas nor precepts. And a generation was to grow up intellectually rootless, as was reflected in the planless, baseless, inconsequent, and sometimes almost capricious course of the years that followed. The people most dedicated to the things of the mind had become intellectually barren—a civilization in a void. It was no wonder that they leaped lightly from ideology to ideology, not understanding before or after why they leaped.

It was no wonder that the suffering inevitable in a time of social change should have been needlessly aggravated.

The disruption in education was made worse by the student movement, as it was called. The scholar class, as has been said before, has always enjoyed prestige and power of decision in Chinese society, and students, as prospective scholars, have also had that status, although in a kind of cadet category. The students had taken the lead in the revolt against the Treaty of Versailles and the cession of part of Shantung to Japan. They had taken the lead in driving out the pro-Japanese Anfu Party and had provided the earliest recruits and most vigorous workers for the Nationalist cause. From the early 1920's onward patriotism became the first business of students in middle schools and universities; learning was second. As the Nationalist movement broadened its object to include salvation of the country by modernization and reconstruction, "Down with Imperialism" and "Down with the Old" became companion rallying-cries. As the strike had been found to be a potent weapon against traitors, so it was put to use against what were called reactionaries. By extension it was applied also against whoever or whatever was deemed unpleasant to the organized students. There were strikes against cabinet ministers not considered patriotic enough, against university presidents and deans not considered sympathetic enough with the new learning, and sometimes against professors whose examinations were considered too difficult. When occasion seemed to call for patriotic parades or processions students simply left their classrooms and the prosaic tasks of study for the more exhilarating exercises of waving banners, singing songs, or making patriotic speeches on the streets. Their motives were laudable but the acts prompted by them resulted after a few years in a virtual paralysis of education above the grade schools. In fact, there were times when the students became a nuisance. When patriotism became a vocation, intellectual growth was stunted, and this was peculiarly unfortunate at a time when China needed all the intellectual resources it could muster for the staggering problems that confronted it in trying to move from one world into another.

It was only one more step to a kind of general dissolution of mores and morals. If the old learning and the old philosophy were outmoded and backward and useless, so were the old restraints, the old unwritten laws that governed all relations—the respect and obedience due elders, the right of the family to final decision in all matters affecting the individual. For the young, especially between 1924 and 1928, when Communist propaganda became most infectious, it became almost a matter of honor to flout parents, to defy discipline, to show contempt for the old laws of manners and morals. Thus one proved one's modernity, one's superiority to the unenlightened slaves of the past. A chasm opened between the generations, always the most tragic breach in human relations, the most prolific of pain. No longer subject to family discipline and lacking in the self-imposed checks operating in societies in which something approaching individual autonomy in conduct is the normal state, the young of both sexes went heedless and headstrong, often to the ruin of their lives. There were some good accompaniments too. There was a degree of emancipation for women. They were no longer confined to association with males only in the home or only if relatives. The two sexes began to meet publicly and to mingle naturally. This alone was a revolution brought to maturity in less than ten years, a healthy, beneficial revolution. Concubinage fell into disrepute, also beneficial. Extramarital alliances did not cease, however. They only became clandestine, which meant that the young girl in the unacknowledged alliance lost the place in the home and the assured status she would have had as a concubine.

In the moral and institutional disruption of the twenty years following World War I there was good as well as bad; but good or bad, the result was the wearing away of the foundation of the civilization and its eventual collapse, a collapse all the more destructive since the civilization had stood stable for so long on so solid a foundation. As it was, the old was gone before there was even a plan for the foundation of the new. Just then it was hard to say what was China.

It should be recorded, however, that notwithstanding what was happening to China internally, its position in the world was improved. As has been said, it was regaining much of what it had lost in the preceding century. Some of the foreign concessions were retroceded, and in many of those that were not the Chinese won more formal representation and, at least as important, informal consideration. In Shanghai some of the more liberal foreign residents proposed as early as 1920 that the Chinese be granted a kind of ex-officio representation on the Municipal Council, the governing body of the International Settlement. The suggestion was received with mingled shock and derision by almost the whole of the foreign community. It was plainly blasphemous. But in 1928 three Chinese were added to the Council membership and later there were to be five out of a total of fourteen. Plainly, too, it was a Chinese show of force that conferred both reasonableness and sanctity. In 1928, also, tariff autonomy was restored to China. Extraterritoriality still existed, but in name more than in fact. By the criteria of what had been, China might be declining, but it was moving toward equality in the world; it is doubtful which impressed the Chinese more.

CHAPTER XXXV

New Spirit in Japan

We left Japan at the close of the Washington Conference in 1922, when it had been called to account for the use it had made of the opportunities created by the preoccupation of the Western Powers in the European war. At Washington, despite some not wholly unconcealed protest, it was forced to give up some of the proceeds of these opportunities. It agreed to withdraw from Siberia and to return to China the former German territorial holdings in Shantung Province awarded to it at the Paris Peace Conference. Also it had to bear with as much grace as it could muster the severance of the Anglo-Japanese alliance. But it did retain the islands in the Pacific that had been German.

Thereupon a new trend seemed to be set in Japan. Indeed, that trend had something to do with the lack of recalcitrance at the Washington Conference. For some of the repercussions of the war were being felt in Japan, too, even if it had been only technically a belligerent, having profiteered politically rather than fought. The unsettling ideas released by the war were stirring in the Japanese people. The Wilsonian message had caught their minds, if less than in other lands, at least enough to produce an effect. The victory of the Allies had even more effect. The Japanese of modern times are abnormally susceptible to the appeal of success; perhaps their self-consciousness about their qualifications for modernity is responsible. Democracy had been victorious, hence it was worthy of emulation. This was not only episodic, the result of the war alone. The temper of the times, the ideas exported from the West in the previous generation, had worked into Japanese thought as it had in the colonial lands, and the spread of education had given those ideas currency. Submission to the willful rule of the minority endowed with unchallengeable power by right of birth was no longer taken as in the natural order, as it had been only a generation before. Parliamentary institutions, if only a caricature of the idea of representative government, had nevertheless opened fissures in the established quasi-feudal order and generated new aspirations—which rightly were called dangerous thoughts.

The war had also upset the economic equilibrium of the country, with all the consequences that produces. Japan had enjoyed a war boom, but its people were no better off. If anything, they were worse off. The Western Powers, including the United States, almost from the beginning of the war had to withdraw from the Far East economically as well as politically. All their resources and energy had to be devoted to producing for war needs. The Japanese therefore had a free field economically as well as politically. The market of almost all of Asia was open and Japan made the most of it. Both its productive facilities and trade increased enormously, beyond all precedent in its history. In 1914 its exports totalled a little less than 600,000,000 yen; in 1919 they were a little more than two billion—a three-fold increase. Significantly, it was in manufactured and semimanufactured goods that the increase was most marked—from 470,000,000 yen in 1914 to 1,800,000,000 yen in 1919. While adjustment must be made for wartime prices, the increase was still notable—nearly 60 per cent. Manufacturing industries increased five-fold in yen value, subject to adjustment for prices. A surer index is the increase in number of workers in factories producing by machinery from a little lower than a million to more than one and a half million in five years. As a result of the war Japan had become an industrialized country years before it would have been in the normal course.

There emerged in consequence a new plutocratic class, as in any war boom. Narikin, they were called—the new-rich. Another consequence was inflation, the normal accompaniment of war booms, and this bore down not only on the middle class but on all who were not in a position to share directly in war profits. It bore down hardest on urban workers and peasants, whose income in no way rose in proportion to the increase in the national income and the rise in prices. Factory workers, not being organized, had no greater protection than peasants. Only during the war were unions formed on any real scale and they were still without power. Discontent became general and progressively sharper. In 1914 there were 50, with 7,900 workers affected; in 1918 there were 417, with 66,000 affected.

There was a more dramatic form of protest, which came to a climax in 1918. The price of rice had shot up without check despite feeble and belated attempts at control. Since rice is the main staple of the Japanese diet, this meant that many were actually short of food; indeed, for those under a certain level of income there was barely enough for sustenance. Protests passed from the vocal to the active, and in the summer of 1918 a wave of riots, starting in a small village, swept over a large part of the country. There was considerable destruction and in some cities troops had to be called out to check disorders. The government had to exercise some caution in measures of suppression, however, since the participants in the riots were a cross section of the people—housewives, artisans, white-collar workers, not proletarians and hooligans. The government did take steps to regulate both the supply and the price of rice. The rice riots left a mark on Japan. While there had been spontaneous, almost elemental peasant violence before in protest against unbearable conditions, these were of a different order, if only because they were more general and were spread over a larger proportion of the populace. They gave both government and people an intimation of what the people could do.

There was still another cause for discontent. This was the Siberian expedition. Seventy thousand Japanese were sent to the continent in what was both to them and to the people an unexplained and fruitless venture. They suffered the hardships of the Siberian climate. They were stung by the hatred of the people among whom they were quartered, who took summary vengeance when they caught small Japanese bands away from their base. These acts produced ruthless punishment by the Japanese command, punishment often inflicted on the innocent and sometimes not without atrocities. These in turn produced more hatred and retaliations from the Siberians. The Japanese troops were both invading and besieged. They did not have the compensation of fighting a people they could consider enemies and in a cause they could understand. Their morale was bad and was reflected in their letters home. It was an unpopular war, if it could be called a war, and it had the effect of aggravating the rancors already caused by harsh economic conditions. This was still further accentuated when the men finally came home. There is no doubt that some of the troops had been influenced by Communist propaganda while in Siberia, their resentment making them not unwilling subjects, and when they were demobilized many of them radiated disaffection.

All these strains mingled to start a strange new tide of feeling. It was then that the "dangerous thoughts" began to be held. It is difficult to describe the content and direction of these thoughts and difficult to avoid taking them too seriously. Their importance was more negative than positive; they signified doubt, insubordination even, rather than rebelliousness or threat against the reality of the Japanese system. Certainly they had too little substance to be considered what later was called subversive, even if they did provoke a kind of hysteria in the Japanese class that had never before experienced defiance or disrespect. It is true that among the young, especially in the universities, there sprang up a kind of "radicalism." The quotation marks are appropriate, since it was generally a quickly acquired, superficial, and not deeply felt set of convictions. They were not unlike the Chinese of a few years earlier, with allowance for a change in the tenor of world thought. The Chinese were dazzled by the glitter of American constitutionalism, the young Japanese a decade later by the glitter of extreme social philosophies. Both were dazzled but not comprehending. It was not unusual in the early 1920's to meet a young Japanese, especially a university student, who blandly and with high complacency informed one that two years before he had been a socialist but that was too tame, so he had become a Communist, but that too constricting, so he was now a philosophical anarchist, which alone comported with a free spirit. Of course, he had once believed in democracy, but that was old hat. There were many such, and their radicalism was as short-lived as it was thin. They were enough, however, to generate, as has been said, virulent repressive movements, repressive first of radicalism and then of liberalism. (That this was not unique to Japan in 1920 will be recognized by Americans who remember 1950.) There was something more substantial to new Japanese ideas, however, than the vagrant intellectual fancyings of young students. There was a drift in opinion that was registered in the country's politics.

Up to the war, government had still been exercised by the old clans, principally the Choshu and Satsuma in alternation. Theirs was a monopoly, though under some restraint as long as the Emperor Meiji was alive. Meiji was a man of strong personality who had ruled since the Restoration and had actively shared in directing the course of the country's modernization. To the synthetic aura of imperial majesty skillfully made for him he added an authentic majesty of his own. His steadying influence had held in check the hot-blooded young military men in the earlier years of the Restoration and his authority over the leaders of the larger clans had held them in check as well. He was succeeded by Yoshihito, who was almost feeble-minded and had to be decorously removed from the throne, being succeeded, first as regent in 1921 and then on his death in 1926 as emperor, by his son Hirohito, who was still on the throne when Japan surrendered in 1945. In all that mattered, however, it was still the clans that had exercised power of government until the European war.

The military, who held the reins almost to the end of World War I, were responsible for the Twenty-one Demands, the series of loans to China to finance a puppet government, and the Siberian expedition. In those years the expansionist policy on the continent crystallized. In 1918, when the first reaction against militaristic policies began to form,

Takashi Hara, leader of the Seiyukai party, succeeded to the premiership. Hara was the first commoner to head a Japanese government. Since he, as the head of his party, was more under party influence than any of his predecessors had been even if nominally affiliated with a party, it was then that the nearest approximation to party government began in Japan. Hara was genuinely a party man, though not conspicuously a liberal in political or social belief. In fact, the Seiyukai was more conservative than its opposition, the Kenseikai, which, because it represented the trading interest, was more inclined to moderation, at least in foreign policy.

If there was party government, it was party government with unique inflections, for the parties themselves could be termed political parties only in free translation. They were not associations of men with a common view of government and political policy. They were rather organized representatives, almost agents, of specific economic interests and groups. In the 1920's it was possible to make a chart showing the affiliation of each of the parties, small as well as large, with one or another of the great holding companies or trusts that had already formed and were to dominate the country's economy at least until World War II. Each party did the bidding of its corporate patron in any matter arising in the Diet that involved the patron's material interest. This did not extend so far as opposition to the military in anything fundamental, for the military had more potent instruments than parties to achieve their purposes. They might be temporarily restrained or even frustrated in minor matters but their position was still impregnable. Even the great trusts did not dare challenge them. Furthermore, the military also had their own affiliations with some of the trusts, which naturally stood to gain by armament programs. The beginning of at least a semblance of party government had this significance then: it marked a breach in the monopoly of the feudal clans and thus shook by a little the dominion of the military, who were inseparably linked, if not identical, with the clans.

Something must be said at this point about the trusts—the Zaibatsu or financial oligarchy. The most important of these were the Mitsui and Mitsubishi companies. These with the lesser corporations, the Sumitomo and Yasuda, held three-quarters of the country's corporate wealth. They had no counterpart anywhere else in the world. They were themselves fiefs in modern guise. Rather, they were empires more than trusts, the Mitsui and Mitsubishi especially. Each owned banks, steamship lines, insurance companies, iron and steel works, machinery-making plants, chemical plants, textile manufactories, mercantile houses, department stores, breweries. There was no area of the economy in which they were not dominant, if not monopolistic. The Mitsui company, a family corporation and the most powerful of the trusts, itself held 15 per cent of the country's corporate wealth, distributed in 120 corporations under its ownership. To speak of the Japanese economy was to mean the Zaibatsu. They and the clans and the military exercised joint dominion over the Japanese Empire, but economically omnipotent though the Zaibatsu were, they were yet less powerful than the military and the clans. They could be overruled; the military could not.

A commoner as premier and a cabinet responsible to a party may have been surface phenomena or at best portents, but they accorded with the atmosphere of the time. This was shown in the general election in 1920, two years after the Hara cabinet took office, when the Seiyukai returned to power with a large majority in the lower house of the Diet. It was with this mandate that Hara, who took up the premiership again, felt secure enough to accept the invitation to the Washington Conference, even if the inclination of the military was to refuse. In November, 1921, however, Hara was assassinated by a fanatic. While no connection with the Washington Conference could be traced, the reaction among the professional patriots which had been generated by the liberal mood of the period probably acted as incitation. Assassination on this motive was to become general later. It was to become the patriots' instrument for national salvation.

Hara's death was followed by a succession of short-lived cabinets, the Seiyukai and Kenseikai alternating, with one or two nonparty cabinets, including one composed exclusively of peers. While the bent of the cabinets' policy varied in the five years after Hara's death, on the whole it was toward the liberal side—liberal, that is, by Japanese standards. It was in this period that Baron Kijuro Shidehara first became Minister of Foreign Affairs. Shidehara, who incidentally was the son-in-law of Baron Iwasaki, head of the family that owned the Mitsubishi company, was the most vigorous and outspoken advocate of moderation toward China. He was opposed to any kind of aggression there, whether political or military, and argued instead for legitimate economic penetration only—export of consumer goods and light manufactured products, purchase of raw materials, and return on investments, all on ordinary business principles. With the good will of China gained, greater benefits would accrue to Japan than encroachment could yield. For Japan's greatest need, he held, was an enlarging market and a source of raw materials, which together would keep its economy prosperous and growing. In the years when Chinese nationalism was at its height and foreigners and foreign rights were being summarily dealt with, it was largely through Shidehara's influence that Japan not only refrained from retaliation but was scrupulously neutral. Shidehara was even making formal statements in the Diet to the effect that China's aspirations were legitimate and that it had a right to choose its own form of government and go its own way without any fear of foreign interference. And as a matter of fact China not only felt gratitude to Japan but there was a feeling almost of friendliness for the first time since the war of 1894.

Mention must be made of a natural disaster, one of the worst in modern times anywhere, that wrought at least physical changes in Japan. This was the earthquake of September 1, 1923. Earthquakes are common in Japan, scarcely a week passing without one that is felt somewhere, although few are serious enough to cause damage. There is no doubt, however, that the Japanese are never without consciousness of earthquakes and the Damoclean threat may have something to do with the tenseness that is one of their dominant traits. It is when this tenseness snaps for one reason or another that the Japanese let themselves go in a wild, hysterical violence that is almost awesome. This may explain the atrocities to which they are prone when at war.

It was noon of a sunny summer day when there was the peculiar grinding crash that signalizes the beginning of an earthquake, and in a few seconds the ground began to heave. A few minutes later buildings began to topple in all parts of Tokyo and Yokohama. This was only the beginning. Fires broke out. Cooking stoves had been overturned. The flimsy wood and paper houses ignited and the flames spread as if blown by a gale. In not many minutes more Tokyo was a blazing furnace. Trapped in their narrow lanes, the inhabitants ran first in one direction and then another, to find themselves cut off by walls of flame on all sides and to perish where they huddled. Some took refuge in open spaces and there found themselves engulfed by fire, the few belongings they brought with them ignited by sparks and providing the fuel that burned them to death. If they took refuge in shallow ponds fire swept over them or they drowned. In Yokohama, the port city, it was even worse than in Tokyo, and in cities to the south for miles it was almost as bad. In twenty-four hours much of central Japan was in ruins. How many died under fallen buildings or were burned to death was never known exactly. The official estimate was more than 150,000. The losses to property were put at $2,500,000,000, too much to be indemnified, since insurance companies were bankrupted.

As in any great disaster there were accompaniments of heroism, but there were also accompaniments of hideousness. Maddened by panic, the Japanese were meet for rumors, however irrational. There was the usual looting and indiscriminate killing to be expected in such circumstances, and there was the desire for scapegoats. One rumor that spread, in the inexplicable way of rumors, was that Korean inhabitants had started the fires. Mobs set out on a man hunt for Koreans. Before they could be checked, several thousand Koreans were slaughtered. So were several hundred Chinese, in some cases because they were mistaken for Koreans and in some cases just because they were foreign. Radicals and socialists were similarly marked out as guilty and the professional patriot organizations went out on a man hunt for them, too. How many of these were killed off has never been known.

The earthquake struck a crippling blow at the country. Much of the profit of the war years was wiped out. Not only profits and property were destroyed. Like wars, great natural catastrophes, too, can act as solvents. Some of the iron restraints of Japanese mores, already weakened by modernity and by the loosening of all ties after the war, began to give. Japan, too, had its jazz age and it struck deeper than conventional morals. As in China at the same time, the tenets of the culture were being challenged—customs, habits, precepts, beliefs. There was never the outright mutiny and the moral anarchy that came to prevail in China. For that Japanese repressions are too strong and respect for authority is too great. Yet there was much that seemed to the older conservatives revolutionary and the end of all things worthy.

The weakening of sanctions in a society is probably always reflected first in control over the young. As in China, young Japanese of both sexes began to rebel at arranged marriages and to insist on taking mates of their own choice. There was the more striking phenomenon of the *moga*. The word is a contraction of the two English words, "modern girl"—*modan garu,* as the Japanese pronounce those two words. Thus, the moga bobbed her hair, wore rather extreme fashions, was pert in her manners, walked out in public with boys and, perhaps worst of all, danced modern dances. Dance halls also became a symbol. They sprang up in all the larger cities. Whereas places of off-color amusement in Japan had always reflected the high aestheticism of the Japanese people, that innate and sure sense of beauty which is one of their distinguishing traits, the dance halls, cafés, and all that clustered around such places were sodden and mangy. It was this that put them in almost as bad repute with the correct and conservative as the moral practices they encouraged. About the last the Japanese have never been oversensitive. Worst of all to the conventional was the barbaric and indecent spectacle of young men and women not married embracing and moving in embrace to the strains of outlandish music. In keeping with such activities there was a change in the strict decorum that governed all personal relations, a decorum perhaps more binding than among any other people in the world. To Japanese manners have been as important as morals, perhaps more so. Manners were the mark not only of the well-bred but of all people not primitive. There is or has been something courtly in the bearing even of a poor and unlettered peasant, or, if not courtliness, poise and simple dignity. Reserve and restraint in movement and speech were the dominant notes. Now there was the kind of abruptness of speech and action, a crudity of word and movement hitherto deemed proper only to the uncivilized—or characteristic of Occidentals, who, despite their other qualities, lacked refinement.

The new and novel came in other forms less objectionable. In the West "modern" architecture was coming into vogue. In the rebuilding of Tokyo therefore modern architecture was widely adopted and, it should be added, adopted very effectively. By the time of the war with the United States there were some excellent buildings in the new style in Tokyo and except in the back streets the capital had the appearance of a Western metropolis.

Western music also was popular—at first because it was a part of the life of advanced countries and therefore must be a part of Japanese life if Japan was to be considered advanced, and later because a genuine feeling for it did seem to develop. A symphony orchestra was organized in Tokyo and later came to give quite creditable concerts. From the windows of middle-class houses could be heard the tinkling of "finger exercises" or even unrhythmic bars of "Anitra's Dance," occasionally off key, doubtless under the minatory watch of the piano teacher. Western pitch does not come easily and naturally to ears trained to an entirely different scale. In student cafés, which in the United States would be playing boogie-woogie on the juke boxes, mechanical record-players were offering the more severe Beethoven quartets. What the students got out of them as they chattered over coffee and tea is not certain, but Western music had come to Japan. Thus in its physical aspect, in social and political organization, in customs and habits, even somewhat in political thought Japan was really beginning to enter the world of the twentieth century; but, again, while simultaneously in many fundamental respects still dwelling in the world of the fifteenth century—the unhealthy paradox of Japan.

In one respect Japan definitely put itself in line with the contemporaneous Western world. Since the granting of the constitution in 1889 there had been only restricted suffrage under the property tax qualification. In the postwar atmosphere agitation began for extension of the right to vote and in a few years it became vigorous. It was vigorous enough by 1925 for concessions to be made, and in March of that year universal manhood suffrage was granted. Thus at one stroke the electorate was increased from about 3,000,000 to 14,000,000. It cannot be said that this made much difference in the spirit or direction of Japanese politics. As some of the more cynical opponents of the measure said, it would only add to the number of voters who had to be bribed. With political parties as limited in power and purpose as they were, the voters' opportunity for effective expression was limited too, but for all that universal suffrage was important for what it signified. A generation before it would have been considered not only revolutionary but blasphemous by those who controlled Japan's destiny.

One event outside Japan did little to fortify the nascent spirit of moderation. This was the passage of a new immigration law in the United States. A mood of antiforeignism was generated in the United States at the end of the war. In its political form this was isolationist, in general it was a kind of rejection of the whole outer world as a recoil from the experience of the European war. One of the corollaries was a strong movement to limit immigration—no more foreign politics, no more foreign ideas, no more foreign persons. With the support of a number of organized groups having a variety of motives a bill was introduced into Congress drastically limiting immigration and introducing the principle of quotas for each country. The basis of the quotas was so fixed as to limit to a trickle immigration from South and East Europe. But the quota was not universally applied. There was a provision in the act by which Oriental immigrants were excluded altogether.

This revived in its touchiest form the Japanese immigration question, which had created sharp friction between the two countries in the years before 1910 but had been allayed by the "gentlemen's agreement." This agreement, made in the administration of Theodore Roosevelt and an understanding rather than a diplomatic instrument, left it to the Japanese government voluntarily to stop emigration to the United States. With some evasions through loopholes the Japanese lived up to their undertaking and the agreement worked satisfactorily. While the Japanese smarted, the wound to their pride was at least assuaged by the fact that the denial was self-imposed.

The issue arose again at the Paris Peace Conference, when the Japanese delegates asked for a declaration of the principle of racial equality. Nothing concrete was involved, but both the American and Australian delegations refused. The Japanese, both at Paris and at home, were plainly galled. Now when word came of the introduction of a law in the United States formally barring them as beyond the pale of American association, there was an outburst of indignation. This was peculiarly unfortunate, since there had been genuine gratitude in Japan for generous American contributions to relief at the time of the earthquake only a year before. In the American government outside Congress there was little enthusiasm for the measure and in some sectors outright disapproval. President Calvin Coolidge and Secretary of State Charles Evans Hughes counselled against the rigid provisions affecting Orientals. It was pointed out that if Japan, for example, were put on the same plane as other countries, its quota would admit fewer than a hundred Japanese immigrants a year. The advocates of restriction argued on their part that if the principle of equality were conceded and the quotas were later liberalized the Japanese would legitimately invoke the principle of equality and claim the right to send a larger number of immigrants.

While the question was under debate in Washington and the Executive department seemed to be having some success in invoking caution, the Japanese Ambassador, Masanao Hanihara, transmitted to the Department of State a note protesting in advance against the passage of the bill. In the note it was said, probably without realization of the usual connotation of the words, that its passage would have "grave consequences." This was construed by Congress as a threat and the bill was passed by an overwhelming majority. President Coolidge signed it but in doing so made the statement that he had no choice, since immigration in general was in question, but if the Japanese exclusion stood alone he would have vetoed it.

The whole episode was unfortunate and the burden of blame rested on the United States. Its right to deal with immigration as it chose was never in dispute, but the way in which it exercised the right was needlessly offensive. The national interest could have been preserved without gratuitously insulting a country with which relations had been strained at the best. The quota principle, in fact, offered an easy way of adopting a policy of restriction of Japanese immigration without giving Japan cause to complain of discrimination. The effect of Japanese exclusion has been much exaggerated, however. The Japanese were embittered no doubt, but, as has been said before, this had little to do with the policy of aggressive expansion they adopted later. They adopted that policy not to retaliate against the United States for a wound to their pride but because they wanted to conquer. America's fault lay not in its politics but in its manners.

In fact, it was after 1924 that Japan seemed most resolutely to renounce aggression. In those years it was exemplary in its conduct toward China. Even in Korea its rule became more lenient. For a time it seemed reasonable to believe that Japan had changed its role in East Asia and would henceforth play the part of good neighbor, taking its compensation in increased economic opportunity. But meanwhile, too, the urge for a "positive policy" in China was quietly germinating and, as has been told, General Tanaka was coming to the fore. When he arrived at power as premier it was clear that Japanese moderation had been transient.

CHAPTER XXXVI

Reaction in Japan: Back to Expansion

The Japanese were becoming restive in their unfamiliar exercise of restraint. Given their history, it was only natural that they should. And what was happening in China and the attitude of the Chinese conduced to make voluntary restraint chafe all the more.

By 1928 China was succeeding beyond all expectation in throwing off foreign controls. It was succeeding all too well—too uncomfortably well—for those Japanese who had their own aspirations on the Asian continent, and these included nearly all the Japanese who had influence in their own land. Moreover, a semblance of unity was recognizable in China and that, too, boded ill for Japanese ambitions. Nationalist success and the appearance of unity together gave point to that "positive policy" which had already been adumbrated under Tanaka's inspiration.

If China was to recover full sovereignty, however, it had to do more than get back residential concessions and settlements, tariff autonomy, legal jurisdiction, and the like. The most serious and important infringements on its sovereignty lay in Hongkong, Manchuria, and Mongolia, and of these the two last were by far the most important. They, too, had to be reincorporated in the Chinese state and plainly the Chinese meant to try to do so. Harsh words signified their intentions, words provocative to those who had the heaviest vested interests at stake—the Russians in Mongolia and north Manchuria, the Japanese in south Manchuria.

In their *élan* the Chinese overestimated their strength and pitched their ambitions beyond their power. They had, it is true, forced the European Powers to retreat. But they forgot that the European Powers were far away and war-weary and America had no colonial interests at stake, whereas Russia and Japan, which had most at stake, were not far away. They were on China's borders, within striking distance; and Japan was not war-weary at all and Russia had emerged from the war in a new incarnation. Of this the Chinese, carried away on the enthusiasm of their successes, seemed to be oblivious, as in the previous century they were still without understanding of the world of their time. Perhaps this was natural in some respects. They had been buffeted by fate so long, had so long been helpless under alien conquerors; now they were able by their own effort to hold their heads high again, perhaps it was inevitable that in the thrill of so doing they should lose balance of judgment.

Their pronouncements were exultant and determined, but there were more than words. The Nationalists' capture of Nanking, despite the efforts of Japanese troops to prevent them from coming through Shantung Province, was itself a challenge to Japan. A more serious challenge came later. Chang Tso-lin, it will be remembered, was killed by a bomb explosion when he retreated in advance of the Nationalists to his stronghold in Manchuria, and there was never any doubt that it was the Japanese who planted the bomb that blew up his train. It can be taken for granted that their object was to prevent the re-establishment of as strong a leadership in Manchuria as Chang could be expected to give it. With Chang out of the way the unregularized status of the Manchurian provinces could be ended and Japan would get substantive control.

Chang Tso-lin was succeeded as military satrap of Manchuria by his son, Chang Hsueh-liang. There was no formal provision for succession. It just came about that way in the dispensation of Chinese warlordism. This itself did not disturb the Japanese unduly, for they had taken the measure of Chang Hsueh-liang, quite correctly, as a weakling. The Young Marshal, as he was called, was military by courtesy only. The Japanese were well aware that the Nationalists had been making overtures to Chang Hsueh-liang and that the young man had given indications of being receptive. After all, he was young, he was Chinese, and those patriotic causes that had won other young Chinese would appeal to him too. As a special inducement the Nationalist government at Nanking gave him soon after his father's death official appointment as head of the administration of the Manchurian provinces and commander of the Manchurian armies. To the discomfiture of the Japanese young Chang declared his allegiance to the Nationalist regime, presumably carrying with him the allegiance of the Manchurian provinces. In paternal urgings the Japanese in Manchuria tried to dissuade Chang from his purposes, but he was firm. They first warned him and then dispatched a high official from Tokyo with China experience, Baron Gonnosuke Hayashi, to reason with him and at the same time promise him financial assistance as a reward. He remained determined, even defiant, and before the end of 1928 raised the Nationalist flag over all official buildings in Mukden.

The Japanese believed they had another string to their bow. It has never been confirmed but is supported by some evidence that they had been cultivating one General Yang Yu-ting, who had been chief of staff to Chang Tso-lin and doubtless did not welcome the elevation of the son as his superior. Whether or not the Japanese intended to execute a coup, evict Chang Hsueh-liang in the same way as his father, and put Yang Yu-ting in his place, young Chang resolved to anticipate them. Early in January, 1929, he invited to a party Yang Yu-ting and one of his military aides. When they arrived they were seized by their host's guards and summarily shot then and there. The Japanese smarted but kept their counsel. Plainly the young man, if weak, was not going to be entirely supine.

There were other ways in which the Chinese were defiant, perhaps even more serious for the Japanese. For years the Japanese had talked publicly about overpopulation, citing the annual increase of some 700,000 a year to press on the tight confines of their little islands. Yet, despite the fact that they had had since 1905 paramount rights in Manchuria, no more than 250,000 Japanese had emigrated there apart from troops and officials. At the same time Chinese had been pouring in, and by 1928 more than nine-tenths of the population of more than 30,000,000 was Chinese, the rest being of original Manchu stock or Mongols. Almost through the whole period of the Manchu dynasty Chinese emigration into the Manchurian provinces had been forbidden, but the prohibition had been evaded to a degree from the middle of the nineteenth century and by 1880 was lifted entirely. The open fertile plains of Manchuria, much like those of the American West and Middle West and almost empty of people, beckoned irresistibly to the over-crowded north China provinces. Chinese peasants began to move across the Great Wall in numbers, at first mainly as farm workers and peddlers and then as tenants, small merchants, and landowners. After 1920 this became a great migration. Between 1920 and 1930 more than 5,000,000 peasants entered Manchuria. Half of them went as seasonal farm workers, returning home when the harvest was in, but the other half remained. Because of the normally high Chinese birth rate Manchuria became Chinese in population, while political control rested with the Russians in the north and the Japanese in the south.

As the years passed from 1900 to 1930 the Chinese in Manchuria took on steadily increasing importance not only in numbers but in the life of the region, especially in the economy. Always industrious, prudent, and commercially shrewd, the Chinese rose in the economic scale, as they always do when given opportunity. Their little hole-in-the-wall stands became small shops, then larger shops, then mercantile establishments. They became the middlemen in the whole process of exchange. From the making of the cheapest commodities by hand they went into manufacturing with simple tools and then into factory production. They started banks which soon took on considerable magnitude. The Japanese owned and controlled the largest-scale enterprises. Almost all else was Chinese.

It was in the sphere of railways, however, that the real clash came between the Chinese and Japanese. It was through their hold on communications in Manchuria, especially the South Manchuria Railway and its branches, that the Japanese could maintain their control of the region. To safeguard this hold they had as early as 1905 compelled the Chinese formally to agree not to build any railways in south Manchuria parallel to their own. Between 1920 and 1930, however, the Chinese built or proceeded to build a number of railway lines there, some of them branching from their own line between Peking and Mukden, which did parallel the South Manchuria Railway. They had plans for others and made no bones about their intentions. The Japanese protested but the Chinese moved on imperturbably.

Thus the Chinese political self-assertion shown in Chang Hsueh-liang's avowed adhesion to the new Nationalist government, the economic competition and growing economic strength in Manchuria, and the construction of railways combined to constitute a direct challenge to Japan's position, the most direct since the Russo-Japanese War. And this in turn, combined with the growing Japanese restiveness from repression of natural instincts for expansion, worked almost chemically to produce a state of explosiveness.

The first test of China's intentions in Manchuria and the relation between its intentions and its power came, contrary to expectation, not between China and Japan but between China and Russia. Neither the Chinese, the Nationalist Chinese, that is, nor the Russians had forgotten the break between them in 1927 and the circumstances that brought it about. The Russians had taken no action, but that they would let the episode go unexpiated was not compatible with Russian communist psychology or the colonial grand strategy laid down by Lenin in 1920. The test came on the status of the Chinese Eastern Railway in North Manchuria connecting the Trans-Siberian Railway with Vladivostok, the part of the original line left to Russia by the peace treaty that concluded the Russo-Japanese War.

Even at the time of the Chinese Nationalist-Russian honeymoon this railway had remained an unsettled issue between them, discreetly left undiscussed but with mental reservations on both sides. One of the first acts of the new Soviet regime, after the pronouncement of the new dispensation of magnanimity and protection for downtrodden colonial peoples, was to denounce all the treaties that had given Russia imperialistic possessions and privileges in China. But one thing was exempted from the application of magnanimity. This was the Chinese Eastern Railway, which incidentally was the most valuable possession the tsar's government had acquired. The Chinese, however, were far from unaware of the omission and pressed the matter, but Russia remained evasive. Indeed, it made much the same arguments in its defense as the frankly imperialistic countries. The Chinese Eastern Railway was essential to national interest, and to the extent of impairing national interest magnanimity did not carry. In the agreement of 1923 between Joffe, representing Moscow, and Sun Yat-sen for the nascent Nationalist regime the question of the railway was left unsettled, which meant that Russia was left undisturbed in possession—while, charmingly, binding itself to help China to recover full independence. In 1924 Russia and the Peking government came to an agreement establishing diplomatic relations. In the agreement were provisions for the railway, which was to remain Russian in ownership but to be jointly managed. There was to be a board of directors composed of five Russians and five Chinese but the actual manager was to be a Russian. To China, however, was reserved the right of civil administration, policing, and administration of justice.

The arrangement would have been a difficult one to make work at best but in the atmosphere of mutual suspicion—the almost simultaneous agreement between Russia and the Canton regime did not allay the Peking government's resentment—it was an almost impossible one. In the desire to recover all rights from usurping foreigners there was little to choose between the Canton Nationalists and the Peking officials, leaving out the pro-Japanese puppets of the Anfu Party. The Chinese in north Manchuria began therefore a process of infiltration, working out from their rights of civil administration. They were especially successful in Harbin in taking over the government of the city, which had been in effective control by Russia for decades. Over the railway there was constant friction. When the Nationalists took over Peking in 1928 and then won Chang Hsueh-liang's allegiance they became more aggressive than their predecessors. One episode led to another. The tension became higher. The Chinese, then sensitive about communist propaganda, accused the Russians of using their position to disseminate it. ·

On May 29, 1929, the Chinese struck. They did so in a way that startled not only the Russians but the rest of the world, in a way that was insensately foolhardy unless they commanded irresistible force. They raided the Russian consulate in Harbin and arrested some eighty officials from all over Manchuria who were attending a conference in the consulate. It was a conference called by the Third International to plan a new propaganda campaign in China, the Chinese said, and probably they were right. Among those arrested were members of the Russian consular staffs and officials of the railway. The Chinese also seized documents from the consular files, with or without justification and in violation of both law and practice in international intercourse. The Moscow government protested but for the moment did no more. Then early in July the Chinese dismissed the Russian general manager of the railway, arrested more officials, closed the headquarters of all Russian organizations, and took over the railway itself.

Now the Russians responded promptly. On July 13 they sent an ultimatum demanding the release of all the arrested Russians and the cancellation of all the other measures taken by the Chinese. There was an exchange of indecisive communications, each side standing by its position. First Russia severed diplomatic relations and then decided to use force. There was more military movement than fighting, Russia hoping by its show of force to bring the Chinese to a compromise. But the Chinese were still confident, for reasons known only to themselves, and Russia struck in earnest. Both Russia and China were signatories of the Kellogg Pact, then only a year old, and the pact was invoked by Henry L. Stimson, American Secretary of State. Russia replied with a sneering snub, telling Mr. Stimson in effect to mind his own business and recalling to his attention that the United States had not yet established relations with the Moscow government and therefore had no right to address it. Russian troops invaded Manchuria. The ensuing proceedings were comic. Chinese resistance crumbled almost before blows were struck. There was not even dummy resistance. Early in December Chang Hsueh-liang accepted the Russian demands in full and Nanking, which had remained inactive and apparently unconcerned, gave approval. Russia's position on the railway was restored. What was most revealing in the incident was that while the other Western Powers—rightly called imperialistic—had made concessions to China without resistance and yielded up a large portion of their privileges, Russia—communist, proletarian, and patron and protector of the disinherited and poor—resorted to the old classical measures for keeping imperialistic perquisites. In fact, it was the only Western Great Power after 1914 to use the old imperialistic methods in China to assert the right of might over the weak and fight to keep the spoils won by might.

China was thus made to seem ludicrous in the eyes of the world. Whether or not it learned a lesson on the danger of overestimating itself, the lesson did not go unremarked by another party—Japan. The Japanese had evidence on which to deduce that it was easy to put China in its place and that the rest of the world would acquiesce. Here lay the real importance of the Russo-Chinese episode, farcical as it was.

Parenthetically, while Russian forces were invading Manchuria and China was nominally defending its soil against an invader, two revolts broke out in China proper against the Nanking government, led by dissident politicians and recalcitrant warlords who did not like the idea of unity and the prospect of losing opportunities for easy loot. The Nanking forces, under Chiang Kai-shek, won in each case, but this, too, gave Japan grounds for comfort and should have given the Chinese grounds for caution.

It may be, however, that by that time China no longer had any choice in what was to happen. Japan had had both warning—in the form of the Chinese seizure of the Chinese Eastern Railway—and assurance— in the form of China's farcical defense combined with the renewal of internal dissension. The first indicated to the Japanese that definite efforts were required if the "positive policy" was to be made good. And the prevailing state of mind of the Japanese military caste left no doubt that the policy would be carried out or, in other words, that China's national- ism would not be further conciliated and Japan would not forswear its goal of continental conquest.

Here something should be said about the so-called Tanaka Memorial, about which so much was written in later years. The memorial, supposed to have been addressed by Tanaka to the emperor, sketched a design for Japanese foreign policy. The theme of the design was world con- quest—first Manchuria, then China, then Siberia and Central and Southeast Asia, then Europe and America. Like all presumably secret documents that are revealed by parties having an interest in revelation, this one was of highly dubious origin. It was brought to light in China, which alone made it suspect. In the second place, it was supposed to have been presented to the emperor, and leaks from the Japanese court were so rare, if they ever occurred at all, that any purported leak would have to be scrutinized with a jaundiced eye. And if there were a leak, the Chinese would be the least likely to receive it. Furthermore, there was internal evidence in the language of the memorial which alone casts doubt on its having been written by a Japanese, especially a Japanese addressing the emperor in the ceremonial court language. But whether or not Tanaka or any other Japanese wrote such a document, insofar as it dealt with the Far East it was a fairly accurate sketch of what Japanese militarists conceived as the destiny of Japan. Not only the most effervescent of them considered that destiny to be mastery of all Asia, at least to the Urals and the frontier of India, with conquest of China, Manchuria, and Mongolia as the first steps.

In any event Japan was confronted with the necessity of a decision on its future in East Asia. China's intention was clear: it would do north of the Great Wall against Russia and Japan as it had done south of the Great Wall against the other Great Powers. If it could, it would recover south Manchuria, north Manchuria, and Mongolia either by economic penetration or military action or both. Japan could not evade for long. Either it could sit by passively and watch south Manchuria pass out of its control, thus permanently thwarting its ambition in East Asia, or it would have to strike in Manchuria to settle the matter once and for all.

The Japanese Empire in 1933

On the whole record of Japan since 1870 and on the evidence of the gathering mood in Tokyo and among the army leaders stationed in Manchuria there could be little doubt what the decision would be. Whatever doubt was held was soon dissolved by the event. There was a succession of minor skirmishes and disputes in Manchuria in 1930 and 1931 involving Chinese, Japanese, and Koreans. In one of them a Japanese officer and his suite were murdered by Chinese. Then there was more than an incident and Japan's decision was revealed.

On the night of September 18, 1931, there was an explosion on the tracks of the South Manchuria Railway near Mukden, very much like the explosion that blew up the train carrying Chang Tso-lin in 1928. As in the case of that explosion, there was no doubt that it had been laid by the Japanese. Such was the finding later of the Lytton Commission sent by the League of Nations to investigate. The purpose of the Japanese was to find a pretext for drastic action, as was confirmed by the fact that a few hours after the explosion troops of the Kwantung Army—the permanent military establishment in Manchuria, commanded by the most aggressive and chauvinistic faction of the Japanese generals —moved in large force on the city of Mukden and took it. Twenty-four hours later they had Changchun, some 250 miles north, and two days after that Kirin, east of Changchun. Clearly the Kwantung Army had made full preparations. It could not have moved so expeditiously and so far otherwise. In a few weeks, as a matter of fact, all of south Manchuria and a large part of the rest was securely in the grip of the Kwantung Army, which was obviously the goal of the explosion. Chinese resistance incidentally was no more effective than it had been against the Russians. The troops of Chang Hsueh-liang melted away and the Nanking government gave no help at all—wisely, since its forces then would have been of little avail against the powerful, well-equipped Japanese army.

And so East Asia entered into its generation of travail. Thus opened the most dramatic phase of its history since the incursion of Genghis Khan seven centuries before, a drama that became a tragedy and finally extended its scope to take in Europe and America. The explosion on the night of September 18, 1931, set off the train of events that led to the death throes of the League of Nations, the invasion of China by Japan, the adhesion of Japan to the Italo-German alliance, the attack on Pearl Harbor, the overrunning of all East Asia (except Siberia) to the Indian border, the crushing defeat of Japan and the destruction of the larger part of its cities, the conquest of China by its Communists and the absorption of China into the Russian bloc, and the release of turmoil and revolution in Southeast Asia. No date in the history of Asia for almost a millennium is as important as September 18, 1931.

CHAPTER XXXVII

Japan Consolidates Its Conquests

As one looks back over the years one knows now that, notwithstanding all the international byplay that followed, whether in Tokyo or Nanking or any of the European capitals or, more especially, at the seat of the League of Nations, Manchuria was destined to become Japanese as from the night of September 18, 1931, unless force was brought from outside to stop Japan. As a matter of fact many of those who had closely observed the affairs of the Far East knew that even then. And since no such force was forthcoming, Manchuria did become Japanese and remained so until force actually was thrown against it in the form of American ships, planes, guns, and men after 1941.

Twenty-four hours after the Japanese had overrun Mukden the situation was brought to the attention of the League, where both the Council and the Assembly were in session. Two days later China formally appealed to the League to compel Japan to withdraw to the position of September 18. The League officially took the case under consideration. The United States, not a member, informed the League that it would co-operate with its efforts and designated an "observer" to sit in League sessions but not participate in its discussions or decisions. It is not necessary to go into the complicated negotiations, debates, maneuvers, evasions—the protracted procedure in which what was left unsaid was more important than what was said. There was frankness on no side. Behind every declaration by whatever party there was a whole body of mental reservations.

The truth is that none of the Powers that dominated the League had any intention of taking action against Japan. Whether there was any justification for their unwillingness, this was their position. There was no doubt a clear realization at the outset that only force would stop the Japanese. Force meant armies and navies and airplanes. Sanctions alone would be futile. Without force they could not be given effect. An embargo by itself would be meaningless. Even if all the great trading Powers abstained from selling to Japan it could get enough from weak neighboring countries to keep going. Only a blockade would serve, and if it threatened to be effective Japan would use its navy to break through it and then there would be war. In 1931, with the world-wide depression nearing its worst, the European Powers were even in less mood for war than in the early 1920's. If at that time they were reluctant to undertake relatively simple punitive expeditions to save their colonial possessions, they were now all the more reluctant to undertake the risky enterprise of a war against a great Power, a strong and militant Power. For the states of the League, then, it was not a question of sanctions to uphold the principles of collective security; it was a question of war or no war. In this they saw more clearly than the United States or at least public opinion in the United States.

The position of the United States was anomalous. The accusation has always been made by one school of ardent League supporters—and few causes in modern times have won more passionate allegiance than did the League among men and women of a certain temperament, those more dedicated to idealism than cognizant of the ways of international politics—that the United States frustrated the League in the Manchurian affair. This is based on the undoubted fact that immediately after the Japanese seized Mukden Secretary of State Stimson counseled moderation. He did so in the belief that the affair was a coup of the Japanese military extremists and the moderate elements might regain control. Interference from without, he feared, would only strengthen the hands of the extremists. But in the first place, there is no evidence that the League would have done anything in those few days even if Mr. Stimson had not given such advice. In the second place, Mr. Stimson not only formally promised full American co-operation in whatever measures the League decided upon but soon made clear that he advocated positive action. And before the end of 1931 he was putting pressure on the League for a more vigorous course. There is even solid ground for the belief that the League would have allowed the whole Manchurian question decorously to fade away if it had not been for Mr. Stimson's vigorous proddings, supported by American public opinion as well as the opinion of League advocates in some of the minor Powers. Indeed, it may be said that such action as was taken can be attributed to American influence, even if the United States was not a League member.

One other thing must be said as well: America pressed for action, but never did any American government official or any influential segment of American opinion indicate that if punitive action taken against Japan was resisted by Japanese force the United States would have thrown in its armed strength. On the contrary, President Hoover made it clear that as long as he was president the United States would not use military means against Japan to enforce the law of nations even if it was guilty of aggression, as he himself believed it was. To that extent the League Powers, Great Britain and France especially, were justified in refusing to commit themselves in more than minatory words.

This may be true, but it is not the whole truth. Nor was it the decisive factor. For even if it had not been true, the British and French would not have supported League action if it called for forcible measures. The idea of international jurisdiction still meant too little to them. Even more, the idea of establishing a precedent for universal injunction against the right of a great Power to administer punishment to a recalcitrant colony was repugnant to them. Great Britain and France were colonial Powers and had their own interests to consider. Encouragement of over-weening ambitions in the weak and ruled was hardly politic. To that extent the reaction against imperialism had not gone. Indeed, in the elements of both countries that carried decision it had not gone far at all. They were still bound by ideas in the old mold. Justice for the Chinese and people like them, no doubt; good treatment, yes; but approbation of the undermining of vested interests, for mutiny against the strong, even if the strong were, like the Japanese, under suspicion— that was another matter. Internationalism was all very well, especially in ceremonial pronouncements; anarchy was anarchy. And clearly any blow at established imperial rights was anarchy.

The resolutions passed in the League were in words and accents of reproof; but to those who read the British, French, and Italian press, where the opinions of the respectable, of those who carried weight, were more frankly exposed, or who heard the private expressions of men in office or positions of influence, it was unmistakably clear that there would be no more than words, that there was no desire for more. The Japanese, whose vigilance for straws in the wind naturally was keen, saw them and interpreted them correctly. They heard the resolutions of reproof and contested them vigorously, if only to keep their public record clear, but they knew they had immunity. They would be condemned but not stopped. And so they went ahead. At the end of 1931 the League dispatched to Manchuria an international commission of inquiry under the chairmanship of Lord Lytton, but by the time it reported, more than a year later, in a judgment that found against Japan, the Japanese had made themselves masters in Manchuria. The incident was closed—for the time.

Meanwhile the conflict had spread, physically in the Far East and politically in the West. While the Nationalist government at Nanking had not lifted a finger to help its Manchurian commander to withstand the Japanese, the Chinese people were aroused. This was China's worst reverse in years, worse even than the Russian affair two years before, since the Chinese had no illusion that Japanese troops would be withdrawn when the fighting was over. They retaliated in a way long familiar to them. They declared a boycott on Japanese goods. The Chinese have long been expert in the use of the boycott and soon Japan was being hurt in a sensitive spot, since it, too, was feeling the effects of the depression. The boycott proved an additional irritant to the Japanese, and in Shanghai, the center of the boycott movement, both the Japanese civilian residents and the naval forces became truculent. In the natural course there were numerous clashes of various kinds, with the two sides equally guilty no doubt. It was the Japanese who had the force, however, and they first made threats and then delivered an ultimatum to the authorities of the Chinese municipality outside the International Settlement. One of the demands stipulated the withdrawal of Chinese troops from the environs of the port. Naval and consular representatives of the Western Powers in Shanghai tried to mediate. The Chinese themselves gave notice of acceptance of the ultimatum. It was too late. The Japanese as usual wanted an excuse for action even if they had to manufacture it.

On the night of January 28, 1932, they attacked in force in Chapei, the northernmost part of the city and one of the most densely populated. They shelled and bombed it, destroying the narrow warrens where thousands dwelt and killing hundreds, perhaps thousands. But here they were due for surprise. Here Chinese troops did not scuttle at the first roar of guns. There had been brought up to Shanghai a few weeks before a southern army commanded by one Tsai Ting-kai, a general of different stuff from most of his kind. His troops met the Japanese attack and stood. They were poorly armed and not too well trained, but they held their ground for weeks despite losses that would have shaken a more professional army. The Japanese used the International Settlement as a base to attack the Chinese—a complete violation of the treaties and usage—while the Chinese were not permitted to do so. Nevertheless the Japanese could not drive through Tsai's army or compel it to surrender. The Chinese held out six weeks and then yielded only when the Japanese brought up a naval force and landed a flanking expedition that moved up from the South. The few of Tsai's troops that survived retreated and the Japanese held Shanghai. Incidentally Chiang Kai-shek sent only a token force to help Tsai and these took practically no part in the fighting. Otherwise Chiang was only a spectator. There was one school of opinion that held that Chiang was not averse to seeing the army of an acknowledged rival military leader destroyed. There was another school that held that Chiang clung firmly to the need of conserving his strength until he could build it up for effective resistance to Japan later. There was a measure of truth in both views. The Japanese had taken Shanghai, although in the final settlement, in which consular representatives of Western Powers acted as mediators, they technically withdrew their troops and turned it back to Chinese jurisdiction.

At almost the same time the United States was taking its own positive action. Whatever may be said about the so-called restraints laid on the League by the United States, in less than four months it was forcing the pace of opposition to Japan. On January 7, 1932, Secretary Stimson issued a statement enunciating what became known as the Stimson Doctrine. The American government formally declared that it would not recognize any situation or treaty between Japan and China brought about by means contrary to the Kellogg Pact or in violation of Chinese integrity or the Open Door Policy. This was given application a few weeks later with the creation of the admittedly bogus state of Manchukuo. Pu-yi or Henry Pu-yi, as he had begun to call himself, the young Manchu who as a child had been deposed as emperor of China, had been living quietly in a foreign concession in Tientsin since he had been driven out of the Forbidden City by Feng Yu-hsiang, the "Christian general." Early in 1932 he was either induced by the Japanese to come to Manchuria or kidnapped by them and taken there—it has never been certain which it was. On February 18, persuaded or submitting to threat, he declared the independence of Manchuria and on March 9 he became head of the state of Manchukuo. The new state was immediately recognized by Japan. Two years later Manchukuo became a monarchy with Pu-yi as emperor.

This squarely put the Stimson Doctrine to the test—a test that the American government met equally squarely. There was an immediate flurry in Geneva and the West European capitals. Just what happened in Geneva and what pressure the American government exercised, if any, have never been established; but on March 12, 1932, the League Assembly resolved that it was "incumbent on members of the League" not to recognize any situation brought about in contravention of the Covenant of the League or the Pact of Paris (Kellogg Pact). Whether this was merely adjuration to the states in the League or constituted a commitment is subject to interpretation and was never put to judgment; but no Great Power except Japan ever did recognize Manchukuo until after the beginning of World War II, when interestingly, Russia did so. It was not one of the "imperialist Powers," although Great Britain and France had their backs to the wall and seemed about to be extinguished, but Russia, paladin of the anti-imperialist, antifascist cause and protector of the downtrodden colonies! How consistent has been Russia's course in East Asia, whether Russia be Red, White, or any other band in the spectrum!

Manchukuo went on nevertheless, nominally as an independent state. It was, of course, a fraudulent affair. Even Japanese officials in Hsinking, the capital (formerly Changchun) could hardly suppress smiles when referring to the "government" of Manchukuo. There was a government structure, with duly appointed officials, all Chinese, behind each of whom stood a Japanese adviser. The Chinese official was informed of his decisions after they were already being put into effect. The poor little emperor issued edicts that he saw for the first time when the Japanese handed them to him. He was indeed a pathetic little figure still in his twenties. While in his 'teens and deprived of his title, he had resolved to learn something of the West and had engaged a British tutor, a former British civil servant. He appears to have acquired something of Western knowledge and Western ways but to have assimilated neither. Unfortunately he was not too bright or resolute in character. While his role may have revolted him, he was truly a very model of a cardboard emperor; he scarcely deserved the contemptuousness with which the Japanese treated him—the Japanese, in their political relations, at least, had all the obtuseness, tactlessness, and heavy-footedness of the militarist mind and character.

Japan was deterred neither by Mr. Stimson's declaration, nor by the League's endorsement, nor by the adoption of the Lytton Commission's recomendation that Manchuria be restored to Chinese sovereignty. On the contrary, it was defiant and scornful. It invaded Jehol in Inner Mongolia and withdrew from the League. The occupation of Jehol was completed in short order, Chinese opposition being negligible, and then the Japanese sent troops south of the Great Wall into north China. While the world looked on shocked but helpless, they advanced on Peiping. But partly because Chinese resistance stiffened and partly because the Japanese felt that taking any of China proper might be too great an affront to the West and perhaps provoke serious retaliation, they agreed to truce negotiations and signed an armistice at Tangku on May 31, 1933. This provided for a so-called demilitarized neutral zone south of the Wall. Since Chinese troops were forbidden to enter the zone while the Japanese were in a position to send their army back into it whenever they chose, the result was to leave north China at Japan's mercy. The first shadow of the eclipse of north China could be discerned. So, too, the shape of a momentous decision began to form for China. It would begin to disappear, segment by segment, or it would have to fight, with whatever strength it could muster and at whatever sacrifice. For America, too, a time of decision was approaching, little as most Americans seemed to be aware of it.

The next few years witnessed the gathering of the storm. On the continent Japan devoted itself to building up in Manchuria the base of an industrial empire and by oblique methods to detaching north China from the rest of the country. Already it was roughly sketching in the plan of a Japan-Manchukuo-north China economic bloc, which was later to be expanded into the Greater East Asia Co-prosperity Sphere running from the northernmost tip of Japan through the Southwest Pacific to the borders of India. At home it was proceeding to fit its already authoritarian mold to the pattern of a modern totalitarian, fascist state, blending native militancy and chauvinism with the highly organized mechanical efficiency of the new European dictatorships, although as it turned out it took over what was ugliest in Europe without the efficiency of European dictatorships.

In China at the same time there was a slowly but steadily mounting passion of hatred, the more virulent for being checked by frustration. A new schism was developing, though one of a different kind from before. On one side were those who were willing to come to terms with Japan and accept what had to be, either because they were fatalistic and saw no hope of successful resistance or because, like the men of the earlier Anfu group, they could see more gain for themselves in serving Japan; arrayed with them, though only temporarily and for different reasons, were those who thought it was better for China to bide its time, swallow humiliation, and use the interval to amass strength for the ultimate test by battle. On the other side were those who, goaded by honest if unreasoning patriotism, wanted to give the challenge to Japan at once. In the government at Nanking were many of both sides. Chiang Kai-shek was determined to stand by the policy of doing nothing for the time, of temporizing, appeasing a little where necessary and proceeding steadily to unify the country, organize and train an army, and develop the resources without which an army could not fight successfully. Despite the vilification to which he was subjected, the accusations of cowardice and self-seeking, he remained resolute. And time was to prove him more right than wrong. In 1937, when war finally came, he was able to make enough resistance to hold up the Japanese until the China-Japan War was merged with the European war. Had he taken the more popular line and perhaps followed his instincts as a Chinese and offered armed resistance in 1933 or 1934, he would have been brushed aside as easily as the Chinese forces in Manchuria and Mongolia.

As for Manchuria, Japan is to be credited there with a remarkable economic achievement. Emphasis must be put on the word economic, for politically Japan never succeeded in winning over or even conciliating the inhabitants. On the contrary, it estranged them needlessly, beyond the necessities of the situation of alien ruler and native subject people. It was needlessly repressive, needlessly brutal, and needlessly crass in its failure to make any attempt to consider the point of view of the inhabitants in its actions. Without jeopardizing any of its ends, military, political, or economic, it could have made concessions to Chinese feelings, aspirations, and interests. It could have given the Chinese at least some opportunity for material betterment, at least a token share in the growing prosperity of the region. The Japanese are probably the most inept colonial rulers in the world. They have never perceived the advantage of letting their subject people have even 2 per cent of the perquisites of their native land; they take 100 per cent for themselves.

Politically the Japanese succeeded only in embittering the people of Manchuria, but economically they performed remarkable feats of transformation. Before 1931 Manchuria was predominantly an agrarian region. It grew food crops—soya beans, wheat, millet, of which the first was by far the most important in the form of either beans, bean cake, or oil. Coal and iron were mined in relatively small-scale enterprises by old-fashioned methods in the main. Production of goods was by handicraft or simple tools. Such machine industry as there was foreigners owned or controlled. The economy was one in which primary products were exchanged for imported consumer goods. The Japanese went in with a conscious plan. While they learned about autarchy from the Germans they also had a foundation of their own on which to build. Their own modernization had been carried out to a considerable extent under central direction, if not government control. Nineteenth-century laissez faire economic theory had been given free play only when it did not interfere with ends determined from above for national reasons. In the Japanese plan Manchuria was to become a subordinate workshop in the enlarged Japanese empire, unlike Korea, which was to remain a supplier of food, lumber, metals, and minerals. In Manchuria were coal and iron and timber. On them heavy industry of the less refined and precise branches could be established, using Japanese capital and technical skill and cheap continental labor, untrained but industrious, intelligent, and adaptable. And here laissez faire was almost completely barred. As early as March, 1933, the "Manchukuo government" laid down a program of economic construction in which it was publicly announced that state control would be established over all "important economic activities." These were not further defined, and the door was left open for complete governmental monopoly in an autarchy.

The South Manchuria Railway was the center around which the whole new economy was built. This was sound enough, for if Manchuria was to be really industrialized, more and better communication and transportation facilities were essential. By 1939, seven years after Manchuria was taken over, 2,650 miles of railway had been built, almost doubling rail capacity. These were planned with two ends in view. The first was strategic. They were so laid as to provide alternative routes from Manchuria to China and from Manchuria to Korea and thence to Japan. Thus troops could be concentrated in any part of Manchuria in case of threat from within or from without and they could be brought from Japan and sent into China or Siberia if the need or opportunity arose. The second purpose was economic. Rail lines were carried to deposits of coal and iron, so as to bring them out more cheaply for use in Manchuria or Japan; they were also carried toward the north and east, where agricultural products, especially soya beans, could be more efficiently gathered for export. In the same way more than 5,000 miles of new highways were built and existing ports enlarged and modernized.

Most of all, a whole industrial complex was set up, with its main center in Mukden. To provide power two great dams were constructed, the one on the Yalu River being on the scale of the Boulder Dam, and generating plants were erected on the same scale. To provide the most essential raw materials there was a phenomenal increase in the production of coal, iron, timber, and cotton. Coal production went up from 9,000,000 metric tons in 1931 to almost 14,000,000 in 1935; iron production rose from 673,000 metric tons in 1931 to 1,325,000 in 1936; timber production increased three and a half times, cotton by a third. With adequate transportation facilities and raw materials, plants were erected comparable in size and capacity to those to be found in Japan proper or even in Western industrial centers. Mukden became a kind of Pittsburgh superimposed on an Oriental city: the technical appurtenances and activities were there but the amenities of a great modern city were lacking. There were steel mills, metal-working mills, and plants producing machinery and machine tools, electrical engineering equipment, industrial chemicals, locomotives, bridge materials, textiles and, of course, a huge arsenal. It was a phenomenal achievement in less than a decade. But the Japanese were too little concerned with what was provided for the inhabitants, mainly Chinese.

Two observations have to be made here, the most important that can be made about Japan in Manchuria. In the first place, the whole development of Manchuria by the Japanese had one purpose and was governed and conditioned by it. That purpose was preparation for war. Japan sought to emancipate itself from the danger of being cut off from supplies of essential raw materials in case of war and in addition to assure itself of an extra arsenal for the production of military supplies. It was creating in Manchuria a military base, not a place for improved life for the inhabitants or even for its own people. Therefore the criterion of economic soundness never was applied to any of the enterprises that entered into Manchuria's development. Many of the enterprises were, indeed, uneconomic; that is, they operated at a loss. Their products could have been bought more cheaply elsewhere, if cost had been the only consideration. But cost was not; the ruling consideration, if not the only one, was utility for war.

The second observation is that, however great the achievement, it was crippling to Japan. Theoretically it might have been sound. In Manchuria there did lie no doubt the potentialities of one of the world's rich and undeveloped regions, one that would yield a high reward on development if—and this should be emphasized—if the country attempting to develop it could afford to sink a huge amount of capital into it before the returns began to come in. And just this Japan could not do. Japan was starting on the career of overreaching itself, the career of trying to be too big for its boots, that was to bring about its ruin.

Had Japan itself been a rich country with a large fund of surplus mobile capital, so that it could have let a large part of the surplus lie dormant for a time, it might have been able to bring off the Manchurian scheme and ultimately enrich itself thereby. But it was not. It was itself still underdeveloped. Uneconomic enterprises for purposes of military aggrandizement were beyond its capacity. Even if they had been themselves economically sound, it could not have afforded them, since it did not have the capital to sink into first costs—the enormous capital outlays required for establishing modern industry. Railways, exploitation of reserves of raw materials, plant and machinery—all these needed huge amounts before returns could even start coming in. It will never be possible to state precisely how much Japan sank into Manchuria even before the plunge into war against the Western Powers, since so much is a matter of accounting and so much more cannot be ascribed directly to the demands of Manchuria but was inescapable nevertheless. The lowest estimate of the amount directly invested in Manchuria between 1932 and 1939 is 3,000,000,000 yen (roughly $1,500,000,000). For a country that was rich at the beginning of the effort that would have been little enough. For Japan it was enormous. One result can be seen in national debt figures—6,000,000,000 yen in 1930, 10,500,000,000 yen in 1937, when China was invaded. It can be seen, too, in balance of trade figures. Imports into Manchuria, consisting mainly of capital goods from Japan, exceeded exports from Manchuria by anywhere from 60,000,000 to 500,000,000 yen a year, all of it financed by Japan. This result was shown in the Japanese economy in increased pressure on domestic capital. The national treasury, banks, insurance companies, and corporations were being drawn fine and by 1937 the strain was beginning to tell.

Nor was this all. There was a still heavier charge on Japan by reason of Manchuria. Japan's aggressive intentions thus signaled, and sustained as the years advanced, had put the rest of the world on guard. China was obviously resolved on restitution and revenge. Russia had massed a large army on the eastern borders of Siberia facing Manchuria; after 1934 there were periodic clashes that at any time might develop into full-scale war. The United States was antagonized, wary, and building up its navy. Japan was itself constrained by its own actions or, rather, pushed forward willy-nilly by a force of its own creation. It had to arm whether it wanted to or not, could afford to or not. Its military leaders could say with justice that the country faced a hostile world. What they did not say was that they had themselves created the hostility.

Nevertheless Japan was compelled to arm, quickly and heavily. On the part of those who already could dictate policy there was no reluctance to do so, of course. Arm it did, however, and the cost of armament was added to the drain on capital to develop Manchuria. By 1936 half of the annual budget was allotted to the army and navy, and even with heavy increases in taxation there was an annual deficit that had to be met by loans. These were in effect forced loans. Under the pressure of the militarists, pressure expressed in threats against both interests and persons, private capital had no option. Japan had gone too far and was facing the consequences, now already beyond its control. It might have had the wealth to develop the resources of Manchuria to the point where they would yield a profit; that is highly doubtful. Or it might have had the wealth to expand and arm itself enough to be able to defend its territorial acquisitions against China or Russia or the United States or even a combination of them; that is even more doubtful. But certainly it did not have the wealth to do both. What it had done was to put itself in a position in which it had to go forward whether it wanted to or not. The resulting tension could not long be borne. It had to fulfill its grandiose designs, to make itself master of the continent while it thought it could, before it broke down under the burden it had taken on. It had to conquer or fall. Naturally it elected to conquer, and it fell.

CHAPTER XXXVIII

Jingoism and Terrorism in Japan

Events moved swiftly in the years between the consolidation of Manchuria into the so-called state of Manchukuo and the outbreak of the war between Japan and China. In both Japan and China they moved continually toward collision. Since Japan was the active agent and China the passive it is better to consider Japan first.

Japan moved steadily forward. As has just been said, it had to; also it wanted to. Its predilections came naturally. Advance was in the blood. That appetite comes with eating is as true in the politics of power as in anything else, and the success Japanese military expansion had won in the preceding years, the demonstration that it could have its way despite the opposition of the Western Powers, had bred desire for further success. The urge to conquest—conquest for its own sake—which had been pushing to the surface since 1868 but was suppressed by the restraint of the clear-headed founders of the new state, could no longer be stemmed. For one thing, those men, the leaders of the Restoration, had with but a few exceptions died. Furthermore, the urge had now become an insensate passion that could no longer be laid. A new class or group had emerged, a dangerous one. It was known as the Young Officer Group and in the main was composed of young army officers, although in their aggressiveness, militancy, and extremism they had the tacit support of some of the leaders of the army. They had the inner drive of Japanese militancy, the belief in force and the right to exercise it. They were also dazzled by the ideas and methods of fascism then current in Europe and tempted by the successes fascism seemed to be gaining. Since a fairly large proportion of them came from the peasant or small landowner class, a class never before allowed to produce officers, they felt the discontent bred in that class by its subordination to the urban and large landowner classes and hence were responsive to the promises of social betterment which European fascism was using to such good effect.

Above all, they wanted to conquer. If in order to get the opportunity to do so they had to suppress those who opposed them at home, they were not only prepared but eager to suppress, by whatever means were required. A kind of inverse social revolution was under way.

There was opposition, of course, if not effective or even resolute. In all the contemporaneous writing about Japan there was much reference to Japanese liberalism and liberals. In this there was a good deal of exaggeration, based in large part on wishful thinking and in some part an adept Japanese propaganda for purposes of protective coloration. The liberalism was not very substantial, and the liberals few and of little influence. Among them were men of the academic and other professions, those who can be roughly described as intellectuals. These had never had much voice in Japan and had even less in the atmosphere then prevailing. Generally included among them, perhaps paradoxically and not entirely accurately, were men of large business interests. There developed, especially in American thinking, a curious interpretation of Japan as a kind of dualism of reactionary militarists and liberal big businessmen, an unexplained variation of the usual social pattern. Yet it contained a measure of truth, not in the sense that the wealthy businessmen shared the body of doctrine commonly described as liberalism, for that they surely did not, but in the sense that they knew too much of the world to believe that the militarists' ambitions were practicable. Their occupations had given them some contact with other countries. They were aware of the strength of Europe and America and the weakness of Japan not only in resources but in industrial and financial underpinning. They recognized the suicidal danger of militarist adventurism. While not particularly opposed to expansion as such—as a matter of fact few of them really believed that China should be permitted full freedom of action if its acts were unfavorable to Japan—they took exception to the time and method of expansion advocated by the extreme militarists. They objected to their heedlessness, perceiving that it would lead to the country's destruction.

Whether they were liberals by conviction or businessmen moved by knowledge and fear, they were ineffectual. The militarists had no comprehension of beliefs arising from knowledge and reflection. They had also the traditional samurai scorn for the men of trade. While welcoming the wealth that trade put at the nation's disposal and even insisting on it, they despised the man who produced it. He was still considered to be of a lower caste. In that, of course, the Japanese militarists did not differ from the European landed aristocracy of two hundred years before.

Nevertheless there was opposition and it was expressed, though diffidently, by administrative officials, parliamentarians, professors, and journalists. It was voiced most often by men of cabinet rank, especially those who had to do with government finance and could foresee the consequences of continued increase in military expenditure. Increase in expenditure was limitless, but to increase in revenue there was a definite limit, especially in a country with not too much surplus capital to begin with. Government borrowing was going on at a rate that was ominous. The service of loans was already a heavy charge on the national income. Successive ministers of finance sought to curb military appropriations and were supported by liberals in the Diet who opposed expansion on principle or because it imposed too heavy an economic burden.

The opposition had to be suppressed. When the military wanted money for expansion, they wanted it, and it had to be provided. The arguments against them they dismissed as negligible, when they understood them. Considerations of economic possibilities, of budgetary soundness, of solvency even, were to them earthy, vulgar, and *infra dig*. They wanted money and it had to come, whether by higher taxes, loans voluntary or forced, levies on capital—it did not matter. The first need therefore was to stifle criticism, whether from cabinet ministers, members of the Diet, the permanent bureaucracy, the press, or individuals. To that end thought control had to be imposed. The definition of dangerous thoughts was broadened and deepened. Public measures to punish those who held and uttered them became more severe, arrests more common, and penalties heavier. Harsh censorship was imposed. Press and public alike became first cautious, then timorous. It was not exactly fascist repression but an approximation thereto.

To win support for such a regime and program it was necessary to work up a fanatical patriotism. This was not difficult. It came easily to Japanese. There had always been wildly chauvinistic secret societies, the Black Dragon Society being probably the best known. In one variant or another all cherished high-blown dreams of conquest, of Japan's mission to rule Asia certainly, the whole world if and when possible. Thus the world would be brought, at length united, under the all-wise and benevolent dispensation of the emperor, the only divine ruler. The societies had never been taken too seriously or included men of any real status in the country, but they did exercise a measure of influence. They were at least feared, for terrorism was not beyond them. There were also organizations of men who had served in the army and navy and young men's leagues which were not unlike the Nazi youth groups. Besides these there were unorganized but numerous hoodlums who could be counted on when violence was called for. A systematic indoctrination of extreme patriotism ever since the Restoration in 1868 left a large proportion of the Japanese people susceptible to the virus of jingoism; certainly their resistance was low, lower than that of any other people in the modern world.

By 1937 jingoism prevailed. It was the national mood—at least no other attitude was articulate or dared to be. The militarists had forged a weapon, and they used it. They used it in the form of intimidation and, when that was not enough, resorted to assassination. Murder became a means of political persuasion. Cabinet ministers, administrative officers, members of the Diet, editors or professors who remained recalcitrant or even openly critical were first threatened and, if that did not suffice, were assassinated, sometimes by hoodlums who were incited to the act and sometimes by military officers in uniform. In one instance two of the highest and most fanatical army leaders were retired by some of the cooler of the generals because of their activities. In retaliation General Nagata, one of the ranking army men who was held responsible for their retirement, was murdered at his desk by one Colonel Aizawa. At Aizawa's trial his advocate pled that what he had done others would have done and would do in the future on the same ground. Four men who had held the premiership were assassinated within six years, always for being "insufficiently patriotic," for "misleading the emperor," for "obstructing the Way of the Gods," on which it was Japan's mission to lead the world. When the assassins were arrested (as they usually were, since they made little effort at concealment), their trials were in the nature of high comedy, even if the material was tragic. The accused freely, even proudly, admitted their guilt. Their counsel argued, often to the applause of the crowded courtroom, that their guilt was exculpated by the purity of their motives. They were safeguarding the sanctity of the Throne, frustrating those who opposed the will of the Divine Emperor. And if they were not acquitted, they were given trivial sentences, again to public applause, for by then mob sentiment had been fired and those who remained rational were perforce silent.

The climax came early in 1936 in the famous February 26 Incident. That night a group of army officers at the head of a picked force of 1,400 men set forth in Tokyo on a coup designed to seize the capital and overthrow the civil government. In a proclamation beginning with the words, "The essence of the nation of Japan as a land of the Gods," they announced: "It is our intention to remove the evil retainers from around the Throne and to smash the group of senior statesmen. It is our duty as subjects of His Majesty the Emperor." Thus they were not rebels. They were loyal protectors of the country. And the moral and emotional state of Japan can be comprehended only if one understands that in this they were wholly sincere. They genuinely believed it and so did a large part of the Japanese people.

The mutineers held the palace gates, and bands of soldiers led by officers rushed through the streets to the houses of cabinet ministers and the most prominent civilian officials, whom they had decided to liquidate. They killed Korekiyo Takahashi, the elderly Finance Minister and one of the most distinguished—and moderate—statesmen of the generation; Admiral Kentaro Suzuki, Grand Chamberlain of the Court; General Jotaro Watanabe, Inspector General of Military Education and one of the three ranking officers of the army and an advocate of discipline, and Admiral Saito, a former prime minister, whose wife was also wounded. All were shot down or cut down with sabers in cold blood. Admiral Okada, the incumbent prime minister, escaped because his brother-in-law was mistaken for him and killed, while he himself was successfully hidden in his garden and later smuggled out to safety dressed as a servant. Others, like Prince Saionji, the Elder Statesman, and Count Makino, one of the emperor's intimate advisers, owed their lives to being away from their houses when the roving bands arrived. For four days the rebels held the public buildings they had seized and defied all attempts to evict them. Finally reliable troops were called out and the rebels surrounded. After an ultimatum threatening to wipe them out to a man unless they surrendered, they gave up. A reaction set in. They had gone too far. Open insurrection was more than all but the lunatic fringe could countenance. The rebels were tried, this time seriously. Fifteen of the leaders were executed and fifty-nine sent to prison. Thereafter open terrorism by violence relaxed but suppression was unabated.

In the same year there was a major political event that showed even more clearly how Japan was moving and that had a deeper and more lasting consequence. The conclusion of the so-called Anti-Comintern Pact with Germany was announced on November 25. In content the pact was relatively innocuous, but in direction it was both revealing and ominous. It provided that the two countries would keep each other informed on the activities of the Communist International, confer on measures of defense deemed to be necessary, and co-operate in such measures as had to be taken. Not only in domestic temper but in international politics Japan was declaring itself. It was now unmistakably arraying itself with the fascist world and European fascism's ambition for world conquest. It was now irreversibly set on its Gadarene plunge.

CHAPTER XXXIX

Desperation and Division in China

In China meanwhile there was a direct reflection of the furies driving Japan. It was shown in the steady, unconcealed Japanese military advance in north China, in the manifest design to do there as had been done in Manchuria. It was shown no less clearly in the hardened determination of the Chinese to resist Japan, a determination formed of desperation but no less firm for that.

In 1934 Japan made the first semiofficial announcement of intended foreclosure. This was the pronouncement of the so-called Amau Declaration. Eiji Amau was a blustering young diplomat who was official spokesman of the Foreign Office. In contrast with most of the Foreign Office officials, who knew the world and knew also the danger of foolhardiness, Amau had concluded that the success in Japan was to the egregious and he had affiliated himself with the extreme militarists and their plans, hoping to rise with their success. With or without the knowledge of his superiors, he suddenly pronounced one day, in pompous, magisterial phrases, a kind of doctrine for future guidance of the world in the Far East.

After the usual grandiloquence on Japan's "mission in East Asia," he declared that "to keep peace and order in the Far East she must act single-handed and on her own responsibility." Therefore joint international efforts to assist China (as, for example, through the League of Nations) would be forbidden. Individual countries might be permitted to make loans to China, provided these were not used for arms or planes or the services of military advisers or had "political use," since such loans would "tend to separate Japan and other countries from China and ultimately would prove prejudicial to the peace of East Asia." This was a Monroe Doctrine in broad extension and free translation. It meant in substance that China was Japan's private preserve, others to enter only by Japan's special permission.

The military remorselessly proceeded to put this principle and program into effect. The demilitarized zone agreed to in the armistice that followed Japan's incursion into North China from Manchuria in 1933 was converted into a so-called autonomous regime, reaching from the Great Wall south to the outskirts of Peiping, which was in effect a puppet regime under the jurisdiction of an obscure and corrupt Chinese general who was a willing tool of the Japanese army. Except in name the whole area was for practical purposes separated from China by 1936. Hopei Province itself, the province in which Peiping lies, had to have a governor sanctioned by the Japanese and all important provincial measures also had to have Japanese assent. It was not inaccurate to say in 1936 that all north China already had the status of south Manchuria before 1931, and the Japanese made no effort to conceal their purpose, which was to construct a separate bloc consisting of the five north China provinces as a buffer region between China proper and Manchukuo—not quite a state but also no longer part of China. The shadow of Japan already lay darkly over north China almost down to the Yangtze Valley.

Not only China was uneasy at all these menacing omens. So only in less degree was Russia, for Siberia's borders marched with Manchuria's and Mongolia's. In addition, the closing years of World War I had evidenced Japan's aspirations to acquire Siberia too, aspirations frustrated only by American pressure at the Washington Conference. Russia perceived the danger no more clearly than China but was better able to take measures to counteract it. Soon after Japan set up the state of Manchukuo, Russia began to move troops into eastern Siberia, to establish military centers and fortified lines there, and to begin constructing industrial centers, so that such military efforts as might be required would not be dependent on the long supply lines to Russia proper. The Japanese were correspondingly resentful and perhaps fearful. While concentrating on the design for China they had not necessarily abandoned hopes for Siberia. Two armed forces were thus confronting each other on the Manchurian border. There were inevitably incidents, some accidental, some provoked. Between 1934 and 1937 there was no little evidence that a Russo-Japanese war was impending. Certainly the inflammables were widely and carelessly strewn and a spark would have sufficed to start a general conflagration. Whether the Japanese restrained themselves out of respect for Russia's potential power or because they had given priority to their aims in China is not certain; but none of the numerous clashes with the Russians was pressed to decision. It may have been only strategic discretion on Japan's part, but discretion there was, and contrary to the expectations of many in the Far East, war did not come.

Russia on its part made preparations by way of men and arms; it did so diplomatically too. One way to ward off the danger from itself was to deflect the main force of Japanese aggression to China. This could be done by encouraging China to resist. If China's resistance politically became too formidable Japan would feel obliged to retort with force and crush China once and for all. If, then, there was war in China, as presumably there would be, Japanese energies would have to be concentrated on China and perhaps eventually spent there. Thereafter Russian propaganda in China and Chinese Communist agitation were devoted to whipping up Chinese bitterness and building up the demand for armed resistance. In 1932 as a matter of fact the Chinese Communist provisional government, then in Kiangsi Province, had already declared war on Japan, an empty gesture at the time, of course. In any event Russian diplomacy after, say, 1934, was devoted to fomenting a China-Japan war.

The Chinese needed little prodding from without. Aside from Japan's obvious designs on the country, there was also the contemptuous and often brutal treatment inflicted on them wherever Japanese troops were stationed. In Shanghai, in Peiping, in Tientsin, swaggering Japanese troops bullied and terrorized, shoving men and women off sidewalks, digging rifle butts into their backs, beating them if the spirit moved, looting if opportunity arose. With the Japanese troops came adventurers and ruffians who were even worse than the soldiers. They not only beat, they plundered. They engaged in smuggling, especially of heroin and other drugs. And they were not restrained or even hindered by Japanese civil or military authorities, for they were a useful weapon of Japanese policy. They were slowly to terrorize the Chinese people into submission, and they did indeed give the Chinese a foretaste of the future in store for them.

It did not, however, beat them into submission. It goaded them to desperation. Natural concern for the land of their birth was hardened by hatred—hatred seared by Japanese brutality and no less malignant for being helpless. The demand for resistance became vocal and organized. As usual organization first took form among the intelligentsia—the professional classes, scholars and students, officials, and the politically conscious among businessmen. An Anti-Japanese National Salvation Association was formed. A Students' National Salvation Union sprang up in the universities. There were other bodies with similar purpose. The movement was not without instigation and incitation by the Communists, but it was also genuine, in the larger part genuine. Memorials, petitions, resolutions began to pour into the government at Nanking. Their burden was uniform and simple: fight Japan. They became so numerous and so clamant, gathering dimension and force as they increased, that they became embarrassing to Chiang Kai-shek. Some of the organizations were suppressed and their leaders arrested and imprisoned on Chiang Kai-shek's orders with or without trial.

Chiang Kai-shek had other purposes or at least another order of priority in his policy. He was moved by two considerations. As already has been said, he perceived—and correctly—that resistance was hopeless until China had acquired and marshalled modern military power. Also, and related to this, he saw as the prime prerequisite to power the effective unification of the country—effective rather than nominal, as was the situation as late as 1936. But in this latter position there was more of passion than of principle, more of emotion than of reason, for what Chiang conceived as the most satisfying aspect of unification was the extinction of the Communists. It was Chiang himself who had brought about the expulsion of the Communists from the Kuomintang in 1927 and decreed the terrible repression after their expulsion. And the Communist leaders who had been driven out by him—or those who survived the blood purge—were still the leaders of the Communist regime in the northwest. Also, as Chiang well knew, they thirsted as parchedly for his blood as he for theirs. It was indeed a blood feud more than a political or ideological conflict.

When the Communists had been driven out those who survived first went underground and then precipitated abortive coups in Canton and northern Kwangtung. These were ill-timed and were crushed easily and with harsh reprisals. The remnants of the Communists then made their way in separate bands to a central point in the hills of Kiangsi Province, north of Kwangtung Province and west of the coast. Taking advantage of the shelter provided by the mountainous country there, a group of the die-hard Communist remnants began to coalesce, drawing to themselves dissident groups and winning support from discontented peasants in the environs. Here the first real center of Communist authority was established. It set up and exercised political authority. A program of agrarian reforms, dispossessing rich landlords, dividing up land, abolishing usury, was instituted. Kuomintang officials were driven out. Inhabitants were forbidden to pay taxes to the Nanking government. It was a government within a government, though a small one. Small though it was, it irked Chiang Kai-shek, not only because it was a rift in national unity but because it represented defiance by his mortal enemies.

The Communists became stronger. Within the bastion of their hills they were training an efficient army, efficient for the kind of guerilla warfare by which alone they had any hope of success. Also the demonstrable amelioration in the lives of peasants under their jurisdiction attracted others, and the sway of their authority was expanding. So also was Chiang's determination to root them out and exterminate them once and for all. When in November, 1931, the first All-China Congress of Soviets was convened at Juichin, in Kiangsi, and the Chinese Soviet Republic was proclaimed, the die was cast. It was not much of a republic and its jurisdiction was restricted enough, but it was a gage of battle nonetheless. And when in April, 1932, it formally declared war on Japan, while Chiang was sitting in Nanking outwardly unperturbed by Japan's aggression, the iron was driven into Chiang's soul.

Chiang had already launched two campaigns on a minor scale against the Communists. They were dismal failures. The Communists employed tactics that were to stand them in such good stead later. Before Chiang's organized expeditions they retreated skillfully, fading away in small groups and blending into the countryside. Then, when Chiang's army was extended too thinly in pursuit, the Communists struck at weak points and destroyed or routed whole detachments, besides interrupting communications and capturing supplies. Each time Chiang's forces were defeated and retired frustrated. Late in 1931 a third offensive was undertaken, this time with 300,000 men, and it met the same fate. So did a fourth in 1933. Meanwhile the Communists were becoming more adept in their own style of warfare. Also their army was increasing in numbers and in armament, though the arms were of the simpler sort.

Chiang Kai-shek then engaged a group of German officers as advisers. They were commanded by General von Seeckt, who incidentally had organized the nucleus of the army on which Hitler was to build his Wehrmacht. A system of blockhouses and fortified points was constructed to encircle the Communist area and, after starving out the Communist forces by a blockade, to destroy them at a blow. In October, 1933, Chiang began the campaign on the new strategy of his German advisers. This time it was to be more successful. The Communists were hemmed in. They could no longer retreat as before. They had to stand and give battle, which would have been hopeless against Chiang's larger numbers and superior armament, or to break out at the cost of losing their political and military base. With considerable skill and some losses they did manage to break out through a weak sector in the circle in the southwest and began their historic retreat across a large part of the East Asian continent.

This was the famous Long March, one of the epic retreats in history. They set out in October, 1934, heading northwest almost 140,000 strong. They crossed perilous mountain passes and rushing rivers, in heat and cold, snow and rain, harassed at almost every point by Chiang's forces and heavy guns, often surrounded and again and again breaking through, though with continuous losses. They suffered hunger and thirst. Their boots were worn through and many marched barefoot over long stretches. Their clothes were worn to shreds. They suffered disease and had little with which to heal wounds and assuage pain. They survived because they lived off the country, and this they could do because they usually had the sympathy of many of the inhabitants in the territory through which they passed. What they lacked in arms they made up in propaganda. The peasants, who were the majority of their army, were convincing advocates. They covered more than 6,000 miles in their serpentine course; twelve months after the start they arrived in the barren, impoverished corner of Shensi Province, the last stage being through eastern Tibet and Kansu Province. Of the almost 140,000 who set out only 20,000 remained. They were the hardened, toughened veterans who made up the core of the force that was to drive Chiang Kai-shek's army of 3,000,000 or more off the continent to the island of Formosa fifteen years later. In 1936 the Communists extended their area of control and set up their capital at Yenan, using caves as administrative offices. There they proclaimed another republic, with the same kind of policy and program as in Kiangsi. It was from Yenan that they set out eastward in 1947 to conquer the whole of China, Mao Tsetung still at their head.

Chiang Kai-shek was mortified in pride but undiminished in determination. The majority of the politically conscious in the country became more insistently vocal in demanding a closing of ranks to confront the enemy from without, but the conflict that called most insistently to the depths of Chiang's being was that against the Communists. To serve his purpose, therefore, it was necessary to suppress internal criticism and he proceeded to do so, much after the Japanese fashion, though not so systematically and with such ferocity. For one thing the Chinese did not lend themselves to regimentation as easily as the Japanese. But newspapers and periodicals were closed down and dissidents were jailed. There was, too, a body of secret police, which used all the methods of secret police everywhere, though with less efficiency than in fascist and Communist countries. This may have silenced criticism but it also made adherents to the Communist cause or at least alienated influential elements from the Kuomintang, a development which the Communists were to capitalize on not so many years after.

Chiang proceeded undeterred, however, against his preferred enemy. He laid plans to drive the Communists out of their lair in the northwest, as he had out of Kiangsi, believing that then they would have no place else for refuge and would be either annihilated or driven out of the country entirely. To drive them out of the northwest, however, he needed forces near the scene of action in addition to his own. He therefore called on the Army of the Northeast, then under command of General Chang Hsueh-liang, the Young Marshal so-called, who had scuttled before the Japanese in 1931. Chiang ordered the Young Marshal to lead his troops against the Communists as the spearhead of another campaign. But many of Chang Hsueh-liang's young officers and to some extent he himself had been moved by the plea sounded ever more eloquently from all parts of the country in words that were almost a chant: "Chinese must not fight Chinese." The Army of the Northeast was patently putting less than full energy into the campaign and in December, 1936, Chiang Kai-shek flew up to Sianfu, in Shensi, which was Chang Hsueh-liang's headquarters, to instill more vigor into the campaign. Then followed an episode, operatic in conception and manner though potentially tragic and certainly historic in its consequences.

On the night of December 12 a group of Chang Hsueh-liang's officers, apparently with his consent, swooped down on Chiang Kai-shek's head-quarters and arrested his staff. Then they made for a resort guesthouse where Chiang himself was staying. He was warned and sought to escape by scrambling over a garden wall but was caught. His captors apparently had intended no harm to his person. It seems that they were detaining him in order to reason with him. Their desire was plain: they wanted him to abandon the fight against the Communists and make war on Japan. Chiang kept his dignity, of which he has a full measure, and demanded that Chang Hsueh-liang be brought to him, since Chang was his subordinate. Chang came.

The captor became the pleader, the captive the accuser and judge in one. Chang argued his cause: the country had to be saved; the civil war must cease; let the country unite and repel the aggressor; he, Chang Hsueh-liang, and his men would then serve Chiang as his obedient subordinates. Chiang was obdurate and uncompromising. He would not discuss the question. He was the head of the state; he would suffer no insubordination. It was not for him to account to his subordinates, especially under duress. Day after day, night after night, the strange dialogue continued. Chang, though Chiang's life was in his power and many of his officers demanded that Chiang be executed, continued to plead; Chiang, knowing his life hung precariously, refused to discuss anything as long as he was a prisoner. Meanwhile Chang Hsueh-liang sent public telegrams to the government at Nanking demanding cessation of the civil war, reorganization of the government to include parties other than the Kuomintang, release of civil prisoners, including those punished for advocating war against Japan, and restoration of civil rights. At Nanking itself there was difference of opinion. One faction wanted to send airplanes at once to bomb Chang Hsueh-liang into submission. Another, realizing that Chiang Kai-shek would then be killed before the planes could have effect, advocated a more conciliatory course. Emissaries who were thought to have influence with Chang Hsueh-liang were sent to Sianfu by plane. T. V. Soong, Chiang's brother-in-law, and Chiang Kai-shek's American-educated wife went.

There was another paradoxical note in an episode already unreal beyond belief. From Yenan came Chou En-lai, one of the veteran leaders of the Communists who was to become prime minister of the Communist government after it took over the country. Chou En-lai did not come to incite Chang Hsueh-liang to kill Chiang, the implacable enemy. On the contrary, he earnestly counseled him to release Chiang. Thus internal peace, unity and effective resistance to Japan could be brought about. And this may have been the decisive factor. On Christmas day Chiang was released, still making no concession. And most paradoxical of all, Chang Hsueh-liang, the captor, went along with Chiang Kai-shek to Nanking as his voluntary prisoner, willing to stand trial for what he had done. And he did stand trial and was convicted and sent to prison, where he remained throughout the war against Japan, accompanying the government as it was driven from point to point by the Japanese. Later he was taken to Formosa, when the Kuomintang government was driven off the continent by the Communists.

Chiang's return to Nanking released something in the Chinese people. His kidnapping, with all its ignominious aspects, had seemed to them the last full measure of humiliation. Not only had it made the country ridiculous in the eyes of the world; it had as well seemed to shatter the slender hope of unity, of nationhood, just at the moment when nationhood seemed about to pass. Another disillusionment had been added to the long succession of disillusionments that had all but broken their spirit. Civil war would start again, with the enemy already within the gates. Then when all hope appeared to be lost, Chiang was freed and returned to Nanking, bringing with him as prisoner the man who had captured him. Deliverance seemed to open for the country. Chiang made a triumphal entry into Nanking. In the larger cities that Christmas night there were demonstrations, spontaneous demonstrations, of the kind the country had not known. It was an outburst of national jubilation, almost a paean of victory. There was hope again.

The significance of the whole episode was not lost on Japan. To Japan it communicated not hope but warning. Even through Japanese military arrogance there penetrated the realization that China was not yet supine, not yet inanimate, soft and pliable, to be moulded to Japan's most high-blown desires. China plainly still had spirit. Internal division could not be counted on as a spearhead for a conquering invader. The years after 1931, when Japanese military panoply had but to show itself and Chinese melted away, would not be repeated. Japan would not win supremacy over China by default.

The realization was reinforced when a few months later delegates of the Kuomintang and the Communist party met and came to an agreement on a united front. It may have been an agreement with tongue in cheek but it was an agreement. Both sides made concessions. Chiang Kai-shek called off the civil war. The Communists renounced all efforts to overthrow the government, to confiscate land, and to carry out any of the other basic points in the orthodox Communist program. Implicit was the consolidation of the united front against Japan. This put a fundamental issue to Japan. Should it abandon the hope of detaching north China? Should it compromise or temporize? Or should it strike before its own impetus was lost and the Chinese became so strong that only a major effort, meaning formal war, would suffice? The answer comes almost by itself. Renunciation, temporization, compromise—these were not in the Japanese mood of the time.

Japan struck. On the night of July 7 there was a minor brush between Chinese and Japanese troops maneuvering in the outskirts of Peiping. Whether the incident was accidental or contrived by the Japanese for a pretext, in accordance with precedent, is not clear. On the evidence and in the light of Japan's revealed aims, the latter is the more credible. At any event the brush at Lukouchiao—the Marco Polo Bridge—was the spark. The conflagration flared. The Japanese sent reinforcements. The Chinese would not yield. Instead they began to move troops toward Peiping from the south.

The war was on. As time was to show, it was not only a China-Japan war. It was a sector in a new world war. Indeed, it was part of World War II from the very beginning. Illogical as it may seem, it may be said in full historical logic that the China-Japan war, which began in 1937, was brought on by the European war, which began in 1939. For Japan was emboldened to defy the rest of the world by an outright attempt to take China because of the immunity it thought was given it, as before in its history, by conflict in Europe. In 1937 Hitler was already frantically and shrilly threatening. The war in Spain was on, Germany and Italy helping Franco, Russia helping the Loyalists, Great Britain and France trying to smooth the international waters. It needed no clairvoyant political insight to perceive that Europe was on the threshold of another war. For practical purposes now if ever Japan had a free field in Eastern Asia. If ever it was to consummate its ambition for mastery of half the Asian continent, now was the time.

CHAPTER XL

Japan Invades

Japan started, too, under a great illusion, a fatal illusion. Despite the warning it was just given, it still believed that China would be an inert mass, large but yielding to pressure and easy to mould. It received a shock from the very outset.

The Japanese militarists had been convinced that the Chinese army, such as it was, would melt away at the first show of Japanese arms, that the clash would be localized in the vicinity of Peiping, that the Chinese government would then yield to the threat of more force, as it always had, and then the north China provinces would be finally separated as a puppet regime. According to the Japanese constitution, the army was obliged to get the authorization of the emperor to send troops abroad. There is considerable evidence that the army leaders assured the emperor that it would not be necessary to send more than two divisions. Even after the first skirmishes showed that the Chinese were still resisting and it was necessary to attack and occupy both Peiping and Tientsin and call for reinforcements, responsible military and civil officials in Tokyo were telling foreign diplomats that this was merely an incident and would be over in a matter of ninety days. Contrary to expectations, it was admitted, the Chinese were being obdurate like naughty children (the newspapers used almost exactly those words) and like naughty children they would have to be chastised. Then they would behave and all would be over. That was in August, 1937. Five years later there would still be almost a million Japanese soldiers in China and while they could advance and win pitched battles they could not consummate victory. They could not get a surrender, they could not stop fighting, and they could get none of the rewards of conquest.

Peiping and Tientsin fell easily to the Japanese, but again as in 1932 Shanghai was drawn into the fighting, this time, however, not through the impulsive entry of one army under a local commander but with the support of the whole country. For this time the clamor for real war against Japan was irresistible, even if Chiang Kai-shek had wanted to abstain. As a matter of fact, when the Japanese struck in the north, a conference with representatives from all parts of the country and all classes was in session with Chiang Kai-shek at Kuling, a summer resort in Kiangsi Province. There the decision was fully and almost unanimously reached for all-out resistance at whatever cost. When the fighting got under way in north China, Chinese troops began moving up from the south along the coast toward Shanghai and Chiang Kai-shek's best divisions started down to Shanghai from Nanking. There were already some Japanese forces there, army as well as navy, and they began to extend their lines in the expectation of quickly dispersing the Chinese.

Serious fighting began in mid-August. The Chinese held firm and when necessary counterattacked. After a few days of hard but indecisive fighting the Japanese were compelled to bring up heavy reinforcements. Still they could not break out of Shanghai. The Chinese not only held but inflicted losses. It was the first time that Japan had known resistance since 1905 in the war with Russia. It was jarring to Japanese pride, but still more divisions had to be called in and finally they were forced to land troops in the south and resort to a flanking attack as in 1932. With Japanese troops in their rear the Chinese had to withdraw but not until mid-November, three months after the battle had begun.

The Japanese then drove toward Nanking, the capital. By now the strength of China's best army was spent and in a little more than a month Nanking was occupied. From the point of view of military strategy Chiang Kai-shek may have erred in sacrificing the core of his army in a single battle, one which in no circumstances could have been won. But from the psychological point of view it was a wise decision. The battle was lost but for China it was a moral victory. It proved to the Chinese people that they could stand up to Japan, that with determination and endurance there was hope of escaping subjection. It was this that steeled the Chinese people to hold out after successive defeats in battles of position, despite loss of half the country, despite the destruction of their cities from the air, despite casualties among combatants and noncombatants running into the millions, despite impoverishment. They could not win, but they could keep Japan from winning, they could bleed it; and there was always hope for intervention from without that would ultimately save them, as it in fact did.

The occupation of Nanking was accompanied by two events more important than the fall of a capital. The first was the Japanese attack on British and American naval vessels in the Yangtze in which the American gunboat "Panay" was sunk, with two killed and forty-three wounded,

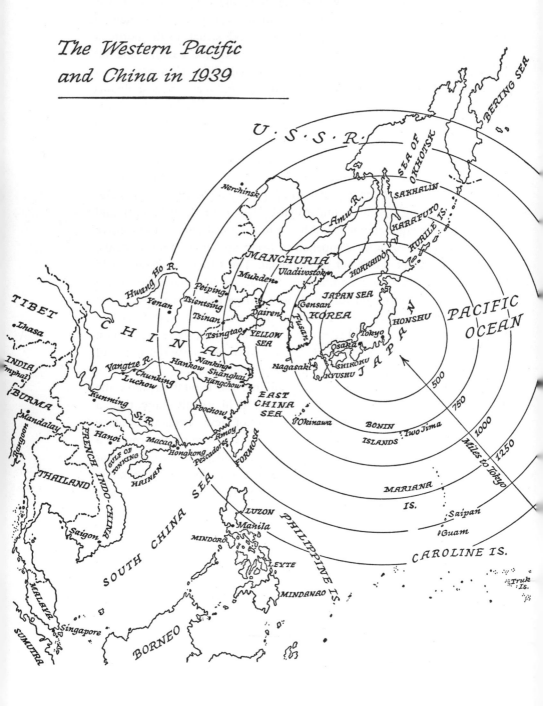

The Western Pacific
and China in 1939

and the British ships "Ladybird" and "Bee" were damaged. Smaller craft, both British and American, also were fired on, three tankers belonging to an American oil company being sunk. It was a deliberate attack. The ships were all clearly marked as British or American. They were first bombed by low-flying planes and then, when they were lying helpless in the water, were raked by shellfire from the shore. American opinion was first stunned and then outraged, but before passions gathered the Japanese government accepted full responsibility and apologized, the apology being almost contrite. Still more eloquent was the demonstration of repentance in Tokyo, where not only officials but ordinary people made pilgrimages to the American Embassy to express regrets. This was palpably sincere and did much to allay American anger, and the incident was allowed to close with the payment of a liberal indemnity, which the Japanese government voluntarily offered. Tension eased but it left a residue of resentment and suspicion.

The second event had a greater effect, though its most direct application was to China. Immediately after the surrender of Nanking there began a kind of blood bath that continued with a sadistic ferocity for almost two weeks. The capital was sacked. Shops and houses were looted. Japanese soldiers rushed about, slaughtering indiscriminately. Whoever crossed their path was shot or cut down—men, women, and children. Young men were rounded up, tied together, led to open fields and mowed down by machine guns. Girls were pursued through the streets, raped, and sometimes bayoneted as well. No effort was made by the Japanese command to check the horrors. Some of the few Europeans and Americans left in the capital went to Japanese headquarters and pleaded for the exercise of control. The Japanese feigned ignorance or were indifferent.

All communications with Nanking had been cut off and the outer world did not know what was going on. When it did there was first incredulity and then shock. Nazi bestialities had not yet occurred to inure men to systematic, sadistic butchery. Everywhere the effect was profound and sentiment turned against Japan. In China it went deeper. It not only implanted a hatred that cannot soon be eradicated; still more, it hardened the determination to hold on, to silence those who believed that some compromise which would save part of the country might be possible.

Whatever the expectation the Japanese had had that the Chinese, once chastised, would repent and promise to behave was now dispelled. The Chinese did not make peace. They refused to consider it. Germany's ambassador tendered offers to mediate. China would not even discuss the matter. Instead the government was moved up the Yangtze to Hankow and there plans were made to carry on resistance. Japan now was beginning to realize, though not openly admit, that it had a real war on its hands, though officially it continued to speak of the "China Incident."

The Western world, too, realized that a major war was in progress in Asia, and this added to the disquiet produced by the storm already rumbling in Europe—the war in Spain was at its height, with Germany, Italy, and Russia participating through "military help," and Germany plainly arming to the full and ready to spring, as it did only a few months later when it moved into Austria. Soon after the fighting began in China there was called a meeting of the signatories of the Nine-Power Pact, together with ten other Powers especially invited. The meeting convened in Brussels on October 6 but Japan refused to attend, as did Germany, and nothing came of it. No country was willing to use force to restrain Japan and, as in 1931, nothing else would have had any use. President Franklin Roosevelt on October 5, 1937, made his "quarantine speech," in which he proposed that aggressor states be quarantined as individuals suffering from any contagious disease were isolated. Even in the United States the response was negative. American opinion was strongly pro-Chinese but not enough to overcome reluctance to get involved in another war.

The war proceeded. The Chinese government withdrew to Hankow and the Japanese began fighting up the Yangtze Valley as well as further north, where Chinese forces had gone into action. At the same time the Communist army in the northwest also had moved, using the guerilla tactics they had already developed. As when they were fighting against Chiang Kai-shek, they never gave formal battle. They retreated, drew out the Japanese lines, then at night gathered at one point where the extended lines were weakest, swooped down quickly, wiped out whole detachments and seized arms and supplies. Then they vanished and the Japanese found themselves pursuing phantoms, using large numbers of men and expending munitions, but never able to destroy the Communists. But slowly the Japanese fought their way north and west. Chiang Kai-shek no longer had the means of effective action. He could use delaying attacks only and on the whole used them effectively for a time. He resisted, then retreated. By early autumn the Japanese were at the gates of Hankow and Wuchang and on October 25 both fell. At the same time Canton also fell, mainly through incompetence. Japan had won the heart of China, but it had suffered heavy casualties and was steadily depleting its strength. And yet there was no end in sight.

Indeed, it could be said that the war was just beginning. China had now adopted the strategy of trading space for time. It would yield territory where necessary but save its army, untrained and badly equipped as the army was. It would keep a foothold, no matter how far into the continent of Asia it was driven. Japan, then, would win territory but it would not win the war. It would not get a surrender, be able to withdraw its forces, check the drain on its resources, and recoup its losses by drawing on the wealth of China. This goal was no nearer than it was a year before. Time was beginning to work in China's favor. An unindustrialized, loosely organized country, it could hold out. There were no arterial centers which, when pressed, would shut off the supply of blood. The peasants could go on tilling their fields and could subsist, though only barely, since they also had to provide food for soldiers. Even in the occupied areas they were still raising crops, however meager. Japan, however, had to maintain a huge army overseas (by October almost a million men), transport them to the battle areas, and supply the requirements of offensive warfare. And for Japan's purpose complicated and costly armament was necessary, the kind of weapons that consumed the raw materials of which it normally has a dearth.

After the fall of Hankow the Chinese government did as it had done after the fall of Nanking. It simply moved on further West, this time to Chungking, more than eight hundred miles further up the Yangtze. In that steamy, muggy bottom of a cup of hills, a rabbit-warren of a city, beautiful yet oppressive in both summer and winter, the capital of unoccupied China remained until the end of the war. To it there began a kind of mass migration of a people's leadership having all the ardors of a pioneering migration. Government officials came first. There being no railways in the Yangtze Valley, they were transported on ships, mainly small, crowded, and uncomfortable ones. Lesser functionaries came by ship or in carts on deeply rutted roads. Archives and records were carried in boxes on poles slung over the shoulders of coolies. Machinery from small plants was taken apart and carried on the backs of coolies. Equipment of commercial houses was similarly transported. Universities moved en masse. Books and laboratory equipment were moved by whatever means offered, on the backs of men as often as not. Professors and students walked—five hundred miles in some instances, a thousand miles or more in others. The universities in Peiping and Tientsin went to Chengtu, west of Chungking, and Kunming, in Yunnan several hundred miles further south. Arrived at their destination, they improvised campuses. Classes, libraries, laboratories, dormitories, and administrative offices were set up in temples, ramshackle government buildings, abandoned courtyards, wherever there was unused space or shelter. Professors and their families lived cramped wherever they could, sometimes in squalor and always without amenities of any kind, often without enough food. And many of them, professors and students alike, came out of the war toughened in spirit perhaps but tuberculous in body. But there at any rate education carried on throughout the war.

The Japanese army never succeeded or even seriously tried to get to Chungking. Its customary foolhardiness and overconfidence did not stretch to the point of extending its lines that far. It tried instead to destroy Chungking from the air and thus drive the Chinese government to the border of Tibet. China's formal defenses against aircraft were all but negligible; geography provided its only protection. For the larger part of the year Chungking lies under a thick cover of fog and the surrounding hills make bomber flights too risky a venture then. But in the few summer months when the sun scorches off the fog the Japanese flew over the city at will, raining explosive and incendiary bombs at their pleasure. The capital, composed mainly of small, flimsy structures, was gutted out by flames. The air raid warning system was highly efficient but even so hundreds, sometimes thousands, were consumed in the flames before they could make their way into hills or caves for refuge. The city was burned out, but the next day masses of laborers cleared the rubble and began its reconstruction. Again and again the process was repeated. The city, pockmarked by empty spaces where material was lacking to rebuild, blotched by jerry-built structures that were eyesores, yet managed to survive. When Japan surrendered and its generals, not yet able to repress the customary swagger, turned over their arms to Chinese commanders, Chungking still stood, scarred and seared but a capital and a monument to China's indestructible will, fortitude under suffering, and resourcefulness in extremity. Whatever dereliction may be charged to China, before, during, and after the war, the wartime life of the people of Chungking belongs in the legends of heroism.

After 1939 the war became a desultory affair, fighting being sporadic rather than continuous. Japan preferred not to take the offensive; China of course was not in a position to do so. From time to time the Japanese sallied forth on an expedition in force, sometimes to destroy the rice crop of an area at harvest time, sometimes to punish guerillas that had become too bold or troublesome. It was a war of attrition, though one of movement. Each was waiting for the other to wear out, the Japanese waiting for China to see the hopelessness of continuing the struggle, the Chinese waiting for Japan to bleed slowly at the pores until hollow within. Technically Japan was by that time victorious but so far as a decision was concerned there was a stalemate.

China's greatest immediately pressing problem was that of getting essential war materials. Cut off from the coast and with the mountainous Asian hinterland behind it, it was under effective blockade even before the outbreak of the European war shut off the trickle of supplies from the West. Russia filtered in some by the arduous Asiatic routes from Europe, and America got in a little before the sea routes were closed entirely. In anticipation of some such contingency China had long contemplated building a highway from Yunnan to the Burma border, which would link it to India and the Western world. At first this was designed mainly for commercial purposes, the section west from Yunnan having been started in 1937. With the war work began in earnest. More than 100,000 men, women, and children were mobilized. Of real road-making machines there was none. There were picks, shovels, spades, and baskets. Thus equipped, men, women, and children swarmed like ants, digging, picking up stones, carrying them off, laying gravel, levelling, surfacing. It was a kind of public works as in ancient Egypt, and it served in the same way. In less than a year there was a highway communicating with the outer world through Burma. It was precarious, tortuous, maintained only by as much effort as went into the making of it. The Japanese bombed it repeatedly, pockmarked it with craters and destroyed bridges and culverts; peasants swarmed over it again and soon the trucks were moving over it once more. At least supplies could come over it until the exigencies of the European war denied it the cargo it could carry. It was another of the prodigious feats of the Chinese under the stimulus of the will to survive.

If there was magnificence in China vis-à-vis Japan, there was also inner deterioration. It was this that was to have such profound consequences after the war, that was, in short, to change the face of East Asia and leave a deep impression on world politics. And only in a minor sense did the deterioration have to do with the war against Japan. It was rather a purely internal deterioration produced by forces of domestic origin. First of all, fissures opened in the united front. The break was between the Kuomintang and the Communists and at the same time within the Kuomintang itself.

Soon after they had taken the northern cities of Peiping and Tientsin and the surrounding area, the Japanese had set up a puppet government. But the men chosen to head it and the dwindling importance of the north as an eddy in the war denied the regime any real prestige. It was unimportant geographically and politically, and it was palpably spurious. The Japanese needed a more imposing front and one with greater depth. But it was difficult to procure and set up and for long they sought in vain. Then Chinese personal rivalries and factional intrigues, which had always cleared the way for the outsider, created opportunity for Japan in the person of Wang Ching-wei, one whom the Chinese would have thought furthest from the role in which he was to be cast.

Wang was one of the most complex and contradictory figures in China's modern political history, a fascinating human case study for a subtle psychologist. He had been schooled in the classical education before the 1911 revolution and had shown singular aptitude as a scholar. He had become one of Sun Yat-sen's disciples in his youth and it was he who threw a bomb at the prince regent and in prison wrote a brilliant essay justifying his act. Before he could be tried and executed the Manchus were overthrown and he was released. As one of Sun Yat-sen's favorite disciples and leading lieutenants, he quickly rose in prestige and standing in the Kuomintang hierarchy. With his intellectual attainments he combined personal charm and moving eloquence, and these made him a national figure.

In the next few years he had a tortuous career. In the main he followed Sun Yat-sen's fortunes but with periodic divagations. There were divagations, too, in his personal philosophy. He followed Sun Yat-sen into the Russian understanding and toleration of Chinese Communists. He was at times on the extreme left, on the very border of the Communist line. Then he shifted to the right wing. He participated in coups both of the right and left, usually unsuccessfully. Most of the time, however, he was in the left Kuomintang. He went with that wing when it broke with the Communists in 1927 and drove out Borodin and the other Russians. Probably his ruling motive was his resentment of Chiang Kai-shek's ascendancy in Sun Yat-sen's favor and in the Kuomintang. To him Chiang was only an illiterate upstart. And for years much of internal Kuomintang politics turned on the rivalry between Wang and Chiang, a rivalry sometimes concealed and sometimes openly virulent.

When the war broke out Wang loyally followed Chiang Kai-shek to Hankow and Chungking but seems to have been consistently relegated to more and more obscure positions. He appears to have become desperate from frustration. Whether it was this that drove him or the sincere conviction that the war was hopeless anyway and he could do more for his country by taking the lead for compromise and conciliation, he yielded to Japanese persuasion, fled from Chungking and suddenly assumed the headship of a government dedicated to peace and friendship with Japan. The government was proclaimed on March 30, 1940, with its capital at Nanking. To the shock of all Chinese and with a crushing blow at their morale Wang—of all people Wang—became Japan's first puppet of any distinction. He was, of course, thereafter—and until his death shortly before the end of the war—never more than a puppet and his government never was more than a paper façade before the Japanese army. It was a sordid rather than tragic end of a distinguished career and the manner of its end hurt the Chinese deeply, hurt their pride in fact more than their war prospects.

The defection of Wang Ching-wei and the setting up of an enemy state within the state may have been serious, but what was more dangerous and more lasting was the degeneration within free China itself, steadfast though it was against Japan. In part this could be accounted for as the natural attrition of war, which always wears on the spirit as well as the body, which depletes morally almost as much as physically. In part this is what was happening in Nationalist China, but only in lesser part. There was more that was not beyond control and that is less easy to understand and to excuse.

Inflation may be taken as an example. Of course there was inflation, there would have been in any country under the same conditions. Currency decreased in value, with the widening discrepancy between mounting war expenditures and diminishing revenue, and there had to be recourse to printing money, so that its value decreased even more. Prices mounted and earnings followed far behind, losing their value, too. Deprivation, harsher with the passing of every year, became the lot of the majority. To a degree this could not have been helped, but it was aggravated by conscienceless hoarding and profiteering by favored groups, favored because of their relations with the highest circles in the Kuomintang and the government. Rice was bought up at the harvest, when it was cheapest, held until there was scarcity and then sold at robber prices. The mass of the people were underfed; the few became fabulously rich. And the point is that without the connivance of men in the government this could not have come about.

Food crops were commandeered from the peasants, ostensibly to feed the army; much of it went into private holdings, also to be sold at robber prices. The pay of soldiers was turned over to army commanders—on padded rolls—and much of it went into the private purse of the commanders. Conscripts were picked up, sometimes right off their fields, roped together and taken to garrisons and then marched off to a camp or presumable battlefield over long distances, with or without food. Many were so weak from hunger that they fell by the wayside and were left to starve. Peasants were exorbitantly taxed; the rich got off scot-free. Corrupt practices were the rule rather than the exception in officialdom, and at their worst they were the practices of locusts rather than of politicians. Nor were they concealed; on the contrary, they were blatantly obvious. They did not have to be concealed, for they had, if not the connivance, at least the indulgence of those who carried the highest authority.

The result was not only to cripple the government and handicap the prosecution of the war but to demoralize the people. The war had begun in a spirit of high dedication. Men of the educated classes, whether scholars, officials, or businessmen, had been fired by patriotism to sacrifice in the cause of national survival. Many followed the government in its trek across the continent, giving up business, homes, and property. They saw what little they brought with them destroyed by bombs. They lived in poverty, sometimes in squalor. They suffered but accepted suffering as worthwhile. Out of it would come deliverance from a brutish invader and rebirth of the nation into a new life—unified, bound together by the consciousness of victory out of suffering and able to take its place in the modern world in keeping with its stature in the past. Then the people saw what was so cruelly visible: callousness, corruption, spoliation, cynicism, impoverishment of the mass and enrichment of the few and, worst of all, subordination of the war to acquisition of power and wealth.

They saw another development. With the motive of prosecuting the war, legitimate at the beginning and then useful as a pretext, there began a process of centralization of political power. The apparatus, the externals of the Russian political structure, still stood. The Kuomintang was a monopolistic party, the sole organism of government. No party congress was held, of course. That pretense had been abandoned in Russia too. Theoretically power rested in the Central Executive Committee of the party in the interval between national party congresses, and there was such a committee in Chungking. It duly met, but with the passing of time it did less and less. It heard reports and accepted them, as it was expected to do. Power rested, then, in the Standing Committee of the Central Executive Committee, a body of twenty-five men, and in that body there was a still smaller group which really wielded power. And that group was composed of Chiang Kai-shek and his own hand-picked immediate associates, which came increasingly to mean Chiang Kai-shek himself. A kind of dictatorship existed, not in name or even open admission but in fact. Yet it was a dictatorship without the advantage of a dictatorship: efficiency.

Also there developed many of the usual accompaniments and instrumentalities of dictatorship: secret police, repression of opinion, suppression of critics. Opposition became an offense. There was a secret police body in Chungking and it came to extend throughout unoccupied China. There were secret arrests, imprisonment without trial, kidnappings, secret executions. Newspapers were closed, or their plants were destroyed, or their editors arrested. Students who demonstrated for more vigorous prosecution of the war, for maintaining the united front, for democratic rights, were arrested and in some cases simply disappeared, never to be heard of again. Before the end of the war the atmosphere was as hideous as in any other dictatorship.

The Chinese people saw all this and inevitably they asked themselves: was it for that they had accepted sacrifice and were suffering as never before? Inevitably there developed a canker of disillusionment and resentment, and it festered. And there began, too, that alienation of the best elements of the country which was to come to the fullest a few years after the war, leaving the government of Chiang Kai-shek without support and opening the way for the Communists. It was in those years, not after 1948, that the Communists began their march to victory.

This brings us to the other aspect of internal deterioration: the break between the Kuomintang and the Communists. In the first two years of the war the united front between the Kuomintang and the Communists worked on the whole satisfactorily. There was no excess of mutual trust. Plainly there were mental reservations on both sides; it was more nearly truce than peace. But the exigencies of the war, with the Japanese advancing in long strides, and the common hatred of the invader, held the two sides together. Both fought, and fought with some regard for each other's activities. But suspicion raised its head. For one thing, Communist guerilla activities were almost too successful for the comfort of the Kuomintang. Guerilla activity to be successful requires support of the population. The Communists, even if they had been moved only by the strategy of the war against Japan, had to extend their influence among the people in order to be assured of food and information. This they could do, since they had always known how to appeal to peasants. Furthermore, the Kuomintang and its armies carried out almost no guerilla activities. The whole area behind Japanese lines therefore became a free field for the Communists. They extended both their influence and their authority, and over a large part of the country wherever the Japanese did not rule they did, they and not the Kuomintang. No doubt this was what they had counted on when they were agitating for war against Japan long before 1937. It has already been pointed out that their motive in those years was compounded of patriotism and party advantage. Chiang Kai-shek and his associates watched the extension of Communist influence with growing uneasiness, and signs of friction began to appear.

Early in 1941 a situation arose that brought the divergent aims to a head and could not be ignored. A Communist force, known as the New Fourth Army, which had been operating with considerable effect behind the Japanese lines in the center of the country nominally under the orders of Chiang Kai-shek, was approaching the Yangtze. Chiang ordered it not to cross. Whether there was a misunderstanding or the order was disobeyed—the evidence is conflicting—the army did cross, met a Kuomintang force and fighting broke out. This developed into a pitched battle and the Communists were completely crushed. They were not accustomed to fighting set battles.

Without open admission on either side the united front ended there and then. It is useless to try to apportion blame. There was right and wrong on both sides. The fact is the united front was broken, never again to be put together. Thereafter the Chungking government shut off the supply of arms and munitions to the Communists and threw up what amounted to a blockade of the Communist region in the northwest. Now China was divided into areas: occupied, unoccupied, and Communist. Communist liaison officers remained in Chungking but their relation with Chungking officials was distant and formal only. The old vendetta had been reopened, its implacability no less deadly for being unavowed. China was invaded from without, divided within. In that atmosphere and condition the Chinese plodded on, their travail already heavy on them and the dark and stormy future that lay ahead all too clearly discernible.

CHAPTER XLI

Pearl Harbor

The stalemate in China was broken but not by anything that happened between China and Japan. It was broken by forces originating outside China. As always in the hundred years since the coming of the West, it was by events and developments in the West, by the nature of international politics in the West, that Far Eastern relations were determined. Not Chinese-Japanese relations but Japanese-American relations and the relations of both Japan and the United States to the European war were to decide when the stalemate in China was to be broken and how.

In one sense there had been a kind of stalemate between the United States and Japan, too, since the affair of the "Panay" had been settled. Neither side pushed its position but also neither side receded. As Japan advanced farther into China it imposed more and more restrictions on the activities of foreigners. With each fresh imposition America voiced protests, which Japan either rejected as groundless or did not heed at all. Meanwhile American public opinion was hardening as sensitiveness to all foreign affairs sharpened with Nazi aggression and the almost stupefying expansion of Nazi power in Europe. There was a growing resentment of all aggression and irritation with the pretensions of militant fascism both East and West. As a direct result the determination to abstain from foreign political affairs (generally but erroneously called isolationism) which had prevailed since World War I was shaken. The world was becoming both too disagreeable and too dangerous to shut American eyes to, let alone keep out of.

It was difficult to decide which half of the world was more disagreeable and dangerous, the East or the West. In East Asia America was more directly involved because of its commitment to the preservation of China's integrity and because of the injurious effect of Japanese restrictions on American interests in China. And the Japanese menace was pointed up more sharply by two acts. In the summer of 1940, Yosuke

Matsuoka, the ebullient, blustering and overvocal Japanese Foreign Minister, made a kind of grand tour of fascist Europe and concluded a German-Italian-Japanese pact which for practical purposes incorporated Japan into the Axis. In 1941 he made another and returned with a Russian-Japanese nonaggression pact. And not long before that Prince Konoye, who doubtless still preferred to be moderate but could be reconciled to extremism when extremism was shown to be profitable and who in any case was too weak to hold out long against military pressure, had proclaimed the "New Order in East Asia." This order, later expanded into the "Greater East Asia Co-prosperity Sphere," was in essence a plan to incorporate all East Asia into a self-sufficient military and economic bloc, a militaristic autarchy organized and conducted for Japanese military power and wealth. It was to be a slightly modified copy of what the Nazis were doing in Europe. Like the Nazi plan, also, it would mean a kind of helotry for the peoples from the Pacific to the borders of India. And, of course, men of all other nationalities would enter only by Japan's leave.

The cumulative effect of Japanese pretensions, threats, and open flouting, its arrogance in speech and aggressiveness in act, was beginning to tell in the United States. From the bombing of the "Panay" through the bombing of helpless Chinese cities, the discriminatory and contemptuous treatment of Europeans and Americans in China, the revelation of intentions in the New Order, the adherence to the Axis, there was added layer on layer to American hostility with a proportionately growing conviction that sooner or later Japan would have to be stopped. As early as mid-July, 1939, the American government freed its hand by giving the required six months' notice of intention to abrogate the standard treaty of amity and commerce between the two countries, which in accordance with international procedure was theretofore automatically renewed. Thus the United States would be able to sever commercial relations whenever it chose. Quite early there had been laid a "moral embargo" on the sale of airplanes to Japan and in 1940 the sale of scrap metals and high octane gasoline for airplanes was legally prohibited; but further than that the United States was yet unwilling to go. It did not want to give Japan a pretext for plunging deeper into Southeast Asia to get oil, thus expanding the Pacific war and drawing in America while Germany was engulfing the West. But public opinion was aroused and there was an insistent demand for retaliatory action against Japan, at least for cessation of the sale of supplies.

Of this trend the Japanese were aware. They were aware, too, of their vulnerability to an embargo. On the Japanese government's initiative, therefore, there began early in 1941 negotiations in Washington between the two governments with a view to finding some basis of accord. There was a succession of meetings extending over a period of months between Secretary of State Cordell Hull and Admiral Kichisaburo Nomura, the Japanese Ambassador. Notes were presented, memoranda exchanged, differences of view argued; but the flow of words and the weight of argument left unmoved and unaffected what lay between the two countries. No doubt, as we now know, it was too formidable to be moved, even to be touched, by words.

Both sides affirmed their desire for peace and a general settlement of Far Eastern problems. Translation of the generalities into concrete terms was impossible. Their aims were not only incompatible but irreconcilable. The issue was China, of course. The United States reiterated its principle of Chinese integrity, of equality of opportunity for all countries there, the principle which it had stated explicitly since 1900 and implicitly since 1840. Japan was not opposed in principle. Application was another matter. To the United States it meant abandonment by Japan of the effort to bring China or any part of it under Japanese control, and from this it followed that Japan would have to withdraw its forces from China. To Japan it meant the New Order in East Asia, in which no doubt the United States would have an equal role with all other Powers except, naturally, Japan which meant no part at all. Most of all, for Japan to have accepted the American position would have constituted confession of failure in the whole China adventure and the writing off of the enormous cost in men and wealth. Even if the Japanese militarists, who made decisions then, were disposed to such an acknowledgment, which plainly they were not, they could not have done so without fatally imperiling their standing at home. Not only their prestige but their power was at stake. To withdraw from China, especially at foreign insistence, would invite the same antimilitarist reaction, though now in much higher degree, as came after 1918. In fact, the army would at least for a time be suppressed. This risk the army would not take, whatever the cost—and to the Japanese army cost, even of human life, never counted for much. It was impossible, then, to come to grips with the issue, no matter how prolonged the negotiations, how skillfully carried out. America would not recede from its position that Japan would have to evacuate China; Japan would not abandon its design to make China a colony.

The issue was cut across by a new and startling Japanese step. On July 23 it was learned that Japanese troops were moving into southern Indo-China in great force. The Japanese had already gone into northern Indo-China the previous summer after the fall of France, nominally to preserve order when French authority could no longer be exercised, and on that pretext had been fastening their control with the unmistakable intention of remaining permanently. By extending their control into southern Indo-China, however, they were doing more than profiteering on France's misfortune. They were in a position from which to spring almost at will across Thailand and Burma to the borders of India, from which they could attack Great Britain in the rear while it was in death grapple with Germany. Now not only resentment but fear was aroused in Washington, and the American government made pointed inquiries of Tokyo, accompanying them with a proposal to neutralize all Indo-China. The Japanese responded by calling up additional troops at home. The American government acted promptly and vigorously. On July 26 President Roosevelt proclaimed the freezing of all Japanese assets in the United States. His action was immediately followed by similar orders on the part of Great Britain, the British Dominions, and the Netherlands. The effect was to cut Japan off from economic intercourse with the rest of the world, since it could get little from its Axis partners, who were themselves shut off by the British naval blockade.

Japan had maneuvered itself into the necessity of a life-and-death choice. It could not remain where it was. To do so was to accept with resignation sentence of death by slow starvation. It had either to retreat entirely, renouncing all the gains it had made, or to go forward. To go forward meant almost certain war, the kind of war it had meant to avoid, since it had counted on being able to get the advantage of conquest and expansion on the cheap. Which Japan would choose was almost foreordained. It would not, of course, wait passively to starve. No nation would, least of all Japan. It would not retreat. Again, the army could not do so without surrendering its ascendancy in the Japanese scheme. It had to go forward. And from July, 1941, it was certain almost with the certainty of astronomical calculations, that, failing some miraculous intervention, war would come in the Pacific. The only question was when and how.

Negotiations continued in Washington nevertheless, but with a marked hardening of attitude and asperity in tone. Japan was becoming more explicit and exigent in its demands. It asked the United States to stop its defensive preparations in the Philippines and cease helping the British and Dutch to do the same in their Pacific and East Asian possessions. More specifically, it asked the United States to stop helping China. The United States on its part was bluntly accusing Japan of unwarranted expansion and demanding that it desist before there could be any prospect of an agreement. More important than conversations in Washington were events in Tokyo. There Prince Konoye, the prime minister, was still trying to hold the military extremists in check or at least to keep them from precipitating disaster. He was pressing them to come further toward meeting the American position. They on their part were insistent on pressing the issue regardless of consequences. There, too, the differences were irreconcilable, and since the army was the stronger Konoye had to give way. He was forced to resign the premiership and on October 17 was succeeded by General Hideki Tojo, one of the most rigid and extreme of the army leaders. What was not known then but came to light when Japanese documents were seized after the surrender was that Tojo and his cohorts soon set a deadline for the negotiations. Either the United States would have to be "sincere," which meant that it would yield, or Japan would strike.

It was in Tokyo that the real negotiations were carried on thereafter. Those who still kept their balance argued for compromise: not complete withdrawal from China but restriction of Japanese forces to a fortified center. America might accept that as a satisfactory settlement. On this point there was protracted debate, with some temporary shifting of positions, but the result was never in doubt. Whatever compromise there would be would have to come from the United States. The deadline was drawing near, though few or none outside Tokyo knew it. As a last effort the Tojo Cabinet sent to Washington Saburu Kurusu, one of the younger diplomats who had, like Matsuoka, hitched his wagon to the militarist star. Kurusu was to take over from Admiral Nomura and try in one last supreme effort to make the American government see reason.

Kurusu arrived in Washington on November 15 and went immediately into session with Secretary Hull. But it was clear that neither side had anything new to add. If there was any difference, it was that Kurusu brought an even more intransigent attitude with him. On November 20 he presented to Secretary Hull a lengthy note containing a set of definite proposals. Japan would withdraw from southern Indo-China to northern Indo-China, the status of the latter to be determined after the restoration of world peace. In return the United States would rescind the order freezing Japanese assets, resume the sale of oil to Japan and, most important, cease giving aid to China. This was November 20. What was not understood then was that that was Japan's last offer.

On November 26 Secretary Hull replied. He proposed a general review of all Far Eastern problems and a set of general principles on which international relations in the Far East would be based. These were, in the main, respect for the sovereignty of all countries in the region, co-operation to maintain peace, maximization of trade, and equality in trade for all countries. On that basis the United States would re-establish commercial relations with Japan, rescinding the freezing order and resuming the sale of oil. Then he appended a list of specific conditions that would have to be met. The most important of these was put succinctly: Japan would evacuate China. It will be seen that the cause for the cessation of economic relations in July, which was the Japanese advance into southern Indo-China, had been removed. But the situation had gone beyond that to what was and always had been the central point of conflict: the status of China. Japan insisted that the United States cease helping China, which would then have no choice except to make peace on Japan's terms. The United States insisted that Japan withdraw from China and abandon all hope of ruling that country. Both sides had committed themselves irretrievably—and irreconcilably.

That was on November 26. On December 7, eleven days later, the bombs fell on Pearl Harbor. The war in the Pacific had come. As a matter of fact the Japanese fleet was already gathering at its rendezvous for the attack on Pearl Harbor when the note of November 20 was presented. Tojo and his associates had made their decision. Given their point of view and their premises, they were right. It was obvious they could no longer conquer a little without conquering all. They had staked too much to be able to withdraw from the game they had themselves started. They could save the stake only by throwing in everything. They had become the prisoners of their own recklessness. They had to go to war now in the hope of riding into success on the general victory of the Axis Powers, sharing in a militarist-fascist division of the world. Whatever the rational among them thought deep within themselves about the chance of success or even of survival, it was too late to think. The past had cast the die for them. Thirty years of heedless adventuring, from the annexation of Korea onward, had led them, step by step. Now it was to be either the heights, that of which the most fanatic among them had dreamed in their wildest dreams, or the precipice, that which the far-sighted had always glimpsed with fear.

For America, too, the past had cut a path from which it could no longer deviate. It had taken on the role of sponsor and guarantor of China's independence, no doubt unwitting when it did so what the consequences might be. Step by step, as the Far Eastern conflict evolved in the decades since the end of the nineteenth century, it found itself more deeply engaged by its commitment. And when that commitment was forcefully and finally challenged, it could no longer extricate itself. For both countries each step constrained it to the next—Japan to advance in expansion, America to immovability in obstruction. Given the nature of the forces that went into the making of the Far Eastern situation, there was no resolution except by war.

CHAPTER XLII

Dark Days After Pearl Harbor

The war opened with melodrama unique even in the record of great wars. It was melodrama with a terrifying note of tragedy for the United States.

December 7 fell on a Sunday. It was a warm, sunny, genial day for December, yet in Washington, always muted and sedate on the Sabbath, there was an air of disquiet. Thick as were the walls of diplomatic secrecy, it had transpired that the impasse with Japan had become more impenetrable in the preceding days. There had been clearly fruitless discussions earlier in the week and then reports that Japan had begun ominous troop movements in Indo-China. On Friday the fifth a long session between the Japanese delegates, Ambassador Nomura and Saburo Kurusu, and Secretary Hull, lasting until the evening, was generally understood to have come to nothing. This understanding was reinforced and quickened when the next day it was announced from the White House that President Roosevelt had sent a direct personal message to the Japanese emperor appealing for the preservation of peace.

Early on Sunday morning the Japanese Embassy telephoned to the State Department asking for an appointment to see Secretary Hull at 1 P.M. Later there was a telephone message asking that the appointment be postponed until 1:45 P.M. Nomura and Kurusu arrived at 2:05 P.M. and were received by Mr. Hull at 2:20. After explaining that they were delayed because a long message from Tokyo had to be decoded, they handed over the message. But forty-five minutes earlier Japanese planes had suddenly descended from the clouds over Honolulu and begun to circle over the naval base at Pearl Harbor, dropping bombs almost at will on the unsuspecting warships clustered there. They sank or damaged eight battleships, three cruisers, and four other vessels. They killed 2,340 men; as many more were wounded or missing. The base itself was all but wrecked. It was the worst military disaster in American history.

What added grimness to the tragedy was that it could have been avoided. Only after the war did it become known that the American government had been forewarned of attack, though not exactly of the time and place. The American intelligence service had broken the Japanese secret code long before and was intercepting and speedily translating messages from Tokyo to the Japanese Embassy. On the night of December 6 a long message began coming in which indicated clearly that Japan was to break relations and hostilities were imminent. It was taken to the highest quarters in the capital in sections and warnings were sent out, to Hawaii and other points, but too late and so phrased as not to make clear that an attack could be expected immediately and that extreme preparations should be taken. Furthermore, early in the morning of the seventh a young radar officer in Hawaii reported the movement of unidentified planes in the vicinity, but this, too, was misconstrued. Thus by a combination of carelessness, misjudgment, accident, misfortune, and chance, a combination that could not be repeated once in a hundred times, the larger part of the American navy was crippled and the whole of the West and South Pacific and Eastern Asia was denuded of defense and left open to Japanese advance.

One factor in the equation of disaster that outweighed any of the others was its implausibility, its unpredictability by any normal political and military calculation. That war would come, that it would come sooner rather than later, was recognized in Washington, even taken for granted. But it was assumed that Japan would push further into Southeast Asia—Thailand or Burma—perhaps even indirectly and subtly, sending in military "training" formations and leaving to the United States the harsh decision on whether or not to go to war. Japan might even attack the Philippines, since it could do so with relative impunity, at least at the outset. But that it would risk an attack on Pearl Harbor, a base nearer the American mainland than Japan and by normal criteria held to be impregnable, that it would rely on the combination of luck, chance, accident, and misjudgment to help bring it off—all that was beyond calculation and still is almost unaccountable.

But the Japanese did bring it off, and with the whole of the South and West Pacific and East Asia open to them, they proceeded to capitalize on their good fortune. Hongkong, the Philippines, and the American-held islands of Guam, Wake, and Midway were attacked simultaneously with Pearl Harbor. All of these fell quickly except Midway and the Philippines. And in the first week of the war another crippling blow was struck at the Western Allies. Great Britain had declared war on Japan on the same day as the United States. A few days later the British battleships "Prince of Wales" and "Repulse," stationed off Singapore,

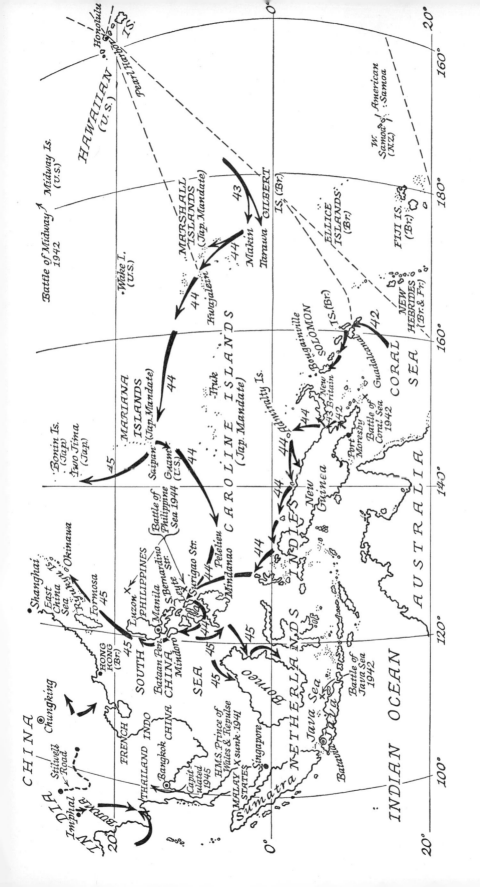

Far Eastern War 1941–45

were sunk by Japanese planes. The Philippines were to hold out for five months, first in the Bataan Peninsula and then in the Corregidor fortress, in both of which small American and Filipino forces, cut off from arms and food and any hope of reinforcement or succor, withstood heroically a relentless siege. General Douglas MacArthur was withdrawn to Australia in March to prepare for the day of counterattack, admittedly a distant day, leaving in command General Jonathan M. Wainwright, who surrendered on May 6.

Thailand had been occupied soon after the opening of the war, and the Japanese swept into the Malay Peninsula. Because of the naval base at Singapore, at the southern tip of the peninsula, probably the strongest naval base in the world aside from Gibraltar, Malaya had been considered reasonably secure. But the base had been designed, on reasoning now hard to fathom, to withstand assault only from the sea, whereas the Japanese came down from the north on land, moving in stages by ship. They were only ineffectually opposed by small British and Australian contingents and to the Western world's consternation Singapore fell on February 15. Early the next month the Dutch East Indies also gave up resistance. The way was open to Burma and by May that, too, was in Japanese possession. In five months Japan had conquered a large part of a continent and stood on the border of India and in islands just north of the coast of Australia.

Yet at that moment, with Japan astride a large part of the world, it could be said with confidence that it was defeated and had laid its own destruction. It was at the top of its form. It could go no further. To have conquered India and Australia, all that was left to it, would have been of little advantage toward ensuring ultimate victory and might have worked to the contrary. Even if it could have succeeded in doing both, which was hardly likely, its lines would have been stretched perilously thin. The most that Japan could hope for was to ride in on the chariot of a complete German victory, one resulting in the mastery of Europe and the paralyzation of the United States, and even that might have gained Japan little, since a Germany flushed with triumph over the world would scarcely be in a mood to let Japan keep a material share of the spoils. Japan could only hope that the United States would, at an early stage, acknowledge defeat and give up the struggle. And this was precisely what Japan had counted on.

For years the Japanese had had a scheme of reasoning as a basis for their larger strategy and overblown hopes. Even the wildest among them recognized that, matching unit of power against unit of power, they could not conquer America in a struggle to the finish. But they derived assurance from a neat, comfortable rationale. As they used to tell foreigners when in an arrogant mood, America had numbers and wealth and resources, but Japan had soul. Americans were inured to luxury and softened by it (not only Japan among militaristic countries so believed) and therefore would not be willing to suffer the self-denial of a long-protracted struggle. They would get tired. They would have no heart for carrying on to a distant conclusion. They would compromise, leaving to Japan most of the fruits of victory. Therefore the sudden crippling blow at Pearl Harbor. Americans would be dismayed at the prospect of building another navy and fighting for years, island by island, across the Pacific. Japan would be triumphant. This may seem fantasy rather than rational calculation, but it was seriously conceived, seriously held and acted on.

As a matter of fact, if the Japanese had gone into Thailand and then acquired Southeast Asia a little at a time, acquiring each part by slow penetration rather than seizure, it is possible that the United States would not have gone into a life-and-death struggle with whole heart. The American people might have considered the issues too remote for the ultimate sacrifice. But when Japan attacked without warning, attacked soil under the American flag, wiped out a large part of the American navy, and killed or wounded several thousand American boys, it drove the iron into America's soul. Humiliated, America was fused into unity as if by chemical action. The "great debate" was stilled. Isolationism was self-expunged. There were no more questions; there would be no doubts. The nation girded for retribution and revenge as it could not have and would not have in any other circumstances. One country or the other had to be destroyed, and unless Germany first destroyed the United States, which was physically impossible, it would be Japan that would lie in ruins.

Thus Japan's doom was already sealed at the height of triumph and glory. It was inevitable in any case that Japan would be victorious at the outset of any war against the United States, with or without a coup such as Pearl Harbor, since its first moves would be in its immediate vicinity against peoples who were weak and could not resist. Geography was its weapon and its shield. By the end of May it had achieved all it ever could. But America had not yet begun to fight. It was only beginning to prepare to fight. Japan could get no stronger. There was no limit to the strength America would amass. The rest was almost mathematical, measured only in time. Japan had nurtured its delusion of grandeur. The delusion was fatal.

It was a long time until the turning, however. A few days after Japan started the war Winston Churchill came to Washington and the grand strategy of the war was laid out, not to be basically altered until the last shot was fired in 1945. It was decided to concentrate at first in the West, to defeat Germany first and only then turn on Japan with the united might of the Western allies. This was bitterly resented by many in the American navy and air force, struggling for years in the Pacific against overwhelming odds and in seeming neglect, but it was justified by the result. The fact is that less than four months after Germany's surrender Japan laid down its arms.

The interval was grim for America, however. The American people, never disposed to patience, had to endure the agonizingly slow passing of time, long day by long day, without sign of progress, waiting for a future not yet visible. There was cause for fear as well as impatience. After all, with the shield of the navy broken, Hawaii lay open to invasion and from there the West coast would be exposed at least to raids. By way of emphasis the Japanese invaded and established bases in the Aleutians early in the summer. Relief from actual fear was to come soon, however, on both sides of the Pacific. On May 4 there opened a naval and air battle in the Coral Sea off the northeast coast of Australia. There were losses on both sides, but after four days the Japanese force was compelled to retreat, having lost an aircraft carrier and two cruisers. Australia was thus saved from immediate invasion. Still more important was the Battle of Midway Island, which opened on June 4 with a large Japanese fleet approaching the island, followed by a landing force. Had the Japanese succeeded, they could have proceeded to the occupation of Hawaii. But they did not. Forewarned, American torpedo and bomber planes went out to meet them. The battle swirled in the air and over the surface of the Pacific for three days. Of the first aerial formations that went out to stop the Japanese fleet as many as nine out of ten men never returned. But the Japanese were stopped before coming in sight of their goal. By the end of the third day they were in full flight, with four aircraft carriers sunk and a number of battleships and cruisers damaged. One American carrier, the "Yorktown," was sunk. This was one of the most decisive battles of the war and the worst naval defeat Japan had ever suffered.

The Midway battle was, in fact, the end of the purely defensive phase of the Pacific war. Japan never again really threatened, and the United States began the long way back, slow and tortuous and bloodied, but sure. The first step was in the extreme southwest Pacific. On August 7 a force of United States Marines landed on Guadalcanal, Tulagi, and Florida in the Solomon Islands, a few hundred miles northeast of Australia. The Japanese had occupied the Solomons earlier in order to sever American lines of communication with Australia. Then began a five months' campaign, small in numbers and scope, but epic in character and terrible in intensity. It was fought by men, ships, and planes day and night almost without respite. The small landing force, numbering at first less than two full divisions, was almost literally cast away on a deserted island, a thousand miles from the nearest American source of support, surrounded by Japanese ships, planes, and men. The first task was to secure an airfield for the landing of arms and supplies. Around this field, Henderson Field as it came to be called, occurred some of the most savage fighting. The Japanese sought, of course, to cut off the Americans and to bring up reinforcements of their own. The day after the American landing a large Japanese fleet caught an Australian-American naval force off neighboring Savo Island, sinking three American cruisers and one Australian cruiser. That was the first of a number of naval battles, both old-fashioned in the sense of ship against ship and modern in the sense of planes and ships against planes and ships. Fortunes were fluctuating, but the balance eventually turned in America's favor, with the most decisive engagement coming in mid-November, when a Japanese fleet escorting transports carrying reinforcements was intercepted and sunk or dispersed. The American marines, later strengthened by the landing of infantry, were at times almost out of food and ammunition, but they held on grimly in an almost primitive struggle of attrition, and in January Japanese resistance ended. America had a taking-off point for the road to Tokyo.

At the same time there was in progress no less fierce fighting in New Guinea. Soon after his arrival in Australia General MacArthur had built an advance base at Port Moresby, on the southern shore of the island nearest Australia. If MacArthur was ever to lead an army back into the Philippines it would be via New Guinea, with the northwestern shore as the jumping-off point. The Japanese had already solidly established themselves on the northern shore of the island opposite Port Moresby and late in the summer of 1942 began an offensive to take that base. To do so they had to come down the Owen Stanley range, mountains standing in malarial swamps and clothed in thick, almost impenetrable jungle. By early September they had come to within almost thirty miles of Port Moresby, but there the defending force, mainly Australian, held. Then the counteroffensive began back across the mountains along the dread Kokoda Trail. The fighting was as mortal as in Guadalcanal and in even worse conditions. Australians and Americans alike suffered as much from disease as from enemy bullets. They first had to make their way up steep mountainsides, sometimes waist-deep in thick mud and with clouds of mosquitoes swarming about them, the Japanese resisting until the last survivor was shot or cut down. Only by November had they got to Kokoda across the mountains and then they had to fight their way to Gona and Buna on the north coast, which had to be cleared if Port Moresby was to be secure. Again the Japanese fought to extermination, and it was not until early December that the Americans closed in on Buna and the Australians on Gona.

The end came in mid-December but only after there were no more Japanese left. They did not surrender even when surrounded and without weapons; they chose to die. Port Moresby was secure; Australia was again reprieved from invasion; the Americans and Australians had opened another road back. But the price paid was awesome. In 1915 at Gallipoli the Australians and New Zealanders, the Anzacs of that ill-fated expedition, had made legend. Now the Australian troops, thousands of whom fell on the Kokoda Trail and before Gona and Buna, had made another that will not fade from their people's memory.

By the end of 1942 practically all the ships sunk or damaged at Pearl Harbor had been raised, repaired, and re-equipped and new ships of all sizes and for all purposes were added. America's prodigious industrial resources had been called into being. The navy was stronger than it had been in 1941. American military power was now arrayed for the advance across the Pacific. At first the two footholds in Guadalcanal and New Guinea had to be broadened to afford a secure permanent establishment. Neighboring islands had to be taken, following preliminary bombardments by ships and planes, naval skirmishes, and hotly contested landings, the Japanese everywhere having to be ferreted out of foxholes and caves.

In the autumn of 1943 the navy was ready for its broadest leap—to Tarawa in the Gilbert Islands, some 1,200 miles northeast of Guadalcanal. With Tarawa in American possession the way would be cleared to the Marshalls and the Marianas, within striking distance of Japan itself. Tarawa was garrisoned by 3,000 Japanese marines, the country's toughest fighting men, and fortified with every resource known to military science. It was to all appearances and to Japan's satisfaction impregnable. After a terrific bombardment from every ship and plane the Americans could muster in order to level the defenses, a bombardment which, incidentally, left most of the defenses intact, the first wave of marines landed on November 20 on the little island of Betio. They were met and held by murderous gunfire; hundreds fell on the beach and in the water before the shore in the first few hours. The losses were harrowing. For a whole day they hung grimly to a toe hold on the beach a few hundred yards wide, with fire pouring down from all sides. But reinforcements were brought up and the beachhead was widened, every yard being contested without quarter. Only after four days was the island wholly in American hands. It was a costly victory but valuable experience in island landings had been gained. At the same time an infantry division had taken Makin, an island to the north, and the Gilberts were secured.

The next stage was in the Marshall Islands, several hundred miles further north and even more formidable than the Gilberts. The attack was launched on Kwajalein, again after days of bombardment. An infantry division landed on the atoll on January 31, 1944, once more against relentless resistance, Kwajalein being garrisoned by three times as many as Tarawa. Americans had acquired both experience and confidence by that time, however, and though the fighting was without quarter as before, in five days the Japanese were wiped out and the island was occupied. Also the American losses were relatively lower despite the ferocity of the fighting—286 killed, 1,230 wounded.

The United States was now solidly established in the mid-Pacific. It had naval and air bases, staging areas for men, arms, and supplies, and a huge fleet free to move with impunity over a large part of the Pacific. The fleet made good use of its opportunity. It started a series of forays against Japanese bases, sinking ships, destroying airstrips and planes, demolishing fortifications. Heavy blows were being struck at Japan in the mid-Pacific. The most successful strike was at Truk in the Carolines, midway between the Marshalls and the Philippines. This was one of Japan's anchor bases in the Southwest Pacific, considered by both Japanese and others to be all but unconquerable. In February carriers swept down on Truk, catching the Japanese by surprise. Squadrons of planes rained demolition and incendiary bombs on the base and left it wrecked, with more than twenty ships sunk and two hundred planes destroyed on the ground or in the air. For practical purposes Truk was useless to the Japanese thereafter. Pearl Harbor was in part avenged.

A little later a similar raid was made on Saipan in the Marianas and much destruction was wrought there, too, though not on the scale of Truk. The raid on Saipan had broader significance, however. Saipan had been Japanese territory since World War I. It was the nearest American forces had come to Japan since Pearl Harbor, except for one not very destructive air raid on Tokyo in 1942. They now proved that they could do so with results serious to Japan. It was a portent.

Meanwhile General MacArthur's army had begun its way west along the north coast of the huge island of New Guinea, starting from Gona and Buna, the two bases won from the Japanese earlier. At first, however, it was necessary to neutralize the enemy base at Rabaul in nearby New Britain, which hampered freedom of movement. The first measure to that effect was taken early in March, 1943, when a fleet of bombers sighted a Japanese convoy making for New Britain and sank almost the whole of it, including transports carrying an estimated 15,000 troops. By September Salamaua and Lae, Japanese strongpoints on the coast opposite New Britain, had fallen and from airfields established there Rabaul was disabled for Japanese use thereafter. The whole of New Britain was subsequently occupied. From there in the spring months of 1944 MacArthur was able to start the leapfrog movements up the coast, one hundred or several hundred miles at a time, leaving Japanese bottled up behind him while he moved up toward the end of New Guinea and the springboard to the Philippines later in the year.

In the same period the road back was being undertaken in Burma. This was even harder, for the jungle was almost impossible to negotiate and the Japanese were numerous and well entrenched. There was political as well as military urgency. When Burma was lost China was cut off from all external sources of supply except the little that could be brought in by the hazardous air route over the Himalayas. China suffered severely and began protesting vigorously in Washington. The Chinese were demanding the reopening of the land route by a campaign to expel the Japanese from Burma. General Joseph W. Stilwell was pressing equally vigorously for the same end. Thus was produced a good deal of acrimony in Chungking and the Western Allied capitals, for the issue of priority among the various theaters of war was squarely put. Washington was shaken at times, but London remained adamant, and in 1942 and 1943, when the Germans were pressing on the Caucasus on one front and toward Cairo on the other, it seemed foolhardy to deflect the slender resources in both sectors to provide for an offensive in Burma that would have only an indirect bearing on the whole war. China was, in consequence, starved of both military and civilian necessities.

Some concessions had to be made to China, however, lest it become too discouraged and drop out of the war or at least cease active resistance to Japan, and guerilla operations were started in Burma with British, Indian, Chinese, and American troops participating at various points. One British commando force led by General Orde C. Wingate, who later fell in action, achieved notable successes, cutting up Japanese troop detachments, destroying supplies and lines of communication, and spreading confusion in the enemy lines. Another force organized and led by General Stilwell and including Chinese troops, who incidentally proved that when properly trained and fed they could be highly effective even against a well-armed enemy, also had favorable results. By the end of 1943 the Japanese hold on Burma was being shaken. In 1944 it became precarious. At the same time American construction battalions had begun hacking a road through the jungle wilderness of North Burma to make a new land highway for supplies to China in the belief, still prevailing then, that eventually a large Allied army would have to strike at Japan through China. It was a harrowing undertaking in a tropical miasma, with men felled by heat and disease rather than bullets, but eventually it was completed, though too late to have much effect on the war.

Stung by these efforts, the Japanese resolved on desperate measures to relieve themselves of danger from India. They decided to attack India itself. They brought up a whole army and in mid-March, 1944, drove toward Imphal, the main base of the British-Indian Fourteenth Army. For the first two weeks the Japanese made progress and threatened to be successful. Imphal was surrounded but the Japanese could neither take it by storm nor force it to surrender. For more than two months Imphal held out, the Japanese meanwhile throwing troops against it with their usual recklessness of human life. When the monsoon rains began and they could no longer sustain losses on so large a scale they called up much of their remaining force for a last do-or-die assault on Imphal. They came on with their usual demoniac fury, literally to do or die, and most of them died. Those remaining were driven back across the Burmese border, leaving behind them 50,000 dead of the 80,000 who started on the expedition. Nor did many of the survivors manage to return to their lines. Without food or arms they, too, were cut down by disease or picked off in small groups by guerillas. From that time it was clear that Japan was doomed to be driven out of Burma.

CHAPTER XLIII

American Offensive: Victory

The time had now come for the United States to take the offensive, to make for the heart of Japan. And it testified to the tremendous power that the United States had amassed in less than three years that it could do so while simultaneously bringing off the landings on the Normandy beaches, the most gigantic military enterprise in the history of war.

On June 15, nine days after British and American troops disembarked under a curtain of German fire on French soil, three American divisions, two of infantry and one of marines, stormed the beaches of Saipan in the Marianas, under as devastating fire as in Normandy. Saipan is only 1500 miles from Tokyo and, being so close to the Japanese home islands, it was a challenge the Japanese could not ignore. They sent a large fleet to Saipan waters immediately after the landing in the hope of destroying the huge assembly of American escort ships and then wiping out the three divisions landed. One of the major naval battles of the war ensued. The Japanese navy was no longer a match for the American in size or skill. The action began on June 19. By the next day what was left of the Japanese fleet scattered in retreat, four aircraft carriers, a battleship, three cruisers and a number of smaller vessels sunk or damaged.

On the island it was not so easy for the American forces. They had to slug it out pillbox by pillbox as in earlier island engagements. It was only after twenty-five days of heavy fighting that they could call the island secured, though small bands of Japanese troops were being hunted down months later. Two weeks after Saipan fell the island of Tinian, slightly to the south, was seized. At the same time another American contingent recaptured Guam, the island held by the United States since the Spanish-American war, which the Japanese had taken soon after Pearl Harbor.

The Marianas were in American hands and the significance was not lost on Japan. Not only was Saipan Japanese territory but American power was now within striking distance of the homeland with the new B-29's. All except the totally uninformed or those drugged by propaganda had a foreboding of what was in store. Later it transpired that influential men in the Japanese upper classes, recognizing the certain prospect of defeat, began to urge consideration of terms on which the war could be ended. And the government of Premier Hideki Tojo, who had been ruling almost as dictator, fell. This itself had the effect of both stunning and warning the people of what was to come. Parenthetically, Japanese official propaganda became increasingly clumsy and transparent as the war went on. Each clash with American forces was blazoned forth in the public prints as a smashing Japanese victory. Again and again the American navy was "annihilated." And each Japanese victory ended with the Americans advancing several hundred miles nearer Japan. Even for Japanese credulity this was too much to be swallowed.

An equally formidable arm of the American pincers was stretching out from further south. MacArthur was continuing his leapfrogging over islands north from New Guinea and by early autumn, 1944, his preparations for revenge for his eviction from the Philippines were coming to fruition. As later revealed, it had been planned to reinvade the Philippines on December 20, but early in September Admiral William F. Halsey, commander of the Third Fleet, after one of his lightning raids on the Philippines recommended that the attack could be speeded up, omitting the operations that had been planned against intermediate islands in order to shorten the leap to the Philippines themselves. A quick decision was taken by the American Joint Chiefs of Staff under General George C. Marshall. The recommendation was approved. MacArthur was instructed to stage his first landing on October 20, two months earlier. He agreed, but one more island still had to be taken to ensure safety in the rear. This was Pelelieu, a powerful Japanese base east of Mindanao, southernmost island of the Philippines. Pelelieu was wrested from the Japanese by September 30 but only after severe fighting. MacArthur now felt he could advance with safety.

On October 19 one of the greatest armadas of modern sea war stretched across the southwest Pacific for hundreds of miles. Making at high speed for the central Philippines, it contained two American fleets, the Third and Seventh, with six battleships, eighteen aircraft carriers, and cruisers and destroyers in proportion. They were escorting six hundred smaller ships of various kinds and sizes packed with the whole of the Sixth Army. Over the whole armada was a protective canopy of more than a thousand planes. As it drew near Leyte, in the central Philippines, hundreds of other bombing planes were pounding Japanese defenses; for days still other bombers had been hammering on Formosa, leading the enemy to believe that island was to be the target.

On the twentieth the Sixth Army stormed ashore, and it should be observed that on that first day 200,000 men went over the beaches of Leyte, more than on D-day in Normandy. As they did, squadrons of planes roamed the skies over the whole Philippines, raining destruction on Japanese troop concentrations, munition dumps, and transportation facilities to interdict the movement of reinforcements to Leyte. As soon as the men had gone ashore the huge carrier fleet steamed out to sea again and sent its planes into the air to watch for any movement by the Japanese navy, which was assumed to be not far away. As a matter of fact, a Japanese search plane had detected the approach of the armada and reported. It was Japan's last and greatest opportunity. A victory would cripple America's striking force for a long time, destroy a great army, and perhaps win a drawn peace. It was Japan's greatest opportunity and also its mortal risk. Defeat would end all possibility of further effective resistance. The Tokyo command decided to accept the risk and seize the opportunity. Three fleets set out for Leyte. Almost the whole of the navy was committed.

The Japanese fleets advanced in formation for a three-pronged attack. They had nine battleships, two carrier-battleships, and four carriers. They were then outnumbered, for more American battleships and carriers had been brought up as a precaution, but two of the Japanese battleships were newly constructed 64,000-ton dreadnaughts mounting more and heavier guns than any in the American fleets. At midnight on the twenty-third one of the Japanese fleets drew into Surigao Strait, at the southern end of the Leyte Gulf. The Americans waited, silent but vigilant, while the Japanese maneuvered themselves into an awkward position, and then caught them in a withering fire from two sides. In a few hours the Japanese were crippled and fleeing. Later a second Japanese carrier fleet steaming down from Formosa was caught by the American carrier force and similarly dispersed, leaving wreckage behind. Then came the critical phase of the battle and of the whole Philippines campaign, truly a historically crucial engagement.

Early in the morning of the twenty-fifth American planes suddenly sighted another large enemy force coming down the San Bernardino Straits toward the Leyte Gulf. As it happened, the Gulf and the Leyte beachhead were at the moment under scant protection, Admiral Halsey and his Third Fleet having struck north in pursuit of the remainder of the defeated enemy carrier force from Formosa. The Japanese came down the San Bernardino Straits with both battleships and cruisers and they were opposed by only a small American force, too small to stop them or even offer much resistance. The Japanese were thus in position to destroy the American fighting ships left in the Gulf, steam into the waters off the beachhead, sink landing craft, supply ships, and transports and cripple the whole expedition. For some reason which has never been satisfactorily explained, however, the Japanese fleet suddenly turned back. Probably its commander had heard of what had befallen the other two fleets and wanted to save something. At any rate the American Third Fleet, which had been summoned back for the emergency, broke off pursuit and steamed at full speed for the Leyte Gulf again. It returned in time to catch some of the retiring Japanese with its carrier planes and inflict further serious damage. The battle was over. In three days Japan had lost forty ships, among them four battleships, fourteen cruisers, and almost all its carriers. Two battleships, eight cruisers and four carriers were actually sunk, the rest were damaged. A still larger number of other classes was damaged. For practical purposes Japan had ceased to be a sea power, and American forces were no longer to be inhibited from the sea in the campaign to reduce Japan to submission.

The American troops on Leyte itself, who naturally had been held up to await the outcome of the naval battle, were now free to proceed. It was a relentless struggle, one of the bitterest Americans had fought. But the naval victory was an asset. The Japanese were handicapped in bringing up reinforcements from the other islands, American planes keeping a constant patrol with devastating results. Mile by mile the Sixth Army pushed ahead. Heavy monsoon rains slowed up progress and added to the misery of the troops. Filipino guerillas, who had been skillfully organized for the opportunity, helped. After two months, but only after two months, could the Sixth Army call Leyte its own. A base had been won from which to proceed into the rest of the archipelago.

The main battle had still to be won, however; with Leyte secured and a foothold gained on the neighboring island of Mindoro, the army was ready for its next and longest step. On January 9, after a number of deceptive movements to confuse the enemy, troops landed on the Lingayen Gulf coast in Luzon, the main island. By evening 68,000 troops had gone ashore and secured a beachhead three miles deep. Here Filipino guerillas were of immeasurable help and progress was swift. Within a month American troops had got to Manila, but there resistance stiffened and they had to fight their way through the city, house by house, for weeks. There, too, there was another instance of the incomprehensible conduct of the Japanese, incomprehensible and hard to forgive or forget. They knew they were beaten. They knew they could not hold the Philippines. Yet they not only brought about the needless devastation of the city but in the Intramuros, the old walled city where a large proportion of the Filipinos themselves still lived, they went berserk and slaughtered helpless noncombatants—men, women, and children— with sadistic, fiendish ferocity, torturing as well as killing. The scar left on Filipino memory will not soon be effaced. It was in vain, of course; Manila fell, and from there American forces spread throughout Luzon and then moved back to Mindanao. By mid-May the whole of the Philippines was cleared. Of something like 300,000 Japanese troops who had been in the islands when MacArthur landed, few were left alive. But the campaign had also cost 60,000 American casualties.

Even while the fighting was still going on in Manila and most of the archipelago was still to be won, the first steps were being taken for a strike even closer to Japan, one which put Tokyo itself within range of American planes. Iwo Jima in the Bonin Islands, 750 miles south of Tokyo, was the next target. Iwo had been pounded from the air almost daily since mid-January, for it was known to be one of the most heavily fortified points in the whole empire. Also the Japanese were bringing up heavy guns and pouring hundreds of tons of concrete for hundreds of pillboxes and bunkers. They were confident that Iwo was to be attacked next and on February 19 it was, three divisions of marines going ashore first.

An inferno of fire met them from cunningly hidden emplacements that had withstood weeks of air bombing and shelling from the sea. It was the worst American troops had yet encountered in the Pacific, as is testified by the fact that 3,600 marines were killed or wounded in the first forty-eight hours. The defenses had to reduced one by one and the defenders bayoneted or burned out by flame-throwers one by one. Yet the fate of the Japanese was sealed. They could not get reinforcements, while American ships brought up and landed more than 100,000 men. It was almost a month before organized resistance ceased, however, and it was, for the size of the battlefield, the most costly American operation, the casualties numbering nearly 20,000, of whom more than 4,000 were killed. But Japan's main cities were now in easy bombing range.

Japan had already been losing its immunity to air attack, however. B-29's based on Saipan had already begun raiding steelworks, dockyards, and similar installations in midsummer, 1944, and by autumn the raids were becoming more frequent and widespread and extended to targets more vital to continued resistance—arsenals, aircraft factories, electrical and metallurgical plants. But it was only after airstrips had been built on the newly captured Iwo that real destruction was to begin. Japanese resistance was at the same time being undermined in other ways than by air raids. Unobtrusively, steadily, and remorselessly American submarines had been sinking ships—the ships that brought from other parts of Asia the raw materials without which Japan could not long go on fighting, no matter how epical the heroism of its soldiers and the stoicism of its civilians. By the end of 1944 not far from a thousand ships had been sent down by submarines, with some being accounted for by American planes flying from bases set up in China. Japan was coming ever nearer to being blockaded, which meant in effect having its war effort starved out. This was confirmed by American air force officers during the occupation. Investigating the results of air operations, they found that numerous large industrial plants were left unscathed by the bombing but had been unable to go on producing for lack of raw materials.

The last and greatest land battle was still ahead. This began on April 1. After naval and aerial bombardment on the scale of the prelude to Iwo, marine and army contingents stormed the beaches of Okinawa in the Ryukyus, off the China coast. This was really bringing the war home to Japan. At first resistance was light, deceptively light, and the American forces secured a beachhead on the west coast relatively easily. They had little difficulty in moving north on the narrow island, but when they turned south to the most populated and heavily fortified part of the island they were soon undeceived. Here struggle took on a ferocity even worse than had been encountered before, and here a new weapon of war entered fully, though it had been foreshadowed in the Philippines. This was the Kamikaze or suicide plane, lightly constructed craft carrying small bombs and designed to crash on American ships and with luck sink them, incidentally blowing up the pilots, who had volunteered for suicide. (Kamikaze means "Divine Wind," and recalls the typhoon winds that miraculously destroyed the Mongol fleets of Kublai Khan who attempted to invade Japan in the thirteenth century.) The Kamikaze did actually wreak a good deal of havoc. Of thirty-three American ships sunk and forty-five damaged, most were the victims of the Kamikaze. Still worse was their distracting and demoralizing effect, since defense against them was difficult, so unorthodox were they as weapons.

The battle lasted just a little less than three months. Only then had resistance ended with the last of the "banzai" charges, those mad flings of the Japanese, who, knowing there was no more hope and sometimes without arms, gathered their surviving remnants and rushed American guns, to be mowed down in a kind of Oriental Wagnerian summons to death. By the end of June American forces held Okinawa and the back of Japanese resistance was broken. There was left only the home islands, which soon would be under siege. At Okinawa, too, almost all of what had remained of the Japanese navy was destroyed. The Japanese lost as well more than 100,000 of their men. The United States also paid. There were some 40,000 casualties, over a quarter of them killed, and a thousand planes had been lost.

Japan was now truly under siege. It was more than the conventional siege of traditional warfare, however. The mighty air arm of the United States was coming into full action. By spring large-scale bombing attacks on Japanese cities had begun. With the surrender of Germany on May 8 the whole weight of American air power, to which British air power was to be added, could be deployed against Japan. In June demolition and incendiary raids were on in full force. The Japanese cities were almost defenseless, most of the planes having been lost before, and large parts of almost every city of any size were reduced to rubble or ashes. Hundreds of American planes, sometimes more than a thousand, were over Japan in a single day, dropping destruction where they chose. Of the fifty-six prefectures in the country only nine escaped relatively unscathed. The small wooden structures that housed family residences and small home industries went up in flames in a few minutes. Fifty square miles of Tokyo itself lay in smoking ruins before the end of June. By July American leaflets were being dropped over Japan warning that certain designated cities would be bombed between certain dates and urging the inhabitants to leave for their own safety. Japanese official estimates put the number of houses destroyed at more than half a million and the number of persons killed at a little less than a quarter of a million. By July, too, American warships were casually drawing up off the coast, shelling ports and industrial towns and sinking ships lying in harbor, including what little was left of the navy. Japan was prostrate.

While publicly the government was still breathing defiance and the headstrong among the military were still admitting nothing, men of some balance, especially those with influence at the imperial court, now less hesitant to speak, were taking counsel on how to extricate the country from the war and escape total destruction. It was decided to ask Russia to mediate. In May it was proposed to send to Moscow Prince Konoye, one-time premier and senior member of the highest aristocratic family outside the court, as emissary. Russia had it own purposes, however, as always. In fact, in April the Russians had given the required twelve months' notice of intention to withdraw from the nonaggression pact with Japan. From this the Tokyo government should have been able to draw deductions. Molotov received the Japanese ambassador and gave inconclusive replies, after the Russian fashion. Pressed by Tokyo to act, Russian representatives alternatively promised, procrastinated, or evaded on one pretext or another. It hardly served Russia's purpose to bring the war to a close until it could win a reward more valuable than

Japan's gratitude. By those who knew the Far East and Russian diplomatic history it had already been taken for granted that nothing could bring Russia into the Far East war until Japan was on the verge of collapse, and when Japan was on the verge of collapse nothing could keep Russia out of the war, for then it would insist on counting itself in on the spoils.

In July the Potsdam conference was convened, with Churchill, Stalin, Truman, and representatives of China present. On July 26 what was tantamount to an ultimatum to Japan was broadcast. It advised Japan to surrender at once or suffer the penalty of complete destruction. The terms of surrender were laid down: Japan would be shorn of all its outlying territory, of all the booty of its aggressions for seventy-five years, and reduced to the four home islands; the country would be occupied by an Allied force; its war-making power would be destroyed; those responsible for leading the country into militaristic conquests would be eliminated from positions of influence in government and, if guilty of war crimes, punished; the country would be disarmed but permitted to retain such industries as were required for the livelihood of the people; all obstacles to democratic government would be removed. When all this was accomplished or assured the occupying forces would be withdrawn. The declaration was not signed by Russia, which was still neutral. The Japanese government made no formal reply. Admiral Suzuki Kantaro, the premier, himself a moderate and aware of the need for peace, felt constrained to assert publicly that the declaration was not worth considering.

Events moved with terrible swiftness to a climax of almost contrived melodrama. On August 6, eleven days after the Potsdam Declaration— a day that mankind is not likely to forget as long as the race exists—a single plane appeared in the morning skies over Hiroshima, a relatively unimportant city of 350,000 in southwest Kyushu. The inhabitants thought little of it. They were accustomed to American planes roaming the skies above them, and a single one did not seem to carry any particular threat. There was a blinding flash, an explosion. The first atomic bomb had been detonated. In a twinkling Hiroshima lay in ruins, one in five of its inhabitants dead, many almost literally blotted out. The world had entered a new era.

That was August 6. Two days later Russia declared war on Japan and sent troops into Manchuria. The next day another atomic bomb was dropped on Nagasaki, the port of Kyushu, though less devastating in effect than in Hiroshima. Japan now faced its fate. The time for overblown army rhetoric had passed.

On August 9 the Supreme Council for the Direction of the War met in special session. It was unable to agree on any action. That evening the emperor summoned an imperial conference, which convened in the palace, with the emperor himself at the head of the table. Present were the prime minister, the president of the Privy Council, the ministers of Navy and War, the chiefs of the General Staffs of the Army and Navy. Debate waxed long and emotional; finally it was decided, the War Minister alone objecting, to accept the terms of the Potsdam Declaration, with one qualification: the prerogatives of the emperor would not be prejudiced.

Acceptance was transmitted to the Allies through the Swiss government on August 10. The Allies sent a joint reply the next day. The emperor could remain on the throne, but his authority would be subject to the orders of the Supreme Commander of the Allied Powers in Tokyo.

There followed two days of moving and dramatic scenes in the imperial palace. Again argument was passionate and inconclusive. To the military representatives, not yet crushed under the weight of events and the ruins that lay about them even in the palace grounds, catastrophe, extinction even, was preferable to the humiliation of the open subjection of the emperor to the orders of an alien conqueror: better to go down in the samurai's death, in a kind of universal banzai charge. The civilians argued for survival rather than glory in death. The emperor listened silently and at length gave judgment. It was his duty to save his people; by surrender alone could they be saved; Japan would surrender. Those around the table bowed assent and burst into sobs.

On August 14 word was flashed to Switzerland that Japan accepted the Allies' terms. And on September 2 on board the U.S.S. "Missouri" in Tokyo Bay, representatives of the Japanese government stood before General MacArthur, flanked by delegates of the Allies, and signed the document of submission. The war was over. Japan's fling in madness had closed in ruins.

CHAPTER XLIV

China: Victorious and Still Divided

China too was victorious, as it were, by co-option. Internally China was almost at its lowest ebb, although, by paradox, in its world position it had risen to its highest status since the middle of the nineteenth century. To understand how this had come about it is necessary to examine events within China and bearing on China in the two years before the end of the war.

The peace settlement as it concerned China had occupied American thought, both official and unofficial, since the beginning of the war. One principle was deemed cardinal. This was the restoration of China's integrity as a sovereign state. As a first application of that principle a Chinese-American treaty was signed in Washington on January 13, 1943, by which all previous treaties between the two countries were abrogated. Thereby extraterritoriality for Americans was abolished and American rights were rescinded in the International Settlements at Shanghai and Amoy and the ports still under foreign jurisdiction. Great Britain signed a similar treaty on the same day and for practical purposes all foreign special rights, privileges, and territorial possessions in China were cancelled. China had become an independent state. But this was only a first step.

More important decisions were to come later. After extensive diplomatic exchanges arrangements were made for a meeting of Churchill, Roosevelt, Stalin, and Chiang Kai-shek in November, 1943, to make political and military plans for the future conduct of the war in both hemispheres. As Stalin and Chiang Kai-shek could not very well meet, since Russia was still neutral in the Far East and did not want to give Japan any pretext for acting in Siberia, it was arranged to hold a meeting in Cairo at which Chiang Kai-shek would be present but not Stalin and another at Teheran at which Stalin would be present but not Chiang Kai-shek.

The meeting with Chiang was particularly sought by President Roosevelt. He had two reasons. The first was concern over China's remaining in the war, on which Americans in Chungking then had considerable doubt. The second was the lack of complete agreement among the Allies, especially between Great Britain and the United States, on China's position in the postwar world. Plainly the President hoped to deal with the second in such a way as to give less ground for the first. Therefore that was given greatest attention at Cairo, where tripartite sessions were held from November 22 to 26. Roosevelt, Churchill, and Chiang Kai-shek quickly came to accord on peace terms in the Far East. Japan would be stripped of all its outlying territories. More specifically, and of most interest to China, Manchuria, Formosa, and the Pescadores Islands would be returned to China. Korea would become free and independent "in due course." Japan would be deprived also of its islands in the Pacific, including those taken from Germany after World War I, but their disposal was left undetermined. These decisions, subsequently known as the Cairo Declaration, were embodied in a statement made public December 1, 1943.

From Cairo Roosevelt and Churchill went on to Teheran, where they were joined by Stalin. They took up the Cairo decisions at once. Stalin gave his assent but there were reservations and intimations of qualification and parentheses of silence that should have foreshadowed what would come later, to the discomfiture of the Western Allies, the roiling of East Asia, and the danger of the world. Whether Roosevelt and Churchill were cognizant of the shadows, especially Roosevelt, or whether Roosevelt, quite well aware of them, preferred not to risk antagonizing Russia when it was bearing the brunt of the war against Germany (the landings in Normandy were still six months off)—on this there is no evidence. But neither side wanted to come to grips with the issues raised or hinted. Stalin did point out that Russia had no ice-free port in the Pacific, Vladivostok being frozen in part of the winter, and indicated the condition was one he would like to see remedied. The position of Dairen, in South Manchuria, was first raised by Roosevelt. When Roosevelt casually suggested that Dairen might be made a free port but under international guarantee, Stalin said that might not be bad, but he did not say it would be good—or enough. The cloud no bigger than a man's hand visible at Teheran became a cloud mass at Yalta and a thunderhead over East Asia a few years later. But at Teheran, too, Stalin repeated the promise he had made to Secretary of State Hull a few months earlier in Moscow that Russia would join the war against Japan.

Here it is best to step out of chronological order and recount what happened at Yalta as it affected the Far East. In sessions first confined to Roosevelt and Stalin the unfinished business of Teheran was brought up. Stalin agreed to go to war against Japan within three months after the defeat of Germany, but then he came to the matter of price. He wanted more than an ice-free port, more than a free port at Dairen under international control. He wanted, in fact, everything that Russia had had in Manchuria before 1914. Both the British and American delegations were jolted and the British counseled refusal, but Roosevelt was under pressure from his military advisers to get Russia into the war even at an exorbitant price. They reasoned that Russian participation would save hundreds of thousands of American lives when the time came for the death blow to Japan. The British position was that the Russians would enter the war in any case, and there was no need to pay a high price. This was doubtless sounder reasoning. But Roosevelt's advisers were pressing, and he yielded. The upshot was that it was agreed that Russia was to get back southern Sakhalin and adjacent islands; it would get back its naval base at Port Arthur and its rights (nominally joint ownership, actually control) on the Chinese Eastern and South Manchuria railways; and Dairen would be internationalized, but "the pre-eminent interests of the Soviet Union would be safeguarded." Russia also agreed to conclude a pact of friendship with Nationalist China. Thus, while China's sovereignty was restored and all special rights cancelled by other Powers, Russia—once more, titular patron of all downtrodden colonial peoples—got back all its classical imperialist tokens. In this respect in the Far East Russia has never acted out of its traditional character since the Bolshevik revolution.

China's relation to the constellation of Powers after the war, more concretely its status in the already projected international organization, was left suspended in lack of concord. On this the United States had strong convictions. These were based partly on its traditional Far Eastern policy and partly on the realization that unless China's status was regularized, formally recognized, and fortified by international prestige, there would probably be confusion in the Far East again and temptation to profiteer on confusion once more. The existence of a strong Communist party in China, the hostility between it and the legitimate government, and the presumptive relation between that party and its Russian ideological forebear underlined the realization. For this reason the United States wanted China's sovereignty restored, its lost territories returned, and itself elevated as one of the main pillars of the international organization, one of the four or five principal founders and guarantors.

Here both Great Britain and Russia were unsympathetic and skeptical, if not opposed. Great Britain and the United States had never seen eye to eye on the importance of China, either to the war itself or in normal international relations. Churchill in his memoirs refers more than once to his failure to understand the value the American government was putting on China when he first went to Washington at the end of 1941. He found that estimate raised rather than lowered on subsequent visits and never could bring himself to agree. Nor, for that matter, did most of his countrymen with any knowledge of world politics and the Far East. He and his countrymen did not think China was or could be a formidable asset in the war or would be able to add to a stable foundation for the postwar order. The British just did not think that China was a Great Power and the Americans did. All the more did American spokesmen, supported by most of American opinion, press for recognition of China as a Great Power while the international order was still malleable. For this there was a certain justification in both logic and politics. Unless China was united and strengthened or, put inversely, if it remained weak enough to tempt rival aggression, there would be renewed conflict in the Far East. Furthermore, with nationalist sentiment clamant through Asia, there would be rancor against the West unless Asia was present, and present with position and dignity, at the council tables of the world. Therefore, on the analogy of the nineteenth-century axiom that if Austria-Hungary had not existed it would have had to be invented, American opinion held that China would have to be a Great Power, even by contrivance.

If that was to come about, however, even if it was to be contrived, China would have to stay in the war against Japan and play an effective part in it. And this became more and more doubtful as the months passed. By the end of 1943 there were large numbers of Americans in China, army men, air corps men, civil advisers, technicians, administrators. Their reports from Chungking were almost in monotone: China was becoming more demoralized month by month, the army more and more ineffectual, the spirit of the people steadily going down, the sole point of concentration, even of attention, being preparation for civil war. America would take care of the Japanese; Chiang Kai-shek would make ready to deal with his real enemies, the Chinese Communists, and the Chinese Communists would make ready to deal with Chiang Kai-shek and the Nationalists. The prospect was dark and the American government was worried. The situation had two phases: the progressive alienation of popular loyalty by the corruption of the Chungking regime and the deepening, broadening chasm between the Nationalist government and the Communists.

The military situation had been becoming steadily worse, although everywhere else Japan was weakening. This had resulted in first creating and then exacerbating a feud between General Joseph Stilwell, American commander in the China-Burma-India theater, and Chiang Kai-shek, his nominal superior. Stilwell was for prosecuting the war against Japan, and in this he was goaded by a single-minded, almost monomaniac fury, to which were added certain qualities of temperament—honor, selflessness, righteous wrath, devotion to a cause, sincerity, repugnance at sloth and evil, and also impatience, irascibility, and perhaps intolerance of the absence in others of his own traits. He had, in short, qualities which unfortunately unfitted him for a situation in which directness and forthrightness were the least likely to get desired results.

There were thus these situations to deal with: the hostility between Chiang Kai-shek and Stilwell, the deterioration in the Chungking government, and the now barely concealed state of war between the Nationalists and the Communists. The Nationalists were deploying more and more of their strength (much of it provided by the United States) for use against the Communists when the inconvenience of Japan was out of the way. The Communists on their part were maneuvering for favorable position against the Nationalist government later. Japan was a secondary consideration to both. It was this last that worried the Americans most, first because they were concerned mainly with the defeat of Japan, and second, because it was considered that a civil war in China after Japan was defeated would nullify America's major end in the Far East.

The first imperative therefore was to try to bring about a settlement between the Nationalists and the Communists or at least to arrive at some compromise which would free both to concentrate against the common enemy—Japan. To this end the United States devoted itself— by exhortation, by moral suasion, by mediation, by everything except threat, which alone might possibly have served. American diplomatic and military officials tried their hands. President Roosevelt thought he might do more by going directly. He decided to send a special mission representing himself and he chose as the head of the mission the second ranking officer of the state—Vice-President Henry A. Wallace. Mr. Wallace went to Chungking in June, 1944, and had long, frank and inconclusive conversations with Chiang Kai-shek. Chiang dealt mainly in recriminations against the Communists, with some parenthetical complaints against Stilwell. To Wallace's urgent advice that the first order of business was the defeat of Japan he agreed but maintained unswervingly that the Communists were the main obstacle, adding that the Communists were only serving Moscow's aims anyway. It was as others before and after had found in dealing with Chiang Kai-shek. He agreed with everything in principle and in generality, and did not change by a hair's breadth in any point of action, however greatly in contradiction to the principle and generality. Mr. Wallace returned to Washington with a report conveying the most depressing outlook.

Events confirmed his findings in full measure. The Japanese were being beaten everywhere else, but in China they were having signal successes. In 1944 they went on a large-scale offensive in China. In part their object was to deal a deadly blow before the Americans and British could come through from Burma, as they were well on the way to doing in 1944. In part it was to clear out a number of American air bases established in China that were punishing Japanese shipping and that would be a mortal threat if American forces should land in China later in the war. The Chinese army gave token resistance at best and the Japanese advanced so rapidly that for a time it seemed that Chungking itself would fall. As it was, a number of American air bases, into which American money and effort had gone, had to be abandoned in haste.

Later in 1944, when the portent of these events was recognized in Washington, President Roosevelt sent as his emissary and later ambassador General Patrick J. Hurley. One of Hurley's first recommendations from Chungking was the removal of General Stilwell, to which Washington acceded, though regretfully. Stilwell was succeeded by General Albert C. Wedemyer, who was instructed to be more conciliatory and who actually was more tactful than his predecessor. Hurley had gone to Chungking via Moscow, where he was assured by Molotov that Russia sought only a settlement in China and that it had no paternal or special interest in the Chinese Communists. Hurley so reported to Chiang Kai-shek. In the hope that Chiang would thus be placated, Hurley began strenuous, if somewhat naïve, efforts to bring the Nationalists and Communists together. He flew to Yenan himself in November, 1944, and there worked out with Mao Tse-tung a series of proposals for settlement to be submitted to Chungking. In essence they provided for a coalition government taking in all parties and based on democratic principles (which were left undefined) and co-operation of Nationalist and Communist armies against Japan.

There followed complicated and tangled negotiations, with refined hair-splitting to conceal that neither side was willing to make concessions to the other. The fact was that neither side believed in the other's good faith, and the fact was, too, that neither side had any reason to do so. Both were right and both were wrong. The Communists had their own independent army and independent administration in the regions in which they had control. This no government could tolerate, and Chiang Kai-shek was justified in not doing so. But whatever Mao Tse-tung may have thought on the matter of principle, he knew that if he incorporated his army into the national army and thus put it under Chiang Kai-shek's orders, Chiang would immediately proceed to scatter it in fragments and then emasculate it, and after that liquidate Mao Tse-tung himself, politically if not physically.

On the other hand, Chiang Kai-shek knew that if he accepted the autonomous status of the Communist armies and administration and incorporated them as a separate entity, they would use the opportunity to expand further at the expense of the government. There was an inexorable fact as an immovable obstacle. Each side wanted above all else to eliminate the other, wanted it more than effective resistance to Japan, for one thing because they both knew by the end of 1944 that Japan was already on the way to defeat. And neither side would let anything stand in its way: the war or American influence or promises of American economic help after the war. Hurley reasoned and pleaded, but in vain. The situation dragged on; China's internal condition became worse. The country stood on a dead center, slowly sinking, when Japan suddenly surrendered.

There was a concrete situation to be faced. The surrender of Japan's armies, numbering a million in China proper and almost as many in Manchuria, had to be taken and the territory they occupied returned to Chinese jurisdiction. The surrender taken by whom—the Nationalists or the Communists? The territory returned to whose jurisdiction— Nationalists or Communists? The situation was one that could not be evaded or dealt with in routine negotiations. Something special was called for.

What was easily predictable happened. Both sides rushed to take over as much territory as they could. The Communists dropped all pretense and claimed the right of a belligerent government and therefore the right to accept surrender of troops, arms, and territory. This was sharply challenged by Chiang Kai-shek and denied by the American government. The American government appealed to Moscow for support but Moscow was noncommittal. The Communists, as it happened, were in a better position than the Chungking government. They controlled a large part of the north and west or had guerila forces that could easily win mastery over nearly all the north and west, while the Nationalist armies were confined to what had been unoccupied China. The Nationalists unfortunately had never resorted to guerila tactics, perhaps because they could not gain the support of the peasantry. Indeed, most of the country outside those parts where Chiang's divisions were stationed held Communist guerillas who in the natural course could have taken over most of the large cities.

The natural course was interrupted by American action, however. In conformity with the United States Army order that Japan should turn over its troops and arms on Chinese soil to the legally recognized government of China, American transport planes flew huge contingents of Nationalist troops to cities such as Shanghai, Nanking, Peiping, Tientsin, more than 100,000 men being thus airlifted. American ships carried additional troops northward. Then and later, as a matter of fact, American ships and planes transported 500,000 Nationalist troops northward.

Both sides raced for Manchuria. Here the Communists had the clear advantage of proximity and the additional advantage of the presence of Russian troops, who had poured into North Manchuria immediately after Moscow's declaration of war and held a large part of the area by the time the Japanese surrender was signed. Russia's position in this regard was complicated by a treaty signed between it and the Nationalist government on August 14, the same day Japan accepted the Allies' terms. The American government had pressed Chungking to enter into negotiations with Russia in order to get its consent to the Yalta arrangement. In the treaty China had agreed to conveying to Russia the stipulated rights in Manchuria, though only after strenuous efforts to safeguard China's rights in the port of Dairen. In exchange Russia pledged itself "to render to China moral support and aid in military supplies and other material resources, such support and aid to be entirely given to the National government as the central government of China." The word "entirely" should be underlined, for it gives an accurate measure of Russia's fidelity to its pledge. Yet the treaty did bind the Russians somewhat in Manchuria. They could not too blatantly turn over the area they occupied to the Chinese Communists and in fact they did not, at least in the beginning, although at points on the coast they did co-operate with the Chinese Communists in preventing American naval transports from landing Nationalist troops. Also it should be recorded here that the treaty did not prevent the Russians from looting and carrying away all the plant and equipment of the great industrial complex of Mukden. Manchuria was thus economically stripped. No single act of depredation by the Nazis was more thorough or more conscienceless. There was a confused situation in Manchuria. The Nationalists on Chiang Kai-shek's orders rushed foolhardily into positions they would later be unable to maintain—against American military advice, as it happened—and the Communists, with some Russian deviousness to help them, consolidated positions wherever they could. At the end of the year two hostile armies confronted each other in Manchuria.

General Hurley meanwhile was desperately working in Chungking for a compromise. In August he flew to Yenan again and induced Mao Tse-tung to return to Chungking with him for direct negotiations with Chiang Kai-shek. The negotiations extended over a period of weeks. They were amicable enough but got nowhere, the two sides again reiterating principles in generalities and yielding nothing. Neither side would waive its position. Chiang did not want to yield anything; Mao thought his position was such that he did not have to. Hurley despaired and went home to report.

So matters stood in China a few weeks after the war's end, and the American government was deeply concerned. Economic conditions throughout China had worsened considerably. Communications were disrupted and trade was paralyzed. Politically there was almost a vacuum, and clashes between troops of the opposing sides were becoming more frequent. The government in Washington decided to make a supreme effort to ward off the danger plainly gathering. President Truman asked General George C. Marshall, just retired as Chief of Staff, to go to China to act as mediator and bring about first a firm truce and then a permanent settlement. General Marshall left for China in mid-December. At the same time President Truman issued a public statement explaining the aims of the government by which General Marshall was to be guided.

The United States wanted a "strong, united and democratic China" as essential to world peace and the success of the United Nations. "A China disorganized and divided either by foreign aggression . . . or by violent internal strife is an undermining influence to world stability and peace." Therefore Marshall was instructed to work for cessation of hostilities and a national conference of all political elements to bring about the unification of the country. The United States hoped for the end of one-party (that is, Kuomintang) government in China but also the elimination of autonomous armies. Meanwhile the United States would continue to give military help in disarming and evacuating Japanese troops (later this was to take the form of transporting huge numbers of Nationalist troops to north China) and if peace was restored the United States was prepared to extend economic aid in large sums for the rehabilitation of the country. But Marshall was told privately to make it clear to Chiang Kai-shek that economic aid was conditional on the establishment of peace and unification.

Supported by his own position and prestige and the authority of the American government, Marshall received a respectful welcome. At first he even attained a measure of success, no doubt because in light of his prestige and the pressure of the American government it was deemed unwise by both sides to flout him too openly. Negotiations turned on the composition of the proposed amalgamated army and national assembly. They were too intricate and complex to be explained briefly. For weeks there was haggling on fractions. At length a truce was arranged, to be supervised by joint Nationalist-Communist-American truce teams. Truce headquarters were to be in Peiping, with a large number of American officers assigned to the post. From there joint teams were sent out to investigate whenever the truce was violated. With the first stage of success seemingly assured, General Marshall went home to report.

The appearance of success was deceptive. In Chungking among the highest of Chiang Kai-shek's advisers a subtle and oblique effort was set afoot to sabotage the truce and the proposed unified government. They knew Chiang, these men, and they worked on him shrewdly, appealing to his old and barely subdued sense of blood-feud and pointing to an opportunity lost: here with America behind them was the chance to deal with the old enemy once and for all. In this the Communists were co-operative. Not handicapped by an excess of good faith, they, too, sought loopholes. And having sources of information in the Chungking government—little, if anything, political is long kept secret in China—they were aware that Chiang was being de-convinced of the wisdom of peace and they sought to forestall the Nationalists.

When General Marshall returned to China the situation had worsened markedly again. Officially the truce was in force; actually it was being violated constantly, sometimes by accident and sometimes by design, sometimes by the Communists but more often by the Nationalists. The capital was moved to its old seat in Nanking in early spring and thereafter it soon became evident that only lip service was being given the truce and only deference to General Marshall prevented an openly avowed break. Negotiations went on without pause. General Marshall carried on with rocklike imperturbability and apostolic patience despite irritations, breaches of faith, and sometimes humiliations. Almost daily he saw first the representatives of Chiang Kai-shek or Chiang himself and then Chou En-lai, the Communist representative stationed in Nanking for the purpose. Sometimes there was curio-shop haggling, sometimes there was agreement in words, to be broken in act the next day. The Communists negotiated as they do everywhere; when there was a sign that their terms would be met they raised their price. The Nationalists on their part were palpably uncompromising except in gesture to soothe General Marshall.

The reasoning of the Chungking leaders was clear and obvious. They were not even averse to communicating it to Americans whom they knew well. Why compromise? Compromise meant meeting American conditions—coalition government, democratic government, termination of monopoly party rule under which they commanded all the offices and all the government enterprises by which they were becoming fabulously rich—this last they did not communicate quite so freely. Why make that sacrifice when, as they thought, they did not have to? They saw the whole state of the world as on their side. America was the strongest Power in the world and they were sure America had to stand behind them. Relations were getting steadily worse between Russia and America and there was certain to be a war. If there was, the United States would need a base in China. Therefore it could not permit China to become Communist. On the contrary, it would have to support the Nationalists whether democratic or not. There was nothing to lose. All that was needed was to humor General Marshall in words, meanwhile soliciting American money and arms to crush the Communists; as an agreeable by-product, they would have done altogether with the heterodox notion called democracy.

Through the spring of 1946, to the accompaniment of pacific conversations in General Marshall's Nanking mansion, friction sharpened and clashes increased in number and seriousness. In June the die was cast. In July there was fighting on a considerable scale. By autumn civil war was on. General Marshall sought to call a halt; he sought in vain. Since the Nationalists were taking the offensive, he tried to put pressure on them by shutting off the supply of American arms which had been continuing to come to them. Acting according to their rationale, they did not think he meant what he said. The Communists by that time were openly bitter at General Marshall and the United States, partly because of the military help to the Nationalists and partly because they were faithfully echoing the voice of Moscow. At any rate the war was on—a war for the control of China, the significance of which was not apprehended outside China and probably not inside China. Blame is impossible to assess with finality. Both sides were guilty. Neither wanted peace enough to pay the price of giving up any of its partisan ambitions. But on the preponderance of evidence that can be corroborated it can be said that the major portion of guilt was the Nationalists'—say three-fifths Nationalist, two-fifths Communist.

General Marshall stayed as long as there seemed to be even remote hope of another truce and permanent settlement. At the end of the year he gave up and returned to Washington—to become Secretary of State, as it happened. On January 7, 1947, as he left China, he issued a public statement on his mission. In it, with almost brutal frankness, he blamed both sides, with a perceptible shade more against the Nationalists. On the Kuomintang or Nationalist side, he said, there was "a dominant group of reactionaries who have been opposed . . . to almost every effort I have made to influence the formation of a genuine coalition government. . . . The reactionaries in the government have evidently counted on substantial American support regardless of their actions." Among the Communists, he went on, there were liberals who "turned to the Communists in disgust at the corruption evident in the local governments" but the party leadership was unwilling to compromise and unscrupulous in its propaganda. But he also stated that the Communists had been less irreconcilable a year previously. "Between this dominant reactionary group in the government and the irreconcilable Communists lay the problem of peace." And there was no peace.

China had escaped subjugation by Japan. It had gained the restoration of sovereignty. It had been elevated to the rank of the five great world Powers. And it was now torn within as it had not been for a century, perhaps never had been. And it had embarked on something the end of which could not even be dimly perceived but which promised— or threatened—decisively to affect the world and perhaps lay it in ruins in a third global war.

CHAPTER XLV

The War's Aftermath in Southeast Asia

The end of the war brought a flux throughout East Asia. All East Asia had been overrun by the Japanese and their surrender left the region not only a vacuum but a scene of turmoil. Of Burma, Thailand, Malaya, Indonesia, Indo-China, the Philippines, and Korea, all except Thailand had been colonial. All had seen their white imperial masters crushed and humiliated, shorn of the prestige that once sustained their rule. With the Japanese no longer able to act there was no functioning administration and economic processes were disrupted.

What was most important was that in almost all of the region there had been guerilla activity against the Japanese. Most of the guerillas had been armed by Americans or British with weapons and munitions dropped from the air or otherwise smuggled in. And as in West Europe under Nazi occupation, the most active, efficient, skillfully organized and courageous guerillas were under Communist leadership, except perhaps in the Philippines. The end of the war thus found everywhere in East Asia compact, armed Communist bodies of experienced fighters devoted to their cause. In the first instance this cause was independence from imperial rule. What else it carried was not yet clear.

In the region that lies between the border of India and Japan Korea must be considered apart and to a degree the Philippines as well. And even within Southeast Asia there are wide divergences. The term Southeast Asia has come to be useful as a general descriptive device but it is accurate only in its geographical connotation. There is no real unity in the area, nothing that all the countries have in common except that they are not white and that all except Thailand have been colonies. One thing more must be said of the region. It is a rich storehouse of raw materials that are not only valuable but essential to Western production and, as much, to the conduct of war—oil, rubber, tin, copra, kapok, among others. World War II proved how the sudden deprivation of these sources could handicap the West.

Thailand can be dealt with quickly. The Japanese evacuated and it was restored to its prewar status, a process made easier because there had been no destruction. Political readjustment also was relatively simple, since the country had not been sharply divided during the war. There were some guerillas and some outright collaborators with the Japanese, but the activities of neither were great enough to carry over into postwar bitterness. And of course there was no nationalist issue to add asperity to all political questions and to break into open violence. The most serious problems were those normal to any country that has been compelled by modern ideas to renounce absolute rule and has had insufficient experience with the democratic process to make representative government function smoothly. There were coups, palace revolts, and minor political upheavals but nothing to add seriously to the perplexities of the postwar world.

To some extent the same was true of the Philippines. In conformance with an act of the United States Congress in 1934 granting independence after a transitional period of twelve years with the status of a commonwealth, the Philippines were duly granted independence on July 4, 1946. It was a right that the Filipinos could claim under law but also had earned by their steadfastness against Japan. Independence was of little use, however, unless life could be sustained. The war had left the whole country disorganized and much of it devastated. Acknowledging an obligation, moral as well as legal, the United States made a grant of $620,000,000 for physical rehabilitation. There was the equally important question of organizing a viable economy for a country of nearly 20,000,000 people. This was not easy, since under the American tariff system, which had been extended to the Philippines under American rule, the economy of the Islands had been linked to that of the United States. Of the foreign trade totalling $234,000,000 in 1939, about 70 per cent was with the United States. Under full independence Philippine exports would have to come into the United States over the tariff barriers, which would mean that they would be negligible in quantity. The economy would have no sound basis. The Philippines would be free but bankrupt.

This situation had already been taken account of in the Hawes-Cutting Bill, which had granted commonwealth status as a step to independence. The bill provided a system of graduated rises in tariff rates against Philippine goods in order to give an opportunity for economic adjustment. This system had to be renewed and extended after the war. There was passed a Philippines Trade Act providing for free trade between the Philippines and the United States for eight years and then for a period of twenty years with small annual rises in tariff rates. There were conditions attached, however. The United States was to enjoy a preferential economic position in the Islands, and in 1947 another treaty was signed by which the United States would give military assistance but would have the right to establish military bases in the Islands. This, of course, aroused no little resentment among the Filipinos.

There were other difficulties. Guerilla activities had left a legacy there too. While the Communists played a less important part in the Philippines than elsewhere in Southeast Asia, there was such a nucleus, and they were as toughened and determined as elsewhere. As usual the rank and file were not conscious Communists, doctrinally convinced, but they were following thoroughly indoctrinated leaders and responding to the usual appeal—follow us and you will get land, fair taxation, and a better living for yourself and your family. The appeal was as cogent as elsewhere. Conditions in the Philippines lent themselves to it. Economically as well as politically the country had been dominated by a minority of about 5 per cent of the population, men of mixed Filipino-Spanish or Filipino-Chinese blood. The rest of the population consisted of poor peasants living on small plots of land, owned or rented, and generally in debt. While the standard of living in general was higher than in other parts of East Asia, it was still low, low enough to generate resentment in a people who had had at least some schooling and had come under the influence of American ideas. If the ruling minority was conscious of this, it was also indifferent to it. Furthermore, among those who not only owned land and big business enterprises but monopolized high government offices corrupt practices were as much the rule as the exception.

In consequence even before the war the Sakdal party, dedicated to social and economic reforms, had been formed and had attained a fair degree of strength. At the close of the war another party was in being, composed mainly of guerillas but including a large number of Sakdalistas. This was the Hukbalahap, and its program was much more consciously and systematically radical because of its Communist leadership. Also it was much stronger—its membership at the end of the war was estimated at 100,000. Well armed with weapons that had been provided by Americans and more militant than the Sakdalistas, it began rallying peasants to its cause with frightening success. For a long time the government's efforts to suppress it were fruitless. The troops sent out against it were neither efficient nor enthusiastic and the kind of reforms that would have weakened the Communist cause were not forthcoming. At length an energetic young officer named Ramon Magsaysay was given command of the punitive expeditions. Because he was energetic, able and honest and, still more, because he had some comprehension of the social questions involved he began to achieve results and the scope of the Hukbalahaps was steadily confined. So impressive was his record that he was elected president in 1953 and, what matters most, was elected on a program of liberal economic and social reforms. Unfortunately, Magsaysay was killed in an airplane crash in 1957, but his successor, Vice-President Carlos García, promised to carry out his policies. There began to be promise of solution in the Philippines, a promise of peace by a better dispensation for the whole of the people and a chance for truly democratic forms.

Burma and Malaya fall in a separate category, since they belonged to the British system and were dealt with primarily by Great Britain. Burma had been a part of India and had been governed by the British raj from 1886, when it was annexed by Great Britain, to 1935, when it was detached from India to become a separate dependency in 1937. In an area of 250,000 square miles, nearly all tropical and much of it mountainous, live 16,000,000 people, of whom two-thirds are Burman and one-tenth Karens, racially somewhat different and generally hostile to the Burmans. There are smaller numbers of Indians, Chinese, and Shan tribesmen. It produces large quantities of rice and smaller quantities of oil and rubber.

The Japanese had been fairly well cleared out of Burma even before the war ended, and the British took over with little difficulty. There was much to be done, however, as the country had been fought over since the beginning and there had been a great deal of destruction. Also there were deep discontents to be laid. Burmese nationalism antedated the war. The contagion had spread from India on one side and China on the other. It flared much higher immediately after the war and the British were confronted by an awkward situation. But a general line of imperial-colonial policy was laid down immediately after the accession of the Labour government in 1945. By one of the most imaginative acts of statesmanship in modern times Great Britain gave India its independence without qualification or restriction—and India voluntarily elected to maintain an affiliation with the Commonwealth as a republic. And, incidentally, the Indian people, almost hysterical in hate against the British before the war, were within five years warmly pro-British. It was difficult, then, to avoid extension to Burma by corollary.

Immediately after the Japanese evacuated there were outbreaks of disorder throughout Burma. Not only nationalistic aspirations were the cause. There were inter-group rivalries in the country as well. One of the groups consisted of Communists, but they themselves were split into two factions. At the end of 1946 the British agreed to meet a Burman delegation to discuss the granting of self-government, but by this time the Burman leaders were no longer satisfied with self-government. In the mood that prevailed in London the government agreed to confer full independence on Burma with the option of remaining in the Commonwealth as an autonomous dominion or contracting itself out. Burma elected full sovereignty outside the Commonwealth and the British consented. In January, 1948, Burma became a sovereign state.

Only one conflict was settled thereby. There were others, even more rancorous. The Communists became more aggressive, though in rival camps. The Karens rebelled. There was hostile intriguing between the conservatives and liberal groups which advocated social reform. There were coups and countercoups, assassinations, plots—too complicated for outsiders to follow. In 1949 civil war broke out or, rather, several civil wars between shifting enemies in shifting combinations. For a long time the country was in turmoil. Neither political nor economic institutions were able to function. By 1950 there was every prospect of anarchy and chaos. Little by little, however, moderate elements of some vigor and insight, animated by a philosophy of gradual social reform, won a grip on the country. The Communists were beaten and, while not eliminated, were driven underground and seriously weakened. The Karens were conciliated. Burma seemed on the way to laying a foundation for a stable order. Peaceful elections could be held and a government functioned normally.

Malaya was much less complicated. It had never been a state or even a single colony. A peninsula pendant to the continent from Thailand, it has consisted of several principalities with slightly different peoples and was acquired by the British over the course of the nineteenth century. Its importance lies in its resources, principally rubber and tin, rubber having been introduced by the British. Before the war one-third of the world's tin and 40 per cent of its rubber came from Malaya. Before 1939 Malaya was governed by the British in several units. There were the Straits Settlements, which included Singapore, the great port and naval base; four Federated Malay States—Perak, Selangor, Negri Semblen, and Pahang; and five unfederated ones—Johore, Kedah, Perlis, Kalantan, and Trengganu. The Straits Settlements were governed as a British Crown Colony. The rest were British protectorates. The population is mixed. Of 6,000,000 inhabitants 40 per cent are Malays, 40 per cent are Chinese, and the remainder are Indian. Europeans are few in number. The Malays cultivated rice on small holdings, having been, at least until the war, uninterested in trade or government or politics. Enterprises of the largest scale were British-controlled. Small enterprises and trade were mainly Chinese, a fact which was to embroil Malaya later.

The Malays, having little consciousness of unity, had had no feeling of nationalism before 1939. The Chinese were of divided loyalties, their homes and the source of their incomes in Malaya and their traditional and emotional allegiance to China. The Indians looked to their homeland. After the war, however, there were stirrings as everywhere else, but, in contrast with India and Burma, the task was simplified for the British by the fact that all three parties were suspicious of each other as well as resentful of British rule. The British first sought to bring about a semiautonomous Malayan Union or tripartite federation, with Singapore still remaining a Crown Colony, but no agreement could be made on the basis of representation for the three groups, the Malays having been granted a preferred position.

Before this could be settled, however, a more powerful factor was injected by the sweep of communism over China. There had been Communists in Malaya before, especially among the Chinese, and the victory in China gave them a strong impetus. The Chinese laborers in the tin mines, on rubber plantations, and on small farms were not without their grievances. Their portion was meager enough—long, cruel work for a reward that barely yielded subsistence. Under British rule Malaya had become, for its size, one of the richest territories in the world, but this did its inhabitants little good. It became ever richer as the growth of the automobile industry increased the demand for rubber, but the inhabitants benefited little thereby. They were scarcely, if at all, better off. It required little propaganda to incite them to action. The promise of a more abundant life was captivating.

Leaders emerged and guerilla bands were formed, consisting mainly of Chinese and copying the tactics that had been successful in China. They were an evanescent force. They never attacked in numbers and in daylight. They ambushed and sabotaged at night and when daylight came took their hoes to the fields and their tools to the mines or plantations. They got their supplies by terrorizing Chinese villages, which became allies perforce. For the British it was like fighting shadows. They finally resorted to the device of rounding up all the Chinese villagers and moving them to new and larger villages constructed for the purpose, which could be fortified and kept under guard, thus cutting the guerillas' sources of supply. This began to show results in time and by 1954 the Communist menace, while not wiped out, became less threatening. The British could resume consultations with Malay, Chinese, and Indian representatives on a permanent form of government. In result Malaya became independent in 1957 and Singapore was placed under a constitution granting effective self-government.

Much more serious was the case of Indonesia—the Netherlands East

Indies, as it was formerly called. The Netherlands Indies, survival of Holland's great age of empire, was one of the world's imperial prizes, an empire in itself. An archipelago, with an area of 730,000 square miles and a population of 75,000,000, it is one of the wealthiest and most densely populated areas in the world. Its rubber, oil, tin, quinine, and copra have been the basis of Holland's prosperity. It is also one of the world's oldest colonies, the Dutch East India Company having won a foothold there early in the sixteenth century. Its history is like that of any other older European colony—development of nature's bounty on a scale far beyond the ability of the indigenous people combined with ruthless exploitation of the indigenous people and complete disregard of their welfare. In the Netherlands Indies as in Malaya the land became prodigiously rich and the natives remained as they were. Toward the end of the nineteenth century Dutch policy modulated. Some attempt was made to give the native people vocational education, to train them to better cultivation of the soil. Also a conscious effort was made to preserve the native culture, in contrast with the effect of colonial rule in other parts of the world. There was, in short, after a long period of exploitation a regime of fairly benevolent paternalism.

No more than exploitation did paternalism serve to stave off the onset of nationalism. Its first manifestation came in Java early in this century, but it did not take serious proportions until after World War I. The Dutch did make concessions in the way of greater local autonomy and some representation in government, but the concessions were belated and did not go far enough. There were disorders and minor uprisings, which were put down with severity. But suppression was, as always, ineffective except as a temporary expedient, and when World War II brought the expulsion of the Dutch officials and residents in the most humiliating circumstances and then the defeat of the Japanese conquerors, there was an almost elemental eruption.

The Netherlands government had anticipated such a development and early in the war sought to stave it off by a declaration of Queen Wilhelmina that after the war the Indies would be admitted into a Dutch Commonwealth as an equal partner. This did not prevent a group of Javanese Nationalists from proclaiming the independence of Indonesia and setting up a provisional government a few days after the Japanese capitulated. Immediately after this proclamation the British landed troops to take the Japanese army's surrender on behalf of the Dutch. The Dutch themselves came a little later and were received with unconcealed hostility. There were numerous brushes as the Dutch sought to spread over Java. The Nationalists retaliated by preventing the release of Dutch women and children from the concentration camps in which they had been held by the Japanese for three years—a cruel retaliation and one which understandably embittered the Dutch.

There was friction, disorder, desultory fighting, and an impasse for a year before a conference was called in the hope of arriving at a compromise. One was arrived at, known as the Linggadjati Agreement, in March, 1946. It seemed a reasonable settlement, providing as it did for the creation of a United States of Indonesia within a Netherlands Union, but including an escape clause permitting any part of the territory to remain outside the Indonesian federation and set up a special relation with the federation and the Netherlands itself. Reasonable or not, the agreement was not effectuated. Each side accused the other of bad faith and there was evidence to support both. There was continued sporadic fighting, and the Dutch sent reinforcements.

In August, 1947, the Indonesian situation was brought into the Security Council of the United Nations, which issued a cease-fire order and proposed arbitration under the auspices of a commission consisting of Australia, Belgium, and the United States. Early in 1948 another compromise agreement was accepted by both sides, with much the same provisions as the first and with much the same results. Again there were accusations of bad faith, again with some ground. By this time Communists had entered the scene, exploiting as always the cause of colonial aspirations for independence and as always gaining adherents thereby. At the end of 1948 the Dutch took matters into their own hands. They put troops in motion, ordered the Indonesian Republic dissolved, and imprisoned its leaders.

Since the question was still within the purview of the Security Council this action antagonized most of the world. The Security Council then spoke firmly. Against the vehement opposition of representatives of the Netherlands it ordered a cessation of the Dutch "police action" and the release of the imprisoned native leaders. The Dutch had to submit, though with unconcealed resentment, and another conference was called to attempt a settlement. This, held at the Hague, was successful. By November, 1949, it had resulted in an agreement to form the United States of Indonesia as a sovereign republican state and an equal partner with Holland under the Crown, a somewhat paradoxical status but not impracticable, although by 1954 the Indonesians contracted themselves out, as did Burma from the British Crown. The future relations between them and the Netherlands remained unsettled; the only thing certain was that they would remain unfriendly. As evidence the Indonesians were soon expropriating Dutch property, a policy they carried to conclusion.

It proved easier, however, to break clear of the Netherlands than to make a viable state. Stretching over 4,000 miles of ocean, a country of countless islands and with a population at a wide range of development and having diverse interests, it would be hard to manage in the most favorable circumstances. But the circumstances were definitely unfavorable. Indonesia had suffered from invasion and civil strife with its former rulers. Its economy was disorganized by years of enemy occupation and then civil war. Several hundred years of colonial rule had left it destitute of men with administrative experience in government, business, or large-scale plantations. There were numerous lines of dissension and factionalism—regional, economic, ideological, religious—conservative, clerical Moslems against Moslems of liberal, secular bent.

Periodic movements to separate started and were suppressed with difficulty. Some of the larger islands, notably Sumatra, which have the largest reserves of natural resources and therefore bring in the largest income, complained that the lion's share of the income was going to Java and only the leavings to themselves. Actual revolt broke out in Sumatra. The Indonesian Republic could still be held together by Sukarno, leader in the struggle for independence and then President of the Republic, but his task was becoming more onerous year by year. Under these conditions the Communists were raising their heads again, as always profiteering on disorder and discontent, and their chance of success seemed better than at the beginning. There was an attempt to restrict democratic privileges—democracy plainly was not working too well—in the interests of greater discipline and efficiency; that, too, was opposed, sometimes on genuine doctrinal grounds and sometimes on the grounds of personal ambition. On the experience of its first few years the future for the Republic of Indonesia did not seem bright.

The aftermath of the war in Korea and Indo-China will be discussed separately later.

CHAPTER XLVI

Civil War in China

We return now to what was the most decisive result of World War II in the Far East, what was to prove one of the most disruptive elements in the whole world in the years after. This was the civil war in China.

Hostilities were unconcealed in the closing months of the war against Japan. The Nationalists were in high mood, buoyed by confident expectation of success. At first their assurance was vindicated. They advanced rapidly—so rapidly indeed that their suspicions might have been aroused: the Japanese had done so too. But all the measurable factors in the equation seemed to be in their favor. They had far more troops than the Communists. The latter numbered roughly 1,000,000 in 1946, while the Nationalists had from 2,000,000 to 3,000,000, of whom many were in divisions trained wholly or in part by Americans during the war. Also the Nationalists were far better armed. They had what had been provided by the United States and what they had taken from the surrendering Japanese. The Communists, it is true, also had taken arms from the Japanese, especially in Manchuria and the north, though without legal right; the Russians had so managed their withdrawal from Manchuria as to let the Chinese Communists come in on their heels and disarm the remaining Japanese. On balance, then, so far as material assets were concerned, the Nationalists were the better equipped for the struggle.

Perhaps emboldened by overconfidence and perhaps for psychological effect on the Chinese people, the Nationalists took the offensive at once. They drove forward in Manchuria and the northwest. By the end of 1946 they were advancing on the Communist capital at Yenan in Shensi. True to their unvarying strategy, the Communists did not meet the attack. As they did against Chiang Kai-shek almost twenty years before and as they did against the Japanese, they risked no engagements in fixed positions. When the enemy advanced in strength they retreated, letting him extend his lines and waiting, patiently but vigilantly, for a weak point on which to swoop. They began to evacuate Yenan.

Chiang took the bait. His armies went ahead rapidly and occupied Yenan to the jubilation of Nanking and other Nationalist centers, which overlooked or misinterpreted the fact that the Communists had not attempted to defend it. Nationalist forces swept on, took city after city, brought thousands of square miles back under their sway and were in high mood. Their objective seemed about to come into their grasp at last: the extirpation of Communists and communism. So it went through a large part of 1947. They were strongly entrenched in Manchuria, in north China, in south China. And this was their weakness, their fatal weakness. They were entrenched in large cities each manned by huge garrisons, and there their main armed force was penned up. The Communists, whose strength had scarcely been touched, let alone exhausted, who had fought little and almost always retreated in good order and with arms and equipment intact, were free to take the initiative, to choose points of attack, to strike when they chose. The tide turned in 1948, slowly but as inexorably as any tide. This did not surprise those who had watched closely and who knew both sides, who had seen their development in previous decades. They had not been taken in by the Nationalists' exultations.

The Communists struck. They took advantage of their mobility. They first severed transportation lines. The Nationalist concentrations of troops in large centers were thus cut off from their sources of supply. They were not permitted by Nanking to give battle; they were ordered to stay within their city fortifications and await organized attacks. The attacks did not come. The Communists were content to maintain informal siege, depending on time to sap their enemy's vitality and morale before they moved in for the kill. There had been in Nanking since early 1946 a large American military mission, its function restricted to advice and training, with participation in actual military activities stringently forbidden. But the senior officers did have personal contact with Chiang Kai-shek and at intervals in 1948 they warned that his lines were dangerously extended and his forces dangerously exposed. They urged him to shorten his lines, retreating if necessary. But Chiang, whose military capabilities did not go far beyond his title of Generalissimo, was either unwilling or unable to see what should have been obvious. He refused, and in city after city his armies became isolated islands in a sea of Communists.

The Communists moved in. By midsummer, 1948, they were no longer afraid of pitched, positional battles. They had the enemy where he was weakest. They laid siege. Chiang's armies called for reinforcements. They had men enough and they had arms enough, but their supplies were running low and the fight had gone out of them, officers and men alike, including many of the generals. Chiang heard their appeals but could do nothing. He was advised to have the garrisons try to break out and to send additional troops to try to cut through to them, but in part he was unwilling and in part the commanders of the garrisons were unwilling. They were probably not competent enough.

The results came swiftly, first in Manchuria and the north. Within two weeks in the latter part of October the Manchurian cities of Changchun, Chinchow, and Mukden fell, the last with several hundred thousand troops, who surrendered meekly. A short time before Tsinan, an important rail center in Shantung Province, had fallen. By December Hsuchow, in Kiangsu Province, capitulated. Hsuchow is only 175 miles from Nanking, the capital. Nationalist China was visibly crumbling.

Then there was a kind of crescendo. The collapse came almost by the force of gravity. Nationalist divisions ran at sight of the Communists and sometimes laid down their arms without firing a shot. In this stage of the war Communist troops were turning up with American arms captured from the Nationalists or just meekly handed over to them. Communist forces entered Peiping and Tientsin in January, 1949. Chiang Kai-shek announced his resignation as President and was succeeded by the Vice-President, Li Tsung-jen. This was transparently a maneuver to win a compromise and thus stave off complete defeat, since it was simultaneous with an appeal for mediation by the Great Powers. It was, of course, futile. The Communists no longer had need to compromise. They knew it and the rest of the world knew it. The rout was on. Panic swept the capital. The Chinese people waited, some with resignation, some with hope, for the arrival of the Communists. Whatever came would be; it could not be worse than what had been. They wanted only an end to the whole affair and a return to peace at long last.

From that point it was only a question of how fast the Communists could travel. In April, 1949, they crossed the Yangtze River and took Nanking, in May they took Hankow and Shanghai. (In Shanghai a few hours before the Communists' arrival the Nationalist garrison commander ordered a public triumphal procession to mark a great Nationalist victory, and then fled.) In October the new People's Republic of China was proclaimed by Mao Tse-tung in Peiping, which again became the capital and was renamed Peking. There was left only the task of mopping up. The rest of the country fell like overripe fruit. Chiang Kai-shek and the faithful among his followers and about 200,000 troops managed to flee to the coast and make their way in small boats across 150 miles of the China Sea to the island of Formosa, where they set up a government and called it the government of China.

China had become Communist. It was a victory which first astounded and then alarmed the whole non-Communist world. But in actuality it was not a victory at all, but an accession by default. It could not be said the Communists had won China but rather that the Nationalists had lost China. The Chinese people were not Communist and did not want communism. They were spectators, neutral observers. Certainly they did not want to fight for the preservation of the Nationalist regime. Not even the Nationalist armies wanted that enough to fight for it. The Chinese people only wanted peace. They had had enough of the old regime. They could only hope that something better could come out of the new. And while it must be said that they were far less surprised at the outcome than the rest of the world, even they had not been prepared for the demonstration of how hollow, how empty, was the whole Nationalist structure. Neither they nor anybody else realized that there was so little within it that it would topple over at the first push. The ancient principle of Chinese political theory was still operating. The Chiang Kai-shek regime had forfeited the mandate of heaven.

And so came about, with postures and gestures that were almost farcical, one of the world's great revolutions, if something with so little dignity in the mode of its advent could be called a revolution. But one-fifth of the human race had been brought under the aegis of communism, or, rather, neo-Marxism Stalin-style, with Oriental variations. The legitimate heir of the historic Chinese Empire was now a rump on an offshore island under the leadership, the quasi-dictatorship, of Chiang Kai-shek. And here something must be said of that tantalizingly puzzling figure.

Even for his closest associates he has always been a man difficult to understand and to appraise. Even their judgments of him have varied over the years. But in one respect the judgment of history can be confidently anticipated. It will be recorded of him that he was one of the most tragic figures in the whole span of China's history. Whatever may have happened to him at the end of his career, however scarring the humiliation with which he was driven out of his country without any manifestations of regret by his people, it will also be said of him that his is the credit for saving his people from the long night of subjection to Japan, his more than any other man's. Without his steadfastness, his determination, the unbending will with which he rejected even thought of compromise in the darkest days from 1939 to 1942, it is more than probable that China would have given up the struggle. Indeed, it is almost certain that there would have been a compromise that saved China's face in words and made it a vassal in actuality. He held his people together when most of them wavered.

Despite the degeneration in the closing years of the war against Japan, despite the loss of prestige and of faith which he shared with his government, when the victory came he was its symbol. The derelictions and abuses, the fall from civic grace, and the infidelity to the traditional sanctions of Chinese political morality would have been forgotten or forgiven as the inevitable corrosion of war. It would have been understood that during the war his initiative was hampered and he was not free to act even for good. He was the symbol of victory and liberation and the hope of regeneration. Had he, then, in the first year of peace taken measures to redeem the past and by acts, acts of palpable benefit to the people, given them visible promise of recompense for the years of trial, had he given tangible evidence that there was a new spirit in government, he would have gone down in China's history as one of its immortal heroes and benefactors.

Chiang first came into prominence in 1923. He was born in 1887 in Chekiang Province, not far from Shanghai. He had little of the classical education and as a youth first attended a military academy in the north and then went to Japan in 1907 to study in a military academy. In Japan he came into contact with the numerous young Chinese who had joined the revolutionary movement and taken refuge there, and he became a follower of Sun Yat-sen. He took a humble part in the 1911 revolution and supported Sun's abortive rising of 1913. When that collapsed he went into hiding and then led an obscure life at odd jobs in Shanghai until the nationalist movement began to gather after World War I.

He joined Sun Yat-sen in Canton, and when Sun made his agreement with Russia he assumed his first important role. He became president of the Whampoa Military Academy, where, under Russian supervision, the young officers who led the Nationalist armies in their victorious march to Peking were trained. Also he was sent to Moscow for further military training and observation of the workings of a revolutionary state. It is a strange quirk of history that it was Chiang Kai-shek who had been in Moscow and had absorbed the revolutionary spirit, while Mao Tse-tung had never been there until after China had become Communist. Not formally but in mind and purpose Chiang had already broken with the Communists by 1926, when he planned and executed a coup in Canton to purge them out of the Kuomintang government. And it was as commander-in-chief in 1927 that he had the major responsibility for the expulsion of the Russians from Hankow, the expulsion of the Chinese Communists from the Kuomintang, and the terrible reprisals in Shanghai.

From 1927 to 1949 Chiang was the dominant figure in the country. Despite the façade of the pseudo-Russian "apparatus" of the Kuomintang monopoly party government his will—or his impulse or his prejudice or his caprice—prevailed. It is not true that he personally decreed everything that was done; but it is true that nothing could be done that he opposed. A man of slight build, mild voice, impassive and not particularly strong face, of no particularly commanding presence, he yet could bend men to his will. He did not always win or hold their loyalty, but from those whose loyalty he held he could and did win obedience.

It used to be said of Chiang by the Chinese in the years of disillusionment with his government, the years of corruption, spoliation and callousness, that he himself was not at fault; it was the men around him who were to blame. This is in part true. The men closest to him have in the main been men similar, in spirit and act, to the worst of the politicians and industrial and financial robber barons of the General Grant era in the United States. But it is also true that there was no law or force that compelled him to choose as his associates the men who surrounded him. With his power he could have drawn to himself men of any stamp he approved or desired.

There has never been any evidence of any desire on Chiang's part for personal enrichment. He is himself neither cynical nor heartless. No doubt he desired the well-being of his people and, according to his lights, hoped to achieve its betterment. The driving force within him was desire for power—personal power—and to that everything had to bend or be bent. And his lights were those of an older, politically darker age. He could repeat words out of the lexicon of democracy when making public speeches or talking to Americans, but he had neither understanding of democracy nor sympathy with it. That there should be division of power was for him beyond real comprehension or, when comprehended, heretical. He may have thought of himself as paternal. He was in fact medieval. He was an authoritarian of the ancient pattern, of the Confucian pattern, without the sanctions and restraints of the Confucian political and moral code.

Chiang owed his success and his power not to any intellectual capacity or an understanding of history or political ideas but to an extraordinary ability to manipulate men and to bring them under his control. He played them against each other, and his personal power against them all, until they submitted themselves to him or could be eliminated, and in elimination he was ruthless. It was thus he reduced the warlords to impotence and civilian politicians to willing or unwilling compliance. Thus he brought about the unstable unification that prevailed for a few years, and for that reason it was unstable. Chiang Kai-shek achieved power and for a time left an impress on his country, but he was also a failure and a tragic figure.

Before going on to discuss the establishment of the Communist regime in China and the changes it brought about in its first few years, it is advisable to take up the transformation in Japan under the Allied occupation and the war in Korea.

CHAPTER XLVII

Occupation of Japan

On August 27, 1945, American troops began landing on an airfield outside Tokyo, vanguard of a force that was to police and supervise the administration of Japan for nearly seven years. Before the end of the occupation there were to be 120,000 of them and an additional 40,000 from the British Commonwealth, half of whom were Australian.

As the transport planes came in over Tokyo Bay, there was grim silence among the occupants, tension in the command. What would the reception be? But a short time before the mass of the Japanese had considered themselves victorious, the pride of Yamato still soaring, the medieval warrior tradition still binding—triumph or death. They had never been defeated in war. No alien soldier had ever set foot on their soil except as a guest. Their land was sacred—abode of the gods, they thought it. Their emperor was, if not divine, then direct representative of Divinity. Their exaltation of the fatherland was not patriotism but frenzy. When the first enemy soldiers landed, those who had wiped out their sons on island after island and devastated their cities from the air and blotted out the inhabitants, would the frenzy become insensate and the maddened mobs rush to tear the invaders to pieces, rushing against the mouths of guns in a racial banzai charge as at Saipan and Okinawa? And then would they in the darkness of night pick off two or three at a time in ambush? The Americans could very well wait, taut and ready to spring, for what would come.

What came was something that can be described as almost a clinical phenomenon in abnormal psychology, incredible, almost inconceivable, to one who knew Japan before. The Japanese people seem to have decided, evidently spontaneously and by self-induced conviction, to do as the emperor had urged in his rescript announcing the surrender— "enduring the unendurable and suffering what is insufferable." They were silent, immobile, docile, to all appearances even deferential as plane after plane spilled its load of heavily armed Americans. It was as if a regiment of an allied country had come for a friendly visit. With allowance for a few small episodes inevitable in any occupation, the atmosphere was one of amity, of mutual liking. The big American lads were strange but friendly uncles. Occupation teams of three or four men lived in villages far from other American troops or any white man and came and went as friendly neighbors.

Not only that: the whole country submitted humbly, awaiting orders, giving obedience. General MacArthur arrived and was received as if a conjoint emperor, if not as imperial senior partner. The emperor called on General MacArthur as if to pay respects. The emperor called! He, on whom no mortals but for the chosen few could look except as he sped by in his maroon limousine, when possibly they caught a glimpse as their heads bowed deep—he called on a foreigner as if to pay respects. And he was received—the emperor was received! And thereafter MacArthur issued decrees and they were dutifully executed, with perhaps slight, subtle modification for purposes not quite of sabotage but of deflection. Officials of the highest rank, those who before had moved only in the centers of omnipotence, came for instructions, from American colonels if need be, took their instructions and departed to carry them out—as Koreans or Chinese in Manchuria used to do for their Japanese rulers.

How explain it? Was it symptom of the psychotic shock of defeat? Were the Japanese so dazed as to react dumbly, even their inflamed chauvinism muted? Was it a sincere manifestation of a realization not only of defeat but of the folly of war? Or was it a policy consciously adopted by shrewd leaders and skillfully inculcated in the masses to lull the Americans, win their good will, gain their confidence, and thus speed their parting? Or was it all of these combined? Probably one will never know. In any case it succeeded. American good will and confidence were won. It was all an extraordinary, if not bizarre episode, its parallel not to be found in history.

As soon as the Occupation was settled and organized it began to put into effect its mandate, given it in the form of the Initial Post-Surrender Policy, a document transmitted to General MacArthur on September 6 as Supreme Commander, Allied Powers. This had been drafted in Washington by the American government alone but was accepted by the other Allied governments and then formally proclaimed by the Far Eastern Commission after it had already gone into effect. By agreement among the principal Powers there was supervisory machinery in the form of an Allied Council for Japan, consisting of representatives of the United States, Russia, China, and the British Commonwealth, which had one representative for the United Kingdom, Australia, New Zealand and India. The Council functioned as the instrument of a Far Eastern Commission, seated in Washington, in which were all the states that had fought against Japan. For practical purposes, however, both the Council and the Commission were a façade behind which General MacArthur exercised dictatorial powers, a fact which generated much friction, principally between MacArthur and the Russian representative and to some degree between MacArthur and the representative of the British Commonwealth.

The Initial Post-Surrender Policy, which may be called the organization of the Occupation, stated a few major ends. They were disarmament and demilitarization, including punishment or purging of war criminals and those who abetted aggression from posts in government, industry, and finance; democratization politically, denoting genuine representative government, freedom of thought and expression, and what is generally comprehended in a Bill of Rights; democratization economically, denoting the dissolution of the great family combines that monopolized the economy and owned most of the wealth; agrarian reform, including a more just distribution of land and relief for tenant farmers, and a fairer distribution of income for urban workers through organized labor and free collective bargaining.

The first object was accomplished relatively easily. Troops were disarmed, arms destroyed, arsenals and naval shipyards dismantled. Also large numbers of both military and civil officers, together with many executives in heavy industries designed for carrying on war, were forced out of political and economic life. Many were prosecuted for war crimes, including General Tojo, who was executed. Prince Konoye committed suicide before he had to pay the penalty. This was a simple procedure and, since it dealt with persons on issues of uncomplicated fact, had no involved ramifications, although it did become evident that purging men high in industry, commerce, and finance tended to paralyze the economy, since there were few who were competent to take their places.

Political democratization was incomparably more difficult. How does one democratize a people, especially a people without any heritage of democratic institutions, without any experience with them, with little understanding of the principles or esteem for the values of democracy? By fiat, by pronouncement, by moral suasion, by evangelical calls to conversion? Especially when the author of the fiat is a conqueror who has just devastated the land and now rules it as conqueror? The slow accumulation of belief in democratic procedures, the slow formation of the habit of its application and acceptance of its results, the gradual rooting and growth of the tradition that makes it part of the natural order—can this come about by order or invocation or intellectual immaculate conception? The Japanese people, who but a few years before had obeyed and respected Tojo, who unquestionably accepted the arbitrament of generals and acclaimed their successful adventures in conquest at the expense of others' suffering—could they acquire in a few months or a few years what had taken the English-speaking countries generations, if not centuries, to acquire?

Could any procedure or program be devised to accelerate the process? For one thing a new constitution was introduced, written by Americans and presented to the Japanese—and adopted by them because it would have been ill-advised to do otherwise and no doubt with mental reservations. The Constitution vests sovereignty in the people, with the emperor the symbol of the state and "deriving his position from the will of the people." The usual guaranties of a Bill of Rights are included, assuring individuals rights as understood in Western democracies. The powers of the Diet were broadened and the emperor's prerogatives were reduced to those of a constitutional monarch. The most novel and startling provision is that by which Japan renounced forever the right to make war or to maintain armed forces. This is probably the most dubious and perhaps inequitable provision of the document. The best comment on its merit and its durability is to be found in the fact that the United States a few years later was putting heavy pressure on the Japanese government to form an army, presumably for defense against Russia.

A broader and probably more solid effort to plant seeds of democracy was made through education. Textbooks were purged of the old chauvinistic legends and myths, of the mysticism about the land of the Gods, of the glorification of the warrior and his deeds. There was a good deal of rewriting of Japanese history (by Americans) and on the whole no doubt the new version was more authentic and verifiable than the one taught before, but how deeply it will penetrate into Japanese belief, how fully be accepted by Japanese as the truthful record of themselves, is hard to say. In all likelihood if any fundamental change is ultimately produced in Japanese attitudes, in the conception of man's status as an individual and the relation between the individual and the state, it will be through the new education rather than through the new constitution or any political structural change by official words.

Economic democratization was incomparably harder to go about, harder to conceive how to bring about, as everywhere else in the world. The problem fell into two parts. The first was breaking the grip on the national economy exercised by the great family trusts, the Zaibatsu. The second was improving the lot of the peasants, approximately half

of the population, mainly by reorganizing the system of land ownership, distribution, and tenure.

The first was attempted early. It was decreed in the officially proclaimed Post-Surrender Policy and General MacArthur had no choice
as Supreme Commander. It was never effected and probably never
could have been. Sixty-seven holding companies were ordered dissolved.
These controlled and operated the most important industrial, financial,
and commercial enterprises in the country. Their securities were turned
over to a Liquidation Commission, which would sell them and with the
proceeds compensate the owners in bonds.

It did not work. In the first place, there were too few people outside
the Zaibatsu who had money enough to buy more than a negligible
part of the securities. In the second place, it was too easy to evade the
order. Unscrambling large, concentrated combines, especially those with
as elaborate and adeptly concealed structures as the Japanese, is always
next to impossible. The heads of great corporations were purged and
the corporations themselves; but behind the scenes the heads of the
corporations still managed them. The corporations were "reorganized"
in smaller and theoretically independent segments, which still worked
together in tacit mutual understanding, and there was nobody to buy
the shares.

Then the whole project drifted into a kind of desuetude, to die slowly
in unspoken recognition that it could not be carried out. Perhaps most
of all, the whole tenor of American thought began to change. American
businessmen began to appear in Tokyo. What they saw smacked of
New Dealism, of "creeping socialism." They had a certain case. Why
sanction in Japan under American auspices what they deemed dangerous heresy at home? And why, moreover, build up the power of
labor in Japan to equal power with ownership, when they considered
this an invitation to revolution at home? Slowly but surely American
policy in Japan conformed to the beliefs of the most influential classes
at home.

The agrarian reforms came off better. After the new Japanese Diet
had failed to produce measures satisfactory to the Occupation authorities, they forced upon it a plan they did consider satisfactory. This was
aimed in general at reducing the number of farm tenants, who numbered
one-third of all farmers, at restricting the amount of land that could be
owned by any individual, at easing the burden of credit and facilitating
marketing. The maximum any working proprietor could own was fixed
at seven and a half acres, with a somewhat larger allotment in Hokkaido,
the northernmost island. Land in excess of that amount, which came

to almost five million acres, had to be turned over to the government for sale to peasants at low rates, with the proceeds payable to owners in bonds. Where there were still tenants crop rent was to be reduced to 25 per cent. Co-operatives were organized. Also, to supervise land transfers there were formed local, prefectural, and national commissions, with landlords, peasant proprietors, and tenants represented.

A degree of success was achieved but only a degree. There were, of course, attempts at evasion. Large landlords, having influential connections, could postpone and soften the blow of divesting themselves of land by various ingenious devices. Fortified by the power and prestige they had exercised locally, they could persuade or overawe peasants, who had little understanding of the new dispensation and its complicated procedures, and for practical purposes many managed to maintain their former status. The commissions were actually the main loophole in the plan. Moreover, less efficient peasants got themselves into difficulty and debt again, and the old relation was re-established. Land transfers were painfully slow, but on the whole there were some concrete results. A principle was established. The peasant got a promise and a grasp of a better life, the agricultural sector of the country a promise of elevation in the social scale.

Meanwhile an extraneous but none the less powerful factor entered —the Cold War. Almost from the beginning of the Occupation there had developed friction between the Russian member of the Allied Council, General Derevyanko, and the American representative, who was usually General MacArthur. The friction was not so much on the merits of issues as a reflection of the worsening relations between the United States and Russia. If the United States proposed something, it was the part of wisdom, patriotism, politics, and ideology for Russia to oppose it, and vice versa. Both sides were uncompromising in about equal measure. Both were compelled to move in courses lying outside Japan, broader than Japan, and beyond its control. And as a matter of fact the softening of the United States toward Japan, the quickening and deepening mood of forgive and forget can be attributed in large part to the Cold War. It was expedient to build up Japan as a potential ally or at least counter to Russia.

As a by-product there openly emerged in Japan a Communist party. It was not new-sprung. Despite the ferocity of governmental suppression that prevailed before the war, there had been an underground nucleus of Communists, both in and out of prison. They were given legitimate opportunity by the Occupation's policy of encouraging free expression of thought and association and freedom of political action. They acted, of course, in conformity with Communist methods everywhere. They made issues for the sake of confusion. They agitated for the advantages agitation begets, regardless of cause. They organized, incited, sabotaged. Rising in equal force with the intensification of the Cold War, Communist activities threatened disruption both of Japanese economic and political processes and the policies of the Occupation. The Occupation first resorted to suppression itself and then gave free rein to repression by Japanese authorities, who welcomed the opportunity and are skilled at suppression of minority beliefs, by whatever doctrine or object inspired. They went to work with gusto and conviction.

That appetite comes with eating is as true of repression as of everything else. The classes that had always practiced it and enjoyed the advantages thereof now had open sesame. They made the most of it. Little by little there emerged, with renewed confidence based on the Occupation's unspoken but unmistakable tolerance, the same groups that had governed Japan before. They were more cautious than before, more discreet, less assertive, and felt their way rather than moved openly; but the trend was visible. Democracy was still professed, but the same men who ruled before were getting into position to rule again. The tendency was to revive the traditional Japanese system. Whether this was equally true of the mass of the Japanese and those who can be described as the intelligentsia, and whether it was wholly acceptable to them, it was too early to know. It may even be doubted.

The tendency was not retarded by the American pressure to rearm. By those who were not dominant before there was a not too resigned bending to the pressure; by most of them it was welcomed, though tacitly and tactfully. But as a sardonic note on the twists of history, even history in short spans, now the politically conscious among the Japanese and the majority of the larger public were opposed and expressed their opposition forcefully. Had they acquired a quick fidelity to the Constitution, to that part that proscribed war and armament forever? Or had they learned that the way of the transgressor is hard, that it is better to be nationally virtuous and safe than nationally triumphant and ruined? One cannot say. But the proposal to rearm had hard sledding and perhaps, if it had not been for America's vigorous prompting, the proposal might have been rejected at the outset.

In September, 1951, after long negotiations among the principal Powers, a treaty of peace was drafted and submitted to an international conference at San Francisco. This was wholly on American initiative and perhaps for that reason was bitterly opposed by Russia. Nor was it received with enthusiasm by the British Commonwealth countries, Australia and New Zealand in particular, which held that in freeing

Japan of all restrictions it was too lenient, since Japan had not yet demonstrated that it could be trusted not to return to militarism. But American influence was irresistible. The treaty was adopted, Russia walking out and India abstaining. It legitimized the separation of territory decreed in the Cairo Declaration and restored Japanese sovereignty. It provided that all Occupation forces be withdrawn ninety days after the treaty came into effect with the deposit of sufficient ratifications. It did come into effect in April, 1952, and all troops were withdrawn.

There was a postscript, a significant and, it may be, ultimately fateful postscript. A supplementary bilateral treaty was negotiated between Japan and the United States. It was a "mutual security" treaty, but its truly important provision gave the United States the right to maintain bases in Japan for land, sea, and air forces "so as to deter armed attack upon Japan." And, further, Japan bound itself not to grant similar rights to any third Power. How the Japanese people regarded this as an exemplification of the democracy that was being inculcated in them has never been openly expressed.

And thus ended the war officially and legally, eleven years after Pearl Harbor. What was the final effect on Japan, the resultant of all the forces old and new playing on it since 1941—the war, the defeat, the Occupation? An episode, a painful, bloody, disastrous episode but an episode only, touching the surface, to be washed off in time and leave Japan to resume its ways in its own land and toward others? Or one which has struck deep in the Japanese people and delivered them to the modern world in ideas and fundamental conceptions as well as material production? A militarism waiting to be resumed or a new democracy? Time alone would tell.

The Japanese people were soon, however, to show their resiliency, fortitude under adversity, and capacity for unified effort for the good of the nation. Their economic state was truly hazardous. Deprived of much of the territory from which they had extracted natural wealth, ravaged by war's destruction, cut off from many of their normal outlets for foreign trade by the chaos of the region, they faced difficulties that seemed unsurmountable. They were helped at the outset by American financial assistance, in some years coming to $300,000,000; but in the main progress was attributable to their own efforts. Factories and shipyards were rebuilt and production flowed again. Trade was hard to find but some was found despite high tariff barriers. But this, too, should be recorded: They were becoming restive under the infraction of their sovereignty represented by American bases on their soil and American occupation of Okinawa. A desire for revindication was being voiced.

CHAPTER XLVIII

The Korean War

The surrender of Japan did not end fighting in East Asia. It only changed the locale of conflict. Before long there was to be not just nationalist and guerilla action but formal war in East Asia—in Korea and Indo-China.

In the Cairo Declaration it had been promised that Korea would regain independence "in due course." The translation given this in the first instance by the principal Powers was trusteeship to last a maximum of five years. In December, 1945, the Foreign Ministers of the United States, the United Kingdom, and Russia, meeting in Moscow, agreed to the setting up of a provisional government in Korea on democratic principles. To help in forming and getting under way such a government a Joint Commission was appointed, composed of representatives of the American and Russian commands in Korea, to plan the necessary steps and make recommendations to the American, British, Russian, and Chinese governments. Also a Russian-American Joint Conference was to consider the most urgent steps required to deal with the serious administrative and economic problems left by the sudden end of the war and the expulsion of the Japanese.

This was the general design. It was frustrated, partly by military events in Korea, partly by the fanatical opposition of Korean leaders to any form of trusteeship or anything short of immediate, unrestricted independence, and, finally, by the deepening of the Russian-American chasm.

As will be remembered, Russia declared war on Japan on August 8, 1945. On August 10 its troops entered Korea. On August 14 Japan laid down its arms. American troops did not arrive in Korea until September 8, almost a month after the Russians. Before then, however, an arrangement had to be made on division of areas between the Russian and American armies, if only for a clear understanding on where each side would accept the surrender of the Japanese forces. By agreement between the two commands this was fixed at the Thirty-eighth Parallel, the Russians on the north, the Americans on the south. It was thus, casually and almost by accident, that the division of Korea came about.

The Russians in their zone proceeded as they do wherever their armies take over. There flocked in at once large numbers of Koreans who had taken refuge in Siberia from the Japanese and had there been indoctrinated with communism. The Russians shut off the area north of the Thirty-eighth Parallel, making that point of division a political and economic barrier instead of a line of military demarcation. Behind that barrier they set about organizing a separate administration with tried and true Communists and those who would accept Communist discipline. Furthermore, they began training an army which would be at the bidding of Communist leaders for Communist purposes, whether Korean or Russian. The economic aspect was no less important, for South Korea is the main source of food supplies for the country and North Korea the main source of raw materials and therefore the industrial center. The future in Korea was already ominously foreshadowed.

The Russian-American Joint Conference to arrange co-ordination of the two zones of Occupation met in January, 1946, and after the fashion of all Russian-American conferences since 1945 dragged out in rigid, arid quibbling over trivial details; after three weeks it adjourned in futility. In March the Joint Russian-American Commission, charged with establishing a provisional Korean government, dragged out for eleven weeks and similarly adjourned in futility. There was evidently hopeless deadlock. The United States had no other recourse than to set up a separate administration south of the Thirty-eighth Parallel. By May, 1947, a South Korean interim government was proclaimed, with Koreans in charge of administration and American army officers functioning in an advisory capacity. Meanwhile fruitless negotiations continued between Washington and Moscow and in September the United States decided to lay the whole Korean problem before the United Nations. In November the United Nations Assembly came to a decision that the Korean people themselves should form a provisional government by free and secret elections in both North and South and a United Nations Temporary Commission on Korea was appointed to observe the election. The Commission arrived in Seoul in January, 1948.

Meanwhile there had been not much less friction in South Korea than between South Korea and North Korea. Immediately after the disarming

of the Japanese, exiled Korean patriots, who had been agitating through-out the world for restoration of Korean independence, flocked back to Korea. There were numerous factions and among them there was as much hostility as between all of them and Japan. They were in accord only in their vehement objection to a trusteeship. Each organized its own party and strove to get the ear of General John R. Hodge, American Army commander. Success fell to Syngman Rhee, who had been in Washington.

Dr. Rhee, already more than seventy years old, had been one of the earliest Korean agitators for Korean reform in the 1890's and then against Japan after the annexation. He had served a prison sentence and endured torture but managed to make his escape from Korea. At Paris in 1919 he tried to present to the peace conference a plea for immediate Korean emancipation but did not get a hearing. He then divided his time between Honolulu and Washington, always agitating, never abandoning hope. After Pearl Harbor he redoubled his efforts. A man of relentless determination to the point of obduracy—and obscurantism —he did manage to impress both himself and his cause wherever he devoted his energies. In October, 1945, he returned to Korea. The prestige given him by his age and long career on his country's behalf won him a prior claim to the loyalty of the Korean people and his knowledge of Washington won him first entree to the Occupation command. This did not abate rivalry with leaders of other factions, however, and there were bickerings, intrigues, assassinations, and sudden deaths only doubtfully attributable to natural causes.

The United Nations Commission had little more success than the Russian-American Conference. It was decided to hold an election in South Korea only, and the election took place on May 10. It was a free election only in the most elastic definition of the word free. It was less an expression of preference by the electorate than a victory of terrorization by violence or intimidation. The Rhee party won and Rhee became Chairman of the National Assembly. It was an unhappy augury for a democratic government. In July the constitution of the Republic of Korea was proclaimed and on July 20 Rhee was elected President of the Republic of Korea. Similar steps were being taken in the North and on September 9 the Democratic People's Republic of Korea was formally established. Thus Korea was formally divided.

The Thirty-eighth Parallel thus became a gap as wide as the sea. It was a gap, however, between likes, two reactionary regimes, each reactionary but of a different stripe. North Korea was an absolutism on the atavistic pattern of all Communist regimes; South Korea was reactionary on the older Oriental pattern. Both were indifferent to human welfare. Both were police states. North Korea, being modeled on Russia, was more efficient but the same principle obtained in both. In North Korea there was the same brutish tyranny of party function-aries as in all Communist states. In South Korea there was the tyranny of the rich, mainly large landowners, those who had been Korea's undoing before the Japanese came. The Americans of the Occupation drafted land reforms on the contemporaneous Japanese model. The reforms were sabotaged in the Assembly, most of the members of which represented large landowning interests directly or indirectly. Those of the Assembly who did not were eliminated or suppressed by terrorization or intimidation. North Korea, having the guidance of Moscow, was the more efficient of the two and therefore in Western eyes more repellent. Both carried little hope or promise for the long-suffering Korean people, who over the centuries have suffered as much as any breed of men on earth.

So matters dragged on until the summer of 1950. There had been rumors and alarms of war throughout the early part of 1950, but there was no verifiable evidence to support them, not even clear indica-tions of which side the attack would come from. Early in the morning of June 25 Korean time (June 24 American time) there was gunfire on the Thirty-eighth Parallel. North Korean troops had struck and had swept across the border in force. At three o'clock on the morning of June 25 (American time) the American government asked for an immediate meeting of the Security Council to act on the incident. A few hours later the Council met and passed a resolution asking for the withdrawal of North Korean forces behind their own side of the line and the cessation of hostilities. On June 27 President Truman ordered General MacArthur, then commanding in Tokyo, to send air and sea forces to Korea to carry out the United Nations' order. He also ordered the United States Seventh Fleet to draw off Formosa to neutralize that island. On the same day the Security Council, noting that its previous resolution had been ignored by North Korea, passed another resolu-tion recommending that all United Nations member states come to the assistance of South Korea. At that time, as it happened, Russia could not veto the resolution because it had withdrawn its delegate to the Council on the ground that the delegate of the Chinese Nationalist regime was still sitting instead of a representative of the Communist regime in Peking. On June 30 President Truman authorized General MacArthur to use ground forces in Korea.

Thus the actual war began in Korea. The succeeding weeks were desperate. The North Korean troops, being better trained and better armed than the South Koreans and with plans well laid in advance, swept through the South Koreans with ease and advanced rapidly down the peninsula. The few American troops brought over from Japan, themselves inexperienced, could do little to stem the advance and also retreated southward. Not until the first week of August could they set up a defense line almost at the tip of the Peninsula—the Pusan perimeter. For a time it seemed that they would be swept into the sea, but they held, grimly and magnificently. Then on September 15, the Tenth United States Army Corps, commanded by General MacArthur, staged a brilliant amphibious landing on Inchon behind the North Korean lines and the tide turned. The North Koreans retreated in confusion and were driven back behind the Thirty-eighth Parallel with heavy losses in killed and captured.

In early October a decision had to be made by the United Nations forces, of which, it may be said, more than 90 per cent were American: to cross the Thirty-eighth Parallel or not to cross. The United Nations did not give a clear-cut answer but a resolution of the Assembly did inferentially authorize crossing the line as a measure to ensure stability in the country, as it was put. With that inferential authorization General MacArthur did cross the line, although India's representatives in Peking and at the United Nations had repeatedly warned that if Mac-Arthur proceeded beyond the Parallel China would enter the war. It was known, too, that Chinese troops had been massing behind the Yalu River, the boundary between Manchuria and Korea.

Then the war entered a new and larger phase, a phase that made it a major war, for by that time the end was near since the North Korean army was all but dispersed. The United Nations forces were in sight of the Yalu when on November 26 the Chinese crossed the river and opened a massive offensive with an estimated 200,000 men. MacArthur was caught with his army inexplicably divided and whole divisions were put to rout and cut up with heavy losses. By January, 1951, the Chinese were back on the Thirty-eighth Parallel and then recaptured Seoul, the South Korean capital. Not until the end of January was the rout stopped. A counteroffensive was then launched by MacArthur and part of the lost ground regained. The Chinese made several new offensives on their part with some gains but they could not recover their earlier momentum. Also their losses had begun to tell, for the "human sea" assaults by which they aimed to win through sheer weight of numbers regardless of casualties had cut heavily into their manpower. China meanwhile had been declared an aggressor by the United Nations.

A stalemate seemed in prospect when Jacob Malik, Russia's delegate to the Security Council, on June 23 made an appeal for an armistice. Representatives of the United Nations, North Korea, and China then met first at a place called Kaesong and then at a place called Panmunjom. The negotiations proceeded as usual with Communists, whether Russian, Chinese, or Korean—bickerings over locale, over the presence of journalists, over order of procedure, over the most trivial details. They were broken off, resumed, broken off again. The most serious issues were the line to be occupied after the cease-fire and the exchange of prisoners. The United Nations representatives (almost entirely American) insisted that every prisoner have the right to choose whether to return to his own country or receive asylum elsewhere. These last seemed impossible of resolution and fighting broke out again, though on a smaller scale than before. Then it was stopped and negotiations taken up again.

This time they bore fruit. Whether the Russians were afraid the Korean War would expand into world-wide conflict or the Chinese had become war-weary and feared continued economic drain, already beginning to tell, cannot be known, but on July 26, 1953, an armistice was finally signed and hostilities ceased the next day. The Chinese and North Koreans yielded on the prisoner issue and many thousand Chinese prisoners elected to desert communism and go to Formosa. The military demarcation line was roughly along the Thirty-eighth Parallel, and thus the situation was similar to what it had been in June, 1950. And there it promised to remain indefinitely, for no sign could be detected of any prospect of a real peace and unification of the country, and the chasm between the two halves, North and South, became wider, deeper, and almost unbridgeable unless world events, world war, or composition of the divergences of the Cold War, served to fill it. Later a mutual defense treaty was contracted between the United States and South Korea. In South Korea itself stability came but it remained under arms and far from democracy in spirit or government.

The Korean War cost 145,000 American casualties, 33,000 of them killed or missing. There were losses, too, in other armies on the United Nations' side. Korea itself was devastated, and the human suffering was harrowing and beyond measure. Few nations have suffered more. There was one other result of the war, one having influence the world over. The United States was galvanized to a gigantic rearmament, the largest program in its history except in the midst of a great war. And sentiment against Russia and the whole Communist world became harder and deeper, almost to the point of unwillingness to compromise. By so much the Korean war served to widen the cleavage cut across the world by the Communist system and its manifest ambition for world dominion. At the same time there developed among the American people for the first time an acrid hostility to China.

CHAPTER XLIX

American Policy Toward Communist China

This is a logical point at which to discuss the tangled, tormented relations between the United States and China after 1948.

It has already been said that even before the civil war in China closed with the Communists' victory, they had already felt and expressed a deep resentment at the United States and had launched a vigorous anti-American propaganda campaign. What they claimed as their main grievance then was that the United States had been partisan in the civil war. In a measure their grievance was justified, for the American government had really helped the Nationalists with money and guns, but they found it expedient to overlook the fact that most of the aid had been given before the civil war began. The propaganda in short was very bitter and not entirely honest.

After the expulsion of Chiang Kai-shek from the mainland and the proclamation of the Communist government (the "People's Republic") there was a concrete and difficult question put to every other state in the world. Would the new regime be recognized as the legitimate government of China and, if recognized, would it be seated in the United Nations as one of the five permanent members of the Security Council with veto power? Great Britain recognized it in short order. It had, as a matter of fact, maintained scrupulous neutrality throughout the civil war, recognizing, no doubt, as did all detached observers in China by mid-1948, that Communist accession was inevitable. The British wanted the new regime to start without active hostility to themselves. But what would really set the direction of China's relations with the rest of the world thereafter was what America would do. This was not only because of America's new role of leadership in world politics but because America had long been a party of prior interest in

China, had been sponsor of its national integrity, and, moreover, had carried almost the whole burden of the war against Japan.

The United States did not recognize the new regime for a combination of reasons. First there was the unfortunate coincidence that just when the decision was being considered, the Chinese were guilty of mistreatment of American persons and property, especially Angus Ward, American Consul in Mukden, and American government property in Peking. This was enough to color thinking on the question and lead to postponement. Important forces opposed to concession of any kind to China, let alone recognition, then had time to gather. These forces were of different make-up and origin.

In the first place there were those—and they were the largest in number if not in direct influence—who had been irritated beyond reconciliation by the ruthlessness of Russian conduct: the cold conquest of Eastern Europe, the Berlin blockade, the brutality of the absorption of Czechoslovakia, the tortuousness of Russian methods of negotiation on any question, whatever its content and however trivial. A hard crust of resentment had formed, and not only among red-baiters—who were, it is true, not few. There were others who were disheartened and chagrined that the sufferings of a large part of the human race in the most terrible of wars had been in vain, that the promise of a genuine peace as recompense for the sufferings was demonstrably delusive. One menace had been laid, another raised. Again America had intervened in a world war, against its will, almost against its instincts, and again its intervention had been barren. And the iron was driven deeper and more painfully into the soul because it was China—China, for which America had stood protector, because of which it had been drawn into war, to save which 250,000 of its young men had been killed or wounded—China which had gone into the camp of the enemy. For Russia was Communist and China was Communist and things equal to the same thing are equal to each other. The axiom may not hold in international politics but it called to the emotions.

There were also those who had a vested interest in China itself— that is, Kuomintang or Chiang Kai-shek China. Many of these were Chinese of great wealth who had taken refuge in the United States, having judiciously sent their money over in advance. Some of them had a genuine loathing of communism as an ugly dictatorship and a denial of human values and human decencies they had taken for granted. Some were cynical. They had made fortunes out of the plums and privileges Nationalist China passed out to the favored few. They wanted to dip into the fleshpots again. They wanted America to restore them to the fleshpots, and so they set out to play skillfully on America's proper resentment against Russia in the hope that it would be extended to Communist China—and perhaps lead to a third world war in which America would win and Chiang Kai-shek and associates could ride back to China on America's coattails, and they could ride back to the fleshpots on Chiang Kai-shek's coattails.

Another vested interest in China was held by missionaries, sincere devoted workers for the Christian faith in China. They had lived in villages in the interior, occupied with their evangelical and healing mission, outside political currents, aware of the movements but only dimly conscious of the sources. Most of them were men and women who came from small communities at home, also sheltered from the raw winds of politics. Therefore, although they may have lived in China for many years, they had acquired little political knowledge and in most cases not even political consciousness. They were in nearly all cases completely naïve about Chinese political affairs and political motives. For them there was not an axiom but a syllogism: Chiang Kai-shek had married a woman of a Christian family and had himself become converted to the faith; Christianity is good; therefore Chiang Kai-shek's government had to be good and the Communists who evicted it had to be evil. And to logic there was added deep emotion as more and more of them were being forced out of the country by the Communists. They felt strongly. Their careers were being cut off in mid-course. The natural expression of their emotion was vehement opposition to having anything to do with the new government—those who had driven out the exponent of their faith, symbol of their victory in bringing light to the land of darkness, and who, besides, had driven them out too.

There was still another vested interest, one less creditable. This was domestic politics. By 1948 domestic politics had taken on an edge of passion that was almost clinical. Passion had already ridden high in the Roosevelt administration. The sense of frustration in the Republican opposition, frustration born of successive defeats, especially the unexpected and humiliating defeat of 1948, had begun to gnaw and erode. And now passion had got a sharper edge from the universal resentment against Russia and the inability to stop its advance. When China became Communist it was not unnatural for fury to be vented on the party in power, more particularly President Truman and his Secretary of State. It was natural but hardly logical, since the Chinese people themselves had not prevented the outcome or even tried to and no American administration could have prevented that outcome short of dispatching an expeditionary force of 250,000 men, and that not even the most ardent advocate of Chiang Kai-shek had ever dared to propose. It was natural and also soon proved to be politically useful. For purposes of domestic politics, too, it was possible to exploit the general anti-Russian feeling.

China became not only a symbol but a stick with which to beat. There was another syllogism to put before the American people: the Truman administration had been in office throughout the Chinese civil war; the civil war had been won by the Communists and China had become Communist; the Truman administration was therefore responsible for the loss of China to Russia. What better reason for repudiating the Truman administration? For those without close knowledge of recent Chinese history, which included nearly all Americans, this was a convincing case and a satisfying one, since it offered a scapegoat for what was plainly unfortunate and dangerous. China thus became a symbol and recognition became a symbol of the China question. Ordinary men and women who never before had thought of China became acutely conscious of it, taking on and being stirred by an emotion that first had been generated spontaneously and then had been skillfully worked up and disseminated for a purpose.

Recognition of China had become a kind of litmus test. Those who opposed it were politically healthy, "pro-American"; those who favored it were by that fact politically dubious and, if not subversive, at least "Communist dupes." Before the end of 1950 the question had passed out of the realm of rational discussion and debate, far beyond the point at which it could be discussed on its merits. It was a measure of men: were they in favor of recognition and therefore in favor of communism or were they against recognition and therefore against communism? As few were in favor of communism it became politically impossible to recognize China.

The United States refused to recognize China, then, and therefore much of the rest of the world refused too, most of it regretfully. For that was the period in which American economic aid was underpinning the economy of more than one country, if not providing the only foundation for the economy, and it was hardly advisable to act flagrantly contrary to American wishes on anything on which the American people felt deeply. As it was, Congress was always threatening to cut off aid to those who were not amenable, by which it meant any who would not do exactly as America wished, regardless of what they thought of the soundness of America's wishes.

China thus was ostracized from decent international society, clearly at American instigation, and it smarted correspondingly. It smarted all the more because, having just been victorious against great odds, having just been admitted to the company of the great as an equal in the councils of the world after a hundred years of a high degree of subjection, it was abnormally conscious of its position and bent on demonstrating that it was no longer what it had been, that it could no longer be kicked about, that it could exact consideration. And smarting, China loosed a more virulent and vicious propaganda campaign than before, lashed out even more violently against America, echoed even more faithfully the anti-American slogans of Moscow, and took reprisals when it could against American persons and American material interests. And this in turn aggravated American rancors, and so each in turn added momentum to the forces driving them apart as potential enemies, hostile but not yet in actual conflict. And it put compromise, even reasonable negotiations, out of the bounds of possibility. The American mind was closed.

The ties between country and country, especially in a crucial period, are always of limited tensile strength. The time comes when the ties can no longer bear additional strain, and pressure at any point, even the lightest pressure, can snap the ties. In February, 1950, Communist China and Russia contracted a thirty-year alliance, which in itself drew the lines tauter. And then came the Korean war, MacArthur's advance to the Yalu and China's offensive into Korea, the first disastrous defeat of American forces, the long-drawn-out war up and down the peninsula, and the exasperating negotiations before an armistice could be agreed on.

Why China intervened in Korea will long be speculated on and never answered with finality. The war itself was a serious setback to it, whatever the outcome might be. It had just got its administration organized, had just succeeded in imposing its authority on the whole country, had just checked currency inflation and laid a foundation for a stable economy, had just laid plans for embarking on the industrialization without which it could not survive in the modern world. Why prejudice all these achievements, remarkable in themselves? Was it genuine fear that the United States would proceed beyond the Yalu into Manchuria and from there threaten China itself because it was now Communist? Was it Russia's instigation and China's subservience to Russia? Was it China's arrogance and overestimation of its own strength, due to exultation at the victory over the Nationalists, as it was in the attack on Russia in Manchuria in 1929? Or was it a desire to retaliate for America's responsibility in decreeing ostracism for China? One will never know with certainty. But there are some grounds for believing that it was the last, for believing that if the United States had established normal relations with China, had agreed to its admittance into the United Nations and not interdicted the Communists' attacking Formosa by the dispatch of the Seventh Fleet to Formosa's waters, then in the autumn of 1950 Chinese

Communist armies would have been fighting in Formosa instead of kill-ing American boys in Korea—and the Korean war would have ended in 1950 instead of 1953. There will always be the heart-breaking ques-tion: was the sacrifice of American boys in Korea in those years need-less?

But American boys were sacrificed. They were killed or wounded or captured and tortured by the Chinese, and it was only human that then American feelings should become bitter, vindictively, intransigently bit-ter. The question of what to do about China was then closed. Advocacy of relations with China, even of settlement with China except on terms of China's complete submission, became almost equated with treason. And this could be and was exploited by the informal fusion of all the groups that wanted Communist China declared out of bounds permanently, if not overthrown, by whatever means required. These groups made up what was known as the China Lobby—an unorganized, amorphous body loosely composed of men of different stripe and motive but homogeneous in purpose. The United States had arrived at the point when any adminis-tration that let it be known it was even considering establishing relations with China would take its political life in its hands. And ten years after the Communists had taken over none had.

CHAPTER L

Communization of China

At this point, too, it is pertinent to discuss briefly the early stages in China's transition to a Communist society—briefly, because the system had not yet been fully formed toward the close of the first decade and because confirmable evidence was hard to come by, since China, too, had gone behind the Iron Curtain.

For one thing, China was driven completely into the arms of Russia, more completely than followed from the 1950 alliance. It cannot be said whether it would have gone there anyway, impelled by ideological affiliation, or whether it was driven there by America's insistence on isolating it. Those who had long known China, especially Britons and Europeans, thought the latter. In any case the association was complete.

The treaty of alliance in itself forged strong bonds certain to have an effect on world politics. Indeed, it was this that made the United States hesitate to carry the campaign into Manchuria by air attack, which would have relieved the pressure on American troops in Korea. The two countries pledged themselves to come to each other's assistance in case of any "act of aggression" by any state against either. Presumably, therefore, if the United States had bombed Manchuria, which is Chinese soil, Russia would have gone into action and World War III would have begun. Aside from that there were no sensational provisions in the treaty. Russia promised to return to China all that it had rewon in World War II and by the Yalta agreement. It also agreed to lend China $300,000,000 in five annual installments toward its industrialization. China on its part agreed—for the first time—to acknowledge the independence of Mongolia—the "Mongolian People's Republic." These probably were less important than the presumable secret clauses and the unwritten acknowledgment that Russia would continue to exercise paramount influence in Manchuria through secret police, "advisers," and a preferred economic position.

Still more important was the fact that there was an influx of Russian advisers, experts, and technicians into every corner of Chinese life. How many there were could not be established—thousands certainly, perhaps tens of thousands. Immediately afterward also the whole lexicon of Chinese public statements was taken outright from the lexicon of Moscow and the Cominform—the same ideas, the same phrases, differing only that they were in Chinese words rather than Russian. At least as far as public declaration was concerned, China's aims and policies were an echo of Russia's aims and policies.

This was true in act as well as statement. Before the Communist accession Mao Tse-tung, leader, strategist, and philosopher of the movement, had made the pronouncement of the "New Democracy." In its essentials and stripped of Communist rubrics he set forth the broad principles and program of the projected Communist state and society. It was not to be in the Russian mould. In its final form it would be a completely Communist system as conceived by Marx and amended by Lenin, but it would proceed to that form by transitional stages. There would not be the dictatorship of the proletariat at once. All classes, "bourgeoisie" included, would be allowed to participate if co-operative. Private property therefore would not be abolished forthwith. It would be allowed to function, although under vigilance and restriction. There would be "democratic centralism," meaning decision at the unchallengeable apex with free discussion below until decision was taken at the top. It was to be, in other words, a modulated dictatorship without the Russian dehumanization that has alienated all those who accept the cumulative restraints of five hundred years of Western civilization.

Without public pronouncement this began to be snuffed out of existence by subsequent acts, especially after the Korean War. The tendency was then toward repetition of Moscow in all things. Pressure was put on private business. Forced loans obtained by intimidation and concealed threat led to gradual expropriation. When persuasion in all things was not effective quickly enough, terror was used. There were killings by official sentence or incited mob attacks—how many it is hard to say, but not few. Land was expropriated from large landowners and divided up among poor peasants—not without justice—and by fair taxation, reduced crop rents, and abolition of usury the peasants' lot was undoubtedly improved. But then came the Korean War. Food had to be mobilized for troops. Also, by all reports, food, insufficient as it normally is in China, was exported to Russia to pay for industrial machinery and armament. Crops were requisitioned in the form of taxation in kind, much as they had been in Chiang Kai-shek's regime. More money had to be levied in the form of "voluntary," "resist the imperialists" loans, both businessmen and small families being drawn on. To get what was required rigid controls had to be imposed. A huge, all-pervasive bureaucracy was created to enforce them, with all the evils of any unchallengeable bureaucracy.

Regimentation in the Russian style was imposed. There were compulsory demonstrations, rallies, and processions. There was thought control. Not only ideas and opinions but phrases were prescribed. Minds had to be "purified," brains "washed." Men were "re-educated." Distinguished professors of architecture or biology had to make public confessions of previous error and "sins" against the Chinese people. If, as distinguished scholars, they had received honorary degrees from American universities, they confessed they had lent themselves to an American imperialistic plot to conquer China and now repented on being shown the light. If they had studied medicine or chemistry or engineering or law at Harvard or Yale or Columbia or Princeton, they confessed they had voluntarily submitted themselves to corruption and served as tools of American imperialism for the subjection of China. So they proclaimed in public meetings in words of abject self-abasement and their confessions were spread in the public prints. It was a continuous, sickening spectacle of degradation of the human spirit. It was Moscow transposed to Peking and other Chinese cities.

In urban factories and handicraft industries Stakhanovism—the Russian speed-up system—was introduced. Workers were driven by all the devices evolved in Russia to make men work harder and produce more but without added compensation. More was got out of them but their real wages remained the same. The Chinese urban laborer had always worked hard but never at a forced pace. Only controls, with fear to enforce them, could make him do so.

Of more significance and lasting effect on the future was the resolute and determined effort to modernize the country by industrialization and agricultural reorganization, both reflecting Russian ideas and methods. Two five-year plans for industrialization were laid down, one expiring in 1957 and the second in 1962. The emphasis was on heavy industry, no doubt with defense in mind. Steel, electric power, coal, railways, and motor vehicles were given priority. The accomplishment of the first five years was impressive and, for China, unprecedented. New means of transportation, pushed into areas hitherto untouched, promised rich returns in raw materials. It was, indeed, a formidable beginning, but only the beginning of the laying of a foundation, and before China could come to maturity in production and distribution (the criteria adopted by the Western world in the twentieth century), several five-year plans would be required. Even before the end of the first period China was beginning to show strain. Too much of its meager capital, even when supplemented by Russian loans, was going into industrial construction, too little for providing consumer goods. Not only was the economy being dislocated but there were indications of discontent in the populace. The people were working too hard and getting too little. On agriculture a definite program of collectivization was started, with co-operatives as the first stage. In the opening years marked progress had been made toward completion, but it was too early to reveal what the effect would be in increasing production and, most of all, in the state of minds of the peasants and their willingness to accept what was essentially a new form of life.

All this was something new in Chinese life. For the first time government was omnipresent and active. Government before had been symbolical and immanent, but it had not ruled. Government was by tradition, by precedent, by what had slowly over the passage of time been accepted as usage. Government officials had to be supported by taxes, but they were almost invisible. Instead of regimentation, there had been a kind of anarchy codified by tradition and custom handed down from generation to generation.

How will the Chinese people take this? Can an old people, a people of an ancient and honored culture, be re-formed in a short time? Can they be made over in their innermost being by fiat? The machinery of a police state can induce compliance for a time, no doubt, but can it forever, especially in a people not given to easy obedience? So long as the exigencies of the international situation, of China's relations with the non-Communist world, America especially, constrain it to close affiliation with Russia for protection, Russian influence will doubtless remain paramount and with it the Russian scheme of life, and the Chinese people will then accept it, taking it as necessary for their preservation as a state. But after that? This is one of the profound questions put to late twentieth-century history, one of earth-shaking consequence, since it involves a fifth of the human race. Now it is possible only to speculate; but unless the past, and in China's case a long, rich, and glorious past, can be nullified in memory as well as existence, it may be ventured that the new constriction to which the Chinese spirit is being subjected will not last. It will be relaxed, adapted to Chinese folkways, or it will be burst through in some terrible elemental convulsion—when, cannot even be guessed.

CHAPTER LI

War in Indo-China

Less serious only than the Communist victory in China was the uprising in Indo-China that ended (tentatively at least) in 1954 with Communists in control of the whole northern half of that colony. As a victory for the Communist system and idea it was next in importance to the Communists' accession in China.

The war in Indo-China belonged in the first instance to the order of colonial revolts for independence and only by extension to the world's ideological conflict, the world schism between Communist and non-Communist countries. Like all the rest of Southeast Asia, Indo-China was left in a vacuum when the Japanese surrendered. The Japanese had really governed it since 1941, and just before they laid down their arms they declared it separated from France with a transparent façade of independence. But there, too, as all over Southeast Asia there had been anti-Japanese guerilla activity and there, too, the most compact and competent guerilla activity was under Communist leadership. As early as 1942 there had been formed the Vietminh or League for Independence of Vietnam, a loose federation of parties and organizations with the common aim of independence from France but not much else in common. On August 22, 1945, a week after Japan had accepted the Allied terms, the Vietminh set up a provisional government at Hanoi to take in Annam, Tongking and Cochin China, where more than four-fifths of the people of Indo-China live. By agreement at Potsdam British and Chinese troops were to occupy Indo-China until the French returned, the British in the south and the Chinese in the north, but when the British arrived early in September the administration of most of the colony was already in the hands of the Vietminh. By the time the French arrived the ground was already laid for struggle.

The nationalist movement was not new in Indo-China. The natives, especially those of Annam, had never been fully reconciled to French rule, which had been imposed between 1860 and 1885. At first protest was unorganized and limited to a few disparate, disconnected groups, mainly among the young and the intelligentsia. The French had taken even less account of indigenous interests and feelings than other colonial Powers. They had organized the colony for their interests and theirs alone. On the most dispassionate analysis there was little to be said for French rule in Indo-China, little to justify it by any criterion, even the most charitable. After World War I the nationalist movement emerged, as in other colonial areas and in reflection of what was happening in China. Indo-China had indeed always reflected Chinese movements and forms while simultaneously resenting the intrusion of the more efficient Chinese colonists into its economic life. China's successes in the late 1920's stimulated the movement to greater boldness in Indo-China, and in 1929 there were serious disorders. These were put down by the French with more than severity and left harsh rancors.

By this time the Communist movement in Indo-China was of little importance; it, too, was a reflection of what was occurring in China. Nguyen Ai Quoc, later better known as Ho Chi Minh, had already come to leadership in it. By the 1930's one of the most influential figures in Asia, he is also one of its haziest figures. Even his date of birth is not certain, though it was probably in 1892, and it is doubtful whether Nguyen Ai Quoc was his real name. He went to Europe as a youth and quite early came into contact with French left-wing socialism. When he became converted to communism is disputed, but it is certain that he went to Moscow in 1923, remained there a few years, and became thoroughly indoctrinated. Whatever may be true of the other leaders of the Vietminh, there is no doubt that Ho Chi Minh is and from the beginning of the Indo-Chinese Communist movement was a convinced and loyal Communist. When communism got its early stride in China he went there, making his headquarters in Canton, and in the late 1920's founded the Indo-China Communist party. He was back in his own country during its Japanese occupation, active in the underground resistance and planning measures to take for independence after the war. When the new state of Vietnam was proclaimed in August, 1946, it was natural that he should assume leadership. And when elections were held throughout Vietnam in January, 1946, and an Assembly was chosen and a constitution drafted, it was natural, too, that he should be elected president.

One thing should be made clear. The Vietminh government at the outset was not predominantly Communist. In fact, the Communists were in a small minority, even among the leaders. The majority were of the middle class, resolved only to free their country from France. If Com-

munists had the same end they were willing to work with them, but by
their class origin few would have welcomed and still fewer approved
communism as such. But as between France and communism they
would at the beginning have evaded choice. As time passed and more
and more of them felt constrained to choose, they became increasingly
resigned to communism, though regretfully.

France had, of course, been contemplating what to do about the
empire even before the war ended. In March, 1945, there was a formal
declaration guaranteeing administrative and economic autonomy to an
Indo-China federation of five states—Tongking, Annam, Cochin China,
Laos, and Cambodia—within a French Union comprising all parts of
the empire. There would be autonomy but the full direction of all parts
of the Union would rest with Paris. There was nothing, it will be seen,
equivalent to the British Commonwealth.

The formation of the Vietnam government under Ho Chi Minh
created a situation that France would have to deal with at once. French
troops arrived in Indo-China early in 1946 and after some difficulties
with the Chinese, who at first refused to evacuate, took over entirely by
the end of February. But the Vietnam government was in being and
there had been some minor skirmishes. On March 6 an armistice was
signed ending hostilities and permitting French troops to occupy Tongking. In the agreement concluding the armistice France recognized the
"Republic of Vietnam as a free state having its own government, parliament, army and finances, forming part of the Indo-Chinese Federation
and the French Union." It was also agreed that a referendum would be
held in Cochin China, where most of French interests and much of the
colony's wealth lay, to determine whether Cochin China should join
the Republic of Vietnam. Also such questions as Vietnam's diplomatic
relations with the entire world would be settled in future negotiations.

These negotiations took place in Fontainebleau from July to September, 1946. To the conference came Ho Chi Minh himself. It should be
observed that at that time Ho was by no means an extremist. He was
then definitely more inclined to compromise even than many of his
subordinates. He did not at that meeting demand all or nothing, but on
some fundamentals he was unyielding. The French on their part were
moderate in principles, rigid on the meaning of principles in action. And
it was soon clear that between generalization and concrete application
there was a gulf too wide to bridge.

There had been apparent accord on the way in which the future of
Cochin China was to be determined. There was supposed to be a referendum, but the French made it clear there would be no referendum. On
one pretext or another, principally the necessity of first re-establishing

law and order, they postponed it and then on their own decision declared
the status of Cochin China to be that of an autonomous republic—
plainly autonomy under French authority. This the Indo-China delegation regarded as a breach of faith. On the status of Vietnam within the
French Union there was an even greater gap. Ho Chi Minh wanted a
literal application of the original proclamation: unity of the whole of
Vietnam as an independent political entity but within the French Union
as an equal partner, with economic and cultural co-operation between
Vietnam and France. But manifestly France was willing to give the show
of independence while keeping the substance of power. It may be that
the government in Paris, having more detachment, more consciousness
of native nationalist movements all over the world and therefore more
discernment, would have been inclined to moderation and compromise.
It may be and probably was that political pressure exercised in Paris
by the French colony in Indo-China through its economic connections
at home prevented the government from using its best judgment. That is
not unusual in the empire-colony relation. The fact is that France would
not recede, Ho Chi Minh would not accept a restoration of colonial subservience, and the conference broke up.

The break caused ferment in Indo-China and nationalists of all stripes
and convictions seethed. The inevitable happened. First France went
into attack and then Vietminh forces attacked Hanoi, one of the most
important cities in Central Indo-China near the east coast. The war was
on. Unrealized at the time, it was to be a war lasting nearly eight years,
a major war in its political consequence, a war that cost 170,000 casualties, including 90,000 dead and missing among French and Vietnamese
loyalists—with Vietminh losses that cannot be estimated—and that cost
France, too, five billion dollars of its scant and sorely needed wealth.

The Vietminh resorted to standard guerilla strategy and tactics. It
fought small, tantalizing engagements, always eluding French forces in
large numbers. The French controlled large urban centers, the guerillas
roamed the rest of the country at will, ruthlessly terrorizing, ambushing,
sabotaging, disorganizing, paralyzing, forcing the French to pursue them
now here, now there, turning up always at unexpected places and conserving their own strength while the French spent theirs. As time went
on and the French showed no desire for accommodation, the native inhabitants became convinced that France was resolved to keep their land
a colony as before. Nationalist groups coalesced. Nationalism became
more widespread and virulent. Ho Chi Minh won ever increasing numbers of adherents. France was uniting the country. And as usual in such
situations, in proportion to the growing strength of the independence
movement grew the power of the Communist leadership, since Com-

munists were a compact group who always knew what they wanted. A definite choice now presented itself: independence even under Communist direction or subjection to France to escape communism—in short, France or Ho Chi Minh. And for a steadily growing number the choice fell on Ho Chi Minh even if the prospects of living under a communist system were unpalatable. It can be said without exaggeration that France made communism in Indo-China.

Slowly, almost imperceptibly, the Vietminh forces were taking over more and more of the country and the French could not stem their advance. In 1949 France at last realized that military measures were not enough and political measures were required, that it could not even maintain itself in Indo-China if the aspirations of the people were not satisfied to some degree. It created the Associated State of Vietnam, nominally independent, actually still to be governed from Paris in all the essentials of government. The titular Emperor of Annam, Bao Dai, was named Head of State. Bao Dai had at first affiliated himself with Ho Chi Minh but then withdrew. France's action was a bid for popular support, but it never attained any real success. It came too late and had too little content, although Bao Dai was not altogether complaisant. Little by little he wrung concessions from the French. Notwithstanding that, Bao Dai won little loyalty from his people. There was no reason why he should. He had never shown any real interest in them. He had spent most of his time living gaily and extravagantly in Paris or on the Riviera, or, when in Indo-China, in his expensive mountain home hunting big game. Even when the conflict in his country was coming to its climax he was hunting in the mountains, apparently unconcerned.

The struggle went on, a struggle in minor engagements, a struggle of nerves as well as arms. The French seemed to be gaining mastery for a while and then they were back where they were. The Vietminh forces seemed to be driven back and then in a little while they were further advanced than they had been. Each cycle closed with their having more of the country under their control than before. The French changed one commander after another, tried one strategy after another. Each promised success at the outset but soon proved as barren of results. The explanation was quite simple. The French had no support in the country except among those directly dependent on them and those whom they could intimidate by their armed presence. Even from those not directly against them they could expect nothing but neutrality. Ho Chi Minh and the Vietminh had the support of the people in increasing proportions. The end was easily predictable, and was predicted by those who knew East Asia.

So the years from 1950 to 1954 passed, the existing trends growing

ever stronger. Meanwhile the United States had intervened at one remove. The prospect of a deeper inroad into East Asia frightened the
government. When it perceived that France could no longer carry the
financial burden—the money spent by France in Indo-China almost
equalled what it obtained from the United States under the Marshall
Plan—the United States took over a large part of the burden. In money,
arms, and supplies it had advanced to France more than a billion dollars
by 1954. In other words, Indo-China had become a sector in the Cold
War. And nevertheless France's hope of putting down the Vietminh
and recovering its former position or the semblance thereof was visibly
fading.

Then came 1954 and a conference of Russia, British, Chinese, and
American Foreign Ministers at Geneva to attempt settlement of the
Korean stalemate and the Indo-Chinese War. So far as Korea was con-
cerned the attempt was abandoned in short order. There was an impasse
and no way out could be devised or even conceived. But events in Indo-
China were focusing that conflict in a dramatic and frightening light.
A few months before the conference the French had established a well-
fortified, heavily manned strongpoint at a place called Dien Bien Phu.
It was designed both for defense and a prospective offensive. The
Vietminh now saw an opportunity both for a military success and a
political demonstration while the Geneva conference was presumably
settling the fate of Indo-China. For the first time they chose to give
formal battle. They brought up several divisions, the largest force they
had ever massed, cut off the French garrison and from the middle of
March laid it under siege.

Another factor then entered. Since Indo-China was a sector of the
Cold War and relations between China and the United States were more
abraded than they had ever been, China also intervened at one remove.
Manpower obviously would not be enough to give the Vietminh victory
against a heavily fortified position such as Dien Bien Phu. The Chinese
therefore provided heavy guns, munitions, and vehicles. Quite likely
these came from Russia via China, but the direct supplier was China.
The days of the French garrison were numbered, cut off as it was from
supplies except what could be precariously flown in from French bases
in the south, in part carried in planes lent by the American government.
The French held out gallantly but on May 7 surrendered.

France could no longer conceal to itself either the fact of the reverse
it had suffered or the consequences the reverse dictated. In dramatic
negotiations in the last hours of the conference it agreed to what constituted surrender of a large part of what had been Indo-China. A truce
was agreed to. The cease-fire was to go into effect along the Seventeenth

Parallel, which meant in actuality that at that line Indo-China was being partitioned. This left France an area of 50,000 square miles, including Cochin China, with a population of 10,000,000. The Vietminh would have a population of 12,000,000 and an area of 77,000 square miles, including the Red River delta, the city of Hanoi, and the port of Haiphong. Laos and Cambodia were to be evacuated by Communist troops and maintain such relations with France as were agreed to in formal documents. Elections were to be held after two years in all Vietnam to determine its future. Meanwhile France would give full independence to what was left in its jurisdiction.

The significance of this was lost on nobody. Communism had advanced another step on the continent of Asia, and the outlook at the time was that it would soon advance another, that the southern half of Indo-China would fall to it with ease as a result of either infiltration or direct attack or both. The new Republic of Vietnam, as the southern half styled itself, was left distressed, chaotic, impoverished. There was no organization, no point of cohesion, no array of groups that a government could base itself on. On the contrary, there were mutually antagonistic elements: private armies and hostile religious sects. In addition, a flood of refugees began to pour in from the Communist north, almost a million of them, and they had to be housed and fed. The prospect was dark indeed.

The reality was surprising. Within three years Vietnam appeared to have laid a foundation as a state. The French had named as head of the new government one Ngo Ding Diem, about whom not much was known except that he was an ardent Catholic and reflective by nature. Certainly the toughness of fiber subsequently revealed was unknown. The reality here too was surprising. The first task Diem set himself was to bring about unification. He proceeded to incorporate or crush two sects with private armies—the Hoa Hao and the Cao Dai—and in addition the Binh Xuyen, a tight organization which controlled vice in Saigon and also had a private army, one which, incidentally, had fought on the side of the French in the civil war. With this feat to lend him prestige, Diem was elected by popular ballot in October, 1955, to the office of president and chief of state. A few months later a constituent assembly was similarly elected. Bao Dai, the nominal emperor, was contemptuously dismissed. Vietnam became independent.

Diem owed much of his success to American support. Military advisers were sent to train his army, arms were supplied, and, equally important, financial aid was given, ranging from $300,000,000 to $500,-000,000 a year, of which most went for military purposes and a smaller amount for economic development. America had thus become the principal prop and sponsor of Vietnam.

The all-Indo-China elections which had been set for 1956 were never held. Diem's regime refused to take part on the ground that the Communist north would never permit free voting. The matter was quietly dropped and Indo-China remained, like Korea, rigidly divided—Vietnam, nominally democratic, in the south, the Vietminh Republic, Communist, in the north. Of the latter little could be learned. Like all Communist regimes, it had gone behind an Iron Curtain. But a full Communist program was in operation, with all the usual accompaniments—some benefits for the poorest classes, totalitarian dictatorship for all. Tight controls were put on commerce, industry, and agriculture. Terrorism was applied when necessary. But some economic development of the country clearly was taking place. It should be added that Vietnam in the south also was only nominally democratic although there was no avowed authoritarianism. Of all Indo-China it could be said that it was a sector of the Cold War.

There was one consequence in international relations. This was the formation of the Southeast Asia Treaty Organization—SEATO—composed of Great Britain, France, the United States, Australia, New Zealand, Pakistan, Thailand, the Philippines. Only two Southeast Asia countries, it should be observed, had renounced neutralism in the Cold War and joined. The formation of SEATO was intended to put the Communist world on notice that a line was being drawn beyond which it could not go with impunity. Whether the Communist world would be deterred by the warning remained to be seen. Thus all Southeast Asia was incorporated in the Cold War.

CHAPTER LII

Conclusion

So we come full circle in East Asia.

The West arrived. The West thrust itself on East Asia with full force and overcame it. But the cycle is closed. The West found the East independent and subdued it; now the East is independent again, once more master of its own destiny. Physically the West has had to recede; in every other way it is there to stay. One might also say that in defeat it has conquered. The East is no longer the East. It is not and never can be like the West in the fullest sense but also it never again can be the East. Between 1800 and 1950 there was more change in East Asia than there had been in the previous two thousand years. The West has been thrust out, but it has left behind its way of life, its forms of organization, its ideas. Both—East and West—both have won, both have lost. The victory and defeat do not quite cancel each other out, because they have been in different arenas. Which has the greater effect history alone can tell.

One thing is definite and indisputable already. In the larger international political sphere, the Far East now stands as the equal of the West. It is no longer a passive agent, waiting to be done by; it will itself be doing, and do in accordance with its own will and its own decision, determined by its own conception of its interests and preferences. East Asia has regained its spirit. It has self-assurance again, confidence in its inner worth and its ability to maintain its position. From the Japanese victory over Russia through China's recovery of national integrity in the 1920's, India's recovery of independence, and the new status gained by Pakistan, Ceylon, Burma, Indonesia, and the Philippines, the East has been proving to itself as well as to others that it need no longer defer, that it is master of its fate. It deals with others on the same plane. It is no longer a pawn in world politics, moved by great Western Powers in a game of high politics, a game of their own for stakes set by themselves, the East being one of the stakes.

This is to say that the countries of the East from Pakistan to Japan will from now on be participants in the system of relations prevailing in international society on the same level with the West, whatever that system may be. This is in itself a form of revolution. For almost a thousand years, except perhaps for a period in which China was at the height of its power, the nature, content, and bearing of world politics was set in and by the peninsula of the Eurasian continent called Europe. That will not be true in the future. The nature, content, and bearing of world politics will from now on be set by a resultant of all the forces in being in Europe, America, and Asia, not in Europe alone. Asia will not just reflect the movement of European high politics. It will contribute itself to the movement of world politics. East and West will now interact in international politics instead of the East being pulled by the magnetic attraction of the West. The status and influence of India in the United Nations and the conspicuous role played by Chou En-lai, Chinese premier, at the Geneva Conference in 1954 are symbolical. So is the part played by China and Southeast Asia in the Cold War. And thereby international relations are not made simpler, easier, and less fraught with danger. On the contrary, they will now be more complex, more difficult, and have more points of friction and potential conflict. The stage of international politics has been broadened. It is as wide as the world: truly a revolution.

Perhaps even more important, East Asia has been brought into the whole social and cultural scheme of the modern world, which in inception was Western. This is to say that it has now entered on the Western way of life. Put otherwise, it has now entered the Machine Age—industrialism—with all that that involves in the way in which life is organized materially, in the institutions that are built around it, in the ideas it releases, in the broader problems it raises.

There must be a new form of government with functions government never had before. There must be means of communication and transportation that give greater mobility to men and things and ideas than has ever been experienced before. There must be universal education with a new and broader content. The family must be organized differently, have a different basis and a looser hold on its members than before. There will be different customs, different habits, new and different conceptions of right and wrong, socially at any rate.

Most difficult of adjustment are the social problems that are raised. It is in this respect as much as in the political that Asia has been incorporated into the ideological conflict and the Cold War. The economic problems, the problem of how an economy shall be organized, the problem of the standard of living yielded by that system of economic organization—this has become or is becoming a political issue in Asia no less than in Europe and America. Not only the spread of communism is responsible. The spread of Western ideas has played a larger if less obviously dramatic part. The people of Asia have learned that abysmal and hopeless poverty is not a decree of nature or of fate but a result of the way society is constituted. Like all human beings they seek material betterment and will strive for it once they have perceived its possibility. They are doing so now, and hence their response to communism. Again, this response is typical of Westernism and modernism rather than communism and would have come about if there had never been a Russian Revolution, once the West had penetrated deeply enough into the East.

The modern history of the Far East, it was said in the beginning, is cultural history. One culture of pulsating vitality struck another of lower vitality. The weaker yielded. It yielded, recovered, and has now found its feet again, though it must grope slowly and painfully for new paths of life. Whether it finds them, and how and with what consequences both to itself and to the outer world, will determine the shape of the history of the next hundred years. The world is not yet one; but its dimensions have shrunk, and by so much its form and its spirit and its forces have changed, and in externals at least it enters on a new being.

SUGGESTED READINGS

On all aspects refer to R. J. Kerner, *Northeastern Asia: A Selected Bibliography* (Berkeley, Calif.: University of California Press, 1939). Also John F. Embree and L. O. Dodson, *Bibliography of the Peoples and Cultures of Mainland Southeast Asia* (New Haven: Yale University Southeast Asia Studies, 1950).

GENERAL AND CHAPTERS I–III

Buck, Pearl S. *The Good Earth*. New York: John Day, 1931.

Clyde, P. H. *The Far East*. New York: Prentice-Hall, 1948.

Fei Hsiao-tung. *Peasant Life in China*. New York, 1939.

Holtom, D. C. *National Faith of Japan: A Study in Modern Shinto*. London: Kegan, Paul, 1938.

Latourette, K. S. *The Chinese: Their History and Culture*. New York: Macmillan, 1945.

———. *A Short History of the Far East*. New York: Macmillan, 1957.

Legge, James. *The Chinese Classics*. London, 1895.

Morse, H. B. *International Relations of the Chinese Empire*. London, 1918.

Morse, H. B., and MacNair, H. F. *Far Eastern International Relations*. Boston: Houghton Mifflin, 1931.

Murasaki, Lady. *The Tale of Genji*. Translated by Arthur Waley. Boston: Houghton Mifflin, 1935.

Reischauer, E. O. *Japan Past and Present*. New York: Knopf, 1946.

Sansom, George B. *Japan: A Short Cultural History*. New York: Knopf, 1932.

———. *The Western World and Japan*. New York: Knopf, 1950.

Tawney, R. H. *Land and Labor in China*. New York: Harcourt, Brace, 1932.

Vinacke, H. M. *History of the Far East in Modern Times*. New York: Appleton-Century-Crofts, 1950.

Williams, S. Wells. *The Middle Kingdom*. New York: 1882.

Winfield, G. F. *China: The Land and the People*. New York: Sloane, 1948.

Zinkin, Maurice. *Asia and the West*. London: Hunt, Barnard, 1953.

CHAPTERS IV–VII

Dennett, Tyler. *Americans in Eastern Asia*. New York, 1922.

Morse, H. B. *International Relations of the Chinese Empire*. London, 1918.

Morse, H. B., and MacNair, H. F. *Far Eastern International Relations*. Boston: Houghton Mifflin, 1931.

Teng, S. Y., and Fairbank, John K. *China's Response to the West*. Cambridge, Mass.: Harvard University Press, 1954.

Williams, S. W. *The Middle Kingdom*. New York, 1882.

CHAPTERS VIII–IX

Borton, Hugh. *Japan's Modern Century*. New York: Ronald Press, 1955.

Cosenza, M. E. *The Complete Journal of Townsend Harris*. New York: Doubleday, 1930.

Dennett, Tyler. *Americans in Eastern Asia*. New York, 1922.

McLaren, W. W. *Political History of Japan during the Meiji Era*. New York, 1916.

Norman, E. H. *Japan's Emergence as a Modern State*. New York: Macmillan, 1940.

Sansom, George B. *The Western World and Japan*. New York: Knopf, 1950.

Walworth, Arthur. *Black Ships off Japan* [the coming of Perry]. New York: Knopf, 1946.

CHAPTER X

Cameron, M. E. *The Reform Movement in China*. Palo Alto, Calif.: Stanford University Press, 1931.

Chang Chih-tung. *Learn*. Translated by S. I. Woodbridge. New York, 1900.

Chiang Monlin. *Tides from the West*. New Haven, Conn.: Yale University Press, 1947.

Hughes, E. R. *The Invasion of China by the Western World*. New York: Macmillan, 1938.

Tan, C. C. *The Boxer Catastrophe*. New York: Columbia University Press, 1955.

CHAPTER XI

Latourette, K. S. *A History of Christian Missions in China*. New York, 1929.

Peffer, Nathaniel. *China: The Collapse of a Civilization*. New York, 1930.

CHAPTER XII

Dennett, Tyler. *Americans in Eastern Asia*. New York, 1922.

Hornbeck, S. K. *Contemporary Politics in the Far East*. New York, 1916.

Joseph Philip. *Foreign Diplomacy in China, 1894–1900*. London, 1928.

Morse, H. B. *International Relations of the Chinese Empire*. London, 1918.

Morse, H. B., and MacNair, H. F. *Far Eastern International Relations*. Boston, Houghton Mifflin, 1931.

Moon, Parker T. *Imperialism and World Politics*. New York, 1926.

Overlach, T. W. *Foreign Financial Control in China*. New York, 1919.

Willoughby, W. W. *Foreign Rights and Interests in China*. Baltimore, Md., 1920.

CHAPTERS XIII–XIV

Borton, Hugh. *Japan's Modern Century*. New York, Ronald Press, 1955.

McLaren, W. W. *A Political History of Japan during the Meiji Era*. New York, 1916.

Norman, E. H. *Japan's Emergence as a Modern State*. New York, Macmillan, 1940.

Sansom, George B. *The Western World and Japan*. New York, Knopf, 1949.

Yanaga, Chitoshi. *Japan Since Perry*. New York, McGraw-Hill, 1949.

CHAPTERS XV–XVII

Langer, W. L. *The Diplomacy of Imperialism 1890–1902*. New York, Knopf, 1935.

Takeuchi, Tatsuji. *War and Diplomacy in the Japanese Empire*. Garden City, New York, Doubleday, 1935.

Tan, C. C. *The Boxer Catastrophe*. New York, Columbia University Press, 1955.

CHAPTERS XVIII–XIX

Dennett, Tyler. *Americans in Eastern Asia*. New York, 1922.

Dennis, A. L. P. *Adventures in American Diplomacy 1896–1906*. New York, 1928.

Dulles, F. R. *America in the Pacific*. Boston, Houghton Mifflin, 1938.

Griswold, A. W. *The Far Eastern Policy of the United States*. New York, Harcourt, Brace, 1938.

Pratt, J. W. *Expansionists of 1898*. Baltimore, Md., Johns Hopkins Press, 1936.

CHAPTER XX

Dennett, Tyler. *Roosevelt and the Russo-Japanese War*. New York, 1925.

Takeuchi, Tatsuji. *War and Diplomacy in the Japanese Empire*. Garden City, N.Y., 1935.

Witte, S. Y. *Memoirs*. Edited by A. Yarmolinsky. New York, 1921.

Zabriskie, E. H. *American-Russian Rivalry in the Far East*. Philadelphia, University of Pennsylvania Press, 1946.

CHAPTERS XXI–XXII AND XXV

Cameron, M. E. *The Reform Movement in China*. Palo Alto, Calif.: Stanford University Press, 1931.

Chien Tuan-sheng. *The Government and Politics of China*. Cambridge, Mass., Harvard University Press, 1950.

Holcombe, A. N. *The Chinese Revolution*. Cambridge, Mass., Harvard University Press, 1930.

Peffer, Nathaniel. *China: The Collapse of a Civilization*. New York, John Day, 1930.

Ross, E. A. *The Changing Chinese*. New York, 1911.

Sharman, Lyon. *Sun Yat-sen, His Life and Its Meaning*. New York, John Day, 1934.

Williams, E. T. *China Yesterday and Today*. New York, T. Y. Crowell, 1939.

CHAPTERS XXIII–XXIV

Iwasaki, U. *The Working Forces in Japanese Politics*. New York, 1921.

McLaren, W. W. *A Political History of Japan during the Meiji Era*. New York, 1916.

Price, E. B. *The Russo-Japanese Treaties of 1907–1916 Concerning Manchuria and Mongolia*. Baltimore, Md., Johns Hopkins Press, 1933.

Quigley, H. S. *Japanese Government and Politics*. New York, Appleton-Century, 1932.

Takeuchi, Tatsuji. *War and Diplomacy in the Japanese Empire*. Garden City, N.Y., Doubleday, 1935.

Uyehara, G. E. *The Political Development of Japan 1867–1909*. London, 1909.

Yanaga, Chitoshi. *Japan Since Perry*. New York, McGraw-Hill, 1949.

CHAPTERS XXVI–XXVII

Buell, R. L. *The Washington Conference*. New York, 1922.

Graves, W. S. *America's Siberian Adventure*. New York, Cape and Smith, 1931.

LaFargue, T. E. *China and the World War*. Palo Alto, Calif., Stanford University Press, 1937.

Reinsch, P. S. *An American Diplomat in China*. Garden City, N.Y., 1922.

Takeuchi, Tatsuji. *War and Diplomacy in the Japanese Empire*. Garden City, N.Y., Doubleday, 1935.

Young, A. Morgan. *Japan in Recent Times, 1912–1927*. New York, 1929.

CHAPTERS XXVIII–XXXIV

Holcombe, A. N. *The Chinese Revolution*. Cambridge, Mass., Harvard University Press, 1930.

Hu Shih. *The Chinese Renaissance*. Chicago, University of Chicago Press, 1934.

MacNair, H. F. *China in Revolution*. Chicago, University of Chicago Press, 1931.

Peffer, Nathaniel. *China: The Collapse of a Civilization*. New York, John Day, 1930.

———. *The White Man's Dilemma*. New York, 1927.

Snow, Edgar. *Red Star over China*. New York, Random House, 1938.

Sun Yat-sen. *The Three Principles of the People*. Translated by F. W. Price. Shanghai, 1927.

Tang Leang-li. *The Inner History of the Chinese Revolution*. London, Routledge, 1930.

CHAPTER XXXV

Borton, Hugh. *Japan's Modern Century*. New York: Ronald Press, 1955.

Reischauer, R. K. *Japan: Government and Politics*. New York: Nelson & Sons, 1939.

Young, A. Morgan. *Imperial Japan 1912–1926*. New York, 1929.

CHAPTERS XXXVI–XXXVIII

Borton, Hugh. *Japan Since 1931*. New York: Ronald Press, 1940.

Byas, Hugh. *Government by Assassination*. New York: Knopf, 1942.

Grew, Joseph C. *Ten Years in Japan*. New York: Simon and Schuster, 1944.

Pollard, R. T. *China's Foreign Relations, 1917–1931*. New York: Macmillan, 1933.

League of Nations. *Report of Commission of Inquiry* [on Manchuria].

Takeuchi, Tatsuji. *War and Diplomacy in the Japanese Empire*. Garden City, N.Y., 1935.

Young, A. M. *Imperial Japan, 1926–1938*. New York: Morrow, 1938.

Young, C. W. *The International Relations of Manchuria*. Chicago: University of Chicago Press, 1929.

CHAPTERS XXXIX–XL

Bisson, T. A. *Japan in China*. New York: Macmillan, 1938.

Grew, J. C. *Ten Years in Japan*. New York: Simon and Schuster, 1944.

Quigley, H. S. *Far Eastern War, 1937–1941*. Boston: World Peace Foundation, 1942.

Stimson, H. L. *The Far Eastern Crisis*. New York: Harper & Bros., 1936.

Taylor, G. E. *The Struggle for North China*. New York: Institute of Pacific Relations, 1940.

U. S. Foreign Relations, *Japan 1931–1941*. Washington, D.C.: Government Printing Office, 1943.

CHAPTERS XLI–XLIII

Butow, R. J. C. *Japan's Decision to Surrender*. Palo Alto, Calif.: Stanford University Press, 1954.

King, Ernest. *United States Navy at War*. Washington, D.C.: U.S. Government Printing Office, 1945.

Lattimore, Owen. *Solution in Asia*. Boston: Little, Brown, 1945.

Marshall, George C. *The Winning of the War in Europe and the Pacific*. New York: Simon and Schuster, 1945.

Morison, S. E. *History of United States Naval Operations in World War II*. Boston, 1948– See volumes relating to Pacific War.

Peffer, Nathaniel. *Basis for Peace in the Far East*. New York: Harper & Bros., 1942.

Pratt, Fletcher. *Fleet against Japan*. New York: Harper & Bros., 1946.

U. S. Foreign Relations, *Japan 1931–1941*. Washington, D.C.: Government Printing Office, 1943.

United States Navy. *Battle Report, Pacific War.* Successive volumes. Washington, D.C.: U.S. Government Printing Office, 1946.

United States Strategic Bombing Survey. Volumes on different aspects of Pacific War. Washington, D.C.: U.S. Government Printing Office, 1946.

CHAPTERS XLIV AND XLVI

Chien Tuan-sheng. *The Government and Politics of China.* Cambridge, Mass.: Harvard University Press, 1950.

United States Department of State. *U.S. Relations with China.* Washington, D.C., 1949.

White, T. H., and Jacoby, Annalee. *Thunder out of China.* New York: Sloane, 1946.

CHAPTERS XLV AND LI

Ball, W. Macmahon. *Nationalism and Communism in Southeast Asia.* New York: Cambridge University Press, 1952.

Emerson, Rupert, Mills, L. A., and Thompson, Virginia. *Government and Nationalism in Southeast Asia.* New York: Institute of Pacific Relations, 1942.

Furnivall, J. S. *Colonial Policy and Practice.* New York: Cambridge University Press, 1948.

Hall, D. G. E. *History of Southeast Asia.* New York: St. Martin's Press, 1955.

Hayden, J. R. *The Philippines.* New York: Macmillan, 1942.

Lasker, Bruno. *Peoples of Southeast Asia.* New York: Knopf, 1944.

Mills, L. A., et al. *The New World of Southeast Asia.* Minneapolis, Minn.: University of Minnesota Press, 1949.

Vinacke, H. M. *Far Eastern Politics in the Post-war Period.* New York: Appleton-Century-Crofts, 1956.

CHAPTER XLVII

Ball, W. Macmahon. *Japan, Enemy or Ally.* New York: John Day, 1949.

Borton, Hugh. *Japan's Modern Century.* New York: Ronald Press, 1955.

Far Eastern Commission. *Report by the Secretary General.* Washington, D.C.: Government Printing Office, 1947 ff.

Martin, E. M. *The Allied Occupation of Japan.* Palo Alto, Calif.: Stanford University Press, 1948.

Quigley, H. S., and Turner, T. S. *The New Japan, Government and Politics.* Minneapolis, Minn., 1956.

Reischauer, E. O. *The United States and Japan.* Cambridge, Mass.: Harvard University Press, 1950.

Wakefield, H. *New Paths for Japan.* London: Oxford University Press, 1948.

CHAPTER XLVIII

Goodrich, L. M. *Korea: Collective Measures against Aggression.* New York: Carnegie Endowment for International Peace, 1953.

Longford, J. H. *The Story of Korea.* London, 1911.

McCune, George M., and Grey, A. L., Jr. *Korea Today.* Cambridge, Mass.: Harvard University Press, 1950.

Osgood, Cornelius. *The Koreans and Their Culture.* New York: Ronald Press, 1951.

CHAPTER XLIX

Department of State. *United States Relations with China.* Washington, D.C., 1949.

Reischauer, E. O. *Wanted, An Asian Policy.* New York: Knopf, 1955.

CHAPTER L

Bodde, Derk. *Peking Diary.* New York: Schuman, 1950.

Fitzgerald, C. P. *Revolution in China.* New York: Praeger, 1952.

Kuo, P. C. *China: New Age and New Outlook.* New York: Knopf, 1956.

Mao Tse-tung. *China's New Democracy.* New York: International Publishers, 1955.

Rostow, W. W. *The Prospects for Communist China.* New York: John Wiley, 1954.

Schwartz, B. I. *Chinese Communism and the Rise of Mao.* Cambridge, Mass.: Harvard University Press, 1951.

Snow, Edgar. *Red Star over China.* New York: Random House, 1938.

Wu Yuan-li. *An Economic Survey of Communist China.* New York: Bookman Associates, 1956.

INDEX